Lecture Notes in Computer Science   1282

Edited by G. Goos, J. Hartmanis and J. van Leeuwen

Advisory Board: W. Brauer   D. Gries   J. Stoer

W0245736

Springer-Verlag Berlin Heidelberg GmbH

David Garlan   Daniel Le Métayer (Eds.)

Coordination Languages and Models

Second International Conference
COORDINATION '97
Berlin, Germany, September 1-3, 1997
Proceedings

 Springer

Series Editors

Gerhard Goos, Karlsruhe University, Germany

Juris Hartmanis, Cornell University, NY, USA

Jan van Leeuwen, Utrecht University, The Netherlands

Volume Editors

David Garlan
Carnegie Mellon University, Computer Science Department
5000 Forbes Avenue, Pittsburgh, PA 15213-3891, USA
E-mail: garlan@cs.cmu.edu

Daniel Le Métayer
IRISA — Campus universitaire de Beaulieu
F-35042 Rennes Cedex, France
E-mail: lemetayer@irisa.fr

Cataloging-in-Publication data applied for

Die Deutsche Bibliothek - CIP-Einheitsaufnahme

Coordination languages and models : second international
conference, coordination '97, Berlin, Germany, September 1 - 3, 1997
; proceedings / [Second International Conference on Coordination
Models and Languages]. David Garlan ; Daniel LeMétayer (ed.). -
Berlin ; Heidelberg ; New York ; Barcelona ; Budapest ; Hong Kong
; London ; Milan ; Paris ; Santa Clara ; Singapore ; Tokyo : Springer,
1997
    ISBN 978-3-540-63383-9

CR Subject Classification (1991): D.1.3, C.2.4,F.1.2, D.2.4

ISSN 0302-9743
ISBN 978-3-540-63383-9   ISBN 978-3-540-69527-1 (eBook)
DOI 10.1007/978-3-540-69527-1

© Springer-Verlag Berlin Heidelberg 1997
Originally published by Springer-Verlag Berlin Heidelberg New York in 1997

Typesetting: Camera-ready by author
SPIN 10547787   06/3142 – 5 4 3 2 1 0   Printed on acid-free paper

Foreword

This volume contains the papers selected for presentation at the second International Conference on Coordination Models and Languages (COORDINATION'97), held in Berlin, September 1 - 3, 1997. COORDINATION was held previously in Cesena (Italy) in 1996, and, given the strong interest of the research community, we expect it to become a regular event.

COORDINATION is devoted to an emerging class of languages and models, which have been variously termed "coordination languages", "configuration languages", and "architectural description languages". Such formalisms provide a clean separation between individual software components and their interaction in the overall software organization. This separation makes large applications more tractable, supports global analysis, and enhances reuse of software. The scope of the conference ranges from theoretical aspects of coordination to languages for coordination and their applications.

In response to the call for papers, 69 papers were submitted to COORDINATION'97, from which 19 regular papers were accepted. Six additional papers were selected as short papers, to be presented at a poster session. Two extra papers that focus on a specific case study proposed by Edwin de Jong (Signaal) are also included in the proceedings. These papers were selected by Edwin de Jong, Jean-Marc Andreoli (Xerox), and Marc Bourgois (Eurocontrol), with the approval of the conference programme committee.

This year's program featured invited talks by Nicholas Carriero, Jeff Kramer, and Doug Lea; summaries of their talks are also included in this volume. In addition, three members of the programme committee agreed to give state-of-the-art reports: Paolo Ciancarini, Oscar Nierstrasz, and Dewayne Perry.

We would like to thank all the contributors, the members of the programme committee, and other paper reviewers. We would like to thank the local arrangements chairpersons Bernd Mahr and Robert Tolksdorf for effectively organizing and publicizing the conference. We are also grateful to Isabelle Ballon for her assistance in processing the referees' reports and preparing the final version of the proceedings. The following organizations provided sponsorship and support for the conference: Sun Microsystems GmbH, Deutschland; JF Lehmanns, Berlin; Deutsche Forschungsgemeinschaft DFG, IKV e V; Berlin; IFV I+K, Berlin. The conference was also supported by the EU-funded working group COORDINA.

June 1997   David Garlan and Daniel Le Métayer

Programme Committee

David Garlan (CMU, USA), co-chair
Daniel Le Métayer (INRIA, FR), co-chair

Jaco de Bakker (CWI, NL)
Maarten Boasson (Signaal, NL)
Luca Cardelli (Digital, USA)
Paolo Ciancarini (Bologna, IT)
Susan Graham (Berkeley, USA)
Chris Hankin (London, UK)
Philippe Kruchten (Rational Soft., CN)
Ugo Montanari (Pisa, IT)
Mark Moriconi (SRI, USA)
Oscar Nierstrasz (Berne, CH)
Dewayne Perry (Bell Labs, USA)
António Porto (Lisbon, P)
James Purtilo (Maryland, USA)
David Schmidt (KSU, USA)
Peter Wegner (Brown, USA)
Alexander L. Wolf (Colorado, USA)

Organizing Committee TU Berlin

Bernd Mahr, co-chair   Markus Andrezak
Robert Tolksdorf, co-chair   Christel Hecht
                             Andreas Knoche

List of Referees

Cecilia Mascolo
Frank van Breugel
Stelvio Cimato
Juan Carlos Cruz
Rocco de Nicola
Roberto Amadio
David Rossi
Jose Legatheaux Martins
Marco Pistore
Franz Achermann
Paolo Ancilotti
Farhad Arbab
Gianluigi Ferrari
Roberto Gorrieri

Didier Buchs
Jetty Kleijn
Theo Dirk Meijler
Gianluigi Zavattaro
Marco Kesseler
Gian Luca Cattani
Juergen Menden
Tamar Richner
Kees Middelburg
Jan Rutten
Pedros Medeiros
Luis Caires
Wiebe van der Hoek

Carla Simone
Antonio Brogi
Stephane Ducasse
Wil van der Aalst
Alessandro Fabbri
Luis Monteiro
Francesca Rossi
Ian Stark
Paola Inverardi
Marcello M. Bonsangue
Gioia Ristori
Mauro Gaspari
Roberto Segala

Contents

Short Papers

From Weaving Threads to Untangling the Web: A View of Coordination from Linda's Perspective

Robert Bjornson, Nicholas Carriero, and David Gelernter

Department of Computer Science, Yale University, New Haven CT 06520, USA
Scientific Computing Associates, Inc., New Haven CT 06510, USA

Abstract. A decade of work with the Linda coordination model in both academic and commercial settings has made clear that the need for coordination arises in a broad range of application domains, from parallel computing to information management. We review how the Linda model has evolved and is evolving to meet the particular demands of these different domains. We conclude by noting that despite this evolution, the underlying conceptual framework has remained unchanged, offering evidence for the existence of a unified approach to the challenges of coordination.

1 Introduction

We present an overview of a decade's work with the Linda coordination model.[1] The work ranges from (very) technically detailed runtime support systems, to user API's, to high-level, abstract computational frameworks in which Linda, and parallelism itself, have been hidden. This span of attention, from the smallest detail to the grand abstraction is itself telling. Perhaps the most important thing we have learned over the last decade is that the need for coordination, and thus for systems to express coordination, is not confined to a narrow and esoteric problem domain. There is a place for arduous, detailed mapping of algorithm to machine; there is also room for abstractions that hide all of these details. What's needed is a coordination model that is as at home at one end of the spectrum as it is at the other, and perhaps more importantly, does a good job of revealing a continuity between discrete points in the spectrum that might otherwise have been overlooked. It is in the space between the points, our experience tells us, that most programmers spend their time and are most productive. Many other models for parallel computing carve out just a part of the spectrum; doing a reasonable job in that context, they nonetheless fail to adapt gracefully to programmers needing more abstraction, or more precision.

This paper follows the spectrum from the detailed to the abstract. Our first task was to prove that a "high-level" coordination model could be implemented efficiently. Having established that, we have moved on to developing and using

---

[1] Throughout this paper, we will use the term "Linda" in two senses. The first sense, illustrated here, relates to a *model* of coordination. The second sense relates to a particular *implementation* of that model.

increasingly higher levels of abstraction based on the basic Linda coordination model.

The work described below combines academic efforts at Yale and commercialization research and development at Scientific Computing Associates. Building and supporting a commercial product has put us into contact with a large number of highly motivated and demanding users; this interplay has encouraged a good deal of the work that follows.

2 Where We've Been and Lessons We've Learned

We begin with a brief review of the development of Linda implementation technology and the evolution of a methodology for developing coordinated applications.

2.1 Implementing Linda

Our initial Linda efforts focussed on systems for parallel programming, not because we thought that that was all Linda was good for, but because parallel programming was an area attracting considerable attention in the early 1980s, and so it was an area rich with opportunities. But, by the very nature of the domain, providing support for parallel programming meant meeting demanding performance requirements. Given that Linda was generally viewed as an appealing design, but one that had little chance of being realized efficiently, our work was cut out for us. ("We choose to go to the moon ...")

The role of compile- and link-time support Fortunately, a couple of critical techniques fell into place to provide a firm foundation for efficient Linda implementations on virtually all MIMD architectures. The first technique exploited compile- and link-time processing to extract and analyze information about how Linda operations were used by any given application. This information made it possible to recast the Linda support problem from providing efficient support for arbitrarily general use of Linda operations, to providing efficient support customized to a particular pattern of use. By focussing on a particular pattern of use, operations could be grouped into non-interfering clusters, based on, for example, the differences in the *type signatures*[2] of the various operations. These clusters induced a fine structure on tuple space that enabled searches to be constrained, that guided locking of sub-spaces on shared memory machines or the distribution of sub-spaces across nodes of a parallel machine, and that allowed for the organization of sub-collections into efficient data structures. As a result, the "look up" problem often assumed to be Linda's Achilles heel was effectively solved (typical Linda programs require, on average, significantly less than two probes of the tuple store to satisfy a tuple request).[4]

---

[2] Roughly the same idea as a function prototype.

Runtime optimizations The second technique embodies the development of a general Linda implementation framework for distributed memory machines that supports a number of runtime optimizations to streamline data transfers and reduce the count of low-level messages needed to accomplish a given Linda operation. This reduction, based on the dynamic detection of patterns of communication, has been particularly valuable in minimizing the cost of supporting Linda's uncoupled, anonymous coordination model on distributed memory machines. The initial distribution of sub-spaces across processors is essentially random. As the computation unfolds, the runtime system tracks statistics that indicate ways in which the random mapping may be improved. If such an opportunity occurs, the runtime reconfigures itself on the fly to the improved mapping. As a result, the runtime actions of Linda codes that engage in message-passing-style point-to-point exchanges often settle down into the pattern of low-level communication activities that would have obtained had the exchange been explicitly encoded in a message-passing system. In other words, for such a case, the high-level Linda operations end up imposing no additional communication costs beyond what a low-level system would have incurred.[2, 6]

Local area networks as parallel machines Having produced efficient Linda support for distributed memory machines like the Ncube, the Intel iPSC and the IBM SP2, the basic blueprint was in place for developing an implementation for "parallel machines" that consisted of nothing more than the typical ethernetted collection of workstations. While this "platform" was decidedly dowdy compared with the "heavy metal" machines that were the darlings of the HPC community, making better use of hardware already bought and paid for turned out to have an enormous impact on parallelism for the masses—an impact whose reverberations are still being felt as parallelism on LANs is periodically rediscovered and rechristened as "NOWs" or "COWs" or whatever.

High-end performance To give a taste for the current state of the art, we present some data for a CRAY T3E[5]. The data is measured using a code that pushes tokens around a ring. In general terms, the performance of Linda is comparable to lower-level systems like MPI. In absolute terms, a simple tuple exchange takes 10μsecs, while bandwidth for large tuples peaks at $\sim$350 Mb/sec for a single transfer, and $\sim$630 Mb/sec aggregate for multiple simultaneous transfers on four nodes.

2.2 A coordination methodology

The work described has spanned more than ten years, and much of it has migrated to or taken place in the commercial realm. During this time, Linda systems have seen considerable use in academic and commercial circles. Out of this experience, certain methodologies have emerged that are in some ways more interesting and more important than the technology under the hood.

Distributed data structures and a methodology for coordination We have found that a methodology of coordination based on the relationship between process and data has been particularly useful. Briefly, if we think of data and process independently, we can identify three relationships:

1. Data "owns" process: a data-centric view in which computation follows from the data.
2. Data and process are co-equal.
3. Process "owns" data: a process-centric view in which data production and consumption follows computation.

Note that the freedom to think about data independent from process is one granted by the "right" coordination model—i.e., it's not surprising that this methodology did *not* arise either out of work with SIMD data parallelism or MIMD message-passing systems.

A core element of this methodology is the notion of a distributed data structure: an entity much like a "normal" data structure, but capable of concurrent modification by multiple threads of control. In the case of the first relationship, the distributed data structure is an ensemble of live data elements that will ultimately resolve into stable elements that form the final data structure. In the second case, distributed data structures are free-floating entities that act as kiosks for the interaction of processes. In the third case, distributed data structures tend to be limited to ordered streams used to "wire" processes together.

This set of relationships encompasses most common forms of parallelism, but in a way that integrates them into a continuous spectrum rather than treats them as discrete points. The first relationship leads more or less immediately to data parallelism, the second to task farm parallelism and the third to functional/pipeline parallelism. This spectrum demonstates that, viewed from the right perspective, these approaches are conceptually related and with the right coordination framework, equally straightforward to express. Because of this, it is, in the abstract, relatively easy to transform from the relationship that most naturally fits an application to one that may run more efficiently—the real heart of the methodology.

Example: rapid parallelization of complex codes We briefly discuss two concrete examples of the methodology and distributed data structures at work. Our experience with applications has involved a number that were "industrial" strength. The size and complexity of these codes precluded any kind of major rewrite to support parallelism, yet it was known that parallelism was latent within the codes. The approach we have developed for these codes starts from the point of view that the data to be processed drives the opportunities for parallelism, and that we just need to introduce a distributed data structure to act as a clearinghouse for making decisions about decomposing the data processing. As such, it involves a variation somewhere between data parallelism and the task farm. We create multiple copies of the code in which each copy does exactly the same thing until a parallel section is reached. At this point, each copy consults a distributed structure to determine if it should skip or compute a portion of the parallel section. The protocol for maintaining the distributed data structure ensures that only one copy is given permission to compute a given portion; all the rest skip it to go immediately to the next portion. At the end of the parallel section, additional distributed data structures are used to bring all copies up to date, at which point all copies resume doing exactly the same thing. Pragmatically, this is quite flexible (it adapts readily to different control flows through the parallel section, to multiple parallel sections, to different policies for parcelling out portions, and to different strategies for updates), performs well, and often requires nearly trivial changes to the original sequential code.

Example: adaptive parallelism The use of distributed data structures to implement task farms is the basis of our second example. Because distributed data structures permit uncoupled and anonymous interactions, there is latent capability in task farms built with them: the cast of characters can change as an application runs. That is, the task manager and the workers do not interact directly but through the distributed data structure kiosks. So the same coordination code works with three, thirty, or 300 workers. Our work on the Piranha system exploited this capability to construct a system to support "adaptive parallelism"—parallel execution in which the population of processes tracks the resources available, growing or shrinking as nodes become free or are taken for other uses.

2.3 Some lessons learned

Looking back, a few clear messages emerge from our early work on coordination:

1. (Efficient) Simplicity can be powerful. The principles underlying Linda can be summed up as: 1) referencing schemes for coordination data should come from within, not be imposed from without; and 2) coordination data should be given a life of its own, not be held captive by processes. From this simplicty flows powerful concepts like distributed data structures and adaptive parallelism.
Simplicity leads to power in another way: the leveraging power of reuse. The same coordination framework can be incorporated in different languages, applied to problems from different domains, and deployed on different hardware.
2. 90%+ of parallel programming[3] isn't a "grand challenge", and isn't *that* hard—with the right tools. The order of intellectual challenge presented by parallelizing a code is often no greater than the challenge presented by designing the original sequential code
3. Because it just isn't that hard, parallel programing increasingly has come to be viewed as not a hard-fought end in itself, but as just another technique among many for improving code performance.

---

[3] One of the 72% of all statistics that are made up.

4. It doesn't pay to place demands on coordination systems that are more stringent than those that have been placed on sequential systems. In the early days when the jury was still out on the tractability of parallel programming, there was a tendency to assume that it was going to be very hard. This gave some currency to a philosophy of saving the programmer from himself that the field hasn't quite shaken. Just as we have managed to grind out interesting sequential codes despite having to overcome the occasional core dump or two, we have and we will continue to produce parallel codes despite having to overcome the odd deadlock here or there.[4]

3 Where We Are Now and the Lessons We Are Learning

One implication of the previous section is that the Linda project spent its energy during the initial years competing with message passing as a way of building parallel programs. Message passing was for many people the self-evident way to program multiple processors; it seemed simple, fit close to the hardware, and required a minimum of imagination. Many of the design choices we drew emerged from this competition; we were trying to do things that MP could do, and as efficiently.

An important impetus to take a wider view came from the commercialization of Linda by Scientific Computing Associates, Inc. (SCA). As Linda was developed by SCA into a suite of commercial products and we saw the sorts of demands that "real world" users were putting on the system, it became clear that our initial implementations had been skewed towards high-performance scientific computing, with its emphasis on expensive iron, speedup/efficiency graphs, highly optimized mapping of algorithms to hardware geometries, and all the rest. The milieu rewarded monolithic, highly tuned, Swiss-watch algorithms. Many of our users, on the other hand, were looking for something quite different; wringing out the last percent of efficiency was much less important to them than overall productivity, adaptivity, and flexibility.

Consider some of the applications that users wanted to build:

An energy company built an enormous spreadsheet to model energy pricing, based on economic and production data. By using Monte Carlo techniques, many individual random variables (spreadsheet cells) could be simultaneously varied over specified random distributions, by repeatedly recalculating the spreadsheet. They wanted to preserve the accustomed GUI (Excel) but spread the calculations over a large number of networked PCs.

A Wall Street trading company wanted to build a system to which tens or hundreds of traders could submit deals to be priced on a network of hundreds of machines acting as calculation engines. The requests would often come in

---

[4] We're not arguing that a seat-of-the-pants approach is the be-all and end-all of programming methodology—just that a better one, desirable as that may be, isn't a prerequisite for parallel programming, any more than it has been for sequential programming.

surges; workflow management, prioritization, and fault tolerance were key requirements.

A bank had a collection of sequential applications that valued securities using different algorithms. They wanted to farm the jobs out to a network of workstations, without having to change the applications, or involve their developers in writing parallel programs.

Another bank had a reporting system that built, priced, and reported on collateralized mortgage obligation deals. The existing system consisted of a number of disjoint programs that communicated via files and ran sequentially as a pipeline. They wanted to distribute the pipeline and parallelize the segments that were bottlenecks by replicating those components dynamically. They also wanted a fault-tolerant system that was easy to monitor.

Looking over these examples, we saw a number of common characteristics that separated them from the sorts of problems traditional to "scientific computing":

Flexibility Users wanted to link together different languages, and different applications. They did not want to change the applications; indeed in many cases they had no ability to change them. They wanted components of their system to exist in different places, at different times.

Complexity hiding The users were interested in running faster or larger, not in the complexities of parallel computing. We had to find ways to hide the starting and stopping of processes, and the communication between them.

Use of modest hardware In strong constrast to the big-iron mentality, many users had large numbers of modest workstations or PCs linked by conventional networks. The machines were not protected in a machine room, nor necessarily administered well.

Incrementally upgradeable or hot-swappable applications Applications, once running, had to be manipulable without bringing down and changing everything.

Large scale A surprise to us was the audacity of many of the commercial projects. The designers routinely called for ensembles of hundreds of machines. In the scientific arena, one saw this scale in grand-challenge problems. Here were companies interested in running very large problems on a daily basis, in production, on mundane machines scattered around offices.

Reliability The users had strong requirements here as well. Calculations were going to be submitted and collected by people such as stock traders, who neither knew nor cared how the calculations were accomplished, but who stood to lose a great deal of time or money if the calculations were not completed on time. Individual failures had to be handled automatically, and the system as a whole had to continue to function in spite of multiple failures.

Fast turnaround Overheads imposed on individual computations had to be kept to a minimum; jobs had to turn around fast. Combining this requirement with running on huge numbers of processors meant that the system had to be persistent, running constantly as a background framework that individual computations could join and leave.

Ensemble style We were seeing ensembles of distinctly different components, rather than large numbers of identical clones. These ensembles included GUI monitors, API libraries, calculation engines, auditing functions, etc., all loosely linked together. Users wanted these disjoint components to function together harmoniously without having to be more closely tied together than necessary.

3.1 Open Linda[5]

The flexible, anonymous communication possible via Linda's tuple space is ideal for these sorts of applications, which are amorphous, shifting, adaptive and lingering, compared to traditional parallel applications. We had long been interested in developing a Linda-based approach targeted to these applications, rather than high-performance ones. We referred to this approach as "Open" Linda because it left open a number of aspects that had been assumed to be "closed" (for efficiency's sake) in the original Linda work. Open Linda systems would simplify the construction of distributed applications that were very difficult to build using a message-passing or RPC style of communication. SCA designed and built an implementation of a new Open Linda specification. The resulting system is marketed under the name *Paradise*[13]. It is important to note that the *same* coordination model underlies both approaches leading to conceptual and practical compatibilities.

We faced a number of issues in redesigning the implementation of tuple space.

Link-time analysis revisited As described previously, closed-Linda systems perform extensive analysis on the use of tuples in a program in order to reduce the searching and matching costs of associative memory lookups. The analysis is remarkably successful at this; it separates tuples into non-interacting disjoint sets and chooses good data structures and lookup strategies for each set. Tuple lookups are reduced to quick accesses to simple data structures.

However, this analysis has the effect of compiling the structure of tuple space into the program at link time. The analysis is so effective precisely because it is static: it knows it won't be surprised by new flavors of tuples. Paradise needs to relax this restriction; we want existing programs to interact with new programs as they are written without requiring the old programs to be relinked or indeed even restarted.

This means that Paradise has to delay some of the analysis and incrementally discover relationships between tuples as they join the computation, rather than doing so all at once during the link phase. Recall that there are two major components to the analysis: forming sets of independent tuple operations, and determining an efficient implementation for each set.

Paradise initializes a new tuple space as a blank slate. As new tuple type signatures arrive, they are compared against the signatures for sets that have

[5] The material in this section describes work done at SCA by Daya Attapatu, Nancy Esposito, Howard Gilbert, Jens Nielsen and Stephen Weston, among others.

already been seen. If any existing set has a compatible signature, the tuple is assigned to that set; if none does, a new set is formed.

Each set is implemented as a hash table, hashing on some subset of fields in the tuple, called key fields. Which fields to use as keys is also discovered dynamically based on the patterns of use that are seen over time. When templates arrive, if they have actual values in all of the key fields, they can be hashed just like tuples and can zero in quickly on potential matches. If, on the other hand, they have formals in one or more of the key fields, they cannot use the hash function, since information is lacking, and must search the entire table.

Therefore, Paradise must determine those template fields that tend to be actual, (and thus should be key fields), and those that are often formal, and should be left out. Each set keeps a ratio of the occurrence of actual vs formal for each field, that decays over time[6]:

$$R_{i+1} = \alpha R_i + (1 - \alpha) isactual(field)$$

Ratios that are sufficently high will cause the field to be hashed. As more templates are seen, fields may need to change from key to non-key or the reverse; this requires rehashing each entry. Paradise includes some hysteresis in the decision to avoid thrashing.

Multiple tuple spaces Because Paradise uses tuples to connect otherwise unrelated applications, possibly written by different programmers, it is vital to provide applications with their own tuple space "sandboxes", distinct from other applications' tuple spaces. This is important for both naming and security. Paradise provides multiple tuple spaces that are explicitly created, referenced and destroyed. Some spaces are private, accessible only within a single application. Others are semi-private, accessed by related applications, while still others are fully public, available to all.

Commensurate with varying degrees of visibility are degrees of access to tuple spaces: processes can have full access, read-only access (like newspapers) or write-only access (like mailboxes) Access to tuple spaces is via handles, which can be duplicated, restricted, and published or passed to other processes. Handles are designed to be hard to forge, and contain within them the capabilities that are permitted on that tuple space.

Fault-tolerance The applications we now see have evolved to be bigger, longer running, and sited on less reliable hardware (often someone's desktop machine), and yet ironically their criticality has increased. This means that fault-tolerant applications are vital. If an application is running for an extended period on several hundred machines, it both extremely likely that one or more will fail, and also extremely unpleasant and unacceptable to have to restart the whole computation when the inevitable failure occurs.

In the Linda model, fault tolerance appears in two guises. Tuple space itself must survive hardware failures, since it is the communication glue. We have been

---

[6] α is a coefficient that determines the rate of decay.

experimenting with mirrored tuple servers, each maintaining identical copies of all the tuples. By choosing the number of replicas and spreading them out appropriately, different degrees of fault tolerance can be achieved at a reasonable cost.

Secondly, application component failures must not cause information to be lost or duplicated. The component processes in a distributed application build up all kinds of state: in memory, in files, in tuples. Linda cannot reasonably hope to guard *all* of a process's state;[7] rather, we aim to make it possible for a process to manipulate tuples in such a way that the sudden disappearance of the process will not leave tuple space in an inconsistent state.

For example, consider a simple counter implemented as a tuple (the ©ts notation specifies which tuple space to use, ts being a handle for the target tuple space):

```
in@ts("counter", ?i);
out@ts("counter", i+1);
```

If the process were to fail between these operations, the counter would disappear, causing all sorts of difficulties. To prevent this, Paradise provides transactions that render multiple tuple space operations atomic and roll the actions back on failure:

```
xaction@ts();
  in@ts("counter", ?i);
  out@ts("counter", i+1);
commit@ts();
```

Persistence In closed-Linda, the tuple space is tied inextricably to the application that creates it: it comes into existence with and is customized for that application, and disappears when the application finishes. In contrast a Paradise tuple space can be persistent (existing until explicitly destroyed) or non-persistent (destroyed automatically when the last active handle to it disappears). Persistent tuple spaces are useful for passing data between one application and another that does not necessarily coexist with the first, or for communicating from one invocation of an application to another, later invocation.

On the other hand, non-persistent tuple spaces can be used to set up secure communication channels between two processes. In a common idiom, a process creats a tuple space A and openly publishes a write-only handle to it. A second process creates another tuple space B and puts a tuple containing the B handle into A, which the first process (and *only* that process) can read. The two processes can then communicate securely via B.

---

[7] Full process checkpointing introduces complexities that we will not pursue here; suffice it to say that it is expensive, non-portable and usually not necessary.

3.2 Coordination skeletons

As our experience with user applications has grown, we have increasingly sought higher-level coordination frameworks (themselves based on Linda) to provide to end-users to make their programming easier and more productive. We present three such models below: each draws heavily from Linda's uncoupled communication style, yet hides many of the tuple usage details from the programmer.

Calculator The distributed calculator (DC) is a framework for running and coordinating multiple instances of sequential applications, without *any* direct involvement with parallelization. The application programmer writes a stand-alone program that reads input from a file and/or invocation parameters and writes the output to another file. A user then submits a set of jobs in the form of a single input file, containing the inputs for all of the runs concatenated together and the name of the program to run. The DC automatically splits the input file into many small files, transfers the input files via tuple space to remote nodes, and starts copies of the desired program on those machines. The results are passed back through tuple space and assembled into a single output file.

The DC is fault-tolerant, because all tuples are protected via transactions. In addition, the overall state of the job is readily visible in the various tuple spaces; we have built monitors that access the information in those tuples and display the progress to the submitter.

Piranha We have mentioned Piranha in 2.2, where it served to illustrate the flexibility of our overall coordination methodology. Here, we discuss it in its role as a template for parallelism. A brief description follows, [3] gives a more complete treatment. As we have noted, Piranha is a variation of the task farm model of parallelism that dynamically reconfigures itself. During a run, a Piranha application executes only on machines deemed to meet "idleness" criteria. This coordination template allows the programmer to specify three entry points:

feeder(): the master routine. It will run on the local machine and will never back off.
piranha(): the worker routine. The piranha system will start copies of the executable at this entry point automatically and opportunistically on remote machines.
retreat(): a routine that will be called automatically by the piranha process when the system forces it to back off, because the machine is no longer idle.

Versions of the piranha model have existed for years but in limited form, due in part to the limitations of the underlying (closed) Linda implementations. For example, changing the collection of nodes that were potential piranha hosts was difficult to do once applications were running, and retreating processes could not always be completely destroyed. In addition, it was difficult to recover from sudden failures since tuples stored on a machine could be lost. The flexibility of the open-Linda model allows true dynamic behavor. For example, piranha executions can flow onto machines that did not exist when the application started.

The piranha support architecture is relatively simple to describe. Each machine runs a piranha daemon that is responsible for monitoring and reporting the state of the machine, starting and stopping piranhas, and cleaning up the system. The daemons coordinate via a private tuple space that contains the list of current applications and the status of each of the machines. When a daemon determines that its machine is free to run a job, it chooses one from the list of available jobs and spawns a child process to run it.

The piranha system has been built to be quite fault tolerant, using transactions on important tuples. Each of the piranha daemons cooperates in keeping the system as a whole running; there is no "master" daemon. All but one of the daemons can suddenly fail without any effect other than applications running more slowly. If all daemons fail, the system becomes dormant, but will begin functioning properly as soon as a single daemon is restarted.

Process Trellis The process trellis is a software architecture for data fusion. An instance of the trellis can refine a number of data streams into an informative overall assessment of a complex system, all in "soft" realtime.

Using the trellis, an application programmer links together individual black-box components to form a directed, acyclic graph. Each component computes a state based on the states of the nodes in the graph inferior to it; its state is then communicated to its superior nodes.

A key component of the process trellis is a scheduler that takes the graph description provided by the application programmer, and a description of the available hardware, and maps the graph nodes to the hardware. The scheduler attempts both to minimize communication between machines and to equalize the computational load; these are often contradictory goals. In addition, given good enough information about both the graph and the hardware, the scheduler can make the soft real-time performance guarantees.

The process trellis has been used to implement an intensive care unit patient monitor[8]. Trellis designs have also been developed for an insider-trading detection system for the stock market and for a weather sensor network.

3.3   Lessons being learned

Our experience with a wider variety of users has taught us:

1. The need for coordination isn't restricted to problems in which the data and the operations on it are largely homogeneous and a coordination "domain" isn't just the ephemeral creation of a run of an application.
2. Modularity is as important for coordination as it is for computation.[8]
3. Such domains persist across runs to serve a variety of purposes.

---

[8] We had an abstract appreciation of this issue from the start, but it took a certain amount of real-world experience to focus our attention on this in practice.

4. While new kinds of applications can be addressed with basically the same coordination model as 2 (or skeletons built on top it), the underlying implementation must respond to a radically different set of concerns.

4 Where We Are Going and What Might Be Learned on the Way

Our thoughts for the future can be divided informally into two groups: those focussed on development projects and those reflecting outstanding conceptual challenges. Clearly these are not independent, but they lead to different kinds of responses.

4.1 Future development

We see a number of opportunities for various coordination models, execution environments and application domains to be extended, modified or flavored by ideas from Linda. The model has a history of inspiring "Linda in the context of X" projects, ranging from language or language-model embeddings through programming environments focussed on particular applications. Adding a dash of Linda isn't much harder than adding a dash of salt; the simplicity of the model encourages hybrid projects. (Linda's simplicity has also worked against it in some contexts; people with complex, fancy or technically demanding requirements often dismiss Linda because they assume that impressively complex problems demand impressively complex solutions. The research community is split on the issue; a significant minority of researchers has always sought the simplest systems available, but many researchers continue to prefer complexity on principle.)

Spreading the benefits of Linda to other coordination models We are currently exploring ways in which some of the basic properties of Linda's coordination model can be migrated to other coordination approaches, in particular message passing systems like MPI[10] and PVM[9].[9] Our goal is to both simplify the use of these systems and to begin constructing a bridge between what are often viewed as incompatible models. The Linda properties currently of interest are a language (as opposed to library) interface and a data store independent of any given process, referenced by a user controlled rather than system imposed addressing scheme. The former simplifies the programming API, enhances semantic bandwidth and affords better support for debugging and tracing. The latter enriches message passing to accommodate simple distributed data structures such as shared variables.

Exploiting recent developments in network computing Two of the most important factors limiting the deployment of Piranha have been incompatibility

---

[9] This work is supported by a DARPA SBIR grant to SCA.

of executable binaries and security concerns. Both of these are to some degree addressed by Java. A marriage of Java and Linda has the potential to be an excellent support environment for adaptive parallelism. Interestingly, a marriage of Linda and Java is appealing for other reasons, including ones that have led JavaSoft to develop a JavaSpaces proposal[12] based on tuple spaces. We are now working on a version of Java-Linda in preparation for an exploration of adaptive parallelism in this setting.[10] Others have been active in this area too (see, for example, [7]).

Expanding the range of application Our work to date has been largely concerned with traditional domains for parallel and distributed applications. Our focus has shifted recently to the groupware/collaborative-computing class of applications, which involve the coordination of people as well as machines.

Consider a newspaper publishing its latest edition. It is using (in concept) a tuple space and not a message operation: the new edition is intended to be read by many clients, and to persist indefinitely; in principle it should also be content-addressable. (Users of Orbis or other news databases ordinarily look up news stories by content, not by name.) The same holds for publications of all kinds (arguably including movies, records and so on).

Of course there are other communication transactions that seem to fit naturally with message passing: when X sends Y a letter (by regular post), X addresses it explicitly and only to Y; likewise when X phones Y. But it's interesting in cases like this to consider the implications of moving to a tuple-space model instead. X would just as soon not need to know Y's address or phone number; it would be convenient to address a letter or make a call by saying "this is for Joe Schwartz, my former college roomate" and leaving it at that. (You'd have to include enough information to identify the recipient uniquely, and the communication attempt would fail if the address proved to be ambiguous.) Letters or phone conversations that persisted in tuple space would continue to be available for reference (which might be, admittedly, a mixed blessing). The security implications here are large, but the point is that tuple space may support existing types of information management more effectively than other models, and may in some cases suggest new types of service too. Recursively nested tuple spaces may be a more appropriate model than the Web for organizing large-scale information sharing.

Concretely, we have found that by building applications like these using the Linda-derived coordination framework Bauhaus[11], it is possible both to simplify development and simultaneously enhance functionality. For example, the well-known Unix `talk` utility, when reimplemented using Bauhaus, requires less code and is far more useful: The exchange of `talk` text blocks becomes a persistent stream of conversation (effectively acting as the "minutes" of a sort of free-form on-line meeting) that any number of agents can join at any time, and can replay from any point.

---

[10] The Yale work on this is supported by ONR Grant # N00014-96-1-0328.

Exploring new coordination skeletons When we create a document, we are executing the first of a potentially unbounded series of coordination operations on that document. Later coordination operations will access the document at times and on behalf of agents that may or may not be known (and may or may not exist) at creation time. A recipient's email alert process is a "known" agent accessing a mail message at a predictable time shortly after the message was created (i.e., after we sent it). We act as unknown (unanticipated) agents, with unanticipated access times, when we rummage through our file-copy mail archives looking for a message we sent last year. Obviously, the same holds for papers, memos, proposals, lectures notes, etc., as well as for other agents acting in the future.

Seen in this light, our electronic world becomes a large coordination problem involving interactions across time with others and (later instances of) ourselves—a world for which our generative coordination approach with its unnamed coordination objects is well suited. Our Lifestreams project employs these Linda concepts and a clean user interface methaphor to tackle the problem of document management and coordination.

We note that in the context of coordination skeletons, the development of more "plastic" coordination interfaces, needed to support plug-and-play software component assembly, becomes an important issue. One of the most promising and least developed tools to emerge from Linda research is the "Linda program builder"[1], which addresses some aspects as this issue. The LPB is potentially applicable in many environments. Our working prototype "semi-automates" the development of coordinated applications in two ways: it captures useful coordination frameworks or skeletons, and full-blown software architectures too. A program builder can save an application developer time, and accumulate higher-level information about an application than a compiler can develop (because the user gives the system higher-level guidance respecting his intentions—tells it, in effect, that a certain data structure is designed for holding tasks or a shared array and so on). It can also accumulate communal experience and wisdom, by caching the coordination frameworks users develop (to the extent they are willing to make them public), together with performance information.

4.2 Conceptual challenges

Data in and of itself doesn't need to be coordinated, but most interesting uses of data do involve coordination. As the context of use changes, or the questions being asked, or the quality of results required, relationships among the data elements themselves and among data and agents change too. These evolving relationships demand coordination. Sometimes a one-off solution is called for, while at other times idiomatic coordination frameworks or skeletons are useful (such as the calculator, trellis and Lifestreams), and at others ... who knows?

When relationships among data are *not* allowed to evolve (tossing in the towel on the coordination problem), the result is a mess like the World Wide Web—a "web" that is growing, but whose pieces are more-or-less static once spun and hold fast random bits, clumps of bytes, and the odd exoskeleton arrayed in a pattern that is of little interest or use to anyone.

Imagine the increased flexibility and functionality that comes from replacing "hard coded" document references with something like

```
<A HREF=//linda:rdⒸts("data tag", ?  page_element)></A>
```

Clearly there is potential here for a "paradigm shift"—a shift from a cyberspace chilled to near absolute zero, where various clumps of data and agents are frozen into the lattice points of a crystal determined by one context of use at one point in time, to a cyberspace warmed to the melting point, where data and agents are free to associate for a passing moment and disassociate the next. More generally, the problem of data overload is driving us towards the discovery of the "fundamentals laws" of coordination that at once dictate, enable and control these associations.

These observations in themselves reflect progress. But our understanding is still incomplete:

What are the fundamentals of the relationship between people and their digital data? The digital data of others?
What, if anything, distinguishes these kinds of coordination?:
 computer with computer
 human with computer
 human with human (including self)
  (computer mediated)
What is "coordination," anyway?

5   Conclusions

It is, perhaps, surprising how ubiquitous the need for coordination is. In ways obvious or not-so-obvious, each of

Parallel computing
Concurrent systems
Distributed programming
Groupware applications
Information management

require coordination support in one form or another. As the on-line world becomes increasingly more complex, it is a safe bet that we will need to cross coordination boundaries between these domains as well.

Given this broad range of coordination problems and the need to cross boundaries, some critical questions arise: How big is the space of solutions? How big does it *need* to be? Certain concepts of computation (e.g., arithmetic and conditionals) have proven useful whether the application is molecular simulation or web browsing. Does the same hold true for concepts of coordination? Although we started at the top of the list, Linda seems to be an increasingly more natural fit as we move *down* the list. The answer that is emerging from more than a decade of Linda work is, "Yes."

References

1. S. Ahmed and D. Gelernter. A CASE environment for parallel programming. In *Proc. Fifth International Workshop on Computer-Aided Software Engineering*, July 1992.
2. R. Bjornson. *Linda on Distributed-Memory Multiprocessors*. PhD thesis, Yale University Department of Computer Science, New Haven, Connecticut, 1992. Department of Computer Science, RR-931.
3. N. Carriero, E. Freeman, D. Gelernter, and D. Kaminsky. Adaptive parallelism and Piranha. *IEEE Computer*, 28(4), Jan. 1995.
4. N. Carriero and D. Gelernter. A foundation for advanced compile-time analysis of Linda programs. In U. Banerjee, D. Gelernter, A. Nicolau, and D. Padua, editors, *Languages and Compilers for Parallel Computing*, number 589 in Lecture Notes in Computer Science. Springer Verlag, Berlin, 1992.
5. N. J. Carriero. An implementation of Linda for a NUMA machine, 1997. Submitted.
6. N. J. Carriero, D. H. Gelernter, T. G. Mattson, and A. H. Sherman. The Linda alternative to message-passing systems. *Parallel Computing*, 20:633–655, Apr. 1994.
7. P. Ciancarini and D. Rossi. Jada: Coordination and Communication for Java agents. In J. Vitek and C. Tschudin, editors, *Mobile Object Systems: Towards the Programmable Internet*, volume 1222, pages 213–228. 1997.
8. M. Factor. *The Process Trellis Software Architecture for Parallel, Real-Time Monitors*. PhD thesis, Yale University Department of Computer Science, 1990.
9. A. Geist, A. Beguelin, J. Dongarra, W. Jiang, R. Manchek, and V. Sunderam. *PVM: Parallel Virtual Machine. A Users' Guide and Tutorial for Networked Parallel Computing*. MIT Press, 1994. ISBN 0-262-57108-0.
10. W. Gropp, E. Lusk, and A. Skjellum. *Using MPI*. MIT Press, 1994. ISBN 0-262-57104-8.
11. S. Hupfer. *Turingware: An Integrated Approach to Collaborative Computing*. PhD thesis, Yale University Department of Computer Science, New Haven, Connecticut, 1996.
12. JavaSoft.
   http://chatsubo.javasoft.com/
           arnold/jse_overview/jse_overview.fm22.html.
13. Scientific Computing Associates, New Haven, CT. *Paradise: User's Guide and Reference Manual*, 1994.

Exposing the Skeleton in the Coordination Closet

Jeff Kramer and Jeff Magee

Department of Computing
Imperial College of Science, Technology and Medicine,
London SW7 2BZ, UK.

{jk,jnm}@doc.ic.ac.uk

Abstract
One of the ways in which we cope with large and complex systems is to abstract away some of the detail, considering them at an architectural level as compositions of interacting components. To this end, the variously termed Coordination, Configuration and Architectural Description Languages (ADL) facilitate description, comprehension and reasoning at that level, providing a clean separation between individual component behaviour and their interaction in a software architecture. However, in the search to provide sufficient detail for reasoning, analysis or construction, many approaches are in danger of obscuring the essential structural aspect of the architecture, thereby losing the benefit of abstraction. In this paper we argue for the use of a concise and simple language explicitly designed for describing architectural structures. This can be used to provide the "skeleton" upon which to add the particular details of concern when necessary. Systems described in this way have an explicit and exposed skeleton which, being shared, helps to maintain consistency between the various elaborated views. To illustrate our approach, we use the Darwin architectural description language and the Tracta approach for compositional reachability analysis.

1. Introduction

For over 15 years we have been involved in research into the design and construction of distributed software systems. Our experience is that structuring systems as interacting components is essential to help deal with the scale, complexity and evolution involved. In particular, the associated use of *compositional* techniques facilitates the use of hierarchies and levels of abstraction in the design process, compositional analysis in the checking and reasoning process, and incremental subsystem construction in the implementation process. We are therefore strong advocates for early consideration of the structural/architectural aspects of a system. Like others [AG94, Bar93, Gol95, GP95, Gra91, Luc95, Pur94, Sh95a], we recognised the need to *separate the structural description* from that of the individual components.

Our first realisation of this approach was in the Conic environment [KMS84, MKS89]. The explicit and separate structural language was referred to as a *configuration language*, describing as it did the component configuration of the system to be constructed. Experience with Conic indicated that the approach was highly beneficial for system comprehension, construction and evolution[KMF90], including dynamic configuration [KM85, KM90]. The principles underlying the approach, termed Configuration Programming [Kra90, KMN89], were articulated as shown in Table 1. As indicated, these principles were also adapted for application to system behaviour specification and analysis. The philosophy here is that the problem of consistency between the system to be constructed and the model to be analysed can be greatly ameliorated if they share a common structure. We illustrate this later in the paper.

Description and Construction	Specification and Analysis
"1. The *configuration language* used for structural description should be separate from the programming language used for basic component programming. 2. *Components* should be defined as context independent types with well-defined interfaces. 3. Using the configuration language, complex components should be definable as a *composition* of instances of component types. 4. *Change* should be expressed at the configuration level, as changes of the component instances and/or their interconnections."	"1. The *configuration language* used for structural specification should be separate from the specification language used for specifying component behaviour. 2. *Component specifications* should specify the visible behaviour at the component interface. 3. Using the configuration language, complex specifications should be definable as a *composition* of component specifications. 4. *Change* should be expressed at the configuration level, as changes of the constituent component specifications and/or their interaction."

Table 1. Configuration Language Principles

Our experience with Conic, and that of our industrial and research users, was very positive. A number of industrial systems were constructed using Conic directly or based on its approach. In addition it was widely used in teaching distributed programming. Its success was undoubtedly due to the use of the separate configuration language and the support for component composition. However, it highlighted a number of shortcomings that needed further investigation. In particular, the Conic configuration language was found to be too closely tied to the implementation level. The configuration language retained a number of dependencies on the programming language (Pascal) which was used for programming the components, defining the interfaces and providing the fixed set of interaction primitives. This lack of independence made the configuration language less suitable as a purely structural specification for the composition of component behaviours.

What was needed was a cleaner and clearer separation of concerns: a purely structural language that could describe system structure in a manner independent of both the computation and the interaction (communication) aspects. This led to Darwin, a language for describing software structure in terms of components and their bindings. Darwin is a pure declarative language, with sound semantics [MDE95, MK96]. Again, we (and others) have had wide experience of its use to describe and construct distributed systems for a number of execution platforms including Regis [MDK94] (our own platform) and CORBA [MTK97]. However, as indicated above, our aim is to use Darwin as the framework for also specifying the component structure and their potential interactions for behaviour analysis. Darwin has therefore been designed to be sufficiently abstract to support multiple views (cf. [Kru95]), two of which are the behavioural view (for behaviour analysis) and the service view (for construction) (Figure 1). Each view is an elaboration of the basic structural view: the skeleton upon which we hang the flesh of behaviour specification or service implementation.

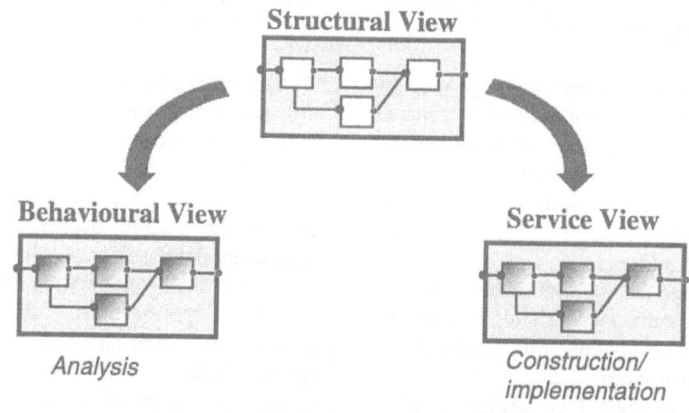

Figure 1. Common Structural View with Service and Behavioural Views

In previous papers we have discussed the use of Darwin to produce the service view, with components providing and requiring services at their interfaces and with implementation elaborations for the primitive components. In this paper we concentrate on the behavioural view using labelled transition systems (LTS) for behaviour specification and analysis. We have chosen to use LTS as it supports the appropriate compositionality (using Compositional Reachability Analysis CRA) with the components specified simply as finite state processes (FSP) [GKC97]. In addition, we have techniques for ameliorating the problem of exponential state explosion [CK96a] and for analysing for both safety [CK96b] and liveness [CGK97] properties. This is supported by software tools which provide for automatic composition, analysis, minimisation, animation and graphical display. Rather than describe the underlying theory or details of the analysis techniques and their relation to Darwin, we use a simple example to illustrate our approach. For the sake of brevity, we make no attempt in this paper to compare our work with that of others. Instead we merely try to indicate some points that we believe are important based on our experience in using Darwin/LTS for specification and reasoning.

2. Architectural Design and Analysis: An Example

In this section we use a small and familiar example to illustrate our approach: the Cruise Control System [Sh95b]. This can be briefly described as follows:

> An automobile cruise control system is controlled by three buttons: *resume, on* and *off*. When the engine is running and on is pressed, the cruise control system records the current speed and maintains the car at this speed. When the accelerator, brake or off is pressed, the cruise control system disengages but retains the speed setting. If resume is pressed, the system accelerates or deaccelerates the car back to the previously recorded speed.

2.1 Design

Any design approach may be used to provide an outline design and decomposition into components. Figure 2 indicates an initial design as an overview diagram. As indicated, the Cruise Controller receives events from the buttons, brake, accelerator and engine. The speed is monitored by counting wheel revolutions over a period. Depending on the circumstances, the Cruise Controller triggers clear speed (Tc) or record speed (Tr), and enables (Es) or disables (Ds) speed control. We can group the

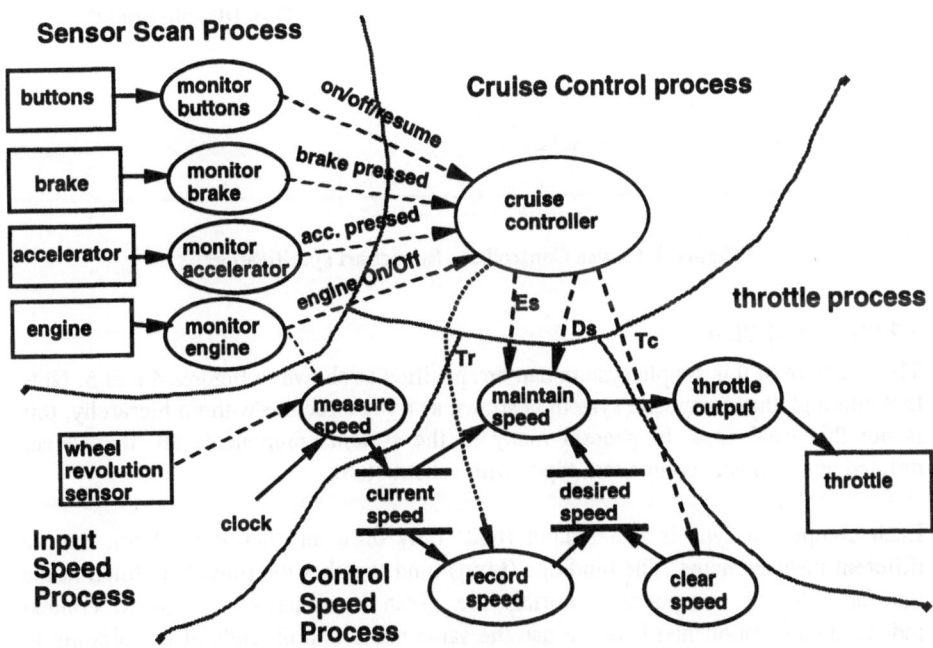

**Figure 2. Cruise control system - overview diagram
partitioned into component processes**

sensor scanning, speed input, speed control, cruise controller and throttle control into process components as shown in Figure 2. In this way, the sensor scan component encapsulates (information hiding) the periodic process of scanning the sensors, the cruise controller encapsulates the decision as to when speed maintenance is activated, and the speed control encapsulates how to maintain speed. The behaviour of the cruise controller component can be specified using a statechart (Figure 3). For instance, this indicates that clear speed is triggered and the cruise controller becomes active when the engine is switched on. Pressing the on button then triggers recording the current speed, enables the speed control and the system is then cruising. Pressing the off button, brake or accelerator disables the speed control and sets the system to standby. Switching the engine off at any time makes the system inactive.

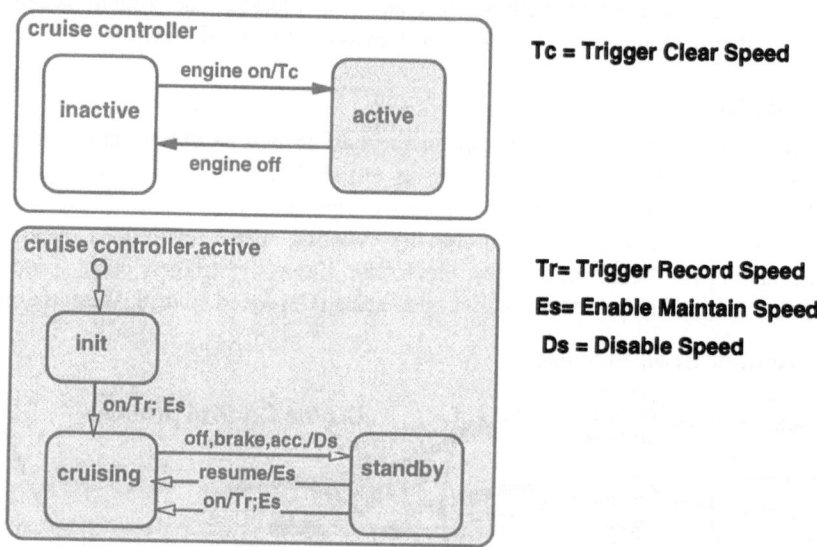

Tc = Trigger Clear Speed

Tr= Trigger Record Speed
Es= Enable Maintain Speed
Ds = Disable Speed

Figure 3. Cruise Controller – Statechart specification.

2.2 Structural View

The structure of this simple system can be specified as shown in Figures 4 and 5. Note that although this composite system is shown as a flat structure with no hierarchy, this is not the usual case. In general many of the system components are themselves defined as composite component types with substructure.

Each component type is instantiated (**inst**) only once and hence need not have a different instance name. The bindings (**bind**) bind together the **portals** defined at the interfaces to the components. Portals are given local names to ensure context independent components; here we use the same name at both ends of the binding to reduce name proliferation as there is no name ambiguity. At this structure level, **interfaces** are simply a set of names referring to the actions or events shared with bound components. Here the interface types are defined as:

```
interface setThrottle { }
interface speed { }
interface prompts {tc; tr; es; ds;}
```

```
interface sensors {engineOn; engineOff; on; off;
                    resume; brake; acc;}
interface engine {engineOn; engineOff;}
```

Darwin can check for any action/event name clashes i.e. a name that is exposed at different component interfaces but is not explicitly shared through a binding.

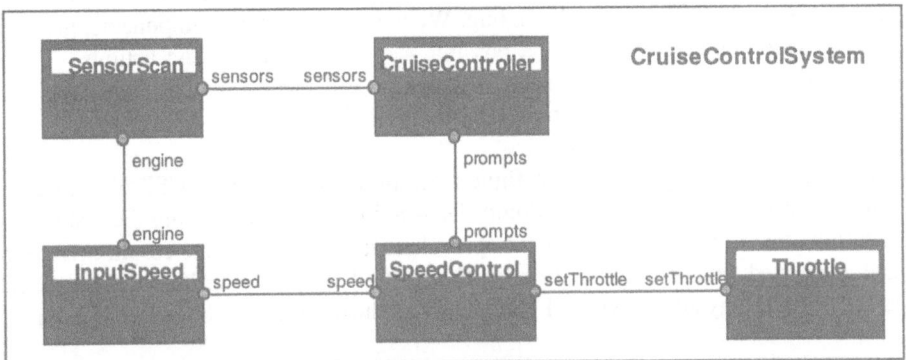

Figure 4. Cruise Control System – Darwin graphical representation

```
component CruiseControlSystem {
    inst
        SensorScan;
        CruiseController;
        InputSpeed;
        SpeedControl;
        Throttle;
    bind
        SensorScan.sensors -- CruiseController.sensors;
        SensorScan.engine -- InputSpeed.engine;
        CruiseController.prompts -- SpeedControl.prompts;
        InputSpeed.speed -- SpeedControl.speed;
        SpeedControl.setThrottle -- Throttle.setThrottle;
}

component SensorScan {
    portal
        sensors;
        engine;
}

component CruiseController {
    portal
        sensors;
        prompts;
}

. . . . . .
```

Figure 5. Cruise Control System – Darwin textual representation.

2.3 Analysis

In order to gain confidence in the correctness of our design, we now provide the behavioural view of our design architecture. Darwin indicates the system structure in terms of component instances and the interconnections by giving the bindings and communicated (shared) actions/events. This can be used to provide renaming of events between processes. This is not necessary in our example as we have used the same names at both ends of each binding. We model each of the components, giving a process specification indicating the possible sequence of events and actions. These are then composed according to an instance of the architecture. In this case, the architecture specifies only one possible instantiation[1].

Each component is specified as a finite state process (FSP) in a CSP-like notation [Hoa85] as shown below[2]. CruiseController is a direct translation from the state chart specification. The events that trigger state chart transitions and the resulting actions and generated events (Figure 3) are all specified as FSP transitions. Component specifications may also be viewed graphically as shown in Figure 6 for InputSpeed.

```
// Sensor Scan Specification
SensorScan =({on,off,resume,brake,acc,engineOn,engineOff} ->
                 SensorScan ).

// Speed Measurement Specification
InputSpeed =( engineOn -> CheckSpeed),
CheckSpeed =( measureSpeed -> speed -> CheckSpeed |
             engineOff -> InputSpeed ).

// Speed Control Specification
SpeedControl = Disabled,
Disabled =    (speed -> Disabled |
       tc -> clearSpeed -> Disabled |
       tr -> recordSpeed -> Disabled |
       es -> enableSpeedControl -> Enabled |
       ds -> disableSpeedControl -> Disabled),
Enabled =
          (speed -> maintainSpeed -> setThrottle -> Enabled |
       tr -> recordSpeed -> Enabled |
       es -> enableSpeedControl -> Enabled |
       ds -> disableSpeedControl -> Disabled).

// Throttle Specification
Throttle = (setThrottle -> Throttle).
```

---

[1] Darwin architectures can include parameterised component types, conditional inst and bind clauses, replication, recursion and even dynamic structures. Thus Darwin generally describes an architecture which can be instantiated to create many possible system instances.

[2] As for Darwin, the FSP and LTS specifications shown here do not illustrate the full power of the specification language which can include parameterised specifications, indexed events and processes, and safety and liveness properties.

```
// Cruise Controller Specification
CruiseController = Inactive,
Inactive    = (engineOn -> tc -> Active),
Active      = (engineOff -> Inactive |
               on -> tr -> es -> Cruising),
Cruising    = (engineOff -> Inactive |
               {off,brake,acc} -> ds -> Standby),
Standby     = (engineOff -> Inactive |
               resume -> es -> Cruising |
               on -> tr -> es -> Cruising).
```

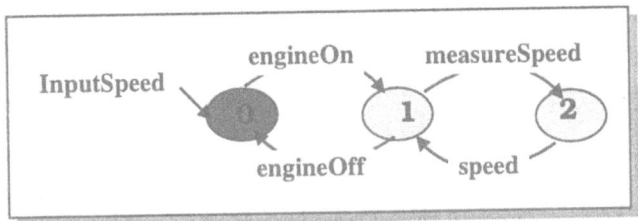

Figure 6. Graphic representation of InputSpeed

As mentioned, Darwin can be used to generate the composite system specification for the system CRUISE including any necessary name hiding and/or renaming. Transition name hiding can be used to hide actions/events not visible at a component interface. The result is a composite LTS which can be subjected to analysis and/or used for animation and experimentation.

```
||CRUISE = (SensorScan || CruiseController ||
            InputSpeed || SpeedControl || Throttle).
```

This system is modelled as an LTS with shared actions to synchronise processes. Although an action/event may be shared by many processes, we usually only share it between two processes. We can check the system for deadlock and for different safety and liveness properties. *How do we know which properties to verify? what test cases to check for?* The *requirements specification* may indicate desired and undesired properties and scenarios. Additionally, *animation* and *experimentation*, which support stepping through the permissible actions/events, may indicate problems and/or properties to be preserved.

We start by composing the cruise control system, using reachability analysis to test for *deadlock*. We can also experiment by stepping through the system using different test scenarios...

- does it enable the system after the engine is switched on and on is pressed?
- does it disable the system when the brake is pressed?
- does it enable the system when resume is pressed?
- does it disable the system when the engine is switched off?

Reachability analysis indicates that there is no deadlock. However, animation of the scenarios indicates that there is a problem with the CruiseController when cruising and the engine is switched off and then on again[3]. This is not obvious when examining the composed state diagram for the system (resulting in 81 states). However, it is clear after hiding some of the internal events and actions - exposing only the user controlled events indicated by operator "@" - and mimimising the resulting LTS (resulting in 6 states as shown in Figure 7):

```
||CRUISEhide = (CRUISE) @ {engineOn, engineOff, on, off,
                                   brake, acc, resume}.
```

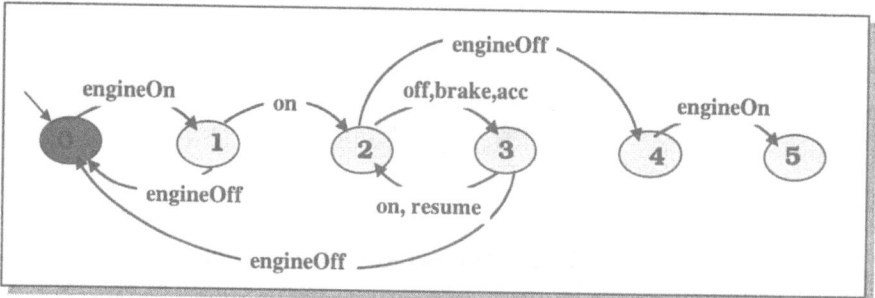

Figure 7. Minimised LTS for the erroneous Cruise Control System.

This undesirable situation can be checked by specifying a safety property that is required from the system. Safety properties are composed with the system [CK96b]; analysis then indicates whether or not the composed property is violated. The safety property required here is that, if the cruise control system is in operation, then it is always disabled if the brake or accelerator is pressed, or if it is switched off, or if the engine is switched off:

```
property SafetyProperty =( {off,acc,brake,engineOff,ds,engineOn}
                                    -> SafetyProperty |
                            {on,resume} -> SafetyCheck),
           SafetyCheck  = ( {on,resume} -> SafetyCheck |
                            {off,acc,brake,engineOff} ->
                                          SafetyAction),
           SafetyAction =   (ds -> SafetyProperty).
```

In this case, testing the cruise system against the property will indicate a violation and provide a trace which leads to that violation.

```
||CRUISEtest = (CRUISE || SafetyProperty).
```

The analysis tool composes the system and produces the following output:

```
Composition:
CRUISEtest = CRUISE || SafetyProperty
```

---

[3] The Cruise Control example has been used for over 3 years for teaching in one of our courses. This rather embarrassing error was only recently discovered while animating the LTS Cruise model.

```
State Space:
 57 * 3 = 171
Composing
 property SafetyProperty violation.
States Composed: 49 Transitions: 120 in 0ms
```

If requested, the analysis tool will also produce a trace that lead to the violation :

```
Trace to property violation in SafetyProperty:
                engineOn
                tc
                on
                clearSpeed
                tr
                recordSpeed
                es
                engineOff
                engineOn
```

We can easily fix the cruise controller by disabling the speed control when the engine is switched off:

```
...
Cruising = (engineOff -> ds -> Inactive |
            {off,brake,acc}-> ds -> Standby),
...
```

If we now reanalyse our cruise system with hiding, we can reassure ourselves that there is now no violation of the safety property, and can also examine the resulting minimised LTS (Figure 8).

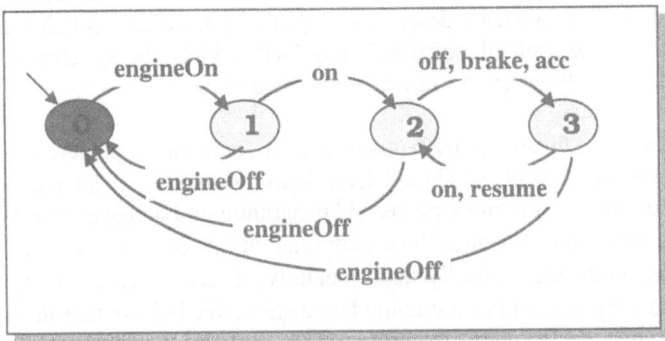

Figure 8. Minimised LTS for the fixed Cruise Control System

2.4 Tool Support

We have briefly and informally demonstrated the process of gaining confidence in a particular Darwin structural architecture and component behaviour. Desired properties can be verified and the system exercised to ensure that it provides the required behaviour. We strongly believe in this process of defining architectural structures, specifying component behaviours and performing behaviour analysis. We believe that it must be easy to do and easy to make changes so as to facilitate experimentation. This demands that there should be tool support which is quick and easy to use. For a number of years we have been working on graphic support tools for Darwin - the System Architect's Assistant [NKM96] – and analysis tools for LTS – the TRACTA tools [GKC97]. These are currently being reimplemented in Java to make them more accessible, easier to use and more flexible so as to support the multiple views. It is beyond the scope of this paper to describe these in detail, but suffice to say that the availability of tools has had a major effect on the utility of the approach and the speed with which new examples and case studies have been specified and analysed.

2.5 Service View - Implementation

The Darwin structural architecture for the cruise control system could now be refined to provide the service view necessary for implementation and construction, possibly as a distributed program with components allocated to machines as desired. Primitive components would be provided with implementations, possibly as CORBA objects [MTK97].

3. Conclusions

In this paper we have argued for the use of a concise and simple language explicitly designed for describing architectural structures. These descriptions must be clear and precise. We should therefore try to avoid the temptation to extend the *language* to include other additional concerns. Rather we believe that it is the system architecture itself that should provide the "skeleton" upon which to add the particular details of concern for that view. Systems described in this way have an explicit and exposed skeleton (hence "exoskeletal software" [Kra94]) which, being shared, helps to maintain consistency between the various elaborated views.

Over 20 years ago Dijkstra [Dij72] made a plea for simple, modest programming languages: "Another lesson we should have learnt from the recent past is that the development of "richer" or "more powerful" programming languages was a mistake in the sense that these monstrosities, these conglomerations of idiosyncrasies, are really unmanageable, both mechanically and mentally. I see a great future for very systematic and very modest programming languages". We believe that this is still true and applies just as strongly to those languages proposed for configuration, coordination or architectural description. It is not a plea for primitive languages, no matter how well founded, but rather for modest, practical languages which can be shown to be useful for the purpose at hand.

We have used the Darwin architectural description language and the Tracta approach for compositional reachability analysis to illustrate the close relationship between the process of composing components to build systems and the process of composing component behaviours for systems analysis. We have argued that tool support is essential in order to make the architectural approach practical. This is particularly important in software evolution and maintenance. We must ensure that it is easier to change the architecture, reanalyse and regenerate the system than it is to hack the code directly. We are continuing to work with our industrial users to test the validity and utility of the approach and tools, and hope to gain more experience with real case studies, particularly in the discovery and specification of system properties.

Acknowledgements

The authors would like to acknowledge discussions with our colleagues in the Distributed Software Engineering Group during the formulation of these ideas. In particular we would like to thank Dimitra Giannakopoulou, Naranker Dulay, Keng Ng and Shing Chi Cheung. We gratefully acknowledge the EPSRC (Grant Ref: SAA GR/J52693 and TRACTA GR/J 87022) and the EU (ARES Framework IV contract 20477) for their financial support.

References

AG94   Allen R. and Garlan D., *Formalizing Architectural Connection*, (Proc. of 16th International Conference on Software Engineering (ICSE 16), Sorrento, May 1994, 71-80.

Bar 93   Barbacci M. et al, *Durra: a structure description language for developing distributed applications*, IEE Software Engineering Journal, Vol. 8, No. 2, March 1993, pp83-94.

CK96a   Cheung S.C. and Kramer J., *Context Constraints for Compositional Reachability Analysis*, ACM Transactions on Software Engineering Methodology TOSEM, 5 (4), (1996), 334-377.

CK96b   Cheung S.C. and Kramer J., *Checking Subsystem Safety Properties in Compositional Reachability Analysis*, (Proc. of 18th IEEE Int. Conf. on Software Engineering (ICSE-18), Berlin, 1996), 144-154.

CGK97   Cheung S.C., Giannakopoulou D., and Kramer J., *Verification of Liveness Properties using Compositional Reachability Analysis*, accepted for (6th European Software Engineering Conference / 5th ACM SIGSOFT Symposium on the Foundations of Software Engineering (ESEC/FSE 97), Zurich, Sept. 1997).

Dij72   Dijkstra E.W., *The Humble Programmer*, Comms. Of the ACM, 15, 10, 859-866, Oct. 1972.

GKC97   Giannakopoulou D., Kramer J. and Cheung S.C., *TRACTA: An Environment for Analysing the Behaviour of Distributed Systems*, (Proc. of 1st ACM SIGPLAN Workshop on Automatic Analysis of Software (AAS '97)), Paris, January 1997, 113-126.

GP95   Garlan D. and Perry D.E., *Introduction to the Special Issue on Software Architecture*, IEEE Transactions on Software Engineering, 21 (4), April 1995, pp 269-274.

Gol95   Goldman, K.J., *The Programmers' Playground: I/O Abstraction for User-Configurable Distributed Applications*, IEEE Trans. on Software Eng., SE-21 (9), (1995), 735-746.

Gra91 Graves, H., *Lockheed Environment for Automatic Programming*, Proc. of KBSE 91, 6th IEEE Knowledge Based Software Engineering Conference, 1991, pp 68-76.

Hoa85 Hoare, C.A.R., *Communicating Sequential Processes*, Prentice-Hall, Englewood Cliffs, N.J., 1985.

KMS84 Kramer J., Magee J. and Sloman M.S. *A Software Architecture for Distributed Computer Control Systems*, Automatica, 20, (1984), 93-102.

KM85 Kramer J. and Magee J., *Dynamic Configuration for Distributed Systems*, IEEE Trans. on Software Eng., SE-11 (4), (1985), 424-436.

KMN89 Kramer J. Magee J. and Ng K., *Graphical Configuration Programming*, IEEE Computer, 22 (10), (1989), 53-65.

KMF90 Kramer J., Magee J. and Finkelstein A., *A Constructive Approach to the Design of Distributed Systems*, (Proc. 10th IEEE Int. Conf'on Distributed Computing Systems, Paris, 1990), 580-587.

KM90 Kramer J. and Magee J., *The Evolving Philosophers Problem: Dynamic Change Management*, IEEE Trans. on Software Eng., SE-16 (11), (1990), 1293-1306.

Kra90 Kramer J., *Configuration Programming - A Framework for the Development of Distributable Systems*, (Proc. of IEEE Int. Conf. on Computer Systems and Software Engineering (CompEuro 90), Tel-Aviv, Israel, 1990), 374-384.

Kra94 Kramer J., *Exoskeletal Software*, (Proc. of 16th IEEE Int. Conf. on Software Engineering (ICSE-16), Sorrento, 1994), 366.

Kru95 Kruchten P.B., The 4+1 Model of Architecture, IEEE Software, 12 (6), Nov. 1995, pp 42-50.

Luc95 Luckham D.C. et al., *Specification and Analysis of Software Architecture using Rapide*, IEEE Transactions on Software Engineering, 21(4), April 1995, pp 336-355.

MDE95 Magee J., Dulay N., Eisenbach S., Kramer J., *Specifying Distributed Software Architectures*, (Proc. of 5th European Software Engineering Conference (ESEC '95), Sitges, September 1995), LNCS 989, (Springer-Verlag), 1995, 137-153.

MDK94 Magee J., Dulay N. and Kramer J., *Regis: A Constructive Development Environment for Distributed Programs*, Distributed Systems Engineering Journal, 1 (5), Special Issue on Configurable Distributed Systems, (1994), 304-312.

MKS89 Magee J., Kramer J., and Sloman M.S., *Constructing Distributed Systems in Conic*, IEEE Trans. on Software Eng., SE-15 (6), (1989), 663-675.

MK96 Magee J. and Kramer J., *Dynamic Structure in Software Architectures*, (Proc. of 4th ACM SIGSOFT Symposium on the Foundations of Software Engineering (FSE 4), San Francisco, October 1996), SEN, Vol.21, No.6, November 1996, 3-14.

MTK97 Magee J., Tseng A., Kramer J., *Composing Distributed Objects in CORBA*, (Third International Symposium on Autonomous Decentralized Systems (ISADS 97), Berlin, Germany, April 9 - 11, 1997.

NMK96   Ng K., Kramer J. and Magee J., *Automated Support for the Design of Distributed Software Architectures*, Journal of Automated Software Engineering (JASE), 3 (3/4), Special Issue on CASE-95, (1996), 261-284.

Pur94   Purtilo J.M., *The POLYLITH Software Bus*, ACM Transactions on Programming Languages, 16(1), January 1994, pp 151-174.

Sh95a   Shaw M., et al., *Abstractions for Software Architecture and Tools to Support Them*, IEEE Transactions on Software Engineering, 21 (4), April 1995, pp 314-335.

Sh95b   Shaw M., *Comparing Architectural Design Styles* IEEE Software, 12 (6), Nov. 1995, pp 27-41.

Tay96   Taylor R. et al, *A Component- and Message-based Architectural Style for GUI Software*, IEEE Transactions on Software Engineering, 22(6), June 1996, pp 390-406.

Design for Open Systems in Java

Doug Lea

State University of New York at Oswego

Abstract. Open systems consist of unbounded collections of objects that may interact in support of any of a number of activities. The features and services provided by each object require various measures of policy control of infrastructure components in order to provide appropriate quality of service for supported activities. This paper surveys some common and emerging Java-based design patterns for establishing and controlling service and application components in open object-oriented architectures.

1 Objects and Activities

The design of object-oriented open systems has two principal foci:

Objects. Encapsulated, typically reactive components with state, identity, and behavior, possibly distributed across space [37,24]. The nature of these components range from ADTs to standard OOP objects to framework-based components to actors[15], and everything in between.

Activities. In various contexts, activities are variously termed threads, sessions [8], (realized) scenarios, scripts, use cases [6], transactions, mobile computations, and distributed algorithms, that flow across a set of objects passing messages to one another in the course of carrying out some kind of functionality.

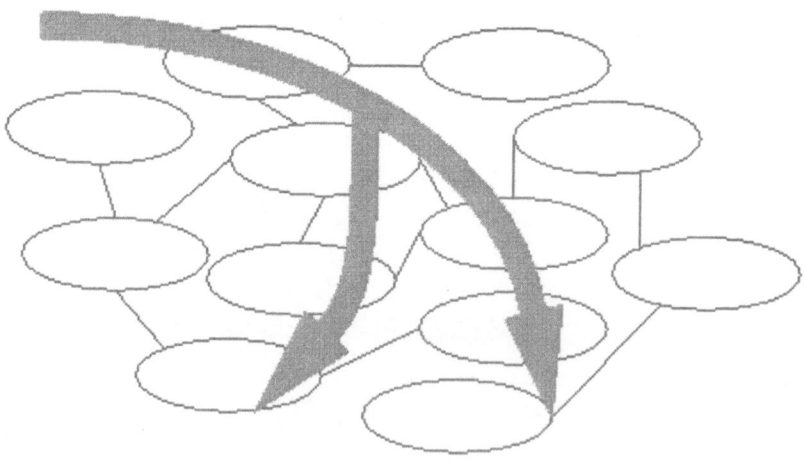

The tension between these two facets of design is captured in the OO notion of *responsibility* [38]. To quote Kent Beck [3]:

> If we're always programming from the outside, how do we ever get anything done? I definitely change gears between "what services does this object provide?" or "how do these services divide between these objects?" to "how am I going to accomplish *that*?", sometimes several times a minute (sometimes days go by).

These concerns apply even to in-the-small OO programming. But they become accentuated in the development of open systems, in particular those developed in Java^{tm}. The Java programming language was created in part as platform for open, distributed, reactive, concurrent applications. Java-based components, frameworks, infrastructures, and systems are currently being rapidly developed and deployed. This paper explores some occasionally disguised aspects of responsibility-driven design seen in the development of Java-based open systems.

2 Encapsulating Services

Activities running on open systems demand a certain *quality of service* (QoS) that increasingly requires that the associated objects support features or *aspects* [20] that improve the reliability, performance, generality, and reusability of their functionality. They include:

Concurrency control	Protocol negotiation	Bandwidth negotiation	UI look and feel
Access Control	Authentication	Versioning	Indexing
Persistence	Memory management	Serialization	Storage layout
Administration	Accounting	Auditing	Mobility
Replication	Transport	Parallelism	Activation
Resource control	Flow control	Scheduling	Prioritization
Media synchronization	Load balancing	Buffering/Caching	Encryption

The presence, nature and control of QoS features differ from those of the basic services provided by higher-level objects. Typically, QoS features are not considered to be part of the interface describing the services provided by application objects (thus differ from application-level features [29,39]), but instead control the ways in which operations are carried out.

In many cases, the development of code dealing with such infrastructure issues represents the majority of effort in supporting an object's desired functionality. However, application-level objects generally do not perform these duties all by themselves, but instead obtain them with the help of infrastructure components.

The main division of responsibility is for infrastructure objects to supply basic mechanism, and for higher level objects to select the policies governing their use. The infrastructure components that help provide adequate QoS represent an extensible microkernel-style [34] computational substrate in which application-level objects choose only those combinations of services that they actually require.

Ideally, this common general architecture enables activities across application-level objects to be scripted using relatively simple protocols, for example those based on push or pull flow, blackboards, etc [23,30,7]. At yet coarser levels of granularity, these may in turn be treated as services.

2.1 The Demise of transparency

One strategy for simplifying the support of QoS features is to hide them via languages, tools, and frameworks that, whenever appropriate, transparently map invocations to remote procedure calls, assignment statements to secure database stores, loops to parallel vector operations, and so on. In Java, this may be arranged in any of several ways; for example:

- Code generation tools
- Preprocessors
- Adherence to special coding rules and conventions
- Specialized compilers
- Bytecode translators that input and output `.class` files
- Just-in-time translators
- Reflection
- Custom virtual machines

No matter how it is arranged, the basic idea is to intercept code (messages, instructions) and map it to alternative code that achieves the desired semantics.

As argued especially by Kiczales [21] and Waldo et al [36], transparency tends not to be a useful property of mappings to most service components. Reasons include:

1. Mappings alter semantics. For the most well-known examples, RPCs and network file accesses can fail in ways that local invocations and local file accesses cannot. Similarly, an invocation that spawns a new thread can introduce concurrency control issues that would not be encountered in a sequential setting. While it may be useful to support a construct that could be mapped to any of a local call or thread-based service or an RPC, folding them all into the same syntactic construct masks semantic differences that are sometimes essential to distinguish in practical applications.

2. More generally, transparency confuses *not caring* with *not knowing*. It is only *usually* possible to program applications that work equally effectively without caring that, for example, field accesses are automatically linked to database operations. However, not knowing if or how these are performed eliminates opportunities to perform other kinds of concurrency control when necessary and to tune performance.

3. Mappings intrinsically entail policy decisions, for example those surrounding failure handling, time-outs, sending copies versus references, optimistic versus pessimistic control, number of active threads, units of atomicity, consensus thresholds, buffer sizes, checkpointing frequency, and access rights. Except in those rare cases where these decisions are known to be optimal, the best general decisions are not always the best decisions in particular instances.

4. Efforts to hide the control information required by underlying services introduces artificial coding requirements and design limitations.
5. It is hard to get the abstractions right. Every implementation has quirks that show through. Developers must then "program between the lines" to deal with idiosyncracies that change over time as the abstractions are refactored and the implementations are improved.
6. Without the ability to tune existing services, developers find themselves essentially recreating entire infrastructures just so they can specialize or optimize certain aspects. Because they must live within existing constraints, these specialized versions are rarely as good or reusable as those built from scratch.
7. The presence or absence of each quality and feature affects high-level design and programming decisions. For example, people write distributed programs differently than they write otherwise equivalent multithreaded non-distributed programs, and write programs based on reliable multicast differently than those based on unreliable protocols.
8. Transparent services can be impossible to integrate with others. Services tend to be established near the bottom layer of translation, requiring exclusive control over the underlying machines, and eliminating opportunities to interpose other functionality. This in turn leads to the development of heavy, monolithic infrastructures, providing inflexibly integrated combinations of services.

In light of such observations and experiences, infrastructure services tend to become less transparent over time, transfering more and more responsibility for policy control to applications. Moreover, allowing explicit control often leads to entire categories of design and implementation techniques. Examples include:

- Distribution: Asynchronous protocols
- Parallelism: Active objects
- Database: Transactional objects
- Location: Mobile agents
- Callers: Authentication
- GUI: Pluggable Toolkits
- System services: Extensible microkernels
- CPU Instructions: RISC

While these trends open up opportunities for developing better software, they also open up new design and programming challenges. The remainder of this paper briefly surveys some emerging design patterns seen in the development of open systems software.

3   Structuring Services

3.1   Bindings

Components and systems supporting flexible policies require programmatic control of the bindings linking high-level invocations to particular mechanisms. There are many roughly similar techniques for structuring services and applications to allow this. Among the best and most common is to use delegation-based approaches (most of which are variants of the Strategy design pattern[12,13]) where:

1. Each service type is described via an interface.
2. Each policy variant is encapsulated as a class implementing one or more service interfaces.
3. Clients (application-level objects) somehow obtain a reference to an appropriate delegate object for each required service.
4. Clients obtain each service by invoking an appropriate method on an appropriate delegate.

For example, an `Account deposit` operation that conceptually just accepts an amount to add to a current balance might be expanded into something like:

```
class Account { // ...
  void deposit(long amount, ...) {
    authenticator.authenticate(clientID);
    accessController.checkAccess(clientID, acl);
    logger.logDeposit(clientID, transID, amount);
    replicate.shadowDeposit(...);
    db.checkpoint(this);
    lock.acquire(...);
    long newBalance = amount + balance;
    lock.release(...);
    db.commit(newBalance, ...)
    UIObservers.notifyOfChange(this);
  }
}
```

Less simple examples include methods for editing documents in groupware systems, approving claims in workflow systems, and estimating current external state in process control applications.

Delegate binding can be indirectly specified. Rather than providing a reference to a delegate, parameterization can be achieved by specifying desired attributes (in which case the closest matching object, or composite of objects[35] is chosen), or selecting from a set of predetermined choices [27], or supplying control constants (e.g., buffer sizes) for a parameterized family of services, or mediating via a Factory[12]. Also, a set of default choices can be provided. Defaults may even vary across time as a result of self-monitoring. Any of these techniques may be used to help ensure that consistent sets of policies are chosen. Ultimately, correctness relies on appropriate component specification and documentation techniques [10].

A few additional variants and alternatives along these lines are mentioned as they arise below. However, without too much loss of generality, subsequent examples illustrate only simple delegation-based bindings.

3.2 Control flow

Invocations of flexible QoS operations need not lead to strictly sequential effects. Outcomes need not even have any direct bearing on the functionality of the object performing the invocation.

Nearly every such invocation serves as a *gate*. Gates may *pass*, possibly returning a value that is needed at another gate, or behave non-procedurally in either of two ways:

1. Block the current activity, waiting for a condition or event to occur, ultimately passing if it does.
2. Fail (normally by throwing an exception)

In open systems, blocking is frequently valuable at the application level, but less so at the infrastructure level [14].

- It is often impossible to state with confidence that a condition change or event performed by some other activity will ever occur, or whether its occurrence will always lead to successful continuation of the current activity.
- Systems cannot afford to tie up resources associated with indefinitely blocked tasks.
- Blocking may reduce service availability
- Detection of deadlocks is often too expensive.
- Failure-based optimistic protocols often outperform conservative blocking protocols.

These concerns lead blocking protocols to be used sparingly in service components, often only for basic synchronization of memory reads and writes.

But even one kind of non-procedural outcome intrinsically adds complexity: Every invocation leads to a potential branch in control. Without compensating effort, many of them lead to *partial* failures of higher level functionality. Most design techniques address this by attempting to replace partial failures with retryable total failures, as seen in transaction frameworks, barrier synchronization algorithms, and reliable network protocols [4]. However, arranging for clean total failure intrinsically requires the involvement of high-level objects, thus contributing additional programmer obligations and code bloat. Additionally, while total failure is a useful goal, it is not always attainable or even desirable:

- Some actions are intrinisically non-reversable, so actions cannot be completely rolled back.
- Programmers of higher-level components are not always able to make well-reasoned judgements about what to do in case of failure, so the infrastructure components themselves must have the ability to provide at least reasonable default handling.
- Some failures are not reliably detectable; detectors can false-alarm.
- Coordination of failure handling across infrastructure components can lead to undesirable couplings among them.

The most flexible solutions entail further parameterization, for example providing continuation callback targets for each failure condition, and, when possible, organizing handlers into larger units. However, this can make the resulting application-level code even harder to write and understand without the use of special development tools that can help organize this kind of event-style processing code, where every method is split into continuations:

```
class App {
  void mainAction(...) {
    local state change;
    delegate1.svc1(..)
  }
  void mainActionSvc1Callback(...) {
    local state change;
    delegate2.scv(...);
  }
  void mainActionSvc1FailureHandler(...) {
    // ...
  }
}
```

3.3 Layering

The ability to choose among and compose different sets of encapsulated services is attractive so long as there are not too many of them. However, classes such as the running `Account` example (especially when expanded out with exception handling) become burdensome to write: There are too many invocations, they must each use compatible policies, and they must be ordered in an appropriate manner.

The traditional solution to such problems is bottom-up layering. For example, starting with a `SimpleAccount` with a `deposit` operation that only updates balances, you could create a `LockableAccount` with a `deposit` operation that arranges before/after [23] locking code via either subclassing or delegation. (Alternatively, layered metaclasses [11] or designs relying on internally executed Command objects [12,17,2] could be used with equivalent effect.) And from there you could define for example a `PersistentLockableAccount`, and so on, to the point where application-level objects surround the next lower layer with only a few lines of processing.

This pure and simple form of layering works well when it applies. However, even in those domains where it has encountered its greatest successes, pure layering tends to apply sparingly. For example, despite ISO protocol stack definitions, common network services tend to have only three well-defined layers: data link, network, and end-to-end [34]. Similarly, layered concurrency control appears effective in practice only at a depth of two or three. [23,16].

Splicing. Some of the limitations of simple layering are addressed in several emerging design patterns and methods. The most common problem is that the conceptual layering of functionality does not always translate into before/after enclosure. Sometimes outer code must be spliced at any of several control points of the inner code. For example, optimistic concurrency control measures often entail four control points at which outer functionality can be invoked. This can be attained by introducing additional callable methods and callbacks in both the inner and the outer classes (introducing yet further parameterization)[26,16,31,10].

However, even these fail to apply when there is not a defensible dominance relation between one service and another (as often seen with security-related services). Program *weavers*, introduced in Aspect-Oriented Programming [20] extend splicing techniques to be usable in such cases via special programming languages and tools. Without such support, developers must provide manually woven solutions of the form illustrated in the above `Account` example.

4 Parameterization

Allocating responsibility for policy bindings emerges as one of the most central design issues in the design of services and components. There are four commonly used techniques for controlling bindings of families of services. Parameterization can be placed at the level of individual methods, objects, classes, and programs.

Methods. Each method can be parameterized with control information. For example:

```
void deposit(long amount,
             Authenticator authenticator,
             Identity clientID,
             AccessController accessController,
             ACL acl,
             TransactionID transID,
             Logger logger,
             FileDirectory workingDirectory, ...);
```

Objects. Each object can maintain references to delegates as instance variables, initialized upon construction. For example:

```
class Account {
  Authenticator authenticator;
  Identity clientID;
  AccessGuard accessChecker;
  ACL acl;
  Logger logger;
  // ...
  Account(Authenticator a, ...) // bind delegates
  void deposit(long amount);
}
```

Such classes may also support tuning interfaces [21,27] that rebind delegates; for example, method `setAuthenticator(Authenticator a)`.

Classes. There are several OO design patterns for parameterizing bindings at the class level. In languages such as C++ and Eiffel, this is usually most easily accomplished via parameterized (template) classes. In Java, the desired effects can be obtained via any of several variants of the *template method* subclassing pattern [12,23]. Each class can contain internal (`protected`) methods that return the appropriate delegate. Different parameterizations are achieved by creating subclasses that provide appropriate definitions of these methods. Among the implementation possibilities is:

```
abstract class AbstractAccount {
  protected abstract Authenticator authenticator();
  // ...
  void deposit(long amount) {
    authenticator().authenticate(...);
    // ...
  }
}

class ConcreteAccount extends AbstractAccount { // ...
  static Authenticator auth;
  protected Authenticator authenticator() { return auth; }
}
```

Programs. Bindings can be established globally, for example via Singletons maintaining delegates used by all objects. For example:

```
class Authenticator {
  static Authenticator theAuthenticator();
}

class Account {
  // ...
  void deposit(long amount) {
    Authenticator.theAuthenticator().authenticate(...);
    // ...
  }
}
```

Simpler forms of this solution are seen, for example in the Java `SecurityManager`.

Each of the above standard solutions are sometimes appropriate and useful. However, each has shortcomings:

- In per-method binding, each caller must explicitly choose parameters, thus mixing program logic with policy control. Each object along the path of some activity must deal with policy issues that it otherwise need not know about. For example, even though a `deposit` method need not deal directly with client IDs or working directory paths, it must relay this information to those components that do need to know. Moreover, there is no intrinsic means for ensuring consistency among control parameters across different objects and methods supporting a given activity.
- The number of per-method control parameters can grow without bound. Adding a parameter causes code in all callers to be changed. (This can be mitigated by defining overloaded versions that omit certain parameters, instead using defaults.)

- Per-object binding wires in information (such as client IDs here) that may cause objects to be too narrowly specialized.
- Allowing per-object bindings to vary dynamically via assignment-based tuning methods can lead to consistency errors if the object is concurrently available. The parameters in force for one activity need not hold for, and may conflict with, those for another.
- Policy control in per-class bindings becomes a compile-time decision. Objects cannot engage in multiple activities requiring different policies.
- Per-program bindings rely on the intrinsic fragility and error-proneness of employing centralized global information, especially in distributed applications, and cannot support multiple concurrent policies.

4.1 Contexts

Some parameterization problems can be addressed by factoring out bindings into distinct *Context* objects that maintain coherent sets of policy control settings. Policy contexts are just maps from names to delegate bindings. Context objects are commonly seen in several guises in open OO systems; for example in registries and naming services such as Java JNDI, in CORBA Contexts that are sent as hidden parameters, and in many objects implementing the Mediator design pattern [12]. While it is possible to support contexts as first-class language constructs [33,9,1], the effects can be obtained in Java without direct syntactic support. For example, a strongly typed version might look like:

```
class BankingContext {
  Authenticator authenticator();
  void setAuthenticator(Authenticator a);
  // ...
}

class Account {
  void deposit(long amount) {
    ctx().authenticator().authenticate(ctx.clientID());
    // ...
  }
}
```

Weakly-typed versions are also possible:

```
class Context {
  Object get(String name);
  void   set(String name, Object val);
  // ...
}
```

```
class Account {
  void deposit(long amount) {
    Authenticator a =
      (Authenticator)(ctx().get("authenticator"));
    a.authenticate(...)
    // ...
  }
}
```

Advantages of context-based control include:

– Isolation of policy control: enables prepackaging of groups of consistent settings.
– Simpler client usage: one parameter versus many.
– Simpler transmission of indirect control settings
– Simpler extensibility: new bindings can be introduced in subclasses (in strongly typed versions) or using new names or subcontexts.
– Simpler support for interpositioning: bindings can be spliced to insert instrumentation, etc.
– Simpler initialization: new contexts can branch off master contexts that provide most default settings.

The ctx() call in the above examples serves as a stand-in for any means of associating a given context object with a particular invocation. Any of the per-method, per-object, per-class, and per-program binding strategies could be employed. Additionally, encapsulation of binding contexts opens up two further options for allocating responsibility for policy control that would be clumsy at best without the use of context objects: per-session and per-group bindings.

Sessions. Contexts can be associated with entire activities, at least when they take the form of *sessions* that have well-defined starting points (and perhaps several branched end-points); for example, a user's session with a bank machine. Per-session context-based control has a diverse and spotty heritage, including:

– Transaction Coordinators
– Session-based network protocols
– Per-thread storage in thread packages
– Mobile agents that preserve dynamic execution state across nodes

Session-based policy control is probably most attractive when objects may support several concurrently available services, each a component of a possibly different activity. Additionally, session-based contexts may be used to capture settings (such as timing information) that become known or further constrained over the course of an activity. (In this sense, session-based contexts are analogous to first-class stack frames, as opposed to the nearly-first-class dispatch tables seen in per-object bindings.)

One tactic for implementing contextual control in non-distributed Java programs is to extend ThreadGroups. Java ThreadGroups can represent a set of subactivities all initiated from a common ancestor. Java supplies a means for any Java code to determine the ThreadGroup it is running under. This could be exploited via code such as:

```
class Account { // ...
  Context ctx() {
    ThreadGroup g =
      Thread.currentThread().getThreadGroup();
    return ((ExtendedThreadGroup)g).bindings();
  }
}
```

This style of session-based contextual control appears useful enough to deserve more direct support. For example, one can imagine a language in which contextual bindings were performed implicitly via a generalization of delegation-based method lookup. (Or viewed differently, as a generalization of transaction control protocols.) However, more elaborate designs are necessary to implement session-based control in distributed settings. These may entail, for example, transfer of bindings across the steps of a mobile computation.

Object Groups. A session is a set of activities all sharing a common ancestor. An object group is a set of objects all perhaps transiently sharing some common (often implicit) characteristics. The notion of a group extends the simple idea of membership in a collection or composite object to encompass common external access policies, common connectivity, common internal policies, and role-specific functionality [4,22]. Groups are sometimes implemented as extended forms of collections that additionally maintain and control shared context. For example, contexts may be managed in tuple spaces [25] such as JavaSpaces[32]. Alternatively, each member can individually replicate shared information when a member of a group, changing contexts when it joins and leaves different groups while assuming different roles.

4.2 Customization

Extensible parameterization of any form has an associated performance cost. However, techniques for optimizing away indirect bindings are well known, and can be applied (albeit with a sometimes large amount of effort) whenever bindings are knowable beforehand for any given method, session, object, group, class, or program. Nearly all of these techniques are based on some form of *customization*: generating special versions of code by partially evaluating with respect to fixed bindings[33,19,28,5]. Special cases include:

1. Exploiting trust among fixed sets of communicating objects optimizes away many security measures.
2. Precomputing fixed control paths across sessions speeds up protocols and enables better resource management.
3. Exploiting fixed known group communication partners enables use of more efficient protocols.
4. Exploiting statically shared context allows explicitly represented state information to be implicitly relied on.
5. Exploiting locality (same thread, machine, network) normally reduces overhead.

6. Exploiting known reachability, containment, and isolation patterns may enable components to be merged.

Tools or manual techniques for carrying these out may operate at any of the levels mentioned above for dealing with mappings. For example, *Configurators* [18] may be used to prearrange settings for incoming service requests, and analogs of the mechanisms that translate slow method lookups to Java *quick* VM instructions could be constructed at the bytecode level.

5 Conclusions

While they are simple at the core, contemporary open system architectures introduce design complexity for the sake of flexibility and extensibility. Several well-established and emerging design patterns represent current best efforts to solve practical design problems encountered in the development of open system components. These patterns may foreshadow advances in languages, methods, and tools that attack these problems more directly.

Acknowledgments. This work was supported in part by a grant from Sun Microsystems Laboratories.

References

1. Abadi, M. and L. Cardelli, *A Theory of Objects*, Springer Verlag, 1996.
2. Atkinson, M., L. Daynes, M. Jordan, T. Printezis and S. Spence, "An Orthogonally Persistent Java", *ACM SIGMOD Record* December 1996
3. Beck, K., posting to *patterns-discussion* mailing list, August, 1995.
4. Birman, K. and R. von Renesse. *Reliable Distributed Computing with the Isis Toolkit*, IEEE Press, 1994.
5. Birman, K., K. Guo, M. Hayden, T. Hickey, R. Friedman, S. Maffeis, R. van Renesse, A. Vaysburd, and W. Vogels, "The Ensemble groupware system", http://simon.cs.cornell.edu/Info/Projects/Ensemble, 1997.
6. Buhr, R. J. A., and R. S. Casselman, *Use Case Maps for Object-Oriented Systems*, Prentice Hall, 1995.
7. Buschmann, F., R. Meunier, H. Rohnert, P. Sommerlad, and M. Stal. *Pattern-Oriented Software Architecture: A System of Patterns*, Wiley, 1996.
8. Chandy, K. M. and A Rifkin, "Systematic composition of objects in distributed systems: Objects and Sessions" *International Conference on System Sciences*, 1997.
9. Dami, L. "A Lambda-calculus for dynamic binding", *Theoretical Computer Science*, 1997.
10. D'Souza, D., and A. Wills, "Composing modeling frameworks in Catalysis", *Communications of the ACM*, 1997.
11. Forman, I., and S. Danforth, "Inheritance of metaclass constraints in SOM", *Proceedings, Reflection 96*, 1996.
12. Gamma, E., R. Helm, R. Johnson, and J. Vlissides. *Design Patterns*, Addison-Wesley, 1994.
13. Garbanito, B., and R. Guerraoui, "Using the strategy design pattern to compose reliable distributed protocols", *Proceedings of the 3rd Conference on Object-Oriented Technologies and Systems*, USENIX, Portland, OR, 1997.

14. Greenwald, M. and D. Cheriton, "The Synergy between non-blocking synchronization and operating system structure", *Proceedings, OSDI*, USENIX, 1996.
15. Hewitt, C., P. Bishop, and R. Steiger, "A Universal Modular ACTOR Formalism for AI", *Third International Joint Conference on Artificial Intelligence*, Stanford University, August 1973.
16. Holmes, D., "Aspects of Synchronization", *ECOOP Workshop on Aspect-Oriented Programming*, 1997.
17. Huni, H., R. Johnson, and R. Engel, "A Framework for network protocol software", *Proceedings OOPSLA 95*, ACM, 1995.
18. Jain, P. and D. Schmidt, "Service Configurator – A Pattern for Dynamic Configuration of Services," *Proceedings of the 3rd Conference on Object-Oriented Technologies and Systems*, USENIX, Portland, OR, 1997.
19. Jones, N. and Nielson, F., "Abstract interpretation: A Semantic-based tool for program analysis". In *Handbook of Logic in Computer Science*, S. Abramsky, D. Gabbay, and T. Maibaum (eds), Clarendon Press, 1995.
20. Kiczales, G. "Aspect-Oriented Programming", *Computing Surveys (online addendum)*, December 1996.
21. Kiczales, G. "Beyond the Black Box: Open Implementation", *IEEE Software*, January, 1996.
22. Lea, D., "Objects in groups", Technical report, *SUNY Oswego*, 1993.
23. Lea, D. *Concurrent Programming in Java*, Addison-Wesley, 1996.
24. Lea, D., and J. Marlowe. "PSL: Protocols and pragamatics for open systems", Technical Report, *Sun Microsystems Labs*, 1995.
25. Leler, W. "Actor-based simulation + Linda = Virtual environments", in C. Laffra, E. H. Blake, V. de May, and X. Pintado (eds). *Object-Oriented Programming for Graphics*, Springer-Verlag, 1995
26. McAffer, J. "Engineering the meta-level", *Proceedings, Reflection 96*, 1996.
27. Maeda, C,. A. Lee, G. Murphy, and G. Kiczales, "Open Implementation analysis and Design, *Proceedings, Symposium on Software Reusability*, 1997.
28. Mosberger, D., and L. Peterson, "Making paths explicit in the Scout operating system", *Proceedings, OSDI*, USENIX, 1996.
29. Prehofer, C., "Feature-Oriented Programming: A Fresh Look at Objects", *Proceedings, ECOOP 97*, Springer-Verlag, 1997.
30. Shaw, M, and D. Garlan. *Software Architecture*, Prentice Hall, 1996.
31. Silva, A.R., J. Pereira, and J. A. Marques, "Object synchronization pattern". *EuroPLoP*, 1996.
32. Sun Microsystems. *JavaSpaces draft specification*, http://chatsubo.javasoft.com, 1997.
33. Ungar, D. "The Self Papers", *Lisp and Symbolic Computation*, 1991.
34. Tanenbaum, A. *Modern Operating Systems*, Prentice Hall, 1992.
35. van Renesse, R., K. Birman, and S. Maffeis, "Horus, a flexible Group Communication System", *Communications of the ACM*, April 1996.
36. Waldo, J., G. Wyant, A. Wollrath, and S. Kendall, "A note on distributed computing" Technical Report, *Sun Microsystems Labs*, 1994.
37. Wegner, P. "Interactive foundations of computing", *Theoretical Computer Science*, 1997.
38. Wirfs-Brock, R., B. Wilkerson, and L. Wiener, *Designing Object-Oriented Software*, Prentice Hall, 1990.
39. Zave, P. "Feature interactions and formal specifications in telecommunications" *IEEE Computer*, August 1993.

Checking Assumptions in Component Dynamics at the Architectural Level

Paola Inverardi[1], Alexander L. Wolf[2], and Daniel Yankelevich[3]

[1] Dipartimento di Matematica
Universitá di L'Aquila
I-67010 L'Aquila, Italy

[2] Department of Computer Science
University of Colorado
Boulder, CO 80309 USA

[3] Departmento de Computación
Universidad de Buenos Aires
Buenos Aires, Argentina

Abstract. A critical challenge faced by the developer of a software system is to understand whether the system's components correctly integrate. While type theory has provided substantial help in detecting and preventing errors in mismatched static properties, much work remains in the area of dynamics. In particular, components make assumptions about their behavioral interaction with other components, but currently we have only limited ways in which to state those assumptions and to analyze those assumptions for correctness.

We have begun to formulate a method that addresses this problem. The method operates at the architectural level so that behavioral integration errors, such as deadlock, can be revealed early in development. For each component, a specification is given both of its own interaction behavior and of the assumptions that it makes about the interaction behavior of the external context in which it expects to operate. We have defined an algorithm that, given such specifications for a set of components, performs "adequacy" checks between the component context assumptions and the component interaction behaviors. A configuration of a system is possible if and only if a successful way of "matching" actual behaviors with assumptions can be found. In effect, we are extending the usual notion of type checking to include the checking of behavioral compatibility.

1 Introduction

A critical challenge faced by the developer of a software system is to understand whether the system's components correctly integrate. While type theory has provided substantial help in detecting and preventing errors in mismatched static properties, much work remains in the area of dynamics. In particular, components make assumptions about their behavioral interaction with other components, but currently we have only limited ways in which to state those assumptions and to analyze those assumptions for correctness.

In previous work [8, 12, 13], we developed a specification and analysis method for software architectures based on the CHAM (CHemical Abstract Machine) formalism [5]. The CHAM formalism had, until then, been used primarily to describe the semantics of various models of concurrency and the semantics of various concurrent programming languages. We showed how it could be used instead to describe actual software systems. The method has proven to be useful for uncovering a variety of errors at the architectural level.

The method as we defined it, however, has a significant shortcoming. This shortcoming limits the method's usefulness when one is developing a system by assembling existing architectural components. In particular, the method depends on the specification and analysis of a system's *global* component interaction behavior. A more appropriate method would permit the specification of the *local* interaction behavior of an individual component. This would include both the actual behavior of the component and the assumptions it makes about the expected interaction behavior of other components. The method would then use the component specifications to discover mismatches among the components at system integration or configuration time.

We have begun to formulate a new method that takes this approach. Although currently based on the CHAM formalism, the method is likely to have wider applicability. In this method, rather than specifying whole systems and their global behavior, we specify individual components and their local behavior. We have defined an algorithm that, given such specifications for a set of components, performs "adequacy" checks between the component context assumptions and the component interaction behaviors. A configuration of a system is possible if and only if a successful way of "matching" actual behaviors with assumptions can be found. In effect, we are extending the usual notion of type checking to include the checking of behavioral compatibility.

In this paper we give an initial demonstration of the feasibility of our approach by describing its application to a system, the Compressing Proxy, first investigated by Garlan, Kindred, and Wing [10], and later by Compare, Inverardi, and Wolf [9]. The system contains incompatibilities between the assumptions and the interaction behaviors of two of its components. Our algorithm successfully reveals the known fact that the error can result in a deadlock.

2 Related Work

Software architectures are structures of individual components that behave independently and interact. Moreover, the dynamics of these structures are of interest. In this line, it is not unexpected that many languages used to express concurrency semantics are borrowed to describe software architectures. Besides CSP and CHAM, other models have been used, such as the Pi Calculus [18] and Posets [14]. We believe that our approach is independent of the particular specification language used, but one advantage of the CHAM formalism is that it has not embedded within it any particular form of interaction. In most other languages, synchronous or asynchronous broadcast, or point-to-point communications are chosen.

From the perspective of Module Interconnection Languages, informal or semiformal languages have been used to describe software architectures [20]. In those cases, it is more difficult to prove properties of the systems. Perry [16] presents a model in which the semantics of connections are taken into account to check when modules match. The semantic information in the modules, given as predicates, is used to verify some properties. However, as it was aimed at modules and assembly of modules, the dynamics of the system are not considered.

The use of sequences of actions associated locally to modules (components) to describe the behavior of the *allowed* interactions was introduced in Path Expressions [7]. In that work, a description of potential behavior is given by a regular expression in which atomic elements represented calls to the module.

The idea of using behavioral equivalence to check the dynamics of a software system at the architectural level has been explored by Allen and Garlan [1, 2]. In their architectural description language Wright [19], each component has one or more *ports* that represent points of interaction with other components. Rather than interacting directly, however, components interact indirectly through special components called *connectors*. Connectors themselves have special ports called *roles*. Interaction occurs between two or more components by placing a connector between them and by associating each port in a component with a role in the connector.

The semantics of ports and roles in Wright are given using a subset of the language CSP [11]. A notion of consistency is introduced via a behavioral equivalence between the CSP agents describing the semantics of corresponding ports and roles. Although roles where introduced explicitly to support connector reuse, the idea is related to our notion of expected behavior. Roles, in a sense, describe the expected behavior for a particular port. However, consistency is checked only at the port level; it is not possible to verify properties that require several ports to interact among them. In other words, the internal behavior of the component is not taken into account, and complex evolutions are not captured by the equivalence. In the example introduced in our paper, we show how the behavior of the component is used in order to find such anomalies.

We can illustrate this point about roles and ports through an analogy that we call the *guest analogy*. Suppose you are invited to a party. You expect the host to receive you at the door and to invite you in. You also expect your host's partner to take you to the living room and to offer you a drink. If your host's partner does not yet know you, then you expect your host to first introduce you to the partner. If both individual behaviors (host and partner) are satisfied, but your host disappears before introducing you to the partner, then you will be in an uncomfortable situation. From your perspective, it is therefore insufficient to have only the behavior of your interaction with the host and your interaction with the partner described, but your assumptions about the global party context—that the host will introduce you to the partner—must also be described.

3 Background

The CHAM formalism was developed by Berry and Boudol in the domain of theoretical computer science for the principal purpose of defining a generalized computational framework [5]. It is built upon the chemical metaphor first proposed by Banâtre and Le Métayer to illustrate their Gamma (Γ) formalism for parallel programming, in which programs can be seen as multiset transformers [3, 4]. The CHAM formalism provides a powerful set of primitives for computational modeling. Indeed, its generality, power, and utility have been clearly demonstrated by its use in formally capturing the semantics of familiar computational models such as CSP [11] and the CCS process calculus [15]. Boudol [6] points out that the CHAM formalism has also been demonstrated as a modeling tool for concurrent-language definition and implementation.

A CHAM is specified by defining *molecules* $m, m', \ldots$ defined as terms of a syntactic algebra that derive from a set of constants and a set of operations, and *solutions* $S, S', \ldots$ of molecules. Molecules constitute the basic elements of a CHAM, while solutions are multisets of molecules interpreted as defining the *states* of a CHAM. A CHAM specification contains *transformation rules* $T, T', \ldots$ that define a *transformation relation* $S \longrightarrow S'$ dictating the way solutions can evolve (i.e., states can change) in the CHAM. Following the chemical metaphor, the term *reaction rule* is used interchangeably with the term *transformation rule*. The transformation rules can be of two kinds: general *laws* that are valid for all CHAMs and specific *rules* that depend on the particular CHAM being specified.

At any given point, a CHAM can apply as many rules as possible to a solution, provided that their premises do not conflict—that is, no molecule is involved in more than one rule. In this way it is possible to model parallel behaviors by performing parallel transformations. When more than one rule can apply to the same molecule or set of molecules, we have nondeterminism, in which case the CHAM makes a nondeterministic choice as to which transformation to perform. Thus, we may not be able to completely control the sequence of transformations; we can only specify when rules are enabled. Finally, if no rules can be applied to a solution, then that solution is said to be *inert*.

When applying the formalism to software architecture, we structure specifications into three parts [12]:

1. a description of the syntax by which components of the system (i.e., the molecules) can be represented;
2. a solution representing the initial state of the system; and
3. a set of reaction rules describing how the components interact to achieve the dynamic behavior of the system.

The syntactic description of the components is given by an algebra of molecules or, in other words, a syntax by which molecules can be built. Following Perry and Wolf [17], we distinguish three classes of components: data elements, processing elements, and connecting elements. The processing elements are those components that perform the transformations on the data elements, while the data elements are those that contain the information that is used and transformed. The connecting elements are the "glue" that holds the different pieces of the architecture together. For example, the elements involved in effecting communication among components are considered connecting elements. This classification is reflected in the syntax, as appropriate.

The initial solution is a subset of all possible molecules that can be constructed using the syntax. It corresponds to the initial, static configuration of the system. Transformation rules applied to the initial solution define how the system dynamically evolves from its initial configuration.

4 The Compressing Proxy Problem

In this section we present the design of the Compressing Proxy system. Our description is derived from that given by Garlan, Kindred, and Wing [10].

To improve the performance of UNIX-based World Wide Web browsers over slow networks, one could create an HTTP (Hyper Text Transfer Protocol) server that compresses and uncompresses data that it sends across the network. This is the purpose of the Compressing Proxy, which weds the **gzip** compression/decompression program to the standard HTTP server available from CERN.

A CERN HTTP server consists of *filters* strung together in series. The filters communicate using a function-call-based stream interface. Functions are provided in the interface to allow an upstream filter to "push" data into a downstream filter. Thus, a filter F is said to *read* data whenever the previous filter in the series invokes the proper interface function in F. The interface also provides a function to close the stream. Because the interface between filters is function-based, all the filters must reside in a single UNIX process.

The **gzip** program is also a filter, but at the level of a UNIX process. Therefore, it uses the standard UNIX input/output interface, and communication with **gzip** occurs through UNIX pipes. An important difference between UNIX filters, such as **gzip**, and the CERN HTTP filters is that the UNIX filters explicitly choose when to read, whereas the CERN HTTP filters are forced to read when data are pushed at them.

To assemble the Compressing Proxy from the existing CERN HTTP server and **gzip** without modification, we must insert **gzip** into the HTTP filter stream at the appropriate point. But since **gzip** does not have the proper interface, we must create an adaptor, as shown in Figure 1. This adaptor acts as a pseudo CERN HTTP filter, communicating normally with the upstream and downstream filters through a function-call interface, and with **gzip** using pipes connected to a separate **gzip** process that it creates.

Without a proper understanding of the assumptions made by each component, a mismatch in the interaction behavior of the components can occur when they become integrated into a single system. Consider the following straightforward method of structuring the adaptor. The adaptor simply passes data onto **gzip** whenever it receives data from the upstream filter. Once the stream is closed by the upstream filter (i.e., there are no more data to be compressed), the adaptor reads the compressed data from **gzip** and pushes the data toward the downstream filter.

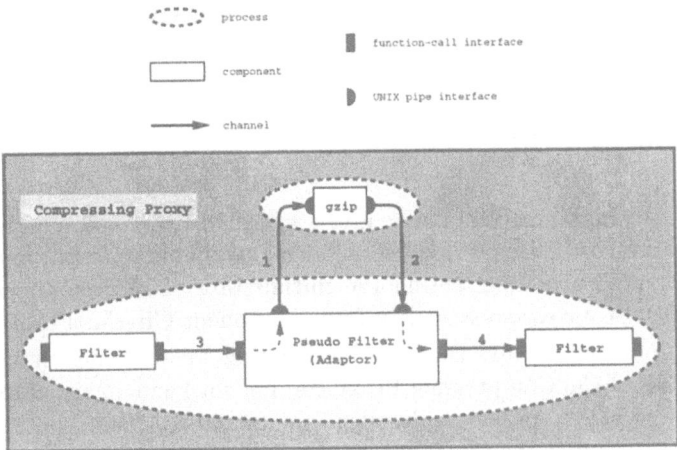

Fig. 1. The Compressing Proxy.

From the perspective of the adaptor, this local behavior makes sense. But it is making assumptions about its interactions with **gzip** that are incompatible with the actual behavior of **gzip**. In particular, **gzip** uses a one-pass compression algorithm and may attempt to write a portion of the compressed data (perhaps because an internal buffer is full) before the adaptor is ready, thus blocking. With **gzip** blocked, the adaptor also becomes blocked when it attempts to pass on more of the data to **gzip**, leaving the system in deadlock.

Obviously, the way to avoid deadlock in this situation is have the adaptor handle the data incrementally and use non-blocking reads and writes. This would allow the adaptor to read some data from **gzip** when its attempt to write data to **gzip** is blocked.

The Compressing Proxy is a simple example with a well understood solution. (We note, however, that the system was indeed initially developed according to the first approach, and the architectural mismatch was not detected until the system was implemented and in use.) Nevertheless, one can see that it is representative of an all-too-common problem in software development.

5 Specifying Component Behavior and Assumptions

In this section we show how to specify the behavior of a component at the architectural level and, from this, how it is then possible to derive a representation of its actual behavior as well as the assumptions that it makes on the external context. In essence, each component is modeled using a separate CHAM, which we refer to as a *component CHAM*. Conceptually, a complete system is specified by combining the separate CHAMs into a single, integrated *system CHAM*. The details of the composition process are beyond the scope of this paper. Here, we are concerned only with how to specify component CHAMs and how they can be checked pairwise for compatibility.

5.1 Component CHAMs

To specify a component CHAM, we give a syntax for the molecules representing the component, rules describing the behavior of the component, and an initial solution of molecules representing the initial state of the component. For the Compressing Proxy we must specify four component CHAMs (Table 1).

It is important to note that the justification for choosing these particular specifications of the Compressing Proxy component behaviors is not germane to the topic this paper. In fact, a detailed understanding of the specifications are unnecessary to follow the discussion below. Therefore, we only give a high-level and incomplete description of the specifications here.

	Upstream CERN Filter (CF$_u$)	**Downstream CERN Filter (CF$_d$)**
Syntax	$M ::= P \mid C \mid M \diamond M$ $P ::= \mathbf{CF_u} \mid \Phi$ $C ::= i(N) \mid o(N)$ $N ::= n_1$	$M ::= P \mid C \mid M \diamond M$ $P ::= \mathbf{CF_d} \mid \Phi$ $C ::= i(N) \mid o(N)$ $N ::= n_1$
Trans. Rules	$T_1 \equiv i(n) \diamond m_1,\, o(n) \diamond m_2$ $\longrightarrow m_1 \diamond i(n),\, m_2 \diamond o(n)$ $T_2 \equiv \mathbf{CF_u} \diamond c \longrightarrow c \diamond \mathbf{CF_u}$	$T_1 \equiv i(n) \diamond m_1,\, o(n) \diamond m_2$ $\longrightarrow m_1 \diamond i(n),\, m_2 \diamond o(n)$ $T_2 \equiv \mathbf{CF_d} \diamond c \longrightarrow c \diamond \mathbf{CF_d}$
Init. Sol.	$\mathbf{CF_u} \diamond o(n_1)$	$\mathbf{CF_d} \diamond i(n_1)$

	GZIP (GZ)	**Adaptor (AD)**
Syntax	$M ::= P \mid C \mid E \mid M \diamond M$ $P ::= \mathbf{GZ} \mid \Phi$ $C ::= i(N) \mid o(N)$ $N ::= n_1 \mid n_2$ $E ::= \mathbf{eof}_i \mid \mathbf{eof}_o$	$M ::= P \mid C \mid E \mid M \diamond M$ $P ::= \mathbf{AD} \mid \Phi$ $C ::= i(N) \mid o(N)$ $N ::= n_1 \mid n_2 \mid n_3 \mid n_4$ $E ::= \mathbf{eof}_i \mid \mathbf{eof}_o$
Trans. Rules	$T_1 \equiv i(n) \diamond m_1,\, o(n) \diamond m_2$ $\longrightarrow m_1 \diamond i(n),\, m_2 \diamond o(n)$ $T_2 \equiv e \diamond m \diamond c \longrightarrow c \diamond e \diamond m$ $T_3 \equiv \mathbf{eof}_o \diamond m_1 \diamond o(n),\, \mathbf{eof}_i \diamond m_2 \diamond i(n)$ $\longrightarrow m_1 \diamond o(n) \diamond \mathbf{eof}_o,$ $m_2 \diamond i(n) \diamond \mathbf{eof}_i$ $T_4 \equiv \mathbf{eof}_i \diamond m \longrightarrow m \diamond \mathbf{eof}_i$ $T_5 \equiv \mathbf{GZ} \diamond m \longrightarrow m \diamond \mathbf{GZ}$	$T_1 \equiv i(n) \diamond m_1,\, o(n) \diamond m_2$ $\longrightarrow m_1 \diamond i(n),\, m_2 \diamond o(n)$ $T_2 \equiv e \diamond m \diamond c \longrightarrow c \diamond e \diamond m$ $T_3 \equiv \mathbf{eof}_o \diamond m_1 \diamond o(n),\, \mathbf{eof}_i \diamond m_2 \diamond i(n)$ $\longrightarrow m_1 \diamond o(n) \diamond \mathbf{eof}_o,$ $m_2 \diamond i(n) \diamond \mathbf{eof}_i$ $T_4 \equiv \mathbf{eof}_i \diamond m \longrightarrow m \diamond \mathbf{eof}_i$ $T_5 \equiv \mathbf{AD} \diamond i(n_3) \diamond m$ $\longrightarrow i(n_2) \diamond \mathbf{eof}_i \diamond o(n_4) \diamond \mathbf{AD}$ $T_6 \equiv \mathbf{AD} \diamond i(n_2) \diamond m$ $\longrightarrow i(n_3) \diamond o(n_1) \diamond \mathbf{eof}_o \diamond \mathbf{AD}$
Init. Sol.	$i(n_1) \diamond \mathbf{eof}_i \diamond o(n_2) \diamond \mathbf{eof}_o \diamond \mathbf{GZ}$	$i(n_3) \diamond o(n_1) \diamond \mathbf{eof}_o \diamond \mathbf{AD}$

Table 1. Component CHAMs for the Compressing Proxy Example.

Consider the upstream CERN filter $\mathbf{CF}_u$. The syntax for molecules M representing this component consists of the set P representing the name of the component's processing element $\mathbf{CF}_u$ and a placeholder Φ to refer to other components with which $\mathbf{CF}_u$ interacts. M also includes the set C representing the connecting elements. The connecting elements for this component are two operations, i for input and o for output, that act on the elements of a third set N. In general, elements of N are used to refer to the channels through which a component communicates with other components. In the case of $\mathbf{CF}_u$ we only need to consider one channel, namely the output channel for this upstream filter. Notice that for $\mathbf{CF}_d$, the downstream filter, we also only consider one channel, in this case the one representing input to the filter. Finally, the syntax includes an infix operator "$\diamond$" used to express the status of the component with respect to its communication behavior. The status is understood by "reading" a molecule from left to right. The left-most position (i.e., the left operand of the left-most "$\diamond$" operator) in the molecule indicates the next action that the molecule is prepared to take. If this position is occupied by a communication operation, then the kind of communication represented by that operation can take place.

The interaction behavior of the upstream filter component is captured using two transformation rules. The first rule is a general inter-element communication rule that generically describes pairwise input/output communication between processing elements. Notice that this same rule is found in all four component CHAMs. The second rule allows $\mathbf{CF}_u$ to iterate its communication behavior.

The initial solution for $\mathbf{CF}_u$ is quite simple. It indicates that the component starts out in a state in which it is waiting to output data. The second transformation rule would have to be applied to this solution before it could actually carry out a communication.

The CHAMs for the other three components follow a similar structure and share similar rules. The critical issue for this example is the interaction behaviors of **gzip** and the adaptor, so we explain them a bit further.

In the specifications of **gzip** and the adaptor, the syntaxes include a set E. The elements of E are used when communications through the adaptor, **AD**, and **gzip**, **GZ**, take place; $\mathbf{eof}_i$ denotes "input end of file", while $\mathbf{eof}_o$ denotes "output end of file". Both component CHAMs share transformation rules T_2 through T_4, which govern the iteration of the input and output behaviors involving data markers $\mathbf{eof}_i$ and $\mathbf{eof}_o$. Rule T_5 of the **gzip** component CHAM describes a simple iterative behavior. The iterative behavior of the adaptor, on the other hand, is more complex, actually changing structure with rule T_6. In particular, it is characterized by a phased behavior in which the component switches from a mode of accepting raw data and then passing the data along (presumably to **gzip**, but in fact to any other component for which it is acting as an adaptor), to a mode of receiving data (again, presumably from **gzip** but also from any adapted component) and then passing the data on down the stream.

As mentioned above, when component CHAMs are integrated to form a system, a certain amount of configuration must occur. For instance, in the Compressing Proxy example, the symbolic communication channels referred to by the individual CHAMs as elements of N are instantiated according to the channel numbers in the diagram of Figure 1, resulting in actual connections being established between the components. Thus, although not obvious from the preceding discussion, the configuration operation would cause the symbolic channel n_1 of the upstream filter and the symbolic channel n_3 of the adaptor to be identified with the actual channel labeled "3" in the diagram.

5.2 Deriving Actual and Assumed Behaviors

In order to check for compatibility between components, we need suitable representations of the actual behavior, AC, of a component, and assumed behavior, AS, of the external context. For each component, we derive these two representations from its component CHAM specification.

The model for both representations is a directed, rooted graph, where both nodes and arcs are labeled. Formally,

$$G = (N, A, so : A \rightarrow N, ta : A \rightarrow N, m : N \rightarrow M \cup \mathcal{N}, l : A \rightarrow \Lambda)$$

where N is the set of nodes, A is the set of arcs, $\mathcal{N}$ is the set of natural numbers, M is the set of node labels taken from the CHAM molecule set, and Λ is the set of arc labels taken from a set that is obtained from the syntax of the components, plus two special labels τ and α. In the Compressing Proxy example, labels are in the set $\Lambda = \{\tau, \alpha\} \cup C \cup E$. The label τ can appear only in AC graphs, while the label α can appear only in AS graphs. In addition to these sets, so is the source node function, ta is the target node function, m is the node labeling function, and l is the arc labeling function. Finally, the graphs are enriched with a relation on arcs called or where $or \subseteq \mathcal{P}(A)$.

AC graphs model behaviors in the following intuitive manner. Nodes represent states of the component and, therefore, are molecules. The root node is the initial state of the component. Note that in the current formulation we do not allow dynamic creation of components. Each arc represents a possible transition into a new state by using a transformation rule of the component CHAM. The label on the arc is the part of the molecule that is deleted or transformed by the rule; we refer to such a label as the *consumed label*. If no other molecule should occur in the transformation, then the label of the arc is τ—that is, the transition can occur without interaction with the external context. An example of such a transformation is rule T_2 of $\mathbf{CF}_u$.

Definition 1 *(AC graph for a component CHAM)*
  AC graphs are defined constructively as follows.

- *The root node is associated with the initial molecule of the component CHAM.*
- *Let ν be a node and let m_ν be the molecule associated with the node ν. Then ν has a child node ν_i if and only if there exists a rule r whose application to a solution s requires m_ν to be in s. The labels and or relation are constructed as follows.*

- *The molecule associated with ν_i is the molecule obtained by modifying m_ν with r.*
- *The arc connecting ν to ν_i is labeled with τ if r can be applied to a solution that contains only m_ν.*
- *The arc is labeled λ if λ is the label consumed by r when applied to m_ν.*
- *If the application of r results in more than one component molecule, then all the arcs connecting ν to a node labeled with a component molecule are identified as* or *arcs.*

Informally, *or* arcs identify alternative subgraphs for the same component. As discussed below, this corresponds to a concurrent (i.e., multi-threaded) behavior of a component. With respect to proving the absence of deadlock, it is sufficient to show that there is at least one "active" alternative subgraph in every derivation.

AS graphs are intuitively the counterpart of AC graphs. They model the assumed behavior of the external context. For each AC graph, therefore, there is a corresponding AS graph that models the behavior of the context required to perform all the derivations modeled by the AC graph. Since in general the context can be provided by several components, AS graphs refer to the behavior of more than one component. It is structured as a graph because, at each step of the actual behavior, a molecule should be present in the context such that the expected transformation in the AC graph can take place. Informally, if AC nodes represent states of a component, AS nodes represent states of the other components that permit a reaction to occur in a solution. Thus, the number of nodes in an AS graph must be the same as the number of nodes in an AC graph. Moreover, there must be a correspondence between a node in an AC graph and a node in an AS graph, since they together describe a subsolution reaction.

In assumption graphs, nodes are labeled differently in order to distinguish the molecules that can participate in each transformation. The graph structure allows us to recover the ordering in which a component asks for molecules from the context. In general, more molecules can participate in producing the required total context. Thus, we identify nodes with numbers, but we can replicate a node whenever a potentially different molecule can provide the required context. In other words, nodes with the same number refer to the same solution, and therefore are associated with the same node in the corresponding AC graph, but they are considered different if the required context can come from different molecules. This helps during the matching phase. If a single molecule produces a subset of the context, then its actual behavior must have the structure of an AS subgraph.

Given an AC graph for a component CHAM we can define the corresponding AS graph. AS graphs have nodes labeled with natural numbers.

Definition 2 *(AS graph for a component CHAM)*
Let G_{ac} be an AC graph for some component CHAM, then the corresponding AS graph, G_{as} is constructed as follows.

- *G_{as} has at least as many nodes as G_{ac}. G_{as} can have replicated nodes.*

- *The root node of G_{as} has the label 0 and is associated with the root node of G_{ac}.*
- *Let ν be a node in G_{as}, let k be its label, and let μ be the associated node in G_{ac}. Then if μ has an outgoing arc to a node μ_1 labeled λ ($\lambda \neq \tau$) due to the application of a rule r, then ν has an outgoing arc to the node corresponding to μ_1 labeled with the conjunction of the labels consumed by r. Each such label corresponds to the consumed label of a molecule required in the context to perform the reaction by r. If the reached node does not already exist, then its label is $k + 1$; if there are already $j - 1$ children of ν. If the outgoing arc in G_{ac} is labeled with τ, then the outgoing arc from ν is labeled with α. In general, the node is replicated unless it is possible to show that the external molecule participating in the reaction is a transformation of the preceding one.*
- *if μ has or arcs, then ν also has corresponding or arcs. If the AC arcs are labeled with τ then the corresponding AS arcs are labeled with α.*

The intuitive meaning of the α label in AS graphs is that of abstracting away from requirements on actual behaviors. That is, an α transition means a *do not care* requirement that can be matched by any sequence of transformations in the actual behavior graph AC. Actually, by construction, one of the purposes of α arcs is to model τ cycles—that is, the fact that a certain molecule can be "spontaneously" offered infinitely many times in the context. The other use of α arcs is to label *or* arcs when the transformation in the actual behavior graph has not required any context.

AC and AS graphs for the component CHAMs of the Compressing Proxy example appear in figures 2, 3, and 4.

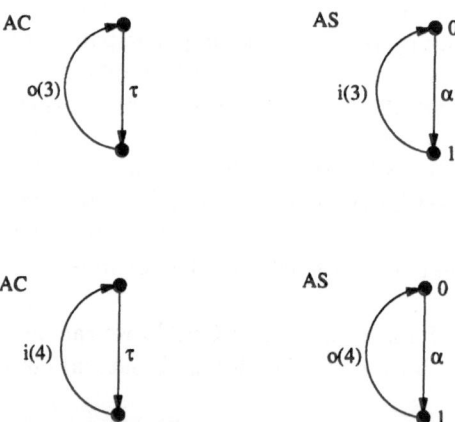

Fig. 2. AC and AS Graphs for the Upstream (top) and Downstream (bottom) Filters.

57

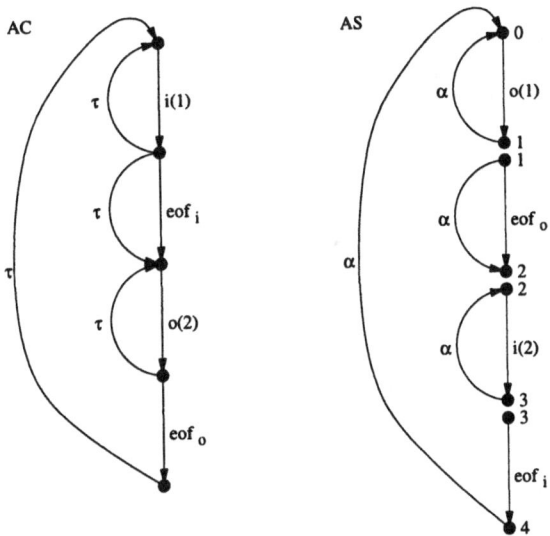

Fig. 3. AC and AS Graphs for **gzip**.

6 Checking Assumptions

The primary goal of this work is to provide a way for an architect to check that a given configuration of components results in a correct system. In essence this means comparing the assumptions on the external context made by one component to the actual behavior exhibited by the components with which it interacts. In this work we have concentrated on deadlock freedom as the correctness criterion and have developed an algorithm that performs the check.

The checking algorithm makes use of an equivalence relation between AC graphs and AS graphs. Informally, the goal of the configuration phase is to find a way to *match* components. This means that all the component's assumptions have to be fulfilled by some other component's actual behavior. In general, of course, multiple actual behaviors can contribute to fulfilling the assumptions of a single component. In our example, this is true for the adaptor component.

If a configuration phase *succeeds*, then the system is deadlock free. If the configuration phase *fails*, then it means that there is no way to satisfy the assumptions of a component—that is, some component will block along some derivation in any possible match of components. This is not enough to conclude that the whole system blocks, but we can iterate the checking phase, reducing the actual behavior of the blocking components. In other words, we can eliminate the part that can block and see how this affects other components.

58

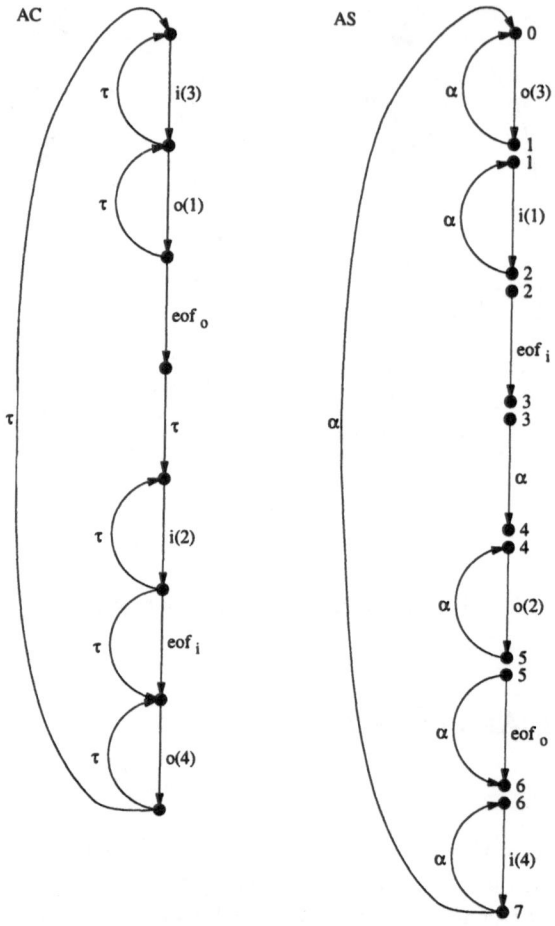

Fig. 4. AC and AS Graphs for the Adaptor.

6.1 Checking Algorithm

The checking algorithm is built upon a notion of equivalence that allows us to compare AC graphs with AS graphs. The equivalence relation allows nodes and arcs to be put in relation. Actually, since an AS graph can be fulfilled by more than one AC graph, we try to put in relation one AS graph with more than one AC graph. The idea is that all the arcs and nodes of the AS graph have to be covered and there should not exist the possibility that an actual behavior cannot provide the required information.

In the following, we denote by $\xrightarrow{\gamma^\bullet}$ any sequence of transformations, suitably labeled, including the empty transformation. We also consider the following equivalence on transformations

$$\nu_i \xrightarrow{\alpha} \nu_{i+1} \xrightarrow{\gamma} \nu_{i+2} = \nu_i \xrightarrow{\gamma} \nu_{i+2}$$

Analogously, the following also holds.

$$\nu_i \xrightarrow{\gamma} \nu_{i+1} \xrightarrow{\alpha} \nu_{i+2} = \nu_i \xrightarrow{\gamma} \nu_{i+2}$$

Definition 3 *Let G_{ac} be an actual behavior graph, G_{as} be an assumption graph, and $\gamma \in \Lambda \setminus \alpha$, then two nodes are related, $\nu_i \simeq \mu_j$:*

- *if $\mu_j \xrightarrow{\gamma} \mu_{j+1}$, then also $\nu_i \xrightarrow{\gamma} \nu_{i+1}$ and $\nu_{i+1} \simeq \mu_{j+1}$;*
- *if $\mu_j \xrightarrow{\alpha} \mu_{j+1}$ then $\nu_i \xrightarrow{\gamma^*} \nu_{i+1}$ and $\nu_{i+1} \simeq \mu_{j+1}$ or ν_{i+1} is already a covered node.*
- *if $\nu_i \xrightarrow{\gamma} \nu_{i+1}$ and $\mu_j \not\xrightarrow{} \mu_{j+1}$ then either there exists a node ν_k such that $\nu_k \simeq \mu_j$ and $\nu_{i+1} \xrightarrow{\gamma^*} \nu_k$ or there exists a ν_k such that if $ta(A) = \nu_k$ then $so(A) = \nu_r$, $l(A) = \tau$, A is an or arc and ν_i is a descendant of ν_r but not of ν_k and $\nu_k \simeq \mu_{j+1}$.*

The two graphs are related if and only if all the nodes in G_{ac} are in relation with G_{as} nodes. The G_{as} nodes in relation are called covered nodes. If the G_{as} nodes are all covered, then the G_{as} graph is completely covered, otherwise it is partially covered. We extend this notion to arcs by saying that an arc is covered when both its source and target nodes are covered.

The above definition allows us to compare AC and AS graphs. Note that in this way we require that an actual behavior must completely match (part of) an assumption.

This definition derives to some extent from the well known Milner bisimulation. Here we do not require complete matching between components and we also have to take into account the potential concurrent behavior of a component. In this respect, the last condition in the above definition says that if an actual behavior performs something that is not required from the assumptions, then this is not harmful if either along that derivation it is possible to reach a solution that allows the required context or if there exists a concurrent component behavior that can actually provide the context.

We can now define the matching algorithm. To do so, let us first define the notion of substitution.

Definition 4 *(Substitution) A substitution is a set of pairs (AC, AS). We denote with ϵ the empty substitution and a generic substitution $\sigma = [AC_1/AS_1, \ldots, AC_n/AS_n]$.*

Given a configuration Γ—that is, a set of components—we identify with the notation $\sigma(\Gamma)$ the system built out of the component in Γ according to the association in the substitution σ.

Definition 5 *(Matching Algorithm)*
Let $\Gamma = \{C1, C2, \ldots, Cn\}$ be a configuration and σ be an empty substitution.

1. If in Γ there are no more AS graphs then $Match(\Gamma) = (true, \sigma)$.
2. Try to find a pair $AC_{Ci} \simeq AS_{Cj}$.
3. If AS_{Cj} is partially covered, obtain a new graph AS'_{Cj} that reflects this partial match by labeling all covered arcs with α; let $\sigma = \sigma \cup \{AS_{Cj}, AC_{Ci}\}$; go to step 2.
4. Remove from Γ the assumptions AS_{Cj}; go to step 1.

The following propositions, which we give here without proof, hold.

Proposition 1 *Let Γ be a configuration if $Match(\Gamma) = (bool, \sigma)$ succeeds—that is, bool = true and $\sigma \neq \epsilon$, then the system $\sigma(C)$ is deadlock free.*

Proposition 2 *Let Γ be a configuration, C be any given component, AS be the assumption graph of C. If there are no or arcs and there is no actual behavior AC in Γ that satisfies the assumptions AS (that is, $AC \not\simeq AS$) then for any possible substitution AC/AS there exists a computation such that C will block.*

Proposition 2 might be generalized to the case with *or* arcs, showing that the algorithm is *complete*. However, the case with *or* arcs is much more complex and requires further, detailed analysis.

Let us now see how we can apply these definitions to our example. The aim is to define a single system out of the four components specified in Table 1. We start with a configuration $\Gamma = \{\mathbf{GZ}, \mathbf{AD}, \mathbf{CF}_u, \mathbf{CF}_d\}$, and we try to apply the algorithm. The first thing to do is try to find a possible pair (AC,AS). We try with the pair $(AC_{\mathbf{CF}_u}, AS_{\mathbf{AD}})$. This pair succeeds, since we can put in relation all nodes of $AC_{\mathbf{CF}_u}$ with nodes in $AS_{\mathbf{AD}}$. We obtain as a result a partially covered assumption graph for the adaptor, $AS'_{\mathbf{AD}}$. Analogously, it happens for the pair $(AC_{\mathbf{CF}_d}, AS'_{\mathbf{AD}})$, thus resulting in the assumption graph $AS''_{\mathbf{AD}}$. Now we can attempt to match the actual behavior of **gzip** with the remaining part of the assumption graph of the adaptor. In this case, we are not able to relate all nodes in $AC_{\mathbf{GZ}}$ to the nodes in $AS''_{\mathbf{AD}}$. Figure 5 illustrates this mismatch problem.

It is worth noticing that the mismatch occurs exactly where the deadlock of the system appears. In fact, we cannot satisfy the assumption of the adaptor that corresponds to the state in which the adaptor requires an eof_o from the context. Thus, the adaptor will be blocked, not producing an eof_i, which in turn will cause **gzip** to block, thus achieving a state of deadlock.

The adaptor can be modified to eliminate the deadlock by introducing parallelism into its behavior, as discussed in Section 4. The modified component CHAM for the adaptor is shown in Table 2. It replaces the phased behavior of the adaptor with non-blocking reads and writes.

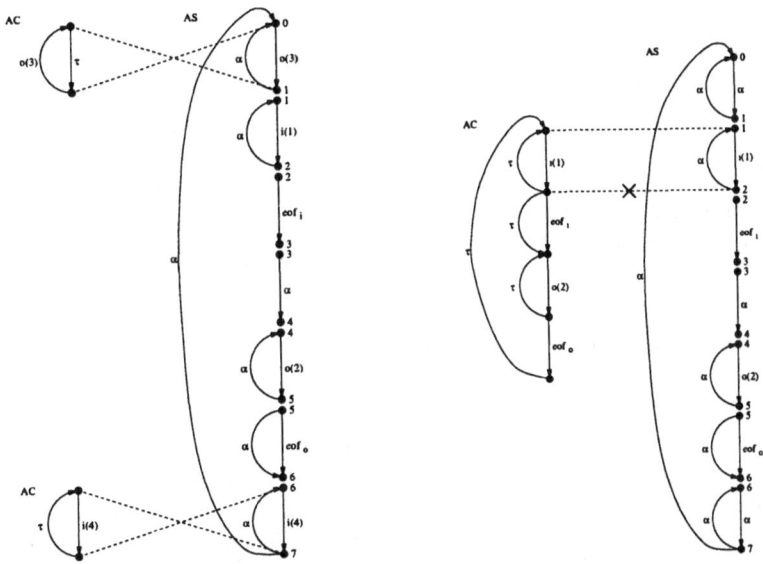

Fig. 5. Mismatch in Actual and Assumed Behavior Leading to Deadlock.

Adaptor (AD)

Syntax	$M' ::= P \mid C \mid E \mid M' \diamond M' \mid M' \parallel M'$ $P ::= \mathbf{AD} \mid \varPhi$ $C ::= i(N) \mid o(N)$ $N ::= n_1 \mid n_2 \mid n_3 \mid n_4$ $E ::= \mathbf{eof}_i \mid \mathbf{eof}_o$
Trans. Rules	$T_1 \equiv i(n) \diamond m_1, \, o(n) \diamond m_2$ $\qquad \longrightarrow m_1 \diamond i(n), \, m_2 \diamond o(n)$ $T_2 \equiv e \diamond m \diamond c \longrightarrow c \diamond e \diamond m$ $T_3 \equiv \mathbf{eof}_o \diamond m_1 \diamond o(n), \, \mathbf{eof}_i \diamond m_2 \diamond i(n)$ $\qquad \longrightarrow m_1 \diamond o(n) \diamond \mathbf{eof}_o, \, m_2 \diamond i(n) \diamond \mathbf{eof}_i$ $T_4 \equiv \mathbf{eof}_i \diamond m \longrightarrow m \diamond \mathbf{eof}_i$ $T_5' \equiv m_1 \parallel m_2 \parallel \cdots \parallel m_k \longrightarrow m_1, m_2, \ldots, m_k$ $T_6' \equiv \mathbf{AD} \diamond m \longrightarrow m \diamond \mathbf{AD}$
Init. Sol.	$i(3) \diamond o(n_1) \diamond \mathbf{eof}_o \diamond \mathbf{AD} \parallel i(n_2) \diamond \mathbf{eof}_i \diamond o(n_4) \diamond \mathbf{AD}$

Table 2. Modified Component CHAM for the Adaptor.

7 Conclusions and Future Work

In this work, we have presented an algorithm to check properties of a system at the architectural level. At this level, the properties of interest are mainly dynamic properties related to the *coordination* of components; one component has a potential behavior, but in order to be successfully integrated in an architecture, it expects the context to behave in some particular way. We introduced the notion of *assumptions* to formalize what a component expects from other components. In other words, in order to work together, components must agree not only on the actual behaviors (e.g., agree on communication protocol, port naming, an the like) but also on the assumptions they make of each other.

The checking algorithm introduced uses the assumptions and actual behavior to verify that the differences between the actual behavior of a component and the assumptions that other components make of what its behavior would be cannot produce a deadlock situation. We have shown how the algorithm works in a case study.

Clearly, this work needs to be generalized. We have introduced the notions needed, and we have presented an algorithm to check a particular problem in a particular situation. The example shows that the algorithm is useful in a real context. However, other properties of interest should be analyzed and algorithms developed to perform verification of those properties.

Moreover, the idea of associating assumptions to components may have interesting consequences, besides deadlock checking. In general, when components are assembled together to form a system, the verification performed is based on type checking of the interfaces. As mentioned in the introduction, some work has been done in checking the dynamics of components. But the notion of checking assumptions against actual behavior may lead to a general way of verifying that the assembly of a system, at the architectural level, is correctly done. The information in the interfaces, besides operations (or ports), types of the operations, and even potential behavior might be enriched by the assumptions that the component makes on how the context behaves. These considerations give additional motivation to generalize the results given in this work.

Acknowledgments The work of A.L. Wolf was supported in part by the National Science Foundation under grant INT-95-14202 and by the Air Force Material Command, Rome Laboratory, and the Defense Advanced Research Projects Agency under Contract Number F30602-94-C-0253. The content of the information does not necessarily reflect the position or the policy of the U.S. Government and no official endorsement should be inferred.

The work of P. Inverardi was supported in part by a CNR/CONICET bilateral project and by the LOMAPS ESPRIT project.

References

1. R. Allen and D. Garlan. Formalizing Architectural Connection. In *Proceedings of the 16th International Conference on Software Engineering*, pages 71–80. IEEE Computer Society, May 1994.
2. R. Allen and D. Garlan. A Case Study in Architectural Modeling: The AEGIS System. In *Proceedings of the 8th International Workshop on Software Specification and Design*, pages 6–15. IEEE Computer Society, March 1996.
3. J.-P. Banâtre and D. Le Métayer. The Gamma Model and its Discipline of Programming. *Science of Computer Programming*, 15:55–77, 1990.

4. J.-P. Banâtre and D. Le Métayer. Programming by Multiset Transformation. *Communications of the ACM*, 36(1):98–111, January 1993.
5. G. Berry and G. Boudol. The Chemical Abstract Machine. *Theoretical Computer Science*, 96:217–248, 1992.
6. G. Boudol. Some Chemical Abstract Machines. In *A Decade of Concurrency*, number 803 in Lecture Notes in Computer Science, pages 92–123. Springer-Verlag, May 1994.
7. R.H. Campbell and A.N. Habermann. The Specification of Process Synchronization by Path Expressions. In *Proceedings of an International Symposium on Operating Systems*, number 16 in Lecture Notes in Computer Science, pages 89–102. Springer-Verlag, April 1974.
8. D. Compare and P. Inverardi. Modelling Interoperability by CHAM: A Case Study. In *Proceedings of the First International Conference on Coordination Models and Languages*, number 1061 in Lecture Notes in Computer Science, pages 428–431. Springer-Verlag, April 1996.
9. D. Compare, P. Inverardi, and A.L. Wolf. Uncovering Architectural Mismatch in Dynamic Behavior. Technical Report CU-CS-828-97, Department of Computer Science, University of Colorado, Boulder, Colorado, February 1997.
10. D. Garlan, D. Kindred, and J.M. Wing. Interoperability: Sample Problems and Solutions. Technical report, Carnegie Mellon University, Pittsburgh, Pennsylvania, In preparation.
11. C.A.R. Hoare. *Communicating Sequential Processes*. Prentice-Hall, Englewood Cliffs, New Jersey, 1985.
12. P. Inverardi and A.L. Wolf. Formal Specification and Analysis of Software Architectures using the Chemical Abstract Machine Model. *IEEE Transactions on Software Engineering*, 21(4):373–386, April 1995.
13. P. Inverardi and D. Yankelevich. Relating CHAM Descriptions of Software Architectures. In *Proceedings of the 8th International Workshop on Software Specification and Design*, pages 66–74. IEEE Computer Society, March 1996.
14. D.C. Luckham, J.J. Kenney, L.M. Augustin, J. Vera, D. Bryan, and W. Mann. Specification and Analysis of System Architecture Using Rapide. *IEEE Transactions on Software Engineering*, 21(4):336–355, April 1995.
15. R. Milner. *Communication and Concurrency*. Prentice-Hall, Englewood Cliffs, New Jersey, 1989.
16. D.E. Perry. The Inscape Environment. In *Proceedings of the 11th International Conference on Software Engineering*, pages 2–11. IEEE Computer Society, May 1989.
17. D.E. Perry and A.L. Wolf. Foundations for the Study of Software Architecture. *SIGSOFT Software Engineering Notes*, 17(4):40–52, October 1992.
18. M. Radestock and S. Eisenbach. What Do You Get From a Pi-calculus Semantics? In *Proceedings of PARLE'94 Parallel Architectures and Languages Europe*, number 817 in Lecture Notes in Computer Science, pages 635–647. Springer-Verlag, 1994.
19. M. Shaw and D. Garlan. *Software Architecture: Perspectives on an Emerging Discipline*. Prentice-Hall, Englewood Cliffs, New Jersey, 1996.
20. A.L. Wolf, L.A. Clarke, and J.C. Wileden. The AdaPIC Tool Set: Supporting Interface Control and Analysis Throughout the Software Development Process. *IEEE Transactions on Software Engineering*, 15(3):250–263, March 1989.

Security Benefits from Software Architecture

C. Bidan and V. Issarny

IRISA / INRIA, Campus de Beaulieu, RENNES Cedex 35042, FRANCE

Abstract. In today's field of distributed software architectures there is a need for environments allowing the easy development of applications consisting of heterogeneous software modules and having various Quality of Service requirements (e.g., timeliness, availability or security). System customization using middleware-services is a promising solution to deal with the coexistence of multiple applications with different Quality of Service requirements.

From the security point of view, the goal for system customization is to permit the interoperation among applications having different, possibly inconsistent security constraints. This paper demonstrates how the software architecture paradigm is beneficial for addressing security issues in distributed systems through system customization. The software architecture paradigm allows the application developer to abstractly specify security-related requirements. Then, our framework takes in charge the system customization to meet these requirements. The practical use of our approach is also addressed by discussing its integration in a *configuration-based* distributed programming environment.

1 Introduction

Due to the progress in computer science, open distributed computing systems are now eligible for supporting a wide class of applications, having different Quality of Service (QoS) requirements (such as timeliness, availability or security). One promising approach to deal with the coexistence of multiple applications with different QoS requirements is system customization using middleware-services [4]. In order to hide the customization process from application developers, we need a framework to specify QoS requirements that takes in charge the system customization by selecting appropriate middleware-services [16]. The software architecture field provides an adequate basis to support such a framework.

The software architecture field has emerged in order to ease the development of complex applications (or software systems) by fostering software re-use, evolution, analysis, and management (e.g., [25, 28]). Although the software architecture field is continuously evolving, the clean separation between software components (e.g. computational units) and their interactions is widely accepted. In that framework, an *Architecture Description Language* (ADL) allows system specifications in terms of the three following abstractions [28]:

(i) Components that abstractly define computational units written in any programming language,

(ii) Connectors that abstractly define types of interactions (e.g., pipe, client-server) among components, and

(iii) Configuration that defines a system structure (i.e., a software architecture) in terms of the interconnection of components through connectors.

Connectors may be viewed as the *glue* that binds the components; they define the set of *roles* that the components must play to communicate, that is to say, the set of *properties* of, and *relationship* among, the components [28, 12]. Reasoning at the level of software architectures provides the adequate abstractions for system customization using middleware-services: QoS properties can be provided by a certain type of connectors in which roles include specifications of QoS-related connector behaviors (i.e., architectural style for connectors that is derived from the QoS requirements [25]). Work in the software architecture research field has been concentrating on the specifications of communication architectures, that is to say, the communication protocol used for handling component interactions (e.g. pipe, RPC, shared memory) [28, 1]. Whereas the referenced work focuses on application communication patterns, we are concerned with the QoS that is guaranteed when using a given connector. QoS-related customization can be achieved as follows. First, the application QoS requirements are defined within the specifications of connectors provided that each interaction is characterized by a unique connector. Dually, *base connectors* (i.e., connectors that are available within the environment) and *system-level software components* (i.e., middleware-services) declare the QoS properties they provide. Then, given the formal specifications of QoS properties, software specification matching [32] is used to retrieve a set of system-level software components together with (base) connectors, so that the conjunction of their QoS properties matches the application requirements [14]. The connector built through the interconnections of selected system-level components and (base) connectors is called a *customized connector* in the following.

Interactions among components, possibly having different QoS requirements, are not taken into account in the above customization model, for which a unique connector is declared for each interaction. However, in open distributed systems interactions among entities may occur dynamically. During the interaction between two components, we must consider requirements of both components (i.e., each component can specify their own connectors). By composing these requirements, we are able to infer the requirements for the interaction according to both components. These latter requirements can be used to build the customized connector. From the security point of view, the complex interactions among components stretch the security problems in open distributed systems [24, 8], and require coping with the coexistence of multiple security constraints.

In this paper, we demonstrate how the software architecture paradigm is helpful for addressing security of open distributed systems: at the compilation time based on the declaration of software components having security requirements (e.g., by *security managers*), a customized connector is built to meet both requirements. After introducing security issues for open distributed systems in section 2, we apply in section 3, system customization to security properties. This allows us to provide a framework enabling *security managers* to implement distributed systems which support multiple security constraints. We then present implementation design in the ASTER configuration-based environment in section 4. Finally, we conclude in section 5 by addressing related work and referring to future work.

2 Security issues for open distributed systems

Security means protection against unauthorized attempts to access information [11, 17, 31]. It is concerned with *confidentiality* (information is disclosed only to users authorized to access it), *integrity* (information is modified only by users who have the right to do so, and only in authorized ways) and *availability* (use of the system cannot be maliciously denied to authorized access). In the remainder, we focus only on the first two constituents of security, the issue of availability being beyond the scope of this paper as it also relates to fault-tolerance issues[1].

Security (i.e., data confidentiality and integrity) is an important issue in any distributed system. Security is enforced using *security functionalities* such as *encryption*, *authentication* and *access control*.

Data encryption consists of making the information either illegible (encryption in order to ensure data confidentiality) or unalterable (digital signature in order to ensure data integrity), or both. Encryption is used for protecting stored and exchanged information (e.g., *via* communication network) against reading or modification.

Authentication permits to ensure the entity's identity, that is to say to verify that the entity (e.g., a user or a process) is actually the one that it claims to be. More specifically, the *authentication protocol* enables to associate each system operation to a unique real user, allowing the checking of whether the operation is authorized or not. An example of *authentication protocol* is given by the UNIX system: it requires the user to enter his name, followed by his password. Let us remark that authentication may be considered as the fundamental security mechanism: if it is not provided, an entity is able to claim to be any entity, and thus access any information.

Access control governs operations on system's entities. For instance, in a file system, access control consists of checking whether users are allowed to access files. More generally, in a large distributed system, access control checks the interactions among entities. By extension, access control also deals with the information flow among entities. Let us remark that access control clearly depends upon authentication, the entity's identity having to be unique and unforgeable.

In open distributed systems, applications which have different security constraints may coexist. This coexistence results from rich and complex interactions

---

[1] Let us notice that this "simplification" is often made in the computer security community through the following phrase: "I don't care if it works, as long as it is secure" [11].

among software components [24], and has led to the need for reasoning about different security constraints: a sound basis for describing the software architecture with respect to the security constraints is needed. This is the scope of this paper in which we use the software architecture paradigm to specify the security requirements, and to provide a system customization approach to build systematically connectors that meet these requirements.

In the above presentation, we have simplified some issues so as to not needlessly complicate this paper. In particular, we have not distinguished between the identification process (associating a user ID with a program) and the authentication process (associating the real user with the user ID), and we have not introduced the delegation process enabling entities (e.g., users) to delegate access privileges to other entities (e.g., program) [18].

To implement security functionalities, some security mechanisms are needed. One fundamental issue of security is proving the correctness of the security mechanisms according to security properties (i.e., the correctness of the system-level components used to implement security functionality) [2]. In the remainder, we assume the existence of a *Trusted Computing Base* (or TCB [9]) which contains "correct" security mechanisms that can be used safely to implement security functionalities.

3 Customized connectors for dealing with security

In traditional distributed systems, an application developer who wants to implement security functionalities has to implicitly manage the corresponding security mechanisms in the application source code (e.g., to implicitly call the encryption and decryption functions). This approach is detrimental to both flexibility and reusability. Besides, the management of interconnected systems is complex indeed impossible. In confined distributed systems, this approach may be considered as sufficient, a unique *security manager* having to manage security issues. On the other hand, the above approach is not suited for open distributed systems. In particular, such a system must support interactions among entities belonging to different *security domains*[2].

Because security issues (in term of encryption, authentication and access control) relate to interactions among software components, it is natural to associate security properties with connectors. We extend the connector specifications so as to include the (application developer) security requirements for the interactions among given software components. At the time of the interaction between any two software components, either a unique connector σ is specified for this interaction, or both software components specify their own connectors σ_1 and σ_2 respectively (i.e., their own security requirements). In the first case, a customized connector is built to meet the requirements specified in the connector σ. In the latter case, we compose the requirements of both connectors σ_1 and σ_2 in order

---

[2] The *security domain* of a given *security manager* is the set of all the system entities he manages [11].

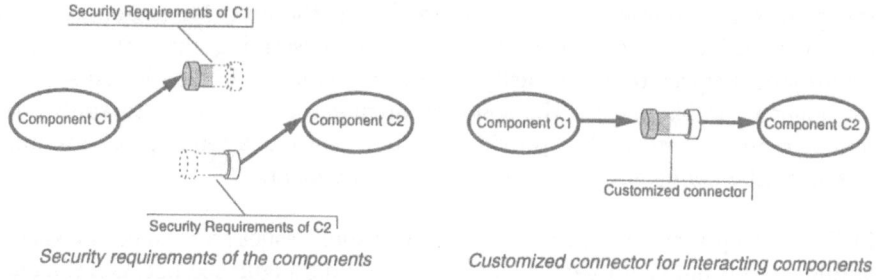

Security requirements of the components   Customized connector for interacting components

Fig. 1. Security requirements and customized connectors

to specify the connector $\sigma_{1,2}$ for the interaction of the software components. The connector $\sigma_{1,2}$ allows one to build the customized connector that meets the security requirements (see figure 1). As discussed in the introduction, the customization process consists of selecting a set of system-level software components that provide security functionalities together with (base) connectors. Note that the system-level components and the (base) connectors have to belong to the TCB.

In order to automatically build customized connectors that meet the security requirements, we have: *i)* to specify security properties for encryption, authentication and access control (i.e., to describe security requirements), and *ii)* to reason about these specifications so as to compose and compare them (i.e., for composing security requirements and for selecting the system-level components).

In the following subsections, we introduce specifications of encryption, authentication and access control which allow us to describe security requirements. We also address comparison and composition of security specifications.

3.1   Encryption specifications

Data is qualified as *plaintext* or *cleartext* when access to this data allows access to the information which is contained. The process of disguising data in such a way as to hide the contained information is *encryption*, and the resulting data is qualified as *ciphertext*. The process of turning ciphertext back into plaintext is *decryption*. An *encryption algorithm* is then composed of an *encryption function* and the corresponding *decryption function*. The encryption function may be used to ensure either confidentiality or integrity.

In general, the encryption and decryption functions are not secret: the security of the encryption algorithm is based on the use of keys. The encryption function takes as input the plaintext and the *encryption key* to compute the ciphertext. In the reverse process, given the ciphertext, the plaintext is computed by using the corresponding *decryption key* and the decryption function (see figure 2)[3].

---

[3] For more details about cryptography, see [27].

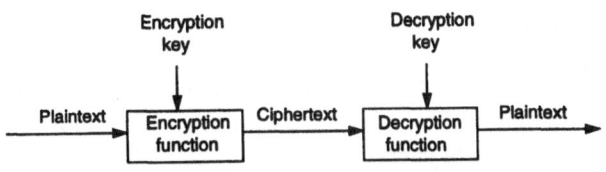

Fig. 2. Encryption and decryption with keys

Specifying encryption requirements Specifying security properties relating to encryption relies on the specification of the encryption algorithm that is used (e.g., by its name: RSA, DES, ...), as well as on the specifications of parameters describing the algorithm behaviors. For instance, parameters may include:

- the algorithm usage, that is to say, if the encryption algorithm is used to cipher the data (for ensuring confidentiality), to sign the data (for ensuring digital signature) or to hash the data (for detecting manipulation);
- the key management, that is to say, the key size (e.g., 512 bits for the RSA algorithm, or 64 bits for the DES algorithm), the support used to find and/or to store the keys (e.g., user's brain, ROM chip or smartcard), the key generation algorithm used to generate secret temporal keys (e.g., random-bit strings algorithms), the lifetime of the secret keys, and so on.

Thus, encryption specification allows one to describe the requirements for encryption as a parameterized encryption algorithm.

As an illustration, an application developer may specify the following requirements for encryption:

Security
    Cipher Algorithm : DES
      Temporal Key : RC4
      Key Size : 64
      Lifetime : 1 hour
    Signature Algorithm : RSA
      Key Size : 512
      Storage : Smartcard

where boldface is used to denote specification keywords. In the above specification, the developer wishes to use the cipher algorithm DES, with 64 bits' temporal keys which are generated for 1 hour by the RC4 algorithm. He requires also the use of the RSA signature algorithm, the 512 bits' keys being stored in smartcard.

In order to decipher data, we must use the decryption function and key, corresponding to the encryption function and key that were used to cipher the original data. During the interaction of two software components, each of them can have encryption requirements. In this context, composing and comparing these requirements are needed so as to ensure that both components use dual encryption algorithms (i.e., to build customized connectors according to encryption requirements of both components).

Composing encryption requirements Due to the symmetry of the encryption and decryption functions, we can not compose and compare two different encryption algorithms (e.g., DES and RSA). However, the composition of encryption requirements can be achieved as follows. We enable the application developer to specify a list of encryption algorithms within connectors. We index each encryption algorithm with the trust degree that the application developer assigns to them [4]. Given two connectors with encryption requirements, the encryption algorithms can be ordered according to the above trust degrees. Then, the encryption algorithm of the connector corresponds to the encryption algorithm (or one of the encryption algorithms) that belongs to both sub-connectors and has the highest trust degree.

Once the encryption algorithm is selected, we are able to reason about its parameters, the connectors being able to specify different values. Like the ordering of encryption algorithms, we define an order on the parameters of encryption algorithms according to the same approach. For instance, let us consider the key size[5]. The application developer may consider that, given an encryption algorithm, the use of 1024 bits' keys instead of 512 bits' keys is acceptable according to the trust degree of the resulting encryption functionality. More generally, the lattice resulting from such an order allows one to compare and compose encryption requirements with respect to the parameter values of the selected encryption algorithm, through specification matching [32].

Given two connectors with encryption requirements (i.e., lists of parameterized encryption algorithms), the (parameterized) encryption algorithm resulting from their composition is the greatest parameterized encryption algorithm *Encrypt* with respect to the trust degree that each application developer (independently) assigns to the encryption algorithms and to their parameter's values. Then, the customization process can be achieved if and only if we can build a customized connector that meets the parameterized encryption algorithm *Encrypt* (i.e., the encryption algorithm of the customized connector is greater than the parameterized encryption algorithm *Encrypt*).

3.2 Authentication specifications

Authentication of entities (e.g., user, process, software component, system) allows to verify that the entities are who they claim to be. An *authentication protocol* specifies the authentication process [6], that is to say, the entities which participate, the exchanged messages among these entities and the format of these messages (i.e., plaintext or ciphertext). Although the main goal of authentication protocols is the authentication of entities, some of them have evolved to deal with additional security properties, such as mutual authentication or temporal key distribution. Authentication protocols needing encryption algorithms

---

[4] In the context of software architectures, the notion of trust degree is close to the notion of weighted properties of the architectural form [25].

[5] An order can also be introduced for any parameter including the lifetime property, the temporal key property (by ordering the generator algorithm according to the trust degree given by the application developer).

for ciphering and/or signing the exchanged messages, another evolutions have consisted of implementing encryption algorithms (for instance, RSA instead of DES). We characterize the former evolution as security semantic evolutions, and the latter evolution as security implementation evolutions.

Let us remark that the authentication protocol resulting from semantic and/or security evolutions may be viewed as an extension of the original protocol, and hence, can be used to implement the original protocol (like the compatibility among the versions of software components). For instance, let us consider an authentication protocol with simple authentication, and suppose that an extended version of this protocol allows to ensure mutual authentication. Then, the latter version can be used to provide simple authentication.

Specifying authentication requirements Authentication specification relies on the specification of the (original) authentication protocol (e.g., Needham-Schroeder protocol, Kerberos protocols, CCITT X.509 protocol [6]). We further parameterize these specifications according to their semantic evolutions (i.e., simple authentication, mutual authentication, key distribution) and their security implementations evolutions (i.e., implementation version, type of encryption algorithms used to cipher and to sign).

Finally, authentication specification also has to include encryption specification in order to describe the encryption algorithm (see §3.1) used to ensure confidentiality and integrity of the exchanged information. Notice that an authentication protocol may use random generator in order to generate temporal keys or to generate timestamps.

As an illustration, authentication specification for a Needham-Schroeder authentication protocol that uses RSA encryption algorithm for both ciphering and signing exchanged message follows:

Security
    Authentication Protocol : Needham-Schroeder
      Semantic :
        Authenticate : Mutual
        Version : *number of the version*
      Encryption
        Cipher Algorithm : RSA
          Key Size : 512bits
          Storage : ROM
        Signature Algorithm : RSA
          Key Size : 512bits
          Storage : ROM

Implementing authentication between two entities requires the use of at least the same authentication protocol. During the interaction of two software components, each of them can have authentication requirements. In this context, composing and comparing these requirements are needed so as to ensure that both components use dual authentication algorithms.

Composing authentication requirements As in the encryption specifications, by enabling application developers to specify an ordered list of authentication protocols within connectors, we are able to compose connectors having different authentication requirements (i.e., different lists of authentication protocols) according to the trust degree that each application developer assigns to each protocol. Given two connectors with authentication requirements, the authentication protocol of the resulting connector corresponds to the authentication protocol that belongs to both of them and has the higher trust degree.

Once the authentication protocol is selected, we are able to reason about its semantic and security evolutions. We order the evolutions according to the trust degree that each application developer assigns to the parameter's values. Then, the lattice resulting from such an order allows us to compare and compose authentication requirements with respect to the parameter values of the selected authentication protocol, through specification matching [32].

Given two connectors with authentication requirements (i.e., lists of parameterized authentication protocols), the (parameterized) authentication protocol resulting from their composition is the greatest parameterized authentication protocol *Authen* with respect to the trust degree that each application developer (independently) assigns to the authentication protocols and to their parameter's values. Then, the customization process can be achieved if and only if we can build a customized connector that meets the parameterized authentication protocol *Authen* (i.e., the authentication protocol of the customized connector is greater than the parameterized encryption algorithm *Authen*).

To summarize, implementing encryption and/or authentication between two software components require to use at least dual algorithms and/or protocol. As a consequence, the composition of security-related requirements amounts to a selection in ordered lists of algorithms and/or protocols specified within connectors (i.e., specification matching with respect to the trust degree that each application developer assigns to them). In addition, ordering the encryption algorithms and authentication protocols according to their parameter values allows also to use specification matching to compare and compose encryption and authentication requirements. With this approach, customized connectors can be built to meet component requirements. According to the connectors with encryption and/or authentication requirements, we are able to select a set of system-level components (which belong to the TCB) and a set of (base) connectors (also belonging to the TCB), in order to construct the customized connectors for the required properties.

3.3 Access control specifications

An *access control policy* (or *ACP*) defines the set of rules, called *access control rules* (or *ACR*), that specify for a pair of entities (ϵ_1, ϵ_2) (e.g. users, processes, files, software components, etc) whether ϵ_1 is authorized to access ϵ_2 or not.

The interaction among entities which do not belong to the same security domain relies on two access control policies, each entity being able to have its own access control constraints. Unlike the encryption and authentication functionalities, the access control does not need symmetric implementation.

Deciding for granting accesses between two entities that belong to different security domains raises the issue of composing the corresponding access control policies: the resulting access control policy (called *composed access control policy* in the following) will allow to check whether the interaction between the entities is authorized. However, various policies can result from the composition of two access control policies, as exemplified below.

Examples Let us consider a file system where we have two sets of users A and C, and two sets of files B and D. We define two access control policies $\mathcal{P}_F^1$ and $\mathcal{P}_F^2$: $\mathcal{P}_F^1$ authorizes users in A to access files in B, and $\mathcal{P}_F^2$ authorizes users in C to access files in D.

First, we compose these sub-policies so as to build the following composed policy, called $\mathcal{P}_F$: the users belonging to both sets A and C (denoted as $A \cap C$) are authorized to access files in $B \cap D$, users in A but not in C (denoted as $A - C$) are authorized to access files in $B - D$, and finally, users in $C - A$ are authorized to access files in $D - B$. $\mathcal{P}_F$ is a *restriction* of the participating policies: some accesses which are authorized in the sub-policies are denied by the $\mathcal{P}_F$ policy.

Let us now compose the sub-policies $\mathcal{P}_F^1$ and $\mathcal{P}_F^2$ so as to obtain the following policy, called $\mathcal{P}_F'$: the users belonging to $A \cap C$ are authorized to access files in B or in D (denoted as $B \cup D$), users in $A - C$ are authorized to access files in $B - D$, and finally, users in $C - A$ are authorized to access files in $D - B$. $\mathcal{P}_F'$ is consistent with both sub-policies: a user is authorized to access a file in $\mathcal{P}_F'$ if and only if the user is authorized to access this file in both $\mathcal{P}_F^1$ and $\mathcal{P}_F^2$.

Another composition of the sub-policies $\mathcal{P}_F^1$ and $\mathcal{P}_F^2$ could result in the following policy $\mathcal{P}_F''$: the users belonging to $A \cup C$ are authorized to access files in $B \cup D$. $\mathcal{P}_F''$ is an extension of the participating sub-policies (i.e.. A's users can access D's files).

Note that all the above composed policies may be regarded as secure in the context in which they are specified. Thus, there is a need for a framework allowing security managers to compose security policies in a controlled and secure way.

To deal with access control composition, our approach relies on the specifications of access control policies and on the definition of composition operators between these specifications.

Specifying access control policies Since in open distributed systems, it is not possible to specify an ACP that takes into account the whole set of the system's entities, we define an ACP not solely in terms of its *access control rules* but also in terms of its *access control domain*, that sets the system's entities to which the policy applies.

The access control domain of a policy is defined in terms of security classifications (i.e., security properties like *secret* entities, *confidential* entities, *unclassified* entities). An access control rule is a set of pairs of system entities verifying an *access control predicate*, i.e. a security property bearing on the system's entities.

So as to illustrate ACP specification, we consider the previous file system example where we omit reflexive accesses. The $\mathcal{P}_F^1$ ACP is defined by:

> **Security**
> > **Access**
> > > **Domain**
> > > > **Classif** Cl-A : Users **with** *PropertyA*
> > > > **Classif** Cl-B : Files **with** *PropertyB*
> > > **Authorized**
> > > > (Entity **in** Cl-A) **to** (Entity **in** Cl-B)

that is to say, the security domain of the policy $\mathcal{P}_F^1$ consists of the users' classification A and the files' classification C. The policy $\mathcal{P}_F^1$ has a single access control rule that authorizes A entities to access B entities.

In our approach, a composed access control policy is built by composing two sub-policies. The domain and rules of the composed policy are defined in terms of the composition of its sub-policies' domains and rules.

Composing access control policies Given two classifications, we define three types of composition: their union, intersection and product. The union of two classifications allows one to extend them. On the other hand, the classification obtained by the intersection is a restriction of the sub-classifications. The product of two classifications permits one to distinguish the entities belonging to a single sub-classification from the entities belonging to both sub-classifications.

The definition of the composition of access control domains follows directly: it amounts to specify the type of composition for each pair of classifications of the sub-domains. Notice that the composed domain can then be composed with another access control domain.

Given two access control rules, we define two composition operators: the *logical or* and the *logical and* between their access control predicates. The *logical or* operator between predicates allows one to compose two access control rules in such a way that the resulting access control rule preserves all the accesses of the sub-rules. On the other hand, the access control rule resulting from the *logical and* operator authorizes access if and only if both sub-rules authorize the access.

Coupling the operators for composing classifications and the ones for composing access control predicates allows one either to restrict or to extend the access control rules of the sub-policies. In particular, using the intersection operator and the *logical and* operator for composing access control predicates, the access control rule resulting from the composition of two sub-rules verifies that the access is authorized if and only if it is authorized by both sub-rules.

Finally, in order to compose two access control policies, we have to specify all the composition operators between their classifications and between their access control rules. Introducing default operators for composing classifications and rules in the access control specifications allows to express the requirements of each connector concerning the operators to be used to compose its ACP with another one. Thus, the composition of two ACPs can be automatically computed: given two connectors with access control requirements, we are able to compose these requirements in order to specify the access control requirements of the composed connector.

We now illustrate the use of composition operators with the file system example. The composed policy $\mathcal{P}_F$ authorizes accesses between $(A - C)$ and $(B - D)$, between $(A \cap C)$ and $(B \cap D)$, and between $(C - A)$ and $(D - B)$.

The specifications of the $\mathcal{P}_F^1$ and $\mathcal{P}_F^2$ policies can be composed to give $\mathcal{P}_F$. The distinction among the classifications $(A-C)$, $(A\cap C)$ and $(C-A)$ (resp. $(B-D)$, $(B \cap D)$ and $(D - B)$) is obtained by the product operator of the classification A and C (resp. B and D). Finally, the use of the *logical and* operator between their access control rules enables us to generate the $\mathcal{P}_F$ access control rules.

We stop at this point in our discussion of ACP specification. In particular, we do not introduce formal denotation that allows to prove the completeness and the soundness of the access control specifications. The interested reader can refer to the companion paper [5] which define formally access control specifications and the aforementioned composition operators, as well as the notion of secure access control policy with respect to the proposed specifications.

Comparing access control specifications The above composition approach provides a basis for building the ACP resulting from the interactions among entities that belong to different security domains. In the context of software system, this approach allows us to compose connectors having different ACP specifications according to the composition operators that each application developer (e.g., *security manager*) has specified.

In order to build the (customized) connector that meets ACP requirements (i.e., the (composed) connector that describes the ACP constraints), we have to compare access control specifications. With respect to relationship between set of entities, the classifications (and then the security domains) can be ordered. Given two classifications Cl_1 and Cl_2, we introduce the *plug-in match* and *exact match* operators defined by:

- under *plug-in match*, the classification Cl_1 matches Cl_2 if and only if $Cl_1 \supseteq Cl_2$, that is to say, any Cl_2's entity belong to Cl_1, and
- under *exact match*, the classification Cl_1 matches Cl_2 if and only if $Cl_1 \equiv Cl_2$.

These operators enable us to compare connectors according to their access control domain specifications. On the other hand, the relation of logical implication provides a basis for comparing access control rules. Given two access control rules λ_1 and λ_2, we define the *plug-in match* and *exact match* notion between accesses:

- under *plug-in match*, the rule λ_1 matches λ_2 if and only if any access which is authorized (resp. denied) by λ_1 is also authorized (resp. denied) by λ_2, and

- under *exact match*, the rule λ_1 matches λ_2 if and only if λ_1 matches λ_2 under *plug-in match* and λ_2 matches λ_1 under *plug-in match*.

Thanks to the aforementioned *plug-in match* and *exact match* operators between classifications and access control rules, we are able to compare access control specification. Then, given the (composed) connector, we can select a set of system-level components (which belong to the TCB) and (base) connectors (also belonging to the TCB), in order to automatically construct the customized connector that meets the access control requirements.

4 Integrating security in ASTER

The preceding discussion has allowed to demonstrate the adequacy of a software architecture approach for specifying and reasoning about security in open distributed systems. Specification matching enables us to build the customized connector that meets security requirements. To gain a practical benefit of this, application developers need a programming environment which allows software components to describe their security requirements in their interfaces. ASTER is such a distributed programming environment (see [14]).

The ASTER environment is a *configuration-based* environment (e.g., [26, 20]). It consists of: *i)* a *Module Interconnection Language* (MIL) [26, 10] which allows the application developers to describe the interfaces of its software components (i.e., the *components* according to ADL's terminology), and the interactions among them (i.e., the *configuration* according to ADL's terminology), and *ii)* the run-time system (i.e., an instantiation of a connector) which is possibly customized to satisfy the needs of a given application (e.g., security requirements) [14]. The ASTER MIL defines the **requires** and **provides** clauses for declaring software component needs and provided properties respectively (i.e., connectors).

The ASTER logical tool is responsible to select the system-level components with the corresponding connectors, that allow to build the *customized run-time system* (i.e., the customized connector) that meets QoS requirements [16].

Example. Figure 3 contains an example of interface declarations of a distributed file system, called FS, using the ASTER MIL. First, the client's interface is declared. The keyword **client** denotes that the specific module issues requests for the declared operation. The declaration of the server's interface follows. The third block contains the construction of the file system application based on the declared interfaces, and is divided in two regions: *i)* the modules that participate, and *ii)* the bindings between requests and services.

We extend the MIL in order to integrate specifications of security constraints (*via* the **Security** clause) within the declaration of software components. For instance, figure 3 gives the interface of the file system, including the specifications

```
interface clt-FS {
    client typeFD read(typeFD fd, typeBUF buf)
    client typeINT write(typeFD fd, typeBUF buf)
}
interface srv-FS {
    typeFD read(typeFD fd, typeBUF buf)
    typeINT write(typeFD fd, typeBUF buf)
}
hierarchical FS-A_users-B_files {
    constituents clt-FS; srv-FS;
    bind
        (clt-FS)read : (srv-FS)read;
        (clt-FS)write : (srv-FS)write;
    requires
      Security
        Access
          Domain
            Classif Cl-A : clt-FS with PropertyA
            Classif Cl-B : srv-FS with PropertyB
          Authorized
            (Entity in Cl-A) to (Entity in Cl-B)
        Authentication Protocol : Needham-Schroeder
          Entities : clt-FS and srv-FS
          Semantic :
            Authenticate : Mutual
        Encryption
          Cipher Algorithm : RSA
            Key Size : 512bits
            Storage : ROM
          Signature Algorithm : RSA
            Key Size : 512bits
            Storage : ROM
}
```

Fig. 3. Declaring FS's software components with security requirements.

of the $\mathcal{P}_F^1$ access control policy; we also specify that mutual authentication of clt-FS and srv-FS components *via* the Needham-Schroeder protocol is needed. Finally, thanks to the operators for composing and comparing security specifications, the logical tool can be directly extended to reason about security requirements.

5 Conclusion

Based on the software architecture paradigm, we have described an approach to specify and compose security requirements of software systems. The integration of this approach in the ASTER *configuration-based* environment provides a framework enabling the application developers (e.g., *security managers*) to specify security requirements of their software components. Thanks to its logical tool, the ASTER environment handles security specifications to build the customized runtime-system that meets these requirements.

The separation between security constraints and implementation issue is helpful not only for *security managers* who have to implement complex applications in a controlled and secure way, but also for *end-users* applications which can specify their own security requirements for interaction among their software components. The resulting runtime-system is then customized to meet the application requirements with respect to the system requirements (specified by *security managers*).

Related Work

The integration of security in large scale distributed systems is not a new concern [22]. The emerging object-based architectures [23, 7] renew the interest in security issues, and lead to the dissociation between implementation and security constraints [24, 8]. However, existing work does not deal with the composition of security constraints, which must be addressed in order to allow the interoperation of software components. On the other hand, recent work uses the object paradigm, and especially the abstract data type so as to ease the security implementation [30], but this work does not propose an automatic customization of the run-time system according to the security requirements.

Various models have been proposed in order to reason about security properties (e.g., see [19] for access control specifications, and [6] for authentication specifications). These models are introduced to check whether the security functionality verifies given security properties. However, these models do not deal with the composition of properties.

Concerning the composition of security properties, and more specifically, composition of access control policies, McLean [21] seems to be the first to propose a formal approach including composition operators: he introduces an algebra of security which enables him to reason about the problem of policy conflict, but he does not resolve the conflict (i.e., he does not allow to compose inconsistent access control policies). More generally, Hosmer [13] has introduced the notion of metapolicies, or "policies about policies", an informal framework for composing *security policies*. Bell formalizes this notion by considering the composition of two access control policies as a function (*policy combiner*) [3]. Our approach to compose access control policies is a practical alternative to Bell's proposal: we clearly identify the set of operators enabling security managers to compose access control policy in a controlled and secure way.

For the past decade, there has been considerable research and development in the area of using formal specification for determining whether two components match. However, to our knowledge, software specification matching has not been used to retrieve software components according to their security properties.

Finally, to our knowledge, using software architecture paradigm to reason about security properties and the integration of security specification in a configuration-based environment is not addressed elsewhere.

Future Work

We are currently working on the implementation of our approach by extending the ASTER logical tool to automatically customized the runtime-system according to the security requirements. We are focusing more specifically on integrating the previous models and composition operators on access control policies. We are also examining the practical use of the ASTER system for integrating security in concrete applications. These include the integration of security issues in a federated distributed file system [15].

Finally, given the treatment of security requirements, one application area for our results is the World-Wide Web (Www). We are currently examining the automatic customization of a base Www platform for ensuring information exchanges in a secure way. We also consider the use of our approach for reasoning about Java-applets, in order to customize the Java Virtual Machine [29] in a controlled and secure way.

References

1. R. Allen and D. Garlan. Formalizing architectural connection. In *Proceedings of the Sixteenth International Conference on Software Engineering*, 1994.
2. J. P. Banâtre, C. Bryce, and D. LeMétayer. Mechanical Proof of Security Properties. In *European Symposium on Research in Computer Security*, November 1994.
3. D. E. Bell. Modeling the Multipolicy Machine. In *Proceedings of the New Security Paradigm Workshop*, pages 2–9, August 1994.
4. P.A. Bernstein. Middleware: a Model for Distributed System Services. *Communication of the ACM*, 39(2), February 1996.
5. C. Bidan and V. Issarny. Dealing with Multi-Policy Security in Large Open Distributed Systems. Submitted for publication, May 1997.
6. M. Burrows, M. Abadi, and R. Needham. A Logic of Authentication. Technical Report 39, Digital Systems Research Center, February 1989.
7. M. Chapman and S. Montesi. Overall Concepts and Principles of TINA. Technical Report TB_MDC.018_1.0_94, TINA-C Document, 1995.
8. R.H. Deng, S.K. Bhonsle, W. Wang, and A.A. Lazar. Integrating Security in CORBA Based Object Architectures. In *Proceedings of the IEEE Symposium on Security and Privacy*, pages 50–61, May 1995.
9. Department of Defense Standard. Trusted computer system evaluation criteria. Technical Report DoD 5200.28-STD, December 1985.
10. F. DeRemer and H. Kron. Programming-in-the-Large versus Programming-in-the-Small. *IEEE Transactions on Software Engineering*, 2(2):80–86, June 1976.
11. M. Gasser. *Building a secure computer system*. Number ISBN 0-442-23022-2. Van Nostrand Reinhold, 1988.
12. D. Gelernter and N. Carriero. Coordination languages and their significance. *Communications of the ACM*, 35(2):97–107, 1992.

13. H.H. Hosmer. Metapolicies II. In *Proceedings of the 15th National Computer Security Conference*, pages 369–378, 1992.

14. V. Issarny and C. Bidan. Aster: A Framework for Sound Customization of Distributed Runtime Systems. In *Proceedings of the Sixteenth IEEE International Conference on Distributed Computing Systems*, 1996.

15. V. Issarny, C. Bidan, and T. Saridakis. Designing an open-ended distributed file system in Aster. In *Proceedings of the 9th International Conference on Parallel and Distributed Computing Systems*, 1996.

16. V. Issarny, C. Bidan, and T. Saridakis. Customizing Middleware to Meet Quality of Service Constraints. Submitted for publication, 1997.

17. P. Janson and R. Molva. Security in open networks and distributed systems. *Computer Networks and ISDN Systems*, (22):323–346, 1991.

18. B. Lampson, M. Abadi, M. Burrows, and E. Wobber. Authentication in Distributed Systems : Theory and Practice. *ACM Transactions on Computer Systems*, 10(4):265–310, November 1992.

19. C. E. Landwehr. Formal models for computer security. *ACM Computing Surveys*, 13(3):247–278, November 1981.

20. J. Magee, N. Dulay, and J. Kramer. A Constructive Development for Parallel and Distributed Programs. In *Proceedings of the International Workshop on Configurable Distributed Systems*, 1994.

21. J. McLean. The Algebra of Security. In *Proceedings of the 1988 IEEE Computer Society Symposium on Security and Privacy*, pages 2–7, April 1988.

22. National Computer Security Center. Trusted network interpretation of the tcsec. Technical Report NCSC-TG-005, July 1987.

23. OMG. The Common Object Request Broker: Architecture and Specification – Revision 2.0. Technical report, OMG Document, 1995.

24. OMG Security Working Group. White Paper on Security. TC Document 94.4.16, OMG, April 1994. Available by ftp at `ftp.omg.org:/pub/docs`.

25. D. E. Perry and A. L. Wolf. Foundations for the study of software architecture. *ACM SIGSOFT Software Engineering Notes*, 17(4):40–52, 1992.

26. J. M. Purtilo. The Polylith software bus. *ACM Transactions on Programming Languages and Systems*, 16(1):151–174, 1994.

27. B. Schneier. *Applied Cryptography, Second Edition: Protocols, Algorithms and Source Code in C*, volume ISBN 0-471-11709-9. John Wiley & Sons, Inc., 1993.

28. M. Shaw, R. DeLine, D. Klein, T. Ross, D. Young, and G. Zelesnik. Abstractions for software architecture and tools to support them. *IEEE Transactions on Software Engineering*, 21(4):314–335, 1995.

29. Sun Microsystems Inc. The Java Virtual Machine Specification. Technical report, Sun Document, 1995.

30. L. van Doorn, M. Abadi, M. Burrows, and E. Wobber. Secure Network Objects. In *Proceedings of the IEEE Symposium on Security and Privacy*, pages 211–221, May 1996.

31. E. Wobber, M. Abadi, M. Burrows, and B. Lampson. Authentication in the Taos Operating System. In *Proceedings of ACM SIGOPS '93*, pages 256–269, 1993.

32. A. M. Zaremski and J. M. Wing. Specification matching of software components. In *Proceedings of the ACM SIGSOFT'95 Foundations of Software Engineering Symposium*, 1995.

Regulated Coordination
in
Open Distributed Systems

Naftaly H. Minsky and Victoria Ungureanu

Department of Computer Science
Rutgers University
New Brunswick, NJ, 08903 USA
Phone: (908) 445-2085
Fax: (908) 445-0537
Email: {minsky,ungurean}@cs.rutgers.edu

Abstract. Modern distributed systems tend to be conglomerates of heterogeneous subsystems, which have been designed separately, by different people, with little, if any, knowledge of each other. A single agent operating within a hybrid system of this kind may have to coordinate its activities with members of several such subsystems, under different coordination policies.

To support coordination in such hybrid systems, we introduce in this paper a new concept of regulated coordination that allows a single agent to engage in several different activities, subject to disparate policies. Coordination policies are *enforced* to ensure compliance with them by all participants. We introduce a toolkit called Moses that can support a wide range of useful coordination policies of this kind, in an efficient and unified manner.

1 Introduction

Industry is undergoing a rapid transition from centralized to highly distributed systems within intranets. Such systems tend to be conglomerates of heterogeneous subsystems, which have been designed separately, by different people, with little, if any, knowledge of each other. A single agent operating within such a hybrid system may have to coordinate its activities with members of several such subsystems, under different coordination policies.

This state of affairs is analogous to the situation of a taxi driver, going about his business in the streets of a city. First, he needs to coordinate with other drivers of his company, and with the dispatcher, according to the company's coordination policy or practices. But he must also coordinate with other car drivers that he encounters, particularly at the intersections between roads. He knows nothing about these drivers, except that they abide by the same traffic laws—another "coordination policy," with a different set of participating agents; and if our driver happens to cross the tunnel from France to England, he would have to adapt himself to a *different* coordination policy for driving. And this may not be all. Our taxi driver may be involved in some other activities that require coordination, such as passing through a toll booth, or calling his friends on his car phone to organize a game of bridge.

There are plenty of computing analogies for this metaphor. For example, all the disparate clients of a given server may be required to abide by the policy governing this service; e.g. they might have to limit the frequency of requests in a certain way—lest the server would be congested, resulting in a denial of services to many clients. While using such a service, an agent may be called to vote on some issue, which may require certain coordination to ensure fair and secret voting. Furthermore, our agent may be involved in an activity that, by a policy of the enterprise in question, is to be monitored—for auditing or for load balancing. (We will elaborate on all these example policies later on in this paper.)

Coordination in such an open and heterogeneous context has two prerequisites. First, the protocol underlying a given coordination policy must be *enforced* on all its participants. This is necessary because we assume no knowledge of the structure and behavior of agents involved in a given policy, or even of the language in which they are programmed[1]—such agents cannot be relied on to observe any given protocol voluntarily. Second, a given agent should be allowed to operate under several disparate coordination policies, which may be independent of each other. We propose to satisfy these two prerequisites by means of the *regulated coordination mechanism* to be introduced in this paper.

We start, in Section 2, with a definition of our concept of *coordination policy*, which underlies our mechanism for regulated coordination. In Section 3 we introduce an implementation of regulated coordination by a toolkit called Moses, illustrating it with a detailed example. This implementation, which uses message passing as the basic coordination primitive, is based on previous work by the authors and their colleagues [11,12]. To demonstrate the range of applicability of Moses we discuss in Section 4 the implementation of two additional coordination policies: for fair voting, and for monitoring. Section 5 places this work in the context of current research on coordination; and we conclude with a thought about some broader implications of this work and directions for future research.

2 The Concept of a Coordination Policy

The term "policy," according to the the American Heritage Dictionary [15], means "a general principle that guides the actions taken by a person or group". According to this definition a policy has three elements: the *actions* guided by the policy, the participating *group*, and the *guiding principles*. Accordingly, we define a coordination policy $\mathcal{P}$ to be the triple $\langle \mathcal{M}, \mathcal{G}, \mathcal{L} \rangle$, where

1. $\mathcal{M}$ is the set of messages, representing the primitive operations of the activity in question. They are called $\mathcal{P}$-messages.

---

[1] In fact, an agent might not be programmed at all—he might be a *person*, and thus inherently unpredictable.

2. $\mathcal{G}$ is a distributed group of *agents*, sometimes called a "policy-group," that are permitted to send and receive $\mathcal{P}$-messages, and thus are the participants in policy $\mathcal{P}$.

3. $\mathcal{L}$ is the set of rules regulating the exchange of $\mathcal{P}$-messages between members of group $\mathcal{G}$. It is called the *law* of this policy.

Here is an example of a coordination policy. Assume that there is a specific issue on which an open and heterogeneous group of agents is asked to vote. Consider the following policy designed to ensure that the vote is fair and confidential; we will call it "electronic vote" policy and denote it by $\mathcal{EV}$:

1. an agent can vote at most once, and only within the time period allotted for this vote;

2. the counting is done correctly; and

3. an agent is guaranteed that nobody else, not even the organizer of the vote, will know how he/she voted.

The components of this particular policy are as follows: the group $\mathcal{G}_{\mathcal{EV}}$ consists of the group of agents that participate in the voting. The set of messages $\mathcal{M}_{\mathcal{EV}}$ consists of all the messages exchanged during the vote including: initiating a vote, casting the vote, and announcing the results; and the law $\mathcal{L}_{\mathcal{EV}}$ is the set of rules described above for $\mathcal{EV}$, written in a given formal language. We introduce such a language in the following section.

Several clarifications of this concept of a policy are in order. First, we take a policy to have an independent existence, separate from the agents participating in it, and independent from any other policy. We provide means for an agent to *join* a given policy $\mathcal{P}$—subject to the law of this policy—which will enable this agent to send and receive $\mathcal{P}$-messages. A given agent may thus join several policies, and be active under them concurrently. Note that by definition different policies cannot be in conflict because the exchange of $\mathcal{P}$-messages is governed solely by $\mathcal{L}_{\mathcal{P}}$, regardless of any other policy the agent in question might belong to.

Second, the law of a policy is expected to be strictly enforced. We insist on enforcement, because complete conformance to the law by all members of a policy-group is often critical to the integrity of the activity in question. And because, in an open context, one cannot rely on the agents belonging to a given policy-group to observe the law voluntarily.

Finally, we point out that although a policy can be formulated without detailed knowledge of the behavior of the prospective participants, an agent involved in a certain policy needs to be familiar with its law, and with the structure of its messages—just as the taxi-driver needs to know the traffic laws. But since the law is enforced, it cannot be violated even by an agent who does not know the law, or who willfully ignores it. This is unlike our traffic analogy, where a driver can drive through a red light, causing much harm to others.

3 Regulated Coordination and its Implementation

We start this discussion by introducing the concept of law—the key aspect of a policy—illustrating it by an example. This is followed with the distributed enforcement mechanism in Section 3.3; a discussion of the mechanism used in Moses for the creation of policies, and for their maintenances is presented in Section 3.4; in Section 3.5 we discuss a refinement of our law by means of a concept of *obligations*, which provide our model with certain *pro-active* capabilities. We conclude this section with a brief discussion of the fault tolerance and scalability of Moses.

3.1 The Law of a Policy

A law $\mathcal{L}$ of a policy $\mathcal{P}$ determines the treatment of $\mathcal{P}$-messages by specifying what should be done when such a message is sent, and when it arrives. More specifically, the law deals with the following two kinds of events that are regulated under Moses[2]:

1. `sent(x,m,y)` — occurs when agent x sends an $\mathcal{P}$-message m addressed to y. If the destination is the keyword `all`, m is multicasted to all members of the group. The sender x is considered the *home* of this event.
2. `arrived(x,m,y)` — occurs when an $\mathcal{P}$-message m sent by x arrives at y. The receiver y is considered the *home* of this event.

We assume no prior knowledge of, or control over, the occurrence of these *regulated events*. But the effect that any given event e would actually have is prescribed by the law $\mathcal{L}$ of the policy in question. This prescription, called the *ruling* of the law for this event, is a (possibly empty) sequence of *primitive operations* (discussed later) which are to be carried out at the home of e, as the immediate response to its occurrence.

Structurally, the law $\mathcal{L}$ is a pair $\langle \mathcal{R}, \mathcal{CS} \rangle$, where $\mathcal{R}$ is a fixed set of rules defined for the entire group $\mathcal{G}$ of the policy in question, and $\mathcal{CS}$ is a mutable set $\{\mathcal{CS}_x \mid x \in \mathcal{G}\}$ of what we call *control states*, one per member of the group. These two parts of the law are discussed in more detail below.

The control state CS_x. This is the part of the law $\mathcal{L}$ that is associated with the individual member x of a group. It is a bag of terms, called the *attributes* of this member. The main role of these attributes is to enable $\mathcal{L}$ to distinguish between different kinds of members, so that the ruling of the law for a given event may depend on its home. Some of the attributes of an agent have a predefined semantics, such as the attribute `clock(t)` where t represents the local time. However, the semantics of attributes is defined, in general, by the law, for a given group. For instance, in the implementation of the electronic voting policy, described in Section 4.1, a term `vote(init(x),end(et))` in the control state of an agent will allow the agent to participate to the vote initiated by x with deadline et.

---

[2] Note that Moses regulates some additional types of events, one of which is treated in Section 3.5, and the others are ignored in this paper.

The Primitive Operations. The operations that can be included in the ruling of the law for a given regulated event e, to be carried out at the home of this event, are called *primitive operations*. They are "primitive" in the sense that they can be performed *only* if thus authorized by the law. These operations include:

1. Operations that change the CS of the home agent. Specifically, we can perform the following operations: (1) +t which adds the term t to the control state; (2) -t which removes the term t; (3) t1←t2 which change term t1 with term t2; and (4) incr(t(v),x) which increments the value v of a term t with some quantity x.

2. Operation forward(m,y,x) emits to the network the message m addressed to y, where x identifies the *sender* of the message. (When a message thus forwarded to y arrives, it would trigger at y the event arrived(x,m,y).) The most common use of this operation is in a ruling for event sent(x,m,y), where operation forward (with no arguments) simply completes the passing of the intended message.

3. Operation deliver(m) delivers the message m to the home-agent. The most common use of this operation is in a ruling for event arrived(x,m,y), where operation deliver (with no arguments) simply delivers the arriving message to the home agent.

The global set of rules $\mathcal{R}$. The function of $\mathcal{R}$ is to evaluate a ruling for any possible regulated-event that occurs at an agent with a given control-state. In our current model, $\mathcal{R}$ is represented by a very simple Prolog-like program—or, if you will, a set of situation-action rules. When this "program" $\mathcal{R}$ is presented with a goal e, representing a regulated event, and with a variable CS, representing the control-state of the home agent, it produces a list of primitive-operations representing the ruling of the law for this event. For the details of this formulation the reader is referred to [14], here we will only illustrate it with the following example.

3.2 Example: Congestion Control Policy

Let s be a server designed to provide certain services to an heterogeneous and open group of agents. Consider the following policy designed to control possible congestion of the server due to large volume of request from its clients; we will call it the "congestion control" policy, denoting it by $\mathcal{CC}$:

1. Every client of s has a quantum of time dt assigned to it, which is to be the *minimal delay* between any two requests sent by this agent to the server.

2. The server can set the delay of an agent to any desired value.

3. If an agent attempts to send a message to s sooner than permitted by his delay, this message is to be blocked. (Later we will remove the harsh edge of this part of our policy.)

The components of policy $\mathcal{CC}$ are as follows: The group $\mathcal{G}_{cc}$ consists of the server s and all its clients. The set $\mathcal{M}_{cc}$ consists of all the messages exchanged

---

Initially: Each client has in its control state: (1) the term clock(T) , where T represents the local current time; (2) a term delay(DT) where DT represents the minimum delay between successive messages sent by the client to the server s; and (3) a term lastCall(Tlast) where Tlast is the time when the last message was sent to the server (initially set to 0).

$\mathcal{R}$1. sent(s,_,_) :- do(forward).

Any message sent by server s is forwarded to its intended destination.

$\mathcal{R}$2. arrived(s,changeDelay(Val),X) :-
      do(delay(DT)←delay(Val)),
      do(deliver(memo(changeDelay(Val)))).

When a message changeDelay(Val) *sent by s arrives at the destination, the* delay *term is changed to* Val*, and a memo is sent to the receiver X to notify it of the change.*

$\mathcal{R}$3. arrived(_,_,_) :- do(deliver).

Any message other than changeDelay *arriving at the destination is delivered without further ado.*

$\mathcal{R}$4. sent(X,M,s) :-
      lastCall(Tlast)@CS,delay(DT)@CS,clock(T)@CS,
      T > (Tlast + DT),
      do(lastCall(Tlast)←lastCall(T)),do(forward).

A message sent to the server s will be forwarded only if the delay condition is satisfied. If the message is forwarded, the term lastCall *is updated to reflect that a message is sent at the current time T.*

Fig. 1. Law $\mathcal{L}_{CC}$ - congestion control policy

between the server and its clients; and the law $\mathcal{L}_{CC}$ mirroring the rules described above, is presented in Figure 1.

We now show how this policy is established by letting this activity be governed by $\mathcal{L}_{CC}$. The set $\mathcal{R}$ of this law consists of four rules. Each is followed with a comment (in italic), which, together with the following discussion, should be understandable even for a reader not familiar with Prolog.[3]

Under this law, server s can send arbitrary messages which are forwarded to the intended destination without further ado (Rule $\mathcal{R}$1). But, this law makes a distinction between the message changeDelay and all other messages sent by s. By Rule $\mathcal{R}$2 , when a changeDelay(val) arrives at some client x it will have the following effects: the value of the term delay is set to val and a memo is

---

[3] For a reader who is familiar with Prolog we point out that the a term t@CS in a rule evaluates to true if the term t is present in the CS of the home agent, and the term do(p) adds the primitive operation p to the ruling of the law.

delivered to x to notify it of the change. Thus, this message provides the server with the ability to adjust at will the delay term of the clients.

The requests made by the clients are governed by rules $\mathcal{R}3$ and $\mathcal{R}4$ as follows. A message sent by a client to the server s is forwarded only if the delay condition between messages is satisfied. By Rule $\mathcal{R}3$ such a message arriving at s is delivered without further ado. If the sender issues its request too early, the message will not be forwarded and is thus effectively blocked.

A major disadvantage of this policy is that clients should be aware of the existence of a minimum delay between messages and cope with its fluctuations. We will show in Section 3.5, how this drawback can be removed.

3.3 The Distributed Enforcement Mechanism

The law for a given policy $\mathcal{P} = \langle \mathcal{M}, \mathcal{G}, \mathcal{L} \rangle$, is enforced in principle as follows: there is a *controller* associated with each member of group $\mathcal{G}$, logically placed between the agent and the communications medium, as is illustrated in Figure 2. All controllers have identical copies of the global set of rules $\mathcal{R}$ of $\mathcal{L}$, and each controller maintains the control states of the agents under its jurisdiction. The steps taken when a member x wishes to send a $\mathcal{P}$-message m to a member y are:

1. x sends m to its assigned controller. The controller evaluates the ruling of the law $\mathcal{L}$ for the event send(x,m,y) and it carries out this ruling. If part of the ruling is to forward a message m' to y'[4], x's controller sends m' to the controller assigned to y'.
2. when m' arrives to the controller of y' it generates an arrived(x,m',y') event. The ruling for this event is computed and carried out. The message m' is delivered to y' if so required by the ruling.

The correctness of the proposed mechanism is based on the following assumptions (1) messages are securely transmitted over the network, and (2) $\mathcal{P}$-messages are sent and received only via correctly implemented controllers, interpreting law $\mathcal{L}$. A presentation of how these requirements are met is outside the scope of this paper, but can be found in [14].

The essential aspect of this architecture is that *all controllers have identical copies of the law*. It is in this sense that the law is said to be global to the group.

Implementation Status. An experimental prototype of the Moses toolkit has been implemented. Our controllers are written in Java, so that Moses toolkit is portable to different platforms. Because our rules do not require the full power of Prolog language, we have built an interpreter for the needed subset of Prolog. This implementation distinguishes between two types of agents:

1. A *bounded agents*, driven by a specific program (which is what "binds" it). These programs use a set of preprogrammed primitives for communication with Moses' controllers. Currently there are versions of these primitives written in C, C++, Java, and Prolog.

---

[4] m' might differ from the original message m, and also the final destination y' might vary from the original destination y.

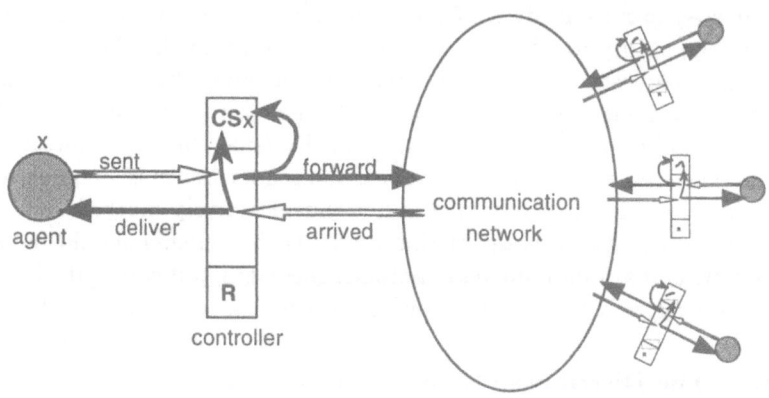

Legend:

a regulated event
a primitive operation

Fig. 2. Enforcement of the Law

2. An *unbounded agent*, which represents a human, not bound by any program. Such an agent communicates with its assigned controller via Netscape, using application specific interfaces consisting of HTML documents with embedded applets. Our choice was motivated by (1) the almost universal deployment of WWW browsers; and (2) the ease of learning to use this interface.

The implementation has been tested on UNIX platform including SunOS and Solaris.

3.4 The Creation of a Policy, and its Maintenance

Under our current implementation of the Moses toolkit, a new policy $\mathcal{P}$ is established by creating a server that provides persistent storage for the law $\mathcal{L}$ of this policy, including the control-states of all members of the policy-group $\mathcal{G}$. This server is called the *secretary* of $\mathcal{P}$, to be denoted by $\mathcal{S}_\mathcal{P}$. The following are some of the services provided by such a secretary.

For an agent x to be able to exchange $\mathcal{P}$-messages under a policy $\mathcal{P}$, it needs to send a connect(g) message to $\mathcal{S}_\mathcal{P}$, asking to be identified with some agent g that is a member of the group $\mathcal{G}$ of $\mathcal{P}$. ($\mathcal{S}_\mathcal{P}$ is likely to require authentication, which can be in form of a password or an X.509 certificate). If the secretary agrees to make the connection, it would assign x to some controller, after providing this controller with the current control-state of g, and with the set of rules $\mathcal{R}$ of the law $\mathcal{L}$ (if the controller does not have these rules already).

Once this connection is made, the interaction of x with the various members of policy $\mathcal{P}$ does not directly involve the secretary $\mathcal{S}_\mathcal{P}$. However, if some event at x ends up changing the control-state of the member g it is associated with, this change would be automatically communicated to S_P.

For example, consider the secretary S_{CC} of our CC policy, at a given moment in time. Let Jones be a currently inactive member of this policy, who has the term delay(dt) in its control-state. And let x be a agent that wishes to operate as Jones under this policy. To do this he sends a connect(Jones) message to S_{CC}, together with an authentication token. After the authentication is performed, x can send CC-messages, as if he is Jones.

Note that nothing prevents a member of one policy-group, such as CC-policy, to join another one, such as $\mathcal{EV}$. Therefore, a given agent may participate in any number of such policy-groups.

The secretary of a policy also acts as a name server for the members of its group $\mathcal{G}$, and it provides means for admitting new members into $\mathcal{G}$, and for removing existing members from it. These operations, which are also subject to $\mathcal{L}$, are not discussed here in detail.

Finally, we note that a policy does not have to be supported by a single secretary. It is possible, in principle, for a policy to have several secretaries, each maintaining a subgroup of $\mathcal{G}$. It is even possible to have an "open policy" that is not supported by any secretary. But the details of such organizations are beyond the scope of this paper.

3.5 Obligations

Note that so far, our law has been purely *reactive*. That is, it prescribes what should be done in response to certain events, but it cannot initiate any action on its own. To provide our model with certain *pro-active* capabilities, in some analogy with the pro-active capabilities proposed by Andreoli et al. [3], we now introduce a concept of "obligation." This concept is based broadly on the societal notion of obligation, and more directly on the concept of *enforced obligation* introduced by Minsky [13], and on the work of Maibaum [10] and of Feather[16], on formal specification of temporal constraints.

Broadly speaking, an obligation imposed on a given agent serves as a kind of *motive force* that *ensures* that a certain action will be carried out at this agent, at a specified time in the future (when the obligation is said to *come due*), provided that a certain condition on the control state of the agent is satisfied at that time.

The primitive operation +obligation(p,dt) carried out at agent x would cause the event obligationDue(p) to occur at x in dt seconds, (provided that this obligation has not been repealed in the meantime, by means of the inverse primitive operation -obligation.) The occurrence of event obligationDue(p) at x, prompts the controller of x to evaluate the ruling of the law for this event, and then carry it out. This ruling is, thus, the action associated with this obligation.

We note that our obligations can be viewed as a kind of triggers. But they are tightly *regulated triggers*, because the imposition of obligations, the action associated with them, and the ability to repeal a pending obligation, are all governed by the law of a group.

The CC Policy Revisited. We illustrate the use of obligation by showing how the CC-policy for preventing server congestion can be modified, freeing clients from having to worry about the delay between messages. Under CC, if the delay condition is not satisfied, the message is blocked, leaving it up to the client to resend the message at a proper time. We now define a variant of this policy, called CC', as follows:

1. Every client of s has a quantum of time dt assigned to it, which is to be the *minimal delay* between any two requests sent by this agent to the server.
2. The server can set the delay of an agent to any desired value.
3' If an agent attempts to send a message to s sooner than permitted by his delay, this message is to be forwarded to the server at the earliest time consistent with the delay, *without client's involvement.*

This is implemented as follows: early messages are buffered[5] in the control state of the client, and obligations are imposed to forward the messages in question at the earliest possible time consistent with the delay condition. While a client may send its requests to s at any rate, these messages will be actually forwarded to the destination at the pace imposed by s, and in their original order.

The only modifications needed to be performed to $\mathcal{L}_{CC}$ are the replacement of Rule $\mathcal{R}4$ by Rule $\mathcal{R}4'$ and adding of Rules $\mathcal{R}5$ and $\mathcal{R}6$. The new rules of $\mathcal{L}_{CC'}$ are presented in Figure 3 and described briefly below. There are three possibilities to take into account when a client attempts to send a message. First if the delay condition is satisfied and there are no buffered messages, then the message is forwarded to server s (Rule $\mathcal{R}4'$). Second, if the delay condition is not satisfied and the buffer is empty, then the message is pushed into the buffer and an obligation is imposed to forward the message at the earliest time that satisfies the delay condition (Rule $\mathcal{R}4'$). Finally, if the delay condition is not satisfied and the buffer is not empty, the the message is added to the buffer in FIFO order (Rule $\mathcal{R}5$).

By Rule $\mathcal{R}6$, when an obligation sendMessage fires the oldest message is removed from the buffer and is forwarded to s. Moreover, if there are still buffered messages, then another sendMessage obligation is set for the earliest time satisfying the delay condition.

3.6 Fault Tolerance and Scalability

Law-governed interaction lends itself to fault tolerant and scalable implementations, as we argue briefly below.

---

[5] This law does not treat the case of buffer overflow, which can be treated however quite easily.

Initially: In addition to the terms clock(T), lastCall(Tlast) and delay(DT) from $\mathcal{L}_{cc}$, each client has now in in its control state a term buffer(L), where L is the list of messages the client sent earlier than required by the delay condition and have not yet been forwarded. L is initially empty.

$\mathcal{R}4'.$

```
sent(X,M,s) :-
        buffer([])@CS, lastCall(Tlast)@CS,delay(DT)@CS,clock(T)@CS,
        T > (Tlast + DT) →
            (do(lastCall(Tlast)←lastCall(T)), do(forward))
            |
            (do(+obligation(sendMessage,Tlast+DT)),
            do(buffer([])←buffer([M]))).
```

A message sent to the server s will be forwarded if there are not buffered messages and the delay condition is satisfied. Otherwise, the message is buffered and an obligation to send the message at the earliest time which satisfies the delay condition is set. In the case the message is forwarded the term lastCall is updated to reflect that a message was sent at the current time T.

$\mathcal{R}5.$
```
sent(X,M,s) :-
        buffer(L)@CS, append(L,[M],L1), do(buffer(L)←buffer(L1)).
```

If there are buffered messages, when a new message M is sent to s, M is appended in FIFO order to the buffer.

$\mathcal{R}6.$
```
obligationDue(sendMessage) :-
        lastCall(Tlast)@CS,delay(DT)@CS,clock(T)@CS,
        do(lastCall(Tlast)←lastCall(T)),
        buffer([M|R])@CS, do(buffer([M|R])←buffer(R)),
        do(forward(M,s)),
        R=[] →
            true
            |
            do(+obligation(sendMessage,T+DT)).
```

When an obligation sendMessage fires the least recent message, M, is removed from the buffer and is forwarded to s. The term lastCall is updated to reflect that a message was sent at current time T. Moreover, if there are buffered messages an obligation sendMessage is set for the earliest time satisfying the delay condition.

Fig. 3. $\mathcal{L}_{cc}$: $\mathcal{CC}'$-policy with obligations

Fault Tolerance. Since Moses assumes nothing about the interacting agents, it is completely tolerant to all their failures, even of a Byzantine kind. But Moses is sensitive to two kinds of failures: (a) the failure of a secretary, which may have a devastating effect on the long term existence of the policy-group, even if it has no effect on the immediate interaction between its members; and (b) the failure of a controller. These failures can be handled by well known methods. Failures of the secretary can be addressed by means of the state-machine approach [17], using a toolkit such as Isis [6] for the active replication of the secretary. Failures of controllers can be analogously handled by replication of each controller. Alternatively, given a reliable secretary, it may be sufficient for the controllers to notify the secretary of all state changes.

Scalability. Since the law is enforced strictly locally, by the controller of each agent, the size of the policy-group has no effect on the interaction between its members. Therefore, Moses is *naturally scalable*, particularly in the case of an *open group*. However, when a group is supported by a single secretary, as in our current implementation, then the size of the group does affect operations such as finding the name of a fellow member of a group, or reporting to the secretary a change of the control state of a given member. But this has a second order effect on the efficiency of interaction under Moses.

4 Examples

To illustrate the expressive power of the proposed coordination mechanism, we present here the implementation in Moses of two disparate policies mentioned previously: the electronic voting policy, and the purchase monitoring policy. Recall that although these policies, and the one discussed in Section 3, are defined by separate laws, unrelated to each other, a given agent may be subject to several of these policies, with respect to different modes of interaction it is involved in.

4.1 Electronic Voting Policy

We introduce here $\mathcal{L_{EV}}$, displayed in Figure 4, which implements the law of the electronic voting policy $\mathcal{EV}$ introduced in Section 2. Under this law every agent in the group can initiate a vote[6] on any issue he chooses, by multicasting the message startVote to all members of the group. The actual voting is to be done by sending castVote messages to the initiator. The law $\mathcal{L_{EV}}$ ensures that the following requirements would be met: (1) a member can vote at most once, and only within the time period allotted for this vote; (2) the counting of the votes is done correctly; (3) nobody else besides the voting agent knows how he voted; (4) agents are notified of the outcome of the vote.

The general exchange of messages between members participating in a vote is described briefly below. First, by Rule $\mathcal{R}1$, a member x of the group can start an electronic vote by multicasting a startVote(issue(i),end(et)) message, where i is a description of the issue subjected to vote, and et is the time when the votes ends. When such a message arrives at a member y a term vote(init(x),end(et)) is added to y's control state, recording the ending time

---

[6] For simplicity reasons, a member can be at a give time the initiator of at most one voting process.

```
R1. sent(X,startVote(issue(I),end(ET)),all) :-
        not(voteInProgress@CS), do(+ yesVotes(0)), do(+noVotes(0)),
        do(+obligation(sendResults, ET + 100)),
        do(+voteInProgress),do(forward).
```

Any member of the group can start an electronic vote by sending a startVote *message to all members. The message contains a description of the issue* I *to be voted and the time* ET *when the vote ends. The initiator incurs an obligation to send the results of the vote to all voters. Note that* X *can initiate a new voting process only if the precedent one organized by him, if any, ended.*

```
R2. arrived(X,startVote(issue(I),end(ET)),Y) :-
        do(+vote(init(X),end(ET))),do(deliver).
```

A startVote *message is delivered to the destination. A term* vote(init(X),end(ET)) *is added to the control state of the receiver recording:* X, *which is the initiator of the vote, and* ET, *which is the time when the voting ends.*

```
R3. sent(Y,castVote(Val),X) :-
        vote(init(X),end(ET))@CS, clock(T)@CS, T < ET,
        do(- vote(init(X),end(ET))), do(forward).
```

A castVote *message containing* Val *the value of the vote, is forwarded to the initiator if the time to vote has not expired. The term* vote(init(X),end(ET)) *is removed from the control state to prevent this agent from voting again.*

```
R4. arrived(Y,castVote(yes),X) :-
        yesVotes(N)@CS, do(incr(yesVotes(N),1)).
R5. arrived(Y,castVote(no),X) :- noVotes(N)@CS, do(incr(noVotes(N),1)).
```

When a message castVote *arrives, the vote is counted, by the controller as an effect of the ruling. The message is NOT delivered to the initiator* X.

```
R6. obligationDue(sendResults) :-
        yesVotes(N1)@CS, noVotes(N2)@CS,
        do(-yesVotes(N1)), do(-noVotes(N2)), do(-voteInProgress),
        do(forward(results(yesVotes(N1),noVotes(N2)),all)).
```

When the time frame allotted for the vote is over, the results of the vote are sent to all group members. Also, the terms which held the count of "yes" and "no" votes, and voteInProgress *are removed from the control state, thus allowing the initiator to start another vote.*

```
R7. arrived(_,results(yesVotes(_),noVotes(_)),_) :- do(deliver).
```

Fig. 4. Law $\mathcal{L}_{\mathcal{EV}}$ for electronic voting policy

of the vote et and the name of the initiator x[7]. As we shall see this term will enable y to cast its vote only once and in the allotted time.

---

[7] At a given time, there can be more than one voting in progress. The name of the initiator serves as an identifier of such a vote process.

Now, a member of the group can vote by sending a message `castVote(val)` to the initiator x, where `val` is the value of the vote (Rule $\mathcal{R}3$). Such a message is forwarded to the destination only if: (1) the agent has in its control state a term `vote(init(x),end(et))`, and (2) the deadline for the vote has not passed yet. Note that the term `vote` is removed from the control state of an agent when the vote is cast, thus preventing him to vote again.

Note that the initiator himself never gets the votes, the counting being done by the controller as *an effect of the ruling*, thus ensuring voters privacy and correctness of the computation (Rules $\mathcal{R}4$ and $\mathcal{R}5$).

Finally, when the time for the vote expires, the result of the votes is multi-casted (Rule $\mathcal{R}6$), as the fulfillment of the obligation the initiator incurred when it started the vote.

4.2 Purchase Monitoring Policy

Consider the following situation: in an organization there is an open group of agents that can issue purchase orders. The following policy, called $\mathcal{PM}$, is imposed to discourage fraud:

1. all purchases whose value exceeds $1000 should be monitored by a prescribed monitor.
2. senders and receivers of purchase orders cannot prevent the monitoring, or subvert it in any way.

The set $\mathcal{M}_{\mathcal{PM}}$ consists of the messages: `purchase(object(o),value(v))`, which is a purchase order for object o with value v; and `monitored(buyer(x),object(o),value(v))`, which carries the information required for auditing. $\mathcal{G}_{\mathcal{PM}}$, the group of agents subject to policy $\mathcal{PM}$, consists of the distinguished monitoring agent m, and the agents that can issue/receive purchase messages.

The law $\mathcal{L}_{PM}$ of this policy is presented in Figure 5 and described briefly below. If an agent x is issuing a purchase order, by Rule $\mathcal{R}1$, the message is forwarded to its intended destination. However, if the value of the purchase is bigger than $1000, a `monitored` message is sent to the distinguished agent m which performs the monitoring.

When a `purchase` message arrives at destination it is delivered (Rule $\mathcal{R}2$).

5 Relationship to Other Coordination Work

Moses differs from other coordination mechanisms mainly in (a) the coordination primitives it uses, and (b) its the target application domain—in a manner summarized below.

Most coordination mechanisms use either *virtually shared space*, as in Linda [7,5], or some form of broadcasting [1], for the interaction between the agents involved, and for the coordination of such interaction. Both means allow for very powerful coordination languages, but are difficult to scale up. We, in contrast,

```
R1. sent(X,purchase(object(O),value(V)),_) :- V > 1000 →
            do(forward(monitored(buyer(X),object(O),value(V)),m))
            |
            true,
        do(forward).
```

A purchase message is forwarded to its intended destination. If the value of the purchase is bigger than $1000, a monitored *message is sent to a distinguished agent* m *which performs the monitoring.*

```
R2. arrived(_,_,_) :- do(deliver).
```
Any message arriving at the destination is delivered without further ado.

Fig. 5. Law $\mathcal{L}_{PM}$ - purchase monitoring policy

assume simple message passing as the base mode for interaction between agents; and our law—i.e., the "coordination program"—is enforced strictly locally, at each agent; although it governs the entire distributed policy-group in question. Consequently, Moses is easily scalable, and lends itself to efficient and fault tolerant implementation. The price is, of course, in expressive power, which is weaker than that of a language like LO [8]. Yet, we believe that the expressive power of Moses is sufficiently rich to be useful, as the examples in this paper hopefully demonstrate.

A possible metaphor for the target application of much of the current co-ordination research, such as [4,1,2], is a *symphonic orchestra* [9,19], in which all players work together to perform a musical piece. In other words, there is a specific task to be performed via the interaction of autonomous, possibly heterogeneous, components; this interaction is to be defined by means of a single "coordination program." We, on the other hand, have in mind the *taxi-driver metaphor*, where a single agent participates in several disparate activities that are subject to different coordination policies. Such a policy may not reflect any particular task to be performed, but–just like the traffic laws—may serve as a constraint on certain actions performed by various agents. It is this type of application that motivated our concept of a coordination policy as an independent entity separate ¿from the agents that may end up participating in it.

6 Conclusion

The concept of regulated coordination presented in this paper allows for an agent to operate under several different policies at the same time, but these policies are completely independent of each other. This is only the first step toward a more comprehensive theory that allows for various relationships between policies, thus supporting coordination between autonomous activities, like for example, workflows. In this context, it was recently noted that "mechanism are needed which allow independent workflows to exchange information and influence each other control flow" [18].

In particular, we are working now on a concept of *policy hierarchies*, which would allow for a set of policies to coexist under a single "super-policy". And we would like to be able to evolve the laws of distinct sub-policies independently of each other.

The main issues to be clarified and resolved here are the *relative jurisdiction* of the law of a super-policy and that of its sub-policies. At the moment it appears that there is no universally useful resolution of these issues. We intend, therefore, to explore several alternatives, hoping to end up with a formulation of a meta-level that allows for the construction of a range of types of policy hierarchies.

References

1. J.-M. Andreoli. Coordination in LO. In J.-M. Andreoli, C. Hankin, and D. Le Metayer, editors, *Coordination Programming*, pages 42–64. Imperial College Press, 1996.
2. J.-M. Andreoli, P. Ciancarini, and R. Pareschi. Interaction abstract machines. In G. Agha, P. Wegner, and A. Yonezawa, editors, *Research Directions in Concurrent Object-Oriented Programming*, pages 257–280. 1993.
3. J.-M. Andreoli, H. Gallaire, and R. Pareschi. Rule-based object coordination. In P. Ciancarini, O. Nierstrasz, and A. Yonezawa, editors, *Object-Based Models and Languages for Concurrent Systems*, Lecture Notes in Computer Science, pages 1–13. Springer-Verlag, 1995. Number 924.
4. J.-P. Banatre and D. Le Metayer. Gamma and the chemical reaction model: Ten years after. In J.-M. Andreoli, C. Hankin, and D. Le Metayer, editors, *Coordination Programming*, pages 3–41. Imperial College Press, 1996.
5. M. Banville. Sonia: an adaptation of Linda for coordination of activities in organizations. In P. Ciancarini and C. Hankin, editors, *Coordination Languages and Models*, Lecture Notes in Computer Science, pages 57–74. Springer-Verlag, 1996. Number 1061.
6. K.P. Birman. The process group approach to reliable distributed computing. *Communications of the ACM*, 36(12):36–53, December 1993.
7. N. Carriero and D. Gelernter. Coordination languages and their significance. *Communications of the ACM*, 35(2):97–107, February 1992.
8. S. Castellani and P. Ciancarini. Enhancing coordination and modularity mechanisms for a language with objects-as-multisets. In P. Ciancarini and C. Hankin, editors, *Coordination Languages and Models*, Lecture Notes in Computer Science, pages 89–106. Springer-Verlag, 1996. Number 1061.
9. M. Cortes and P. Mishra. DCWPL: A programming language for describing collaborative work. In *Conference on Computer Supported Cooperative Work*, pages 21–29, 1996.
10. S.J.H. Kent, T.S.E. Maibaum, and W.J. Quirk. Formally specifying temporal constraints and error recovery. In *Proceedings of the IEEE Int. Symp. on Requirement Engineering*, pages 208–215, San Diego, CA, January 1993.
11. N.H. Minsky. The imposition of protocols over open distributed systems. *IEEE Transactions on Software Engineering*, February 1991.
12. N.H. Minsky and J. Leichter. Law-governed Linda as a coordination model. In P. Ciancarini, O. Nierstrasz, and A. Yonezawa, editors, *Object-Based Models and Languages for Concurrent Systems*, number 924 in Lecture Notes in Computer Science, pages 125–146. Springer-Verlag, 1995.

13. N.H. Minsky and A. Lockman. Ensuring integrity by adding obligations to privileges. In *Proceedings of the 8th International Conference on Software Engineering*, pages 92–102, August 1985.

14. N.H. Minsky and V. Ungureanu. Unified support for heterogeneous security policies. Technical report, Rutgers University, LCSR, February 1996.

15. W. Morris. *The American Heritage Dictionary of the English Language*. Houghton Mifflin Company, 1981.

16. Feather Martin S. An implementation of bounded obligtions. In *Proceedings of the 8th Knowladge Based Software Engineering Conference*, pages 114–122, Chicago, Ill, September 1993.

17. F.B. Schneider. Implementing fault tolerant services using the state machine approach. *ACM Computing Surveys*, 22(4):300–319, 1990.

18. F. Schwenkreis. Workflow for the German Federal Government - a position paper. In *NSF Workshop on Workflow and Process Automation in Information Systems*, May 1996.

19. A. Werner, M.Polze and M. Malek. The unstoppable orchestra: A responsive distributed application. In *Third International Conference on Configurable Distributed Systems*, pages 154–160, May 1996.

Debugging Distributed Applications Using a Coordination Architecture

Pieter A. Olivier

olivierp@wins.uva.nl

University of Amsterdam,
Programming Research Group,
Kruislaan 403,
NL-1098 SJ Amsterdam, Netherlands

Abstract. Most distributed systems consist of a number of sequential processes running in parallel. We present a language-independent debugging framework for the debugging of these distributed systems.

Over the years, a lot of effort has been invested in the construction of debuggers for sequential programs. The majority of these debuggers work by abstracting the behaviour of the program being debugged into *events*, and visualizing these events.

We utilize these sequential debuggers to generate language-independent debugging events about the sequential execution of the processes in the distributed system. The underlying *coordination architecture* is used to generate debugging events dealing with the interaction between processes. These sequential and process interaction related debugging events are then processed by a separate distributed system that implements the high-level language-independent debugging functionality.

We also present a powerful multilingual distributed debugger based on our framework.

1   Introduction

Debugging is the process of locating and fixing errors (*bugs*) in software systems. A debugger is a software tool that can help understand a system being debugged by visualizing different aspects of the execution of the system.

Most debuggers work by gathering *primitive events*, filtering or clustering them, and presenting the results to the user. Details on how to gather events, which filtering or clustering algorithms to use, and when and how the results are presented differ in each case. Unfortunately, when it comes to distributed debugging, every system seems to 'reinvent the wheel' in the area of primitive event gathering. Solutions ranging from hardware assisted compiler instrumented code[AY91], to manually inserted event generation calls[BW83] can be found in the literature.

Although multilingual sequential debuggers have been around for quite some time[Bea83, SP91], many distributed debugging tools are based on support from a single experimental operating system or language environment[For89]. This calls for an interface between distributed and sequential debuggers, in order to combine the two fields[WHCM90] and reuse existing implementations. We have designed such an interface, and subsequently build a powerful, multilingual debugger for distributed systems.

In a typical distributed system, most components are written in traditional, sequential languages. The majority of the underlying language implementations support some kind of event reporting for a traditional sequential debugger. Our primary goal is to unify this existing work. We decided to focus on unifying the techniques already available instead of implementing yet another event reporting technique from scratch.

We have combined the power of the TOOLBUS coordination architecture (see Section 2) with existing low level debugging interfaces for sequential programming languages. The resulting framework consists of language-dependent debugging interfaces, based on the native debugging support of existing language environments, coupled with language-independent debugging components. This approach is based on our earlier work that focused on the debugging of simulated embedded systems where the simulator generated the primitive debugging events[Oli96].

To show the feasibility of our approach, we have constructed a debugger for distributed applications. The debugger offers a uniform graphical user interface for inspecting both the communication behaviour of the system being debugged, and for tracing the source level execution of the components of the system. Our debugger is both extensible in the set of languages it can handle, as well as in the debugging functionality it has to offer, because of the debugging framework it is based on.

In this paper, we propose a framework for distributed debugging that is build on top of the native debugging interfaces of most modern language implementations. We use these sequential debugging interfaces to report (sequential) primitive debugging events. By adding event reporting for the parallel medium we use (the TOOLBUS[BK96b]), the resulting set of primitive events is rich enough to build a solid distributed debugging environment.

In section 2 we will introduce the TOOLBUS coordination architecture on which our framework is based. In Section 3 we introduce our basic framework. In section 4 we present the notion of event rules that play a central role in our framework. In Section 5 we show how these event rules can be used to implement some of the functionality that is typically found in traditional sequential debuggers. In section 6 a prototype debugger implementation is presented, based on our framework.

2   ToolBus

The TOOLBUS[BK96a, BK96b] is a software coordination architecture that utilizes a scripting language based on process algebra[BW90] to describe the communication between software tools. A TOOLBUS *script* describes a number of processes that can communicate with each other and with *tools* existing outside the TOOLBUS (Figure 1). A tool is more or less equivalent to an operating system process. A language-dependent adapter that translates between the internal TOOLBUS data format and the data format used by the individual tools makes it possible to write every tool in the language best suitable for the task(s) it has to perform.

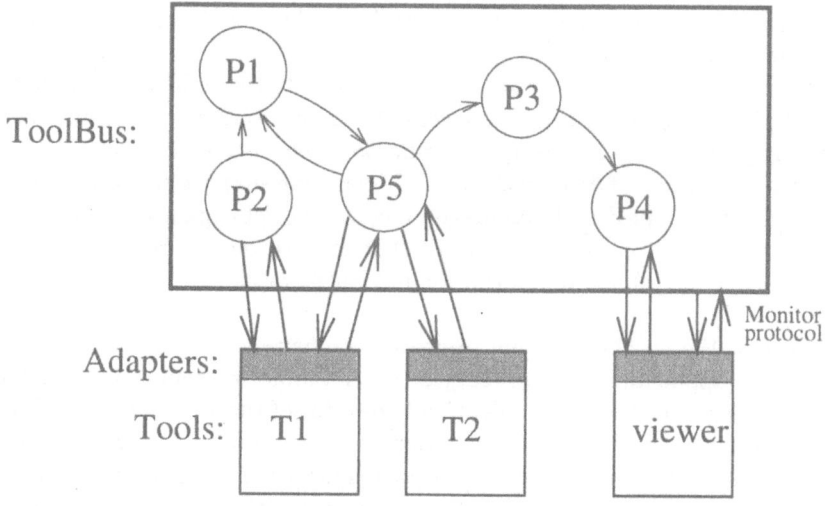

Fig. 1. The TOOLBUS software application architecture

ToolBus processes are described as expressions which are built using the TOOLBUS primitives and process composition operators. The following sections give an overview of the most important TOOLBUS primitives and operators. For a more complete description of TOOLBUS expressions see [BK96b].

2.1 Communication inside the TOOLBUS

There are two mechanisms available for processes in the TOOLBUS to communicate with each other, message passing and selective broadcasting. A process can synchronously send a *message* using the snd-msg primitive which must be received by another process using the rec-msg primitive. A process can send a *note* using snd-note to all processes that have subscribed, using subscribe, to that particular note type. The receiving processes read notes asynchronously using rec-note, at low priority. Transmitting notes amounts to *asynchronous selective broadcasting*.

2.2 Communication between TOOLBUS and tools

A TOOLBUS process can initiate communication with a tool by sending a message to a tool using snd-do, or snd-eval when an answer is expected. A process can receive the answer to a `snd-eval` request using the `rec-value` action.

A tool can initiate communication by sending an *event* to the TOOLBUS. A TOOLBUS process receives this event using the `rec-event` primitive and must acknowledge the event using the `snd-ack-event` primitive.

The execution and termination of the tools attached to the TOOLBUS as well as their connection/disconnection can be controlled explicitly by appropriate primitives.

2.3   Process composition

More complex processes can be created using process composition operators for *choice* (+ operator), *sequential composition* (. operator), *parallel composition* (|| operator), *iteration* (∗ operator) and *guarded (conditional) execution* (the `if-then-fi` operator). The *process creation* primitive `create` can be used to create new processes.

2.4   Types and variables

All terms within the TOOLBUS are *typed*. The TOOLBUS defines a number of basic types for booleans, integers, reals, strings, and binary strings. Complex types can be formed using a list constructor or function application. The type `term` is a supertype of all other types. The `let-in-endlet` construction makes it possible to declare variables.

2.5   A small example

To familiarize the reader with the syntax and semantics of TOOLBUS scripts, this section contains a small example. In this example a TOOLBUS script is presented that connects two tools, a calculator tool that calculates expressions and a user interface tool that asks the user for an expression and presents its value as result.

This TOOLBUS script contains two processes, a UI process that handles user interface events and a CALC process communicating with the calculator tool.

In addition to these processes, two tool types are introduced by *tool declarations*, which make it possible for the TOOLBUS to find and execute tools. A tool declaration also introduces a new type, that can later be used to declare tool identifier variables of that type.

```
tool ui is { command = "wish-adapter -script ui.tcl" }
```

The USER-INTERFACE process uses three variables. The first one, UI, is a tool identifier of type ui. The second variable E contains any expressions to be calculated, the third variable V contains the calculated result.

The USER-INTERFACE process first starts the user interface tool. The variable UI is a *result occurrence* of UI, because it is followed by a ?. When a variable is used as a result variable a value is assigned to it, in contrast with a *value occurrence* of a variable (without a following ?), when the current value of the variable is substituted. In this case, the tool identifier for the new instance of the user interface tool (ui) is assigned to UI.

After starting the ui tool, the UI process enters a loop waiting for expr events from the newly created user interface tool. Such an event is generated when the user enters an expression and wants to evaluate it. At this point the user interface tool generates an expr event, for instance expr("3+4"). The expression "3+4" is assigned to the variable E, and send to the CALC process for evaluation using the snd-msg action. The result is received in the rec-msg action and returned to the user interface tool using snd-ack-event.

The loop continues until the user interface tool generates a quit event, for instance when the user pressed the Quit button.

```
process USER-INTERFACE is
let
  UI : ui,
  E : str,
  V : str
in
  execute(ui, UI?) .
  ( rec-event(UI, expr(E?)) .
    snd-msg(calc, expr(E)) .
    rec-msg(calc, expr(E, V?)) .
    snd-ack-event(UI, expr(E, V))
  ) *
  rec-event(UI, quit) .
  snd-ack-event(UI, quit) .
  shutdown("Goodbye!")
endlet
```

The CALC process starts the calculator tool and waits for calculation requests. It relays them to the calculator tool and sends the result back.

Because the delta action is never executed, it can effectively be used in combination with the iteration operator to implement an endless loop.

```
tool calculator is { command = "calc" }

process CALC is
let
  Calc : calculator,
  E : str,
  V : str
in
  execute(calculator, Calc?) .
  ( rec-msg(calc, expr(E?)) .
    snd-eval(Calc, expr(E)) .
    rec-value(Calc, expr(E, V?)) .
```

```
      snd-msg(calc, expr(E, V))
   ) * delta
endlet
```

The last construct of every TOOLBUS script is the TOOLBUS configuration that starts a number of processes in parallel. In this case the processes UI and CALC are created and execution begins.

```
toolbus(UI,CALC)
```

2.6 Debugging TOOLBUS applications

An important feature of the TOOLBUS is the builtin monitor protocol, which is an extension of the normal communication protocol between TOOLBUS and tools. Based on this protocol, a tool which acts as a viewer tool can be connected to the TOOLBUS. Using the monitor protocol, the viewer tool is notified of state changes in the TOOLBUS. For instance, whenever a new TOOLBUS process is created, the viewer tool is informed of the name and process-id of the new process.

The current TOOLBUS distribution contains a viewer tool written in the user interface scripting language Tcl/Tk[Ous94]. This tool implements a debugging interface consisting of a source window and a TOOLBUS window. In the source window, the TOOLBUS script being executed is displayed, and actions that are executed are highlighted. The user can run or step through the execution of processes, and can set breakpoints by double clicking on a specific source line. In the TOOLBUS window a picture is drawn of the current processes and tools connected to the TOOLBUS. In this picture, arrows are drawn indicating communication taking place between tools and processes. Double clicking on a process in the TOOLBUS window opens a new window containing the variables of the selected process and their current values.

3 A TOOLBUS framework for debugging distributed applications

Although the debugging approach described in Section 2.6 has proved very useful, it has two drawbacks:

1. The main debugging component, the viewer, is a monolithic piece of Tcl/Tk code and is therefore hard to extend.
2. Only the external communication behaviour of the tools can be observed. The tools connected to the TOOLBUS are treated as *black boxes*. There is no way to inspect the local state of tools.

The majority of distributed systems consist of a number of sequential processes running in parallel. We present a debugging framework for distributed systems which is based on the events generated by native debuggers for these

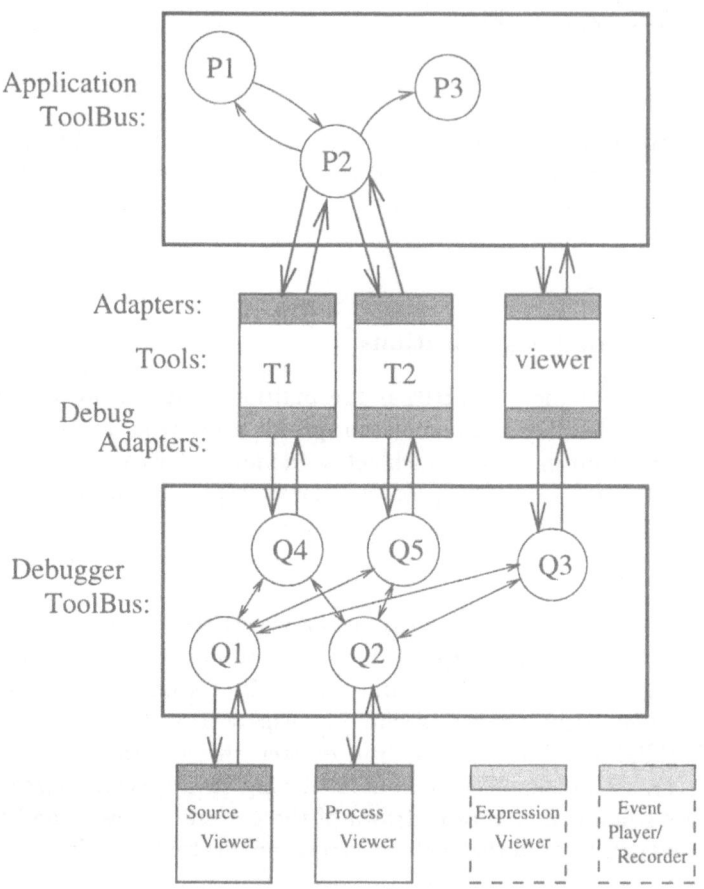

Fig. 2. Framework overview

sequential processes. These processes may either be the tools connected to the TOOLBUS, or the processes within the TOOLBUS. The native debugger events are translated into language-independent debugging events. The events generated by the TOOLBUS monitor protocol are used to generate special events about the interaction between processes. The combination of language-independent debugging events and process interaction events are used to synthesize high-level debugging facilities not found in the underlying native debuggers. Examples of these facilities are:

- A uniform graphical user interface for debugging all processes, independent of the language they are written in.
- Full conditional breakpoint and watchpoint support, based on the expressions discussed in Section 4.2.
- Breakpoints and watchpoints that can be set on any type of event, not just on specific locations in the source code. For example, watch the value of a variable whenever a certain message is send.

– Execution tracing of components by highlighting the appropriate area in the source code.

The first step towards this new architecture is to introduce a second TOOL-BUS which actually implements the debugger. We will call the TOOLBUS system being debugged the *application bus*, and the debugging TOOLBUS the *debugger bus*.

In the old situation, the viewer tool immediately visualized the events as they came in. In our architecture, the viewer tool acts as a gateway between the application bus and the debugger bus. The actual debugging functionality is implemented using a number of cooperating tools, for instance, a source code browser and a TOOLBUS process viewer.

This architecture not only solves the first problem mentioned above, it opens up the possibility to solve the second problem as well. As we mentioned in the introduction, we are interested in reusing the low level debugging interfaces of the components of the application bus. Examples include the debugging interfaces of languages like *Java*[GJS96], *Python*[AWA96], *Tcl/Tk*[Ous94], and *C* (using *gdb*).

In section 2, we described that a tool is connected to the TOOLBUS using a TOOLBUS *adapter*, which is basically a piece of interface code that establishes a connection with the TOOLBUS, and converts between TOOLBUS terms and the internal data format of the tool. By combining an existing TOOLBUS adapter with the low level debugging interface of a tool, we create a *debug-adapter*. A debug-adapter can capture debugging events and send them to the debugger bus for processing. Figure 2 shows an overview of this framework.

4 Event rules

Most debuggers gather primitive events and use these to inform the user of what is going on in the program. Our framework uses these native debugging components to do this event gathering. The primary task of the debug adapters introduced in Section 3 is to unify and filter these events in order to make our framework language-independent.

We do this unification and filtering of low level debugging events by using *event rules*. All interactions between the debugger bus and application bus are based on event rules. An event rule consists of an *event port*, an *event condition*, a list of *event actions*, and an *event rule lifetime*. The event port indicates at which points during the execution of a program an event rule is *activated*. When an event rule is activated, its event condition is evaluated to see if the event rule must be *triggered*. Triggering the event rule consists of executing its event actions. The event rule lifetime determines if an event rule is only triggered once and then destroyed automatically, or if it can be triggered a number of times until it is destroyed explicitly.

4.1 Event ports

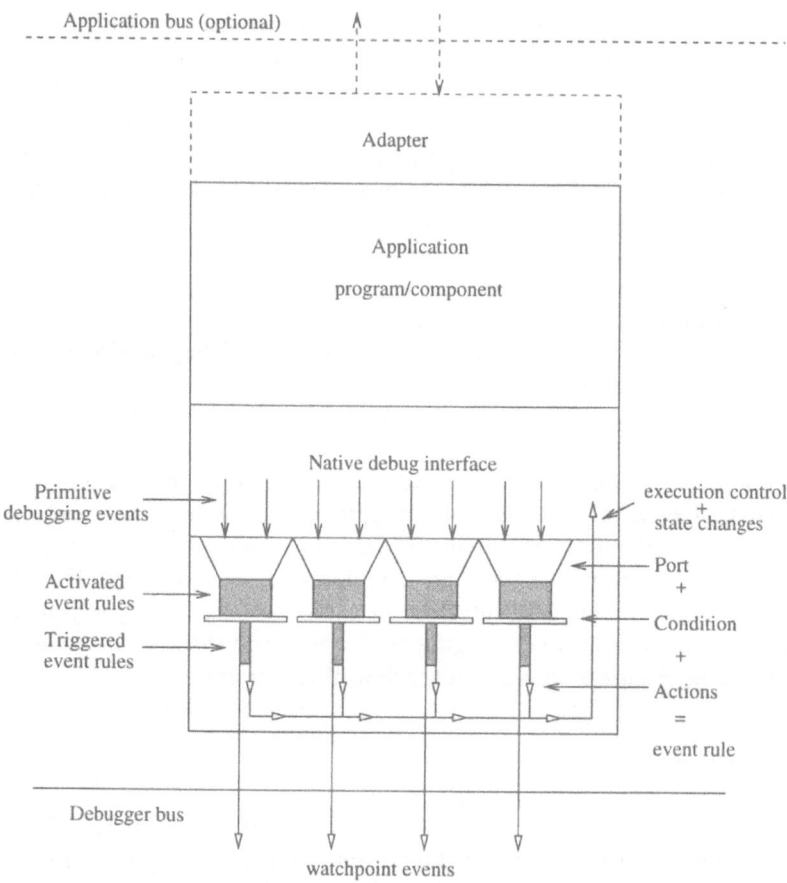

Fig. 3. Event processing inside a debug adapter

The event port is used to bind a set of native debugging events to an event rule. The name *event port* is derived from the standard Prolog 4-port tracer. The ports call, exit, redo, and fail are directly based on their Prolog counterparts. The event port of an event rule can be:

- call(*name*): Activate the event rule when the function/predicate *name* is called.
- exit(*name*): Activate the event rule on function/predicate exit.
- redo(*name*): Activate when backtracking occurs.
- fail(*name*): Activate when a function/predicate fails.
- stopped: Activate the event rule when execution stops.

- **started**: activate when execution starts (again).
- **location**(*loc*): Activate the event rule when the specific location in the source code indicated by *loc* is reached.
- **variable-change**(*var*): When the value of a variable changes.
- **exception**(*name*): When an exception or error occurs.
- **always**: Whenever a statement is executed.

The remaining four event port types are based on process interaction events:

- **process-creation**: Activate the event rule when a process is created.
- **process-destruction**: Activate the event rule when a process ceases to exist.
- **send**(*pattern*): Activate the event rule when a process sends a message matching with *pattern* to another process.
- **receive**(*pattern*): Activate the event rule when a process receives a message matching with *pattern* from another process.

The event port can also have a modifier indicating whether the event rule is activated before or after the port is reached. This modifier can be:

- **before**: Activate the event rule before the port is reached. For instance, stop the execution of a process before a specific source line is executed.
- **after**: Activate the event rule after the port is reached. For instance, show the value of a variable after a message has been received.

4.2 Event conditions

Event conditions are used to filter uninteresting events locally. This prevents the debugger bus from getting swamped with events, and protects the user from an excessive amount of information that he or she did not ask for. For instance, by implementing conditional breakpoints when the underlying native debugger only supports unconditional breakpoints.

The event condition is an expression that is evaluated when the event rule is activated. The event rule is only triggered when this expression evaluates to *true*. The debug adapter decides which terms are considered to be equivalent to *true* and which are not.

In our framework, there are two places where we use expressions:

- In the condition of event rules.
- In the arguments of actions of event rules.

Unfortunately, the syntax and semantics of expressions are different in every programming language. To make things even worse, not every debugger supports the evaluation of these 'native' expressions.

Our framework offers the user *mixed expressions* in order to overcome the inadequacy of some debuggers in this area. Our expression language consists of prefix functions that are evaluated whenever their value is needed.

These expressions are called *mixed*, because there is a special function `eval`, which takes a single string argument. This string is passed to the native debugging interface for evaluation, effectively providing an escape to the language under consideration. Although the result type of most functions is predefined, the result of `eval` is left to the debug adapter. For instance, if it can determine that the result is of type `integer`, an integer is returned. It can always return a string representing the result when there is no other sensible TOOLBUS term equivalent.

A host of other functions can be used in expressions, including functions to analyze terms, dissect lists, and perform simple calculations. Other functions return information about the process that invoked the observation point, like its execution state or process id. A complete overview of these functions is beyond the scope of this paper. Section 5 presents some of these functions in more detail, and shows how they can be used to implement some common debugger features.

The event port and event condition can be used by the debug adapter to configure the underlying native debugger. In this way, events can be filtered in an early stage, using hardware or operating system support when possible.

4.3 Event actions

When an event rule is triggered, a list of actions called *event actions* associated with the event rule is executed. Every event action is either:

- An action that changes the (execution) state of a process.
- An action that generates a watchpoint event for the debugger bus.

Which actions are allowed depends on the particular debug adapter, but most debug adapters support at least these actions:

- `watch(expr)`: Evaluate *expr* and generate a TOOLBUS `watch` event so the debugger bus can visualize the current value of *expr*. An event rule that has a `watch` action associated with it is called a *watchpoint*.
- `change-exec-state(state)`: Change the execution state of a process. Possible values for *state* are:
  - `step`: Execute a single instruction.
  - `step-over`: Execution a single instruction, but if this instruction happens to be a function, execute the entire function.
  - `run`: Run the process at full speed, only interrupt it when an event rule is activated.
  - `stop`: Stop executing the process.
- `break`: An abbreviation for `change-exec-state(break)`. This actions stops the execution of a process. An event rule that has a `break` action associated with it is called a *breakpoint*.

Some debug adapters support the `execute(code)` action. *code* is a string that is executed as native code in the context of the process that triggered the event rule. This execution can have side effects, changing the internal state of the process.

4.4 Event lifetime

Some event rules are no longer needed after they have been triggered. Such a rule has a lifetime of one-shot. These rules are typically used in cases where the user wants to take action immediately, like stopping the execution of a program, or changing the value of a variable. Other rules have a longer lifetime, and have to be removed explicitly. These rules have a persistent lifetime.

4.5 The event rule ToolBus process

Figure 3 shows the event processing inside a debug adapter. First the event port is used to determine which event rules are activated. Then the event condition is used to filter these activated event rules. Finally, triggering the event rule results in the execution of actions that either change the (execution) state of the process that generated the original primitive event, or actions that generate watchpoint events for the debugger bus.

Because the interaction between a debug adapter and the debugger bus is completely based on event rules, the interface between them can be described using the EVENT-RULE TOOLBUS process given below.

By unifying all primitive debugging events using event rules, the interaction between the debug adapters and the debugger bus can be described in one simple TOOLBUS process. This process can:

- Create a new event rule. After creating the event rule, a message is broadcasted to inform all debugger bus components that a new event rule exists.
- Destroy an existing event rule. A message is broadcasted to inform everyone the event rule no longer exists.
- Receive and broadcast watchpoint events. When a watchpoint is triggered, a message is broadcasted so all tools that depend on this watchpoint can update their view.

```
process EVENT-RULES(D:debug-adapter) is
let
   P       : term,   %% list of process-id's, or 'all' indicating all
                     %% processes controlled by the debug adapter.
   Port    : term,   %% event port and modifier
   Cond    : term,   %% event condition
   Life    : term,   %% lifetime of an event rule
   Acts    : list,   %% event actions
   Rid     : int,    %% event rule identifier
   Expr    : term,   %% Watchpoint expression
   Value   : term,   %% Value of an evaluated watchpoint expression
   Result: term      %% ok or error(<str>)
in
   ( rec-msg(proc(D,P?), create-rule(Port?,Cond?,Acts?,Life?)) .
     snd-eval(D, create-rule(P, Port,Cond,Acts,Life)) .
     rec-value(D, create-rule(P, Port,Cond,Acts,Life,Rid?)) .
     snd-note(event(proc(D,P), rule-created(Port,Cond,Acts,Life,Rid)))
```

```
        +
        rec-msg(proc(D,P?), destroy-rule(Rid?)) .
        snd-do(D, destroy-rule(P,Rid)) .
        snd-note(event(proc(D,P), rule-destroyed(Rid)))
        +
        rec-event(D, watchpoint(P?,Rid?,Expr?,Value?)) .
        snd-note(event(proc(D,P), watchpoint(Rid,Expr,Value))) .
        snd-ack-event(D, watchpoint(P,Rid,Expr,Value))
    ) * delta
endlet
```

5   Example event rules

In this section, we will show how some well known debugger features can be implemented using special event rules. Our debugger implementation (Section 6) implements these features using the event rules described in this section.

5.1   Instruction highlighting

Most debuggers can visualize the execution of a program by highlighting instructions as they are executed. This instruction highlighting can be found in two flavours:

- Highlight on halt.
- Execution animation.

Both flavours can be implemented using event rules that utilize the function cpe that returns the current point of execution of a process in source coordinates.

To highlight the current instruction whenever the execution is halted, we use a persistent event rule with port stopped, no condition, and as only action watch(cpe).

By changing the port from stopped to always, the event rule is triggered with the execution of every instruction. This enables the debugger to animate the execution of the process, but this slows down execution by at least an order of magnitude.

5.2   Watching variables

To watch the current value of a set of variables whenever the execution of a process stops, we use the function var(*name*) that retrieves the current value of a variable. By creating a persistent event rule with port stopped, no condition, and as actions var(*name*), the value of the variable is updated whenever the process stops.

We could also change the port from stopped to variable-change to animate the value of the variable during program execution, again slowing down the execution.

5.3 Simple breakpoints

Almost every debugger enables the user to set a breakpoint at a specific location in the source code. When the execution of the program reaches this location, the execution is halted. In our framework, this kind of breakpoints are called 'simple breakpoints'. A simple breakpoint is implemented by creating an event rule with port location(loc), where loc is the location at which to break given in source coordinates. The event rule has no condition, and the list of actions only consists of break.

5.4 Direct execution control

The user must also be able to start and stop processes at will. This can be done using event rules of class always, with no conditions, and a one-shot lifetime. Using the change-exec-state action, the execution state of the process can be influenced directly. Because the event rule has a lifetime of one-shot, it disappears after executing the actions.

6 The Toolbus Integrated Debugging Environment

To prove the feasibility of our framework, we have implemented a debugger called TIDE: the Toolbus Integrated Debugging Environment. It offers impressive advantages over 'standard' debugging environments:

- TIDE can debug distributed systems based on the TOOLBUS.
- TIDE operates in any operating environment that is supported by the TOOLBUS. This includes most modern unix operating systems.
- When the distributed system to be debugged is based on the TOOLBUS, TIDE can display a graphical representation of the processes and communication in the system.
- Even in non-TOOLBUS based distributed or stand-alone systems, TIDE can trace sequential components at the source level, as long as the component is executing using one of the language environments supported by TIDE.
- Support for a new source language only requires a new debug adapter to interface with the TIDE system. Because these adapters are build on top of the native debugging interface of the language implementation in question, it is typically very small (300-600 lines of source code).

Although TIDE is not finished yet, it is already a powerful, multilingual distributed debugger. Figure 4 shows a screenshot of a debugging session. In the upper left corner an overview of the application bus is show using the *process viewer* tool. The system being debugged consists of five TOOLBUS processes and two native processes (TOOLBUS tools), one written in C and one written in Tcl.

The remaining three windows are maintained by the *source viewer* tool, and are used to track the execution of all processes of the application bus. The debug adapter that is in charge of the application bus (the viewer tool in Figure 2) controls *several* processes, namely all TOOLBUS processes in the application bus.

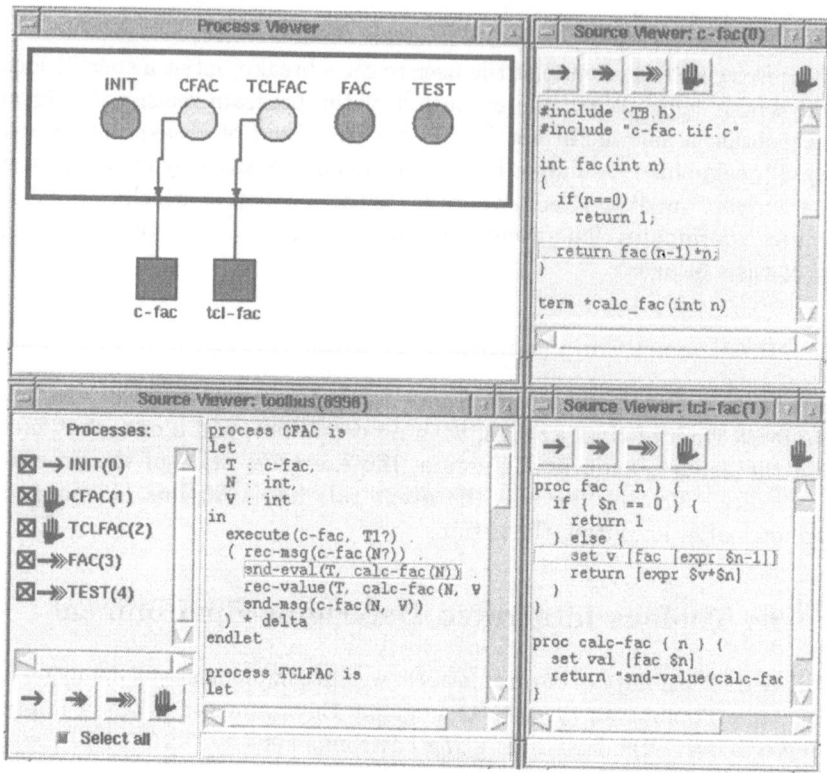

Fig. 4. Debugging a distributed system using TIDE

Because of this, the source viewer in the lower left corner not only displays the TOOLBUS script that controls the application bus, but also the list of TOOLBUS processes running in the application bus. The current state of execution of each process (stopped, running, or single-stepping) is also shown next to the process name.

In the upper right corner, the source code of the C tool is displayed. In the lower right corner the source code of the Tcl tool is displayed. Because the debug adapters that control these last two tools only supports a single process, no list of processes is displayed next to the source code.

The TIDE implementation currently supports the following features:

- Source level execution tracing, both in animation mode or only when the system is stopped.
- Execution control over all processes that are debugged.
- Full breakpoint support, including conditional breakpoints. Breakpoint locations can be specified by clicking on the desired position in the source browser.
- Full watchpoint support, including conditional watchpoints. As explained in Section 4.2, both the conditions of break- and watchpoint, and the watch-

point expressions can be a mixture of "native" expressions and special debugger functions.
- Visualization of the interprocess communication in the system. All processes can be displayed in a *process viewer* window. Active processes are highlighted, and communication between them is visualized by directed arrows.
- Support for languages like Java, C, Tcl/Tk, and Python.

7 Main results

We have introduced a framework for distributed debugging, by systematically building on well known sequential debugging techniques and implementations. The resulting distributed debugger prototype is unique, both in its simple design and in its flexibility towards the support of new source languages.

The performance is comparable to that of sequential debuggers, because primitive events are filtered locally when there is no interest in them. Only interesting events are processed in a distributed fashion.

Because of the modularity and simplicity of our framework, we believe it to be a solid base for future experiments.

Before starting any new experiments however, we need to add support for more source languages, especially for languages based on paradigms other than the imperative paradigm, like logical and functional languages.

We also would like to extend the framework to allow *event abstraction* by grouping basic events into combined "abstract events". By visualizing these abstract events[Kun95], we could offer more help in understanding the distributed system being debugged at the application level rather than at the implementation level.

References

[AWA96] Guido van Rossum Aaron Watters and James Ahlstrom. *Internet Programming with Python*. MIS Press/Henry Holt publishers, 1996.

[AY91] D.K. Arvind and D. Yokotsuka. Debugging concurrent programs using static analysis and run-time hardware monitoring. In *Third IEEE Symposium on Parallel and Distributed Processing*, pages 716–719. IEEE Computer Society Press, 1991.

[Bea83] Bert Beander. An interactive, symbolic, multilingual debugger. In *Symposium on High-Level Debugging, 1983*, pages 173–180. ACM SIGSOFT/SIGPLAN, 1983.

[BK96a] J.A. Bergstra and P. Klint. The discrete time toolbus. In *Algebraic Methodology and Software Technology (AMAST'96)*, volume 1101 of *LNCS*, pages 286–305. Springer-Verlag, 1996.

[BK96b] J.A. Bergstra and P. Klint. The toolbus coordination architecture. In P. Ciancarini and C. Hankin, editors, *Coordination Languages and Models (COORDINATION)*, volume 1061 of *LNCS*, pages 75–88. Springer-Verlag, 1996.

[BW83]   Peter C. Bates and Jack C. Wileden. High level debugging of distributed
            systems: The behavioral abstraction approach. *Journal of Systems and
            Software, 3(4)*, pages 394–399, 1983.

[BW90]   J.C.M. Baeten and W.P. Weijland. *Process Algebra*. Cambridge Tracts in
            Theoretical Computer Science 18. Cambridge University Press, 1990.

[For89]   Alessandro Forin. Debugging of heterogeneous parallel systems. In *Work-
            shop on Parallel and Distributed Debugging, 1988*, pages 130–140. ACM,
            1989.

[GJS96]   James Gosling, Bill Joy, and Guy Steele. *The Java Language Specification*.
            Addison-Wesley, 1996.

[Kun95]   Thomas Kunz. High-level views of distributed executions. In *Proceedings
            of the 2nd International Workshop on Automated and Algorithmic Debug-
            ging*, 1995.

[Oli96]   P.A. Olivier.   A simulator framework for embedded systems.   In
            P. Ciancarini and C. Hankin, editors, *Coordination Languages and Mod-
            els (COORDINATION)*, volume 1061 of *LNCS*, pages 436–439. Springer-
            Verlag, 1996.

[Ous94]   John Ousterhout. *Tcl and the Tk Toolkit*. Addison-Wesley Publishing,
            1994.

[SP91]   R.M. Stallman and R.H. Pesch. Using gdb: A guide to the gnu source-level
            debugger, July 1991.

[WHCM90] James P. Black Wing Hong Cheung and Eric Manning. A framework for
            distributed debugging. *IEEE Software*, pages 106–115, 1990.

Coordinating Durative Actions[(*)]

I. Nunes

J.L.Fiadeiro

Department of Informatics
Faculty of Sciences, University of Lisbon
Campo Grande
1700 Lisboa, Portugal
{in,llf}@di.fc.ul.pt

W.M.Turski

Institute of Informatics
Warsaw University
ul. Banacha 2
02-097 Warsaw, Poland
wmt@mimuw.edu.pl

Abstract. A computing paradigm is presented for coordinating the execution of durative actions, i.e. actions which, although executed atomically on a private local state, have a duration in the sense that the system state in which they finish executing is not necessarily the same in which they started. Just as in traditional coordination languages, the coordination model that is responsible for controlling the interference between the actions is independent from the computation model in which actions execute. This coordination model is formalised through an operational and a denotational semantics, both parameterised by those of the underlying computational model.

1. Introduction

The behavioural paradigm developed in [11,12] for supporting multiprocessor computing is presented as a coordination model for controlling the execution of durative actions, i.e. actions which, although executed atomically on a private local state, have a duration in the sense that the system state in which they finish executing is not necessarily the same in which they started. Systems of durative actions arise naturally from the need to coordinate the behaviour of individual programs that can access a shared data space, namely to achieve interoperability of, possibly heterogeneous, components in the context of reuse-based and incremental system development, and for which the atomicity imposed through the use of a single processor executing a single program at the time is simply unrealistic and undesirable.

The proposed coordination model relies on a small set of primitives that support, on the one hand, local computations without interference of the environment and, on the other hand, the decoupling between the global states in which actions are launched and the global states in which they find the system when they finish executing.

[(*)] This work was partially supported by JNICT through contracts PRAXIS XXI 2/2.1/MAT/46/94 (ESCOLA), PCSH/OGE/1038/95 (MAGO) and PRAXIS XXI 2/2.1/TIT/1662/95 (SARA).

Like in (more) traditional coordination languages, the coordination model that is responsible for controlling the interference between the actions is independent from the computation model in which actions execute. That is to say, it does not really matter if the computations performed locally by the actions are programmed in a, say, imperative or functional style.

In section 2, we present the behavioural paradigm in detail, from an operational, but informal point of view, and compare it to (more) traditional coordination models. In section 3, behavioural programs are formalised as sets of coordination primitives used to relate programs written in some programming language whose details are considered irrelevant. In section 4, we formalise the rules that provide an operational semantics for behavioural programs. In section 5, we formalise the relationship between this operational semantics and a denotational semantics defined over Durative Transition Systems – an extension of labelled transition systems introduced in [7,8] to cope with action duration.

2. Coordination in the behavioural paradigm

It seems hard to improve on the characterisation of the distinction between *computation* and *coordination* that was proposed in [5]: "[A] computation model allows programmers to build a single computational activity: a single-threaded, step-at-a-time computation; [a] coordination model is the glue that binds separate activities into an ensemble".

The aim of this paper is to present a computing paradigm proposed in [11,12] – the *behavioural paradigm* – which explores this very distinction between coordination and computation, and proposes primitives for coordinating the interference between actions which perform computations over a common state space.

In order to understand the essence of the behavioural paradigm, consider the chemical reaction metaphor which is at the base of coordination formalisms, namely Gamma [1]:

Reaction condition → Action

Execution consists in removing from the "chemical solution" (the multiset that provides the global state space) the elements that satisfy the reaction condition, replacing them by the results of the action. Evaluation of the reaction condition and computation of the effects of the action are done atomically ("test and set") in the sense that the state of the system (the multiset) does not change between the evaluation of the condition and the computation of the action. The computation of the action is also done atomically in this sense: its effects are going to update the same state that was used for evaluating the condition and determining the course of the computation.

One of the characteristics of the behavioural paradigm is the relaxation of the assumption on the atomicity of the execution of the action. More precisely, the action computes in a local copy of the relevant part of the state of the system and, hence, atomically in the sense that the computation proceeds without interference from the environment. However, while the computation proceeds on the local copy, the state of the system may change because other actions may have terminated. Hence, the state in which the computation induced by the action ends is not necessarily the same in which the execution started.

Because the state in which the reaction condition is evaluated is still the same in which the execution starts, this relaxation implies that the conditions that lead to the execution of the action are not necessarily met when the execution ends. Hence, it may well be true that the effects computed locally are no longer of interest. To determine whether the global state should or should not be updated with the effects computed by the action, the behavioural paradigm relies on a second condition – the *post-guard* – which is evaluated when the local execution of the action ends (the so-called *accepting state*). The global state is updated iff the post-guard evaluates to *true*. The evaluation of the post-guard and the update of the global state are done atomically ("test and set").

The other important characteristic of the behavioural paradigm is that it addresses *multiprocessor computing*. Systems evolve in an environment populated by one or more agents which are identical in their ability to perform (local) programs, except perhaps, for efficiency. Agents are equipped with memories in which they execute the actions that they are assigned. For that purpose, they are able to *load* into their memories the relevant part of the state of the system when the execution of an action is assigned, and to *discharge* their local states into the global state of the system when the execution of an action ends and the corresponding post-guard is true. Loading and discharging are instantaneous.

All actions that *can* be initiated in a given state *are* initiated, regardless of any possible future conflict; conflicts are resolved in the accepting states. Moreover, no agent is allowed to idle in a system state in which a reaction condition (*pre-guard* in the terminology of the behaviour paradigm) is satisfied. In particular, several copies of the same action can be launched if there is more than one agent free or if an agent becomes free while the pre-guard of the action remains true. This is justified by the fact that some agents may be slower than other agents; the first to terminate gets the chance to update the global state of the system if the post-guard is true; the effects of the action may falsify the post-guard thus preventing the agents performing the other copies of the action to terminate productively. But, as in nature, success may be reserved for some slower agent that gets its chance from changes performed in its environment. The "waste" of computations is only apparent because, on the one hand, all that is done is to keep busy agents that would otherwise be idle (pre-guards that are false can only become true due to the termination of some action, which automatically frees an agent) and, on the other hand, the more the copies in execution the better the chances of success become. (Again, nature is very good at launching several processes in concurrency even if it is known that at most one will be successful!) Besides, it is assumed that actions are assigned to agents in a fair way: when more than one can be assigned, the actual choice is unbiased. Moreover, as processors become cheaper and cheaper, multiprocessor environments can be easily populated with a fair number of agents.

The model that we have just described also justifies that, unlike the tuple space model with generative communication used by coordination languages [2,4], where agents communicate by putting and consuming tuples in the tuple space, the only moment when, in the behavioural paradigm, the state of the system is modified is at discharging, which can be seen as a substitution of some values for other ones. That is, evaluation of a pre-guard (reaction condition) does not change (consume from) the global state. This happens precisely to allow for existing free agents to get a chance of picking another instance of the launched action.

A behavioural program is an initial condition together with a set of rules where each rule is called a double guarded action – *dga* – and takes the form

(pre-guard,postguard) → [loading | program | discharging]

By *loading* and *discharging* we are denoting lists of attribute symbols. These are the names of the attributes of the system (the "program variables") which, in the behavioural paradigm, can be typed as usual in programming languages. This is a departure from the multiset / (tuple space) representations typical of coordination languages, but not an essential one.

The loading and discharging lists account for the attributes whose values an agent has to load into its local state when assigned to perform the action, and the attributes that it has to update when it discharges its local state. Loading lists are optional in the sense that the full state of the system could be loaded each time an action is launched. The same does not hold for the discharging list. This list performs an important role in determining the global state of the system that results from the acceptance of an action (see below).

In order to illustrate the coordination model just described, consider the "dining philosophers". The following specification is that of a given philosopher (this example is taken from [11]).

$$(LOT \wedge ROT \wedge \neg H)$$

$$(\neg H, \neg H) \quad \rightarrow \quad [\quad | think | H]$$

$$(H \wedge PR \wedge PL, H \wedge PR \wedge PL) \quad \rightarrow \quad [\quad | eat | H, PR, ROT, PL, LOT]$$

$$(H \wedge PL \wedge \neg PR \wedge \neg ROT, \neg ROT) \quad \rightarrow \quad [\quad | rel\_L | PL, LOT]$$

$$(H \wedge PR \wedge \neg PL \wedge \neg LOT, \neg LOT) \quad \rightarrow \quad [\quad | rel\_R | PR, ROT]$$

$$(H \wedge LOT, H \wedge LOT) \quad \rightarrow \quad [\ | \ take\_L \ | \ PL, LOT]$$

$$(H \wedge ROT, H \wedge ROT) \quad \rightarrow \quad [\ | \ take\_R \ | \ PR, ROT]$$

where the propositional symbols are used with the following meanings:

H   –   the philosopher is hungry

LOT –   the left fork is on the table

ROT –   the right fork is on the table

PL   –   the philosopher possesses the left fork

PR   –   the philosopher possesses the right fork

The condition $(\neg H \wedge LOT \wedge ROT)$ defines initial states: when program execution begins, the philosopher must not be hungry and both left and right forks must be on the table.

In this example all loading lists are empty. This means that the computations performed locally by each action do not depend on the state in which the action is launched.

The intended semantics of the rel_L action specification, for example, is the following. When a philosopher is hungry (H), possesses the left fork (PL) and does not possess the right fork ($\neg$PR), and the right fork is not on the table ($\neg$ROT), he will release the left fork (the action is launched because the pre-guard is true). This is so specified in order to prevent deadlock. If, while our philosopher is in the process of releasing his left fork, the philosopher at his right releases his left fork (our philosopher's right fork), then our philosopher should not bring about the action. This is expressed through the post-guard: if the right fork is on the table (ROT) when the philosopher finishes executing the release, the action is rejected. The pre-guard of the action *take_R* is now true and so the process of picking-up the right fork is launched.

The only situation for which no action is specified is the one where the philosopher is hungry, holds no fork and no fork is on the table. This is not, fortunately, a stable state: the missing forks are held by neighbours, and they will eventually release them. For all other situations well-defined actions are prescribed; if the results of these actions are not accepted at any time it is because a neighbour successfully completes an action of his own. In a system composed of several philosophers this means that some action is accepted in each state. Thus this specification is deadlock free.

It is perhaps worthwhile to observe that this specification avoids deadlocks without referring to any information on the actual state of the philosopher's neighbours. As soon as the information on neighbours is explicitly available and used, a conspiracy to starve a common neighbour becomes possible. In our design, where this information is not available (nor needed), starvation is possible either because of a gross heterogeneity of philosophers, or as a chance phenomenon. Even if the philosophers are roughly similar, a pattern of fork movements preventing one or more of their number from eating would not be inconsistent with the design, just as an arbitrarily long run of heads is not inconsistent with repeated tossing of a fair coin. This seems unavoidable, but practically irrelevant.

We have deliberately omitted the definition of the program executed locally by each action to remind that the behavioural paradigm is all about coordinating durative actions and not about programming their effects. This is achieved through the pre and post-guards and by the loading and discharging lists. Naturally, these local programs have to be supplied for the behavioural program to be complete. For instance, in the case of rel_L, this could be

PL:=false; LOT:=true

assuming that the programming language in which rel_L is given uses local attributes with the same names as the global attributes of the system. But it could well be that rel_L uses different attributes, in which case the discharging of the local state has to be a bit more than a simple copy. However, it is essential that discharging (as well as loading) are atomic (and efficient!).

3. Coordination Primitives + Programs = Behavioural Programs

Summarising the informal discussion of the previous section, the behavioural paradigm is characterized by a collection of primitives whose aim is to control the interference between durative actions, and which clearly separates computation concerns from coordination ones:

- The programming language in which computations are programmed is not constrained to any particular one: we rely on an interface that is provided by the loading and discharging operations;

- Pre- and post-guards stand for activation/permission criteria to coordinate the execution and productivity of actions.

A behavioural program is a set of double-guarded actions (*dgas*), each of which includes two guards – the pre and post-guards – two lists of attributes – the loading and the discharging lists – and the program executed locally by the action.

In other words, a behavioural program is a collection of individual programs implicitly related through some coordinating and comunication primitives. These are the guards and the interface lists of attributes. The guards control *why* and *what* is to be made active in the system, as reactions to the system state. The loading list defines what an agent has to know about the system state in order to execute an action. The discharging list defines to what extent does an accepted action change the system state.

In order to formalize the notion of behavioural program we begin by defining the concept of system signature which consists of a declaration of the specific vocabulary symbols that are relevant for that system description.

For simplicity, we shall assume that a collection of data types has been fixed which provides a data signature $U=(S,F)$, where S is a set of sorts and F is an $S^* \times S$-indexed family of function symbols.

Definition 3.1: A signature Θ is a pair (At,Ac) where:

- At is an S-indexed family of sets of attribute symbols,
- Ac is a set of action symbols equipped with two mappings L and D providing, for each action $g \in Ac$, its loading (L_g) and discharging (D_g) lists, each of which is an S-indexed family of sets of attribute symbols. ◆

Definition 3.2: The language $\mathcal{L}(At)$ for Θ of state formulas, is defined by:

$$e_s ::= p|f(e_{1s_1}, ..., e_{ns_n})$$

where $p \in At_s$ and $f:s_1,...,s_n \rightarrow s \in F$

$$A ::= e_{1s} = e_{2s}|\neg A| A_1 \supset A_2 \qquad\qquad ◆$$

We will use the traditional propositional constants and connectives tt, ff, $\wedge$, $\vee$, $\equiv$, defined through the usual abbreviations.

As already mentioned, the behavioural paradigm is not characterised by a specific syntax for its programs but through a collection of primitives whose aim is to coordinate durative actions. In particular, the durative actions may be programmed in any programming language, subject to some restrictions. These restrictions, or assumptions, on the nature of the language that can be used for programming actions, constitute what we call a *context*. In so far as this section is concerned, we only need to know about syntactical aspects, which we call a *programming context* for a given signature.

Definition 3.3: A programming context $\mathcal{T}_p(\Theta)$ for a signature Θ is a language PL. ◆

No assumption is made on the actual syntax of the programming language PL besides the fact that it has to work over the data types defined in the signature. The idea is that, to coordinate durative actions, we do not need to know explicitly how their internal computations are programmed. Instead, we rely on an interface that is provided through the global attributes At and the loading and discharging lists for each action.

Definition 3.4: Given a programming context $\mathcal{T}_p(\Theta)$ for a signature $\Theta=(Ac,At)$, a behavioural program is a pair BP = (I,BDY) where I is an initial condition and BDY assigns, to every $g \in Ac$, a triple (A_g,P_g,C_g) where:

- A_g and P_g are formulas of $\mathcal{L}(At)$, standing for the pre- and the post-guard of action g, respectively;

- C_g is a program in the language PL.

Each such triple is called a *dga* (double-guarded action specification). ◆

4. An operational semantics for behavioural programs

Here we present an operational semantics as a set of rules which describe, formally, execution in the behavioural paradigm. These rules specify how expressions are evaluated and how *dgas* are executed.

Before proceeding we must define the notion of state for a signature. Again, we assume a fixed U-algebra $\mathcal{U} = (S_\mathcal{U}, F_\mathcal{U})$ that interprets the data types corresponding to U, where $S_\mathcal{U} = \{s_\mathcal{U} | s \in S\}$ and $F_\mathcal{U} = \{f_\mathcal{U} : s_{1\mathcal{U}} \times \ldots \times s_{n\mathcal{U}} \to s_\mathcal{U} | f : s_1, \ldots, s_n \to s\}$.

Definition 4.1: A state σ for a signature $\Theta = (At, Ac)$ is an S-indexed family $(\sigma_s : At_s \to s_\mathcal{U})$ $s \in S$ where, for every $s \in S$, σ_s assigns a value over its domain to each attribute in At_s. The notation σ_Ω stands for the projection of state σ in set Ω, where $\Omega_s \subseteq At_s$ for all $s \in S$. The notation $\sigma[p]$ stands for the value of attribute p in state $\sigma \in \Sigma$. The notation $\sigma'[\sigma_\Omega / \Omega]$ stands for the state that is equal to σ' except for the values of attributes in Ω whose values are given by σ_Ω. ◆

State formulas as defined in 3.2 can be evaluated over such states:

Definition 4.2: The value of an expression $f(e_1, \ldots, e_n)$ at σ – written $\sigma[f(e_1, \ldots, e_n)]$ – is $f_\mathcal{U}(\sigma[e_1], \ldots, \sigma[e_n])$. ◆

Definition 4.3: We define the satisfaction relation $\vDash_\Theta : \Sigma \times \mathcal{L}(At)$ inductively as follows:

$\sigma \vDash_\Theta e_1 = e_2$	iff	$\sigma[e_1] = \sigma[e_2]$
$\sigma \vDash_\Theta \neg A$	iff	$\sigma \nvDash_\Theta A$
$\sigma \vDash_\Theta A_1 \supset A_2$	iff	$\sigma \vDash_\Theta A_1$ implies $\sigma \vDash_\Theta A_2$	◆

Now that we already have a precise notion of state we may extend the programming context with the denotational semantics of all programs of actions of Ac.

Definition 4.4: An extension $\mathcal{T}_d$ of a programming context $\mathcal{T}_p = PL$ for a signature Θ consists of a pair $(PL, \{ \llbracket C_g \rrbracket | g \in Ac \})$ where,

- $\llbracket C_g \rrbracket : (\Sigma_{Lg} \to \Sigma_{Dg})$ is a denotational semantics for program C_g; we denote by Σ_{Lg} the set $\{\sigma_{Lg} | \sigma \in \Sigma\}$ and by Σ_{Dg} the set $\{\sigma_{Dg} | \sigma \in \Sigma\}$;

We also call such an extension $\mathcal{T}_d$, a *denotational context* for Θ. ◆

At the local level, we see that, because they are deterministic, actions are functions and, because they are atomic, they are functions from a local state to another local state.

Local computations are executed by agents which have an identity. That is, agents may be referred to, even though a given agent does not need to know the identity of the agents with which it cooperates. Each agent works over a (local) private state.

When an agent is assigned an action, a *loading* of the values it needs to accomplish its task is performed into its private state and the agent starts execution. If the system is receptive at the time the agent finishes executing the action, that is, the post-guard of the action is satisfied by the system state, then a *discharging* of its output values must be done (from its private state).

The need for the loading and discharging operations results from the fact that we allowed each agent to have its own states. Hence, the loading operation defines how the attributes in L_g are *loaded*: whether they are just copied or translated in some way to define a local state is a detail that is not relevant. Whatever the loading operation is, it should be a simple one because it needs to be performed atomically. The discharging operation gives to the system attributes in D_g a value computed by action g. As with the loading operation, the details of the discharging operation are not relevant here.

In order to define the operational semantics of behavioural programs, we need to extend programming contexts as defined in 3.4 to account for the executing agents and the loading and discharging operations as well as the operational semantics of the language used to program actions.

Definition 4.5: An operational extension of a programming context $\mathcal{T}_p$=PL for a signature Θ consists of a tuple $(PL, Pr, \{\Sigma_a | a \in Pr\}, \{(l_g^a, d_g^a, \xrightarrow{a}) | (a,g) \in Pr \times Ac\})$ where,

- Pr is a set of agent symbols that stand for the existing executing agents;
- Σ_a is the local state space (memory) of agent a;
- $l_g^a : \Sigma_{Lg} \to \Sigma_a$ gives semantics to the *loading* operations;
- $d_g^a : \Sigma_a \to \Sigma_{Dg}$ gives semantics to the *discharging* operations;
- $\xrightarrow{a} : (PL \times \Sigma_a \to \Sigma_a)$ is an operational semantics for comands in PL, for agent a.

We also call such an extended context $\mathcal{T}_o$, an *operational context* for Θ. ◆

Definition 4.6: An operational $\mathcal{T}_o = (PL, Pr, \{\Sigma_a | a \in Pr\}, \{(l_g^a, d_g^a, \xrightarrow{a}) | (a,g) \in Pr \times Ac\})$, and a denotational $\mathcal{T}_d = (PL, \{[\![C_g]\!]_g | g \in Ac\})$ contexts for a signature Θ are said to *agree* iff

for every $\sigma \in \Sigma, a \in Pr$, $[\![C_g]\!]\sigma_{Lg} = d_g^a(\xrightarrow{a} (C_g, l_g^a(\sigma_{Lg})))$ ◆

That is to say, the program C_g, whose denotational semantics is given by $[\![C_g]\!]$, is *implemented* by each agent a according to a "local" operational semantics $\xrightarrow{a}$ that, given program C_g and an agent a's private state (the one resulting from applying a's *loading* operation to $[\![C_g]\!]$ argument – σ_{Lg}), returns another private state of agent a (if we apply a's *discharging* operation to this local state, we obtain $[\![C_g]\!]\sigma_{Lg}$ result – σ_{Dg}).

At the operational level, transitions between *configurations* are defined, that is, the several steps of the execution of a behavioural program BP are reflected in the global state of the system (updating it whenever an agent discharges the results of its task) and in the several configurations of the agents (updating them whenever an action is assigned to an agent, and whenever an agent becomes free, whether having discharged the results of its task or not).

Definition 4.7: Given an operational context T_0 for a signature Θ, a *configuration* for Θ and Pr is a pair $<\sigma,\alpha>$ whose first component is a state for Θ and whose second component is a Pr-indexed set of agent configurations $\alpha = \{<st_a,ac_a,ls_a>|a \in \text{Pr}\}$ where:

- $st_a \in \{idle, busy, ready\}$ stands for the activity state of agent a, that is,
  - a is *idle* if a is unoccupied (with no action assigned to it);
  - a is *busy* if a is assigned an action and executing it;
  - a is *ready* if a has finished executing the action it was assigned to and it is waiting to become free (with or without discharging);
- $ac_a \in \text{Ac}$ stands for the action agent a is assigned to;
- $ls_a \in \Sigma$ stands for the state in which the system was in when the action in ac_a was assigned to agent a, that is, the action launching state. ◆

Configurations do not contain a program part because a behavioural program is a reactive program, that is, it does not "consume" itself when executing. Therefore, all *dga*s are always active in the sense that the program reacts to the environment at all times according to them.

Given a behavioural program BP and an operational context T_0 for a signature Θ, we define a relation $\rightarrow \subseteq C \times C$, where C is the set of all configurations for Θ and Pr, by

$$\text{for all } c,c' \in C, \quad c \rightarrow c' \text{ iff } c \rightarrow_{np} c' \text{ or } c \rightarrow_p c'$$

We represent by $<\sigma_1,\alpha_1> \rightarrow_{np} <\sigma_2,\alpha_2>$ the *non-productive* reaction of BP to configuration $<\sigma_1,\alpha_1>$, resulting in configuration $<\sigma_2,\alpha_2>$; *non-productive* means that no discharging of locally computed values happens in the transition from $<\sigma_1,\alpha_1>$ to $<\sigma_2,\alpha_2>$, and so, the system state σ_2 is the same as σ_1. A transition $<\sigma_1,\alpha_1> \rightarrow_p <\sigma_2,\alpha_2>$ represents a *productive* transition, that is, one where a discharging over the system state is done. This does not mean, however, that σ_1 is necessarily different from σ_2; it may happen that the discharge did not change the global state. These relations will be defined below through rules which provide an operational semantics for the behavioural paradigm.

The rules of the operational semantics have to control the launching and acceptance of actions according to the behaviour paradigm. With respect to launching, whenever the pre-guard of an action g is true of the system state, action g is assigned to an idle agent a (changing its configuration accordingly).

With respect to acceptance, whenever an agent a finishes executing an action g, which is signaled through the change of its state of activity to *ready*, and if the system state verifies the post-guard of g, it *discharges* the results computed locally by g into the system state according to g's discharging list. After this, agent a returns to an *idle* state of activity.

If the system state does not verify g's post-guard, agent a returns to an *idle* state of activity without discharging g's results.

It can be the case that a configuration is reached such that the system state does not verify none of the action pre-guards and, moreover, it does not verify the post-guards of none of the pending actions: the executing actions (the ones that are assigned to *busy* agents) and the already executed ones (assigned to *ready* agents). In this case we say that the system reached a *terminal* configuration because no more productive transitions are possible. We will denote *terminal* configurations by $<\sigma,\alpha>\sqrt{}$.

Definition 4.8: Given a Pr-indexed set α of agent configurations,

- $\alpha(a)$ stands for the configuration of agent a, that is, $<st_a,ac_a,ls_a>$
- $\alpha(a).x$ stands for the value of x in a's configuration, where x can be one of *st,ac* and *ls*
- $\alpha[<v_1,v_2,v_3>/a]$ represents the set of configurations that results from α by assigning $<v_1,v_2,v_3>$ to the configuration of agent a . When any of the v_i is not made explicit, it means that its value is not relevant in that context; $\alpha[<v_1, , >/a]$ stands for the set of configurations that results from α by assigning v_1 to the *st* component of agent a . $\quad\blacklozenge$

The operational semantics of a behavioural program is given over an operational context.

Definition 4.9: Given $\mathcal{T}_o = (PL,Pr,\{\Sigma_a|a \in Pr\},\{(l_g^a,d_g^a,\overset{a}{\to})|(a,g) \in Pr \times Ac\})$ – an operational context for a signature $\Theta = (At,Ac)$ – the following set of rules provides an operational semantics for a behavioural program $BP = (I,\{(A_g,P_g,C_g)|g \in Ac\})$:

1. $$\frac{\sigma \vDash_\Theta A_g \quad \alpha(a).st=idle}{<\sigma,\alpha> \to_{np} <\sigma,\alpha[<busy,g,\sigma>/a]>}$$

2. $$\frac{\sigma' \vDash_\Theta P_g \quad \alpha(a)=<ready,g,\sigma> \quad <C_g,l_g^a(\sigma_{Lg})> \overset{a}{\to} \sigma^a}{<\sigma',\alpha> \to_p <\sigma'[d_g^a(\sigma^a)/D_g],\alpha[<idle, , >/a]>}$$

3. $$\frac{\sigma' \nvDash_\Theta P_g \quad \alpha(a)=<ready,g,\sigma>}{<\sigma',\alpha> \to_{np} <\sigma',\alpha[<idle, , >/a]>}$$

4. $$\frac{\bigwedge_{g \in Ac}(\bigwedge_{a \in Pr}((\alpha(a)=<ready,g, > \vee \alpha(a)=<busy,g, >) \supset \sigma \vDash_\Theta P_g) \wedge \sigma \nvDash_\Theta A_g)}{<\sigma,\alpha> \to_{np} <\sigma,\alpha>\sqrt{}}$$

$\blacklozenge$

The rules for the evaluation of state formulas are as defined in 4.3.

The first rule says that whenever there is an action g whose pre-guard is true of the system state and there is an available agent a, action g is assigned to idle agent a and a copy of the system state is kept on a's configuration. The system state remains the same. This is a non-productive transition.

The second rule says that whenever the system state satisfies the post-guard of some *locally executed* action (the agent which executed it is *ready*), the results of that action are *discharged* to the system attributes in D_g while the attributes in $\mathcal{A}\backslash D_g$ keep their values. The set of agent configurations also changes insofar as the activity of the discharging agent is set to *idle*. This is a productive transition.

Notice how the duration of action execution is simulated: when an agent is assigned an action its state of activity is set to *busy*. The acceptance of its results is only considered when the agent is in a *ready* state of activity. This acts like some flag the agent waves when it ends its task. The actual transition from *busy* to *ready* is performed locally within the state of the agent. Because we are only concerned with the coordination model, this transition has to be determined according to the underlying computation model, and is not made explicit in the rule. The premiss $<C_g, l_g^a(\sigma_{Lg})> \xrightarrow{a} \sigma^a$ is the witness of the result of some local operational semantics and acts as interface between the computation and the coordination models.

Notice that the values of the attributes of the system – At – in the resulting state of a given action g, are completely determined. The values for attributes in D_g are given through the execution of C_g and depend on the values of the attributes in L_g at launching time (g is executed locally over the local state that is the result of *loading* the launching state. This launching state is the one that was stored in the agent's configuration at the time of the assignment); the other attributes – in $At\backslash D_g$ – depend on "what went on" in the system while g was executing, that is, they keep the value they had in the accepting state.

The third rule, a non-productive one, says that if the system state does not satisfy the post-guard of some locally executed action, the results of that action are ignored: the system state does not change. Only the set of agent configurations changes: the activity of the given agent is set to *idle*.

The fourth rule is the one that relates configurations for which no more productive transitions are possible, with the special terminal configuration.

5. A denotational semantics for behavioural programs

The rules for operational semantics usually define labelled transitions systems (e.g. as in [6] and [10]). These are pairs $<\Sigma, \{\xrightarrow{g} | g \in Ac\}>$ where Σ is a non-empty set (of states), Ac is a set (of actions/labels) and, for each $g \in Ac$, $\xrightarrow{g} \subseteq \Sigma \times \Sigma$ is the transition relation (a partial function if actions are deterministic). Given $\sigma, \sigma' \in \Sigma$, $\sigma \xrightarrow{g} \sigma'$ means that action g takes the system from state σ to state σ'. In this context, each transition within the system is completely defined by an action and two states, the launching and the resulting ones.

In the behavioural paradigm, observable transitions relate not two but three states: the launching, the accepting and the resulting ones. We consider that the behaviour of a program obtains from productive transitions only, that is, we do not consider the assignment and deassignment of agents as part of the observable behaviour. Notice that, although we ignore the agents changes of activity, the information about which action they execute and the corresponding launching state is used in order to determine the resulting state of a given transition. The *ls* component of a *ready* agent represents the state the system was in when the action it executes was launched. This launching state is crucial, together with the accepting one, to determine the resulting state.

We are going to show how the operational semantics given in 4.9. defines an extended version (by inclusion of an initial state) of *durative transition systems* in the sense of [7,8] – $<\Sigma,\sigma_0,\{\xrightarrow{g}|g\in Ac\}>$ – where each *durative transition* – $\xrightarrow{g}:(\Sigma\times\Sigma)\rightarrow\Sigma$ – is the set of triples composed by the launching, accepting and resulting states of all instances of action g.

We shall need the following auxiliary definitions in order to define durative transitions:

Definition 5.1: Given an operational context $\mathcal{T}_0$ for a signature Θ we call α_{idle} the set of agents configurations where all agents are idle. ♦

Definition 5.2: A configuration $<\sigma,\alpha>$ is said to be *reachable from* a configuration $<\sigma_1,\alpha_1>$ in a given program BP iff it is possible to obtain $<\sigma,\alpha>$ from $<\sigma_1,\alpha_1>$ by successive application of the operational rules, that is,

$$<\sigma_1,\alpha_1> \rightarrow^* <\sigma,\alpha> \qquad ♦$$

Given a behavioural program BP = (I,BDY), let a productive rule be applied to a configuration $<\sigma',\alpha>$, where agent *a* is such that $\alpha(a)=<ready,g,\sigma>$, changing it to $<\sigma'',\alpha[<idle, , >/a]>$. Let configuration $<\sigma',\alpha>$ be reachable from $<\sigma_0,\alpha_{idle}>$ where σ_0 is a state where I holds; then we know that there was a transition which assigned action *g* to agent *a* – because g's pre-guard was true of the system state – and stored that launching state in *a*'s configuration. Then, the triple $(\sigma,\sigma',\sigma'')$ represents the launching, accepting and resulting states of an instance of action g. The durative transition $\xrightarrow{g}$ is composed of all triples $(\sigma,\sigma',\sigma'')$ under these circumstances.

Definition 5.3: The durative transition system $\mathcal{D} = <\Sigma,\sigma_0,\{\xrightarrow{g}|g\in Ac\}>$ *defined by* a behavioural program BP = (I,{(A_g,P_g,C_g)|g∈ Ac}) is such that:

- $\sigma_0\vDash_\Theta I$
- $(\sigma,\sigma',\sigma'')\in\xrightarrow{g}$ iff for every $<\sigma',\alpha>$ s.t.

   $<\sigma',\alpha>$ *reachable from* $<\sigma_0,\alpha_{idle}>$ and for some *a*, $\alpha(a)=<ready,g,\sigma>$,

   $<\sigma',\alpha> \rightarrow_p <\sigma'',\alpha[<idle, , >/a]>$ ♦

The operational semantics just presented is shown to agree with an *extended* version of the denotational semantics presented in [8] by inclusion of the initial state.

Definition 5.4: Given a *denotational* context $\mathcal{T}_d = (PL, \{[\![C_g]\!] | g \in Ac\})$ for a signature Θ the denotational semantics of a program $BP = (I, \{(A_g, P_g, C_g) | g \in Ac\})$ for Θ is the durative transition system $\mathcal{D} = <\Sigma, \sigma_0, \{\mathcal{M}(A_g, P_g, C_g)]\!] | g \in Ac\}>$ where,

- $\sigma_0 \vDash_\Theta I$
- $\mathcal{M}(A_g, P_g, C_g)]\!] = \{(\sigma, \sigma', \sigma'') | \sigma \vDash A_g, \sigma' \vDash P_g, \sigma'' = \sigma'[[\![C_g]\!](\sigma_{Lg})/D_g]\}$

$\mathcal{M}(A_g, P_g, C_g)]\!]$ is the denotation of the *dga* (A_g, P_g, C_g). ◆

When the operational and denotational contexts for a given signature agree with each other as defined in 4.6, that is, the first *implements* the second and the second *abstracts* the first, the durative transitions defined operationally, that is, the triples of states $(\sigma, \sigma', \sigma'')$ where σ is the state the system is in when an agent is assigned an action, σ' is the state the system is in when the results of that action are accepted and σ'' is the resulting state, are the same as the ones obtained by the denotation of *dgas*.

Proposition 5.5: Given $\mathcal{T}_o = (PL, Pr, \{\Sigma_a | a \in Pr\}, \{(l_g^a, d_g^a, \xrightarrow{a}) | (a,g) \in Pr \times Ac\})$ and $\mathcal{T}_d = (PL, \{[\![C_g]\!] | g \in Ac\})$ – an operational and a denotational contexts for a signature $\Theta = (At, Ac)$ – which agree with each other, the *dts* defined by a behavioural program $BP = (I, \{(A_g, P_g, C_g) | g \in Ac\})$ is its denotation $\mathcal{D} = <\Sigma, \sigma_0, \{\mathcal{M}(A_g, P_g, C_g)]\!] | g \in Ac\}>$. ◆

6. Concluding remarks

The behavioural paradigm developed in [11,12] for supporting multiprocessor computing was presented as a coordination model for controlling the execution of durative actions, i.e. actions which, although executed atomically on a private local state, have a duration in the sense that the system state in which they finish executing is not necessarily the same in which they started.

In the proposed framework, each action has two associated guards. On the one hand, a pre-guard that characterizes the states of the system in which the action is desirable. As long as there are free processors, all actions that should be launched are launched regardless of any possible future conflict. Conflicts are resolved at acceptance time. This is achieved through a post-guard which characterises the system states in which an already "locally-executed" action is acceptable.

The interface between the global space of the system and the local space in which each action executes is made through two atomic operations of loading and discharging. When an action is launched, an atomic loading of the attributes that it needs to read is performed into the local state of the processor (agent) to which the action was assigned, and execution starts. When local execution ends, and if the post-guard of the action is satisfied by the system state, an atomic discharging of the effects computed locally is performed into the global state.

The proposed collection of primitives controls the interference between durative actions and clearly separates computation concerns from coordination ones as in [5]. The programming language in which computations are programmed is not constrained to any particular one: we rely on an interface that is provided by the loading and discharging operations. Pre- and post-guards stand for activation/permission criteria to coordinate the execution and productivity of actions.

Operational and denotational semantics were proposed for this paradigm which support, through context parameterisation, the separation between the coordination model and the computation model in which individual actions are programmed. The operational model formalises a multiprocessor environment through a collection of agents. The denotational semantics, which was proved to be equivalent to the operational one, is based on durative transition systems, an extension of labelled transitions systems proposed in [7,8] for capturing the notion of duration used in the behavioural paradigm. An axiomatic semantics is also available based on Durative Transition Logic, a modal logic introduced in [7] which is complete for durative transition systems. See [8] for further details.

Further work is under way for exploring the relationship between the behavioural paradigm and traditional coordination models in more detail, namely in what concerns multiset/ tuple space representations as well as the deductive approach to the operational semantics [9]. Applications to software architectures are also envisaged, for which we intend to integrate the behavioural formalisms in the categorical approach developed in [3].

References

1. J.P.Banâtre and D.Le Métayer, "Programming by Multiset Transformation", *Communications* ACM16, 1 pp. 55-77, 1993.

2. P.Ciancarini, C.Hankin, "Coordination Languages and Models", LNCS 1061, Springer-Verlag, 1996.

3. J.L.Fiadeiro and A.Lopes, "Semantics of Architectural Connectors", *Theory and Practice of Software Development*, M.Bidoit and M.Dauchet (eds), LNCS 1214, pp. 505-519, Springer-Verlag, 1997.

4. D.Gelernter, "Generative Communication in Linda", ACM *Trans. Prog. Lang. Syst.* 7, 1, pp. 80-112, 1985.

5. D.Gelernter, N.Carriero, "Coordination Languages and their Significance", *Communications* ACM 35, 2, pp. 97-107, 1992.

6. Z.Manna, A.Pnueli, *The Temporal Logic of Reactive and Concurrent Systems*, Springer-Verlag 1991.

7. I.Nunes, J.L.Fiadeiro and W.M.Turski, "A Modal Logic of Durative Actions", in *ICTL97*, Kluwer, in print, 1997.

8. I.Nunes, J.L.Fiadeiro and W.M.Turski, "Semantics of Behavioural Programs", Research Report, Department of Informatics, Faculty of Sciences, University of Lisbon, December 1996.

9. A.Porto, V.Vasconcelos, "Truth and Action Osmosis (the TAO Computational Model)", in J.M.Andreoli, C.Hankin and D.LeMetayer (eds), *Coordination Programming, mechanisms, models and semantics*, pp. 65-97, Imperial College Press, 1996.

10. C.Stirling, "Modal and Temporal Logics", in S.Abramsky, D.Gabbay and T.Maibaum (eds), *Handbook of Logic in Computer Science* 2, pp. 477-563, 1992.

11. W.M.Turski, "On Specification of Multiprocessor Computing", *Acta Informatica* 27, pp. 685-696, 1990.

12. W.M.Turski, "Extending the Computing Paradigm", *Structured Programming* 13, pp. 1-9, 1992.

Communication-Passing Style for Coordination Languages

Suresh Jagannathan

Computer Science Research, NEC Research Institute, 4 Independence Way,
Princeton, NJ 08540, *suresh@research.nj.nec.com*

Abstract. Coordination languages for parallel and distributed systems specify mechanisms for creating tasks and communicating data among them. These languages typically assume that (a) once a task begins execution on some processor, it will remain resident on that processor throughout its lifetime, and (b) communicating shared data among tasks is through some form of message-passing and data migration. In this paper, we investigate an alternative approach to understanding coordination. *Communication-passing style* (CmPS) refers to a coordination semantics in which data communication is always undertaken by migrating the continuation of the task requiring the data to the processor where the data resides.

Communication-passing style is closely related to continuation-passing style (CPS), a useful transformation for compiling functional languages. Just as CPS eliminates implicit call-return sequences, CmPS eliminates implicit inter-processor data communication and synchronization requests. In a CmPS-transformed program, only continuations (i.e., control contexts) are transmitted across machines; all synchronization and data communication occurs locally. Besides providing significant optimization opportunities, CmPS is a natural representation for implementations on networks of workstations.

This paper presents an operational semantics for a coordination language that supports first-class distributed data repositories. The computation sublanguage considered is an untyped call-by-value functional language similar to pure Scheme. Optimizations and implementation issues that arise from using a CmPS-driven coordination language are also described.

1 Introduction

Implementations of functional languages often first transform the source program into *continuation-passing style* (CPS) [1, 16]. In a CPS'ed program, every procedure is supplied an extra argument, its *continuation*, that represents the "rest of the computation" following a call to this procedure. When a procedure is applied, the supplied continuation conceptually represents the return point to which control should be transferred upon completion of the procedure body. The most important advantage of the CPS transform is that it makes all control-flow in a program explicit, thus simplifying and enabling various source-level optimizations.

Communication-passing style (CmPS) is a natural extension of CPS in a distributed context. Assume a collection of tasks executing on some collection of processors, and assume some distribution of shared data on these processors. In a CmPS-transformed program, inter-processor communication is always undertaken by *migrating* the continuation of a task to the processor where the shared data it requires resides. Just as CPS eliminates implicit call-return sequences, CmPS eliminates implicit inter-processor data communication and synchronization requests. In a CmPS-transformed program, only continuations (i.e., control contexts) are transmitted across machines; all synchronization and data communication occurs locally. Just as CPS can be thought as transforming procedure calls to gotos, CmPS can be thought as transforming data communication to task migration.

Using a communication-passing style transform, the responsibility of the programmer is restricted to devising reasonable data distribution among the computing elements available; issues of global consistency and synchronization are no longer relevant. Shared data remains resident on the node where it was created, and tasks migrate as needed among those nodes containing the shared data they require.

Networks of commodity workstations (NOWs) are likely soon to become the preferred platform for building long-lived parallel and distributed programs. Programs written under existing languages, however, appear ill-suited to execute on such platforms. In traditional languages, tasks usually have a great deal of control over *what* they compute, but rarely have any power in determining *where* or *how* their computation is exercised. Thus, while a program creating many tasks may be able to specify where these tasks should be initially allocated, the executing process usually does not have the capability of efficiently altering or refining this mapping as computation progresses. Yet, it is precisely this feature that is crucial when executing parallel and distributed programs in a loosely-coupled, potentially time-shared environment, such as a NOW.

Furthermore, typical implementations in this environment require data shared among tasks running on different machines to be copied back-and-forth to ensure global consistency. Locality often suffers if the primary accessor of the data executes on a machine different from where the data actually resides. In addition to ensuring global consistency of multiple copies of a shared object, implementations must also overcome bandwidth limitations if shared data is accessed by many tasks on many different machines.

In this paper, we consider the integration of a coordination language loosely based on Linda [4] into a simple untyped call-by-value higher-order computation language. Rather than tuple-spaces, our coordination language supports first-class *address spaces*. An address space defines a separate locus of execution that may contain globally visible shared-data. Instead of distributed data structures, our coordination language supports *naming environments* implicitly defined with each address space. Tasks may deposit, retrieve, or remove bindings on any address space, blocking if a desired binding is not found. Within this context, we consider a formal language specification and abstract implementation that supports CmPS-style coordination.

The paper is organized as follows. The next section presents a direct-style formal operational semantics for the kernel language using a CEK-machine [7, 8] formulation. Section 3 provides further motivation for communication-passing style through a series of simple examples. Because the semantics is presented in direct-style, continuations are implicitly managed by the machine, and not exposed in the source program. In the context of a higher-order computation language, a CmPS strategy, like CPS, can be expressed entirely as a source-to-source transformation; this transform is described in Section 4. Section 5 discusses some optimizations in the context of the semantics that may significantly reduce the bandwidth requirements needed to support a CmPS-based implementation. Sections 6 and 7 provide comparison to related work and conclusions.

2   The Language

In this section, we define a simple parallel and distributed language L. We proceed to give a small-step operational semantics for L in terms of the CEK^T machine, a parallel extension of the CEK-machine [7]. We regard the specification of this machine as a state transition system whose objects of interest include expressions, environments, continuations, threads, and shared environments.

The source language for L, whose grammar is shown in Figure 1, consists of two parts. L's computation component is a simple untyped call-by-value lambda-calculus with constants, variables, conditionals, single-argument functions, recursion, applications, and (primitive) applications. Like Scheme, the computation language is latently typed—no static typing discipline is imposed on programs.

L's coordination language supports the creation of multiple threads of control and multiple address spaces. An address space defines a new logical locus of execution; when a new address space is created, resources on some machine in a network ensemble maybe allocated for it. We leave unspecified the manner in which the mapping between address spaces and physical machines is chosen. New threads are always created on a specific address space. Evaluating (makeAS) creates a new address space, and evaluating the expression, (spawn $AS\ e$) creates a new thread on address space AS to evaluate e. Associated with each address space is a shared environment accessible to expressions evaluating on other address spaces. We provide three operations on this environment: (put $AS\ [x\ v]\ e$) deposits a binding $\langle x, v \rangle$ that binds variable x to value v in the environment associated with address space AS and evaluates e once the binding has been deposited; this binding shadows any previous binding for x in AS. The expression, (rd $AS\ [x]\ e$) reads a binding for x from AS, and binds x in e. If no binding for x is available, evaluation of the expression blocks until a put operation to deposit a binding for x is executed by some other thread. Similar to rd is get which reads and then *removes* the appropriate binding from the target environment. Note that because synchronization is tied to name lookup, variables associated

$$e \in E \quad ::= \quad Comp \mid Coord$$

$$c_\lambda \in Comp \quad ::= \quad c \mid x \mid \lambda x.e \mid \mu f.\lambda x.e$$
$$\mid \quad (e_1\, e_2)$$
$$\mid \quad (p\, e_1 \dots e_n)$$
$$\mid \quad (\text{if } e_1\, e_2\, e_3)$$

$$c_\pi \in Coord \quad ::= \quad (\text{put } e\,[x\, e_a]\, e_b)$$
$$\mid \quad (\text{rd } e\,[x]\, e_b)$$
$$\mid \quad (\text{get } e\,[x]\, e_b)$$
$$\mid \quad (\text{spawn } e_a\, e_b)$$

$$p \in Primop \quad ::= \quad + \mid\ -\ \mid \dots \mid \text{makeAS} \mid \text{spawn}$$

Fig. 1. The language.

with bindings found in shared environments cannot be renamed in the contexts in which they are referenced.

Readers familiar with Linda [4] will see obvious similarities between these operations and Linda's support for distributed data structures via tuple-spaces. We believe the coordination operators defined here can be easily generalized to support associative matching in the style supported by Linda, but such extensions are orthogonal to our motivation for investigating the semantics of communication-passing style transformations, and thus not included here.

2.1 Semantics

To specify a CEK^T-machine, we define a set of states, *State*, and a binary transition relation, $\longrightarrow$, on states. A particular state includes the state of all threads in all address spaces, and the contents of the shared environment in each address space. The domain definitions for states are shown in Figures 2 and 3.

$$s \in State \quad = ThreadMap \times SharedEnv$$
$$T \in ThreadMap = AspaceUid \times ThreadUid \to ThreadState$$
$$\rho \in SharedEnv \ = AspaceUid \to Env$$
$$\alpha \in AspaceUid$$
$$\tau \in ThreadUid$$

Fig. 2. CEK^T-machine Thread and Address Space States

$$
\begin{aligned}
t \in \textit{ThreadState} &= \textit{ControlState} + \textit{ReturnState} + \textit{HaltState} \\
\langle e, r, k \rangle \in \textit{ControlState} &= \textit{Exp} \times \textit{Env} \times \textit{Cont} \\
\langle k, v \rangle \in \textit{ReturnState} &= \textit{Cont} \times \textit{Value} \\
\mathbf{halt}(v) \in \textit{HaltState} &= \textit{Value} \\
r \in \textit{Env} &= \textit{Var} \to \textit{Value} \\
k \in \textit{Cont} &= \textit{Frame}^* \\
\textit{frame} \in \textit{Frame} &= \textit{CompFrame} + \textit{CoordFrame} \\
\textit{frame}_\lambda \in \textit{CompFrame} &= \textit{ArgFrame} + \textit{FunFrame} + \\
&\quad \textit{PrimFrame} + \textit{IfFrame} + \textit{CoordFrame} \\
\textit{frame}_\pi \in \textit{CoordFrame} &= \textit{SpawnFrame} + \textit{PutArgFrame} + \\
&\quad \textit{RdArgFrame} + \textit{GetArgFrame} + \textit{PutBodyFrame} \\
\mathbf{arg}\langle e, r \rangle \in \textit{ArgFrame} &= \textit{Exp} \times \textit{Env} \\
\mathbf{fun}\langle v \rangle \in \textit{FunFrame} &= \textit{Value} \\
\mathbf{cond}\langle e_t, e_f, r \rangle \in \textit{IfFrame} &= \textit{Exp} \times \textit{Exp} \times \textit{Env} \\
\mathbf{spawn}\langle e, r \rangle \in \textit{SpawnFrame} &= \textit{Exp} \times \textit{Env} \\
\mathbf{prim}\langle p, r, \vec{v}, \vec{e} \rangle \in \textit{PrimFrame} &= \textit{Primitive} \times \textit{Env} \times \textit{Value}^* \times \textit{Exp}^* \\
v \in \textit{Value} &= \textit{Constant} + \textit{Closure} + \textit{AspaceUid} + \textit{ThreadUid} \\
\lambda x.\,e, \mu f.\lambda e. \in \textit{Closure} &= (\textit{LambdaExp} \times \textit{Env}) + (\textit{RecExp} \times \textit{Env})
\end{aligned}
$$

Fig. 3. CEK^T-machine Thread States

In the following, we write $X + Y$ and $X \times Y$ to mean the cartesian sum and product of sets X and Y, resp. We write $X \to Y$ to denote the set of partial functions from X to Y. The notation $f[x \mapsto v]$ denotes the function that is identical to f on all elements except x for which it returns y; f/x denotes the function identical to f on all elements except x for which it is undefined. We write X^* to denote the finite sequences of elements of X. If x ranges over X, then $\vec{x}$ denotes a list of elements drawn from X. We write "$v_1 @ \vec{v}$" to indicate the list whose head is v_1 and whose tail is $\vec{v}$.

Machine States A *state* in our semantics is a pair consisting of a *ThreadMap*, T, and a global shared environment, ρ. T is a function that maps pairs of address spaces and threads to thread states. The shared environment is a map from address spaces to environments. We assume all address spaces and threads are associated with a unique identifier that names them.[1]

A given thread τ may be in one of three states. If τ is in *control state*, $\langle e, r, k \rangle$, it means τ is currently evaluating expression e in environment r. If τ is in a *return state*, it has computed a value for a subexpression that must now be passed to continuation. When τ completes, it enters a *halt state*.

The continuation k of e is the "remainder" of the computation to be performed by this thread after evaluation of e. Continuations are represented as a stack of frames. There are two kinds of continuation frames, those that deal

---

[1] We freely denote address spaces and threads by their uids when obvious from context.

with the computation sublanguage and those that deal with the coordination sublanguage. For the computation sublanguage, an *ArgFrame* is used to hold the argument value of a function call while the expression in the function position of the call is evaluated; a *FunFrame* is used to combine the function found at a call with its arguments; a *PrimFrame* is used to collect arguments to primitives; and, an *IfFrame* is used to hold the true and false branches of a conditional while the test is being evaluated. For the coordination sublanguage, a *SpawnFrame* is used to hold the expression to be spawned while the value of the address space in which this thread should evaluate is being computed; *PutArg* frames and *PutBody* frames are used to hold intermediate results of subexpressions in a put operation; and, *RdArg* and *GetArg* frames serve similar purposes for rd and get operations, respectively.

The language supports four kinds of values: constants, closures, and tagged unique identifiers for address spaces and threads. Note that there is mutual reference in the definition of *Env*, *Closure*, and *Value*. Rather than appealing to a domain-theoretic interpretation of these structures, we simply choose the smallest sets satisfying the desired equations; the empty environment serves as the base case.

In order to define $\longrightarrow$, we assume a partial function to apply primitive operations to constants:

$$\mathcal{P} : Primitive \times Constant^* \to Constant$$

Transition Relation We can think of $\longrightarrow$ as an implementation of an interpreter for this language. The interpreter chooses some thread to evaluate, matches the current state with a left-hand side of a rule, and "transforms" the state to the right-hand side. At any point during evaluation, there may be many thread states that satisfy the left-hand side of a rule; any one of these threads may be chosen for evaluation. The only dependencies among threads are those induced by lookups and updates of shared environments. Thus, any two threads not involved in a communication event via a shared environment may be evaluated concurrently; the semantics imposes no conditions on the *order* in which threads are evaluated. The semantics makes no assumptions about fairness or liveness.

However, the semantics must guarantee that for any given thread, there is at most one rule that satisfies the thread's current state. Moreover, a thread in a state whose evaluation is associated with a rule that has side-conditions, must satisfy these conditions before it can be evaluated to the right-hand side. If no thread in the machine can be further reduced, and not all threads are in a halt state, the program is deadlocked.

Given CEK^T, we define *eval*, a partial function that maps a program to a pair $\langle \rho', \{v_0, v_1, v_2, \ldots, v_n\} \rangle$ where ρ' is a shared environment, and v_i represents the value yielded by evaluating thread with uid τ_i. Let $\overset{*}{\longrightarrow}$ be the reflexive transitive closure of $\longrightarrow$. Then, the semantics of a program P is given by:

$$eval(P) = \langle \rho', \{v_1, v_2, \ldots, v_n\} \rangle \Longleftrightarrow$$

$$\langle T_\perp[\langle \alpha_0, \tau_0 \rangle \mapsto \langle P, r_\perp, k_\perp \rangle], \rho_\perp \rangle \xrightarrow{*}$$
$$\langle T_\perp[\langle \alpha_0, \tau_0 \rangle \mapsto \mathbf{halt}(v_0), \ldots, \langle \alpha_n, \tau_n \rangle \mapsto \mathbf{halt}(v_n)], \rho' \rangle$$

The transition relation consists of four kinds of rules. The first group describes actions on the global state; these rules define the creation of new address spaces and threads. The second group of rules defines the semantics of the coordination language, and describes how shared environments are manipulated. The third and fourth group of rules defines the action of the machine on control and return states, and describe single-threaded behavior. The first two groups of rules are given in Figures 4 and 5. The latter two are shown in the appendix.

There are three "top-level" rules that specify how new threads and address spaces are added to the global state. To create a new thread, we first determine the address space on which the thread will be evaluated, pushing the expression to be spawned along with the current environment on the continuation stack. Provided that the address space exists, a new uid is associated with this thread, and the thread is instantiated with an initial state consisting of the thread body, the environment in which the **spawn** expression is being evaluated, and the empty continuation. Thus, threads do not inherit the dynamic control context of their parent. Creating a new address space involves generating a new address space uid α', augmenting the thread map to include a reference to the new address space, and augmenting the shared environment to map α' to an initial empty environment.

$$\langle T[\langle \alpha, \tau \rangle \mapsto \langle (\mathbf{spawn}\ e_1\ e_2), r, k \rangle], \rho \rangle \longrightarrow \langle T[\langle \alpha, \tau \rangle \mapsto \langle e_1, r, \mathbf{spawn}\langle e_2, r \rangle : k \rangle], \rho \rangle$$

$$\langle T[\langle \alpha, \tau \rangle \mapsto \langle \alpha', \mathbf{spawn}\langle e_2, r \rangle : k \rangle], \rho \rangle \longrightarrow$$
$$\langle T[\langle \alpha, \tau \rangle \mapsto \langle k, \tau' \rangle, \langle \alpha', \tau' \rangle \mapsto \langle e_2, r, k_\perp \rangle], \rho \rangle$$
provided $\alpha' \in Dom(\rho)$ and τ' fresh

$$\langle T[\langle \alpha, \tau \rangle \mapsto \langle \mathbf{makeAS}, r, k \rangle], \rho \rangle \longrightarrow$$
$$\langle T[\langle \alpha', \tau_0 \rangle \mapsto \mathbf{halt}(v_0), \langle \alpha, \tau \rangle \mapsto \langle k, \alpha' \rangle], \rho[\alpha' \mapsto \lambda x.\ undef] \rangle$$
provided $\alpha' \notin Dom(\rho)$ and α' fresh

Fig. 4. Transition rules for threads and address spaces.

The rules defining the semantics of the coordination sublanguage are also divided into two groups. The first group defines the order of evaluation of subexpressions on the coordination operators; the second defines how the shared environment and thread map are manipulated. Consider a put operation executing as part of thread σ on address space AS_s. Let AS_t be the target address space where the generated binding $\langle x, v \rangle$ is to be deposited. To perform this operation, the machine extends the shared environment on AS_t with $\langle x, v \rangle$, and "migrates" σ to AS_t. Migration is expressed by executing a transition that yields a new thread map which removes the current thread from AS_s and installs a new thread (with the same thread uid) on AS_t.

A similar transition is performed for rd and get operations. The relevant transition rules for these operators also have side-conditions that guarantee that the transition is satisfiable only when the relevant binding is available on the appropriate shared environment. Note that the introduction of a new computation sublanguage will not entail any modification to the semantics of the coordination sublanguage.

The CmPS-transform is expressed explicitly in the semantics (and *implicitly* in the coordination language) by manipulating threads and their continuations. Since continuations are manifest in the semantics, and since, by definition, there is a unique continuation associated with every executing thread, it becomes straightforward to specify the act of migrating a continuation from one address space to another in terms of simple restrictions and extensions on the global thread map. Moreover, because each transition is atomic, and because thread uids are globally unique, the machine will never enter a state in which the same thread is concurrently executing on multiple address spaces.

$\langle (\text{put } e_a\,[x\,e_x]\,e_b), r, k \rangle \longrightarrow \langle e_a, r, \mathbf{putArg}\langle x, e_x, e_b, r \rangle : k \rangle$
$\langle (\text{rd } e\,[x]\,e_b), r, k \rangle \longrightarrow \langle e, r, \mathbf{rdArg}\langle x, e_b, r \rangle : k \rangle$
$\langle (\text{rd } e\,[x]\,e_b), r, k \rangle \longrightarrow \langle e, r, \mathbf{getArg}\langle x, e_b, r \rangle : k \rangle$

$\langle \mathbf{putArg}\langle x, e_x, e_b, r \rangle : k, v \rangle \longrightarrow \langle e_x, r, \mathbf{putBody}\langle x, e_b, v, r \rangle : k \rangle$
$\langle T[\langle \alpha, \tau \rangle \mapsto \langle \mathbf{putBody}\langle x, e_b, v, r \rangle : k, v_a \rangle], \rho \rangle \longrightarrow$
$\quad \langle T/\langle \alpha, \tau \rangle[\langle v, \tau \rangle \mapsto \langle e_b, r, k \rangle], (\rho\,v)[x \mapsto v_a] \rangle$

$\langle T[\langle \alpha, \tau \rangle \mapsto \langle \mathbf{rdArg}\langle x, e_b, r \rangle : k, v \rangle], \rho \rangle \longrightarrow \langle T/\langle \alpha, \tau \rangle[\langle v, \tau \rangle \mapsto \langle e_b, r[x \mapsto v_x], k \rangle], \rho \rangle$
$\quad$ provided $x \in Dom((\rho\,v))$ and $((\rho\,v)\,x) = v_x$

$\langle T[\langle \alpha, \tau \rangle \mapsto \langle \mathbf{getArg}\langle x, e_b, r \rangle : k, v \rangle], \rho \rangle \longrightarrow \langle T/\langle \alpha, \tau \rangle[\langle v, \tau \rangle \mapsto \langle e_b, r[x \mapsto v_x], k \rangle], \rho' \rangle$
$\quad$ where $\rho' = (\rho\,v)/x$, $x \in Dom((\rho\,v))$ and $((\rho\,v)\,x) = v_x$

Fig. 5. Transition rule for coordination sublanguage

---

3   An Example

To motivate communication-passing style, consider the simple example shown in Figure 6. To make the presentation more readable, we use pure Scheme as the computation sublanguage, and italicize operators belonging to the coordination sublanguage.

```
(letrec ((tree
          (lambda (AS v)
            (cond ((leaf?) (put AS [val (leaf v)] v))
                  (else (let ((left (makeAS))
                              (right (makeAS)))
                          (spawn left (tree left (left-part v)))
                          (spawn right (tree right (right-part v)))
                          (put AS [val (C (rd left [val] val)
                                          (rd right [val] val))]
                               val)))))))
  (tree (makeAS) initial-val))
```

Fig. 6. A simple tree-structured parallel program.

This program creates a tree of address spaces, with a single task running on each address space. All tasks communicate via shared variable val that has a potentially different binding value on each address space. A leaf task simply deposits a binding for val in its associated address space. A non-leaf task creates two child address spaces, and spawns a thread on each of them. These threads simply perform a recursive call, using some portion of the initial value supplied to the root of the tree as their argument. A non-leaf task waits for its children to supply a binding-value for val on their corresponding address spaces, combines these values, and deposits the result as its binding-value for val on its address space.

Consider a straightforward implementation of this program. Each address space would be mapped to some physical node in a network ensemble. Every non-leaf task would initiate two messages for each of C's rd arguments. The first message is a request for val's binding-value on the target address space; the request may be enqueued if the value is not present. The second is the reply containing the data. For any non-leaf task T, the bandwidth requirements imposed by T is the sum of the sizes of the binding-values for val in its descendents.

Now, consider a CmPS implementation. For a non-leaf task, the rd operation on the left child will cause the continuation of the parent to migrate to the address space on which the left child resides. Once val has been read on this address space, a continuation migrates to the right child, and finally returns back to the parent. Unlike the implementation sketched above, three messages (rather than four) are initiated by each non-leaf task. Moreover, using a safe-for-space implementation of continuations [1, 21], the bandwidth requirement needed to support this migration is neglible since the only data referenced in the migrating continuation is an empty shared environment. As a result, we may expect significant performance improvement over the non-CmPS implementation.

In this simple program, consistency issues were not critical since every binding in a shared-environment is read and written exactly once. Figure 7 is a slightly more sophisticated version of the same program. Instead of shared data being read exactly once, each non-leaf task spawns three new threads which read a given piece of shared data multiple times. The first thread performs some computation that repeatedly reads val's binding-value on the left-child; the second performs the same computation except it reads val's binding value multiple times on the right-child; and, the third repeatedly refines val's binding-value on the current address space. Thus, instead of a single communication event between parent and child tasks, there are multiple events, and instead of a single unique value computed for each task, there is effectively a stream of values produced.

```
(letrec ((g (lambda (AS) perform repeated calculation on (rd AS [val] val)))
         (h (lambda (AS)
               perform repeated calculation on
               (put AS [val (C (rd AS [left-val] left-val)
                                (rd AS [right-val] right-val))]
                    val)))
         (tree (lambda (AS v)
                 (cond ((leaf?) (put [val (leaf v)] v))
                       (else
                         (let ((left (makeAS))
                               (right (makeAS)))
                           (spawn left (tree left (left-part v)))
                           (spawn right (tree right (right-part v)))
                           (spawn AS (put AS [left-val (g left)]
                                           left-val))
                           (spawn AS (put AS [right-val (g right)]
                                           right-val))
                           (spawn AS (put AS [val (h AS)] val)))))))))
  (tree (makeAS) initial-val))
```

Fig. 7. A simple tree-structured parallel program.

In this example, consistency of shared data becomes an important issue. In order to be faithful to the semantics, a non-CmPS implementation which chooses to cache the value yielded by rd on its local address space must ensure that the address space is notified whenever the read value is updated. Rather than implementing a sophisticated consistency protocol, an implementation may choose to have every rd operation on a remote address space entail a remote communication event.

In a CmPS-implementation, on the other hand, the computation of a call to g will always occur on either the left or right child. The size of the continuation is again neglible because it includes only a reference to the current address space. This is because spawned threads begin execution in an empty continuation. Unlike the earlier example, the continuation corresponding to the two threads responsible for computing left-val and right-val are sent to two different address spaces, namely the address spaces corresponding to the left and right child. When the call to g is finished, these continuations migrate back to their parent, updating the shared environment appropriately with a new binding for left-val and right-val. Thus, exactly four communication events occur between a non-leaf node and its two children. In contrast, a non-CmPS implementation will incur a number of communication events proportional to the number of iterations performed by g.

For fine-grained programs such as these, a CmPS-style communication model would appear to be significantly more effective at reducing bandwidth requirements, than implementations based on more traditional data-migration [15] or RPC-style [2] semantics. Nonetheless, it is clear that the effectiveness of this communication strategy depends upon the size of the continuations being migrated. If these continuations are large, bandwidth requirements may in fact exceed what would have been necessary in a more traditional implementation. In Section 5, we examine some simple optimizations and alterations to our semantics that address this concern.

4   A Source-Level Transformation

The direct-style semantics given in Section 2 manipulated continuations as part of the machine specification dealing with the creation and coordination of threads. For example, whenever a coordination operator accesses an address space AS, its continuation is migrated to AS. These actions are not manifest in the source program, but defined explicitly in the transitions undertaken by the machine. Given that the computation sublanguage we are considering is higher-order, however, it is straightforward to express this behavior as a source-level transformation. Demonstrating this transform is illustrative because it provides further motivation for why we regard the specification of task migration in this language to be closely related to a continuation-passing transformation.

Figure 8 shows the CmPS source-level transformation for the coordination sublanguage. We omit presentation of the transform for the computation sublanguage since it would be identical to an ordinary CPS [1, 10] translation.

Assume a thread τ executing on address space AS has continuation k and is to evaluate a put expression. The CmPS-transform for this expression evaluates the operator's first argument to an address space, v_{AS}, evaluates the binding-expression to get value v_{arg}, and creates a new thread on v_{AS} that deposits a binding on the address space associated with v_{AS}. Finally, k is applied to the CmPS-transformed value of put's body. The continuation of the call to k is the continuation of the spawn operator, which we have defined in our CEK^T specification to be the empty continuation. Thus, no further evaluation of τ takes place on AS; the rest of τ's computation is undertaken by its proxy on v_{AS}.

$\mathcal{C}[\![(\text{put } e_{AS} [x\ e_a]\ e_b)]\!]\ k = (\text{let } ((k_1\ (\text{lambda } (v_{AS})$
$\qquad\qquad\qquad\qquad (\text{let } ((k_2\ (\text{lambda } (v_{arg})$
$\qquad\qquad\qquad\qquad\qquad\qquad (\text{let } ((k_3\ (\text{lambda } (z)\ (k\ z))))$
$\qquad\qquad\qquad\qquad\qquad\qquad\qquad (\text{spawn } v_{AS}\ (\text{put } v_{AS} [x\ v_{arg}]$
$\qquad\qquad\qquad\qquad\qquad\qquad\qquad\qquad\qquad \mathcal{C}[\![e_b]\!]\ k_3))))))$
$\qquad\qquad\qquad\qquad\qquad \mathcal{C}[\![e_a]\!]\ k_2))))$
$\qquad\qquad\qquad \mathcal{C}[\![e_{AS}]\!]\ k_1)$

$\mathcal{C}[\![(\text{rd } e_{AS} [x]\ e_b)]\!]\ k = (\text{let } ((k_1\ (\text{lambda } (v_{AS})$
$\qquad\qquad\qquad\qquad (\text{let } ((k_2\ (\text{lambda } (z)\ (k\ z))))$
$\qquad\qquad\qquad\qquad\qquad (\text{spawn } v_{AS}\ (\text{rd } v_{AS} [x]\ \mathcal{C}[\![e_b]\!]\ k_2))))))$
$\qquad\qquad\qquad \mathcal{C}[\![e_{AS}]\!]\ k_1)$

$\mathcal{C}[\![(\text{get } e_{AS} [x]\ e_b)]\!]\ k = (\text{let } ((k_1\ (\text{lambda } (v_{AS})$
$\qquad\qquad\qquad\qquad (\text{let } ((k_2\ (\text{lambda } (z)\ (k\ z))))$
$\qquad\qquad\qquad\qquad\qquad (\text{spawn } v_{AS}\ (\text{get } v_{AS} [x]\ \mathcal{C}[\![e_b]\!]\ k_2))))))$
$\qquad\qquad\qquad \mathcal{C}[\![e_{AS}]\!]\ k_1)$

Fig. 8. A source-level CmPS transformation for the coordination sublanguage. Italicized variables are fresh.

This transformation produces the desired behavior: the body of the put expression as well as put's continuation evaluate on v_{AS}. Moreover, there is no further evaluation of τ on AS. The transformation for rd and get are similarly defined. In these cases as well, the body of the operator along with the operator's continuation are evaluated in a new thread instantiated on the address space where the relevant binding exists. Like CPS, this transform makes all control-flow explicit. It now becomes syntactically apparent that coordination operations introduced by the transformation all occur as arguments to spawn. Moreover, the target address spaces for these operators (i.e., the address space on which the desired binding is to be deposited or retrieved) is the same as the address space on which the thread instantiated by the enclosing spawn begins execution.

Note that the body of the spawn expression for all three operators is a *non-transformed* variant of the input to $\mathcal{C}$. The meaning of these expressions is as shown in Figure 5. Since the evaluation of these expressions occur on the same address space as the bindings they manipulate, there is no observable effect on the thread map when they are evaluated. Indeed, we can simplify the transition rules for the coordination sublanguage by assuming the existence of this transformation. These simplified rules are shown in Figure 9.

$$\langle(\mathbf{put}\ e_a\,[x\ e_x]\ e_b),r,k\rangle \longrightarrow \langle e_a,r,\mathbf{putArg}\langle x,e_x,e_b,r\rangle : k\rangle$$
$$\langle(\mathbf{rd}\ e\,[x]\ e_b),r,k\rangle \longrightarrow \langle e,r,\mathbf{rdArg}\langle x,e_b,r\rangle : k\rangle$$
$$\langle(\mathbf{get}\ e\,[x]\ e_b),r,k\rangle \longrightarrow \langle e,r,\mathbf{getArg}\langle x,e_b,r\rangle : k\rangle$$

$$\langle\mathbf{putArg}\langle x,e_x,e_b,r\rangle : k,v_{AS}\rangle \longrightarrow \langle e_x,r,\mathbf{putBody}\langle x,e_b,v_{AS},r\rangle : k\rangle$$
$$\langle T[\langle\alpha,\tau\rangle \mapsto \langle\mathbf{putBody}\langle x,e_b,v,r\rangle : k,v_a\rangle],\rho\rangle \longrightarrow$$
$$\quad \langle T[\langle\alpha,\tau\rangle \mapsto \langle e_b,r,k\rangle],(\rho\,\alpha)[x \mapsto v_a]\rangle$$

$$\langle T[\langle\alpha,\tau\rangle \mapsto \langle\mathbf{rdArg}\langle x,e_b,r\rangle : k,\alpha\rangle],\rho\rangle \longrightarrow \langle T[\langle\alpha,\tau\rangle \mapsto \langle e_b,r[x \mapsto v_x],k\rangle],\rho\rangle$$
$$\quad \text{provided } x \in Dom((\rho\,\alpha)) \text{ and } ((\rho\,\alpha)\,x) = v_x$$

$$\langle T[\langle\alpha,\tau\rangle \mapsto \langle\mathbf{getArg}\langle x,e_b,r\rangle : k,\alpha\rangle],\rho\rangle \longrightarrow \langle T[\langle\alpha,\tau\rangle \mapsto \langle e_b,r[x \mapsto v_x],k\rangle],\rho'\rangle$$
$$\quad \text{where } \rho' = (\rho\,\alpha)/x,\ x \in Dom((\rho\,\alpha)) \text{ and } ((\rho\,\alpha)\,x) = v_x$$

Fig. 9. Transition rule for coordination sublanguage assuming a CmPS source-level transformation.

5 Computation Migration

The effectiveness of communication-passing style depends greatly on the size of continuations of coordination operations. The larger these continuations, the greater the bandwidth requirements imposed. Moreover, if a continuation is closed over a large structure that never happens to be accessed on the address spaces to which the continuation migrates, efficiency is likely to be significantly impacted. As an example, consider the following program fragment:

```
(let ((z big object))
  (lambda (AS-list)
    (map (lambda (AS) (cons z (rd AS [x] x)))
         AS-list)))
```

The procedure returned by this expression maps over a list of address spaces AS-list, pairing a large locally-defined structure z with the value of shared variable x on each address space in AS-list. The continuation of the rd expression includes z. Using a CmPS-based implementation defined earlier, this continuation would migrate to each address space in the list, performing the pairing on the remote site.

Note that in this example, no interesting portion of rd's continuation, other than the topmost frame, is necessary to evaluate the operation's body. Suppose only this piece of the continuation were sent as the context within which the rd operation evaluates on AS, with the rest of the continuation resident on the sender S. In this case, the value of x found on the different address spaces in AS-list would be sent back to S whereupon the pairing within z would be performed. Communication costs would be significantly reduced since z would not be unnecessarily copied as the part of the migrated continuation.

The tradeoff here is added communication: whereas the CmPS scheme described earlier would migrate the task's continuation to each address space in AS-list in turn, this reduced copying scheme would cause the task's continuation to always return back to the original address space before migrating to the next address space in the list because of the need to perform the pairing on the sender. Conceptually, this scheme suggests that a continuation be distributed among a collection of address spaces. If control ever passes through the base of a migrated continuation, the continuation below the base is resumed. Thus, falling off the end of a migrated continuation is tantamount to shifting control back to the address space where the suspended portion resides. This approach, sometimes referred to as *computation migration* [13] reduces bandwidth requirements while potentially increasing the number of remote communication events.

To support computation migration, we extend the coordination language with one new operation. The expression, (! *e*) marks the top frame of the current continuation stack, and returns the result of evaluating *e*. The specification of the abstract machine is now changed to ensure that no continuation frames below the most recently marked "frozen" frame are migrated. This annotation is closely related to "prompts" [6], a mechanism to delimit the extent of continuation-capturing operations.

To achieve the desired degree of migration, the above expression could be rewritten thus:

```
(let ((z big object))
  (lambda (AS-list)
    (map (lambda (AS) (cons z (! (rd AS [x] x))))
         AS-list)))
```

The freeze operation ensures that the continuation within which the rd expression evaluates on AS is a single *ArgFrame* to hold the result of the second argument to cons. When control passes back to the suspended continuation on the caller address-space, the result is supplied as the continuation's argument. Further evaluation of this expression now proceeds on the sender.

As another example, consider a slightly different implementation of the above program:

```
(let ((z big object))
  (lambda (AS-list)
    (map (lambda (elt) (cons z (list elt)))
         (! (map (lambda (AS) (rd AS [x] x)) AS-list)))))
```

In this program, the values of x are first explicitly collected before being paired with z. The expression surrounded by "!" performs a series of rd operations on the address spaces found in AS-list. Each of these operations involve migrating a continuation to a new address space. The program ensures that the continuation sent to perform the rd does not include z. This implementation is quite unlike the previous one, which caused every remote rd operation to return its result back to the sender. In this version, rd's continuation appends to the list built by map, and executes a recursive call on the next address space in the list. Consequently, control moves among the address spaces found in AS-list, and returns to the sender only after all distributed members have been collected.

As this example illustrates, judicious use of the "freeze" annotation can make a computation migration strategy an effective optimization in a CmPS-based implementation, and may significantly reduce the bandwidth requirements of communication-intensive applications.

$$\langle (!\ e), r, k \rangle \longrightarrow \langle e, r, \mathbf{freeze}\langle \rangle : k \rangle$$

$$\langle \mathbf{freeze}\langle \rangle : k, v \rangle \longrightarrow \langle k, v \rangle$$

$$\langle (\mathbf{put}\ e_a\ [x\ e_x]\ e_b), r, k \rangle \longrightarrow \langle e_a, r, \mathbf{putArg}\langle x, e_x, e_b, r \rangle : k \rangle$$

$$\langle (\mathbf{rd}\ e\ [x]\ e_b), r, k \rangle \longrightarrow \langle e, r, \mathbf{rdArg}\langle x, e_b, r \rangle : k \rangle$$

$$\langle (\mathbf{get}\ e\ [x]\ e_b), r, k \rangle \longrightarrow \langle e, r, \mathbf{getArg}\langle x, e_b, r \rangle : k \rangle$$

$$\langle \mathbf{putArg}\langle x, e_x, e_b, r \rangle : k, v \rangle \longrightarrow \langle e_x, r, \mathbf{putBody}\langle x, e_b, v, r \rangle : k \rangle$$

$$\langle T[\langle \alpha, \tau \rangle \mapsto \langle \mathbf{putBody}\langle x, e_b, v, r \rangle : k^* : \mathbf{freeze}\langle \rangle : k, v_a \rangle], \rho \rangle \longrightarrow$$
$$\langle T[\langle \alpha, \tau \rangle \mapsto \mathbf{suspend}\langle\ k \rangle, \langle v, \tau' \rangle \mapsto \langle e_b, r, k^* : \mathbf{migrate}\langle\ \alpha, \tau \rangle \rangle], (\rho\, v)[x \mapsto v_a] \rangle$$
$$\text{where } \tau' \text{ is fresh, } k^* = k_1 : \ldots : k_n \text{ and } k_i \neq \mathbf{freeze}\langle \rangle, 1 \leq i \leq n$$

$$\langle T[\langle \alpha, \tau \rangle \mapsto \langle \mathbf{rdArg}\langle x, e_b, r \rangle : k^* : \mathbf{freeze}\langle \rangle : k, v \rangle], \rho \rangle \longrightarrow$$
$$\langle T[\langle \alpha, \tau \rangle \mapsto \mathbf{suspend}\langle\ k \rangle, \langle v, \tau' \rangle \mapsto \langle e_b, r[x \mapsto v_x], k^* : \mathbf{migrate}\langle\ \alpha, \tau \rangle \rangle], \rho \rangle$$
$$\text{where } \tau' \text{ fresh, } x \in Dom((\rho\, v)), ((\rho\, v)\, x) = v_x,$$
$$k^* = k_1 : \ldots : k_n, \text{ and } k_i \neq \mathbf{freeze}\langle \rangle, 1 \leq i \leq n$$

$$\langle T[\langle \alpha, \tau \rangle \mapsto \langle \mathbf{rdArg}\langle x, e_b, r \rangle : k^* : \mathbf{freeze}\langle \rangle : k, v \rangle], \rho \rangle \longrightarrow$$
$$\langle T[\langle \alpha, \tau \rangle \mapsto \mathbf{suspend}\langle\ k \rangle, \langle v, \tau' \rangle \mapsto \langle e_b, r[x \mapsto v_x], k^* : \mathbf{migrate}\langle\ \alpha, \tau \rangle \rangle], \rho \rangle$$
$$\text{where } \tau' \text{ fresh, } \rho' = (\rho\, v)/x, x \in Dom((\rho\, v)), ((\rho\, v)\, x) = v_x,$$
$$k^* = k_1 : \ldots : k_n, \text{ and } k_i \neq \mathbf{freeze}\langle \rangle, 1 \leq i \leq n$$

$$\langle T[\langle \alpha, \tau \rangle \mapsto \langle \mathbf{migrate}\langle\ \alpha', \tau' \rangle, v \rangle, \langle \alpha', \tau' \rangle \mapsto \mathbf{suspend}\langle\ k \rangle], \rho \rangle \longrightarrow$$
$$\langle T/\langle \alpha, \tau \rangle[\langle \alpha', \tau' \rangle \mapsto \langle k, v \rangle], \rho \rangle$$

Fig. 10. Transition rules to support computation migration.

Figure 10 shows the modifications to the state machine necessary to support computation migration. We add three new continuation frames: a *Freeze Frame* marks a continuation point below which continuation frames will not be migrated; a *Suspend Frame* marks that portion of a continuation which is suspended pending a return of control-flow from a migrated sub-continuation; a *Migrate Frame* records the address space and thread containing a suspended continuation. To evaluate the body e_b of a coordination expression, a new thread is created on the target address space. This thread begins evaluation of e_b using a continuation containing a series of frames whose bottom-most frame is a *Migrate Frame*. The size of this continuation depends upon freeze points currently on the continuation stack. When the machine encounters a *Migrate Frame*, **migrate**$\langle\,\alpha,\tau\,\rangle$, it enters a new state in which the suspended continuation on α is resumed using thread τ. The thread executing the *Migrate Frame* is also removed since control has now shifted back to α. When the machine encounters a *Freeze Frame*, it simply pops the frame and proceeds with the continuation below it.

It should be obvious that the behavior of any terminating program implemented using computation migration will be observationally equivalent to one using just CmPS. This is because there are no transitions from a suspended continuation, and a continuation embedded inside a *Suspend Frame* can only be extracted by a thread evaluating a *Migrate Frame* whose arguments uniquely identify the suspended computation.

6 Related Work

Most closely related to the coordination language developed here is Linda [4]. Piranha [11] is a Linda implementation of master-worker style parallelism targeted for networks of workstations. If any node becomes unavailable due to system load, Piranha causes the Piranha processes executing on that node to *retreat*. Retreating involves executing a user-supplied procedure that cleans up intermediate state generated by these processes. Because Piranha does not consider migration of full-fledged control-contexts, programmers are required to structure their programs so that intermediate computation can be easily moved by the retreat procedure.

Olden [20] supports thread migration for a distributed dialect of C. To make the implementation tractable, Olden restricts pointers into the runtime stack; thus migrated tasks are guaranteed not to have remote references into their local data stack. Prohibiting pointers into the stack, however, is likely to greatly impact expressivity in C. Like CmPS, task migration in Olden is initiated whenever a task attempts to access data resident on another processor. Olden also uses a migration scheme similar to computation migration that faults only the top-most frame of the runtime stack. It does not provide linguistic extensions to delimit the effect of a migration operation. Rather than devising separate coordination and computation sublanguages, Olden specifies parallelism using continuation-capturing operations based on futures [12] and lazy task creation [17].

Flanagan and Felleisen [9] and Moreau [18] present a CEK-based operational semantics for parallel languages supporting the *future* construct [12]. Unlike the semantics described here, neither of the above reports consider implementation issues or language extensions to handle distributed computation. Jagannathan and Weeks [14] present an abstract interpretation of a core language similar to the one described here. The language analyzed did not include continuations, however. The formal exact semantics was given in direct-style, and thus is not well-suited to specifying issues related to task migration as done here.

Process migration [19] and computation migration [13] are two approaches to moving threads in distributed environments. We have presented the semantics of computation migration using a well-specified operational semantics. A pleasant property of our formal description of computation migration is that only minor modifications to the machine state domain used by the original semantics, which migrates full continuations, is necessary to specify computation migration. We believe ours is the first attempt to present a precise operational characterization of computation migration for a coordination language.

Obliq [3] and Kali [5] are two implementations of higher-order distributed languages that would form a natural basis on which to implement the coordination language described here. Indeed, we have incorporated the ideas presented here into Kali and expect to report on its practical utility in the near future.

7 Conclusions

As networks of workstations (NOWs) become increasingly the platform of choice for parallel and distributed systems, language abstractions tailored to the particular characteristics of a NOW are required. In this paper, we have developed a semantics for a coordination language with this idea in mind. The language, based loosely on Linda, supports first-class address spaces. Address spaces can serve as virtual processors closed over a shared naming environment in a NOW ensemble.

We have presented an operational semantics in which all communication events are treated by migrating the continuation of the task initiating the event to the address space where the desired data resides. We have argued that this strategy, called CmPS, can significantly reduce communication costs in a loosely-coupled, high-latency environment such as a NOW. Furthermore, we have shown that when embedded within a computation sublanguage supporting first-class procedures, CmPS can be expressed entirely as a source-level transformation on top of a more traditional implementation. Finally, we have also sketched an optimization that may significantly reduce communication costs by allowing programmers to delimit the dynamic context of migrating continuations.

References

1. A. Appel, *Compiling with Continuations*, Cambridge University Press, 1992.
2. A. D. Birrell and B. Nelson, *Implementing remote procedure call*, ACM Transactions on Computer Systems, 2 (1984), pp. 39–59.
3. L. Cardelli, *A Language with Distributed Scope*, in Proceedings of the 22nd ACM Symposium on Principles of Programming Languages, New York, 1995, ACM, pp. 286–298.
4. N. Carriero and D. Gelernter, *Linda in Context*, Communications of the ACM, 32 (1989), pp. 444 – 458.
5. H. Cejtin, S. Jagannathan, and R. Kelsey, *Higher-Order Distributed Objects*, ACM Transactions on Programming Languages and Systems, 17 (1995), pp. 704–739.

6. M. Felleisen, *The Theory and Practice of First-Class Prompts*, in 15th ACM Symposium on Principles of Programming Languages, 1988, pp. 180–190.

7. M. Felleisen and D. Friedman, *Control Operators, the SECD-machine, and the Lambda-calculus*, in 3rd Working Conference on the Formal Description of Programming Concepts, North-Holland, 1986, pp. 193–219.

8. ———, *A Calculus for Assignments in Higher-Order Languages*, in Proceedings of the 14th ACM Symposium on Principles of Programming Languages, 1987, pp. 314–325.

9. C. Flanagan and M. Felleisen, *The Semantics of Future and Its Use in Program Optimization*, in Proceedings of the 12nd ACM Symposium on Principles of Programming Languages, 1995, pp. 290–220.

10. C. Flanagan, A. Sabry, B. Duba, and M. Felleisen, *The Essence of Compiling with Continuations*, in 1993 ACM Symposium on Programming Language Design and Implementation, 1993, pp. 237–247.

11. D. Gelernter and D. Kaminsky, *Supercomputing out of Recycled Garbage: Preliminary Experience with Piranha*, in Proceedings of the 6th ACM International Conference on Supercomputing, July 1992, pp. 417–427.

12. R. Halstead, *Multilisp: A Language for Concurrent Symbolic Computation*, Transactions on Programming Languages and Systems, 7 (1985), pp. 501–538.

13. W. Hsieh, P. Wang, and W. Weihl, *Computation Migration: Enhancing Locality for Distributed-Memory Parallel Systems*, in The 4th ACM SIGPLAN Symposium on Principles and Practice of Parallel Programming, New York, May 1993, ACM, pp. 239–249.

14. S. Jagannathan and S. Weeks, *Analyzing Stores and References in a Parallel Symbolic Language*, in Proceedings of the 1994 ACM International Conference on Lisp and Functional Programming, 1994, pp. 294–305.

15. E. Jul, H. Levy, N. Hutchison, and A. Black, *Fine-Grained Mobility in the Emerald System*, ACM Transactions on Computer Systems, 6 (1988), pp. 109–133.

16. R. Kelsey and P. Hudak, *Realistic Compilation by Program Transformation*, in Proceedings of the 16th ACM Symposium on Principles of Programming Languages, 1989, pp. 281–292.

17. R. Mohr, D. Kranz, and R. Halstead, *Lazy Task Creation: A Technique for Increasing the Granularity of Parallel Programs*, in Proceedings of the 1990 ACM Conference on Lisp and Functional Programming, June 1990.

18. L. Moreau, *The Semantics of Scheme with Future*, in Proceedings of the 1996 ACM International Conference on Functional Programming, 1996, pp. 146–156.

19. M. Powell and B. Miller, *Process Migration in DEMOS/MP*, in Proceedings of the 9th ACM Symposium on Operating Systems Principles, New York, 1983, ACM, pp. 110–119.

20. A. Rogers, M. Carlisle, J. Reppy, and L. Hendren, *Supporting Dynamic Data Structures on Distributed-Memory Machines*, ACM Transactions on Programming Languages and Systems, 17 (1995), pp. 233–263.

21. Z. Shao and A. Appel, *Space-Efficient Closure Representations*, in Proceedings of the 1994 ACM Symposium on Lisp and Functional Programming, 1994, pp. 150–161.

A Transition Rules for the Computation Language

To describe transitions dealing only with L's computation sublanguage, it is often convenient to write $t \longrightarrow t'$
to mean $\langle T[\langle \alpha, \tau \rangle \mapsto t], \rho \rangle \longrightarrow \langle T[\langle \alpha, \tau \rangle \mapsto t'], \rho \rangle$ where $\langle \alpha, \tau \rangle \in Dom(T)$.

There are two groups of rules for the computation sublanguage. The first group describes transitions on control states; the second group describes transitions on return states. The machine immediately evaluates constants, variables, and abstractions, transferring the result to the current continuation. For applications, a frame holding the value of the argument to the call is pushed on the stack while the function position is evaluated. Primitives and conditionals are treated similarly.

Return states manipulate the continuation stack. The machine enters such a state when a continuation must be applied. This event occurs whenever the machine reduces an expression to a value and must transfer control to the current continuation. To illustrate, consider the actions that the machine must perform to handle a function call. Assuming that the function position yields a closure, the top frame of the current continuation will hold the argument to the call. To evaluate this argument, the machine executes a transition to a new control state in which the argument frame has been popped, and the argument expression is now the next expression to be evaluated. A new frame holding the value of the closure is also pushed. At some later point, when the argument is also reduced to a value, the body of the closure becomes the current expression, the environment in which the expression is evaluated is augmented with a binding for the formal to the value yielded by evaluation of the argument, and the function frame is popped from the continuation stack.

$$\langle c, r, k \rangle \longrightarrow \langle k, c \rangle$$
$$\langle x, r, k \rangle \longrightarrow \langle k, (r\,x) \rangle$$
$$\langle \lambda x.\,e, r, k \rangle \longrightarrow \langle k, \langle \lambda x.\,e, r \rangle \rangle$$
$$\langle \mu f.\lambda x.\,e, r, k \rangle \longrightarrow \langle k, \langle \mu f.\lambda x.\,e, r \rangle \rangle$$
$$\langle (e_1\ e_2), r, k \rangle \longrightarrow \langle e_1, r, \mathbf{arg}\langle e_2, r \rangle : k \rangle$$
$$\langle (p\ e_1\ \vec{e}), r, k \rangle \longrightarrow \langle e_1, r, \mathbf{prim}\langle p, \langle \rangle, \vec{e}, r \rangle : k \rangle$$
$$\langle (\mathbf{if}\ e_1\ e_2\ e_3), r, k \rangle \longrightarrow \langle e_1, r, \mathbf{cond}\langle e_2, e_3, r \rangle : k \rangle$$

$$\langle \langle \rangle, v \rangle \longrightarrow \mathbf{halt}(v)$$
$$\langle \mathbf{arg}\langle e', r \rangle : k, v \rangle \longrightarrow \langle e', r, \mathbf{fun}\langle v \rangle : k \rangle$$
$$\langle \mathbf{fun}\langle \langle \lambda x.\,e, r \rangle \rangle : k, v \rangle \longrightarrow \langle e, r[x \mapsto v], k \rangle$$
$$\langle \mathbf{fun}\langle \langle \mu f.\lambda x.\,e, r \rangle \rangle : k, v \rangle \longrightarrow \langle e, r[x \mapsto v,\ f \mapsto \langle \mu f.\lambda x.\,e, r \rangle], k \rangle$$
$$\langle \mathbf{prim}\langle p, \vec{v}, \langle \rangle, : \rangle k, v \rangle \longrightarrow \langle k, \mathcal{P}(p, v@\ \vec{v}) \rangle$$
$$\langle \mathbf{prim}\langle p, \vec{v}, \vec{e} : e, : \rangle k, v \rangle \longrightarrow \langle e, r, \mathbf{prim}\langle p, v : \vec{v}, \vec{e}, : \rangle k \rangle$$
$$\langle \mathbf{cond}\langle e_t, e_f, r \rangle : k, \mathbf{true} \rangle \longrightarrow \langle e_t, r, k \rangle$$
$$\langle \mathbf{cond}\langle e_t, e_f, r \rangle : k, \mathbf{false} \rangle \longrightarrow \langle e_f, r, k \rangle$$

Software Architecture for Large Control Systems: A Case Study Description

Edwin de Jong

Hollandse Signaalapparaten B.V.
P.O. box 42, 7550 GD Hengelo, The Netherlands
edejong@signaal.nl

Abstract. A case study description is presented that can be used as a reference in studying or comparing the properties of software architectures. The case study is centred around a railroad control system. Care has been taken to keep the problem simple, yet containing all the issues a real-world, industrial-quality system has to face. Besides functional requirements, the case study addresses real-time, fault-tolerant, and adaptive behaviour.

1 Introduction

The architecture of a system defines its organization, in terms of components and their possible interconnections and interactions, as well as its fundamental properties. Over the past years many different architectural styles have been developed (see e.g. [1]), each with its own set of properties and applications. The choice for a particular software architecture is one of the earliest to be made during the system development process, and therefore embodies one of the most critical design decisions as it defines a framework within which future design decisions will have to be made.

This paper presents a case study description that can be used as a reference in studying or demonstrating the properties of software architectures, or in comparing different architectural styles. The case study is centred around a railroad control system and is described in detail below. Care has been taken to keep the problem simple, yet containing all the issues a real-world, industrial-quality system has to face. Besides functional aspects, the case study addresses a set of requirements related to real-time, fault-tolerant, and adaptive behaviour. The problem description can be used, for instance, to examine the effect of a particular software architecture (e.g. the choice of components, their interaction, and their coordinated behaviour) on the final solution, to study models and languages for describing software architecture and coordination, or to assess related tools and development environments.

2 Background

In everyday life (embedded) control systems are gaining an ever more important role. They are encountered in many modern consumer electronics products, such as washing-machines, televisions, and audio equipment. Also on-board control systems in

151

automobiles, trains, and aircrafts are becoming pervasive, and increasingly control systems are used in larger and more critical applications, such as process control, air and other types of traffic management, and military command-and-control. The common feature of these systems is that they co-exist as an integral part of some larger product or environment.

Generally, a control system performs the following tasks: (1) processing the raw data obtained from the environment through sensing devices, (2) determination of model parameters describing the environment, (3) tracking discrepancies between desired state and perceived state, (4) taking corrective action, and (5) informing the operator or team of operators about the current and predicted state of affairs, and in case the system does not act autonomously, assisting the operators in the decision making process.

In addition to the functional requirements of these systems, many non-functional requirements, such as a high degree of availability and robustness, geographical distribution over a possibly wide variety of different host processors, and adaptability and extendibility, place constraints on the design freedom that are very difficult to meet. In practice, there are many interrelated system aspects that need to be considered. A schematic overview is given in Fig. 1, which illustrates that systems' design is in fact a multi-dimensional problem. A methodology for the design of control systems should provide (a basis for) a solution for the combination of these problems. However, although solutions are available for many of the problems in isolation, incompatible, or even conflicting, premises make it very difficult to cover all design aspects by a coherent solution. It is often necessary to sacrifice optimality in many, if not all of the separate dimensions.

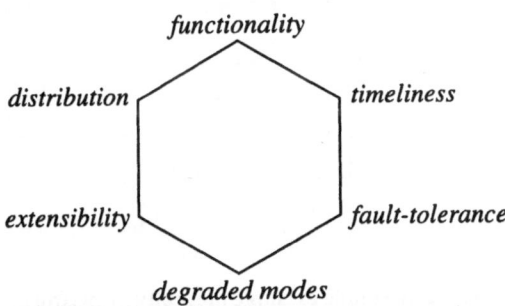

Fig. 1. Some aspects of the multi-dimensional design problem.

3   Problem Description

Consider a railway network consisting of railway tracks, junctions, and stations. A number of trains is expected to traverse the network in accordance to a global schedule. For each train the schedule determines the route that is to be traversed and a timetable, that specifies the expected times of arrival and departure for each station along the route.

It is required that a control system be developed for a given railway network. The primary objective of the system is to avoid collisions between trains. The secondary objective of the system is to respect the timetables as much as possible. A third objective is to make travelling as comfortable as possible, which means that trains should try to avoid abrupt changes in speed.

Below, the problem is explained in more detail. Note, however, that the description is by no means precise or complete. If required, the reader is free to make additional assumptions, as long as these assumptions can be justified as being realistic.

3.1 The Railway Network

The railway network consists of a two-dimensional map of railway tracks. Wherever two or more tracks meet, there is a junction. A railway station is situated along one or more parallel tracks. At each track a platform allows passengers and cargo to enter or leave the train (see Fig. 2). Tracks, platforms, as well as trains have a certain length. Consequently, platforms and railway tracks can hold but a limited number of trains.

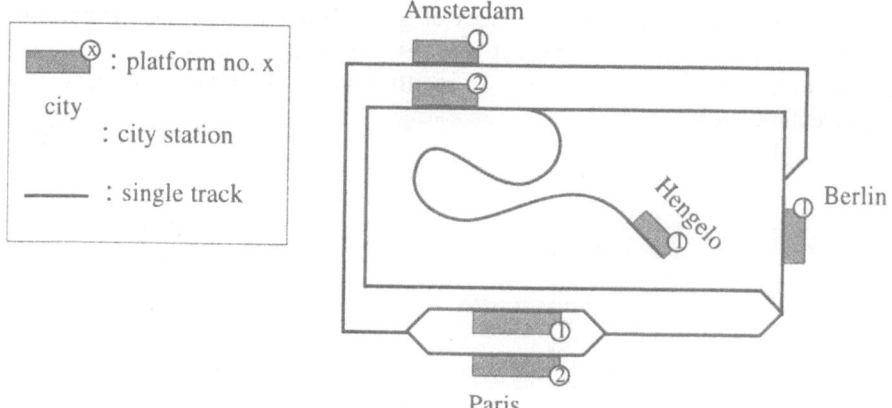

Fig. 2. A simple example of a railway network.

The tracks are bidirectional, i.e. trains may move in either way. However, trains cannot pass each other on a single track, and two trains that keep moving in opposite directions towards each other on the same track will eventually collide.

3.2 Schedules

Each train travels according to a - possibly infinite - schedule that lists the stations it subsequently has to arrive at (these are not necessarily neighbours). In addition, the schedule specifies for each of the listed stations, the platform the train should stop at, and the time of arrival and departure. Trains should adhere to this schedule as much as possible. They may arrive earlier, and depart later than specified, but one should take into account that this might delay other trains. The exact route a train has to follow is left unspecified, so given the current situation, the railway control system may choose any suitable path for a train to reach its next destination.

3.3 Trains

Trains have both a maximum speed and a maximum acceleration/deceleration. In addition, they have a certain length. Trains are fragile objects: if at any time they fail to keep a safe distance, they collide and break down. The latter means that both trains instantly stop and block the track (possibly causing more collisions). When a collision has occurred, the track will be cleared after some period of time.

3.4 Infrastructure

Communication between the trains and the railway control system is established by means of a mobile wide area network (MWAN). The network supports at least broadcasting of messages, but also multicasting and point-to-point addressing can be used, if so desired. The communication network has limited bandwidth and messages are subject to some maximum latency. The MWAN is typically used to transfer information from the trains to the control system, and conversely, to relay commands from the control system to the trains.

4 System Requirements

Repeatedly the railway control system has to perform the following tasks.

(1) Monitor the position of each of the trains (speed, acceleration and direction should at least be derivable from this). At all times, a train is capable of determining its own position.

(2) Assess the current situation, predict future developments, and if necessary, prepare corrective actions in order to meet the three objectives of the system: avoiding collisions, respecting the timetables as much as possible, and arranging a comfortable journey. Basically there are two possible actions. The speed of one or more of the trains can be adjusted, either by acceleration or deceleration. Alternatively a train can be rerouted, for instance along a faster route, or to make way for another train to pass by.

(3) Execute the planned actions. Using the communication network, the planned actions are made available to the trains. A certain amount of time has to be reserved for the execution of actions, since neither communication nor the actions themselves occur instantaneously.

Besides the functional requirements of the system, a number of additional aspects must be taken into account.

4.1 Timing

Deadlines of different importance have to be taken into account. Firstly, potential collisions must be resolved before they become unavoidable, and secondly, actual rerouting should take place before arrival at the corresponding station or junction.

4.2 Scalability

The control system must be scalable. Ideally, a control system should work without modifications for a railway network of any size, and for any (feasible) schedule. In practice this will not be possible, due to real-time constraints. With respect to this, one should be able to assess the ability of a certain configuration to handle particular networks and schedules.

Perhaps needless to say, processors do not have an infinite amount of processing power, while communications have to face a limited bandwidth and some maximum latency.

4.3 Extendibility

The railway control system should support anticipated changes in its environment. Since railway services must continue to be available at all times, the system must allow upgrading on-line, i.e. during operational use.

In reality, nothing is ever fixed. In our world, merely three things may change.

(1) The railway network topology may be altered. This means either that new tracks and/or stations get inserted in the network, or that some get removed. Removal of a station implies modifications of all schedules that contain that station.

(2) The parameters of a train, i.e. its maximum speed and acceleration/deceleration, and its length, may change. For instance, this may occur when a train is replaced by a new model. These changes only occur at the railway stations.

(3) The schedule may get altered. This includes the addition of extra trains to the cup final, or removal of trains that are considered too expensive because very few passengers use it (as soon as a train has no schedule, it will be removed). Trains may also be delayed at a station, for example because of some sort of unexpected maintenance. Trains will only be removed when they are at a station (unless accidents occur and trains are removed at the location of the accident). Likewise, new trains will only be inserted at a station, after having made sure that this will not lead to *inevitable* collisions.

4.4 Fault-tolerance

In reality both the railway control system and its environment may exhibit unexpected behaviour due to failures. Despite these failures, however, the system should be able to continue operating, at least in a degraded mode where the safety-critical functions, related to collision avoidance, are retained.

We distinguish between three different types of failures.

(1) Trains may fail for numerous reasons at unpredictable times (e.g. someone pulling the emergency brake). In our world, a broken train typically decelerates as quickly as possible to a full stop, effectively blocking the railway track for other trains. A broken train will get fixed after some period of time and will proceed on its journey.

(2) The communication network that is used for information exchange between the control system and the trains, is unreliable. Messages will not be corrupted, but they tend to get lost at unpredictable times. So, there is no guarantee that messages will arrive. This is one of the most fundamental problems that the system has to deal with. (Solutions that employ an abundant duplication of messages to increase reliability will have to make some realistic assertions concerning the necessary bandwidth.)

(3) The processor, or processors, of the computing system that hosts the railway control system, are prone to failure. Whenever a processor fails, it immediately stops executing without further notice. By incorporating redundant hardware the control system should be able to continue operating, either fully or in a degraded mode.

5 Concluding Remarks

This volume contains two papers that address some of the issues raised by the case study description. The paper by A.A. Holzbacher, M. Périn, and M. Südholt [2] discusses the dynamic evolution of software architectures. Using graph grammars a class of architectures for the railroad control system is defined, ensuring several desirable properties by construction. Dynamic evolution is modelled by graph transformation rules. An implementation is derived from the formal specification in the coordination language ConCoord.

The paper by S. Stuurman and J. van Katwijk [3] shows how different architectural styles can be instantiated from a model of the railroad control system. Three architectural styles (a global state, a layered, and a data flow architecture) are evaluated with respect to a number of properties.

References

1. *IEEE Software*, special issue on architecture, November 1995.
2. A.A. Holzbacher, M. Périn, and M. Südholt, Modeling railway control systems using graph grammars: a case study, *proc. Coordination'97*, Springer Verlag LNCS, this volume.
3. S. Stuurman, J. van Katwijk, Evaluation of software architectures for a control system: a case study, *proc. Coordination'97*, Springer Verlag LNCS, this volume.

Evaluation of Software Architectures for a Control System: A Case Study

Sylvia Stuurman and Jan van Katwijk

Delft University of Technology

Abstract. In this paper, we give our view on the software architecture phase in the development process. During this phase, we distinguish modeling and structuring activities. A system is modeled according to a certain approach, and this model is used to instantiate a certain architectural style. In general, the activities are intertwined.

The choice for a certain software architecture has implications on the non-functional properties of the system. We illustrate our view with a case study of a software controller for a (toy) railroad system which we have available in our software lab. Several models of this system, expressed in formal specification languages, were made in the past, so we are able to produce a software architecture for the system while carrying out both activities separately.

The resulting software architectures are evaluated with respect to timing aspects, scalability, fault-tolerance, and extendibility. Extendibility of a software system is especially important for domains were changes should be applicable on-line. Design for change should start at the software architectural level.

1 Introduction

In this paper, we illustrate our view of the software architecture phase in the development process and the implications of the choice for a certain architectural style within that phase, with a case study of a railroad system. The essence of our view is that we distinguish modeling and structuring activities. The choice for a certain software architecture primarily has an impact on the non-functional requirements of the system. Therefore, when evaluating different architectures for a certain system, one should take into account the non-functional properties that are relevant. Roughly said, one addresses the functional requirements during the modeling activities, and the non-functional requirements during the structuring activities.

A software architecture-driven development process consists of a Requirements Analysis phase, a Software Architecture phase, a Construction phase, and a Maintenance and Change phase. During the Software Architecture phase, one models the system, chooses a software architecture style, instantiates this style, and refines the instantiation either by adding detail or by decomposing components or connections (again going through modeling, choosing a style, instantiation and refinement). This process should result in an architecture which is

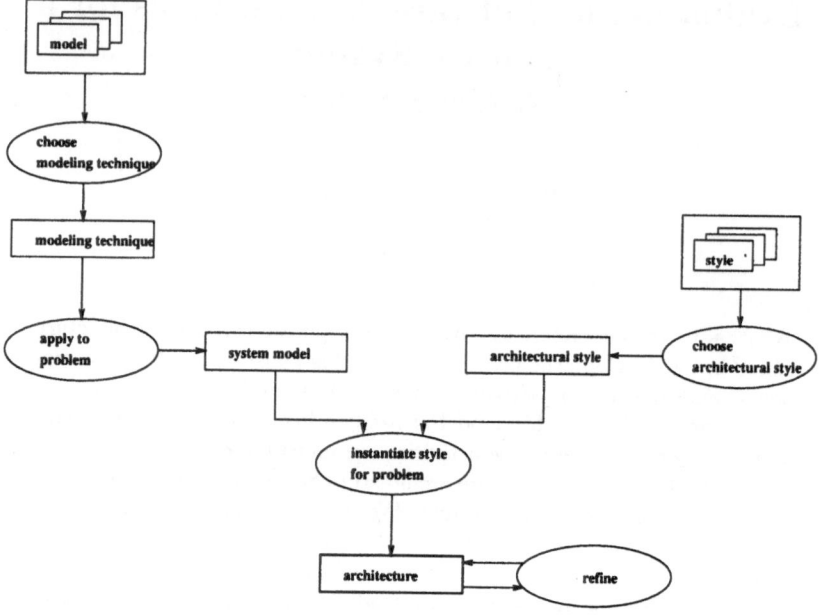

Fig. 1. software architecture in the development process

defined with so much detail that either reusable components and connections can be fitted, or components and connections can be designed and implemented. Note that this view does support a sequential as well as an iterative or an incremental development process, and that in general, the modeling and structuring activities are intertwined. The Software Architecture phase as we view it is depicted in Fig. 1. In this figure, ovals denote activities, while boxes represent products. Input for all activities are the requirements (not shown).

An architectural style is a pattern in the organization of software ([12]), or, somewhat more precisely, "a set of design rules that identify the kinds of components and connectors that may be used to compose a system or subsystem, together with local or global constraints on the way the composition is done" ([11]). Architectural styles are categorized in taxonomies in order to provide guidelines mapping classes of problems onto classes of solutions ([11]).

In [2], Boasson argues that at the highest level, two fundamentally distinct approaches towards software architectures can be discerned: the data-centered and the function-oriented approach. To relate this statement with our view of the Software Architecture phase in the development process, one could say that a data-centered or a function-oriented model each leads to different sets of software architectural styles.

We describe two software architectures on a high level of abstraction, based on two different approaches for system modeling for a (toy) railroad system which we have available in our software lab. In [1], a data-centered model of the system is given, described in the formal specification language AE-VDM. A function-oriented model of the railroad system, described in PAISLey, is given in [15]. The railroad network described in the case study differs at some points from our toy railroad system, so we had to adapt the models.

For each architecture, we derive the implications they have on those quality properties that are important for a railroad controller:

Timing : The requirements of a real-time system usually contain temporal constraints. In the case of the railway network, there are strict temporal constraints because of safety reasons, and less strict temporal constraints with respect to the schedules. Performance with respect to these constraints can only be measured when all design decisions have been made. It is highly desirable to decrease this gap between temporal constraints and performance at the architectural level. We discuss time aspects of each proposed architecture.

Scalability : Both the toy railroad system and the railway network presented in this case study are scale models of real-life situations. Therefore, scalability is a requirement for a software architecture.

Fault-Tolerance : One of the problems of controlling a physical system is that such a system often does not behave exactly according to whichever model we use to represent it. Reliability addresses the behaviour of a system in an environment behaving according to the model; robustness addresses behaviour of the system in "abnormal" circumstances. Behaviour in abnormal circumstances is often indicated with the term "incident handling". In each architecture, we indicate which changes are needed to incorporate incident handling, in order to achieve a certain degree of robustness. Incidents are not only formed by unexpected events in the railway network, but also by failing communication and hardware.

Extendibility : Requirements are not as static and final as they are usually treated. They change, either as a result of an inaccurate modeling of the environment, or of a changing world. The answer to changing requirements is a changing system. In a system like the railway network presented here, it is necessary to apply changes on-line.

Two possible mechanisms for on-line changes of software found in literature are:
- A change at the architecture level, consisting of adding or destroying components and connections. A model for "dynamic change management" along these lines is presented by Kramer and Magee in [6].
- A change at source code level. Frieder and Segal described a scheme for procedure replacement in [3].

In our opinion, design for change should start at the architectural level. When evaluating an architecture, one should bear in mind that the first mechanism should be applicable in the changes one can think of.

The two architectures are proposed and discussed in Sects. 2 and 3. The last section contains conclusions and suggestions for future research.

2 Data-Centered Approach: A Global State Architecture

The first type of architecture that we analyze is based on a data-centered model of the railroad controller for our toy railroad system, described in detail in [1]. The solution given below is meant as an example of the global state architecture; we don't pretend to propose an optimal solution.

2.1 Event-Action Model

According to e.g. Parnas ([9]), the behaviour of reactive systems can successfully be modeled in terms of events and actions. Events can be defined in terms of changes in the global state of the system, including time. Actions consist of computations resulting in changes in the global state. Similarly, the functionality of the railway system can be described in rules, specifying an action for each discerned event.

In the first place, the speed behaviour of each individual train is modeled by a finite state machine, shown in Fig. 2. In state HALT, a train is stopped (temporarily). State ACC is the state of a (gently) accelerating train; state DEC for a gently decelerating one. A train in state CONST drives with a certain constant speed. A train in state EMERGENCY stops as soon as possible.

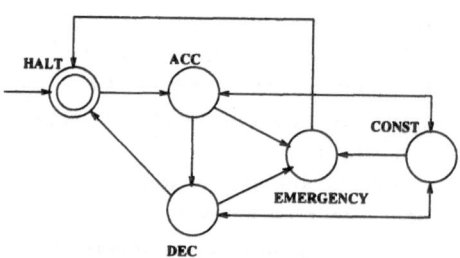

Fig. 2. state diagram for a train

The transitions in the finite state machine are described by action-event rules, stating the events that trigger a transition (Table1). These events involve information about the desired speed for each train, to be generated on-the-fly from the schedule of the train. The "before" column shows the state before the transition; the "after" column the state after the transition; the "event" column describes the event that triggers the transition.

Another finite state machine is used to model the overall behaviour of a train (Fig. 3).

Five states are discerned: in the STATION state, a train is situated at a station; in state START, the route to the next station is (being) determined; in

Table 1. speed of a train

	before	event	after
1	HALT, CONST, ACC or DEC	|desired speed| > | actual speed|	ACC
2	HALT or DEC	desired speed = actual speed = 0	HALT
3	ACC, CONST or DEC	|desired speed| = | actual speed|	CONST
4	ACC, CONST or DEC	|desired speed| < | actual speed|	DEC
5	ACC, CONST or DEC	state of train is Error	Emergency
6	EMERGENCY	actual speed = 0	HALT

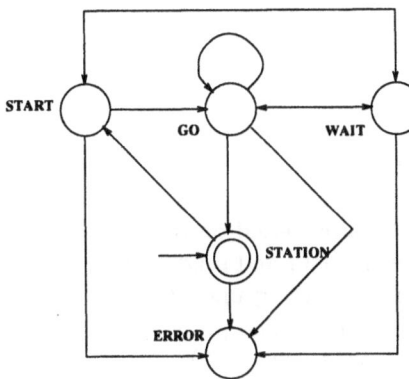

Fig. 3. state diagram for a train

state GO, the train is driving; in state WAIT, the train is stopped somewhere along the route; state ERROR is used for cases of failures. We have assumed that in the initial state, a train is always positioned at a station. The transitions are showed in Table 2.

Table 2. behaviour of a train

	before	event	after
1	STATION	departure time reached	START
2	START or GO	next part of route free	GO
3	START or GO	next part of route blocked	WAIT
4	GO	destination reached	STATION
5	WAIT	next part of route free	GO
6	WAIT	deadlock occurred	START
7	all states	error occurred	ERROR

Data such as the desired speed is set as a side effect of state transitions. Table

3 shows a simple way of setting the desired speed. Other side effects consist of determining the route to be taken, and the setting of switches in the railway network.

Table 3. setting the desired speed

	state transition	desired speed
1	START → GO	desired speed + maximum speed
2	GO → WAIT	desired speed = 0
3	GO → STATION	desired speed = 0

2.2 Software Architecture

Figure 4 shows an architecture, based on this model. A central data store component contains the relevant data and sends events, representing changes in the state or time, to components acting upon these events. These components are able to read and write the data. The proposed architecture can be seen as an instantiation of the blackboard style ([12]).

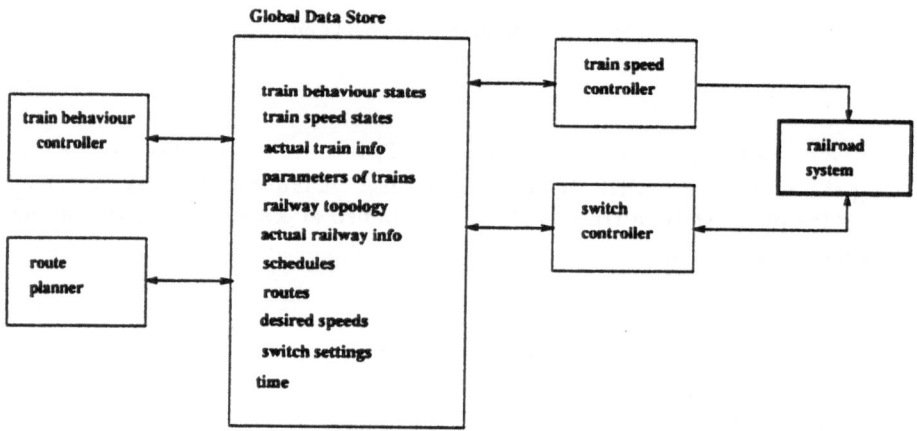

Fig. 4. global state architecture

The Global Data Store: is used to store the global state. Essential of this architecture is the fact that all data are stored globally. As a result, all data needed by components are found in the global data store.

Information kept in the global data store consists of the state of the behaviour and speed of each train, of the actual information (about speed and position) of each train, the parameters of the trains, the schedules, the derived routes and desired speed, the topology of the railway, the switch settings, and the time.

Certain transitions in the global state represent events.

The Train Behaviour Controller: carries the responsibility of maintaining the finite state machine representation of the behaviour of the trains, according to the rules described in Table 2. The information it needs consists of the train behaviour states, the schedules, time, the positions, speed and directions of other trains, and the train parameters. The component modifies the train behaviour states, the desired speed, and the switch settings.

The Route Planner: is responsible for determining the route to be taken to the next station mentioned in the schedule of the train.

One may implement a deadlock avoiding route planner , or one that does less planning ahead. In the last case, a second task of the route planner is deadlock detection (and consequently determine new routes).

Information needed by the route planner consists of the schedules, the railway topology, and of the positions, speed and direction of the trains.

The Train Speed Controller: is responsible for maintaining the desired speed in a comfortable way, according to the rules in Table 1. Another task of this component is to update information about the actual position, speed and direction of the trains.

Changes in the desired speed for a train, and the transition to behaviour state ERROR, form events of interest for train speed controller.

The Switch Controller: has the task of updating information about the state of the switches and setting them.

Multiplicity of Components: The architecture as it is proposed here does not state anything about the multiplicity of the components. Obviously, there is only one data store. On the other hand, each train might have its own behaviour and speed controller, and route planner. Multiplicity of the switch controller is a possibility as well. Multiplicity of these components is an open design decision in this architecture.

2.3 Implications on Properties

Timing: To be able to analyze the timing behaviour of a system implemented along these lines, the components performing the functionality should be implemented as cyclic, asynchronously communicating processes. These processes poll the global data store to obtain information about the relevant data. Consequently, restrictions to the cycle time can be derived from the temporal constraints and the speed and duration of the connections and computations.

Scalability: In the case that routes for the trains are generated decentrally, on the fly, the possibility of deadlocks is present. With an increasing number of trains driving on a railway network, deadlocks will occur more frequently. The introduction of deadlock avoidance may become necessary, though this will have implications on the timing aspect. However, whether deadlock avoidance is chosen or not, the architecture as we have presented it here suits both solutions. Because the global state contains the data of all trains, a deadlock avoiding algorithm can be introduced very easily.

For scalability reasons, it should be possible to parallelize the computation. As we have seen, the train behaviour and train speed controller can be parallelized (one for each train). The train speed controller can be split into a component maintaining the speed, and a component polling the train for actual speed, position and direction information.

The route planner might be parallelized as well, but in that case, deadlock avoidance is better performed by a separate component. In both cases, computation time increases with an increase of the complexity of the railway network.

Another possible bottleneck is formed by the access on the global data store. The introduction of (parallel) agents detecting changes in parts of the state, and able to read and write data, might be needed with an increase of the railroad system.

Extendibility: Changes in the topology of the network are introduced as changes in the data of the global state. A component, responsible for deriving new schedules, might be introduced. In this case, the timing issue (components should not make use of the new data too soon or too late) is rather trivial: a physical change in the railway network topology will always take place with trains at a safe distance, so the new situation will be read by the controller components by the time that a train has reached a new situation.

Changes in the parameters of trains are to be introduced in the same way, by changing the data in the global data store. When the changes are applied when the train is in state STATION at a station, the new parameters will be used in time.

The same applies for changes in the schedules of trains: the schedule is read by the route planner component when the train is going to leave the station, so the new data will be used on time.

In general, the conclusion is that the proposed architecture is an easily extendible architecture. Data can be changed fairly easy, and an extension of the functionality can be done by adding or changing components, and adding or changing data in the global data store. No big changes in the architecture are needed, because components never communicate directly.

Prerequisites are that changes in the global data store can be applied from outside, and that components and new data and datatypes can be added at run-time.

Fault-Tolerance: A failing train should result in an emergency stop. In our model, this will be effectuated when the event "error" occurs in the global data state

(Table 2). Error-detection might be an extra task of the train speed controller (actual speed differs too much from the expected speed), or by a new component.

Incident handling requires an overall view of the system. In the global state architecture, each component conceptually has such an overview. As a result, one can add components with intelligent incident handling capacities fairly easy.

A failing communication network is another source of problems. We can discern different type of data in the data store: information that is updated frequently, such as the actual position, speed and direction of the trains, and information representing a state, where each change is a major difference with the old data.

The loss of messages containing the first type of data is not really a problem: as long as the time restrictions are not too tight, a decision based on information that is slightly older than it should be will do no harm.

Messages containing information about an event or a state transition may not get lost. A solution might be to handle this kind of information in the same way as continually updated information: instead of waiting for an event, components poll the data in the global data store. Each time when they poll, they update the state information (or data changed as a side effect) in the global data store.

To make the system fault-tolerant, the global data store should be duplicated and/or distributed on different hardware. In the case that all information is stored in the global data store, setting an extra processor with one or more components at work when another fails is easy, because local data don't exist.

3 Function-Centered Approach: A Data Flow Architecture

The second software architecture is loosely based on a PAISLey model for the railroad controller, described in [15]. This PAISLey model is based on two computation models: asynchronously interacting concurrent processes and functional programming. A specification written in PAISLey requires a process structure and a definition of the structure of interprocess communication, and therefore can be mapped almost directly onto a software architecture.

The PAISLey specification of the railroad controller consists of cyclic, asynchronously communicating processes.

3.1 Software Architecture

The dataflow architecture depicted in Fig. 5 is an instantiation of the control-loop architectural style ([10]). The position of the train is the process variable to control. The actual position is compared to the desired position, and differences between them trigger speed or direction commands. The desired position is computed by consulting the route (which contains time information) and the parameters for the train. The actual position is obtained by polling the trains.

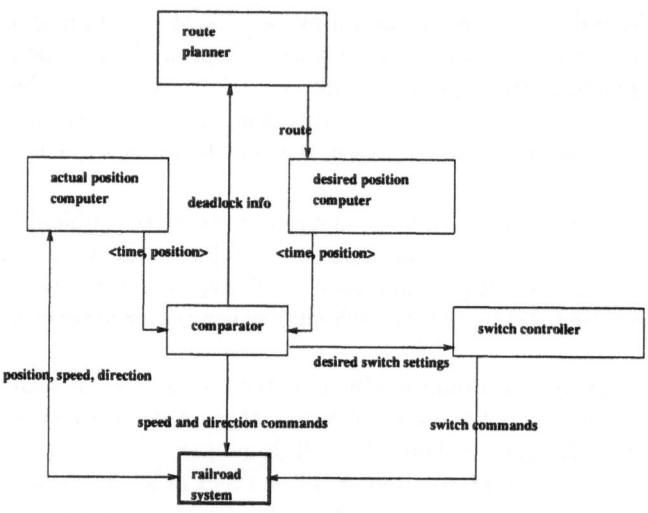

Fig. 5. a dataflow architecture

The Route Planner: computes the route for the trains. Data local to this component are the schedules. In the case of a deadlock, the route planner gets a message
from the Comparator, whereupon it computes new routes.

The Comparator: compares the actual and desired position. To simplify comparison, positions are attributed with an indication of time. A difference between
positions at a same time indicates the need for control, to be executed in the
form of speed and direction commands for the train, and sometimes commands
to set a switch.
    Information needed by the Comparator consists of the position and speed of
all the trains and the state of the switches in the railway network.

The Actual Position Computer: polls the trains and derives <time, position,
speed> for the trains.

The Desired Position Computer: derives the desired position for each train from
the route, sent by the route planner.

The Switch Controller: keeps track of the state of the switches in the railroad,
and sets them according to the messages of the Comparator.

Multiplicity of Components: Both position computers and the comparator in
this architecture can have multiple instances, i.e. one for each train. For the
route planner , this is less obvious. Introducing deadlock avoidance in a system
with one route planner for each train will be difficult, and will require severe

communication between the different components. In a system where the routes for all trains are computed by one component, the information needed to avoid deadlocks is available at the right place.

3.2 Implications on Properties

Timing: The comparator and the switch controller are triggered by both position controllers, which are the "drivers" of the system. From the cycle time of the processes, the speed of the connections and the time needed for different computations, one can analyze whether the system will respect the temporal constraints.

Again, there is the question of deadlock avoidance or detection. Deadlock avoidance should be performed by the route planner. In that case, there should be one route planner for the whole system.

The most logical place for deadlock detection is the comparator, because it receives information about the position of each train. However, the computation time needed for deadlock detection might conflict with the temporal constraints for the comparator. In that case an extra component should be introduced.

Scalability: As we have seen, parallelization can be introduced for both position computers and for the comparator. Inherent to this solution is that the computation time of the comparator increases with an increase of the number of trains: to determine whether a train is able to go on or should stop, the comparator needs information about the speed and position of all trains. An extra component, filtering the relevant information for the comparator, might be needed when upscaling the system.

The same applies for the route planner: its computation time increases with an increase of the complexity of the railway system.

Extendibility: A change in the railway topology network should be applied to data in all four components. Changes in the parameters of a train should be applied in the comparator for the train. New schedules are to be added in the route planner.

In general, because data and computation are intertwined in this architecture, as opposed to the previous one, one should, for each change in data, determine which of the components make use of the information. In the case of an extension of the functionality, one should determine which information is needed for a to-be-added component, and from which components this information can be derived.

Therefore, changes are inherently harder to apply than in the previous architecture.

Fault-Tolerance: A failing train can be detected by the comparator (because of an increasing difference between the actual and desired position). Because the system is based on the comparison between the desired and the actual situation, no extra measures are needed to take failing trains into account. The comparator is the component that has an overall view of the system, because it receives speed and position information of all trains. However, this component is not the appropriate one to be charged with incident handling, because it should perform under strict temporal constraints. Adding incident handling is another case of adding functionality, and as has been said above, this is less straight-forward in the dataflow architecture as in the global state architecture, because in this case, components communicate directly, and data and functionality are not separated.

The connections between the components are of the dataflow type in some cases (continuously updated information): this is the case for the connection between the railroad system and the actual position computer, and for the connection between both position computers and the comparator. The other connections are used for commands, or for information that is delivered once (a new route, a deadlock situation). When these connections fail to deliver a message, the result may be a disaster. An obvious solution is to deliver these kind of messages multiple times.

Failing processors in this system are harder to replace than in the previous architecture. Every component has local data. The only way to be able to replace a processor is to keep track of these local data on the redundant hardware.

4 Conclusion and Future Work

4.1 Conclusion

Software Architecture in the Development Process: In this paper, we illustrated our view on the software architecture phase in the development process, sketched in Fig. 1, with a case study of a railroad controller in software. Concerning the development process, we can make the following remarks:

- In this case study, the software architecture phase was carried out sequentially: modeling the system took place first, and then a style was chosen and instantiated. The reason for this order was that several models of the system were already available.
  In general, system modeling and the choice and instantiation of an architectural style are carried out at the same time.
- The case study clearly shows the existence of relations between the activities within the software architecture phase. The choice of a model influences the choice of an architectural style, and vice-versa. The adequacy of different approaches toward system modeling for different architectural styles should be added to taxonomies of styles.
- Architectural styles differ more in the degree with which they satisfy the non-functional requirements than the functional requirements.

Implications of Architectural Styles on Non-Functional Requirements: Here, we summarize the effects of the proposed architectures on the quality properties that we found important.

Timing: Whether temporal constraints can be met or not can only be determined in a fully implemented system. In both architectures, we were able to reason under which conditions timing analysis would be possible, and we could reason about possible bottlenecks. At the level of abstraction of both proposed architectures, difference between the solutions with respect to timing issues cannot be found.

Scalability: A big difference between both proposed architectures is that in the global data store architecture, information is always available to every component. As a result, it is easy to divide the functionality of one component between several others. In the dataflow architecture, when breaking one component into several ones, according to functionality or to components of the controlled system, one should always bear in mind how the newly created components get their information.

Fault-Tolerance: Introducing incident handling requires on the one hand the possibility for a component to run in a separate thread, and on the other hand the possibility to gather information about the global state of the system. In the global state architecture, this requires a decision for multiple threads. In the dataflow architecture, multiple threads are part of the style. On the other hand, extending the functionality in this architecture is less easy, because components communicate directly (so one has to determine where the necessary information should be obtained).

Failing hardware is handled more easily in the global state architecture, because the state is always available. The global state itself however, should be duplicated.

Extendibility: Changes of data (topology of the railroad network, parameters of the trains, schedules) are very easy to apply in the global data store architecture. In the dataflow architecture, one should always determine which of the components store such information locally.

In general, changes to the functionality of the system are much easier to apply in the global data store architecture, because there is no need to analyze where the information, needed for each component, is to be obtained.

A requirements for the possibility of on-line changes is that it should be possible to add components, data and data-types on-line.

4.2 Future Directions

On-line system evolution in real-time systems is considered one of the future challenges in this area ([13]). A promising approach would be to explore the possibilities of the global state architecture with this respect. Changes in functionality within this architecture can be applied by adding or substituting components. In addition, facilities to change the global state, and the generation and distribution of events, should be developed.

Even without facilities to change the global state, it is comparatively easy to handle failing processors when using the global state architecture, assuming the global state component is fail-proof: components performing computation may be substituted by other components without a loss of data.

The description of an architecture evokes a static view of components and connections. Architectures with possibilities for on-line system evolution are dynamic. Apparently, techniques to describe and analyze the dynamics of architectures are lacking. Representation of the dynamics of architectural styles and instantiations form an interesting subject for future research.

References

1. T. Biegstraaten, K. Brink, J. van Katwijk, and H. Toetenel. A simple railroad controller: A case study in real-time specification. Technical Report 94-86, Delft University of Technology, Department of Technical Mathematics and Informatics, 1994.

2. M. Boasson. The artistry of software architecture. *IEEE Software*, 12(6):13–17, November 1995.

3. O. Frieder and M.E. Segal. Dynamic program updating in a distributed computer system. In *Proceedings of the IEEE Conference on Software Maintenance*, Phoenix, Arizona, October 1988.

4. B. Hayes-Roth, K. Pfleger, P. Lalanda, P. Morignot, and M. Balabanovic. A domain-specific software architecture for adaptive intelligent systems. *IEEE Transactions on Software Engineering*, 21(4):288–301, April 1995.

5. K. Jeffay. The real-time producer-consumer paradigm: A paradigm for the construction of efficient, predictable real-time systems. In *Proceedings of the 1993 ACM/SIGAPP Symposium on Applied Computing*, pages 796–804, Indiana, February 1993. ACM Press.

6. J. Kramer and J. Magee. The evolving philosophers problem: Dynamic change management. *IEEE Transactions on Software Engineering*, 16(11):1293–1306, November 1990.

7. P. Kruchten. The 4+1 view model of architecture. *IEEE Software*, 12(5):42–50, November 1995.

8. R.T. Monroe, A. Kompanek, R. Melton, and D. Garlan. Architectural styles, design patterns and objects. *IEEE Software*, 14(1), January 1997.

9. D.L. Parnas, A.J. van Scouwen, and S.P. Kwan. Evaluation of safety-critical software. *Communications of the ACM*, 33(6):636–648, September 1990.

10. M. Shaw. Beyond objects: A software design paradigm based on process control. *ACM Software Engineering Notes*, 20(1), January 1995.

11. M. Shaw. A field guide to boxology: Preliminary classification of architectural styles for software systems. manuscript, http://www.cs.cmu.edu/afs/cs/project/compose/www/html/Publications/1.html, 1996.

12. M. Shaw and D. Garlan. *Software Architecture: Perspectives on an Emerging Discipline*. Prentice-Hall, 1996.

13. J.A. Stankovic. Real-time and embedded systems. Group Report of the Real-Time Working Group of the IEEE Technical Committee on Real-Time Systems, at http://www-ccs.cs.umass.edu/sdcr/rt.ps, 1996.

14. A.S. Tanenbaum. *Structured Computer Organisation*. Prentice-Hall, 1976.

15. J. van Katwijk and H. Toetenel. Experience using paisley for real-time specification. Technical Report 95-29, Delft University of Technology, Department of Technical Mathematics and Informatics, 1995.

Modeling Railway Control Systems Using Graph Grammars: A Case Study

A. A. Holzbacher[1], M. Périn[2], M. Südholt[2]

[1] IRISA/INSA Rennes, Département d'Informatique, Campus de Beaulieu, 35042 Rennes Cedex, France, aholzbac@insa-rennes.fr
[2] IRISA/INRIA Rennes, Projet Lande, Campus de Beaulieu, 35042 Rennes Cedex, France, {mperin,sudholt}@irisa.fr

Abstract. In this paper we develop in three phases a railway control system following the requirements of [2]. We are mainly concerned with the *software architecture* of the control system and its *dynamic evolution*; we do not discuss here the implementation details of the components forming the control system. First, we informally discuss our design proposal for the architecture of the control system: a hierarchy of controllers whose leaves are local controllers connected in a network that mimics the underlying railway topology. Second, we formally define by means of particular *graph grammars* a style of software architectures for the railway control system consisting of two complementary *views* and ensuring several desirable properties by construction. The dynamic evolution of the architecture is modelled by a set of *coordination rules* which define graph transformations and are *verified* with respect to to the graph grammar. Third, using a coordination rule as a formal specification of a dynamic modification of the railway control system, we derive its implementation in ConCoord, a programming environment for concurrent coordinated programming. With regard to software engineering, the two first phases belong to the system design while the third one forms the first implementation step.

1 Introduction

In this paper, we propose a design for a railway control system following the requirements of [2]. We have added one assumption to the problem definition: we require for each train a detailed schedule which defines its timetable and its route giving *all* the places that it must traverse, *i.e.* tracks, junctions and platforms. This schedule is defined off-line. During program execution, a train schedule may be subject to corrective actions by the control system. With regard to the requirements defined in the case study [2], the solution we present addresses at a high-level of abstraction most requirements except for the fault-tolerance aspects. In the software architecture we propose next, the functionalities of the railway control system are distributed among its components in a manner that promotes real-time responsiveness. We do not discuss here the implementation details of the system components. It is worth noticing that in a programming environment with a separate definition of the system architecture and the component codes (*e.g.* in ConCoord), each component code can be expressed in the programming language which better suits its functionality, for instance real-time aspects.

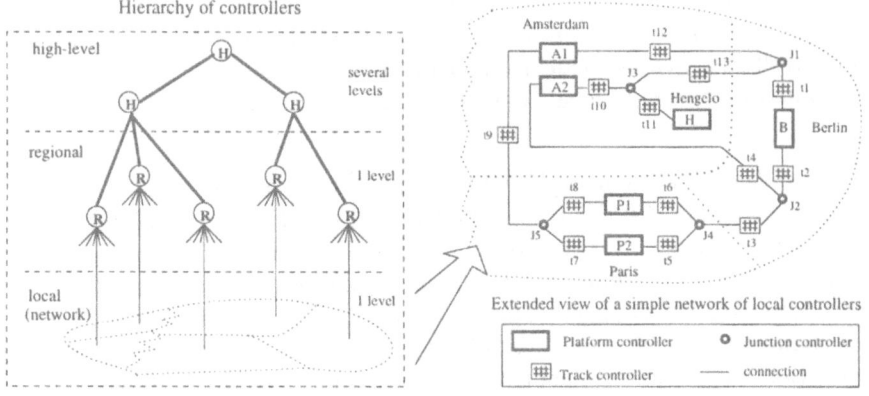

Fig. 1. Architecture of the Railway Control System

The paper is structured as follows. First, we informally discuss our design proposal for the railway control system (Section 2). Second, we formally define the style of the software architecture of the control system using graph grammars and we describe the dynamic evolution of the architecture in terms of coordination rules (Section 3). Third, we implement a coordination rule in ConCoord [5] (Section 4). Finally, we discuss the limitations of our approach in terms of ease of use and expressiveness.

2 An Informal Design of the Railway Control System

Complex system can be seen as a set of individual components and an architecture defining their links and interactions. An explicit description of a system architecture provides a global high-level view of the system which facilitates the different phases of software engineering [4,9]. Here, we present the first design phase of a railway control system: the informal definition of its components and its software architecture. We propose a solution in which control of the railway is first distributed among local controllers connected in a network and then centralised using a control hierarchy (see Figure 1 left).

Local Controllers. We define a local controller for each track, junction and platform of the railway network (*cf.* Figure 1 right). A local controller for a railway device communicates in real-time with the trains currently at the device and may modify their detailed schedule. A track controller may modify the speed of trains currently on the track; a junction controller may redirect trains through the junction to resolve potential collisions; a platform controller may delay trains and handles the addition and removal of trains in the railway network. We do not provide local controllers for stations; a train at a station is managed by the controller of the station platform where it is.

Whenever possible, schedule constraints are solved by local controllers in order to promote real-time responsiveness. This distribution of control between local controllers provides means for concurrency and thus naturally leads to a distributed execution of local controllers on a computer network.

Network of Local Controllers. Local controllers have a view of the system state which is limited to the trains currently at the device they control. In order to decide corrective actions on schedules, a local controller may require information about the trains located at neighbouring devices. Thus, it may interact with the controllers managing its neighbouring devices. A track controller communicates with two junction controllers, two platform controllers or a junction and a platform controller. A junction controller interacts with three track controllers. For simplicity, we only consider junctions linking three tracks which can serve to model junctions linking more than three tracks. A platform controller communicates with one or two track controllers. The interactions between local controllers define a software architecture which mimics the topology of the railway network.

Control Hierarchy. Due to their limited view of the system state, local controllers are not able to resolve all constraints on the trains schedules. Moreover, the monitoring of the system also requires a more centralised view of the system state. For these reasons, we superimpose a hierarchy of regional and high-level controllers over the network of local controllers. First, we partition the railway network into regions connected by tracks. A regional controller centralises state information and controls decisions corresponding to a region of the railway network. It interacts will all local controllers of the region, requesting their state, getting their alarms and sending them commands with corrective actions. Each local controller in the railway control system communicates with a single regional controller. Second, we develop on top of the regional controllers a hierarchy of high-level controllers in which controllers at consecutive levels interact in the same way that local and regional controllers do. If a local controller cannot resolve a constraint, this is propagated upwards in the control hierarchy until a controller which can handle it is found. For example, a high-level controller may solve schedules constraints for trains crossing a region frontier.

The monitoring of the system state is realised by the regional and high-level controllers. The users interact with the railway control system through these controllers, in order to request, for example, a modification on the topology of the railway network, such as the addition of a platform on an existing track. The number of levels of the hierarchy is critical for the system performance. Its value at system start-up depends on the initially foreseen load for each control region of the railway network. During system execution, load balancing can be done by dynamically adding/removing controllers to/from the hierarchy.

3 Formal Definition using Graph Grammars

In this section we introduce a formal framework based on graph grammars for the description of software architectures [8]. We generalise it to include *multiple architectural views* in order to separately define then relate two views: the network of local controllers and the control hierarchy. This formal description permits us to study the dynamic evolution of the software architecture.

3.1 Graph Grammars

The formal framework proposed in [8] introduces the use of graph grammars for the definition of *architecture styles*, *i.e.* sets of architectures that have similar structure and meaning.

Graph Representation. We describe architectures in terms of graphs which share some resemblance with the "box and line" drawing used in informal descriptions. Nodes of the graph stand for system components and edges represent interactions between components. We see graphs as multisets (which enables us to define graph transformations as multiset rewrite rules) of relations of the form $R(c_1, \ldots, c_n)$, where R denotes an n-ary relation over the component names $c_1, \ldots, c_n$. We distinguish two kinds of relations. A relation with a capitalized letter, such as **Process**(c_1), defines a node c_1 of the architecture graph representing a component of type **Process**. A relation with only lower-case letters represents a link between components, *e.g.*, **pipe**(c_1, c_2) denotes an edge of the graph labeled by **pipe** between two components.

Graph Generation using Grammars. Using the multiset/graph correspondence, we now introduce graph grammars to describe sets of correct architectures. We consider context-free graph grammars with variables representing names of system components (denoted by c_i). We represent a grammar by its set of production rules where the axiom, that initiates the production process, is marked with the symbol '▷'. The production rules form a multiset rewrite system. Given a multiset M, the application of a rule ($lhs \rightarrow rhs$) consumes the lhs term from M and adds the rhs terms to M, thus yielding a new multiset. In a production rule, all variables that only appear on the rhs receive a fresh name, *i.e.* not already used in the multiset. We are exclusively interested in the *terminal* multisets produced by a grammar G, *i.e.* the multisets containing only terminal terms, since the terminals terms form the graph of the architecture. Terminals, such as **Process**(c_1) and **pipe**(c_1, c_2), and non-terminals are obvious from the production rules. Consider the grammar shown below which defines the style of pipeline architectures. **Process**(c_1) and **pipe**(c_1, c_2) represent a process component and a pipe between two components, respectively. Pipeline architectures are derived from the *Pipeline* axiom by application of Rule 1 that introduces a **Process** component with a fresh name. Rule 2 is used to add new pipeline connections and process components. Rule 3 adds the last connected process component.

▷ *Pipeline* $\rightarrow_1$ **Process**(c_1), *Pipe*(c_1)
   Pipe$(c_1) \rightarrow_2$ **pipe**(c_1, c_2), **Process**(c_2), *Pipe*(c_2)
   Pipe$(c_1) \rightarrow_3$ **pipe**(c_1, c_2), **Process**(c_2)

The Pipeline Style.

Architecture Style. A grammar is a finite representation of the infinite set of terminal graphs that it can produce. A software architecture belongs to the style defined by a grammar if its corresponding graph can be produced by the grammar. Thus, the architecture style defined by a grammar G can be defined as (see [8]):

$$ArchStyle(G) = \{M \mid \{Axiom_G\} \rightarrow_G^* M \text{ and } M \text{ is terminal}\}$$

We extend this definition to include multiple architecture views since we use two views for the case study: the local network of controllers and the hierarchy of controllers. Each view, say V_i, has its own style defined by a grammar G_i and is related to the set T_i of terminals of G_i. The overall style is defined by a tuple of grammars $(G_1, \ldots, G_n)$ as follows. An architecture represented as a multiset M of terminals in $T_1 \cup \ldots \cup T_n$ belongs to $ArchStyle((G_1, \ldots, G_n))$ if, for each view V_i, M restricted to T_i belongs to the style defined by G_i.

$$ArchStyle((G_1, \ldots, G_n)) = \{M \mid \bigwedge_{i=1,\ldots,n} (M \cap T_i \in ArchStyle(G_i))\}$$

Coordination Rules. The dynamic evolution of software architectures is described in terms of *multiset rewrite rules*, henceforth called *coordination rules* and denoted by *lhs* $\Rightarrow$ *rhs*. Their semantics is the same as that for rewrite rules of context-free graph grammars but, in contrast, there are no restrictions on the *lhs* number of terms. The rule shown below, *e.g.*, reduces a pipeline by discarding a process and replacing the two pipes connected to it by a new pipe.

$$\textbf{pipe}(c_1, c_2), \textbf{Process}(c_2), \textbf{pipe}(c_2, c_3) \Rightarrow \textbf{pipe}(c_1, c_3)$$

An application of this rule to a pipeline architecture always yields a pipeline and thus preserves the pipeline style. This notion of the preservation of architecture style is at the core of our approach and can be checked *statically* by verifying the correctness of a coordination rule with respect to a grammar G using the algorithm defined in [3]. In the process of the formal definition of architectures, this algorithm can also be used to check *statically* that a given architecture M belongs to the style defined by a grammar. The algorithm has been implemented and is currently under testing. It is restricted to single view architectures but its extension to multiple views is straightforward: coordination rules must be checked with respect to each grammar related to a view of the multiple view architecture style.

3.2 Railway Topology View and Control View

As discussed in Section 2, the software architecture of the railway control system consists of two related structures: a network of local controllers and a control hierarchy (*cf.* Figure 1). In this section we define these structures by means of graph grammars. The formal definitions are expressed using standard notations from the field of rewrite systems with three extensions. First, $R\{(x_1, x_2), (y_1, y_2)\}$ is syntactic sugar for $R(x_1, x_2)$, $R(y_1, y_2)$. Second, $[C]: lhs \Rightarrow rhs$ is equivalent to $lhs \cup C \Rightarrow rhs \cup C$. Third, $n \times R(x)$ is equivalent to n occurrences of the term $R(x)$.

Definition of the Network of Local Controllers. As suggested in Section 2, we have three kinds of local controllers: platform, junction and track controllers. In terms of multisets, these controllers are represented using unary relations and their connections using a binary relation. **Platform$_n(p)$** represents a platform controller p with n connecting ports ($n \in \{1, 2\}$). **Junction(j)** represents a junction controller j with three connecting ports. **Track(t)** represents a track controller t with two connecting ports. All links are of type **connection(t, e)** representing a connection between a port of the track controller t and a port of the local controller e (where e is a platform or a junction controller). Consequently, there are no (direct) connections between two track controllers or between a platform and a junction.

Graph Grammar G_1 and its Properties. In Figure 2, we define the grammar G_1 for the network of local controllers and represent graphically five of its rules. For example, Rule 7 provides a way of adding a dead end platform to a network using a junction, whereas Rule 8 introduces a split/merge of a path using two junctions (and corresponding paths). The network defined in the case study [2] and illustrated in Figure 1 belongs to the style of Grammar G_1. Its derivation using rules of Grammar G_1 can be found in [6].

Grammar G_1 ensures that all networks belonging to its style obey two *connectivity properties* by construction. First, it respects the cardinality of connections for each kind of local controller, and thus can not produce a local controller which is disconnected from all other local controllers. For example, a track is always connected to *exactly* two controllers because a terminal **Track** can be produced only by applying Rule 5, which connects the track to two other controllers at the same time. Second, the grammar guarantees that the network is well-formed in the following sense: it cannot produce junctions and platforms which are not directly connected. There must be at least an intermediate track.

Definition of the Control Hierarchy. We superimpose a hierarchy of regional controllers (henceforth R-controllers) and high-level controllers (HL-controllers) on the network of local controllers (L-controllers) in order to

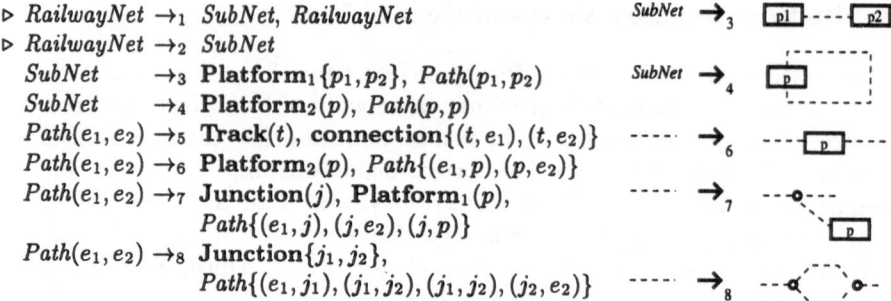

$\triangleright$ *RailwayNet* $\rightarrow_1$ *SubNet, RailwayNet*
$\triangleright$ *RailwayNet* $\rightarrow_2$ *SubNet*
SubNet $\rightarrow_3$ **Platform$_1\{p_1,p_2\}$, **Path(p_1,p_2)
SubNet $\rightarrow_4$ **Platform$_2(p)$, **Path(p,p)
Path(e_1,e_2) $\rightarrow_5$ **Track(t), **connection$\{(t,e_1),(t,e_2)\}$
Path(e_1,e_2) $\rightarrow_6$ **Platform$_2(p)$, **Path$\{(e_1,p),(p,e_2)\}$
Path(e_1,e_2) $\rightarrow_7$ **Junction(j), **Platform$_1(p)$,
$\qquad$ **Path$\{(e_1,j),(j,e_2),(j,p)\}$
Path(e_1,e_2) $\rightarrow_8$ **Junction$\{j_1,j_2\}$,
$\qquad$ **Path$\{(e_1,j_1),(j_1,j_2),(j_1,j_2),(j_2,e_2)\}$

Fig. 2. Grammar G_1 for the Railway Topology

resolve constraints which cannot be handled by local controllers. A R-controller supervises a region in the railway network by communicating with its L-controllers. HL-controllers supervise R-controllers or other HL-controllers.

Graph Grammar G_2 and its Properties. Grammar G_2 (Figure 3) defines the architecture of the control hierarchy of the railway control system (*cf.* Figure 1 left). In this grammar, a R-controller and a HL-controller are denoted by **R-Ctrler** and **HL-Ctrler**, respectively. A HL-controller c interacts with either a HL-controller or a R-controller c' trough a link **supervise**(c,c'). The terminal **ctrl**(c,l) denotes a link between a R-controller c and a L-controller l. We use special relations **HL-freelink**(c) to count the free control links of a HL-controller. Each HL-controller is created with *max* links (both **HL-freelink** and **supervise**), where *max* is a constant that must be set as part of the definition of the grammar. The free links allow us to know how many controllers a HL-controller manages. Rules 6–8 use the same technique to bound to *max'* the number of L-controllers a R-controller manages. For a R-controller, free links are denoted by **R-freelink**. Rules 9–12 enumerate the type of controllers which can be linked to a R-controller. Note that we could have associated to a HL-controller a list of the controllers it manages using the list representation of [3]. This would have made obsolete the constraint on the bound *max*, but does not seem suitable for realistic railway control systems.

Grammar G_2 ensures three properties: first, the simplest control hierarchy consists of one R-controller. Second, an R-controller must have exactly one HL-controller, *i.e.* in a correct system, R-controllers are related to the global control. Third, the grammar does not produce R-controllers or HL-controllers which control nothing, since at creation, both **HL-Ctrler** and **R-Ctrler** control at least one subcontroller (Rule 3 and Rule 6).

Relating the Local Control Network and the Control Hierarchy.
Grammars G_1 and G_2 provide two different and complementary architectural

179

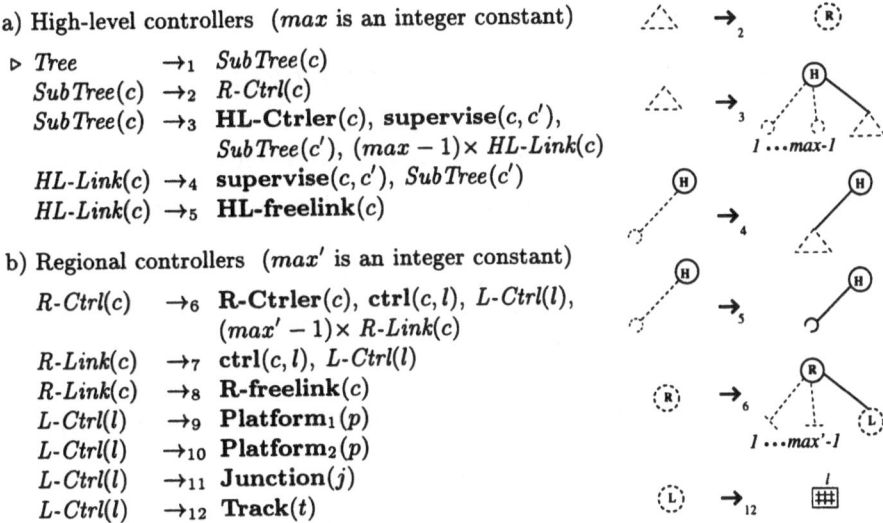

a) High-level controllers (*max* is an integer constant)

▷ *Tree* $\to_1$ *SubTree(c)*
  SubTree(c) $\to_2$ *R-Ctrl(c)*
  SubTree(c) $\to_3$ **HL-Ctrler(c), supervise(c, c'),**
    SubTree(c'), *(max* $-$ 1) $\times$ *HL-Link(c)*
  HL-Link(c) $\to_4$ **supervise(c, c')**, *SubTree(c')*
  HL-Link(c) $\to_5$ **HL-freelink(c)**

b) Regional controllers (*max'* is an integer constant)

  R-Ctrl(c) $\to_6$ **R-Ctrler(c), ctrl(c, l), L-Ctrl(l),**
    (max' $-$ 1) $\times$ *R-Link(c)*
  R-Link(c) $\to_7$ **ctrl(c, l), L-Ctrl(l)**
  R-Link(c) $\to_8$ **R-freelink(c)**
  L-Ctrl(l) $\to_9$ **Platform$_1$(p)**
  L-Ctrl(l) $\to_{10}$ **Platform$_2$(p)**
  L-Ctrl(l) $\to_{11}$ **Junction(j)**
  L-Ctrl(l) $\to_{12}$ **Track(t)**

Fig. 3. Grammar G_2 for the Hierarchic Control Structure

views of the railway control system. The former represents the neighbour relationship between the network devices managed by the L-controllers; the latter enables the distribution/centralization of control by means of a control hierarchy. These two views are related by their common terms. Assume that the overall architecture of the railway control system, represented by the multiset *RCS*, belongs to the style defined by (G_1, G_2). Then terms of *RCS* generated by both G_1 and G_2 are the same in the two views. In our case, common terms are terminals representing L-controllers (*i.e.* using names in $T_1 \cap T_2$). Therefore the coherence of the two related views and the property of Grammar G_2 ensures that each L-controller is linked to exactly one R-controller. Views can also be extracted. For example, if we are only concerned with the L-controllers defined by Grammar G_1, we filter the *RCS* multiset with respect to the set of terminals T_1, hence hiding the terminals of Grammar G_2: **HL-Ctrler, supervise, R-Ctrler, ctrl, HL-freelink.**

3.3 Definition of Dynamic Architectural Changes

We define now a set of coordination rules governing dynamic changes of the network of L-controllers and the control hierarchy. Correctness of these rules with respect to the two grammars ensures preservation of the style defined by (G_1, G_2). Therefore properties which rely on the style still hold after dynamic modifications through correct coordination rules.

In Figure 4 we show the coordination rules governing the dynamic changes to the network of L-controllers (*i.e.* insertion/elimination of controllers) which mimic transformations on the devices of the railway topology. In order to

a) correct introduction rules

$$\mathbf{Track}(t\langle e_1, e_2\rangle) \qquad\qquad \Rightarrow_1 \mathbf{Platform}_2(p),\ \mathbf{Track}\{t_1\langle e_1, p\rangle, t_2\langle p, e_2\rangle\}$$

$$\mathbf{Track}(t\langle e_1, e_2\rangle) \qquad\qquad \Rightarrow_2 \mathbf{Junction}\{j_1, j_2\},$$
$$\mathbf{Track}\{t_1\langle e_1, j_1\rangle, t_1'\langle j_1, j_2\rangle, t_2'\langle j_1, j_2\rangle, t_2\langle j_2, e_2\rangle\}$$

$$\mathbf{Platform}_1(p) \qquad\qquad \Rightarrow_3 \mathbf{Platform}_2(p),\ \mathbf{Track}(t\langle p, p'\rangle),\ \mathbf{Platform}_1(p')$$

$[\,\mathbf{Platform}_1\{p_1, p_2, p_3, p_4\}\,]:$
$$\mathbf{Track}\{t\langle p_1, p_2\rangle, t'\langle p_3, p_4\rangle\} \Rightarrow_4 \mathbf{Junction}\{j_1, j_2\},\ \mathbf{Track}(t''\langle j_1, j_2\rangle)$$
$$\mathbf{Track}\{t_1\langle p_1, j_1\rangle, t_2\langle j_1, p_2\rangle, t_1'\langle p_3, j_2\rangle, t_2'\langle j_2, p_4\rangle\}$$

b) correct elimination rules

$$\mathbf{Track}\{t_1\langle e_1, j_1\rangle, t_2\langle j_2, e_2\rangle, t_1'\langle e_3, j_1\rangle, t_2'\langle j_2, e_4\rangle\} \Rightarrow_5 \mathbf{Track}\{t\langle e_1, e_2\rangle, t'\langle e_3, e_4\rangle\}$$
$$\mathbf{Junction}\{j_1, j_2\},\ \mathbf{Track}(t''\langle j_1, j_2\rangle)$$

$[\,\mathbf{Platform}_2\{p_1, p_2\},\ \mathbf{Track}(t'\langle p_3, e\rangle)\,]:$
$$\mathbf{Platform}_2(p_3),\ \mathbf{Junction}(j), \qquad\qquad \Rightarrow_6 \mathbf{Platform}_1(p_3),$$
$$\mathbf{Track}\{t_1\langle p_1, j\rangle, t_2\langle j, p_2\rangle, t''\langle j, p_3\rangle\} \qquad\qquad \mathbf{Track}(t\langle p_1, p_2\rangle)$$

c) two incorrect rules

$$\mathbf{Track}(t\langle e_1, e_2\rangle) \qquad\qquad \Rightarrow_7 \epsilon$$

$$\mathbf{Track}\{t\langle p_1, p_2\rangle, t'\langle p_3, p_4\rangle\} \Rightarrow_8 \mathbf{Junction}\{j_1, j_2\},\ \mathbf{Track}(t''\langle j_1, j_2\rangle)$$
$$\mathbf{Track}\{t_1\langle p_1, j_1\rangle, t_2\langle j_1, p_2\rangle, t_1'\langle p_3, j_2\rangle, t_2'\langle j_2, p_4\rangle\}$$

Fig. 4. Coordination Rules for the Network of Local Controllers

make coordination rules more readable, we will denote the linking of a track controller t to two controllers e_1 and e_2 by $\mathbf{Track}(t\langle e_1, e_2\rangle)$ instead of the notation $\mathbf{Track}(t)$, $\mathbf{connection}(t, e_1)$, $\mathbf{connection}(t, e_2)$. Similar simplifications will be applied in the graphics in order to make them more intuitive: we shall no more explicitly represent track controllers. Expressed in graphical form, the coordination rules are quite easy to understand. Figure 5 left shows the graphical representation of Rules 4 and 6. Rule 4 relates two tracks (each track joined two platforms) using two junctions. Rule 6 destroys a connection between three platforms by removing a junction. The coordination rules of Figure 4a,b preserve the style specified by Grammar G_1; this can be proven *statically* using the algorithm referred to in Section 3.1. Therefore these coordination rules preserve the connectivity properties of Grammar G_1. Elimination rule 6, for instance, removes a path between the platform p_3 and platforms p_1 and p_2 but ensures that p_3 remains connected to another part of the network (through e). Note that when a rule changes the number of connections of elements, it indicates the change explicitly using different terminals (*cf.* Rule 3).

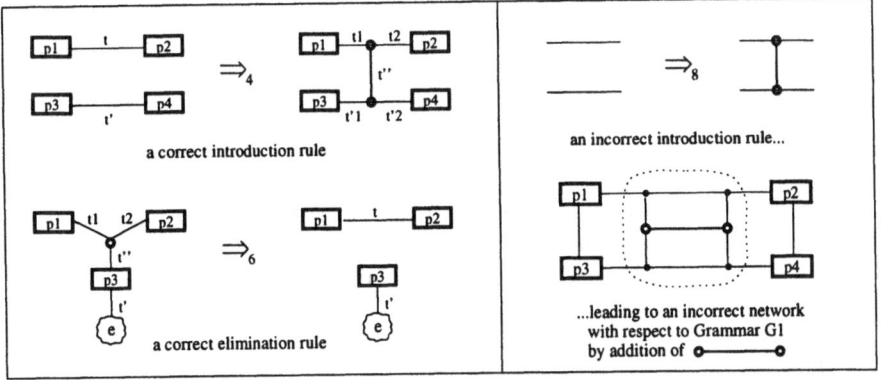

Fig. 5. Graphical Representation of Correct and Incorrect Coordination Rules

There are a many (possibly quite natural) *incorrect rules* whose application destroys the underlying style. Consider, for instance, the rules of Figure 4c. Rule 7 may obviously disconnect a L-controller by removing the last track connected to it and thus does not preserve the style defined by Grammar G_1. Rule 8 is trickier. Analogous to Rule 4, it connects two tracks by introducing two junctions (*cf.* Figure 5 right), however it can be applied in much less restricted contexts and can be used, for instance, to create the network shown in Figure 5 right which does not belong to the style defined by Grammar G_1. The two incorrect rules (7 and 8) are rejected by the verification algorithm.

The correctness of Rules 1–6 with respect to Grammar G_1 guarantees that we meet the requirements set by the ground level of the architecture, namely the connectivity properties. We are now interested in verifying another important property: each L-controller must be controlled by exactly one R-controller. In our design, this requirement depends on the second architectural view, the hierarchy of controllers. So Rules 1–6 must be completed with terminals of Grammar G_2 when they have an impact on the control hierarchy. Consider for instance Rule 1 of Figure 4 – the insertion of a platform on an existing track. We augment this rule with information about controllers of the hierarchy by linking each L-controllers to an R-controller, yielding the following Rule 1':

[R-Ctrler(c), **ctrl**$\{(c, e_1), (c, e_2)\}$ **]** :
ctrl(c, t), $2 \times$ **R-freelink**(c) $\Rightarrow_{1'}$ **ctrl**$\{(c, t_1), (c, p), (c, t_2)\}$,
Track(t),$\qquad\qquad\qquad\qquad$ **Track**(t_1), **Platform**$_2(p)$, **Track**(t_2),
connection$\{(t, e_1), (t, e_2)\}$ $\qquad$ **connection**$\{(t_1, e_1), (t_1, p), (t_2, p), (t_2, e_2)\}$

This new rule must be checked with respect to Grammars G_1 and G_2. Correctness with respect to the Grammar G_1 still holds because the restriction of Rule 1' to the G_1-view yields the initial rule. In order to ensure the correctness with respect to the whole architecture, it is therefore sufficient to check the augmented rule 1' against Grammar G_2. With decomposition into architectural views, we can define richer and richer coordination rules, step by step, while ensuring their correctness separately with respect to each view.

For the control hierarchy, a set of *coordination rules* offering facilities to reorganize the tree of controllers can be found in [6]. Here we only show an example of a rule to split an overloaded HL-controller by introducing a new HL-controller with at least one sub-controller to supervise.

$$[\,\mathbf{HL\text{-}Ctrler}(c),\ \mathbf{supervise}(c,c_1'),\ \mathbf{HL\text{-}Ctrler}(c_1'),\ \mathbf{supervise}(c_1',c_1'')\,]:$$

$$\begin{array}{ll}\mathbf{HL\text{-}freelink}(c), & \Rightarrow \quad \mathbf{supervise}(c,c_2'),\ \mathbf{HL\text{-}Ctrler}(c_2'),\\ \mathbf{supervise}(c_1',c_2'') & \quad \mathbf{supervise}(c_2',c_2''),\ \mathbf{HL\text{-}freelink}(c_1'),\\ & \quad (max-1)\times\mathbf{HL\text{-}freelink}(c_2')\end{array}$$

4 Implementation in ConCoord

The formal specification of the railway control system developed in the previous section serves as a basis to derive an implementation of the control system. In this section, we implement the first coordination rule of Figure 4 in its augmented version (Rule 1') which models the addition of a platform to an existing track in a railway region. In order to remain at the same abstraction level as the graph grammars, we use ConCoord's *coordination language*: CCL [5]. This allows us to express the modifications of the control network and hierarchy described in Rule 1' referring solely to the interfaces of the involved local and regional controllers (these interfaces appear below). The implementations of these controllers are not needed in the rule description and thus they are not shown here. Each controller implementation can be written in a different *computation language* which is a sequential language with a few extensions for communication.

```
component<t_device> L_Ctrler(int id,int n_neigh,L_init<t_device> init)
{ inoutport<t_neigh> neigh[n_neigh];
  inoutport<t_reg> reg;
  states no_train (int[n_neigh]);
}

component R_Ctrler(int id,int max_local,R_init init)
{ inoutport<t_reg> local[max_local];
  inoutport<t_high> higher;
  states add_platform (int,int,L_init<track>,int,L_init<platform>,
                       int,L_init<track>);
}
```

The Interfaces of Local and Regional Controllers. In ConCoord, a system component is an instance of a type called *component* whose interface may declare generic and initialisation parameters, ports and states. One gives values to generic and initialisation parameters when instantiating a component. Above, we declare a generic parameter t_device in L_Ctrler which allows us to parameterise the behaviour of instances of L_Ctrler by the type of device to be controlled (*i.e.* track, platform or junction). For instance, we denote a local track controller by L_Ctrler<track>. A local controller is initialised with a unique identifier id, the number of its neighbouring devices (n_neigh) (*e.g.* two for a track controller) and state information init (*e.g.* a track length for a track controller). A regional controller, *i.e.* an instance of R_Ctrler, is initialised with a unique identifier id, the maximum number of local controllers forming its region (max_local) and state information init (*e.g.* starting topology of the region). Initialisation parameters related to component interactions like n_neigh and max_local are derived from the graph grammars; others like the generic parameter t_device are proper to the implementation.

An instance of a *component* interacts with other system components via its ports *inoutport* by sending/receiving messages whose type is defined between angle brackets in the code shown above. A local controller for a railway device interacts with the local controllers for its neighbouring devices by the port array neigh (one element per neighbouring controller) and with its region controller via the port reg. A regional controller interacts with its region local controllers via the port array local (one element per potential local controller) and with its higher-level controller by means of the port higher. Though ConCoord does not actually provide a port type *inoutport*, we use it here to remain at the same level of abstraction as the graph grammars. In a ConCoord implementation, we would build each *inoutport* defined above in terms of various input or output ports (see [6] for more details).

In the previous section, we have defined architectural modifications of the railway control system by means of coordination rules whose *lhs* refers to the system architecture but not to its component states. In practice, the execution of such rules is triggered by both the system structure and its component states. In the declaration *states* of L_Ctrler and R_Ctrler, we define execution states which are relevant in the triggering of the addition of a platform to a railway region. It seems reasonable to require that no trains are currently on the devices affected by this modification; this information is provided by a state variable no_train in L_Ctrler which indicates the existence/absence of trains moving from a device towards its neighbouring devices. As already said, the monitoring of the railway control system and thus its interfacing with users occurs through the hierarchy controllers. In particular, a user requests to a regional controller the addition of a platform to its region; this information is represented in R_Ctrler by a state variable add_platform whose parameters provide sufficient information to execute the platform addition as we detail below. A system designer must foresee the component states associated to dynamic architectural modifications when specifying coordination rules. Such states can be included in the *lhs* of coordination rules but they are meaningless for the verification algorithm.

Addition of a Platform. In Rule 1′, the addition of a platform to an existing track in a railway region is modelled as the replacement of a track controller t by a track controller t1, a platform controller p and a track controller t2. The scope of the modification is a single region supervised by a regional controller c. The track controller t is neighbouring two local controllers named e1 and e2. As e1 and e2 can manage trains at either a platform or a junction, four CCL conditional statements are necessary to express this rule. In the statement *when* below e1 and e2 are two platform controllers. This statement defines a condition on the controller states and the system structure which triggers the execution of architectural actions.

```
when (c,t,e1,e2,e1_id,e2_id):(R_ctrler c;L_Ctrler<track> t;
                              L_Ctrler<platform> e1,e2; int e1_id, e2_id|
            // Condition on the state of system components
    c.add_platform(t_id,t1_id,t1_init,p_id,p_init,t2_id,t2_init)
    and e1.no_train(e1_nt) with (e1_nt[1]==0)
    and t.no_train(t_nt) with (t_nt[0]==0 and t_nt[1]==0)
    and e2.no_train(e2_nt) with (e2_nt[0]==0)
            // Condition on the system architecture
    and c.local[t_id]--t.reg and c.local[e1_id]--e1.reg
    and c.local[e2_id]--e2.reg
    and e1.neigh[1]--t.neigh[0] and t.neigh[1]--e2.neigh[0])
            // Architectural Modification
      => forall (c,t,e1,e2,e1_id,e2_id)
        { kill t;
          create    track t1(t1_id,2,t1_init), platform p(p_id,2,p_init)
                    track t2(t2_id,2,t2_init),
          bind      e1.neigh[1]--t1.neigh[0],t1.neigh[1]--p.neigh[0],
                    p.neigh[1]--t2.neigh[0],t2.neigh[1]--e2.neigh[0],
                    c.local[t1_id]--t1.reg,c.local[p_id]--p.reg,
                    c.local[t2_id]--t2.reg;
        };
```

The first part of the condition queries on the state add_platform of the regional controller c which indicates the existence of a user request for the addition of a platform in the region. Its parameters provide the identification of the track controller t_id onto which the platform has to be placed and values for the initialisation parameters of the track and platform controllers to be created (see statement *create*). The state no_train of the local controllers e1, t and e2 ensures the absence of trains moving from (to) the platform controlled by e1 via the track controlled by t to (from) the platform controlled by e2. We use the indices 0 and 1 to refer to the left and right neighbouring sides. The second part of the condition queries on the system architecture defined in the *lhs* of Rule 1′. In ConCoord, a channel between two ports is represented by the binding symbol '−−' and is mandatory for communication to happen via these ports. The regional controller c manages the local controllers t, e1 and e2 (see above 'local[]−−reg' representing **ctrl** of Grammar G_2). The reader should notice that t is identified by t_id from add_platform. The track controlled by t is neighbouring the platforms controlled by e1 and e2 (see above 'neigh−−neigh' representing **connection** of Grammar G_1). The second part of the statement *when* (following '=>') details the architectural modifications: the removal of the track controller t, the creation of the controllers t1, p and t2 (initialised using the parameters of add_platform) and the binding of their ports as defined by the *rhs* of the coordination rule. In the statement *when* above, we have directly transcribed the *lhs* and *rhs* of coordination Rule 1' into architectural conditions and actions. This step can be fully automated. In a second step we have refined the coordination rule introducing the notion of controller states.

5 Discussion of our approach

In this paper, we have discussed three successive phases of the development of a railway control system: an informal design, a formal definition of its architecture style using graph grammars and the dynamic evolution of the architecture, and a first stage of implementation in terms of ConCoord.

From a software engineering viewpoint, the formal framework we have presented has several advantages. It supports the static verification of some structural properties of a system, those which rely on the architecture style. It is sufficiently powerful to permit the definition of complex systems in terms of various complementary architectural views. Similar to the $4 + 1$ view model of architectures [7], views can be used to represent (partial) aspects of an architecture, but unlike the $4 + 1$ model our views are completely formalized. Moreover, the architecture of a railway control system presented here is fully scalable and extensible in the sense required in [2]: the architecture style defined using the two graph grammars captures arbitrarily complex architectures and the coordination rules enable the dynamic extension of an architecture. Finally, the formal definition of a system architecture and its dynamic evolution provide a strong basis for the derivation of an implementation of the system.

This case study has revealed some shortcomings of our framework that require future work to facilitate its use. First, establishing the relationship between a set of possible architectures and its description as a graph grammar is not always intuitive. We believe that it is possible to develop tools for producing instances of minimal size of an architecture style from a graph grammar. This would be helpful to grasp the architectures that a grammar can produce. Second, we had to prove by induction on the production rules the properties of Grammar G1 and G2 that we announce in subsection 3.2. Since these properties are expressible and decidable in monadic second order logic [1], we would like to verify them automatically ; however no practical tools exists.

One of the most attractive features of the formal framework we use is the static verification of coordination rules with respect to graph grammars. This feature requires the graph grammars to be context-free. This restriction limits their expressiveness. For example, it is not possible to describe a hierarchy with an unbounded number of siblings and arbitrary interactions between them. With such a structure, we could represent a control hierarchy in which siblings R-controllers collaborate in the same manner that L-controllers of the control network do, without the participation of HL-controllers. Such a control hierarchy could be described using context-sensitive instead of context-free grammars, but would require an adaptation of the verification algorithm in order to ensure its termination for context-sensitive grammars.

In the formal framework, the coordination rules express local changes and cannot deal with global conditions on the system structure, such as the existence of a path between to given platforms. For example, consider an elimination rule that removes a track. We would like to impose this rule to be applicable only if it does not remove the only track between two subnets of the railway topology. However, this condition cannot be tested when dealing only with local information since it is equivalent to ask for the existence of another path between the two subnets. This notion of locality is a prerequisite for the automatic verification algorithm, facilitates the understanding of coordination rules and enables the simultaneous application of rules in disjoint parts of the system.

References

1. B. Courcelle. *Graph rewriting: an algebraic and logic approach*, chapter 5 in: Handbook of Theoretical Computer Science. Elsevier, 1990.
2. E. de Jong. Software architecture for large control systems: a case study. In *Proc. of COORDINATION '97*, LNCS, this volume. Springer Verlag, 1997.
3. P. Fradet and D. Le Métayer. Structured gamma. TR 989, IRISA, Rennes, 1996.
4. D. Garlan. Research Directions in Software Architecture. *ACM Computing Surveys*, 27:257–261, June 1995.
5. A. A. Holzbacher. A Software Environment for Concurrent Coordinated Programming. In *Proc. of the Conference on Coordination Models, Languages and Applications*, LNCS 1061, pages 249–266. Springer-Verlag, 1996.
6. A. A. Holzbacher, M. Périn, and M. Südholt. Modeling railway control systems using graph grammars: a case study. TR 1100, IRISA, Rennes, 1997.
7. P. B. Kruchten. The 4 + 1 view model of architecture. *IEEE Software*, pages 42–50, November 1995.
8. D. Le Métayer. Software architecture styles as graph grammars. In *In Proc. of the ACM SIGSOFT Symposium of the foundations of Software Engineering*, pages p.15–23, 1996.
9. M. Shaw and D. Garlan. Formulations and Formalisms in Software Architecture. In *Computer Science Today, Recent Trends and Developments*, LNCS 1000, pages 307–323. Springer-Verlag, 1995.

On What Linda Is:
Formal Description of Linda as a Reactive System

David Gelernter   Lenore Zuck

Department of Computer Science
Yale University

1 Introduction

Linda is a *coordination language*—it's the glue that allows modules expressed in ordinary "computation" languages to be cemented into parallel programs. The term "coordination language" is seeing increasingly general use to designate a variety of parallel environments, but we introduced it specifically to designate systems that were supported by compilers—to designate *languages*, in other words, and not mere communication libraries.

Communication in Linda takes place via distributed data structures in a logically shared memory. The fact that distributed data structures in a logically shared memory are a natural, readily understood programming paradigm is implicit in the fact that *all* programming is based on (ordinary) data structures in an (ordinary) memory. Those ordinary data structures are no good for parallel programming, of course—a mere physical shared memory in itself is useless—because of the communication and synchronization problems that arise in the presence of concurrency. But Linda represents a conceptually minimal adaptation of well-understood, standard programming paradigms.

Because Linda is a useful coordination language, it would be worth knowing exactly what Linda means. If we knew, we would be able to tell whether Linda implementations really do what they ought to; we would also be able to use Linda in new ways, which have seemed interesting and attractive for some time but don't make sense without a formal Linda semantics. Because the Linda operations are simple and powerful, they seem like a good basis for a specification-level coordination language—a language designed not for building coordinated systems but for specifying how they should behave. Linda's clarity, simplicity and power suggest that specifications in Linda would be relatively simple to build and understand—and of course they could easily be executable, if that were desirable. The following presentation is designed to pin down the meaning of the tuple-space operations; we show also by means of a simple but substantial example how they could be used (once we understand their meaning) as a specification language for coordinated systems.

There have been (surprisingly few) previous attempts at supplying Linda with formal semantics. Most of those attempts have not dealt strictly with Linda (e.g., [12]), are not operational (e.g., [5]), and do not deal with the possibility of infinite computations in Linda (e.g., [7]). The semantics we present here deals strictly with Linda, is fully operational, and deals explicitly with infinite computations.

This paper is organized as follows. In Section 2 we briefly review the coordination language Linda and the formal model we use for defining its semantics. We also present an example of a C-Linda code that finds all the primes between 1 and some given n. This example is used throughout the paper. Section 3 defines an "Abstract Linda System," that is, a theoretical system that defines the Linda interface of a Linda system. Section 4 uses the formal abstract system of Section 3 to define when a real system qualifies as a Linda system. Section 5 is a case study of a Linda program that demonstrates the main point discussed in the previous sections. Section 6 discusses some applications of the formal Linda semantics, while Section 7 elaborates on one such application by presenting formal specification for LifeStream using Linda. We conclude with Section 8.

2 Basics

A Linda system is a finite system of processes, running under some sequential host language, that share a "tuple space" and that communicate with the tuple space using Linda operations. Linda tuples are k-ary sequences over some predefined domain of ground elements, and the tuple space is a multilist of tuples. A "template" is a set of tuples, each element of which is said to "match" the template. There are four Linda operations. 1) Out adds a tuple to the tuple space. 2) In takes a template as an argument and removes a matching tuple from the tuple space, which it returns. 3) Rd is a non-destructive version of In: given a template it returns a matching tuple without affecting the contents of the tuple space. 4) Eval generates tuples in parallel; it takes as an argument k functions, and starts in parallel k processes, each evaluating one of the k functions. The values returned by these processes are combined to add a (k-ary) tuple into the tuple space. Both the In and the Rd operations block until a matching tuple is found, while the Eval operation does not cause its caller to block; it returns without waiting for the child processes to finish.

See Section 5.1 for an example of a C-Linda program.

The semantics of Linda is specified using trace semantics as appears in [1], which is based on the works in [13, 15, 10]. A brief summary follows.

We use the term *reactive system* to describe computational entities which exhibit an ongoing activity, interacting with their environment and possibly not terminating. (Cf. [9].) Intuitively, a reactive system is a black box which from time to time performs externally visible atomic (indivisible) activities called "actions". An observer may record the history of a run by writing down the sequence of visible actions as they occur. Obviously, after the system performs a finite number of steps, the observed sequence is finite. We call it a "partial trace". A "trace" is the sequence observed when the system is allowed to run forever. Traces can be finite or infinite. We call an occurrence of an action in a trace an *event*.

For many purposes, how the traces are developed is of no interest; all that matters is the set of possible traces. We call the description of a system's possible traces the "behavior" of the system, and we often identify a system with its behavior. Formally, a *behavior* consists of a set of actions and a set of traces – finite and infinite sequences over the set of actions.

See Section 5.2 for an example of a "real" system, namely the one presented in Section 5.1, as a reactive system.

3 An Abstract Linda System – ALS

We define an abstract Linda system, or *ALS* for short, which is a reactive system that represents the abstraction of Linda in any Linda system. Roughly speaking, for given sets of ground elements, tuples over the ground elements, templates over the the tuples, and processes we define an ALS whose actions are the invocations and the responses of all the Linda operations performed by the given set of processes using the tuples and the templates.

Section 3.1 describes the set of tuples, templates, and processes. Section 3.2 defines the set of actions given the sets of tuples, templates, and processes. Section 3.3 defines a *tuple space* at the end of a finite sequence of ALS actions, that is used to define the set of the ALS traces in Section 3.4.

Thus, for given sets of tuples, templates, and processes, this section presents a unique ALS that corresponds to these sets.

3.1 Tuples, Templates, and Processes

Let G be a set of *ground elements*, and let $T \subseteq G^+ = \bigcup_{k \geq 1} G^k$ be the set of *tuples*. The set T is associated with a set $\bar{T} \subseteq 2^T$ of *templates*. The tuples in each template are said to *satisfy* or to *match* the template.

Let $\mathcal{P}$ be the set of processes. Processes come in two varieties: *autonomous* processes that are started by external actions, and *eval* processes that are started as the result of an **Eval** operation. Let $\mathcal{P}_a$ denote the set of autonomous processes, and let $\mathcal{P}_e$ denote the set of eval processes. The eval processes are further partitioned into *process groups*. Each process group P corresponds to a possible execution of a single **Eval** operation. It consists of one process for each of the arguments of that **Eval** operation[1]. We assume that each process group is *owned* by a unique process, namely the process that can activate it.

Let P be the process group corresponding to the execution of **Eval**$(f_1, \ldots, f_k)$. Hence $|P| = k$. Assume that $P = \{p_1, \ldots, p_k\}$, and that each p_i is to compute f_i. (We assume that the identity of each p_i includes all the information required to derive i and f_i.) If the computation that p_i performs terminates, it returns its result $g_i \in G$ by means of a special **Finish** action. When all of the processes

---

[1] We model the processes as if they are non-recyclable, in particular, each eval process may be activated only by its owner, and only to perform a certain function in the evaluation of a certain eval expression.

in P return their results, the system adds a copy of the tuple $(g_1, \ldots, g_k)$ to the tuple space.

Note: the correctness of each process, i.e., whether g_i is indeed the result of f_i, is of no relevance to us, since the processes are provided by the user and are not in the control of the system.

Given the sets G, T, $\bar{T}$, and $\mathcal{P}$ (with its partitions), an *abstract Linda system over* G, $\bar{T}$, *and* $\mathcal{P}$, or $ALS(T, \bar{T}, \mathcal{P})$, is a reactive system that does all that the Linda portion of a Linda system can do using the same tuple space, templates, and processes. In the rest of this section we formally define the behavior of $ALS(T, \bar{T}, \mathcal{P})$ by describing its actions and its traces.

For an example of an ALS see Section 5.3; the tuples, templates, and processes are described in Section 5.3.

3.2 ALS's Actions

Given sets G, $\bar{T}$, and $\mathcal{P}$ as above, the actions of $ALS(T, \bar{T}, \mathcal{P})$ are all those described in Table 1. The first and second columns of each entry describe a family of actions by their common name and sets of arguments. The third column describes the intuitive meaning of the action, and the fourth describes the process(es) that the action is local to—the process, or processors, that have the action in their local set of actions in their view of the trace.

Action	For every	Explanation	Local To:
Invoke-Rd(p, T)	$p \in \mathcal{P}$, $T \in \bar{T}$	used by p to initiate a Rd operation with template T	p
Invoke-In(p, T)	$p \in \mathcal{P}$, $T \in \bar{T}$	used by p to initiate a In operation with template T	p
Invoke-Out(p, t)	$p \in \mathcal{P}$, $t \in T$	used by p to initiate an Out operation with tuple t	p
Respond-Rd(p, t)	$p \in \mathcal{P}$, $t \in T$	used by the system to return t to p as a result of a Rd	p
Respond-In(p, t)	$p \in \mathcal{P}$, $t \in T$	used to return t to p as a result of an In	p
Start(p, p)	$p \in \mathcal{P}_a$	used to start a process p that is activated externally	p
Start(p, P)	$p \in \mathcal{P}$ and $P \subseteq \mathcal{P}_e$ owned by p	issued by p, activates every process in P	$\{p\} \cup P$
Finish(p, g)	$p \in \mathcal{P}_e$, $g \in G$	used by p to return g and halt	p

Table 1. Actions of $ALS(T, \bar{T}, \mathcal{P})$

For every process p, let p's *local actions in* $ALS(\mathcal{T}, \bar{\mathcal{T}}, \mathcal{P})$ be the set of actions that are local to p. Note that only $\texttt{Start}(p, P)$ actions may be local to more than one process.

3.3 ALS's Tuple Space

The tuple space of a Linda system evolves over time, hence, it makes sense to define it at each point of a trace, or, more formally, at the end of each partial trace.

Consider some tuple $t \in \mathcal{T}$. Copies of t are added to the tuple space either explicitly, as the result of an $\texttt{Invoke-Out}(-, t)$ action, or implicitly, as the result of the finishing of every eval process in some process group whose combined result is t. Copies of t are removed from the tuple space only as a result of a $\texttt{Respond-In}(-, t)$ action.

Consider now a finite sequence α over $ALS(\mathcal{T}, \bar{\mathcal{T}}, \mathcal{P})$'s actions. Let $mult(t, \alpha)$, the *multiplicity of t at the end of* α, be the difference between the number of α events that cause a copy of t to be added into the tuple space and the number of α events that cause a copy of t to be removed from the tuple space.

More formally, assume $\alpha = \alpha_1, \ldots, \alpha_n$, and $t = (g_1, \ldots, g_k)$. For every process group P with cardinality k, we say that P *computes t in* α if there is a $\texttt{Finish}(p_i, g_i)$ event in α for every $i = 1, \ldots, k$ and p_i that computes the ith element in the eval expression. We now define:

$$mult(t, \alpha) = |\{i : 1 \leq i \leq n \text{ and } \alpha_i = \texttt{Invoke-Out}(-, t)\}| +$$
$$|\{P : P \text{ computes } t \text{ in } \alpha\}| -$$
$$|\{i : 1 \leq i \leq n \text{ and } \alpha_i = \texttt{Respond-In}(-, t)\}|$$

(The second term in the addition captures the notion that process groups are disposable—each eval operation spawns a "fresh" process group.)

The *tuple space at the end of* α is the function $mult(t, \alpha)$ that maps for every tuple $t \in \mathcal{T}$ its multiplicity at the end of α.

3.4 ALS's Traces

An ALS trace is a sequence of ALS actions whose behavior is consistent with Linda. In this section we define exactly what "being consistent with Linda" means.

We distinguish between three types of properties of ALS's traces: local, safety, and liveness. Local properties refer to the local view of a trace by individual processes. Safety properties are properties that can be violated by finite prefices of traces, and are not local. Liveness properties are trace properties that are not local and cannot be violated by finite prefices. prefices of traces. E.g., consider a trace where a certain process invokes a **Rd** which is returns and then a **In** that blocks, local properties require that the result of the **Rd** is a tuple that satisfies the template, and that the process performs no actions after the **In**. Safety properties require that the tuple returned by **Rd** is indeed in tuple space when it is returned. Liveness properties state that indeed the In is allowed to block.

For the rest of this section, fix some T, $\bar{T}$, and $\mathcal{P}$, and a (possibly infinite) sequence α over $ALS(T, \bar{T}, \mathcal{P})$'s actions. For a process p in $\mathcal{P}$, let α_p be p's local view on α, i.e., α_p is the restriction of α to p's local actions in $ALS(T, \bar{T}, \mathcal{P})$.

Local Properties of Traces Let p be a process in $\mathcal{P}$. The sequence α satisfies local properties with respect to p if α_p satisfies the following: 1) every response is immediately preceded by a matching invocation; 2) if an invocation is not immediately followed by a response it is the last event (of α_p); 3) the first event is an appropriate Start event, and every other Start event starts a process group that is owned by p; and 4) if p returns a value, then it is an eval process, and this return of value is the last event in p local history.

Formally, α *satisfies the local properties with respect to p* if α_p satisfies:

1. every Respond-Rd(p, t) event (respectively, Respond-In(p, t)) is immediately preceded by an Invoke-Rd(p, T) (respectively, Invoke-In(p, T)) event where $t \in T$;
2. every Invoke-Rd (respectively, Invoke-In) event is either the last event or is immediately followed by a Respond-Rd (respectively, Respond-In) event;
3. if α_p is not empty then its first event is Start(p) if $p \in \mathcal{P}_a$ and Start$(-, P)$ if $p \in \mathcal{P}_e$ and P is the (unique) process group that includes p. Every other Start event in α_p is of the form Start$(p, -)$;
4. if there is a Finish event in α_p, it is the last event in α_p and $p \in \mathcal{P}_e$.

Safety Properties of Traces The only safety properties of α are that it returns correct values, i.e., values that are in the tuple space.

Formally, we say that α *satisfies the safety properties* if for every prefix $\alpha'; a$ of α, where a is either a Respond-Rd$(-, t)$ or a Respond-In$(-, t)$ event, $mult(t, \alpha') \geq 1$.

Liveness Properties of Traces The liveness properties of an ALS trace define when operations may and may not block. As is often the case with such properties, traces that satisfy liveness are those that give "non-blocking" a fair chance, or, in other words, where enough attempts are made to respond to an invocation.

The Linda model allows for some latitude in the choice of fairness assumptions on traces. Examples include allowing blocking for operations whose template eventually permanently cannot be matched, or for for operations whose templates cannot be matched infinitely many times, or for operations for whom every tuple that is in the template either is eventually never in the tuple space or is removed from the tuple space infinitely many times. All these properties are fairly easy to express formally. E.g., the first property defines α to be fair if for every Invoke operation in α with template T, either there is a matching

Respond or for some prefix α' of α, for every prefix α'' of α that extends α, $mult(t, \alpha'') = 0$ for every $t \in T$.

Whatever definition of fairness is used, one must be able to define precisely what it is along the lines of the example above. With the definition, it is possible to define when the sequence α is fair.

An ALS Trace Putting it all together, the sequence α is an $ALS(\mathcal{T}, \bar{\mathcal{T}}, \mathcal{P})$-trace if it satisfies the local property with respect to every process $p \in \mathcal{P}$, it is safe, and it is live.

4 Linda Systems

Our goal is to determine whether a given system is a Linda system. We accomplish this by:

1. Expressing the "real" system as a reactive system (see Section 5.2 for an example);
2. Defining an ALS that corresponds to the real system;
3. Defining a mapping between traces of the real system to sequences of of the ALS actions, and testing the sequences the traces map to are ALS traces.

Let S be a system that is a candidate for a real Linda system, i.e., a multiprocess system, with each of the processes capable of running a code in some host language, and communicating with the tuple space using the Linda constructs: **In**, **Rd**, **Out**, and **Eval**. The system S may be a program (as we show in our example in Section 5), a set of programs, or a compiler. The processes of S should not be able to communicate with their surroundings (including their peer processes) in any other way but their Linda communication with the tuple space. If this is not the case, then obviously S is not a good candidate for being a Linda system.

We first have to express S as a reactive system, where all the Linda operations, and the return of processes generated by eval functions, are in the set of actions. We expect this set of actions to include all the internal actions of processes, including the operations of the host language.

The second step is to map an ALS $\mathcal{A}_S$ to S. For that purpose, it suffices to identify the set of tuples, templates, and processes of $\mathcal{A}_S$. Given S, the set of ground elements, tuples, and templates is fairly straightforward to define since they are all parameters to S's operations. The set of processes may be somewhat tricky to define, since the identity of autonomous and eval processes in the real system is not a priori known; neither is it a priori known which processes in the real system may spawn others. Thus the precise definition of the set of processes may only be known at run-time. Some attention should also be paid if S's processes are recycled, since ALS doesn't allow recyclying. However, given the set of S's traces it is possible to define the set of processes. See Section 5.3 for an example of such definitions.

Once the set of tuples, templates, and processes is defined, the set of actions follows trivially. For practical purposes, one may restrict this set to the actions that actually correspond to S's actions. See Section 5.3 for an example of a restricted set of actions.

The last step in the mapping is to map S traces into sequences of $\mathcal{A}_S$ actions. Let τ be an S-trace. Consider now the sequence $\mu(\tau)$ obtained from τ by the following procedure:

1. For every process p, for every Rd (resp. In) action of p that does not block, add the action Respond-Rd(p, t) (resp. Respond-In(p, T)) to $\mu(\tau)$ just before the next p-action in $\mu(\tau)$, where t is the tuple returned by the Rd (resp. In) operation.
2. Remove any internal actions from τ, so the only actions there are Linda related operations;
3. For every autonomous $\mathcal{A}$ process p, add the action Start(p, p) to the beginning of $\mu(tau)$;
4. Rename the actions in $\mu(tau)$ according to Table 2; (Attention should be paid here to the names of the process groups and the eval processes).

old action name	new action name
Eval$(f_1, \ldots, f_k)$ issued by p to Q	Start(p, Q)
Rd with template T by p	Invoke-Rd(p, T)
In with template T by p	Invoke-In(p, T)
Out with tuple t by p	Invoke-Out(p, t)
return of v by p	Finish(p, v)

Table 2. Renaming Actions of an S-Trace

Notes: a) In 1) we assume that it is always possible to determine whether an operation blocks; b) Since the value of returned tuples may only be determined from the local variables, step 1) is performed before step 2), otherwise information about the values returned may be lost; c) It is easy to see that the final $\mu(tau)$ is indeed a sequence over $\mathcal{A}_S$ actions.

The system S is a *correct implementation of Linda* if for every S-trace τ, the sequence $\mu(\tau)$ is an $\mathcal{A}$-trace.

The formal definition of when R is a correct implementation of Linda ignores issues of "correctness" of S. A system that, for example, allows blocked processes to continue their local computations, or processes to communicate directly, may still be considered a correct Linda implementation according to this definition. This, however, is acceptable since the purpose of the definition is to capture when the Linda portion of a system is correct. If one chooses to construct a system whose processes don't compute the functions they are assigned to, or where blocked processes perform operations (note that if the system is a correct

implementation of Linda then these cannot be Linda operations), the system is
incorrect, regardless of whether it is a correct Linda implementation. A correct
Linda system is merely one that performs its Linda tasks well.

5 PrimeFinder: An Example

We use the PrimeFinder program of [6] to demonstrate most of the ideas above.

5.1 PrimeFinder: A C-Linda Program

Consider the C program shown in Figure 1. The program constructs an N element vector where the jth entry is 1 if j is prime and 0 otherwise. The output of the program is the number of primes in between 1 and N.

```
# define N 1000

real_main()
{
    int      count=0, i, is_prime(), ok;
    for (i=2; i <= N; ++i) eval (''primes'', i, is_prime(i));
    for (i=2; i <= N; ++i) {
        rd(''primes'', i, ? ok);
        if (ok) ++count;}
    printf(''%d.\n'', count);
}

is_prime(me)
    int      me;
{   int      i, limit, ok;
    double   sqrt();
    limit = sqrt((double) me) + 1;
    for (i=2; i <= limit; ++i) {
        rd(''primes'', i, ? ok);
        if (ok && (me%i == 0)) return 0;}
    return 1;
}
```

Fig. 1. PrimeFinder

To build a vector in in tuple space, PrimeFinder uses tuples of the form
(''primes'', i, is_prime(i)). Hence, each tuple-element of the vector is labelled with the vector name ''primes'' and the index of the element. To read

the jth element of the vector, the program issues a rd(''primes'', j, ? ok) command, and, when it returns, the variable ok contains the value of the jth element of primes. The templates the program uses are of the form (''primes'', j, ? ok), and the set of tuples that matches such a templates is the set of tuples that corresponds to the jth entry of the vector primes. Obviously, we expect this set to include at most one tuple.

To generate the vector elements, the program issues eval commands. Each eval has three arguments, the first two are identity functions of the string "primes" and the index of the element, say i, and the third is the integer function *is_prime(i)* that returns either 0 or 1, depending on whether i is prime or not. It does so by checking the remainder of the division of i with every prime integer between 2 and $\sqrt{i}$.

5.2 PrimeFinder: A Reactive System

We describe PrimeFinder, for any (natural) value of N as a reactive system by describing the set of actions and the set of traces. The set $acts_{PF}$ includes the Linda actions and output actions. For simplicity of the exposition, we choose to include in $acts_{PF}$ the return of values by eval processes.

More formally, for every $i \geq 2$ let t_i denote the tuple *("primes", i, prime(i))*, and T_i denote the (singleton) template $\{t_i\}$, referred to in the program text as (''primes'', i, ? ok). Let e_i denote the eval tuple *("primes", i, is_prime(i))*. Then $acts_{PF}$ includes the following:

1. The actions $\mathrm{Rd}^j(T_i)$ for $i \geq 2$, $j \geq 1$. The action $\mathrm{Rd}^1(T_i)$ is an action of the main process. The action $\mathrm{Rd}^j(T_i)$ is a $\mathrm{Rd}(T_i)$ action initiated the process executing is_prime(j), i.e., the third process generated by Eval(e_j).
2. the actions Eval(e_i) for $i \geq 2$;
3. the actions *return(i; "primes")*, *return(i)*, and *return(i;b)* for every $i \geq 2$ and $b = 0, 1$. The action *return(i; "primes")* is the return action of the first eval process of Eval(e_i); the action *return(i)* is used by the second eval process of Eval(e_i), and the action *return(i;b)* is used by the third eval process of Eval(e_i), where b is the value returned.
4. the local actions of the processes, including the print actions increments actions, testing, and setting of variables. Note that this includes the actions that sets value of the (local) variable(s) ok.

A trace in $traces_{PF}$ is composed by interleaving $3 \times N - 2$ local traces, one for the main process and $3 \times (N - 1)$ for the processes generated by each Eval. The trace of the main process, assuming no blocking occurs, is

$$\iota^* \mathrm{Eval}(e_2), \iota^*, \ldots, \iota^* \mathrm{Eval}(e_N), \iota^* \, \mathrm{Rd}^1(T_2), \ldots, \iota^*, \mathrm{Rd}^1(T_N), \iota^* \qquad (1)$$

where every ι^* denotes a finite sequence of internal actions, the last of which ends with a *print(c)* actions (where c is the number of 1 entries in the table). If blocking does occur, the trace of the main process is a prefix of Trace 1 that ends with a Rd action.

Each $\mathtt{Eval}(e_i)$ generates three processes. The trace of the first one is

$$return(i, \text{"primes"});$$

the trace of the second one is
$$return(i);$$

the trace of the third one is either

$$\iota^*, \mathtt{Rd}^i(T_2), \ldots, \iota^*, \mathtt{Rd}^i(T_{\lfloor\sqrt{i}\rfloor}), \iota^* return(prime(i))$$

if no blocking occurs, of a prefix of it that ends with a $\mathtt{Rd}$ if a blocking occurs.

A trace τ of PrimeFinder is obtained by interleaving the above $3 \times N - 2$ traces so that no action of a process generated by an $\mathtt{Eval}$ occurs before the $\mathtt{Eval}$, and no $\mathtt{Rd}$ returns (and the next action of the process issuing the $\mathtt{Rd}$ occurs in τ) before the tuple it reads is in tuple space, i.e., the corresponding three *returns* occur.

Thus, the PrimeFinder system consists of the set of actions described above, and the traces that includes, for every $N \geq 2$, all traces that satisfy the trace definition above.

5.3 $\mathcal{A}$: An ALS for PrimeFinder

We describe an ALS $\mathcal{A}$ that can run PrimeFinder, and is minimal in the sense that each of its member sets—the set of tuples, templates, processes, and actions— is a subset (modulo renaming) of the corresponding member set of any other ALS in which PrimeFinder can run.

$\mathcal{A}$'s Tuples, Templates, and Processes The set G^A of ground elements consists of the string "primes" and the set of non-negative integers. The set of tuples is $T^A = \{t_i : i \geq 2\}$, and the set of templates is $\bar{T}^A = \{T_i : i \geq 2\}$.

There is one autonomous process in the system, P_1, that runs the main program. For every $i \geq 2$, there is one process group, $P_i = \{P_i^1, P_i^2, P_i^3\}$, the role of each is the role of the first, second, and third processes in Section 5.2. of p_i^1, p_i^2, and p_i^3 above. The differences between the processes here and those of Section 5.2 is their respective sets of actions, since ALS actions differ from "real" program actions. The set $\mathcal{P}^A$ of processes consists of P_1 together with the set of $\{P_i^j : i \geq 2, 1 \leq j \leq 3\}$.

$\mathcal{A}$'s Actions and the set $acts'$ The set $acts(\mathcal{A})$ is straightforward to define since it is uniquely defined by the tuples, templates, and processes. Note, however, that PrimeFinder requires a strict subset of the actions (this is also obvious from $acts_{PF}$) and let $acts'$ denote that minimal set. Then $acts'$ includes $\mathtt{Invoke\text{-}Rd}(P, T)$ and $\mathtt{Respond\text{-}Rd}(P, t)$ for every process $P \in \mathcal{P}^A$, template $T \in \bar{T}^A$, and tuple $t \in T^A$, $\mathtt{Start}(P_1, P_1)$, $\mathtt{Start}(P_1, P_i)$ for process group P_i, $i \geq 2$, and the $\mathtt{Finish}$ actions: $\mathtt{Finish}(P_i^1, \text{"primes"})$, $\mathtt{Finish}(P_i^2, i)$ and $\mathtt{Finish}(P_i^3, prime(i))$ for every $i \geq 2$.

5.4 𝒜-Traces

The definition of 𝒜-traces follows immediately from the definition of traces in Section 3. Here we present a discussion of some of the properties of the ALS traces.

All of 𝒜's that are not in *acts'* are actions that do not correspond to actions in $acts_{PF}$. Consequently, many 𝒜-traces do not have corresponding runs of PrimeFinder. There are also many 𝒜-traces that are over *acts'* that do not have corresponding runs of PrimeFinder. E.g., consider a program similar to PrimeFinder, only where entries to the table are read by processes in reverse order. This new program has 𝒜 for its ALS, whose set of actions can be restricted in the same way. Yet the traces that correspond to it are different that those corresponding to PrimeFinder. There are other programs that share the same ALS. The construction of the ALS guarantees some abstract system that captures the program. In fact, the ALS we construct is minimal in the sense described above. However, it allows all possible traces over its actions, thus, we expect it to include traces that have no corresponding runs in the system that is abstracts.

5.5 Mapping *traces*$_{PF}$ to 𝒜-traces

Let τ be a trace of PrimeFinder as described in Section 5.4. We construct a sequence $\mu(\tau)$ over $acts_A$ that corresponds to τ following the procedure outlined in Section 4.

1. For every $\mathrm{Rd}^j(T)$ in τ that is not the last local action of its issuing process P (P_1 or P_j^3 if $j > 1$), add the action $\mathrm{Respond\text{-}Rd}(P, t)$ to $\mu(\tau)$ just before the next action of p, where t is the tuple *("primess", i, ok)* with *ok* denoting the value set to the variable *ok* of P after the Rd.
2. Remove from $\mu(\tau)$ all the local ι actions.
3. Rename actions in $\mu(\tau)$ according to Table 3.

τ action	$\mu(tau)$ action
Eval(e_i)	Start(P_1, P_i)
Rd^1(T_i)	Invoke-Rd(P_1, T_1)
Rd^j(T_i)	Invoke-Rd(P_i^3, T_i)
return(i, "primes")	Finish(P_i^1, "primes")
return(i)	Finish(P_i^2, i)
return(i, b)	Finish(P_i^3, b)

Table 3. Renaming actions in τ'

4. Add the action $\mathrm{Start}(P_1, P_1)$ at the beginning of of $\mu(\tau)$.

From the discussion in Section 5.2 and the construction of $\mu(tau)$ it follows that $\mu(\tau)$ satisfied the safety and local properties of traces. If, in addition, τ are fair (under any reasonable defintion of fairness), thus no blocking occurs, then it is east to see that $\mu(\tau)$ is also fair. Thus, if τ is fair, then μ maps it into an $\mathcal{A}$-trace.

6 Applications

First and foremost, having a formal semantics to Linda allows determining whether the many systems that have been suggested as Linda systems are indeed so. All that is required is to verify that the system satisfies the axioms described by the requirements of the ALS traces.

The power of Linda is that it separates the coordination aspects of a system from its computational aspects. Temporal logic is a powerful verification tool for concurrency, hence it only makes sense to use temporal reasoning for the Linda part of a Linda system—exactly the part that our semantics captures. See, e.g., [4] for examples of temporal properties of Linda computations.

Ideally, we would like to use (linear-time propositional) temporal logic [14] for formal reasoning about Linda programs. Having a trace semantics for Linda makes this seem feasible. However, the theory of unordered message buffers in temporal logic is highly undecidable (Π_1^1-complete) ([17]), that is, the problem of determining whether a temporal logic formula is satisfied by all sequences of read and write actions to an unordered message buffer is highly undecidable. Thus, a complete axiom system for Linda is not feasible. In fact, it is not even possible to specify the necessary safety and liveness axioms in temporal logic (see, e.g., [8]). Yet, in many Linda applications that we are aware of, the Ins and Outs have some structure that often result in systems that do lend themselves to temporal verification. We will present more details about temporal reasoning for Linda systems in [18].

Our semantics also sheds light on many issues that were a source of confusion in the past. We list here two examples. More will be given in the full version of this paper.

The first example is that of the nature of blocking operations. The meaning of non-blocking operations is straightforward—they merely have to produce a correct result. There is, however, some confusion in the Linda community as to when operations are allowed to block. A common way of avoiding the issue is to allow only for finite traces (see, e.g., [7]). However, reactive systems in general and Linda systems in particular are expected to be able to carry out lengthy interactions with their environment that is, for any practical purpose, infinite. (After all, we don't really expect our ATM machine, or our operating system, to stop periodically.) The Linda systems developed at Yale have a $fair_2$ fairness. We would like to believe that every Linda system has a fairness property that describes when operations can block. If one is to attribute meaning to blocking, this fairness property should be made explicit.

The second example is that of pairwise communication. In the past, Linda has been set apart as a model that allows only for symmetric coordination, and does not allow for pairwise communication, and consequently, for secure communication (see, e.g., [3, 16, ?]). However, this is an oversight, since one can define the templates such that pairwise communication is allowed. Security can also be obtained, at least at the level that any known digital cryptosystem allows. To see this, observe that, while in most cases templates are expressed by (anti-) tuples that have either actual values that have to be matched, or formal values whose type has to match, there is no requirement that this always be the case. We can have a tuple that, for example, has a "lock" in one of its fields. For a template to match this tuple, the template much have the appropriate "key." Using this simple lock-key in its many variations, one can guarantee that only certain processes may Out, and only certain processes may In or Rd some tuples.

The last application of the formal Linda semantics is that Linda is quite useful as a specification language. Its formal semantics allows for formal semantics for the system it specifies. The next section is an example of one such system.

7 LifeStream and its Linda Specification

A LifeStream is a free-floating cyberspace data structure designed to capture an entire electronic life. A *free-floating cyberspace data structure* (or cyberstructure) is a collection of information that can be reached from any internet-connected computer. Cyberstructures are successors to the "distributed data structures" supported in Linda. Linda supports data structures that are directly accessible from within arbitrarily-many disjoint address spaces, and can be safely shared by arbitrarily-many concurrent processes; a cyberstructure has the same characteristics, with respect to any collection of net-connected nodes. A user can "tune in" his personal cyberstructure from his Unix machine at work, Mac at home, generic PC at the supermarket and so on. A present-day LifeStream is designed to capture all the documents a user creates online, all that he sends and receives, and any other bits of information, from rolodex cards to appointment reminders to Web bookmarks, that are stored online. It is also designed to organize and store the much greater volume and variety of data that will exist online in the near future, from utility bills through birth certificates.

In a LifeStream, every chunk of information belonging to some user (every document, every piece of email) is stored on a single time-ordered stream. When you tune in the system, you see a stream of documents receding into the distance; farther away in imaginary space means farther back in time. When you create a new document or when one arrives (via email, for example) from elsewhere, a new document pops up at the end of the stream. To create a new document, you press the "new" button to get an empty box ready to fill, or clone, an old document to get a new copy that can be altered. You don't need to name documents (although you can); documents are located by attribute and chronology, not by name. The "find" button creates a substream—you can ask for "all documents that mention Sheboygan," "all letters to Schwartz," "my last letter to Schwartz" and so on. In response, the system shows you the sub-portion of the stream consisting only of the documents you've specified. Substreams persist until you kill them; a newly-arriving letter from Schwartz gets dumped in the main stream and also appears in the "letters to Schwartz" substream. When you press the "squish" button you get a one-screen summary of a substream, where the type of summary depends on the type of information in the substream. Sending email consists of copying from one stream to another. To run an application, you create a new window as you do for a new document; the application runs inside, and the output it generates is stored and retrieved like any other document. The stream has a future as well as a past; appointments and calendar items are stored there, and become visible when their creation-times arrive (or when you go to the future on purpose to look around).

The simplicity of LifeStreams' formal structure (i.e., the fact that it's merely a "class", etc.) suggests that it ought to be possible to specify the behavior of the system formally. The goal in doing so isn't to prove theorems about the system, but to explain in a simple but precise way what the system is and how it behaves. Because a central characteristic of the system is the fact that it defines a "cyberstructure", Linda proves to be a good basis for a formal LifeStreams specification.

7.1 Linda Specifications for LifeStreams

A LifeStream is a set of tuples over which the primitives *append* and *scan* are defined. The set T of tuples is partitioned into:

1. LifeStream-*elements:* 3-ary tuples of the form

   (LSid, index, value)

   where LSid is taken from a set of LifeStream identifiers, **index** is some positive integer, and **value** is some legal entry in a LifeStream (e.g., a document), and

2. LifeStream-*tails:* 3-ary tuples of the form

   (LSid, TAIL, number)

   where LSid is a valid LifeStream identifier, TAIL is a special symbol occurring only in the second position of LifeStream-tails, and **number** is some non-negative integer denoting the current length of the lifestream LSid. Initially, the tuple space contains a (single) copy of the object **(LSid, TAIL, 0)** for each lifestream.

Not every tuple space over T is valid; each element of T must have a multiplicity of at most one, and, if a lifestream's tail defines its length to be some $k > 0$, then the tuple space must include all the first k elements of the lifestream (and no element beyond that). The requirements of valid LifeStream tuple spaces are defined implicitly in the Linda-based definitions of the LifeStream primitives below.

Append adds a tuple to a lifestream. If a lifestream has a tail (length) **MAX**, then **Append(LSid, NewDoc)** adds **NewDoc** to the the stream and increments **Max**. In general, **Append(LSid, NewDoc)** is expressed by the following sequence of Linda commands:

```
In      (LSid, TAIL, ?x)
Out     (LSid, x, NewDoc)
Out     (LSid, TAIL, ++x)
```

where "**(LSid, TAIL, ?x)**" is a template matching a tuple of type LifeStream-*tails* whose first field is **LSid** (for valid lifestreams there is only one such tuple) and whose third field is stored in the formal parameter x.

Read returns a specific tuple from a lifestream. If the lifestream contains at least k elements, then **Read(LSid, k)** returns the kth element. **Read(LSid, k)** is expressed by the following Linda command:

```
Rd (LSid, k, ?val)
```

These are the only primitives that we need to define LifeStreams. It is assumed that invocations of these primitives are all serializable [2]. Roughly speaking, this means that any execution of these operations is indistinguishable from some execution where each primitive is performed atomically. This amounts to requiring that no two **Appends** to the same LifeStream interleave.

All of the LifeStream operations, *New, Clone, Find, Copy* and *Squish*, are straight forward to express with **Append** and **Read**.
New is defined by:

```
proc New(LSid, NewDoc)
{
    Append (LSid, NewDoc)
}
```

Clone is defined by:

```
proc Copy(LSid, k)
{
    NewDoc := Read (LSid, k)
    Append (LSid, NewDoc)
}
```

Find is defined by:

```
proc Find(LSid, SQ)
{
    List substream
    In (LSid, TAIL, ?len)
    for i := 1 to len
        if (SQ(Read(LSid, i))) add_to_list(substream, i)
    return substream
}
```

here *Find* iterates over the stream LSid, applying the search query to each document. The result is a list of element (document) identifiers that make up the substream.[2]

Copy is defined by:

```
proc Clone(S_LSid, D_LSid,  k)
{
    Doc := Read (S_LSid, k)
    Append (D_LSid, Doc)
}
```

and *Squish* is defined by:

```
proc Squish(LSid, SQ)
{
    summarize_SQ (Find (LSid, SQ));
}
```

where **summarize_SQ** is an appropriate summary type for the search query SQ. Summarize works by iterating over the documents in the substream (created by the search query SQ) and combining the data into an overview.

8 Future Directions

We have presented a simple, operational, trace-based, semantics to Linda. This allows us to tell tell whether Linda implementations really do what they ought to; it sheds light on some issues that were unclear before: the meaning of blocking operations and Linda's general communication mechanisms; it also enables one to use Linda in new ways, which have seemed interesting and attractive for some time but don't make sense without a formal Linda semantics. Linda's clarity, simplicity and power suggest that specifications in Linda would be relatively simple to build and understand—and of course they could easily be executable, if that were desirable.

In the future we are planning to investigate whether other interesting coordination systems can be defined with Linda — previous work [11] (along with our own) leads us to believe that Linda is a useful model beyond its traditional use in parallel systems. We also plan extend our formal Lifestream model in incorporate the new "future" time, mutable documents, and a rich form of search queries.

References

1. Y. Afek, H. Attiya, A. Fekete, M. J. Fischer, N. A. Lynch, Y. Mansour, D. Wang, and L. D. Zuck. Reliable communication over unreliable channels. *Journal of the ACM*, 41(6):1267–1297, 1994.

---

[2] In actual implementation more efficient means would be used.

2. P.A. Bernstein, V. Hadzilacos, and N. Goodman. *Concurrency Control and Recovery in Database Systems*. Addison-Wesley, 1987.
3. S. Bijnens, W. Joosen, and P. Verbaeten. Sender-initiated and recevier-initiated coordination in a global object space. In O. Ciancarini, O. Nierstrasz, and A. Yonezawa, editors, *Object-Based Models and Languages for Concurrent Systems*, pages 14–28. Springer Verlag, LNCS 924, 1994.
4. N. Brown. Conrrectness-preserving transformations for the design of parallel programs. In O. Ciancarini, O. Nierstrasz, and A. Yonezawa, editors, *Object-Based Models and Languages for Concurrent Systems*, pages 29–48. Springer Verlag, LNCS 924, 1994.
5. P. Butcher. A behavioral semantics for Linda-2. *IEEE Software Engineering Journal*, 6(4):196–204, 7 1991.
6. N. Carriero and D. Gelernter. *How to Write Parallel Programs: A First Course*. MIT Press, 1990.
7. P. Ciancarini, K. K. Jensen, and D. Yankelevich. On the operational semantics of a coordination language. In O. Ciancarini, O. Nierstrasz, and A. Yonezawa, editors, *Object-Based Models and Languages for Concurrent Systems*, pages 77–106. Springer Verlag, LNCS 924, 1994.
8. E.A. Emerson. Temporal and modal logic. In J. van Leeuwen, editor, *Handbook of Theoretical Computer Science, Volume B: Formal models and Semantics*, pages 995–1072. The MIT Press/Elsevier, 1990.
9. D. Harel and A. Pnueli. On the development of reactive systems. In K. R. Apt, editor, *Logics and Models of Concurrent Systems*, Lecture Notes in Computer Science, pages 477–498. Springer-Verlag, 1985.
10. C. A. R. Hoare. *Communicating Sequential Processes*. Prentice-Hall, Englewood Cliffs, NJ, 1985.
11. S. Hupfer, D. Kaminsky, N. Carriero, and D. Gelernter. Coordination applications of Linda. In *Proceedings of Irisa/Inria Conference on Research Directions in High-Level Parallel Programming Languages*. Mont Saint-Michel, June 1991.
12. S. Jagannathan. Semantics and analysis of first-class tuple-spaces. Technical Report DCS/RR-783, 4 1990.
13. Gilles Kahn. The semantics of a simple language for parallel programming. In *Information Processing, 74*, pages 471–475, Amsterdam, 1974. North Holland.
14. Z. Manna and A. Pnueli. *The Temporal Logic of Reactive and Concurrent Systems (Specification)*. Springer-Verlag, 1992.
15. Robin Milner. *A calculus of Communicating Systems*, volume 92 of *Lecture Notes in Computer Science*. Springer-Verlag, New York, 1980.
16. N. H. Minsky and J. Leichter. Law-governed linda as a coordination model. In O. Ciancarini, O. Nierstrasz, and A. Yonezawa, editors, *Object-Based Models and Languages for Concurrent Systems*, pages 125–146. Springer Verlag, LNCS 924, 1994.
17. A. P. Sistla, E. M. Clarke, N. Francez, and A. R. Meyer. Can message buffers be axiomatized in linear temporal logic? *Infomation and Control*, 63(1/2):88–112, 1984.
18. L. Zuck. Temporal reasoning of Linda system. In preparation, 1997.

Three Semantics of the Output Operation for Generative Communication*

Nadia Busi[1]   Roberto Gorrieri[2]   Gianluigi Zavattaro[2]

[1] Dipartimento di Matematica, Università di Siena,
Via del Capitano 15, I-53100 Siena, Italy
e-mail: busi@cs.unibo.it
[2] Dipartimento di Scienze dell'Informazione, Università di Bologna,
Mura Anteo Zamboni 7, I-40127 Bologna, Italy
e-mail: {gorrieri,zavattar}@cs.unibo.it

Abstract. A simple, yet Turing powerful, calculus based on generative communication is introduced; among its primitives, it contains a conditional input operation that tests for presence (or absence) of an output, reminiscent of the *inp* predicate of Linda. We study three different operational semantics for the output operation, called *instantaneous, ordered* and *unordered*. The associated behavioural semantics are obtained as the coarsest congruence contained in the corresponding strong barbed semantics. We prove that when the output operation is *instantaneous*, the obtained semantics is a sort of asynchronous bisimulation; on the contrary, for the *ordered* semantics, as well as for the *unordered* one, the resulting semantics is a small variant of the classic (synchronous) bisimulation. A further result is that the language under *unordered* semantics is no more Turing powerful, hence the language becomes strictly less expressive.

1 Introduction

Generative communication, realized by means of the insertion and withdrawal of elements from a shared multiset, is the peculiar feature of a family of coordination languages [GC92], of which Linda [Gel85] is the most prominent representative. This communication mechanism is based on the following principles: a sender communicates with a receiver through a shared data space (called *tuple space*, TS for short), where emitted messages are collected; the receiver can consume the message from TS; a message generated by a process has an independent existence in the tuple space until it is explicitly withdrawn by a receiver; in fact, after its insertion in TS, a message becomes equally accessible to all processes, but it is bound to none. Hence, the communication is asynchronous because the sender may proceed just after performing the emission of a message to the TS. Similarly, the receiver can input a message present in TS at any time: a handshake synchronization between TS and the receiver completes the communication

---

* Work supported by Esprit Working Group Coordina.

between the sender and the receiver, with the side-effect of removing the message from TS.

Besides the non-blocking output operation $out(a)$ (that sends message a to the tuple space) and the blocking input operation $in(a)$ (that removes message a from TS), Linda also offers a conditional input predicate, called $inp(a)$, that checks the current status of TS; if the required message a is absent, the value $false$ is returned; on the contrary, if the message is found, its behavior is the same as the in operation and the value $true$ is returned. We represent this predicate by means of an $if\text{-}then\text{-}else$ construct $inp(a)?P_-Q$; it directs the flow of control to P or to Q, depending on the presence or absence of message a in TS.

The main aim of this paper is an investigation about possible semantics for generative communication in a process algebraic setting, with particular care to the output operation that, in our opinion, has not yet received enough attention.

Conceptually, the execution of the Linda-like output primitive $out(a)$ can be seen as composed of two phases: the $emission$ of the message a (sending a to the TS) and the $rendering$ of a (actual presence of a in the TS, we denote with $\langle a \rangle$). The three semantics we are going to investigate are inspired by previous related proposals (e.g., of the asynchronous object calculus of [HT91]), as well as by the informal semantics of Linda reported in the reference manual [SCA95]. The three different semantics may be summarized as follows:

- $Instantaneous$: With $out(a)$ we mean that the message is already in the TS. Hence, $out(a).P = \langle a \rangle | P$, where $|$ is the parallel composition operator. For instance, consider a process P that wants to input a and a process $out(a)$; if composed in parallel, P can immediately input message a. This approach has been adopted in the asynchronous π-calculus [HT91, Bou92]; it is obtained by means of a simple syntactic restriction to that language: outputs cannot be used as prefixes. Consider processes $P = \mu.out(a_1)$ and $Q = \mu.(out(a_1)|out(a_2)| \ldots |out(a_n))$, where μ is any non output prefix; in one single $atomic$ step, P executes action μ and puts $\langle a_1 \rangle$ in the TS, while Q executes action μ and puts messages $\langle a_1 \rangle, \ldots, \langle a_n \rangle$ in the TS.
- $Ordered$: The emission and the rendering of one message form together one single autonomous atomic action: $out(a).P$ becomes in one (internal) step the agent $\langle a \rangle | P$. In this way, the order of emission is respected by the rendering order. The implementation of $out(a)$ is simple: the sender sends the message a and then waits for the acknowledgement from the TS; hence, the emission of a message is realized by means of a synchronous hand-shake communication between the sender and the TS. This approach has already received an operational treatment in [HKH95] and [CGZ96].
- $Unordered$: The emission and the rendering of one message are distinct autonomous actions. Hence, $out(a).P$ emits message a becoming the agent $\langle\langle a \rangle\rangle | P$ in one (internal) step, where P is free to proceed, but message a is not yet present in the TS; indeed, $\langle\langle a \rangle\rangle$ takes one further internal step to become $\langle a \rangle$. The implementation of the $out(a)$ operation is trivial: the process $out(a).P$ sends the message a to the TS, and proceeds without waiting

for the message to reach the TS; hence, the emission is realized by means of an asynchronous communication between the sender and the TS. Thus the order of emission may not to be respected by the rendering order: for instance, if a process executes the sequence $out(a).out(b)$, then a may be rendered before or after the emission of b, or even after the rendering of b. To the best of our knowledge, we do not know of any other papers studying the semantics of this approach.

In Section 2 we introduce the syntax of our process algebra and the three operational semantics for the *out* primitive, comparing their differencies with one instructive example.

Section 3 studies the behavioural semantics for the three operational semantics, following the approach of [MS92]: firstly, identify the internal transitions, then define the observable actions, and finally find the coarsest congruence contained in the barbed semantics (a very coarse equivalence that equates processes that are bisimilar on internal actions and offer, at any pair of related states, the same observable actions).

The main results of the paper are that a variant of the asynchronous bisimulation [ACS96] is the right semantics for the instantaneous semantics, while the correct semantics for the other two cases is a variant of the classic (synchronous) bisimulation [Mil89], where inputs and outputs are treated symmetrically. All the resulting three congruences are different and not included one in the others.

Section 4 discusses the expressiveness of our calculus under the three semantics. We show that, for the instantaneous and ordered semantics, it is possible to encode a Random Access Machine (RAM) [SS63], a Turing equivalent formalism. On the contrary, it is possible to prove that our calculus is not Turing powerful under the unordered semantics [BGZ97b].

Finally, Section 5 reports some conclusive remarks.

2 The Language and its Operational Semantics

The syntax of our language is defined by the following grammar:

$$P ::= \langle a \rangle \mid C \mid P|P \mid P \backslash a$$
$$C ::= 0 \mid out(a).C \mid in(a).C \mid inp(a)?C\_C \mid C|C \mid X \mid rec\,X.C$$

Agents, ranged over by P, Q, ..., consist of the parallel composition of the messages already in the TS (each one denoted by one agent $\langle a \rangle$ where a, b, ..., are used to range over the possible messages) and the concurrent programs denoted by C, D, ..., sharing the tuples. We use also a restriction operator in order to have the possibility of defining the scope of message names. A program C can be a terminated program 0 (which is usually omitted for the sake of simplicity), a program starting with a coordination primitive (*in*, *out*, and *inp*), or the parallel composition of two programs.

The coordination primitives $out(a)$ and $in(a)$ can be represented as usual prefixes, while $inp(a)$ requires a sort of *if-then-else* construct. In fact, $inp(a)?C\_D$

$$
\begin{array}{ll}
(i) & P|Q \equiv Q|P \\[2mm]
(ii) & (P|Q)|R \equiv P|(Q|R) \\[2mm]
(iii) & P|0 \equiv P \\[2mm]
(iv) & rec\,X.P \equiv P[rec\,X.P/X]
\end{array}
$$

Table 1. Structural congruence.

is a program which requires the message a to be consumed; if a is present, it is removed and the program C is executed, otherwise D is chosen. Recursively defined programs are also considered, by allowing program variables (denoted by X, Y, ...) and by introducing an operator for closed and guarded recursion $rec\,X.C$. In the following *Agent* denotes the set containing all possible agents.

We present three different operational semantics for our language, one for each kind of output prefix introduced in the previous section. The semantics are presented in two steps. First, we define *structural congruences* over agents; this relations capture the fact that, for example, the order of the terms in a parallel composition has no effects on its behaviour. Next, we define *labeled transition systems* specifying how agents evolve by means of the actions performed by some program in it.

The structural congruence for the *instantaneous* semantics $\equiv_i$ is the smallest congruence satisfying the rules (i), ..., (iv) of Table 1 and (v) of Table 3. The structural congruences for the *ordered* and *unordered* semantics denoted with $\equiv_o$ and $\equiv_u$ are instead defined both as the smallest congruence satisfying only (i), ..., (iv).

The labelled transition systems are of the kind (*Agent*, *Label*, $\longrightarrow$) where $Label = \{\tau, a, \overline{a}, \neg a\}$ (ranged over by α, β, ...) is the set of the possible labels. The labelled transition relation $\longrightarrow_i$ for the *instantaneous* semantics is the smallest one satisfying the axioms and rules from (1) to (10) in Table 2; $\longrightarrow_o$ for the *ordered* semantics is the one satisfying (1)...(10) and the axiom (11) of Table 3; while $\longrightarrow_u$ for the unordered semantics considers the axioms and rules (1)...(10), (12) and (13). The indexes i, o, and u distinguishing the three structural congruences and transition relations, are omitted when they are made clear by the context.

Axiom (1) shows that the tuple $\langle a \rangle$ is able to give its contents to the environment, by performing an action labeled with $\overline{a}$. Axioms (2) and (3) define the possible input actions on the message a (action labeled with a), according to the execution of an *in* or a successful *inp* operation, respectively. If a process executing an *inp* does not find the required message a, it can guess its absence by performing an action labeled with $\neg a$ (axiom (4)). Rule (5) states that no

(1)	$\langle a \rangle \xrightarrow{\bar{a}} 0$	(2)	$in(a).P \xrightarrow{a} P$

$$(3) \quad inp(a)?P\_Q \xrightarrow{a} P \qquad\qquad (4) \quad inp(a)?P\_Q \xrightarrow{\neg a} Q$$

$$(5) \quad \frac{P \xrightarrow{\alpha} P'}{P\backslash a \xrightarrow{\alpha} P'\backslash a} \quad \alpha \notin \{a, \bar{a}, \neg a\} \qquad (6) \quad \frac{P \xrightarrow{\neg a} P'}{P\backslash a \xrightarrow{\tau} P'\backslash a}$$

$$(7) \quad \frac{P \xrightarrow{\neg a} P' \quad Q \xrightarrow{\bar{a}}\!\!\!\!\not\;\;}{P|Q \xrightarrow{\neg a} P'|Q} \qquad\qquad (8) \quad \frac{P \xrightarrow{a} P' \quad Q \xrightarrow{\bar{a}} Q'}{P|Q \xrightarrow{\tau} P'|Q'}$$

$$(9) \quad \frac{P \xrightarrow{\alpha} P'}{P|Q \xrightarrow{\alpha} P'|Q} \quad \alpha \neq \neg a \qquad (10) \quad \frac{P \equiv Q \quad Q \xrightarrow{\alpha} Q' \quad P' \equiv Q'}{P \xrightarrow{\alpha} P'}$$

Table 2. Operational semantics.

actions containing the name a can be performed by the agent $P\backslash a$. When an agent P willing to perform a $\neg a$ operation is restricted on the name a, its $\neg a$ operation becomes a local step of computation (i.e. labeled with τ) because no further agents can offer message a; in other words, the search for a has finished because it has become a local name (rule (6)). On the other hand, if P is composed in parallel with another agent Q, the executability of $\neg a$ by $P|Q$ depends on the inability of Q to offer message a. Otherwise, the guess of P is wrong and this $\neg a$ operation cannot be executed (rule (7)). The other rules are the usual for synchronization between complementary actions (8), local actions in parallel composed agents (9), and possibility of executing the same actions for structurally congruent agents (10). There are no rules for recursion because its semantics is defined by the congruence rule (v) which applies one unfolding step to a recursively defined program.

Rule (7) uses a negative premise; it's easy to see that our transition system specification is strictly stratifiable [Gro93], thus there exists a unique transition system agreeing with it.

Instantaneous:	(v)	$out(a).P \equiv \langle a \rangle | P$
Ordered:	(11)	$out(a).P \xrightarrow{\tau} \langle a \rangle | P$
Unordered:	(12)	$out(a).P \xrightarrow{\tau} \langle\langle a \rangle\rangle | P$
	(13)	$\langle\langle a \rangle\rangle \xrightarrow{\tau} \langle a \rangle$

Table 3. Three semantics for the *out* primitive.

The rules which differentiate the three semantics are presented in Table 3. Following the *instantaneous* approach messages have to be considered already available at the moment an output operation has to be performed. This is obtained by introducing a further rule for the structural congruence stating that a program starting with the prefix *out(a)* is the same as putting the tuple ⟨a⟩ in parallel with the continuation of the program.

In the *ordered* approach the output operation consists of one local non-blocking action labeled with τ which creates the tuple ⟨a⟩. In this way, when a sequence of output is executed, the messages are rendered in the same order they are emitted.

In the *unordered* approach, the execution of an output operation emitting the message a does not directly generate the corresponding tuple ⟨a⟩, but it creates an agent which will make message a available only after a non predictable delay. This agent, denoted by ⟨⟨a⟩⟩,[3] is only able to perform an internal action labelled with τ becoming ⟨a⟩.

Example 1. An example, inspired by [SCA95], allows us to show the differences among the three semantics. Consider P and Q below where the only difference between them is the order of emission of the messages a and b:

$$P \stackrel{def}{=} (out(a).out(b) \mid in(a).inp(b)?C\_D)\backslash a\backslash b$$
$$Q \stackrel{def}{=} (out(b).out(a) \mid in(a).inp(b)?C\_D)\backslash a\backslash b$$

The message names a and b are considered as local names in order to be sure that the *in* and *inp* operations on these names are executed locally.

In the *instantaneous* semantics the messages a and b becomes available in the same instant, hence when the testing process consumes a and executes the *inp(b)* primitive the required message is found and consumed. Hence, the *inp* continuation is C for both P and Q.

Under the *ordered* semantics the messages a and b become available in the same order they are emitted. In this case the test performed by the *inp* operation in P and Q gives rise to two different results. The presence of the message b is ensured only in Q, where b becomes available before a; hence the continuation of the *inp* operation is D. Instead, in P the presence or the absence of the tuple b at the instant the *inp* is executed, depends on the order of execution of the operations: if the *inp* primitive is performed before the *out(b)* operation, then the message b is not found (the continuation is D), otherwise it is found and consumed (the continuation is C).

The *unordered* semantics shows a third kind of behaviour because the messages a and b become available in an unpredictable order, hence the search performed by the *inp* operation can give rise to a success or a failure in both P and Q.

---

[3] The syntax for the agents P is extended in the case of unordered output semantics by allowing P to be also the agent ⟨⟨a⟩⟩.

211

The behaviours of the agents P and Q under the three different semantics are summarized by showing the possible continuations of the *inp* operator:

	Instantaneous	Ordered	Unordered
P	C	C/D	C/D
Q	C	C	C/D

∎

3 Behavioural Semantics

In this section the problem of defining observational semantics for the three different operational semantics is considered. The approach we follow consists in investigating the coarsest congruence contained in the *barbed bisimulation* [MS92] for the three semantics. In order to define barbed bisimulation we have to introduce the notion of *reduction* and *commitments*.

In our language, we consider as reductions not only the usual derivations labeled with τ, but also those labeled with $\neg a$. In fact, a derivation $P \xrightarrow{\neg a} P'$ indicates that P can become P' if no tuples $\langle a \rangle$ are available in the external environment. Hence, if P is stand–alone (i.e. without external environment), it can be considered able to become P'. Indeed, the label $\neg a$ has been introduced only for helping an SOS formulation of the semantics, while it is conceptually an internal step. Formally:

$P \longrightarrow P'$ iff $P \xrightarrow{\tau} P'$ or $P \xrightarrow{\neg a} P'$ for some a

As in [ACS96] the notion of commitments is defined taking care that we are dealing with a calculus having asynchronous communication. The fact that an observer has no direct way of knowing if the message he has sent has been received is reflected by imposing that only *output* commitments are taken into account.

$P \downarrow \bar{a}$ iff $P \xrightarrow{\bar{a}} P'$ for some P'
$P \Downarrow \bar{a}$ iff $P \longrightarrow^* P'$ and $P' \downarrow \bar{a}$ for some P'

We also define a *weak* commitment $\Downarrow \bar{a}$ in order to be able to denote the possibility of a certain commitment after some reduction steps.

Definition 1. A binary, symmetric relation $\mathcal{R}$ on *Agent* is a *barbed bisimulation* if $(P, Q) \in \mathcal{R}$ implies:

- if $P \longrightarrow P'$ then there exists Q' such that $Q \longrightarrow Q'$ and $(P', Q') \in \mathcal{R}$;
- if $P \downarrow \bar{a}$ then $Q \downarrow \bar{a}$.

Two agents P and Q are *barbed bisimilar*, written $P \overset{\bullet}{\sim} Q$, if there exists a barbed bisimulation $\mathcal{R}$ such that $(P, Q) \in \mathcal{R}$. ∎

As already stated we investigate the coarsest congruence contained in the barbed bisimulation for the three semantics. In the *instantaneous* case we have obtained the following *asynchronous ¬-bisimulation*.

Definition 2. A binary, symmetric relation $\mathcal{R}$ on *Agent* is an *asynchronous* ¬-*bisimulation* if $(P, Q) \in \mathcal{R}$ implies:

- if $P \xrightarrow{\bar{a}} P'$ then there exists Q' such that $Q \xrightarrow{\bar{a}} Q'$ and $(P', Q') \in \mathcal{R}$;
- if $P \xrightarrow{\tau} P'$ then there exists Q' such that
    - either $Q \xrightarrow{\tau} Q'$ and $(P', Q') \in \mathcal{R}$
    - or there exist b and Q'' such that $Q \xrightarrow{\neg b} Q'$, $(P', Q') \in \mathcal{R}$, $Q \xrightarrow{b} Q''$ and $(P'|\langle b \rangle, Q'') \in \mathcal{R}$;
- if $P \xrightarrow{\neg a} P'$ then there exists Q' such that
    - either $Q \xrightarrow{\neg a} Q'$ and $(P', Q') \in \mathcal{R}$
    - or $Q \xrightarrow{\tau} Q'$ and $(P', Q') \in \mathcal{R}$
    - or there exist b and Q'' such that $Q \xrightarrow{\neg b} Q'$, $(P', Q') \in \mathcal{R}$, $Q \xrightarrow{b} Q''$ and $(P'|\langle b \rangle, Q'') \in \mathcal{R}$;
- if $P \xrightarrow{a} P'$ then there exists Q' such that
    - either $Q \xrightarrow{a} Q'$ and $(P', Q') \in \mathcal{R}$
    - or $Q \xrightarrow{\tau} Q'$ and $(P', Q'|\langle a \rangle) \in \mathcal{R}$
    - or there exist b and Q'' such that $Q \xrightarrow{\neg b} Q'$, $(P', Q'|\langle a \rangle) \in \mathcal{R}$, $Q \xrightarrow{b} Q''$ and $(P'|\langle b \rangle, Q''|\langle a \rangle) \in \mathcal{R}$.

Two agents P and Q are *asynchronous* ¬-*bisimilar*, written $P \sim_a Q$, if there exists an asynchronous ¬-bisimulation $\mathcal{R}$ such that $(P, Q) \in \mathcal{R}$. ∎

In the standard bisimulation [Mil89], a step can be matched only by a step having the same label; in the asynchronous bisimulation [ACS96] an *in* step can be matched also by a τ labelled transition under some conditions. These conditions are the same presented in the final item of the definition of our asynchronous ¬-bisimulation; that is why we call it asynchronous. All the other new matchings allowed by the asynchronous ¬-bisimulation are due to the fact that we deal also with the new kind of label ¬a (that is why we have introduced the symbol ¬ in its name). These matchings can be understood considering P and Q as below, where a is a name not appearing in R:

$$P \stackrel{def}{=} inp(b)?out(b).R\_R$$
$$Q \stackrel{def}{=} (\langle a \rangle | in(a).R) \backslash a$$

The agents P and Q cannot be distinguished under *instantaneous* semantics because they both perform an internal step of computation having no influence on the environment, and then become R.

In order to equate the agents above, the asynchronous ¬-bisimulation must introduce several new matchings. One of them, for example, allows a τ-step to be matched by a transition labeled with b. This is possible if the tuple $\langle b \rangle$ is generated immediately after having consumed it, and if an equivalent continuation can be chosen also if the message b is not present in the environment.

Proposition 3. *For the* instantaneous *semantics* $\sim_a$ *is a congruence.* ∎

Theorem 4. *For the* instantaneous *semantics* $\sim_a$ *is the coarsest congruence contained in* $\overset{\bullet}{\sim}$.

Proof (hint). *As $\sim_a$ is a congruence, it is sufficient to show that for every P and Q barbed bisimilar in every context, there exists $\mathcal{R}$, $\neg$-bisimulation such that $(P, Q) \in \mathcal{R}$. Let $n(S)$ denote the message names appearing in the agent S and $L = n(P) \cup n(Q)$. We use $\prod_{i \in \{1...n\}} P_i$ as a shorthand for $P_1 | \ldots | P_n$. The $\neg$-bisimulation $\mathcal{R}$ is defined as:*

$$\mathcal{R} = \{(P, Q) \mid P|R \overset{\bullet}{\sim} Q|R \text{ and } n(P), n(Q) \subseteq L\}$$

where R is the following context:

$$R = \prod_{l \in L} rec\, X.in(l).out(a_l).in(a_l).X \mid$$
$$\prod_{l \in L} rec\, X.out(b_l).in(b_l).out(l).out(c_l).in(c_l).X$$

where the names a_l, b_l, c_l for all $l \in L$ are supposed to be distinct and fresh. ∎

We now consider the *ordered* and *unordered* semantics. The barbed congruence is no more the asynchronous $\neg$-bisimulation, but a lot of possible matchings between *equivalent* steps are lost.

Definition 5. A binary, symmetric relation $\mathcal{R}$ on *Agent* is a $\neg$-*bisimulation* if $(P, Q) \in \mathcal{R}$ implies:

- if $P \overset{\alpha}{\longrightarrow} P'$, with $\alpha \neq \neg a$, then there exists Q' such that $Q \overset{\alpha}{\longrightarrow} Q'$ and $(P', Q') \in \mathcal{R}$;
- if $P \overset{\neg a}{\longrightarrow} P'$ then there exists Q' such that $(Q \overset{\neg a}{\longrightarrow} Q'$ or $Q \overset{\tau}{\longrightarrow} Q')$ and $(P', Q') \in \mathcal{R}$.

Two agents P and Q are $\neg$-*bisimilar*, written $P \sim Q$, if there exists a $\neg$-bisimulation $\mathcal{R}$ such that $(P, Q) \in \mathcal{R}$. ∎

Proposition 6. *For* ordered *and* unordered *semantics* $\sim$ *is a congruence.* ∎

Theorem 7. *For the* ordered *and* unordered *semantics* $\sim$ *is the coarsest congruence contained in* $\overset{\bullet}{\sim}$.

Proof (hint). *The proofs are similar to the one of Theorem 4, with the context R defined in a different way:*

$$R = \prod_{l \in L} rec\, X.in(l).out(a_l).in(a_l).X \mid$$
$$\prod_{l \in L} rec\, X.inp(l)?out(b_l).X_{-}$$
$$out(l).out(c_l).rec\, Y.inp(b_l)?out(l).Y_{-}in(c_l).X$$

∎

It is interesting to note that the restriction operator is not used in the definition of the context R in both the theorems, hence the results presented in Theorems 4 and 7 are correct also if the restriction operator is eliminated from the language.

A comparison among the equivalences

The equivalence $\sim_a$ on the *instantaneous* semantics and $\sim$ on the *ordered* and *unordered* semantics, infer three different equivalences on the language:

$P \sim_1 Q$ iff $P \sim_a Q$ in the *instantaneous* semantics
$P \sim_2 Q$ iff $P \sim Q$ in the *ordered* semantics
$P \sim_3 Q$ iff $P \sim Q$ in the *unordered* semantics

We show by examples that the three congruences are all different and no one of them is included in the others.

Example 2. Consider the following agents:

$$P \stackrel{def}{=} (out(a).out(b) \mid in(b).inp(a)?out(c)\_out(d))\backslash a\backslash b$$
$$Q \stackrel{def}{=} (out(b).out(a) \mid in(b).inp(a)?out(c)\_out(d))\backslash a\backslash b$$
$$R \stackrel{def}{=} (out(a).out(b) \mid in(b).in(a).out(c))\backslash a\backslash b$$

Under *instantaneous* semantics the three agents are equivalent; $P \sim_1 Q \sim_1 R$ because the unique behaviour the three agents can have is the one in which both the messages a and b are consumed and the new message c is emitted. In the case of *ordered* semantics only P and R are equivalent; $Q \not\sim_2 P \sim_2 R \not\sim_2 Q$ because Q can generate the message d (i.e. $Q \Downarrow \bar{d}$) while P and R can only emit c (i.e. $P, R \not\Downarrow \bar{d}$). In the *unordered* semantics only P and Q are equivalent; $R \not\sim_3 P \sim_3 Q \not\sim_3 R$ because P and Q can generate the message d (i.e. $P, Q \Downarrow \bar{d}$) while R can only emit c (i.e. $R \not\Downarrow \bar{d}$). ∎

This example shows that $\sim_1 \not\subseteq \sim_2$, $\sim_1 \not\subseteq \sim_3$, and $\sim_2 \not\subseteq \sim_3$. The following example shows that also the inverse inclusions are false.

Example 3. In this example a τ prefix and an internal choice $\tau.P + \tau.Q$ operator are used. The agent P containing τ-prefixes and Q containing internal choices, are defined as follows, where a_i are considered to be distinct and fresh names:

$$P \stackrel{def}{=} (P' \mid \langle a_1 \rangle \mid \ldots \mid \langle a_n \rangle)\backslash a_1 \backslash \ldots \backslash a_n$$
where P' is obtained by substituting $in(a_i)$ for the ith τ in P

$$Q \stackrel{def}{=} (Q' \mid \langle a_1 \rangle \mid \ldots \mid \langle a_n \rangle)\backslash a_1 \backslash \ldots \backslash a_n$$
where Q' is obtained by substituting $in(a_i).R_i + in(a_i).S_i$
for the ith internal choice $\tau.R_i + \tau.S_i$ in Q

Consider the following agents:

$$P \stackrel{def}{=} (out(a).out(b) \mid in(b).inp(a)?out(c)\_out(d))\backslash a\backslash b$$
$$Q \stackrel{def}{=} \tau.(\tau.\tau.\tau.\tau.\tau.out(c) + \tau.(\tau.\tau.\tau.\tau.out(c) + \tau.(\tau.\tau.\tau.out(c) +$$
$$\tau.(\tau.\tau.out(c) + \tau.(out(d)\mid\tau)))))$$

It is not difficult to see that under the *unordered* semantics P and Q have the same possible computations; hence $P \sim_3 Q$. Instead, they can not be equivalent in the case of *instantaneous* or *ordered* semantics because $Q \Downarrow \bar{d}$ while $P \not\Downarrow \bar{d}$ in both the cases.

We also prove that $\sim_2 \not\subseteq \sim_1$. Let:

$$P \stackrel{def}{=} (out(a).out(b) \mid in(a).inp(b)?out(c)\_out(d))\backslash a\backslash b$$
$$Q \stackrel{def}{=} \tau.(\tau.\tau.\tau.out(c) + \tau.(\tau.\tau.out(c) + \tau.(\tau.out(d) + out(d).\tau)))$$

In the case of *ordered* semantics P and Q have the same possible computations; hence $P \sim_2 Q$. Instead, under *instantaneous* semantics P and Q can not be considered equivalent because $Q \Downarrow \overline{d}$ while $P \not\Downarrow \overline{d}$. ■

4 Expressiveness of the Language

In this section we analyze the expressive power of our small calculus under the three possible semantics. We show that our language is Turing powerful (under the *instantaneous* and *ordered* semantics) because it is expressive enough to model a Random Access Machine (RAM) [SS63]. In the case of *unordered* semantics, the RAM is not implementable because the language is no more Turing powerful.

A RAM is a computational model composed of a finite set of registers that can hold arbitrary large natural numbers and by a program, that is a sequence of simple numbered instructions, like arithmetical operations on the contents of registers or conditional jumps.

To perform a computation, the inputs are provided in registers $r_1, \ldots, r_n$; if other registers are used in the program, they are supposed to contain the value 0 at the beginning of the computation. The execution of the program begins with the first instruction and continues by executing the other instructions in sequence, unless a jump instruction is encountered. The execution stops when an instruction number higher than the length of the program is reached; this happens if the program was executing the last instruction of the program and this instruction does not require a jump, or if the current instruction requires a jump to an instruction number not appearing in the program. If the program terminates, the result of the computation is the content of the registers specified as outputs.

In [Min67] it is shown that the following two instructions are sufficient to model every recursive function:

- $Succ(r_j)$: add 1 to the content of register r_j;
- $DecJump(r_j, s)$: if the contents of register r_j is not zero, then decrease it by 1 and go to the next instruction, otherwise jump to instruction s.

For example, the following program computes the sum of registers r_1 and r_2, putting the result in register r_1 (note that the third instruction corresponds to an unconditional jump, because register r_3 contains the value 0 at the beginning of the computation and its contents is never modified by the program):

    $1 : DecJump(r_2, 4)$
    $2 : Succ(r_1)$
    $3 : DecJump(r_3, 1)$

In the translation of the RAM in our language, we model the contents of registers and the program counter by means of tuples: if register r_j contains the number n, then n tuples $\langle r_j \rangle$ are in the tuple space; if the next instruction to execute is the ith, then TS contains the tuple $\langle p_i \rangle$.

To model the instruction we proceed in the following way: a *Succ* instruction on register r_j at position i is represented by an agent that consumes the "program counter tuple", adds a tuple $\langle r_j \rangle$ and updates the program counter by adding a tuple $\langle p_{i+1} \rangle$; an instruction $DecJump(r_j, s)$ at position i is modeled by an agent that, after consuming the "program counter tuple", performs an *inp* on message r_j; if the operation succeeds, then a tuple $\langle r_j \rangle$ has been withdrawn from the tuple space and the agent updates the program counter by adding $\langle p_{i+1} \rangle$, otherwise a jump to the sth instruction is performed by adding $\langle p_s \rangle$. The use of the recursion operator in the representation of the instructions permits to reuse them.

$$[\![i : Succ(r_j)]\!] \stackrel{def}{=} rec\, X.(in(p_i).out(r_j).out(p_{i+1}).X)$$

$$[\![i : DecJump(r_j, s)]\!] \stackrel{def}{=} rec\, X.(in(p_i).inp(r_j)?(out(p_{i+1}).X) \_ (out(p_s).X))$$

The agent modeling the program $I_1 \ldots I_k$ with inputs $n_1, \ldots, n_m$ is:
$$\langle p_1 \rangle | \underbrace{\langle r_1 \rangle | \ldots | \langle r_1 \rangle}_{n_1 \text{ times}} | \ldots | \underbrace{\langle r_m \rangle | \ldots | \langle r_m \rangle}_{n_m \text{ times}} | [\![I_1]\!] | \ldots | [\![I_k]\!]$$

The unordered case

The implementation of the RAM we have presented, is not correct for the unordered semantics because of problems in updating the program counter. Consider an execution of a program with instructions:

$\quad i \qquad : Succ(r_j)$
$\quad i+1 : DecJump(r_j, s)$

in which the register r_j is empty at the moment the ith instruction is executed. The implementation of the $Succ(r_j)$ instruction creates two tuples: $\langle r_j \rangle$ and the new "program counter tuple" $\langle p_{i+1} \rangle$. If the tuple $\langle p_{i+1} \rangle$ becomes available before $\langle r_j \rangle$, the following $DecJump(r_j, s)$ instruction could execute the jump because no tuple $\langle r_j \rangle$ is available. In the *instantaneous* and *ordered* semantics this kind of problems cannot arise because the "program counter tuple" becomes available simultaneously (in the instantaneous case) or only after (in the ordered case) the tuple $\langle r_j \rangle$. Under *unordered* semantics the order of rendering of the tuples is not predictable, hence the wrong jump could be performed.

We not only say that the implementation we have presented is not correct under *unordered* semantics, but we also assert that the RAM is not implementable in any way. In fact, under this semantics, the language is no more Turing powerful; in [BGZ97b] we show that the problem of termination is decidable under the unordered semantics. The proof is divided in two steps: we first define a net semantics in terms of contextual P/T nets (i.e., P/T nets extended with arcs testing for presence or absence of tokens in a place; see, e.g., [MR95, BP95]). This semantics, defined following the style of [BG95, BGZ97a], preserves the interleaving behaviour, hence also the possibility of deadlock. Then, given the contextual P/T net semantics, we present a mapping on finite (standard) P/T nets that preserves deadlock. As deadlock is decidable on finite P/T nets, we conclude that the termination problem is decidable under the unordered semantics.

5 Conclusion and Future Research

A formal semantics for three different interpretations of the output operation is studied, providing each of them with an operational and a corresponding behavioural semantics. We think this is a first necessary step in order to equip languages like Linda with a formal semantics, currently non-available.

In the reference manual [SCA95] it is often unclear which is the real interpretation of the *out* primitive. As an illustrative example, consider $Q = (out(b).out(a) \mid in(a).inp(b)?C\_D)$. If we assume the ordered semantics, then the input of a is possible only if $\langle b \rangle$ is already in TS; hence, the execution of *inp* will always enable C. Differently, if we assume the unordered semantics, then no guarantee is given that $\langle b \rangle$ is in TS; hence, it is sometimes possible that D is executed instead. The choice between the two semantics is not solved in [SCA95] and other similar publications (e.g., [Nar90]). For instance, on page 2-6 of [SCA95] we can read: "*out* returns after the tuple has been added to tuple space", hence supporting the claim that the intended semantics is ordered. On the contrary, on page 2-26 of [SCA95] a comment to a program reported on page 2-25 expresses a concern very similar to the above about the possible executability of D, hence validating that the intended semantics is the unordered one. Similar contradictions can be found in [Nar90]: on lines 19-20 of page 4 it is said that, in shared memory implementations, it is not ensured that "an out followed by a predicate operation on the same tuple will succeed", hence supporting that the intended semantics is unordered. Instead, on lines 7-9 of the same page we can read: "The time at which the tuple is visible to other processes is indeterminate. In the existing shared memory implementations, the operation is completed immediately.", hence validating the ordered semantics approach, at least for shared memory implementations.

The expressiveness of the three semantics has been also studied, at least in relation to the problem of Turing equivalence. However, we plan to study further this issue in order to provide formal support to the reasoning on the implementations of Linda-like languages. One relevant question is the following: is it possible to use one semantics as an implementation for another one? In this direction, we have already one result: the instantaneous and ordered semantics cannot be implemented in the unordered one (by contradiction, if it was possible, then the language under the unordered semantics would be Turing powerful).

We would like to mention that we have left for future research the investigation of further, interesting implementations of the output operation like, e.g. [Nar90], according to which the tuple generated by a process by means of an *out* operation "will be visible to the same process by the time the next Linda operation executes", while the tuple "is not guaranteed to be visible to another process until some variable latency period has past".

The study carried out in this paper can be extended to cope with further coordination primitives, as, e.g., the rd and rdp Linda operators, that have been already studied in [BGZ97c], for the ordered case only.

References

[ACS96] R. Amadio, I. Castellani, and D. Sangiorgi. On Bisimulations for the Asynchronous π-Calculus. In Proc. *CONCUR'96*, volume 1119 of *LNCS*, pages 147–162, Springer Verlag, 1996.

[Bou92] G. Boudol. Asynchrony and the π-calculus. Technical Report 1702, INRIA, Sophia–Antipolis, 1992.

[BG95] N. Busi and R. Gorrieri. A Petri Net Semantics for π–calculus. In Proc. *CONCUR'95*, volume 962 of *LNCS*, pages 145–159, Springer Verlag, 1995.

[BGZ97a] N. Busi, R. Gorrieri, and G. Zavattaro. A Truly Concurrent view of Linda Interprocess Communication. Technical Report UBLCS-97-02, Department of Computer Science, University of Bologna, February 1997.

[BGZ97b] N. Busi, R. Gorrieri, and G. Zavattaro. On the Turing Equivalence of Linda Coordination Primitives. Technical Report UBLCS-97-05, Department of Computer Science, University of Bologna, May 1997.

[BGZ97c] N. Busi, R. Gorrieri, and G. Zavattaro, A Process Algebraic View of Linda Coordination Primitives. To appear in *Theoretical Computer Science*. Available as Technical Report UBLCS-97-06, Department of Computer Science, University of Bologna, May 1997.

[BP95] N. Busi and G.M. Pinna. A Causal Semantics for Contextual P/T nets. In Proc. *ICTCS'95*, 311–325, World Scientific, 1995.

[CGZ96] P. Ciancarini, R. Gorrieri, and G. Zavattaro. Towards a Calculus for Generative Communication. In Proc. *1st IFIP Conf. on FMOODS'96*, pages 283–297. Chapman & Hall, 1996.

[Gel85] D. Gelernter. Generative Communication in Linda. *ACM Transactions on Programming Languages and Systems*, 7(1):80–112, 1985.

[GC92] D. Gelernter and N. Carriero. Coordination Languages and their Significance. *Communications of the ACM*, 35(2):97–107, 1992.

[Gro93] J.F. Groote. Transition system specifications with negative premises. *Theoretical Computer Science*, 118:263-299, 1993.

[HKH95] M. Hansen, J. Kleist, and H. Hüttel. Bisimulations for Asynchronous Mobile Processes. In Proc. *Tbilisi Symposium on Language, Logic, and Computation*, 1995.

[HT91] K. Honda and M. Tokoro. An Object Calculus for Asynchronous Communication. In Proc. *ECOOP '91*, volume 512 of *LNCS*, pages 133–147. Springer Verlag, 1991.

[Mil89] R. Milner. *Communication and Concurrency*. Prentice-Hall, 1989.

[MS92] R. Milner and D. Sangiorgi. Barbed Bisimulation. In Proc. *ICALP'92*, volume 623 of *LNCS*, pages 685–695, Springer Verlag, 1992.

[Min67] M. L. Minsky. *Computation: finite and infinite machines*. Prentice-Hall, Englewood Cliffs, 1967.

[MR95] U. Montanari and F. Rossi. Contextual Nets. *Acta Informatica*, 32(6):545–596, 1995.

[Nar90] J. E. Narem. An Informal Operational Semantics of C-Linda V2.3.5. Technical Report YALEU/DCS/TR-839, Department of Computer Science, Yale University, December 1990.

[SCA95] Scientific Computing Associates. *Linda: User's guide and reference manual.* Scientific Computing Associates, 1995.

[SS63] J. C. Shepherdson and J. E. Sturgis. Computability of recursive functions. *Journal of the ACM*, 10:217–255, 1963.

Coordinating Mobile Agents
via Blackboards and Access Rights*

Rocco De Nicola[1]   GianLuigi Ferrari[2]   Rosario Pugliese[1]

[1]Dipartimento di Sistemi e Informatica, Università di Firenze
[2]Dipartimento di Informatica, Università di Pisa

Abstract. LLinda (Locality based Linda) is a variant of Linda which supports a programming paradigm where agents can migrate from one computing environment to another. In this paper, we define a type system for LLinda that permits statically checking access rights violations of mobile agents. Types are used to describe processes intentions (read, write, execute, ...) relatively to the different localities they are willing to interact with or they want to migrate to. The type system is used to determine the operations that processes want to perform at each locality, to check whether they comply with the declared intentions and whether they have the necessary rights to perform the intended operations at the specific localities.

1   Introduction

Network computing is calling for new programming paradigms and languages for network applications. In these new paradigms, the interactions among clients and servers take place by means of *mobile agents*. Programs are transported and executed at the client site. Java [18] has popularized this paradigm. Beside it, other programming languages support the mobile agents paradigm (e.g. [2, 9, 17, 21]) that pushing forward this approach permit tighter interactions of processes over the nets.

Security, i.e. *privacy* and *integrity* of data, is a key issue in the development of mobile applications. One can easily imagine malicious mobile agents attempting to access private information. A server receiving a mobile agent for execution needs then to put strong requirements to ensure that the agent will not violate privacy and put integrity of information at risk. Similarly, mobile agents must ensure that their execution at the server site will not damages them or compromise their security.

Programming languages for mobile agents support policies (both at compilation and run–time) which restrict privileges and capabilities of mobile agents

---

* Work partially supported by EEC: HCM project EXPRESS and Esprit Working Group *CONFER2*, by CNR Integrated Project "Metodi e Strumenti per la Progettazione e la Verifica di Sistemi Eterogenei Connessi mediante Reti di Comunicazione" and Progetto Speciale "Modelli e Metodi per la Matematica e l'Ingegneria", and by Istituto di Elaborazione dell'Informazione CNR, Pisa.

more than needed (e.g. Java [18]). This, unnecessarily, reduces the expressive power (and the capabilities) of the agents. Moreover, it is not guaranteed that certain desired security properties are enforced by the language implementation. More generally, there is a lack of formal foundations through which it is possible to express and prove that classes of programs satisfy desired security properties.

We have in mind the results in the area of functional programming where *type systems* permit avoiding programming errors by checks at compile time. Types are used to define the notion of *well–behaved* programs and only programs which comply with the requirement of the type system are considered for execution.

The main goal of this paper is to show that types and type systems can be used to statically enforce security properties for languages of mobile processes. We take the LLinda language (Locality based Linda) [6] as our starting point and define a type system that permits checking whether the operations processes intend to perform over the sites of a net do comply with their access rights.

LLinda supports a programming paradigm where programs can migrate from one computing environment to another. The language consists of a core Linda language [8, 3] with multiple tuple spaces and of a set of operators, borrowed from Milner's CCS [12], for building processes. LLinda naturally supports programming with explicit localities. Indeed, tuple spaces are distributed over (allocated at) different localities and Linda operations are indexed with the tuple space they operate on. This allows programmers to distribute/retrieve data and processes over/from different nodes directly. Localities are first-class data (they can be manipulated just as any other data), but programmers share control over them with what we call the *net coordinator*. All issues related to location scoping and mobility of processes (e.g. the visibility of localities, the allocation policies of tuple spaces) are managed by the net coordinator.

For instance, a system composed by a process *Server* and two identical processes *Client* can be programmed in LLinda as follows.

$$Server \stackrel{def}{=} \mathbf{out}(l)@\mathbf{self}.\mathbf{nil}$$

Server makes available a tuple, that contains the locality l, in its local tuple space referred to via **self**, then evolves to the stopped process **nil**.

$$Client \stackrel{def}{=} \mathbf{read}(!\,u)@l_S.\mathbf{eval}(P)@u.\mathbf{nil}$$

Client accesses the tuple space located at l_S to read an address u, then sends process P in execution at u, finally evolves to **nil**.

The net coordinator allocates *Server* on the site s (**self** is bound to s) and the two processes *Client* on sites s_1 and s_2. At both sites, care is taken that l_S is bound to s; this allows both clients to interact with the server and to send process P for execution at u.

The typing analysis of LLinda programs is structured in two phases reflecting the two–level syntax of LLinda.

The first phase of the typing analysis deduces process intentions (read, write, withdraw, execute, ...) relatively to the different localities they are willing to interact with or they want to migrate to. This is done by an inference system which assigns types to processes, and also checks whether these behave in accordance with their declared intentions. To explain the outcome of the first stage of typing analysis, let us consider the example above. Assume that process P has type δ. Then, process *Client* is typed by

$$\delta_c = l_S \longmapsto \langle \{r\}, \phi \rangle, u \longmapsto \langle \{e\}, \delta \rangle$$

A process type is a function stating process's intentions over localities. In particular, δ_c states that *Client* intends to perform a **read** operation at locality l_S and intends to send a process with type δ for execution at locality u.

The second phase of the typing analysis checks whether each process has the necessary rights to perform the intended operations, i.e. it does not violate the access rights as granted by the net coordinator. In our running example, assume that the net coordinator gives the following access rights (again represented as functions) to the sites s_1 and s_2 where *Client* is duplicated,

$$\delta_{s_1} = s \longmapsto \langle \{r\}, \phi \rangle, u \longmapsto \langle \{e\}, \delta \rangle \qquad\qquad \delta_{s_2} = s \longmapsto \langle \{r\}, \phi \rangle$$

then, only processes allocated at s_1 have the right of sending processes with type δ for execution at u.

The language we consider in the paper, actually, is a variant of LLinda, called TLLinda (typed LLinda), that has been obtained by annotating LLinda programs with explicit types. Our main result is a *soundness* theorem, stated with respect to TLLinda semantics, which ensures that well–typed TLLinda programs can never fail during the execution for misuse of access rights. For instance, the soundness theorem ensures that the client allocated at s_2 cannot send a process for execution on the site whose address is given by u; only the client allocated at s_1 has the right to send P for execution at u.

2 Overview of LLinda

In this section, we briefly review LLinda [6] and illustrate how to use it for programming mobile applications.

2.1 Processes

We will rely on the syntactic categories listed below; all of them are followed by the symbols we will use (possibly with indexes) to refer to their elements.

- S (s) is a set of *sites* (or *physical localities*). A site can be considered as the address of a node where processes and tuple spaces are allocated.
- Loc (l) is a set of *localities*. A locality may be thought of as the symbolic name for a site. Localities permit structuring programs over distributed environments while ignoring the precise allocation of processes and data. A distinguished locality **self** ($\in Loc$) is assumed, that processes use for denoting their execution site.

- *VLoc* (*u*) is a set of *locality variables*.
- *Val* (*v*) is a set of basic values.
- *Var* (*x*) is a set of value variables.
- *Exp* (*e*) is the category of *value expressions*. These are built up from values and value variables, by using a set of operators (which we do not specify).
- Ψ (*A*) is a set of *process constants*, each with a fixed *arity*.
- χ (*X*) is a set of *process variables*.

For simplicity, we will use ℓ for denoting either a locality or a locality variable. Moreover, $\tilde{\ell}$ will indicate sequences of localities and $\{\tilde{\ell}\}$ the set of localities in $\tilde{\ell}$. A similar notation will be used throughout the paper to deal with sequences.

Substitution works as expected and we will use the standard notation $e[e'/x]$ to indicate the substitution of the value expression e' for the variable x in e ($e[\tilde{e'}/\tilde{x}]$ will denote the simultaneous replacement of each $x \in \tilde{x}$ with the corresponding $e' \in \tilde{e'}$ in e).

The LLinda *terms* are given by the abstract syntax below:

$$P ::= \mathbf{nil} \qquad \text{(null process)}$$
$$| \quad a.P \qquad \text{(action prefixing)}$$
$$| \quad P_1 \mid P_2 \qquad \text{(parallel composition)}$$
$$| \quad P_1 + P_2 \qquad \text{(choice)}$$
$$| \quad X \qquad \text{(process variable)}$$
$$| \quad A(\tilde{X}, \tilde{u}, \tilde{x})\langle \tilde{P}, \tilde{\ell}, \tilde{e}\rangle \qquad \text{(process invocation)}$$
$$a ::= \mathbf{out}(t)@\ell \mid \mathbf{in}(t)@\ell \mid \mathbf{read}(t)@\ell \mid \mathbf{eval}(P)@\ell \mid \mathbf{newloc}(u)$$
$$t ::= e \mid P \mid \ell \mid !x \mid !X \mid !u \mid t_1, t_2$$

The Linda operations to generate tuples (**out**), to spawn a new process (**eval**), to read tuples (**read**), and to withdraw tuples (**in**) are located. New sites are created through the prefix action **newloc**(*u*). This operation calls for the creation of a "fresh" site that will be accessed via the locality variable *u*. LLinda adopts a *static binding* discipline for the execution of **out** operations (i.e. their argument tuples are evaluated within the local allocation environment) and a *dynamic binding* discipline for the execution of **eval** operations (i.e. the meaning of localities used by processes spawned at remote sites depends on the allocation environments of those sites).

Tuples are sequences of actual fields (i.e. expressions, processes, localities or locality variables) and formal fields; these are denoted by "!*var*", where *var* is a generic variable. We shall use *fields*(*t*) to denote the set of fields of *t*.

The prefixes **in**(*t*)@ℓ._ and **read**(*t*)@ℓ._ act as binders for variables in the formal fields of *t*. The prefix **newloc**(*u*)._ binds the locality variable *u*. A *process* is a term whose variables are all bound. Both processes and localities are first-class data and can be manipulated just as any other data.

Process constants are used in recursive process definitions. It is assumed that each process constant *A* has a *single* defining equation $A(\tilde{X}, \tilde{u}, \tilde{x}) \stackrel{def}{=} P$; all free (value, process and locality) variables in *P* are contained in $\{\tilde{X}, \tilde{u}, \tilde{x}\}$ and all occurrences of process constants in P are *guarded* (i.e. each process constant occurs within the scope of a **in/read** prefix). Without loss of generality, we assume a fixed order for the classes of formal parameters in process definitions and invocations. Finally, process invocation uses a *call–by–need* parameter passing mechanism.

2.2 The Coordination Level: Nets of Processes

Given a finite set of sites, a LLinda *net* of processes is a map that associates a node to each site. A *node* is a pair (P, ρ) where ρ is the local *allocation environment*, i.e. a (partial) function from *Loc* to S. In what follows $\mathcal{E}$ will denote the set of environments, ϕ the empty environment and $[s/l]$ the environment which maps the locality l to the site s. Finally, if $\rho_1, \rho_2 \in \mathcal{E}$, then $\rho_1 \bullet \rho_2$ stands for the environment defined by:

$$\rho_1 \bullet \rho_2\,(l) = \begin{cases} \rho_1(l) & \text{if } l \in dom(\rho_1) \\ \rho_2(l) & \text{otherwise} \end{cases}$$

Let S be a finite subset of $\mathcal{S}$ and $\mathcal{N}$ be the set of nodes; a *net over S* is a map $N_S : \mathcal{S} \longrightarrow \mathcal{N}$ such that

- $N_S(s)$ is defined if and only if $s \in S$,
- $N_S(s) = (P, \rho)$ implies $range(\rho) \subseteq S$ and $\rho(\texttt{self}) = s$.

Each node in a net has a unique site, thus we can consider a net just as a set. We write $s ::_\rho P$ (when $N_S(s) = (P, \rho)$) for an element of a net (N_S), and $N_S, s ::_\rho P$ for the net given by $N_S \cup \{s ::_\rho P\}$ (with the implicit side condition that $s \notin S$).

A net provides a mechanism for coordinating the allocation of processes which interact via multiple tuple spaces distributed over the sites of S. Processes at each site can potentially access any other site of the net; however, site visibility is (locally) controlled by the local allocation environment. A site s is *visible* at the node (P, ρ) only if $s \in range(\rho)$.

2.3 Mobile LLinda agents and the electronic marketplace

In this section, by means of a simple scenario for the electronic marketplace (essentially borrowed from [22]), we illustrate how to use LLinda for programming mobile agents. More examples about the LLinda pragmatic can be found in [6].

Assume that a client (process) P wants to buy a specific camera, c. To decide where to purchase the camera, P activates a migrating agent A and passes the following information to it:

- c, the make and the model of the camera P has chosen,
- loc_D, the locality of the directory of the electronic marketplace, and
- a length measure, which will be used for identifying the geographical area for which P wants pricing information,

and expects that A returns the name, address and telephone number of the camera shop closest to its site with the lowest price for c within the chosen area. Thus, the following could be part of the behaviour of P

$$P \stackrel{def}{=} \ldots \mathbf{eval}(A(x,u,y)\langle c, loc_D, length\rangle)@\mathbf{self}.\mathbf{in}(c, !x, !y)@\mathbf{self}.\ldots$$

where x will retain the name, address and telephone number of the camera shop from where to buy c at cost y.

The agent A behaves as follows:

- Obtains the site where P is located, which will be used both for returning the outcome of the query and for identifying the geographical area which is of interest for pricing information. This is done by putting a tuple containing $\mathbf{self}$ into a new tuple space u', in order to force the evaluation of $\mathbf{self}$ within the local tuple space, and by withdrawing the tuple.
- Migrates to the site of the marketplace directory where it asks for and obtains the list of all camera shops whose location is close to the site of P. Each item in the list contains name, address and telephone number of a camera shop; a function l will return the locality information within an item.
- Visits each camera shop in turn and obtains the local price for c. The agent retains information about the shop only if it offers a price lowest than that currently stored.
- After visiting all the camera shops in the list, it sends back to the site of P the information about the shop that offers the lowest price for c and terminates.

For the sake of simplicity, in defining agents we assume LLinda provides a conditional construct (actually, it can be simulated by using the dynamic creation of new sites and the choice operator) and a data type $list$ (with the usual operators hd, tl and $empty$).

$$A(x,u,y) \stackrel{def}{=} \mathbf{newloc}(u').\mathbf{out}(\mathbf{self})@u'.\mathbf{in}(!u'')@u'.$$
$$\mathbf{eval}(B(x,u,y)\langle x,u'',y\rangle)@u.\mathbf{nil}$$

$$B(x,u,y) \stackrel{def}{=} \mathbf{out}(cshop,u,y)@\mathbf{self}.\mathbf{in}(cshop, !list)@\mathbf{self}.$$
$$\text{if } empty(list) \text{ then } \mathbf{out}(x, nocloseshop, -1)@u.\mathbf{nil}$$
$$\text{else } I(x,y,u,u''')\langle x, list, u, l(hd(list))\rangle$$

$$I(x,y,u,u''') \stackrel{def}{=} \mathbf{eval}(\mathbf{read}(x, !cost)@\mathbf{self}.$$
$$R(x,y,w,z,u)\langle x,y,cost,hd(y),u\rangle)@u'''.\mathbf{nil}$$

$$R(x,y,w,z,u) \stackrel{def}{=} \text{if } empty(y) \text{ then } \mathbf{out}(x,z,w)@u.\mathbf{nil}$$
$$\text{else } C(x,y,w,z,u,u''')\langle x, tl(y), w, z, u, l(hd(tl(y)))\rangle$$

$$C(x,y,w,z,u,u''') \stackrel{def}{=} \mathbf{eval}(\mathbf{read}(x, !cost)@\mathbf{self}.\text{if } cost < z$$
$$\text{then } R(x,y,w,z,u)\langle x,y,cost,hd(y),u\rangle$$
$$\text{else } R(x,y,w,z,u)\langle x,y,w,z,u\rangle)@u'''.\mathbf{nil}$$

The following will be part of the behaviour of each camera shop S_i

$$S_i \stackrel{def}{=} \ldots |\mathbf{out}(c, price(c))@\mathbf{self}.\mathbf{nil}| \ldots$$

Let D denote the marketplace directory process. The net could be initially structured as follows

$$\{ \, s_P ::_{\{s_P/\text{self},s_D/loc_D\}} P, s_D ::_{\{s_D/\text{self},s_1/cs_1,\ldots,s_n/cs_n\}} D,$$
$$s_1 ::_{\{s_1/\text{self}\}} S_1, \ldots, s_n ::_{\{s_n/\text{self}\}} S_n\}$$

3 TLLinda: Typed LLinda

In this section we enrich LLinda with types, that carry information about processes intentions (downloading a tuple, activating a process, creating a new tuple space, ...).

3.1 Types

We will use $\{r, i, o, e, n\}$ to indicate the set of process *capabilities*, where each symbol stands for the operation whose name begins with it; r denotes the capability of executing a **read** operation, i the capability of executing an **in** operation, and so on.

Polarities are non–empty subsets of $\{r, i, o, e, n\}$. We use Π, ranged over by π (possibly indexed), to denote the set of all polarities. Polarities are used differently by processes and net coordinators. The polarity of a locality or of a locality variable, say ℓ, within a process carries information about the operations the process intends to perform at ℓ. A net coordinator uses polarities to fix access rights. Type checking will guarantee that only intentions that match access rights as granted by the coordinator are allowed.

Orderings between polarities can be used to model hierarchies of access rights. Obviously, if a process is able to perform an **in** operation at ℓ then it is also able to perform a **read** at ℓ. Also, type checking should ensure that, if a process has capabilities π, then it can execute all operations that require capabilities smaller than π. These intuitions lead to the *subpolarity relation*, obtained as the least reflexive and transitive relation induced by the following rules:

$$\{i\} \sqsubseteq_\Pi \{r\} \qquad \frac{\pi_1 \subseteq \pi_2}{\pi_2 \sqsubseteq_\Pi \pi_1} \qquad \frac{\pi_1 \sqsubseteq_\Pi \pi_1' \quad \pi_2 \sqsubseteq_\Pi \pi_2'}{(\pi_1 \cup \pi_2) \sqsubseteq_\Pi (\pi_1' \cup \pi_2')}$$

One could think of associating a polarity to each process or to each locality to completely characterize processes intentions and localities rights. It is not difficult to see that this would be insufficient for taking into account process migrations and different access rights of the different localities.

An obvious choice, for assigning types to a process, would be that of associating to it a single polarity describing all the operations it intends to perform, while ignoring the specific localities it refers to. But in this way, we would not characterize different intentions relative to different localities. Also associating polarities to each of the localities referred to within a process would be unsatisfactory. It hinders the possibility of keeping track of the capabilities of remotely executed processes, that might be different from those of sender processes. As an example, consider a process that does not have the right of accessing a remote tuple space (e.g. a database), but it has the right of sending a process for remote execution at a (server) node that has the needed right.

To take into account remote executions (*migrations*) of processes, we need to further structure our types and to associate to each locality not just a polarity but also the type that is required for the processes executed at that locality.

A *type* is a finite map that assigns pairs consisting of polarities and types to localities and to locality variables. The first component of the pair associated to ℓ describes the polarity of ℓ while the second describes the types of the processes executed at ℓ.

The set of types, Δ, ranged over by δ, is defined by the following domain equation

$$\Delta = Fin((Loc \cup VLoc) \longmapsto (\Pi \times \Delta))_\perp \tag{1}$$

The construction of Δ rests on the following construction over *complete partial orders* (cpo). Let $\langle D, \sqsubseteq_D \rangle$ be a cpo. Define H to be:

$$H(D) = Fin((Loc \cup VLoc) \longmapsto (\Pi \times D))_\perp$$

ordered by

1. $\perp \sqsubseteq_{H(D)} f$, for all $f \in H(D)$
2. $f \sqsubseteq_{H(D)} g$ when
   - $dom(g) \subseteq dom(f)$, and
   - $\forall \ell \in dom(g) : f(\ell) \sqsubseteq_{\Pi \times D} g(\ell)$, where $\sqsubseteq_{\Pi \times D}$ is the obvious ordering on $\Pi \times D$.

$H(D)$ is the set of partial functions with finite domain from $Loc \cup VLoc$ to the cpo $\Pi \times D$. The ordering $\sqsubseteq_{H(D)}$ states that the more defined the partial function the smaller it is. It is not difficult to show that if $\langle D, \sqsubseteq_D \rangle$ is a (ω–algebraic) cpo then also $\langle H(D), \sqsubseteq_{H(D)} \rangle$ is a (ω–algebraic) cpo [2].

Let $\langle \Delta, \preceq \rangle$ be the initial solution of the recursive domain equation (1); $\preceq$ is called the *subtype relation*. As usual, $\sqcup$ shall denote the least upper bound and ϕ shall denote the element of Δ with empty domain. Moreover, if $\delta \in \Delta$, then $\delta^i(\ell)$ is used to denote the i-th component of the pair $\delta(\ell)$.

---

[2] The construction H on cpos may be straightforwardly turned into a functor $\mathcal{H}$ in the category $\mathbf{CPO}^{\mathbf{E}}$, the category of cpos with embeddings as morphisms. The action of the functor $\mathcal{H}$ on cpos is defined as for H. If $i : D \lhd D'$ is an embedding, $\mathcal{H}(i) : \mathcal{H}(D) \longrightarrow \mathcal{H}(D')$ (the action of the functor on embeddings) is obtained as:

$$(\mathcal{H}(i))(\perp) = \perp \qquad (\mathcal{H}(i))(f) = i \circ f.$$

By using standard techniques, we can prove that $\mathcal{H}$ is a continuous and covariant functor in $\mathbf{CPO}^{\mathbf{E}}$ which preserves ω–algebraicity [10]. Therefore, the theory in [15] ensures the existence and uniqueness in $\mathbf{CPO}^{\mathbf{E}}$ of the initial fixed point of the functor $\mathcal{H}$, i.e. the initial solution of the recursive domain equation (1).

3.2 TLLinda

The abstract syntax of TLLinda *terms* (*processes*, as usual, are closed terms) is reported below. We recall that ℓ stands for a generic locality or locality variable. To avoid name clashing and thus overloading of types, we will assume that *Vloc*, the set of locality variables, is partitioned into two subsets, *NVloc* and *TVloc*. Variables in *NVloc* are used as arguments of **newloc**, and variables in *TVloc* are used as formals of tuples, to bind localities.

$$P ::= \mathbf{nil} \mid a.P \mid P_1 \mid P_2 \mid P_1 + P_2 \mid X \mid A(\widetilde{X} : \widetilde{\delta}, \widetilde{u} : \widetilde{\delta}, \widetilde{x})\langle \widetilde{P}, \widetilde{\ell}, \widetilde{e} \rangle$$

$$a ::= \mathbf{out}(t)@\ell \mid \mathbf{in}(t)@\ell \mid \mathbf{read}(t)@\ell \mid \mathbf{eval}(P)@\ell \mid \mathbf{newloc}(u : \delta)$$

$$t ::= e \mid P \mid \ell \mid !x \mid !X : \delta \mid !u : \delta \mid t_1, t_2$$

$$\delta ::= \phi \mid \ell \longmapsto \langle \pi, \delta \rangle \mid \delta_1, \delta_2 \mid \nu \mid rec\ \nu.\delta$$

Notice that we introduced an explicit syntax for types pointing out their recursive structure throughout the *rec* operator (ν is a type variable).

We now type the process P presented in Section 2.3. We can assume that process P can perform any operation both at the site where it is located (addressed by **self**) and at the site it dynamically creates (namely u'). It seems also reasonable to assume that when (a process activated by) P migrates in the site of the marketplace directory (addressed by loc_D), it can perform both local **out** and **in**, remote **out** at u'' for returning the outcome of the initial query, and can migrate to u''' (the site of a camerashop). Finally, when running at the site of a camerashop, (a process activated by) P can perform local **read** (for reading the local price for the camera c), remote **out** at the original site of P, and can migrate to the sites of other camerashops. Such requirements can be formally expressed by means of the following TLLinda types

$$\delta :\ rec\ \nu.(\mathbf{self} \longmapsto \langle\{o,i,e,n\}, \nu\rangle, u' \longmapsto \langle\{o,i,e,n\}, \nu\rangle, loc_D \longmapsto \langle\{e\}, \delta'\rangle)$$

$$\delta' :\ \mathbf{self} \longmapsto \langle\{o,i\}, \phi\rangle, u'' \longmapsto \langle\{o\}, \phi\rangle, u''' \longmapsto \langle\{e\}, \delta''\rangle$$

$$\delta'' :\ rec\ \nu.(\mathbf{self} \longmapsto \langle\{r\}, \phi\rangle, u'' \longmapsto \langle\{o\}, \phi\rangle, u''' \longmapsto \langle\{e\}, \nu\rangle)$$

We now introduce the formal syntax of TLLinda nets, whose rôle is allocating and coordinating processes, and assigning access rights. The type of sites is similar to that of processes; it associates pairs ⟨polarity, type⟩ to localities and locality variables. This is declared by means of two functions, Λ and Υ. For each site s, Λ describes the access rights of s on the other sites, while Υ describes the constraints on the locality variables used by processes located at s.

A TLLinda *net* is a triple $N_S : \langle\Lambda, \Upsilon\rangle$ where N_S is a LLinda net, and Λ and Υ have the following structure: $\Lambda : S \longrightarrow (S \longrightarrow \Pi)$ and $\Upsilon : S \longrightarrow (VLoc \longrightarrow \Pi)$.

4 Process Semantics

In this section, first we present an inference system that assigns types to processes, then describe the evolution of processes in isolation. The type system records the operations that processes are willing to perform at specific localities and to check whether the intended operations comply with the declared types of the variables.

4.1 Static Semantics: Type Inference System

Type contexts γ are functions mapping process variables and constants into types. In what follows, ϕ will denote the empty context. The auxiliary function *update*, defined structurally over tuples syntax, will be used for updating type contexts. *update* is the identity for all fields but $!X : \delta$. Formally, it is defined by:

$$update(\gamma, t) = \begin{cases} update(update(\gamma, t_1), t_2) & \text{if } t = t_1, t_2 \\ \gamma[\delta/X] & \text{if } t = !X : \delta \\ \gamma & \text{otherwise} \end{cases}$$

The type judgments for processes take the form $\gamma \vdash P : \delta$ where γ is a type context giving the type of process variables and constants of P. We can read $\gamma \vdash P : \delta$ as asserting that P capabilities are those of δ, within the context γ.

The simplest process (the null process) has no capability and hence its behaviour is consistent in any type context.

$$\gamma \vdash \mathbf{nil} : \phi$$

The process $\mathbf{out}(t)@\ell.P$ puts the tuple t in the tuple space whose address is specified by ℓ and then behaves like P. The typing rule of the out operation

$$\frac{\gamma \vdash P : \delta}{\gamma \vdash \mathbf{out}(t)@\ell.P : \delta[(\delta^1(\ell) \cup \{o\})/\delta^1(\ell)]}$$

states that the type of $\mathbf{out}(t)@\ell.P$ (possibly) extends that of P at ℓ with capability o. Since **out** is not a binder, P is typed within the same context (γ) as $\mathbf{out}(t)@\ell.P$.

The typing rules for **read** and **in** update the context with the types of the process variables they bind. The second half of their premises checks whether process P does not misuse the locality variables bound by **read** and **in**. Thus, for each locality variable u with type δ_u it is checked that the remote operations of P at u ($\delta^2(u)$) do respect δ_u. The resulting type is obtained by extending the type of P at ℓ with the corresponding capability (r or i) and the type of P at each of the locality variables bound by **read** and **in** with the corresponding type declarations.

$$\frac{update(\gamma, t) \vdash P : \delta \qquad (!u : \delta_u) \in fields(t) \Rightarrow \delta_u \preceq \delta^2(u)}{\gamma \vdash \mathbf{read}(t)@\ell.P : \delta[(\delta^1(\ell) \cup \{r\})/\delta^1(\ell)][\widetilde{\delta_u}/\delta^2(u)]}$$

$$\frac{update(\gamma, t) \vdash P : \delta \qquad (!u : \delta_u) \in fields(t) \Rightarrow \delta_u \preceq \delta^2(u)}{\gamma \vdash \mathbf{in}(t)@\ell.P : \delta[(\delta^1(\ell) \cup \{i\})/\delta^1(\ell)][\widetilde{\delta_u}/\delta^2(u)]}$$

where $\{\widetilde{u}\}$ are all the locality variables bound by **read** and **in**.

The typing rule of **eval** extends the type of P at ℓ with e and records that the remote operations of P have to be extended with those (δ') of the spawned process Q.

$$\frac{\gamma \vdash P : \delta \qquad \gamma \vdash Q : \delta'}{\gamma \vdash \mathbf{eval}(Q)@\ell.P : \delta[(\delta^1(\ell) \cup \{e\})/\delta^1(\ell), (\delta^2(\ell) \sqcup \delta')/\delta^2(\ell)]}$$

The typing rule for **newloc** extends the type of P at **self** with n and at u with the type δ' declared for u, while checks whether the operations that P is willing to perform at u ($\delta^2(u)$) comply with δ'.

$$\frac{\gamma \vdash P : \delta \qquad \delta' \preceq \delta^2(u)}{\gamma \vdash \mathbf{newloc}(!\,u : \delta')@\ell.P : \delta[(\delta^1(\mathtt{self}) \cup \{n\})/\delta^1(\mathtt{self})][\delta'/\delta^2(u)]}$$

The typing rules for parallel composition and choice state that the intentions of the composed processes are just the union, formally the least upper bound, of those of the components. The binding context is left unchanged.

$$\frac{\gamma \vdash P : \delta_1 \qquad \gamma \vdash Q : \delta_2}{\gamma \vdash P+Q : \delta_1 \sqcup \delta_2} \qquad\qquad \frac{\gamma \vdash P : \delta_1 \qquad \gamma \vdash Q : \delta_2}{\gamma \vdash P \,|\, Q : \delta_1 \sqcup \delta_2}$$

The type of a process variable is always determined by the type context, γ, that has been set up by the other inference rules. Definedness of $\gamma(X)$ is guaranteed by the fact that processes are closed terms. Each time a process variable is "freed" the rules take care that its type is recorded in the type context.

$$\frac{}{\gamma \vdash X : \gamma(X)}$$

The typing rule for (possibly recursive) process definition, first, updates the type context with the types declared for the process variables that occur as parameters in the definition and with the binding between the process constant and a type variable ν. The resulting context is used for inferring a type δ for P; ν may possibly occur in δ. Then, as in the rules for **in** and **read**, for each formal locality variable u_i, it is checked that the operations of P at u_i (i.e. $\delta^2(u_i)$) match the type declaration δ_{u_i}. Finally, the inferred type is given by the least fixed point of the function $rec\ \nu.\delta[\widetilde{\delta_u/\delta^2(u)}]$. Note that $\delta^2(u_i)$, the type of the formal locality variable u_i inferred within the type system, is replaced by δ_{u_i}, the type specified in the definition of the process constant.

$$\frac{\gamma[\widetilde{\delta_X/\widetilde{X}}][\nu/A] \vdash P : \delta \qquad u_i \in \widetilde{u} \Rightarrow \delta_{u_i} \preceq \delta^2(u_i)}{\gamma \vdash A(\widetilde{X} : \widetilde{\delta_X}, \widetilde{u} : \widetilde{\delta_u}, \widetilde{x}) : rec\ \nu.\delta[\widetilde{\delta_u/\delta^2(u)}]} \qquad A(\widetilde{X} : \widetilde{\delta_X}, \widetilde{u} : \widetilde{\delta_u}, \widetilde{x}) \overset{def}{=} P$$

The typing rule for process invocation, first, determines the type of the process constant and those of the process arguments: then, checks whether each of the types inferred for the process arguments agrees with that of the corresponding formal parameter. No requirement is imposed on the other arguments. Locality variables are controlled when one of the rules for **in**, **read** and **newloc** is applied. Localities are controlled when well–typedness of nets is checked. Actually, this is a consequence of the fact that the type of the process invocation is obtained from that of the process constant by replacing the formal locality variables with the corresponding actual parameters.

$$\frac{\gamma \vdash A(\widetilde{X} : \widetilde{\delta_X}, \widetilde{u} : \widetilde{\delta_u}, \widetilde{x}) : \delta \qquad P_i \in \{\widetilde{P}\} \wedge \gamma \vdash P_i : \delta_i \Rightarrow \delta_{X_i} \preceq \delta_i}{\gamma \vdash A(\widetilde{X} : \widetilde{\delta_X}, \widetilde{u} : \widetilde{\delta_u}, \widetilde{x})\langle \widetilde{P}, \widetilde{\ell}, \widetilde{e} \rangle : \delta[\widetilde{\ell}/\widetilde{u}]}$$

4.2 Dynamic Symbolic Semantics

The labelled transition system of the symbolic semantics describes abstractly the possible evolutions of TLLinda processes without providing the actual allocation of processes and tuple spaces. For this reason, the corresponding operational semantics is called *symbolic* in that neither expressions nor tuples are evaluated.

To describe the effects of the evaluation of processes which are placed within tuples fields, (see Section 5.2), we introduce the auxiliary term $P\{\rho\}$ that indicates the process P packaged with the allocation of localities specified by ρ; the mapping ρ is an evaluation environment and $P\{\rho\}$ is a *closure*.

The structural rules of the symbolic semantics are reported in Table 1. Labels of transitions are pairs $\langle \mu, \rho \rangle$ which provide an abstract description of the activities performed in process evolution. For instance, $\mu = s(t)@\ell$ describes the output (sending) of tuple t in the tuple space specified by ℓ. Similarly, $\mu = n(u : \delta)@\texttt{self}$ can be thought of as the request of binding a fresh site of type δ to the variable u. The environment ρ records the local bindings that must be used when evaluating μ. The interpretation of the structural rules of Table 1 is somehow straightforward.

5 Net Semantics

In this section, we present the criteria for establishing whether a net is well–typed and describe the dynamic operational semantics of nets. For type checking, it will be required that the types of the processes in a net agree with those of the sites where they are located. More specifically, the types of the processes, as determined by the type inference system, are checked against those fixed by the net coordinator, while taking into account where each process has been located.

5.1 Static Semantics

The rôle of a net is to allocate and coordinate a set of processes. Hence, beyond addressing all the issues related to physical distribution, the net coordinator assigns privileges to the sites where processes are allocated. The pair of functions,

$$\text{out}(t)@\ell.P \xrightarrow[\phi]{s(t)@\ell} P \qquad \text{eval}(Q)@\ell.P \xrightarrow[\phi]{e(Q)@\ell} P$$

$$\text{in}(t)@\ell.P \xrightarrow[\phi]{i(t)@\ell} P \qquad \text{read}(t)@\ell.P \xrightarrow[\phi]{r(t)@\ell} P$$

$$\text{newloc}(u:\delta).P \xrightarrow[\phi]{n(u:\delta)@\text{self}} P$$

$$\dfrac{P \xrightarrow{\mu}_\rho P'}{P+Q \xrightarrow{\mu}_\rho P'} \qquad \dfrac{P \xrightarrow{\mu}_\rho P'}{Q+P \xrightarrow{\mu}_\rho P'}$$

$$\dfrac{P \xrightarrow{\mu}_\rho P'}{P\mid Q \xrightarrow{\mu}_\rho P'\mid Q} \qquad \dfrac{P \xrightarrow{\mu}_\rho P'}{Q\mid P \xrightarrow{\mu}_\rho Q\mid P'}$$

$$\dfrac{P \xrightarrow{\mu}_{\rho'} P'}{P\{\rho\} \xrightarrow{\mu}_{\rho'\bullet\rho} P'\{\rho\}} \qquad \dfrac{P[\widetilde{P}/\widetilde{X},\widetilde{\ell}/\widetilde{u},\widetilde{e}/\widetilde{x}] \xrightarrow{\mu}_\rho P'}{A(\widetilde{X}:\widetilde{\delta_X},\widetilde{u}:\widetilde{\delta_u},\widetilde{x})\langle\widetilde{P},\widetilde{\ell},\widetilde{e}\rangle \xrightarrow{\mu}_\rho P'} A(\widetilde{X}:\widetilde{\delta_X},\widetilde{u}:\widetilde{\delta_u},\widetilde{x}) \stackrel{def}{=} P$$

Table 1. The Structural Rules of Symbolic Semantics

Λ and Υ, introduced in Section 3 associate a type to each site. It is this the type that is compared with that of located processes (that expresses their expected behaviour) for checking whether the net is well–typed.

Given a net $N_S : \langle\Lambda,\Upsilon\rangle$, the type δ_s of each site $s \in S$ is obtained as: $\forall \ell \in (dom(\rho_s) \cup dom(\Upsilon(s)))$:

$$\delta_s(\ell) = \begin{cases} \langle\Lambda(s)(\rho_s(\ell)),\delta_{\rho_s(\ell)}\rangle & \text{if } \ell \in dom(\rho_s) \\ \langle\Upsilon(s)(\ell),\delta_s\rangle & \text{if } \ell \in dom(\Upsilon(s)) \cap NVloc \\ \langle\Upsilon(s)(\ell),\bot\rangle & \text{if } \ell \in dom(\Upsilon(s)) \cap TVloc \end{cases}$$

The first item above uses the allocation environment ρ_s of s to determine the site associated to ℓ, hence the relative polarity and type. The second item uses $\Upsilon(s)$ to determine the polarity of ℓ; moreover, it says that a new site (denoted by ℓ) inherits the rights of the creating one. The final item uses $\Upsilon(s)$ similarly to the second one, but does not impose any static requirement on the type of the sites that will be bound (as a result of a communication) to ℓ.

Definition 5.1 A net $N_S : \langle\Lambda,\Upsilon\rangle$ is *well–typed* if $\forall s \in S$, $N_S(s) = (P,\rho)$ and $\phi \vdash P : \delta$ imply $\delta_s \preceq \delta$.

5.2 Dynamic Coordination Semantics

The operational semantics of nets is presented in Table 2. To avoid cumbersome notations, in the operational rules we use ℓ to denote localities, locality variables and sites and, suppose that allocation environments are extended to sites and act as the identity function over sites.

The evaluation function for tuples, $\mathcal{T}[\ ]$, makes use of an allocation environment for resolving locality names. $\mathcal{T}[\ ]$ is inductively defined over the syntax of tuples. There is only one non–trivial case, namely the evaluation of a process, say $\mathcal{T}[P]\rho$, which yields a process closure, i.e. $P\{\rho\}$.

As in [7, 16], we model tuples as processes but find it convenient to introduce auxiliary processes for denoting *evaluated tuples* (referred to as *et* possibly indexed) placed in one of the tuple spaces. Thus TLLinda syntax is extended with the process **out**(et) whose symbolic structural rule is

$$\mathbf{out}(et) \xrightarrow[\phi]{o(et)@\mathtt{self}} \mathbf{nil}.$$

Each node in a net has a unique site, thus we can consider a net just as a set. We write $s ::^\delta_\rho P$ for an element of a net, and $N_S, s ::^\delta_\rho P$ for the net given by $N_S \cup \{s ::^\delta_\rho P\}$ (with the implicit side condition that $s \notin S$).

The structural rules of the operational semantics specify the outcome of both local and remote operations performed by located processes. Thus, for each Linda primitive, we have two structural rules.

For instance, the evaluation of an **out** operation modifies a tuple space. Rule (1) adds a new tuple to the local tuple space of the process. Rule (2), instead, adds a new tuple to the remote tuple space located at s_2; the evaluation of the tuple t depends on the allocation environment $\rho \bullet \rho_1$. This corresponds to having a *static scoping* discipline for the remote generation of tuples. Moreover, if the tuple t contains a field with a process, the corresponding field of the evaluated tuple *et* contains a closure. Hence, processes in a tuple are transmitted together with their local allocation environment.

A *dynamic scoping* strategy is adopted for the **eval** operation, described by rules (3) and (4). In this case the process spawned at the remote node is transmitted *without* the local allocation environment, and its execution is influenced by the remote allocation environment ρ_2.

Rules (1)–(9) may modify the structure of the nodes of the net but cannot introduce new sites. The creation of a new node is described by rule (10). The environment of a new node is obtained from that of the creating one (with the obvious update for the **self** locality). The underlying idea is that the new node inherits all the knowledge about localities of the creating node.

The pattern–matching function for tuples that takes types into account is reported in Table 3. The rule ensures that if **read/in** looks for sites with type δ then only sites with type δ' such that $\delta' \preceq \delta$ would be accepted; while if **read/in** looks for processes with type δ then only processes with type δ' such that $\delta \preceq \delta'$ would be accepted.

6   Properties

In this section, we show that typing is sound, i.e. well–typed TLLinda nets (and processes) never encounter run–time errors due to misuse of access rights.

$$\frac{P \xrightarrow[\rho']{s(t)@\ell} P' \qquad s = \rho' \bullet \rho(\ell) \qquad et = \mathcal{T}[\![t]\!]_{\rho' \bullet \rho}}{N_S, s ::_\rho^\delta P \rightarrowtail N_S, s ::_\rho^\delta P' \mid \mathbf{out}(et)} \tag{1}$$

$$\frac{P_1 \xrightarrow[\rho]{s(t)@\ell} P_1' \qquad s_2 = \rho \bullet \rho_1(\ell) \qquad et = \mathcal{T}[\![t]\!]_{\rho \bullet \rho_1}}{N_S, s_1 ::_{\rho_1}^{\delta_1} P_1, s_2 ::_{\rho_2}^{\delta_2} P_2 \rightarrowtail N_S, s_1 ::_{\rho_1}^{\delta_1} P_1', s_2 ::_{\rho_2}^{\delta_2} P_2 \mid \mathbf{out}(et)} \tag{2}$$

$$\frac{P \xrightarrow[\rho']{e(Q)@\ell} P' \qquad s = \rho' \bullet \rho(\ell)}{N_S, s ::_\rho^\delta P \rightarrowtail N_S, s ::_\rho^\delta Q \mid P'} \tag{3}$$

$$\frac{P_1 \xrightarrow[\rho]{e(Q)@\ell} P_1' \qquad s_2 = \rho \bullet \rho_1(\ell)}{N_S, s_1 ::_{\rho_1}^{\delta_1} P_1, s_2 ::_{\rho_2}^{\delta_2} P_2 \rightarrowtail N_S, s_1 ::_{\rho_1}^{\delta_1} P_1', s_2 ::_{\rho_2}^{\delta_2} Q \mid P_2} \tag{4}$$

$$\frac{P_1 \xrightarrow[\rho']{i(t)@\ell} P_1' \quad s = \rho' \bullet \rho(\ell) \quad P_2 \xrightarrow[\phi]{o(et)@\text{self}} P_2' \quad match(\mathcal{T}[\![t]\!]_{\rho' \bullet \rho}, et)}{N_S, s ::_\rho^\delta P_1 | P_2 \rightarrowtail N_S, s ::_\rho^\delta P_1'[et/\mathcal{T}[\![t]\!]_{\rho' \bullet \rho}] \| P_2'} \tag{5}$$

$$\frac{P_1 \xrightarrow[\rho]{i(t)@\ell} P_1' \quad s_2 = \rho \bullet \rho_1(\ell) \quad P_2 \xrightarrow[\phi]{o(et)@\text{self}} P_2' \quad match(\mathcal{T}[\![t]\!]_{\rho \bullet \rho_1}, et)}{N_S, s_1 ::_{\rho_1}^{\delta_1} P_1, s_2 ::_{\rho_2}^{\delta_2} P_2 \rightarrowtail N_S, s_1 ::_{\rho_1}^{\delta_1} P_1'[et/\mathcal{T}[\![t]\!]_{\rho \bullet \rho_1}], s_2 ::_{\rho_2}^{\delta_2} P_2'} \tag{6}$$

$$\frac{P_1 \xrightarrow[\rho']{r(t)@\ell} P_1' \quad s = \rho' \bullet \rho(\ell) \quad P_2 \xrightarrow[\phi]{o(et)@\text{self}} P_2' \quad match(\mathcal{T}[\![t]\!]_{\rho' \bullet \rho}, et)}{N_S, s ::_\rho^\delta P_1 | P_2 \rightarrowtail N_S, s ::_\rho^\delta P_1'[et/\mathcal{T}[\![t]\!]_{\rho' \bullet \rho}] \| P_2} \tag{7}$$

$$\frac{P_1 \xrightarrow[\rho]{r(t)@\ell} P_1' \quad s_2 = \rho \bullet \rho_1(\ell) \quad P_2 \xrightarrow[\phi]{o(et)@\text{self}} P_2' \quad match(\mathcal{T}[\![t]\!]_{\rho \bullet \rho_1}, et)}{N_S, s_1 ::_{\rho_1}^{\delta_1} P_1, s_2 ::_{\rho_2}^{\delta_2} P_2 \rightarrowtail N_S, s_1 ::_{\rho_1}^{\delta_1} P_1'[et/\mathcal{T}[\![t]\!]_{\rho \bullet \rho_1}], s_2 ::_{\rho_2}^{\delta_2} P_2} \tag{8}$$

$$\frac{N_S, s ::_\rho^\delta P_1 \rightarrowtail N_S, s ::_\rho^\delta P_1'}{N_S, s ::_\rho^\delta P_1 | P_2 \rightarrowtail N_S, s ::_\rho^\delta P_1' | P_2} \tag{9}$$

$$\frac{P \xrightarrow[\rho']{n(u:\delta')@\text{self}} P' \qquad s \notin S \cup \{s'\}}{N_S, s' ::_\rho^\delta P \rightarrowtail N_S, s' ::_\rho^\delta P'[s/u], s ::_{[s/\text{self}] \bullet \rho}^{\delta'} \mathbf{nil}} \tag{10}$$

plus the symmetric of rules (5), (7) and (9)

Table 2. The Structural Rules of Nets Operational Semantics

$$
\begin{array}{ccc}
match(v,v) & match(P,P) & match(s,s)
\end{array}
$$

$$
match(!\,x,v) \qquad \dfrac{\phi \vdash P : \delta' \quad \delta \preceq \delta'}{match(!\,X : \delta, P)} \qquad \dfrac{\delta_s \preceq \delta}{match(!\,u : \delta, s)}
$$

$$
match(v,!\,x) \qquad \dfrac{\phi \vdash P : \delta' \quad \delta \preceq \delta'}{match(P,!\,X : \delta)} \qquad \dfrac{\delta \preceq \delta_s}{match(s,!\,u : \delta)}
$$

$$
\dfrac{match(et_1, et_2) \quad match(et_3, et_4)}{match((et_1, et_3), (et_2, et_4))}
$$

Table 3. The Matching Rules

We start by stating two properties of the type inference system for processes. The first one says that each process has a type and type inference terminates in a finite number of steps; the second says that typing is monomorphic.

Proposition 6.1 For each process P, there is a type δ such that $\phi \vdash P : \delta$ can be derived in a finite number of steps.

Proposition 6.2 If $\phi \vdash P : \delta_1$ and $\phi \vdash P : \delta_2$, then $\delta_1 = \delta_2$.

An easy consequence of the above properties is that given a process P and a type δ it is decidable whether P has type δ.

Corollary 6.3 Given a process P and a type δ, the type assignment $\phi \vdash P : \delta$ is decidable.

The following theorem establishes an important relationship between the operational semantics and the static semantics of TLLinda nets; the simple idea is that well–typedness is an *invariant* of the operational semantics. This result is essentially a variant of standard *subject reduction*, that takes into account the fact that new sites can be dynamically created. This calls for the following definition.

Given a net $N_S : \langle \Lambda, \Upsilon \rangle$ and a site $s \notin S$, we say that $\langle \Lambda', \Upsilon' \rangle$ is a *conservative extension* of $\langle \Lambda, \Upsilon \rangle$ over $S \cup \{s\}$ when

- for all $s' \in S$, $\Lambda'(s') = \Lambda(s')$ and $\Upsilon'(s') = \Upsilon(s')$, and
- there exists $s' \in S$ such that $\Lambda'(s) = \Lambda(s')$ and $\Upsilon'(s) = \Upsilon(s')$.

Conservative extensions guarantee that dynamically created nodes inherit the access rights of the creating ones.

Theorem 6.4 If $N_S : \langle \Lambda, \Upsilon \rangle$ is well–typed and $N_S \rightarrowtail N'_{S'}$ then

- $S' = S$ and $N'_{S'} : \langle \Lambda, \Upsilon \rangle$ is well–typed, or

– there exist $s \notin S$ such that $S' = S \cup \{s\}$, and $\langle \Lambda', \Upsilon' \rangle$ conservative extension of $\langle \Lambda, \Upsilon \rangle$ over $S \cup \{s\}$ and $N'_{S'} : \langle \Lambda', \Upsilon' \rangle$ is well–typed.

As a simple corollary of Theorem 6.4, the soundness follows. Indeed, since well–typedness is an invariant of the operational semantics, then it can never be the case that from a well–typed one a non well–typed net is obtained.

Corollary 6.5 If $N_S, s ::_\rho^\delta P$ is well–typed then process P cannot fail for misuse of access rights.

The last result states that the operational semantics of well–typed TLLinda nets is in agreement with that of the corresponding LLinda nets [6].

Theorem 6.6 If $N_S : \langle \Lambda, \Upsilon \rangle$ is a TLLinda well–typed net and we remove all of the type annotations, the resulting net has the same operational semantics as the LLinda net N_S.

7 Concluding Remarks

We have developed a type system for a language of mobile agents, that permits using type information for statically detecting violations of security properties related to capabilities and access control. The issue of "traditional" data typing was not addressed.

We consider the paper as a first step towards the ambitious goal of demonstrating that typing information can be systematically used to guarantee that well–typed processes always enjoy classes of security properties. We plan to extend the work by introducing a notion of multi–level security (e.g. structuring localities into levels of security) and by introducing *keys* to model dynamic transmission of access rights.

We also plan to develop observational semantics for TLLinda as foundation for programming logics and verification techniques. To this purpose, our starting point will be the testing framework developed for a process calculus based on Linda in [7, 16]. Other observational semantics for Linda based process calculi have been proposed in [5, 4, 1].

Type systems have been already proposed for calculi of mobile processes. Among those reminiscent of ours, although not addressing security issues, we mention the work of Pierce and Sangiorgi [14] and that of Kobayashi, Pierce and Turner [11]. In [14], a type system is developed for the π-calculus [13] that uses types of channels to record information on whether channels are used to *read* or to *write*. This type system has been extended in [11] by associating *multiplicities* to types for describing how many times each channel can be used. The main difference with our approach lies in the treatment of localities and, more importantly, in the rôle played by type information at the level of net coordinator to check and enforce access rights of processes.

The present work shares parts of its motivations with the work of [20]. However, they only concentrate on a *sequential* procedural language and their type system is used to guarantee that programs enjoy a *non interference* security property.

References

1. N. Busi, R. Gorrieri, G. Zavattaro. A Process Algebraic View of Linda Coordination Primitives. *Theoretical Computer Science.* (to appear)
2. L. Cardelli. A language with distributed scope. *Computing Systems*, 8(1):27-59, MIT Press, 1995.
3. N. Carriero, D. Gelernter. Linda in Context. *Communications of the ACM*, 32(4):444-458, 1989.
4. P. Ciancarini, R. Gorrieri, G. Zavattaro. Towards a Calculus for Generative Communication. Proc. FMOODS'96, pp.283-297, Chapman & Hall, 1996.
5. P. Ciancarini, K.K. Jensen, D. Yankelevich. On the Operational Semantics of a Coordination Language. Proc. Object–Based Models and Languages for Concurrent Systems, *LNCS* 924, pp.77-106, Springer, 1995.
6. R. De Nicola, G.-L. Ferrari, R. Pugliese. Locality based Linda: programming with explicit localities. Proc. TAPSOFT'97, *LNCS* 1214, pp.712-726, Springer, 1997.
7. R. De Nicola, R. Pugliese. A Process Algebra based on Linda. Proc. COORDINATION'96, *LNCS* 1061, pages 160-178, Springer, 1996.
8. D. Gelernter. Generative Communication in Linda. *ACM Transactions on Programming Languages and Systems*, 7(1):80-112, 1985.
9. A. Giacalone, P. Mishra, S. Prasad. Facile: A symmetric integration of concurrent and functional programming. *Int. Journal of Parallel Programming*, 18(2), 1989.
10. A. Ingolfsdottir. Semantic Models for Communicating Processes with Value–Passing. *Ph.D. Thesis*, University of Edinburgh, 1994.
11. N. Kobayashi, B. Pierce and D. Turner. Linearity and the π-calculus. In Proc. POPL'96, 1996.
12. R. Milner. *Communication and Concurrency*. Prentice Hall Int., 1989.
13. R. Milner, J. Parrow, D. Walker. A calculus of mobile processes, (Part I and II). *Information and Computation*, 100:1-77, 1992.
14. B. Pierce and D. Sangiorgi. Typing and subtyping for mobile processes. Proc. LICS'93, IEEE-Press, 1993 (to appear in *Mathematical Struct. in Comp. Science*)
15. G.D. Plotkin. Lectures notes in domain theory. University of Edinburgh, 1983.
16. R. Pugliese. Semantic Theories for Asynchronous Languages. Ph.D. Thesis VIII-96-6, Univ. di Roma "La Sapienza", Dip. Scienze dell'Informazione, 1996.
17. J. Reppy. Higher Order Concurrency. Ph.D. Thesis, Cornell University, 1992.
18. Sun Microsystems. The Java Language: A white paper. White Paper, 1994.
19. B. Thomsen, L. Leth, A. Giacalone. Some Issues in the Semantics of Facile Distributed Programming. REX Workshop "Semantics: Foundations and Applications", LNCS 666, Springer, 1992.
20. D. Volpano, G. Smith. A typed-based approach to program security. Proc. TAPSOFT'97, *LNCS* 1214, pp.607-621, Springer, 1997.
21. J.E. White. Telescript Technology: The Foundation for the Electronic Market Place. General Magic White Paper, 1994.
22. General Magic. Telescript Technology: Mobile Agents. White Paper, 1996.

Modeling Coordination via Asynchronous Communication

Antonio Brogi[1] and Jean-Marie Jacquet[2]

[1] Dipartimento di Informatica, Università di Pisa
Corso Italia 40, 56125 Pisa, Italy
brogi@di.unipi.it
[2] Institut d'Informatique, Facultés Universitaires de Namur
rue Grandgagnage 21, 5000 Namur, Belgium
jmj@info.fundp.ac.be

Abstract. The paper proposes a theoretical study of coordination languages. A language that embodies the essential features of coordination languages is considered. The language includes Linda's asynchronous communication primitives, as well as several composition operators. Computations in this language are described by means of an operational semantics, reporting the whole traces of executions. The non-compositionality of this intuitive operational semantics motivates the design of a compositional and fully abstract denotational semantics, can be exploited for studying program equivalence in this setting.

1 Introduction

Modern computer systems consist of large numbers of software components that interact one another. The process of software construction is more and more centered on the composition of generic existing packages to construct complex systems. Moreover, the rapid expansion of computer networks is highlighting the need for integrating and coordinating hetereogeneous components, which rely on different computational models and are physically distributed on the net.

Carrero and Gelernter [3] first pointed out the relevance of defining *coordination* models and languages for combining separate computational activities into asynchronous ensembles and for supporting communication among them. Linda [2] was the first coordination language, presented as a set of inter-agent communication primitives which can be virtually added to any programming language.

The interest for coordination models and languages is rapidly growing, and several coordination-based systems are under development or already available [4]. The study of models and languages for coordinating separate activities of software components is therefore of primary importance in this scenario. The scope of this paper is to contribute to setting the theoretical foundations of the growing field of coordination languages.

In this paper we will consider a simple language $\mathcal{L}$ that embodies the essential features of coordination languages based on generative communication à la Linda

239

[2]. The language includes Linda's out, in, and rd primitives for adding, deleting and checking the presence of an object in a shared dataspace. The language also includes sequential and parallel composition operators, as well as a choice operator in the style of CCS [7].

We will first describe the operational semantics of the language in the SOS style [9]. We will consider as observable behaviour of programs, for all possible computations, the sequences of states of the shared dataspace generated by computations. We will then define a denotational semantics and study the properties of compositionality and full abstraction with respect to the operational model of the language.

The definition of the denotational model is inspired by the denotational models for *nonuniform* concurrent languages proposed by Horita, de Bakker and Rutten in [6]. However, whereas in [6] the state of the computation is represented by the values of individual variables and is changed by assigning variables, in our setting the state of the computation is represented by the content of the shared dataspace and is changed by out and in primitives. In both cases the meaning of a process needs to represent the possible interactions between the process itself and the environment. Simply recording the initial and final states of computation sequences does not provide a compositional description of processes. We will therefore employ sequences of states which contain *gaps* between steps to represent possible interactions with the environment.

The denotational model of the language is defined in a *compositional* way. First the denotation of atomic agents (viz., communication actions) is given. Then the denotation of sequential, parallel and choice compositions of agents is defined by means of homomorphic operations on the denotations of agents. As the denotational semantics preserves the observational equivalence of agents, we have that denotationally equivalent programs are indistinguishable, that is, they exhibit the same observable operational behaviour in any possible context. We then show that the obtained denotational model is also *fully abstract* with respect to the operational model of the language. Intuitively speaking, this means that operationally indistinguishable programs are equivalent in the chosen denotational semantics.

The properties of compositionality and full abstraction of the denotational semantics establish firm foundations for reasoning about programs and program transformations. Let A be an agent which is part of a larger system, or context, denoted by $\mathcal{C}[A]$. Suppose that A' is an alternative, possibly more efficient, version of A obtained for instance by applying some program transformation technique to A. If A' is denotationally equivalent to A, that is if $\mathcal{D}(A) = \mathcal{D}(A')$, then the property of compositionality ensures that the substitution of A' for A does not affect the observable behaviour of the whole system, that is $\mathcal{O}(\mathcal{C}[A]) = \mathcal{O}(\mathcal{C}[A'])$. While compositionality ensures that any pair of denotationally equivalent agents can be substituted one another without affecting the observational behaviour of a system, full abstraction establishes that *only* denotationally equivalent programs satisfy such a property.

The paper is organised as follows. The language $\mathcal{L}$ is introduced in Section 2, where syntax and operational semantics of the language are presented. A fully abstract denotational semantics for $\mathcal{L}$ is defined in Section 3, while Section 4 contains some concluding remarks.

2 The $\mathcal{L}$ language

2.1 Syntax

We shall consider a simple language $\mathcal{L}$ embodying the essential features of coordination languages. Consequently, it has as basic elements Linda's out, in, and rd primitives, for putting an object on a shared space, getting it and checking its presence, respectively. $\mathcal{L}$ also includes sequential and parallel composition operators as well as a choice operator in the style of CCS [7]. However, for simplicity purposes, only finite processes are treated here, under the observation that infinite processes can be handled by extending the results of this paper in the classical way, exemplified, for instance, in [6].

The language $\mathcal{L}$ is formally defined by the following grammar.

Definition 1.

1. Let *Stoken* be an infinite set, the elements of which are subsequently called *tokens* and are typically represented by the letters t and u, possibly subscripted.
2. Define the set of agents *Sagent* by the following rules, where t is a token, A is an agent and c denotes a communication action.

$$c ::= tell(t) \mid ask(t) \mid get(t)$$
$$A ::= c \mid A \; ; \; A \mid A \parallel A \mid A + A$$

3. Define the language $\mathcal{L}$ as the above set *Sagent*.

2.2 Operational semantics

Configurations. $\mathcal{L}$ computations may be modelled by the following transition system written in Plotkin's style. Following intuition, most of configurations consist of an agent to be solved together with a multi-set of tokens denoting the tokens currently available for the computation. To easily express termination, we shall introduce particular configurations composed of a special terminating symbol E together with a multi-set of tokens. For uniformity purposes, we shall abuse language and qualify E as an agent. However, to meet the intuition, we shall always rewrite agents of the form $(E \; ; \; A)$, $(E \parallel A)$, and $(A \parallel E)$ as A. This is technically achieved by defining the extended set of agents as follows. In particular, simplifications are operated by imposing a bimonoid structure.

Definition 2. Define the extended set of agents *Seagent* by the following grammar

$$Ae ::= E \mid c \mid A\,;\,A \mid A \parallel A \mid A\,+\,A$$

Moreover, we shall subsequently assert that the structure $(Seagent, E, \,;\, , \parallel\,)$ is a bimonoid and simplify elements of $\mathcal{L}$ accordingly.

Definition 3. Define the set of stores *Sstore* as the set of finite multisets with elements from *Stoken*.

Definition 4. Define the set of configurations *Sconf* as *Seagent* × *Sstore*. Configurations are denoted as $\langle A \mid \sigma \rangle$, where A is an (extended) agent and σ is a multi-set of tokens.

Transition rules. The transition rules defining the operational semantics of the language are reported in Figure 1.

(T) $\qquad \langle tell(t) \mid \sigma \rangle \longrightarrow \langle E \mid \sigma \cup \{t\} \rangle$

(A) $\qquad \langle ask(t) \mid \sigma \cup \{t\} \rangle \longrightarrow \langle E \mid \sigma \cup \{t\} \rangle$

(G) $\qquad \langle get(t) \mid \sigma \cup \{t\} \rangle \longrightarrow \langle E \mid \sigma \rangle$

(S) $\qquad \dfrac{\langle A \mid \sigma \rangle \longrightarrow \langle A' \mid \sigma' \rangle}{\langle A\,;\,B \mid \sigma \rangle \longrightarrow \langle A'\,;\,B \mid \sigma' \rangle}$

(P) $\qquad \dfrac{\langle A \mid \sigma \rangle \longrightarrow \langle A' \mid \sigma' \rangle}{\begin{array}{l}\langle A \parallel B \mid \sigma \rangle \longrightarrow \langle A' \parallel B \mid \sigma' \rangle \\ \langle B \parallel A \mid \sigma \rangle \longrightarrow \langle B \parallel A' \mid \sigma' \rangle\end{array}}$

(C) $\qquad \dfrac{\langle A \mid \sigma \rangle \longrightarrow \langle A' \mid \sigma' \rangle}{\begin{array}{l}\langle A\,+\,B \mid \sigma \rangle \longrightarrow \langle A' \mid \sigma' \rangle \\ \langle B\,+\,A \mid \sigma \rangle \longrightarrow \langle A' \mid \sigma' \rangle\end{array}}$

Fig. 1. The transition rules.

Rule **(T)** states that an atomic agent $tell(t)$ can be executed in any store σ, and that its execution results in adding the token t to the store σ. Rule **(A)** states that an atomic agent $ask(t)$ can be executed in any store containing the token t, and that its execution does not modify the current store. Rule **(G)** also states that an atomic agent $get(t)$ can be executed in any store containing an occurrence of t, but in the resulting store the occurrence of t has been deleted. Rules **(S)**, **(P)**, and **(C)** describe the operational meaning of sequential, parallel and choice operators in the standard way [7].

242

Observables. A reasonable notion of observables consists of reporting, for all possible computations, the sequence of states the computations produce. It is defined subsequently as the semantics $\mathcal{O}_h$ to stress this notion of history of states. Another reasonable notion of observable would consists of focusing on the results of the computations only. It is however considered to be outside the scope of this paper and will be studied in future work.

We will use the following notation to represent sequences of elements and their concatenation. Given a set A, the set of finite sequences of elements of A is denoted by $A^{<\omega}$. The concatenation of two sequences q_1 and q_2 is denoted by $q_1.q_2$. Also if S_1 and S_2 are two sets of (finite) sequences we put:

$$S_1.S_2 \;=\; \{q_1.q_2 \mid q_1 \in S_1 \wedge q_2 \in S_2\}.$$

Definition 5.

1. Let δ^+ and δ^- be two fresh symbols denoting respectively success and failure. Define the set of histories *Shist* as the set of finite sequences ending by one termination mark: $Stoken^{<\omega}.\{\delta^+,\delta^-\}$.
2. Define the *"history semantics"* $\mathcal{O}_h : Sagent \to \mathcal{P}(Shist)$ as the following function: For any agent A,

$$\mathcal{O}_h(A) = \{\sigma_0.\cdots.\sigma_n.\delta^+ : \langle A_0 \mid \sigma_0\rangle \to \langle A_1 \mid \sigma_1\rangle \to \cdots \langle A_n \mid \sigma_n\rangle,$$
$$A_0 = A, \sigma_0 = \emptyset, A_n = E, n \geq 0\}$$
$$\cup$$
$$\{\sigma_0.\cdots.\sigma_n.\delta^- : \langle A_0 \mid \sigma_0\rangle \to \langle A_1 \mid \sigma_1\rangle \to \cdots \langle A_n \mid \sigma_n\rangle \not\to,$$
$$A_0 = A, \sigma_0 = \emptyset, A_n \neq E, n \geq 0\}$$

On compositionality. It is here worth noting that the operational semantics $\mathcal{O}_h$ is not compositional. For instance, taking $t \neq u$, we have that:

$$\mathcal{O}_h(get(t)) \;=\; \mathcal{O}_h(get(u)) \;=\; \{\emptyset.\delta^-\}$$

whereas

$$\mathcal{O}_h(tell(t) \parallel get(t)) = \{\emptyset.\{t\}.\emptyset.\delta^+\}$$
$$\mathcal{O}_h(tell(t) \parallel get(u)) = \{\emptyset.\{t\}.\delta^-\}$$

Hence, $\mathcal{O}_h$ is not compositional.

The purpose of the next section is precisely to define a compositional semantics for $\mathcal{L}$ which is correct with respect to the history operational semantics but which also contains a "minimal" amount of information to be compositional. In other words, we shall try to define a fully abstract (compositional) semantics.

3 Fully abstract compositional semantics for histories

There are two main reasons why the history semantics $\mathcal{O}_h$ is not compositional. First, the execution of a computation step produces a store which is not necessarily empty. A compositional semantics should therefore account for initial stores of any content. Second, as shown from the transition system, the computation of the agent $A \parallel B$ amounts to interleaving execution steps of A and B. A compositional semantics should thus allow for transition steps made by the environment.

Following [6], we shall model transition steps in the form of pairs of input and output stores and take as semantic domain sets of sequences of such pairs. These sequences possibly contain gaps, accounting for actions of the environment. Moreover, they will start with any store, allowing previous steps to result in a possibly non-empty store.

3.1 Notation

Before proceeding, it is convenient to introduce some notation.

Definition 6. Define *Shhist* as the set $(Sstore \times Sstore)^{<\omega} \times (Sstore.(\{\delta^+, \delta^-\}))$.

Notation 7

1. Let S be a set of histories of *Shhist* and p be a sequence of $(Sstore \times Sstore)^{<\omega}$. Then
$$S[p] = \{h : p.h \in S\}$$

2. Let S be a set of histories of *Shhist*. Then,
$$S^a = \{h : h = (\sigma, \tau).h' \in S\}$$
$$S^+ = \{h : h = (\sigma, \delta^+) \in S\}$$
$$S^- = \{h : h = (\sigma, \delta^-) \in S\}$$

3. Let h be an history of *Shhist*. Then
$$init(h) = \begin{cases} \sigma & \text{if } h = (\sigma, \tau).h' \\ \sigma & \text{if } h = (\sigma, \delta), \delta \in \{\delta^+, \delta^-\} \end{cases}$$

4. For $n \geq 0$ and $\delta \in \{\delta^+, \delta^-\}$, let $h = (\sigma_1, \tau_1). \cdots .(\sigma_{n-1}, \tau_{n-1}).(\sigma_n, \delta)$, be an history of *Shhist*. Then
$$diff(h) = (\sigma_1 \setminus \tau_1) \cup (\tau_1 \setminus \sigma_1) \cup \cdots \cup (\sigma_{n-1} \setminus \tau_{n-1}) \cup (\tau_{n-1} \setminus \sigma_{n-1})$$

where $\cup$ and $\setminus$ denote, respectively, multiset union and difference. Abusing notation, we shall lift $diff$ to sets of histories in the natural way: For any set S of histories of *Shhist*,
$$diff(S) = \bigcup \{diff(h) : h \in S\}$$

Definition 8. An history $h \in Shhist$ is *continuous* iff it has the form

$$(\sigma_0, \sigma_1).(\sigma_1, \sigma_2). \cdots .(\sigma_{n-1}, \sigma_n).(\sigma_n, \delta)$$

with $\delta \in \{\delta^+, \delta^-\}$. In that case, $\overline{h}$ denotes the following sequence of stores

$$\overline{h} = \sigma_0.\sigma_1. \cdots .\sigma_n.\delta$$

3.2 Denotational semantics

Defining a compositional semantics consists of, on the one hand, specifying the meaning of elementary statements and, on the other hand, providing an operator at the semantic level for each syntactic operator. We start with this second task in the following section. A compositional semantics, called denotational in view of the compositionality property, is defined next. It is then proved correct with respect to the history operational semantics $\mathcal{O}_h$, and finally it is established to be fully abstract.

Semantic operators. There are three syntactic operators to combine elementary agents: Sequential composition, parallel composition, and choice. Let us examine each of them in turn.

Sequential composition. Since semantic histories may include gaps and begin with any input store, composing the meaning of two agents which are sequentially composed amounts to concatenating their histories. This is achieved by the following operator, where further care is taken in the expected manner for the termination marks.

Definition 9. Define $\tilde{;} : \mathcal{P}(Shhist) \times \mathcal{P}(Shhist) \to \mathcal{P}(Shhist)$ as the following function: For any subset S_1, S_2 of $Shhist$,

$$S_1 \,\tilde{;}\, S_2 = \{h_1.h_2 : h_1.(\sigma, \delta^+) \in S_1, h_2 \in S_2\}$$
$$\cup \{h_1.(\sigma, \delta^-) : h_1.(\sigma, \delta^-) \in S_1\}$$

Parallel composition. Parallel composition is modelled in an interleaving fashion. Consequently, composing in parallel two semantic histories amounts to taking their merge. Again, care has to be taken for termination marks, as formalised below.

Definition 10. Define the parallel composition of two histories as the function $\tilde{\|}_h : Shhist \times Shhist \to \mathcal{P}(Shhist)$ defined inductively by the following equalities, where δ stands either for δ^+ or δ^-.

$$(\sigma_1, \tau_1).h_1 \,\widetilde{\|}_h\, (\sigma_2, \tau_2).h_2 = \{(\sigma_1, \tau_1).h : h \in h_1 \,\widetilde{\|}_h\, (\sigma_2, \tau_2).h_2\}$$
$$\cup \{(\sigma_2, \tau_2).h : h \in (\sigma_1, \tau_1).h_1 \,\widetilde{\|}_h\, h_2\}$$

$$(\sigma_1, \tau_1).h_1 \,\widetilde{\|}_h\, (\sigma_2, \delta_2) = (\sigma_2, \delta_2) \,\widetilde{\|}_h\, (\sigma_1, \tau_1).h_1$$
$$= \{(\sigma_1, \tau_1).h : h \in h_1 \,\widetilde{\|}_h\, (\sigma_2, \delta_2)\}$$

$$(\sigma_1, \delta_1) \,\widetilde{\|}_h\, (\sigma_2, \delta_2) = \begin{cases} \{(\sigma_1, \delta^+)\}, & \text{if } \sigma_1 = \sigma_2 \text{ and } \delta_1 = \delta_2 = \delta^+ \\ \{(\sigma_1, \delta^-)\}, & \text{if } 1)\ \sigma_1 = \sigma_2 \text{ and} \\ & \quad\ 2)\ \delta_1 = \delta^- \text{ or } \delta_2 = \delta^- \\ \emptyset, & \text{if } \sigma_1 \neq \sigma_2 \end{cases}$$

Definition 11. Define the parallel composition of two sets of histories as the natural lifting of function $\widetilde{\|}_h$, namely as the function $\widetilde{\|}$: $\mathcal{P}(Shhist) \times \mathcal{P}(Shhist) \to \mathcal{P}(Shhist)$ defined as follows: for any subset S_1, S_2 of $Shhist$,

$$S_1 \,\widetilde{\|}\, S_2 = \bigcup \{h_1 \,\widetilde{\|}_h\, h_2 : h_1 \in S_1, h_2 \in S_2\}.$$

Choice. Choice is modelled as an internal choice, namely an agent formed from the choice of two agents can proceed as any of its components. As before care has to be taken for termination marks. The composed agent fails if the two components do so, it succeeds if at least one of the two components does.

Definition 12. Define $\widetilde{+}$: $\mathcal{P}(Shhist) \times \mathcal{P}(Shhist) \to \mathcal{P}(Shhist)$ as the following function: for any subset S_1, S_2 of $Shhist$,

$$S_1 \,\widetilde{+}\, S_2 = S_1^a \cup S_2^a \cup S_1^+ \cup S_2^+ \cup (S_1^- \cap S_2^-).$$

Definition. Given the operators $\widetilde{;}$, $\widetilde{\|}$, and $\widetilde{+}$, defining the denotational semantics amounts to specifying the semantics of the basic constructs *tell*, *ask*, and *get*. This is achieved according to the intuition given by their operational behaviour.

Definition 13. Define the denotational semantics as the following function $\mathcal{D}_h$: $Sagent \to \mathcal{P}(Shhist)$: for any token t, for any agents A_1, A_2,

$$\mathcal{D}_h(tell(t)) = \{(\sigma, \sigma \cup \{t\}).(\tau, \delta^+) : \sigma, \tau \in Sstore\} \tag{1}$$

$$\mathcal{D}_h(ask(t)) = \{(\sigma, \sigma).(\tau, \delta^+) : \sigma, \tau \in Sstore, t \in \sigma\} \tag{2}$$
$$\cup \{(\sigma, \delta^-) : \sigma \in Sstore, t \notin \sigma\}$$

$$\mathcal{D}_h(get(t)) = \{(\sigma, \sigma \setminus \{t\}).(\tau, \delta^+) : \sigma, \tau \in Sstore, t \in \sigma\} \tag{3}$$
$$\cup \{(\sigma, \delta^-) : \sigma \in Sstore, t \notin \sigma\}$$

$$\mathcal{D}_h(A_1 ; A_2) = \mathcal{D}_h(A_1) \,\widetilde{;}\, \mathcal{D}_h(A_2) \tag{4}$$

$$\mathcal{D}_h(A_1 \| A_2) = \mathcal{D}_h(A_1) \,\widetilde{\|}\, \mathcal{D}_h(A_2) \tag{5}$$

$$\mathcal{D}_h(A_1 + A_2) = \mathcal{D}_h(A_1) \,\widetilde{+}\, \mathcal{D}_h(A_2) \tag{6}$$

Properties. It is easy to observe that the semantics $\mathcal{D}_h$ is compositional by construction. It is also correct with respect to the semantics $\mathcal{O}_h$ in the sense that the latter can be obtained from $\mathcal{D}_h$. Indeed, it is sufficient to take the continuous histories from $\mathcal{D}_h$ starting in the empty store to get those produced by $\mathcal{O}_h$.

Proposition 14. *Let* $\alpha : \mathcal{P}(Shhist) \rightarrow \mathcal{P}(Shhist)$ *be defined as follows: For any subset* $S \subseteq Shhist$,

$$\alpha(S) = \{\overline{h} : h \in S, h \ continuous, init(h) = \emptyset\}.$$

Then

$$\mathcal{O}_h = \alpha \circ \mathcal{D}_h.$$

Proof By structural reasoning. ∎

Proposition 14 establishes that if two agents A_1 and A_2 have same denotation, viz. $\mathcal{D}_h(A_1) = \mathcal{D}_h(A_2)$, then they are indistinguishable in any context. Note that, as a corollary of this proposition every operational history $\emptyset.\sigma_1.\cdots.\sigma_n.\delta$ is in a one-to-one correspondence with a continuous denotational history starting in the empty store: $(\emptyset, \sigma_1).\cdots.(\sigma_n, \delta)$.

The denotational semantics can also be characterised in terms of the operational semantics as follows.

Proposition 15. *Extend the denotational semantics to the empty agent* E *as follows:*

$$\mathcal{D}_h(E) = \{(\sigma, \delta^+) : \sigma \in Sstore\}.$$

Let A *be an agent and* σ, τ *be stores such that* $\mathcal{D}_h(A)[(\sigma, \tau)] \neq \emptyset$. *Moreover, let* $B_1, \ldots, B_m$ *be all the agents such that*

$$\langle A \mid \sigma \rangle \rightarrow \langle B_i \mid \tau \rangle$$

Then,

$$\mathcal{D}_h(A)[(\sigma, \tau)] = \mathcal{D}_h(B_1) \cup \cdots \cup \mathcal{D}_h(B_m).$$

Proof By structural reasoning. ∎

Note that $\mathcal{D}_h(B_1) \cup \cdots \cup \mathcal{D}_h(B_m)$ is similar to $\mathcal{D}_h(B_1 + \cdots + B_m)$. The two sets actually differ by the treatment of immediately failing computation: All of them are registered in $\mathcal{D}_h(B_1) \cup \cdots \cup \mathcal{D}_h(B_m)$ while only those common to $B_1, \ldots, B_m$ appear in the denotational semantics of $B_1 + \cdots + B_m$.

The next property to ask is whether $\mathcal{D}_h$ contains the least amount of information necessary to be compositional and correct. That corresponds to a full abstraction result. This result is so involved that it deserves a complete section, which is done in the next section.

As a preliminary result, it is interesting to observe that for any agent A, the denotational semantics $\mathcal{D}_h(A)$ is *extensible* in the following sense.

Proposition 16. *For any agent A, any stores σ, σ_1, ..., σ_n,*

1. *there is a continuous history in $\mathcal{D}_h(A)$ starting in σ*
2. *if $\mathcal{D}_h(A)[(\sigma_1, \sigma_2). \cdots .(\sigma_{n-1}, \sigma_n)] \neq \emptyset$ then there is a continuous history in $\mathcal{D}_h(A)$ of the form $(\sigma_1, \sigma_2). \cdots .(\sigma_{n-1}, \sigma_n).h'$*

Proof By structural reasoning. ∎

3.3 Full abstraction

Definitions.

Definition 17. Let □ be a fresh symbol. Define the set of contexts *Scontext* by the following rules, where A is an agent.

$$C ::= \square \mid A \mid C\,;\,A \mid A\,;\,C \mid C \parallel A \mid A \parallel C \mid C + A \mid A + C$$

The application of a context C to an agent A is defined as the new agent obtained by replacing the place holder □ in C, if any, by A. This is subsequently denoted as $C[A]$.

Definition 18. The semantics $\mathcal{D}_h$ is fully abstract with respect to the semantics $\mathcal{O}_h$ iff the following property holds: for any agents A_1, A_2, the following assertions are equivalent
  i) for any context C, $\mathcal{O}_h(C[A_1]) = \mathcal{O}_h(C[A_2])$;
  ii) $\mathcal{D}_h(A_1) = \mathcal{D}_h(A_2)$.

Intuition. The compositional property of $\mathcal{D}_h$ together with proposition 14 establish the implication $(ii) \Rightarrow (i)$. It thus remains to prove the converse $(i) \Rightarrow (ii)$. To that end, we shall proceed by contradiction. Given two agents A_1, A_2 such that

$$\mathcal{D}_h(A_1) \neq \mathcal{D}_h(A_2)$$

we shall construct a context C such that

$$\mathcal{O}_h(C[A_1]) \neq \mathcal{O}_h(C[A_2])$$

The two semantics reporting sets, the construction amounts to constructing from a denotational history h of one agent, say A_1, which is not in the denotation of the other A_2, a context C and an operational history in $C[A_1]$ but not in $C[A_2]$. In view of the relation between $\mathcal{O}_h$ and $\mathcal{D}_h$ as shown by α in proposition 14, this amounts to establishing the existence of a continuous denotational history, starting in $\emptyset$, which is in $\mathcal{D}_h(C[A_1])$ and not in $\mathcal{D}_h(C[A_2])$. To that end, following

[6], we shall construct from h a new history h' and an agent T such that h' is in the denotation of $A_1 \parallel T$ and not in the denotation of $A_2 \parallel T$.

The proof basically proceeds by induction on the length of h.

In the base case, h takes the form (σ, δ) with δ being either δ^+ or δ^-. The tester T then essentially constructs a continuous sequence yielding σ from the initial store $\emptyset$ in a way that, on the one hand, prevents A_1 and A_2 to do any intermediary step, and, on the other hand, forces A_1 and A_2 to do the last step (σ, δ). By hypothesis, this is possible for A_1 and not for A_2.

In the non basic case, h takes the form $(\sigma, \tau).h^*$ for some history h^*. Two cases are possible: either there is no history starting by (σ, τ) in $\mathcal{D}_h(A_2)$ or those which start by (σ, τ) cannot end by h^*. In the first case, the proof proceeds as in the base case. In the second case, the proof uses induction. However, the induction should be applied for h^* in $\mathcal{D}_h(A_1)[(\sigma, \tau)]$ and not in $\mathcal{D}_h(A_2)[(\sigma, \tau)]$. As stated by proposition 15, these sets turned out to be basically but not exactly the denotations $\mathcal{D}_h(A_1')$ and $\mathcal{D}_h(A_2')$, of some agents A_1' and A_2'. We shall consequently generalise a bit the induction to sets of denotational histories. This extension being discarded here for the sake of simplicity, we thus apply the induction hypothesis for h^*, A_1' and A_2'. It points out a tester T' and an history h'' which is in $\mathcal{D}_h(A_1' \parallel T')$ and not in $\mathcal{D}_h(A_2' \parallel T')$. From there we should construct a tester T and an history h''' in $\mathcal{D}_h(A_1 \parallel T)$ and not in $\mathcal{D}_h(A_2 \parallel T)$. Basically, the step (σ, τ) has to be done before h'' and since h''' needs to be continuous, h'' has to start in a possibly non empty store. Hence, we have to generalise the theorem and construct in general from h an history h' which start in any initial store. Given this generalisation, the tester T basically consists of first making the steps necessary to produce σ from the given initial store, then of making an auxiliary transition from τ to some τ' chosen so as to ensure that A_1 and A_2 have to do the step (σ, τ), and finally consists of T'.

Auxiliary concepts. The above intuition points out an auxiliary task which consists of making, by means of an auxiliary agent, the steps necessary to produce a given target store τ from a given initial store σ. These steps are subsequently achieved by means of the following agent $Ag_{\sigma \to \tau}^V$.

Definition 19. Let V be a finite set of tokens, and σ and τ be two stores. Let

$$\sigma \setminus \tau = \{g_1, \cdots, g_m\}$$
$$\tau \setminus \sigma = \{t_1, \cdots, t_n\}$$

with $m, n \geq 0$. Let $a_1, \ldots, a_{m+n}$ be tokens not in V, σ, and τ. Abusing language by forgetting in the notation about these a_i's, we denote by $Ag_{\sigma \to \tau}^V$, the agent

(actually one of the possible such agents)

$$get(g_1); tell(a_1);$$
$$\cdots$$
$$get(g_m); tell(a_m);$$
$$tell(t_1); tell(a_{m+1});$$
$$\cdots$$
$$tell(t_n); tell(a_{m+n});$$
$$get(a_1); \cdots; get(a_{m+n})$$

Moreover, we note by $\Sigma^V_{\sigma \to \tau}$ the associated sequence of states

$$(\xi_0, \gamma_1).(\gamma_1, \xi_1).$$
$$\cdots$$
$$(\xi_{m-1}, \gamma_m).(\gamma_m, \xi_m).$$
$$(\xi_m, \tau_1).(\tau_1, \xi_{m+1}).$$
$$\cdots$$
$$(\xi_{m+n-1}, \tau_n).(\tau_n, \xi_{m+n}).$$
$$(\rho_0, \rho_1).\cdots.(\rho_{m+n-1}, \rho_{m+n})$$

where

$$
\begin{aligned}
&\xi_0 = \sigma \\
&\rho_0 = \xi_{m+n} \\
&\rho_{m+n} = \tau \\
&\gamma_i = \xi_{i-1} \setminus \{g_i\} && (1 \le i \le m) \\
&\xi_i = \gamma_i \cup \{a_i\} && (1 \le i \le m) \\
&\tau_j = \xi_{m+j-1} \cup \{t_j\} && (1 \le j \le n) \\
&\xi_{m+j} = \tau_j \cup \{a_{m+j}\} && (1 \le j \le n) \\
&\rho_k = \rho_{k-1} \setminus \{a_k\} && (1 \le k \le m+n)
\end{aligned}
$$

Obviously, $Ag^V_{\sigma \to \tau}$ can perform the history $\Sigma^V_{\sigma \to \tau}.(\rho_{m+n}, \delta^+)$. If V is suitably chosen, it also has the property of being responsible for making the steps of $\Sigma^V_{\sigma \to \tau}$ when placed in parallel with another agent.

Proposition 20. *Let σ and τ be two stores. Let A be an agent and let V contain the tokens present in the tell, get and read communication primitives of A.*

1. *Any history $h = \Sigma^V_{\sigma \to \tau}.h'$ in $\mathcal{D}_h(Ag^V_{\sigma \to \tau} \parallel A)$ is in the set $\Sigma^V_{\sigma \to \tau}.(\gamma, \delta^+) \; \widetilde{\parallel}_h \; h_a$ for some store γ and some history $h_a \in \mathcal{D}_h(A)$.*
2. *For any agent B, any history $h = \Sigma^V_{\sigma \to \tau}.h'$ of $\mathcal{D}_h((Ag^V_{\sigma \to \tau} \; ; \; B) \parallel A)$ is of the set $\Sigma^V_{\sigma \to \tau}.h_b \; \widetilde{\parallel}_h \; h_a$ for some histories $h_a \in \mathcal{D}_h(A)$ and $h_b \in \mathcal{D}_h(B)$.*

Proof Let us establish the first part of the proposition, the proof of the other part being similar.

By definition 13, if h is in $\mathcal{D}_h(Ag^V_{\sigma \to \tau} \parallel A)$, there are $h_1 \in \mathcal{D}_h(Ag^V_{\sigma \to \tau})$ and $h_2 \in \mathcal{D}_h(A)$ such that $h \in h_1 \; \widetilde{\parallel}_h \; h_2$. Moreover, in view of $Ag^V_{\sigma \to \tau}$, h_1 is necessarily of the following form:

$$(\alpha_1, \alpha_1 \setminus \{g_1\}).(\beta_1, \beta_1 \cup \{a_1\}).$$
$$\cdots.$$
$$(\alpha_m, \alpha_m \setminus \{g_m\}).(\beta_m, \beta_m \cup \{a_m\}).$$
$$(\alpha_{m+1}, \alpha_{m+1} \cup \{t_1\}).(\beta_{m+1}, \beta_{m+1} \cup \{a_{m+1}\}).$$
$$\cdots$$
$$(\alpha_{m+n}, \alpha_{m+n} \cup \{t_n\}).(\beta_{m+n}, \beta_{m+n} \cup \{a_{m+n}\}).$$
$$(\pi_1, \pi_1 \setminus \{a_1\}).$$
$$\cdots$$
$$(\pi_{m+n}, \pi_{m+n} \setminus \{a_{m+n}\})$$

Let us first progressively establish that $h_1 = \Sigma^V_{\sigma \to \tau}.h'_1$ for some history h'_1.

Using the notations of definition 19, we first observe that h_2 cannot be of the form $(\xi_0, \gamma_1).h'_2$. Indeed, if this was the case, then, in view of the merge operator $\|_h$, either $h_1 = (\gamma_1, \xi_1).h'_1$ or $h'_2 = (\gamma_1, \xi_1).h''_2$. However, both cases are impossible. In the first case, in view of the above form of h_1, one would have $\xi_1 = \gamma_1 \setminus \{g_1\}$ and thus $a_1 \notin \xi_1$ since $a_1 \notin \gamma_1$ whereas by definition of ξ_1, $a_1 \in \xi_1$. In the second case, since a_1 cannot be told by A by choice of a_1, then again $a_1 \notin \xi_1$ whereas by definition of ξ_1, $a_1 \in \xi_1$. Hence,

$$h_1 = (\xi_0, \gamma_1).r_1$$

Moreover, as just explained, by its choice, a_1 cannot be told by A and consequently, h_2 cannot be of the form $h_2 = (\gamma_1, \xi_1).h'_2$, for some h'_2. It follows that

$$h_1 = (\xi_0, \gamma_1).(\gamma_1, \xi_1).r_2$$

By similar reasoning, h_1 can be proved to be of the form

$$h_1 = (\xi_0, \gamma_1).(\gamma_1, \xi_1).\cdots.(\xi_{m-1}, \gamma_m).(\gamma_m, \xi_m).(\xi_m, \tau_1).(\tau_1, \xi_{m+1}).$$
$$\cdots(\xi_{m+n-1}, \tau_n).(\tau_n, \xi_{m+n}).r_3$$

Now, since by definition A cannot get any a_i, h_1 must further be of the form

$$(\xi_0, \gamma_1).(\gamma_1, \xi_1).$$
$$\cdots$$
$$(\xi_{m-1}, \gamma_m).(\gamma_m, \xi_m).$$
$$(\xi_m, \tau_1).(\tau_1, \xi_{m+1}).$$
$$\cdots$$
$$(\xi_{m+n-1}, \tau_n).(\tau_n, \xi_{m+n}).$$
$$(\rho_0, \rho_1).\cdots.(\rho_{m+n-1}, \rho_{m+n}).r_4$$

Summing up, the agent $Ag^V_{\sigma \to \tau}$ has made all the $2(m+n)$ steps and thus has reached completion successfully. It follows that r_4 should be (γ, δ^+), for some store γ. ∎

Proposition 20 can be extended to more general sets of denotational histories.

Definition 21. A set S of denotational histories is called *coherent* if it is extensible (in the sense of proposition 16) and if the set $diff(S)$ is finite.

Proposition 22. *Let σ and τ be two stores. Let S be a coherent subset of $Shhist$ and let V contain $diff(S)$.*

1. *Any history $h = \Sigma_{\sigma \to \tau}^{V}.h'$ in $\mathcal{D}_h(Ag_{\sigma \to \tau}^{V}) \, \widetilde{\|} \, S$ is in the set $\Sigma_{\sigma \to \tau}^{V}.(\gamma, \delta^+) \, \widetilde{\|}_h \, h_s$ for some store γ and some history $h_s \in S$.*
2. *For any agent B, any history $h = \Sigma_{\sigma \to \tau}^{V}.h'$ in $\mathcal{D}_h(Ag_{\sigma \to \tau}^{V} \, ; \, B) \, \widetilde{\|} \, S$ is in the set $\Sigma_{\sigma \to \tau}^{V}.h_b \, \widetilde{\|}_h \, h_s$ for some histories $h_s \in S$ and $h_b \in \mathcal{D}_h(B)$.*

Proof Similar to that of proposition 20. ∎

Key proposition.

Theorem 23. *Let S_1, S_2 be two coherent subsets of $Shhist$ such that $S_1 \setminus S_2 \neq \emptyset$. Then, for any store α, there is an agent T and a continuous history $h \in (S_1 \, \widetilde{\|} \, \mathcal{D}_h(T)) \setminus (S_2 \, \widetilde{\|} \, \mathcal{D}_h(T))$ which starts in α.*

Proof The proof is conducted by induction on the minimum Lg of the length of the histories which are in S_1 and not in S_2.

Case I: $Lg = 1$. Then there is an history $h \in S_1 \setminus S_2$ which is of the form (σ, δ^+) or of the form (σ, δ^-).

Subcase i: $h = (\sigma, \delta^+)$. Let us first examine the case where $h = (\sigma, \delta^+)$. By hypothesis, $(\sigma, \delta^+) \notin S_2$. Let V be the set $diff(S_2)$. Consider $T = Ag_{\alpha \to \sigma}^{V}$. Obviously, $h = \Sigma_{\alpha \to \sigma}^{V}.(\sigma, \delta^+)$ is a continuous history belonging to $S_1 \, \widetilde{\|} \, \mathcal{D}_h(T)$. To conclude in this case, let us prove that it does not belong to $S_2 \, \| \, \mathcal{D}_h(T)$. Indeed, if so, by proposition 22, h should come from the following merge:

$$h \in \Sigma_{\alpha \to \sigma}^{V}.(\gamma, \delta^+) \, \widetilde{\|}_h \, h_s$$

for some store γ and some history $h_s \in S_2$. Moreover, since h ends after $\Sigma_{\alpha \to \sigma}^{V}$ by (σ, δ^+), one should have, by definition of the merge (see definition 10), $\gamma = \sigma$ and $h_s = (\sigma, \delta^+)$. Therefore, (σ, δ^+) should belong to S_2, which contradicts the hypothesis on A_2.

Subcase ii: $h = (\sigma, \delta^-)$. The case where $h = (\sigma, \delta^-)$ can be treated similarly with the proof ending by noting that $h_s = (\sigma, \delta^-)$ should belong to S_2, which contradicts the hypothesis.

Case II: $Lg > 1$. Let us now consider the case where the minimum of the lengths of the histories of $S_1 \setminus S_2$ is greater than 1. In that case, let h be such an history of minimum length. It is thus of the form $h = (\sigma, \tau).h'$ for some stores σ, τ and some history h'. There are two cases to be considered: either $S_2[(\sigma, \tau)] = \emptyset$ or $S_2[(\sigma, \tau)] \neq \emptyset$ but $h' \notin S_2[(\sigma, \tau)]$.

Subcase i: $S_2[(\sigma, \tau)] = \emptyset$. If $S_2[(\sigma, \tau)] = \emptyset$, then let us first observe, by proposition 16, that there is a continuous history of the form $(\sigma, \tau).h_r$ in S_1. Let us then consider V and $T = Ag_{\alpha \to \sigma}^V$ as above. Obviously, $h^* = \Sigma_{\alpha \to \sigma}^V.(\sigma, \tau).h_r$ is a continuous history starting in α. Moreover, if (ω, δ) is the last pair of the sequence h_r, then h^* belongs to the merge of the histories $\Sigma_{\alpha \to \sigma}^V.(\omega, \delta^+)$ and $(\sigma, \tau).h_r$, and consequently to $S_1 \, \widetilde{\|} \, \mathcal{D}_h(T)$. To conclude, let us establish that it does not belong to $S_2 \, \widetilde{\|} \, \mathcal{D}_h(T)$. Indeed, otherwise, following proposition 22, h^* should then come from the merge of two histories of the form $\Sigma_{\alpha \to \sigma}^V.(\gamma, \delta^+)$ and h_s with $h_s \in S_2$. According to the definition of the merge operation, one would then have $h_s = (\sigma, \tau).h_r$ and thus $S_2[(\sigma, \tau)]$ would be non-empty, which contradicts the hypothesis.

Subcase ii: $S_2[(\sigma, \tau)] \neq \emptyset$ *but* $h' \notin S_2[(\sigma, \tau)]$. In that case, by hypothesis $h' \in S_1[(\sigma, \tau)] \setminus S_2[(\sigma, \tau)]$ and the minimum of the length of those histories which are in $S_1[(\sigma, \tau)]$ and not in $S_2[(\sigma, \tau)]$ is strictly less than Lg. We are thus in the position of applying the induction hypothesis. For an arbitrarily given store α' — to be specified in a moment — it delivers a tester T' and a continuous history h_r^* starting in α' and which is in $(S_1[(\sigma, \tau)] \, \widetilde{\|} \, \mathcal{D}_h(T')) \setminus (S_2[(\sigma, \tau)] \, \widetilde{\|} \, \mathcal{D}_h(T'))$. The proof then consists of prefixing T' by some actions, yielding T, and h_r^* by a suitable sequence, yielding h^*, such as h^* starts, as required, in α, is continuous, and is in $S_1 \, \widetilde{\|} \, \mathcal{D}_h(T)$ and not in $S_2 \, \widetilde{\|} \, \mathcal{D}_h(T)$. Applying the previous technique, T should start by $Ag_{\alpha \to \sigma}^V$ to bring the store α to σ, then leave S_1 and S_2 do the step (σ, τ) and then resume by doing T'. In order to force the S_i's to do so, we need a trick which basically consists of adding in h^* after (σ, τ) a step that can only be made by T. Hence, let t be a fresh token not appearing in $diff(S_1)$, $diff(S_2)$, and in the tokens used by $Ag_{\alpha \to \sigma}^V$ and let α' be $\alpha \cup \{t\}$. Moreover, let us take $T = Ag_{\alpha \to \sigma}^V$; $tell(t)$; T' and $h^* = \Sigma_{\alpha \to \sigma}^V.(\sigma, \tau).(\tau, \alpha').h_r^*$. Then, h^* is in $S_1 \, \widetilde{\|} \, \mathcal{D}_h(T)$. Indeed, as $h_r^* \in S_1[(\sigma, \tau)] \, \widetilde{\|} \, \mathcal{D}_h(T')$, there is $h_1 \in S_1[(\sigma, \tau)]$ and $h_t \in \mathcal{D}_h(T')$ such that $h_r^* \in h_1 \, \widetilde{\|}_h \, h_t$. Therefore, $(\sigma, \tau).h_1 \in S_1$ and $\Sigma_{\alpha \to \sigma}^V.(\tau, \alpha').h_t \in \mathcal{D}_h(T)$. It follows that $h^* \in (\sigma, \tau).h_1 \, \widetilde{\|}_h \, \Sigma_{\alpha \to \sigma}^V.(\tau, \alpha').h_t$ is in $S_1 \, \widetilde{\|} \, \mathcal{D}_h(T)$.

To conclude, it remains to be established that $h^* \notin S_2 \, \widetilde{\|} \, \mathcal{D}_h(T)$. Let us proceed by contradiction as before. Otherwise, in view of proposition 22, h^* should be in the set $\Sigma_{\sigma \to \tau}^V.h_t \, \widetilde{\|}_h \, h_s$ for some histories $h_t \in \mathcal{D}_h(tell(t) \, ; \, T')$ and $h_s \in S_2$. Moreover, T cannot be responsible for the step (σ, τ) i.e., restated in formal terms, h_t cannot be of the form $h_t = (\sigma, \tau).h_t'$. Indeed, if this was the case, then $\tau = \sigma \cup \{t\}$, whereas by definition $t \notin \tau$. Hence, $h_s = (\sigma, \tau).h_s'$ for some history h_s'. Note that, since $h_s \in S_2$, $h_s' \in S_2[(\sigma, \tau)]$. Moving one step further in h^*, again, thanks to the choice of the token t, S_2 cannot perform the step (τ, α') ie h_s' cannot rewrite as $h_s' = (\tau, \alpha').h_s''$. Therefore, $h_t = (\tau, \alpha').h_t'$.

Summing up, $h_r^* \in h_t' \, \widetilde{\|}_h \, h_s'$ for some histories $h_t' \in \mathcal{D}_h(T')$ and $h_s' \in S_2[(\sigma, \tau)]$ and consequently, $h_r^* \in S_2[(\sigma, \tau)] \, \widetilde{\|} \, \mathcal{D}_h(T')$, which contradicts the fact that by construction h_r^* is in $(S_1[(\sigma, \tau)] \, \widetilde{\|} \, \mathcal{D}_h(T')) \setminus (S_2[(\sigma, \tau)] \, \widetilde{\|} \, \mathcal{D}_h(T'))$. ∎

Proof of the full abstraction property. We are now in a position to establish the full abstraction property.

Theorem 24. *The semantics $\mathcal{D}_h$ is fully abstract with respect to the semantics $\mathcal{O}_h$.*

Proof Following definition 18, two following properties should be established equivalent:

    i) for any context C, $\mathcal{O}_h(C[A_1]) = \mathcal{O}_h(C[A_2])$;

    ii) $\mathcal{D}_h(A_1) = \mathcal{D}_h(A_2)$.

The implication ii) $\Rightarrow$ i) follows directly from proposition 14.

The other implication i) $\Rightarrow$ ii) is proved by contradiction. Assume $\mathcal{D}_h(A_1) \neq \mathcal{D}_h(A_2)$. Then, since both $\mathcal{D}_h(A_1)$ and $\mathcal{D}_h(A_2)$ are sets, there is an history h which is in one set and not in the other one. Without loss of generality, we may assume that $h \in \mathcal{D}_h(A_1)$ and $h \notin \mathcal{D}_h(A_2)$. Then $\mathcal{D}_h(A_1) \setminus \mathcal{D}_h(A_2) \neq \emptyset$ and, consequently taking as coherent sets $S_1 = \mathcal{D}_h(A_1)$, $S_2 = \mathcal{D}_h(A_2)$, and $\emptyset$ as initial store α, theorem 23 establishes that there is an agent T and a continuous history $h \in (\mathcal{D}_h(A_1) \,\widetilde{\|}\, \mathcal{D}_h(T)) \setminus (\mathcal{D}_h(A_2) \,\widetilde{\|}\, \mathcal{D}_h(T))$ which starts in $\emptyset$. Note that, by definition 13, $h \in \mathcal{D}_h(A_1 \| T) \setminus \mathcal{D}_h(A_2 \| T)$. Therefore, by proposition 14, $\overline{h}$ is an operational history of $\mathcal{O}_h(A_1 \| T)$ which is not in $\mathcal{O}_h(A_2 \| T)$. There is thus a context $C = \square \| T$, such that $\mathcal{O}_h(C[A_1]) \neq \mathcal{O}_h(C[A_2])$, which concludes the proof. ∎

4   Concluding Remarks

We have considered a simple language that embodies the essential features of coordination languages based on generative communication à la Linda.

The definition of a fully abstract compositional semantics for the language sets a firm foundation for reasoning about agents and agent compositions in a coordination-oriented setting. For instance, the denotational semantics induces a number of semantic equalities among agents. The following proposition reports a few classical ones.

Proposition 25.

$$(C1) \qquad X + X = X$$
$$(C2) \qquad X + Y = Y + X$$
$$(C3) \qquad X + (Y + Z) = (X + Y) + Z$$

$$(P1) \qquad X \| Y = Y \| X$$
$$(P2) \qquad X \| (Y \| Z) = (X \| Y) \| Z$$

$$(SC) \qquad (X + Y) \,;\, Z = (X \,;\, Z) + (Y \,;\, Z)$$

$$(E1) \qquad X \,;\, E = X$$
$$(E2) \qquad E \,;\, X = X$$
$$(E3) \qquad E \| X = X$$

254

Proof   Direct from definitions 9, 10, 11, 12, and 13.   ∎

It is worth noting that, on the other hand, the equality

$$X \; ; \; (Y \; + \; Z) = (X \; ; \; Y) \; + \; (X \; ; \; Z)$$

does not hold.

Future work will be devoted to develop and analyse semantics-preserving program transformation techniques in this setting.

As we already pointed out in the Introduction, our denotational semantics is inspired to the denotational models for concurrent languages proposed by Horita, de Bakker and Rutten in [6]. In [6] the problem of defining fully abstract denotational semantics for concurrent languages is studied in the context of a concurrent imperative setting based on assignments of variables and if-then-else constructs as basic operations. Our contribution has been to show that whereas the concurrent language $\mathcal{L}$ differs substantially from this setting, the denotational model proposed in [6] can be applied to characterise $\mathcal{L}$. Namely, the idea of employing *gaps* in state sequences to represent possible interactions of agents with the state and the testing technique allow us to obtain a fully abstract compositional denotational semantics for $\mathcal{L}$.

A general framework embodying a variety of concurrent languages all based on asynchronous communication is studied in [5]. Among others, a full abstraction result similar to ours is claimed however without many details. Our contribution was to show how the peculiarities of the $\mathcal{L}$ language can be used to actually establish the claim in a restricted setting.

Full abstraction for a shared variable parallel imperative language is also studied in [1]. However, the observables are composed of the final states of the computation along with termination marks. They thus substantially differ from what is returned by the semantics $\mathcal{O}_h$ and hence so are the denotational semantics, although traces are also used in [1].

De Nicola and Pugliese defined in [8] a testing scenario for a process algebra based on Linda's primitives. The language considered in [8] is richer than the language $\mathcal{L}$ considered in this paper, in that the former includes several other composition operators and allows infinite processes. The work by De Nicola and Pugliese however differs from ours in the type of description chosen to model Linda-based coordination languages (testing vs. denotational semantics).

Acknowledgements
This work has been partially supported by the cooperation project 95.12 "Coordination languages: From theory to practice", funded by C.G.R.I., F.N.R.S. and the Italian Foreign Ministry.

References

1. S. Brookes. Full Abstraction for a Shared-Variable Parallel Language. In *Proceedings of the Eighth Annual IEEE Symposium on Logic in Computer Science*, pages 98–109, Montreal, Canada, June 1993. IEEE Computer Society Press.
2. N. Carriero and D. Gelernter. Linda in Context. *Communications of the ACM*, 32(4):444–458, 1989.
3. N. Carriero and D. Gelernter. Coordination Languages and Their Significance. *Communications of the ACM*, 35(2):97–107, 1992.
4. P. Ciancarini and C. Hankin, editors. *Proceedings of The First International Conference on Coordination Models and Languages*, number 1061 in LNCS. Springer-Verlag, 1996.
5. F.S. de Boer, J.N. Kok, C. Palamidessi, and J.J.M.M. Rutten. The Failure of Failures in a Paradigm of Asynchronous Communication. In J.C.M. Baeten and J.F. Groote, editors, *Proc. 2nd Int. Conf. on Concurrency Theory (Concur'91)*, volume 527 of *Lecture Notes in Computer Science*, pages 111–126, Amsterdam, The Netherlands, 1991. Springer-Verlag.
6. E. Horita, J.W. de Bakker, and J.J.M.M. Rutten. Fully abstract denotational models for nonuniform concurrent languages. *Information and computation*, 115(1):125–178, 1994.
7. R. Milner. *A Calculus of communucating systems*. Springer-Verlag, 1980.
8. R. De Nicola and R. Pugliese. A process algebra based on Linda. In P. Ciancarini and C. Hankin, editors, *COORDINATION 96*, number 1061 in LNCS. Springer-Verlag, 1996.
9. G. Plotkin. A structural approach to operational semantics. Technical Report DAIMI-FN-19, Aarhus University, 1981.

Partial Order and SOS Semantics for Linear Constraint Programs[*]

Eike Best[1], Frank S. de Boer[2] and Catuscia Palamidessi[3]

[1] Fachbereich Informatik, C.v.O.-Universität Oldenburg, Germany.
e.best@informatik.uni-oldenburg.de
[2] Vakgroep Informatica, Universiteit Utrecht, The Netherlands.
frankb@cs.ruu.nl
[3] DISI, Università di Genova, Italy. catuscia@disi.unige.it

Abstract. In this paper we consider linear constraint programming
(lcp), a non-monotonic extension of concurrent constraint programming
(ccp) which allows to remove information. The entailment relation of a
linear constraint system, in terms of which linear constraint programs are
defined, is based on the main underlying idea of linear logic: hypotheses
in a logical derivation represent physical resources which are consumed,
once used in the entailment relation.
We give a semantical analysis of this extension of ccp in terms of the
causal relations among occurrences of basic actions (i.e. events). Using a
partial order based history model, we define truly concurrent operational
and partial order semantic models of lcp. They allow us to compare –
and classify – various sublanguages of the proposed extension of ccp
(including ccp itself) from the point of view of the degree of parallelism
they generate. The two main results of the paper are consistency and
completeness of the partial order model with respect to the operational
semantics, and thus – as we will argue – its adequacy.

1 Introduction

In the concurrent constraint paradigm [18, 20, 21] (ccp, for short) parallel processes interact via a common store, represented by a constraint or a set of constraints, which expresses some partial information on the values of the variables
involved in the computation. One of the most characteristic features of the ccp
paradigm is a formalization of the basic operations which allow to update and
to query the common store, in terms of the logical notions of consistency, conjunction and entailment supported by a given underlying constraint system.
An update of the common store consists of adding (consistently) a constraint,
whereas a query consists of checking whether the current store entails some constraint. Thus the computational model of ccp gives rise to a monotonic evolution
of the store: more and more information is added in the course of the computation. Moreover, since the definition of the entailment relation of a constraint

[*] This work has been supported by the HCM Project EXPRESS and by the Esprit
Research Project CALIBAN.

system is based on classical logic, it is difficult to envisage extensions of ccp which allow, for example, to *remove* constraints from the common store. Such extensions would greatly enhance the expressive power of ccp and would allow very compact solutions to programming problems which in a purely monotonic setting require considerably elaborate programming techniques.

One of the main contributions of [4] has been the introduction of an operator in ccp which consists of removing some constraint from the common store, and which thus gives rise to non-monotonic computations; the resulting paradigm is called *linear constraint programming* (lcp). The concept of store becomes thus similar to the notion of *blackboard* used in Linda [9, 5] and in Shared Prolog [2]. In the paper [1], it is shown that the underlying linear constraint system of lcp is closely related to a subclass of high-level Petri nets, and this relation is used to investigate the complexity of the entailment relation. In the present paper, correct and complete operational and partial order semantics of lcp are given. They are based on a specific history model which allows constraints, events, and their interdependencies, to be described formally.

The structure of this paper is as follows. In section 2 we define the notion of a linear constraint system, upon which rests the mechanism of information removal. Then, in section 3, we describe the lcp language as a suitable process algebra defined on top of a given linear constraint system. Parallel agents operate on a common store by adding and removing tokens. Adding tokens is modeled basically as in ccp by *tell* actions. Tokens can be removed by the execution of a *get* action of the form $get(c)$, where c is a token of the underlying linear constraint system. The execution of a $get(c)$ with respect to a given store consists of removing those tokens from which c can be derived. Thus in a sense we identify an occurrence of c with a multiset of tokens from which c can be derived. If the current store does not contain a multiset of tokens which entails c, then the get action suspends waiting for parallel processes to add the necessary information. On the other hand in case the store contains different multisets entailing c one is nondeterministically selected and subsequently removed.

In sections 4 and 5, we give a semantical analysis of the proposed non-monotonic extension of ccp in terms of the *causal* relations among occurrences of basic actions (*events*). Such a semantical description is of interest because it allows to treat parallelism as a primitive concept, whereas most semantical models describe parallelism in terms of interleaving and thus reduce it to a form of non-determinism.

In section 4 we define a history model with some specific features that allow executions of a linear constraint program to be described. In this model, the elements of a store (i.e. constraints) and the events, as well as their read/write interdependences, are represented explicitly. The set of histories associated with a linear constraint program is defined in SOS (structured operational semantics) style. By abstracting, we derive an operational semantics, which allows us to observe temporal order and simultaneity of actions, from the set of histories.

In section 5 we define our partial order model, the construction of which is based on the basic distinction between two kinds of causal relations among actions: dependencies based on the 'flow of control' and dependencies based on the 'flow of data'. The control dependencies can be derived in a straightforward manner from the structure of the program (they derive mainly from the sequencing operator). The data dependencies are obtained from the histories, 'at run-time', and are defined in terms of the entailment relation of the underlying linear constraint system. In order to evaluate the adequacy of the description of the causal dependencies we show correctness and completeness with respect to the observational semantics defined in section 4. This is the main difference with respect to other approaches to the true concurrent semantics of ccp [11, 12, 17]. In those works the adequacy of a partial order model is established with respect to an *interleaving* operational semantics.

Finally, in section 6, we show that our semantical model allows us to compare various sublanguages of the proposed extension of ccp (including ccp itself) from the point of view of their degree of parallelism.

Other approaches to combine ccp with linear logic concepts have been proposed in [8, 19]. In general, these works are directly based on the framework of linear logic, i.e. the operators of the language are interpreted as operators of linear logic, and its operational semantics is expressed in terms of the proof theory of linear logic. The approach of this paper, on the contrary, is based on a separation among *the data* (the constraints), whose theory has some linear logic flavour, and *the programming language*, whose operational semantics is defined in terms of a transition system in the usual SOS style. The advantage of our approach is that it gives more freedom in the definition of the language operators. For instance, it is not clear what would be the correspondent in linear logic of the typical ccp actions *ask* and *atomic tell*.

2   Linear constraint systems

As announced in the introduction, the aim is to model a constraint as a physical resource, which can be produced in several copies and each copy of which disappears once it is consumed, i.e. used as a hypothesis in the entailment relation. In order to represent the idea that the same resource can have multiple copies, it is natural to define the elements of the constraint system to be multisets instead than sets. Furthermore the underlying logic must be modified. The derivation of a (basic) constraint by the entailment relation *consumes the hypothesis*, hence, if the derivation of a constraint uses twice the same information, then this information must be represented twice in the hypothesis. Therefore the entailment relation must be defined from multisets of constraints to constraints.

Thus, we first recall some basic notions about multisets. Given a set $(c, d, \ldots \in$ $) S$, a multiset of elements of S is a mapping $M: S \to \mathbf{N}$ where $\mathbf{N}$ is the set of natural numbers. In the following we will sometimes use the extensional notation: for instance, the multiset M such that $M(c) = 2$, $M(d) = 1$ and $M(e) = 0$ for $e \notin \{c, d\}$, will be represented by $M = \{c, c, d\}$. We denote by $\mathcal{M}(S)$ the set of the multisets on S, and by $\mathcal{M}_F(S)$ the set of the *finite* multisets on S.

A useful notion is *multiset inclusion*, denoted by $\subseteq$, and defined as

$$M \subseteq M' \text{ iff } \forall c \in S.\ M(c) \leq M'(c).$$

The *multiset sum* is a (total) function $\oplus \colon \mathcal{M}(S) \times \mathcal{M}(S) \to \mathcal{M}(S)$ defined as

$$(M \oplus M')(c) = M(c) + M'(c).$$

The *multiset difference* is defined as a function $\ominus \colon \mathcal{M}(S) \times \mathcal{M}(S) \to \mathcal{M}(S)$ such that for each $c \in S$

$$(M \ominus M')(c) = \begin{cases} M(c) - M'(c) & \text{if } M(c) \geq M'(c) \\ 0 & \text{if } M(c) < M'(c). \end{cases}$$

Definition 1. [1, 4]

- A *basic linear constraint system* is a pair $\langle B, \vdash_B \rangle$ where B is a set of *basic constraints* and the *basic entailment relation* $\vdash_B \subseteq \mathcal{M}_f(B) \times B$ satisfies:
  (i) $\{c\} \vdash_B c$,
  (ii) if $\mu_1 \vdash_B c_1, \ldots, \mu_n \vdash_B c_n$ and $\{c_1, \ldots, c_n\} \vdash_B d$, then $\mu_1 \oplus \ldots \oplus \mu_n \vdash_B d$.
- The *linear constraint system* induced by $\langle B, \vdash_B \rangle$ is the structure $\langle \mathcal{M}(B), \vdash \rangle$, where $\vdash \subseteq \mathcal{M}(B) \times \mathcal{M}(B)$ is the minimal relation such that

$$\text{if } \forall i \in I.\ \mu_i \vdash_B c_i \quad \text{then} \quad \bigoplus_{i \in I} \mu_i \vdash \bigoplus_{i \in I} \{c_i\}.$$

A linear constraint system does not have all the properties of a (usual) constraint system; it is not a complete algebraic lattice and not even a lattice (for instance it does not necessarily have a minimum element). However it is a preorder (see [1] for a proof), and therefore can be transformed into a partial order by factorising it with respect to the associated equivalence relation. The relation $\vdash$ is generally infinite, even when B is finite, and even when restricted to $\mathcal{M}_f(B)$ modulo equivalence.

3 The language

In order to compare our language with previous ccp paradigms, we consider a sort of 'superlanguage' $\mathcal{L}$ embodying the main mechanisms for communication and synchronization which have been proposed: the *eventual tell* (*tell*), the *atomic tell* (*atell*), the *ask*, and also the *removing ask* (*get*) which is our present proposal. A sublanguage $\mathcal{L}_G$ of $\mathcal{L}$ will be characterized by the set G of basic actions which are available in it. For instance, *atomic ccp* [20] corresponds to $\mathcal{L}_{\{atell, ask\}}$, and *eventual ccp* (or ccp, [20, 21]) corresponds to $\mathcal{L}_{\{tell, ask\}}$. In the last section we will compare these two languages and the language we propose, $\mathcal{L}_{\{tell, ask, get\}}$, from the point of view of potential parallelism and expressiveness.

We assume given a linear constraint system $\mathbf{L} = \langle \mathcal{M}(S), \vdash \rangle$, with tokens $c, d, \ldots \in S$ and elements $M, M' \ldots \in \mathcal{M}(S)$. The description of the language is parametric with respect to it.

The actions listed above have an argument which is a token. We could be more general and admit a finite multiset as argument, but this would give rise to some technical complications when building the partial order model of the language, possibly deflecting the attention from what we consider to be the main ideas and results of that construction. We will indicate later how this generalisation can be incorporated.

The basic actions operate on a common *store*, which ranges over $\mathcal{M}(S)$. Intuitively, the effect of *tell*(c) consists of simply adding (in the multiset sense) the token c to the current store. The action *atell*(c) has the same effect, but it can be executed only if the resulting store is consistent. Otherwise, we say that *atell*(c) is *not enabled*. The action *ask*(c) is a test on the current store and its execution does not modify the store: *ask*(c) is *enabled* in the store M iff $M' \vdash c$, for some $M' \subseteq M$. The action *get*(c) differs from *ask*(c) because, when enabled, it removes information from the current store. More precisely, it removes from the current store a multiset of tokens $d_1, \ldots, d_m$ that entail c.

The following grammar defines the syntax of the language $\mathcal{L}$. Every program P consists of a (possibly empty) list of procedure declarations D followed by an agent A. In the syntax, g stands for one of the four elementary actions mentioned above.

$$
\begin{array}{lll}
\textit{Programs} & P ::= & A \mid D \,;\, P \\
\textit{Declarations } D & ::= & p(x) \text{:-} A \\
\textit{Agents} & A ::= & stop \mid g \to A \mid A + A \mid A \,\|\, A \mid p(x).
\end{array}
$$

The agent *stop* represents successful termination. An agent $g \to A$ executes g, if g is enabled, and then it behaves like A. If g is not enabled, then execution is *suspended*, waiting for other (parallel) agents to add information to the store. The choice operator in $A + B$ selects nondeterministically one of the agents A and B (if it is enabled, that is, the current store allows it to perform one of its initial actions). If neither the agent A nor B is enabled then the composite agent $A + B$ is suspended. Parallel composition is represented by $\|$. Finally, the agent $p(x)$ is a procedure call, where p is the name of the procedure and x is the actual parameter. The meaning of $p(x)$ is given by a procedure declaration of the form $p(y) \text{:-} A$, where y is the formal parameter.

The parameter passing is modeled by renaming the formal parameter y in the body A by the actual parameter x. This is formally expressed by substituting every token c occurring in A by $c[x/y]$. The result of this substitution we denote as $A[x/y]$. Concerning the local variables of the body, we assume a mechanism which takes care of renaming them into fresh ones, thus avoiding possible clashes with the global variables of the store.

4 Operational semantics and the history model

In this section we introduce a transition system which allows the construction of a partial order model describing the *causal dependencies* and the *weak causal dependencies* among (occurrences) of actions. In order to describe the *data de-pendencies* among actions, we represent a history as a pattern of occurrences of those actions which have been executed, together with the resources (con-straints) they have produced or consumed. This history associates with each action the set of its 'causes', namely, those actions in the store that enabled it. As a model of histories, we use a combination of the *causal nets* of net theory [15] and the *composets* of Janicki and Koutny [6]. Our nets are a particular case of *contextual nets*, which have been introduced by Montanari and Rossi [14] and used in [13] for modeling ccp.

Formally, a *history* is an object (R, E, λ, F, G) where R are the resources, E are the events $(R \cap E = \emptyset)$, λ is a labelling function from R to S (set of constraints or, as we will say exchangeably, tokens) and from E to the set $\{tell(c), atell(c), ask(c), get(c) \mid c \in S\}$, the relation F is a subset of $(R \times E) \cup (E \times R)$, and the relation G is a subset of $(R \times E)$ such that $(F \cup G)^*$ is a partial order relation on $(R \cup E)$ and $F \cap (R \times E)$ and $F^{-1} \cap (R \times E)$ are partial functions. Two histories are isomorphic if they differ only in the (names of) elements of R and E. As usual, we consider isomorphic histories as equal.

The basic intuition behind the labelling is as follows. $\lambda(r)$ denotes the con-straint associated with the resource r; a constraint can be produced and con-sumed several times during an execution, and resources are a means of distin-guishing these productions and consumptions. Similarly, $\lambda(e)$ denotes the action of which e is an execution. There may be many events which are executions of the same action.

The basic intuition of the relations F and G is as follows. $(e, r) \in F$ could be read as 'event e produces the resource r'; this could be true, for instance, if $\lambda(e)$ is a $tell(c)$ and $\lambda(r)$ is c. $(r, e) \in F$ could be read as 'event e consumes the resource r'; this could be true, for instance, if $\lambda(e)$ is $get(c)$ and $\lambda(r)$ belongs to a multiset M over S such that $M \vdash c$. $(r, e) \in G$ could be read as 'event e reads the resource r'; this could be true, for instance, if $\lambda(e)$ is $ask(c)$ and $\lambda(r)$ belongs to a multiset M such that $M \vdash c$.

We use the letter χ for histories, and we use decorations consistently. Thus, if χ_1 is some history, then R_1, E_1, etc., are the sets belonging to χ_1, and if χ' is a history then R', E', etc. are its sets, and so on. The empty history is defined as $\emptyset = (\emptyset, \emptyset, \emptyset, \emptyset, \emptyset)$. The union of two histories, $\chi_1 \cup \chi_2$, is defined as the componentwise union of the constituent sets. For a history χ, the substructure (R, E, F) (without λ and G) is a causal net in the Petri net sense [15].

Example 1. Let $\chi_1 = (R_1, E_1, \lambda_1, F_1, G_1)$, such that $R_1 = \{r, \bar{r}\}$, $E_1 = \{e_1, e_2, e_3\}$, $\lambda_1 = \{(r, c), (\bar{r}, \bar{c}), (e_1, tell(c)), (e_2, ask(c)), (e_3, get(c))\}$, $F_1 = \{(e_1, r), (r, e_3), (e_3, \bar{r})\}$ and $G_1 = \{(r, e_2)\}$. This history is shown on the left-hand side of Figure 1, with elements of F_1 being drawn as solid arrows and elements of G_1 (actually, only one such element) as broken arrows. Intuitively speaking, it represents a history in which a $tell(c)$ action (actually, more precisely, an event representing an ex-ecution of a $tell(c)$ action) first produces constraint c (actually, more precisely, a resource representing a constraint c) which is then both read (by an $ask(c)$ action on account of $\{c\} \vdash c$) and removed (by a $get(c)$ action, also on account

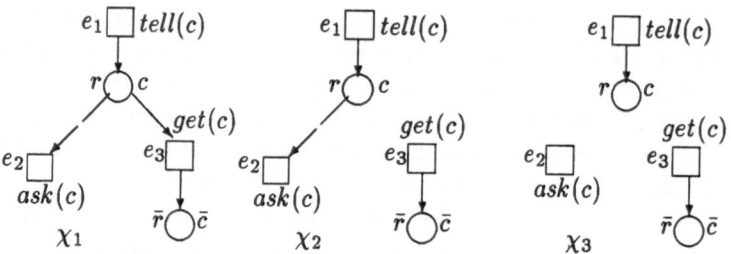

Fig. 1. Three histories χ_1 (left), χ_2 (middle) and χ_3 (right)

of $\{c\} \vdash c$). If the underlying constraint system would also allow the inference $\emptyset \vdash c$ (which might be the case as nothing in the definition of a constraint system prevents it) then a history χ_2 – shown in the middle of Figure 1 – which differs from χ_1 only by deleting the element (r, e_3) from F_1, is also a history consisting of a $tell(c)$ action followed by an $ask(c)$ action (on account of $\{c\} \vdash c$) and a $get(c)$ action (on account of $\emptyset \vdash c$). The history χ_3 arising from χ_2 by deleting (r, e_2) from G_2 – shown on the right-hand side of Figure 1 – is then also a history describing a $tell(c)$, an $ask(c)$ and a $get(c)$, where all three events are concurrent.

We will call a resource r in a history χ *unconsumed* iff $r \notin dom(F)$. We call the set of unconsumed resources $R_u(\chi)$ or just R_u if the particular history χ to which it refers is understood. The *store* associated with χ, called $store(\chi)$, is the multiset

$$store(\chi) \;=\; \bigoplus_{r \in R_u(\chi)} \{\lambda(r)\} \,.$$

Notice that this is indeed an element of $\mathcal{M}(S)$, where the constraints are counted as many times as they occur as labels of unconsumed resources. Later, for reasons of brevity, we abbreviate such a multiset by $\lambda(R_u(\chi))$.

We now give the operational semantics of the language using as basic configurations pairs $\langle A, \chi \rangle$ where A is an agent and χ is a history. Since the intended model is *true concurrent*, we allow also transitions which represent concurrent execution of more than one action, provided they are independent, that is, *steps* denoted by α. Hence in general a transition will be labeled by multisets of actions. Thus a transition has the following format:

$$\langle A, \chi \rangle \xrightarrow{\alpha} \langle A', \chi' \rangle$$

where A and A' are agents, α is a finite multiset of actions $tell(c)$, $atell(c)$, $ask(c)$, and $get(c) \mid c \in S\}$, and χ and χ' are histories. The basic intuition underlying this transition can be described as follows:

A, with a starting history χ, evolves by executing the step α into A', with a resulting history χ' (of which χ will be a prefix).

A1 $\langle tell(c) \to A, \chi \rangle \xrightarrow{\{tell(c)\}} \langle A, \chi \cup \chi_{new} \rangle$

where $\chi_{new} = (\{r\}, \{e\}, \{(r,c),(e, tell(c))\}, \{(e,r)\}, \emptyset)$,
and r and e are not already in χ.

A2 $\langle atell(c) \to A, \chi \rangle \xrightarrow{\{atell(c)\}} \langle A, \chi \cup \chi_{new} \rangle$

where $\chi_{new} = (\{r\}, \{e\}, \{(r,c),(e, atell(c))\}, \{(e,r)\}, \{(r_1,e),\dots,(r_n,e)\})$
and r and e are not already in χ,
and $r_1, \dots, r_n$ are all unconsumed resources of χ,
and $store(\chi \cup \chi_{new})$ is consistent.

A3 $\langle ask(c) \to A, \chi \rangle \xrightarrow{\{ask(c)\}} \langle A, \chi \cup \chi_{new} \rangle$

where $\chi_{new} = (\emptyset, \{e\}, \{(e, ask(c))\}, \emptyset, \{(r_1,e),\dots,(r_n,e)\})$,
and e is not already in χ,
and $r_1, \dots, r_n \in R_u(\chi)$ such that $\{\lambda(r_1),\dots,\lambda(r_n)\} \vdash c$.

A4 $\langle get(c) \to A, \chi \rangle \xrightarrow{\{get(c)\}} \langle A, \chi \cup \chi_{new} \rangle$

where $\chi_{new} = (\{\bar{r}\}, \{e\}, \{(e, get(c)),(\bar{r}, \bar{c})\}, \{(r_1,e),\dots,(r_n,e),(e,\bar{r})\}, \emptyset)$,
and e and $\bar{r}$ are not already in χ,
and $r_1, \dots, r_n \in R_u(\chi)$ such that $\{\lambda(r_1),\dots,\lambda(r_n)\} \vdash c$.

Table 1. Basic Actions.

R1 $\dfrac{\langle A, \chi \rangle \xrightarrow{\alpha} \langle A', \chi' \rangle}{\langle A+B, \chi \rangle \xrightarrow{\alpha} \langle A', \chi' \rangle}$ and $\dfrac{\langle B, \chi \rangle \xrightarrow{\beta} \langle B', \chi' \rangle}{\langle A+B, \chi \rangle \xrightarrow{\beta} \langle B', \chi' \rangle}$

R2 $\dfrac{\langle A, \chi \rangle \xrightarrow{\alpha} \langle A', \chi' \rangle, \ \langle B, \chi \rangle \xrightarrow{\beta} \langle B', \chi'' \rangle}{\langle A\|B, \chi \rangle \xrightarrow{\alpha \oplus \beta} \langle A'\|B', \chi' \cup \chi'' \rangle}$ where $\chi' \cup \chi''$ is a history and $atell(\alpha) = \emptyset \vee atell(\beta) = \emptyset$

R3 $\dfrac{\langle A[y/x], \chi \rangle \xrightarrow{\alpha} \langle A', \chi' \rangle}{\langle p(y), \chi \rangle \xrightarrow{\alpha} \langle A', \chi' \rangle}$ where $p(x) :\!\text{-} A$ is the declaration for p.

Table 2. The transition system L.

$$\mathbf{I}\ \langle A, \chi \rangle \xrightarrow{\ \emptyset\ } \langle A, \chi \rangle$$

Table 3. The idling step.

Table 1 describes the transition rules for the basic actions. The rules for the choice and parallel operator and recursion are given in Table 2. Table 3 shows an auxiliary rule. The rules are explained in turn.

A $tell(c)$ action (Rule **A1**) gives rise to a new event e that neither reads nor consumes resources ($G(e) = \emptyset$ and $F^{-1}(e) = \emptyset$), but produces a new resource r labelled c (by $F(e) = \{r\}$). The $atell(c)$ is like the $tell(c)$ except that it also reads (but does not consume) all unconsumed resources, since the entire store has to be checked for consistency. The $ask(c)$ reads, but does not consume, resources that entail c.

The $get(c)$ operation is more involved. If we would be interested in the subset of the language with no atomic tell, then $get(c)$ could be modeled like $ask(c)$ except that after reading it also consumes the resources. Formally, the distinction would only be in the use of the relation G for the former and F for the latter. However, in the presence of atomic tell, things are more complicated. For instance, consider the agent

$$(tell(c) \rightarrow get(c) \rightarrow stop) \parallel (atell(d) \rightarrow stop)$$

where d is inconsistent w.r.t. c. If the first action to be executed is $tell(c)$, then $atell(d)$ can only be executed after $get(c)$. One way to enforce this dependency is to assume that $get(c)$ "produces" a special token, which we call $\bar{c}$, on which $atell(d)$ will depend. This special token is of course neutral w.r.t. the constraint system, in the sense that it neither entails, nor is entailed by, any other contraint.[4]

Note that for $tell$ we have essentially a disjoint union of histories while the union is disjoint in the case of ask and get only if $n = 0$ (we do allow this special case), and for $atell$ it is disjoint only if its initial store $store(\chi)$ is empty.

The more general case that the actions do not have a single constraint, but a finite multiset of constraints as parameters, can be incorporated in these rules as follows. Let us only consider the action $tell(\{c_1, \ldots, c_n\})$. The rule **A1** needs to be modified such that a single new event e and n new resources $r_1, \ldots, r_n$

---

[4] Another possibility would be to consider inhibitory arcs ([7]). The idea would be that a resource c inhibits every $atell(d)$ with d inconsistent w.r.t. c. Then the dependency of an action $atell(d)$ upon an action $get(c)$ would be derived by an analysis of the inhibitory relation and the F relation. This solution is perhaps more intuitive and natural, but would complicate the derivation of the dependency relation, hence we do not consider it here.

with labels $c_1, \ldots, c_n$ are added to χ, and the new F relation consists of all pairs (e, r_i) for $1 \leq i \leq n$. The other rules can be extended similarly (where rules **A3** and **A4** need no real extension).

The most interesting rule of Table 2 is **R2**, for concurrent composition. The other two rules **R1** and **R3** are essentially standard. Note that Rule **R2** has the same initial history, χ, for both A and B in its premise. This models the fact that the store is shared and that two parallel programs A and B pursue parts of a common history. The premise of **R2** allows A to change χ into a new history χ' and B to change χ into a possibly different history χ'', but χ is a common prefix of both, and therefore also of the – elementwise – union $\chi' \cup \chi''$ which is the result of $A\|B$, evolving in parallel from χ. It is assumed that the events and resources newly chosen in the separate evolutions of A and B are different; for instance, if A starts with a *tell(c)* action and B also starts with a *tell(c)* action, then the two new events chosen according to the two applications of rule **A1** are different (although their labels are the same), and the same is true for the two new resources (whose labels are, of course, also the same, namely c).

Note that the requirement that $\chi' \cup \chi''$ be a history amounts to require that F and F^{-1} in $\chi' \cup \chi''$ be partial function. In general this would not be guaranteed. For instance, if in the premise of Rule **R2**, A and B both execute a *get(c)* action, and χ contains only one unconsumed resource r labelled c. Then A would add a new event e' with $(r, e') \in F'$ in χ' and B would add another event e'' with $(r, e'') \in F''$ in χ''. The above condition forces the unconsumed resources R_u of χ to be partitioned in R_A and R_B, so that the resources consumed in the step $\langle A, \chi \rangle \xrightarrow{\alpha} \langle A', \chi' \rangle$ belong to R_A while the resources consumed in the step $\langle B, \chi \rangle \xrightarrow{\beta} \langle B', \chi'' \rangle$ belong to R_B.

The other condition (applied recursively) implies that all *atell* actions in the computation will be sequentialised. This is necessary because by definition an atomic tell should always prevent inconsistency of the store, hence we cannot allow two atomic tell to be executed in parallel since they could add inconsistent constraints to the store.[5]

Note that Rule **R2**, as it stands, forces all parallel agents to make a transition step at the same time (synchronous cooperation). In order to allow each component to proceed 'at its own speed', we allow an agent to perform an *idling step*, which is described by the axiom **I** of Table 3. Intuitively, an idling step represents the fact that the agent 'skips a turn'.

The behaviour of the get operation can be best understood in terms of a 'ring architecture', in which tokens circulate freely among the nodes where the process reside. Note that in this way get actions can be executed in parallel since disjoint access to the common store is automatically guaranteed.

---

[5] In our language inconsistency might still arise by the execution of an atomic tell in parallel with an eventual tell. This is not very elegant, but it is only for the sake of generality that we are considering a syntax which has both kinds of tell. In general, in a language, it does not make sense to have both atomic and eventual tell.

Example 2. Consider the agent

$$tell(c) \rightarrow ((ask(c) \rightarrow stop) \| (get(c) \rightarrow stop)).$$

If the underlying constraint system does not contain the entailment $\emptyset \vdash c$, then χ_1 (given previously as an example) is a possible history of this agent, starting with the empty history. If, on the other hand, the underlying constraint system does allow $\emptyset \vdash c$, then χ_2 and χ_3, in addition to χ_1 (as defined previously), are also possible histories of that agent, starting with $\emptyset$.

Note that the operational rules only add more elements to a given history and that they do not remove elements. Thus, in an evolution, histories grow monotonically, as it should be.

From the transition system L we derive the operational semantics and the notion of observable. In this paper, we restrict ourselves to finite maximal behavious only.

Definition 2. The operational semantics of an agent A, $\mathcal{O}(A)$, is defined as follows:

$$\mathcal{O}(A) \;=\; \{\, \chi \mid \langle A, \emptyset \rangle \xrightarrow{\alpha_1} \ldots \xrightarrow{\alpha_n} \langle B, \chi \rangle \not\rightarrow \,\},$$

where $\langle B, \chi \rangle \not\rightarrow$ indicates that the agent B, starting with history χ, can perform only idling steps.

Note that due to the possible existence of deadlocks, a maximal history is not necessarily a complete one (i.e. it might be the case that not all processes have evolved into *stop*).

Definition 3. The *observables* of an agent A, $Obs(A)$, are defined as follows:

$$Obs(A) \;=\; \{\, \alpha_1 \ldots \alpha_n \mid \langle A, \emptyset \rangle \xrightarrow{\alpha_1} \ldots \xrightarrow{\alpha_n} \langle B, \chi \rangle \not\rightarrow \,\}.$$

Note that we are assuming that the observer is capable to observe actions which are performed at the same time (represented as a multiset). The semantics $Obs(A)$ represents a significant abstraction from $\mathcal{O}(A)$; all resources, intermediate stores, and identities of events are forgotten.

5 Control flow and partial order semantics

Histories χ describe the data dependencies between events, and the operational semantics restricts histories to those that start with the initially empty history and end in a final state. These histories do not describe the control dependencies. For instance, the agent $A = tell(c) \rightarrow (tell(c) \rightarrow stop)$ generates in $\mathcal{O}(A)$ the unique (up to renaming of resources and events) final history

$$\chi = (\{r, r'\}, \{e, e'\}, \{(r, c), (r', c), (e, tell(c)), (e', tell(c))\}, \{(e, r), (e', r')\}, \emptyset)$$

which contains two concurrent events, while control flow dictates that the events should be in sequence.[6]

We proceed as follows. First we give a definition which allows the control dependencies to be obtained statically from an agent, again in the form of a partial order or a set of partial orders η with a simpler structure than χ. The two partial orders χ and η are not immediately comparable, but we will make them comparable in a second step by extending η and restricting χ suitably. Then, in a third step, the partial order model for agents is constructed by combining control dependency orders η and data dependency orders χ, essentially by forming the union of the two respective relations.

As announced, control dependencies can be derived statically from the structure of the agent. We use *partial words* [23] which can also be viewed as traces [10]. A partial word, for our purposes, is a triple $(E, \lambda, \prec)$ such that E is a (finite) set of events, λ is a function from E to the set $\{tell(c), atell(c), ask(c), get(c)\}$ (both with the same interpretation as before), and $\prec$ is a partial order on E called the *precedence relation*. $\emptyset = (\emptyset, \emptyset, \emptyset)$ is the empty partial word, and union is defined componentwise. Disjoint union between two partial words, $\eta_1 \uplus \eta_2$, is defined by first making the two event sets disjoint (if they are not already) and then forming the union. As with histories, we consider isomorphic partial words as equal.

Definition 4. Let A be a agent. Define $\mathcal{C}(A)$ as the smallest collection of partial words satisfying the following five properties:

(1) If $A = stop$ then $\mathcal{C}(A) = \{(\emptyset, \emptyset, \emptyset)\}$.
(2) If $A = g \to A'$ then $\mathcal{C}(A) = \{(\emptyset, \emptyset, \emptyset)\} \cup g.\mathcal{C}(A')$,
   where for some set $\mathcal{E}$ of partial words, we define
   $$g.\mathcal{E} = \{(\{e_g\} \uplus E, \{(e_g, g)\} \cup \lambda, (\{(e_g, e) \mid e \in E\} \cup \prec)) \mid (E, \lambda, \prec) \in \mathcal{E}\},$$
   that is, we prefix every partial word in $\mathcal{E}$ by a new event labelled g.
   Notice that $g.\{(\emptyset, \emptyset, \emptyset)\} = \{(\{e_g\}, \{(e_g, g)\}, \emptyset)\}$.
(3) If $A = A_1 + A_2$ then $\mathcal{C}(A) = \mathcal{C}(A_1) \cup \mathcal{C}(A_2)$.
(4) If $A = A_1 \| A_2$ then $\mathcal{C}(A) = \{\eta_1 \uplus \eta_2 \mid \eta_1 \in \mathcal{C}(A_1) \wedge \eta_2 \in \mathcal{C}(A_2)\}$.
(5) If $A = p(y)$ and $p(x) :\text{-} A'$ is the declaration of p then $\mathcal{C}(A) = \mathcal{C}(A'[y/x])$.

Lemma 5. (Well-definedness) *Set set $\mathcal{C}(A)$ is well defined.*

Proof. (Sketch.) The only interesting case is (5). We may limit ourselves to immediate recursion, i.e. recursion at most in a single process. Other kinds of recursion (two or more processes calling themselves recursively) can be treated by standard methods. Let $A = p(y)$ with $p(x) : -A'$. Let $A'' = A'[y/x]$. Define a function f, depending on A'', from sets-of-partial-words to sets-of-partial-words, by

$$f(\mathcal{E}) = \mathcal{C}(A'')[\mathcal{E}[z/y]/p(z)],$$

---

[6] Note, however, that $Obs(A_0)$ contains a two-element sequence in addition to a one-element sequence.

where $[\mathcal{E}[z/y]/p(z)]$ means that the occurrences of $p(z)$ in A'' are substituted, in the computation of $\mathcal{C}(A'')$, by $\mathcal{E}$. Then f is monotonic since $\mathcal{E}_1 \subseteq \mathcal{E}_2$ clearly implies $\mathcal{C}(A'')[\mathcal{E}_1[z/y]/p(z)] \subseteq \mathcal{C}(A'')[\mathcal{E}_2[z/y]/p(z)]$. Hence f has a unique minimal fixpoint, which in case recursion is guarded is the limit of the sequence $\emptyset$, $f(\emptyset)$, $f(f(\emptyset))$, ... Define $\mathcal{C}(A)$ as this least fixpoint of f and observe that this satisfies the properties in the previous definition. $\qquad\square$

Now, we turn to combining data flow objects in $\mathcal{O}(A)$ (which are histories χ) with control flow objects in $\mathcal{C}(A)$ (which are partial words η) to yield the partial order semantics of A. First, consider a given history χ. Our intention is to abstract from the resources R and to lift F and G to a precedence between the events of χ. However it is not reasonable to abstract χ directly to a partial word, for the reason illustrated by the following example.

Example 3. Consider again the agent

$$tell(c) \to ((ask(c) \to stop)\|(get(c) \to stop)).$$

Assume $\emptyset \not\vdash c$. Then the observational semantics of this agent contains the sequences $\{tell(c)\}\{ask(c), get(c)\}$ and $\{tell(c)\}\{ask(c)\}\{get(c)\}$, but not the sequence $\{tell(c)\}\{get(c)\}\{ask(c)\}$.

As is well known [6, 7], partial words are not rich enough to discriminate such behaviour. Following [7] (and similarly to [17], but with differences as discussed there), we introduce *weak precedence* as an additional form of precedence. Thus, we associate with $\chi = (R, E, \lambda, F, G)$ an object $\xi = \xi(\chi) = (E, \lambda, \prec, \gamma)$, which we call an *event history*, defined by:

$$e \prec_{aux} e' \iff \exists r \in R : (e, r) \in F \wedge (r, e') \in F \cup G$$
$$e \gamma_{aux} e' \iff \exists r \in R : (r, e) \in G \wedge (r, e') \in F$$

as well as $\prec = \rho^* \circ \prec_{aux} \circ \rho^*$ and $\gamma = \rho^+$ with $\rho = (\prec_{aux} \cup \gamma_{aux})$. The relations $\prec$ and γ are called *precedence* and *weak precedence*, respectively. Note that by this definition, weak precedence is induced when some resource is read by some event and consumed by another event. The intuition is that if $e \prec e'$ then e occurs before e' and if $(e, e') \in \gamma$ then e' does not occur before e. (We will make this intuition precise later, in the definition of the set *Lin*.)

For an arbitrary event history $\xi = (E, \lambda, \prec, \gamma)$, the substructure $(E, \lambda, \prec)$ (without γ) is a partial word and the substructure $(E, \prec, \gamma)$ (without λ) is a relational structure in the sense of [7]. It turns out that for agents A, all associated structures are always stratified in the sense of [7], i.e. they are composets in the sense of [6].

By these definitions, data dependency partial orders and control dependency partial orders are made comparable and can now be combined. We first need to introduce the following definition: Given an arbitrary event history $\xi = (E_d, \lambda_d, \prec_d, \gamma_d)$ and an arbitrary partial word $\eta = (E_c, \lambda_c, \prec_c)$, let $f : E_d \to E_c$ be a bijection. Then ξ and η are compatible with respect to f, *compatible*(ξ, f, η), iff f is label-preserving, that is, $\forall e \in E_d: \lambda_d(e) = \lambda_c(f(e))$ and, moreover, f is weakly order preserving, i.e. the transitive closure of the relation

$$\prec_d \cup \gamma_d \cup (f \circ \prec_c \circ f^{-1})$$

is irreflexive. Intuitively, this means that the function f identifies the events of ξ and η in a consistent way, i.e. the union of the dependency relations does not contain cycles.

If $compatible(\xi, f, \eta)$ holds, then the combination $combine(\xi, f, \eta)$ is well-defined and it is the following event history:

$$combine(\xi, f, \eta) \;=\; (E_d, \lambda_d, (\prec_d \cup (f \circ \prec_c \circ f^{-1}))^+, \gamma_d).$$

Definition 6. The partial order semantics of an agent A, $\mathcal{P}(A)$, is defined as follows:

$$\mathcal{P}(A) \;=\; \{\, \xi \mid \exists \chi \in \mathcal{O}(A), f, \eta \in \mathcal{C}(A): \\ compatible(\xi(\chi), f, \eta) \wedge \xi = combine(\xi(\chi), f, \eta) \,\}.$$

Notice that all elements of $\mathcal{P}(A)$ are finite.

The question now arises whether the above definition of the set of partial orders associated with an agent adequately captures the degree of parallelism. More precisely, the question is whether the degree of parallelism given by the partial order model is neither too restrictive nor too liberal. As we have mentioned, we will answer this question by comparing the semantics $\mathcal{P}(A)$ with the observational semantics $Obs(A)$.

Formally, we define the set of all linearisations of a (finite) event history $\xi = (E, \lambda, \prec, \gamma)$ as follows:

$$Lin(\xi) \;=\; \{\, \lambda(X_1) \ldots \lambda(X_m) \mid \\ \textstyle\bigcup_{i=1}^{m} X_i = E \text{ and } X_1, \ldots, X_m \text{ are mutually disjoint} \\ \text{and } e \prec e' \text{ implies } e \in X_i, e' \in X_j \text{ for some } i < j \\ \text{and } (e, e') \in \gamma \text{ implies } e \in X_i, e' \in X_j \text{ for some } i \leq j \,\}.$$

If ξ is empty then $Lin(\xi) = \{\varepsilon\}$. Note that the definition of $Lin(\xi)$ treats the two precedence relations $\prec$ and γ of ξ slightly differently according to their interpretation given above. Notice also that every element of the set $Lin(\xi)$ is a finite sequence of multisets of actions (since this set is the codomain of λ), and hence the two sets of sequences $Lins(A)$ and $Obs(A)$ are comparable, where

$$Lins(A) = \bigcup_{\xi \in \mathcal{P}(A)} Lin(\xi).$$

Correctness of the partial order model, i.e., the guarantee that it is not too liberal, is ensured by the fact that all linearisations of a partial order associated to an agent represent valid observations.

Theorem 7. (Correctness) *For any agent A we have $Lins(A) \subseteq Obs(A)$.*

Proof. (Sketch.) Let $\alpha_1 \ldots \alpha_n \in Lins(A)$. Then there exists an event history $\xi \in \mathcal{P}(A)$ with $\alpha_1 \ldots \alpha_n \in Lin(\xi)$. $\xi \in \mathcal{P}(A)$ means that there is a history $\chi \in \mathcal{O}(A)$, a function f and a partial word $\eta \in \mathcal{C}(A)$ such that they are compatible and ξ is their combination. Such η represents a possible abstract unfolding of the agent, abstract in the sense that the guards are not tested. The fact that there is an event history compatible with η implies that there is a way, compatible with such unfolding, of executing the actions of η so that they will produce and consume the resources in the way needed to activate the guards. Thus we derive from η one of the possible (maximally parallel) computations of the agent, from which we derive $\alpha_1 \ldots \alpha_n$ as an observable. $\qquad\square$

The reverse inclusion which we call *completeness*, guarantees that our partial order model is not too restrictive.

Theorem 8. (Completeness) *For any agent A we have $Obs(A) \subseteq Lins(A)$.*

Proof. (Sketch.) Let $\alpha_1 \ldots \alpha_n \in Obs(A)$. Then there exists some χ such that $\langle A, \emptyset \rangle$ goes by $\alpha_1 \ldots \alpha_n$ to $\langle A, \chi \rangle$. We need to combine χ with some good (i.e. compatible) $\eta = (E, \lambda, \prec)$, to yield a good ξ. Such an η can be constructed by enriching the operational rules with a way of construction (inductively) also this η, and then applying this enriched set of rules to the above sequence $\alpha_1 \ldots \alpha_n$ which yields χ out of the empty history. For instance, we may define rules such as

$$\langle tell(c) \to A, \eta \rangle \xrightarrow{\{tell(c)\}} \langle A, \eta_{new} \rangle,$$

where η_{new} is defined in an analogous way as the corresponding history. We may then define η by $\langle A, \emptyset \rangle \xrightarrow{\alpha_1} \ldots \xrightarrow{\alpha_n} \langle A, \eta \rangle$; note that given $\alpha_1 \ldots \alpha_n$, this is a good definition, though in order to be able to combine the η so obtained with χ, $\alpha_1 \ldots \alpha_n$ may need to be re-linearised using the silent step axiom (I). $\qquad\square$

A similar result is stated in [11], but with an essential difference: in [11] the observations of an agent consist of sequences of basic actions generated by an *interleaving* operational semantics (and, correspondingly, linearisations are sequences of actions instead of sequences of sets of actions).

We argue that, having an operational semantics which allows us to observe simultaneity of actions, our result is stronger. In fact, in an analogous process algebraic setting, consider the agent $A = a \parallel b$, where a and b are some basic actions. If we would consider an interleaving operational semantics, then it would follow that a partial order semantics $\mathcal{P}'(A)$ containing only the two posets with $a \prec b$, and $b \prec a$, is correct and complete (according to the formulation of completeness in [11]). On the other hand, having the possibility to observe the simultaneity of actions, we have a way to rule out that semantics as *incomplete*.

However, also our formulation of completeness does not identify an *optimal* semantics. More precisely, consider the following definition:

Definition 9. Let $\mathcal{P}'$ be a function which maps agents into sets of partial orders. We say that $\mathcal{P}'$ is a *correct interpretation* iff for any agent A, $Lins(A) \subseteq Obs(A)$ holds.

Now, if we take the interpretation

$$\bar{\mathcal{P}}(A) = \bigcup \{\mathcal{P}'(A) \mid \mathcal{P}' \text{ is a correct interpretation}\}$$

we have that $\bar{\mathcal{P}}$ is correct and complete in the above sense, but it does not coincide (in general) with the model $\mathcal{P}$. For instance, in the case of $A = a \parallel b$, the model $\mathcal{P}$ would contain only the poset where a and b are not related, whereas $\bar{\mathcal{P}}$ contains also the other two posets with with $a \prec b$ and $b \prec a$.

However the model $\mathcal{P}$ should be 'more general'. In what sense precisely is a topic of future research.

6 Language comparison

The model we have presented in the previous sections allows us to compare the various sublanguages of $\mathcal{L}$ from the point of view of potential parallelism. In particular we are interested in comparing ccp and atomic ccp with $\mathcal{L}_{\{tell, ask, get\}}$, which we call ccp$_{get}$.

We can see that ccp$_{get}$ presents an intermediate degree of parallelism: less than ccp, but more than atomic ccp. This is formally justified by the following proposition:

Proposition 10. *Let A be an agent, let $\chi \in \mathcal{O}(A)$, let $\xi(\chi) = (E, \lambda, \prec, \gamma)$, let $e, e' \in E$ and $g = \lambda(e), g' = \lambda(e')$. Then*

- *If g, g' are atomic tell actions, then either $e \prec e'$ or $e' \prec e$.*
- *If g, g' are tell actions, then neither $e \prec e'$ nor $e' \prec e$.*
- *If g, g' are ask actions, then neither $e \prec e'$ nor $e' \prec e$.*

This proposition states that two atomic tell actions are always executed in interleaving, and two tell or two ask actions are always independent, hence they can be performed simultaneously. Concerning two get actions, they can be always independent (which happens when the resources they need are disjoint), or not. In the second case, they can still be performed in parallel if the store is 'rich enough' to entail both of them.

Concerning other dependencies, ask and get actions depend in general on some tell or atomic tell actions. Atomic tell actions can depend on some get actions. In fact the removal of information might eliminate some item which is inconsistent with the constraint to be added. Note that a get action is also capable to restore consistency.

The presence of the ask actions in ccp$_{get}$ might seem redundant, since $ask(c)$ would be equivalent, concerning the results in all possible contexts, to two consecutive actions $get(c)$ and $tell(c)$. However, on the basis of the above discussion, we see that from the point of view of the distributed efficiency it is more convenient to use $ask(c)$.

Let us now consider also one of the main important features of a programming language: its expressiveness. With no doubts, atomic ccp is more expressive than ccp (for a formal proof see [3]), but the necessary sequentialisation of atomic tell actions is a serious drawback for distributed implementation. On the other hand, ccp is very suitable for distributed implementation, but many distributed algorithms, which can be easily expressed in atomic ccp, require complicated adaptations in ccp, and it is often necessary to use an arbiter or some kind of centralized control. We argue that ccp_{get} could be a reasonable compromise also in terms of expressiveness.

Let us consider the problem of the dining philosophers, which, according to Dijkstra, can be regarded as a benchmark of expressiveness. This problem has a very simple distributed solution in atomic ccp, which can be obtained by translating the Concurrent Prolog program proposed by Shapiro [22]. In ccp, a solution can be obtained by translating the PARLOG program proposed by Ringwood [16]. This solution, which is rather complicated (70 lines of code), uses a series of agents to implement each state a philosopher can occupy–thinking, preparing to eat, and eating. Philosophers circulate along data streams among these process-states. The agents representing the states can be regarded as a sort of central entity which control the overall situation.

In ccp_{get} a simple, natural and distributed solution can be obtained as follows. Assuming that there are n philosophers, we initialize the store with $n-1$ tokens, representing available tickets, and n tokens representing the forks. When a philosopher wants to eat, he must first get a ticket. If he succeeds (i.e. if there are tickets still available), then he can get the forks, when available. When he has eaten, he releases (by tell actions) forks and ticket. This algorithm, which is inspired by [5], is proved to be deadlock-free.

Acknowledgments

We wish to acknowledge helpful comments by Walter Vogler and by the anonymous reviewers.

References

1. E. Best and C. Palamidessi: Linear constraint systems as high-level nets. Proc. CONCUR'96. Springer LNCS **1119** (1996) 498–513
2. A. Brogi and P. Ciancarini: The concurrent language Shared Prolog. ACM TOPLAS **13** (1991) 99–123
3. F.S. de Boer and C. Palamidessi. Embedding as a Tool for Language Comparison. Information and Computation **108** (1994) 128–157
4. F.S. de Boer, C. Palamidessi and E. Best: Concurrent Constraint Programming with Information Removal. Proc. First Int. Workshop on Concurrent Constraint Programming, Venice (1995) 1–13
5. N. Carriero and D. Gelernter: Linda in context. Comm. ACM **32** (1989) 445–458
6. R. Janicki and M. Koutny: Structure of Concurrency. Theoretical Computer Science **112** (1993) 5–52
7. R. Janicki and M. Koutny: Semantics of Inhibitor Nets. Information and Computation **123** (1995) 1–16

8. N. Kobayashi and A. Yonezawa: ACL–A Concurrent Linear Logic Programming Paradigm. Proc. of the International Logic Programming Symposium (1993) 279–294

9. D. Gelernter: Generative Communication in Linda. ACM TOPLAS **7** (1985) 80–112

10. A. Mazurkiewicz: Trace Theory. Petri Nets: Applications and Relationships to Other Models of Concurrency, Advances in Petri Nets 1986, Part II. Springer-Verlag, LNCS **255** (1987) 279-324

11. U. Montanari and F. Rossi: True concurrency in concurrent constraint programming. Proc. of the International Logic Programming Symposium (1991) 694–716

12. U. Montanari and F. Rossi: Graph rewriting for a partial order semantics of concurrent constraint programming. Theoretical Computer Science **109** (1993)

13. U. Montanari and F. Rossi: Concurrent Semantics for Concurrent Constraint Programming via Contextual Nets. V.J. Saraswat and P. Van Hentenryck (eds.) Constraint Programming (1995)

14. U. Montanari and F. Rossi: Contextual nets. Acta Informatica **32** (1995)

15. W. Reisig: Petri Nets. An Introduction. EATCS Monographs on Theoretical Computer Science **3** (1985)

16. G.A. Ringwood: Parlog86 and the dining logicians. Comm. ACM **31** (1988) 10–25

17. F. Rossi: *Constraints and Concurrency.* PhD thesis, University of Pisa (1993)

18. V.A. Saraswat: *Concurrent Constraint Programming.* PhD thesis, Carnegie-Mellon University (1989) Published by The MIT Press (1993)

19. V.A. Saraswat and P. Lincoln: Higher-order, linear concurrent constraint programming. Technical report, Xerox PARC (1992)

20. V.A. Saraswat and M. Rinard: Concurrent constraint programming. Proc. of the seventeenth ACM Symposium on Principles of Programming Languages (1990) 232–245

21. V.A. Saraswat, M. Rinard, and P. Panangaden: Semantics foundations of concurrent constraint programming. In *Proc. of the eighteenth ACM Symposium on Principles of Programming Languages* (1991) 333–353

22. E. Shapiro: Embedding Linda and other joys of concurrent logic programming. Technical Report, The Weizmann Institute of Science (1989)

23. P.H. Starke: Processes in Petri Nets. Elektronische Informationsverarbeitung und Kybernetik **17** (1981) 389–416

Programmable Coordination Media

Enrico Denti, Antonio Natali, Andrea Omicini

LIA - DEIS - Università di Bologna
Viale Risorgimento, 2 - 40136, Bologna (Italy)
Ph.: +39 51 6443087 - Fax: +39 51 6443073
mailto:{edenti,anatali,aomicini}@deis.unibo.it
http://www-lia.deis.unibo.it/Staff/

Abstract. The design, development and maintenance of multi-component software systems often suffer from the lack of suitable coordination abstractions. The aim of this paper is to show the benefits of coordination models based on global communication abstractions whose behaviour is not fixed, but is extensible so as to accomplish the intended behaviour of the whole system. Accordingly, we propose the notion of *programmable coordination medium* as an abstraction provided by the coordination model around which the global behaviour of a coordination architecture can be designed. As an example, we show how a Linda-based approach can be empowered by exploiting the notion of programmable tuple space, as supported by the $\mathcal{ACLT}$ coordination model.

Keywords: Coordination Models, Programmable Coordination Media, Reactions, Tuple Spaces, Multi-Agent Systems

1 Introduction

Component technology is radically altering the way software systems are designed: for instance, today typical WWW servers are built by simply assembling and extending existing components like HTTP servers, DB managers and e-mail applications. Generally speaking, most current multi-component systems are designed by mapping each service to be provided into a single component, often adding new components as soon as new functionalities are needed: the whole system is conceived to be nothing more than the sum of its parts.

Correspondingly, current models for component interaction (like COM/OLE-ActiveX [3], CORBA [13], CGI interface protocol) are usually based on message passing and point-to-point communication, thus providing no real coordination. When designing composite software system, these models lack the adequate abstractions needed to achieve an intelligent and flexible behaviour of the overall system. Whenever a change to the *global* system behaviour is needed, for instance, they require *local* modifications to (possibly all) the components of the system. This is why these systems are usually designed around special components (monitors, coordinators) embodying the core of the global behaviour of the overall system, so that a change to one such a component affects the whole system.

Coordination models like the blackboard based ones, instead, provide for a global, explicit communication abstraction (a blackboard, a tuple space), around which a multi-component system is naturally to be built. However, how these coordination media work is usually set once and for all by the coordination model, and cannot be modified or extended according to the intended overall system's behaviour. Thus, coordination entities have to take charge of the interaction protocol, and cannot abstract from the coordination policy.

The main aim of this paper is to discuss the benefits of designing multi-component software systems around a global communication abstraction whose behaviour can be extended and tailored to the system needs. To this end, we suggest the notion of *programmable coordination medium* as a kernel for coordination models whose flexibility and expressive power lies in the extensibility of the coordination medium itself. In particular, we propose that extensibility be the result of embodying computational properties typically in charge of the components into the communication abstraction.

As a case study, Section 2 shows how a shared communication device à la Linda can work as the core of a flexible coordination architecture in the Linda-based $\mathcal{ACLT}$ [14] coordination model. $\mathcal{ACLT}$ tuple spaces are enhanced so as to be *reactive* to communication events, rather than to communication state changes only. Reactions to communication events can be defined through a logic-based specification language, making $\mathcal{ACLT}$ tuple spaces *programmable*.

As a typical example of a coordination architecture designed around a programmable coordination medium, we discuss a simple case of a multi-agent system based on the $\mathcal{ACLT}$ coordination model. As suggested in [8], it can be desirable to design the observable behaviour of agents of a multi-agent system according to a quite abstract and straightforward pattern, while most of the global properties of the system are naturally placed in the global communication abstraction. In this way, a change to the coordination policy requires no modifications to the interaction protocol of a single component of the system. Correspondingly, Section 3 shows how a multi-agent architecture can be built around a programmable coordination medium by extending the behaviour of $\mathcal{ACLT}$ tuple spaces through reaction programming.

2 Programmable tuple spaces

In order to show the effectiveness of an approach to coordination based on the notion of *programmable coordination medium*, this Section discusses some peculiar aspects of the Linda-based $\mathcal{ACLT}$ coordination model [14]. Linda [10] introduces the notion of *generative communication* and promotes the separation between the computation model and the coordination model [12], based on a shared memory communication abstraction called *tuple space*. In this paper, we will take the Linda coordination model as known, as well as its most common extensions (like the predicate, non-blocking in_noblock and rd_noblock primitives).

The $\mathcal{ACLT}$ coordination model (first presented in [14]) extends the basic Linda model with the notions of *logic tuple space* (see also [4,5]), *multiple tuple spaces*[1] [11], and *reactive tuple space* [7]. In the $\mathcal{ACLT}$ model, communication takes place through a multiplicity of named logic tuple spaces, which are collections of first-order unitary clauses, uniquely identified by a ground term. In particular, a logic tuple space may be given a twofold interpretation, either as a simple communication device, or or as a knowledge repository. According to the latter reading, a logic tuple space can be used as a logic theory, where deductive activities over the communication state can be performed. For this purpose, $\mathcal{ACLT}$ provides for a family of *demo* primitives, along with a coherent notion of logic consequence in a time-dependent environment [14].

What is relevant here is the $\mathcal{ACLT}$ notion of *programmable tuple space*. The first idea is to raise observability at the system level from tuples to (communication) operations over tuples. Correspondingly, $\mathcal{ACLT}$ tuple spaces are *reactive*, since they are provided with the capability to react to *communication events* rather than just to the *communication state changes* only, as in standard Linda [7].

A simple *specification language* allows communication events to be associated to *reactions*, which are sequences of operations executed atomically in response to specific communication primitives performed over tuple spaces. In other terms, a reaction can be thought as an event-handler catching communication events, and having full access to both the whole information concerning the specific communication event, and the current communication state, as represented by the tuple space.

By programming reactions, the effect of the execution of a communication operation can be extended as needed. Moreover, thanks to the reaction execution model, all the results due to a single communication operation (its own effect, and the effects of all the reactions associated to it) are made visible to the coordination entities as a single transition of the state of the communication abstraction. As a consequence, the behaviour of the coordination medium can be made as complex as desired at the component's perception level.

In principle, since the specification language is founded on the same communication pattern exploited for agent interaction (that is, logic tuples and basic operations over tuple spaces), components may be allowed to manipulate the communication abstraction behaviour. Along with the chance of performing deductions on the current coordination state provided by the $\mathcal{ACLT}$ notion of tuple space as a full-fledged logic theory, this opens the way to systems able to reason about themselves, and possibly self-modify their behaviour dynamically, according to the system goals.

---

[1] Although $\mathcal{ACLT}$ exploits multiple tuple spaces, we will henceforth leave this feature aside, since it is not relevant in the context of this work. Thus, we will always refer any communication primitive to a sort of "default tuple space", without specifying any tuple space name.

2.1 The reaction model

$\mathcal{ACLT}$ (Linda-like) primitives have the same semantics as Linda ones. However, the behaviour of an $\mathcal{ACLT}$ tuple space can be extended by exploiting reactions to add new effects to communication events.

The $\mathcal{ACLT}$ reaction model is based on the idea of making communication events observable at the system level. For this purpose, any *physical* (communication) *event* can be associated with one or more *logical events*, each denoted by a unique name. Multiple logical events can be connected to the same physical event, as well as multiple physical events can correspond to the same logical event. The association between communication events and logical events is set by a special tuple of the form map(*Operation*, *Event*), which captures the idea that each time *Operation* is performed on the tuple space, a logical *Event* occurs.

The $\mathcal{ACLT}$ tuple space's programming model is based on the notion of *reaction*, triggered in response to logical events' occurrence, and specified through tuples of the form react(*Event*,*Body*). The *reaction body Body* is the collection of the primitive operations to be executed when the logical *Event* occurs, and is syntactically defined as a conjunction of *reaction goals*. A reaction goal is either a state primitive (current_agent/1, current_op/1, ...), a term predicate (term equality/inequality, term unifiability/non-unifiability, ...), or a communication primitive (out_r, in_r, rd_r)[2]. In the special but frequent case that a single physical event is mapped onto a single logical event, a simplified shortcut syntax can be used, avoiding the map/2 clause and expressing the reaction by means of a single reaction(*Operation*,*Body*) tuple.[3]

Reactions are executed only after the corresponding logical event has actually occurred: so, in particular, when a reaction to an out(*Tuple*) primitive is triggered, the emitted *Tuple* is already in the tuple space. Instead, in and rd communication primitives can be seen as made of two distinct communication events: the first query phase, when a tuple template is provided (the *pre* phase), and the subsequent answer phase, when a unifying tuple is eventually returned to the querying agent (the *post* phase).[4] According to that, $\mathcal{ACLT}$ allows different reactions to be associated to each of these two phases [7], by means of the pre/0 and post/0 predicates, which succeed only in the corresponding phase. So, for instance, when the reactions possibly associated to the the *post* phase of an in(*Tuple*) primitive are executed, the returned tuple (i.e., the one uni-

---

[2] These are the only communication primitives which can occur inside a reaction: out_r works as a conventional out, while in_r and rd_r correspond to in_noblock and rd_noblock, respectively. Consequently, blocking primitives are not allowed inside reaction goals.

[3] Although in the following examples we will exploit only the simplified reaction/2 syntax, the map/2 + react/2 syntax may come to be useful whenever the same reaction body ought to be repeated as a response to many different physical events, as in the case of the tracer presented in [7].

[4] Correspondingly, the current_tuple primitive returns the tuple template in the first phase, and the unified tuple in the answer phase.

278

fying with *Tuple*) is no longer in the tuple space, while it is still there during the execution of reactions possibly associated to the the *pre* phase of the **in** primitive.

Because reaction goals are actually executed sequentially, their relative order may influence the result of the reaction [8]. Since multiple **react/2** tuples can be specified for a given logical event - as well as multiple **reaction/2** for the same communication primitive -, multiple reactions may be triggered at the same time: in principle, such reactions are executed as mutually-independent actions, in a non-deterministic order.

2.2 Reactions as transactions

A *successful reaction* is one whose reaction goals are all executed successfully. Instead, if even one reaction goal fails, the reaction aborts. Only successful reactions produce effects, while failed reactions yield no results at all. If, for instance, the default tuple space contains no **value/1** tuple, the reaction body

```
in_r(value(X)), out_r(value(1)), out_r(value(s(X)))
```

fails and produces no effect, while the reaction body

```
out_r(value(1)), in_r(value(X)), out_r(value(s(X)))
```

succeeds, and eventually adds the tuple **value(s(1))** to the default tuple space.

At the system level, $\mathcal{ACLT}$ reactions are executed atomically with a transaction semantics: the (potentially multiple) effects of a successful reaction are carried out in a single transition of the tuple space state. Consequently, outside a reaction there is no way to perceive the multiplicity of effects possibly produced by the sequential execution of the reaction itself. So, in the case the reaction succeeds, all its side-effect operations are realised simultaneously, leading to a single observable state transition. Instead, a failed reaction is virtually cancelled, as if it had never been executed, and yields no effect at all. Consider, for instance, the following reaction:

```
map(out, event).
react(event, ( current_tuple(p(_)),
        in_r(p(a)), in_r(p(X)), out_r(pp(a,X)) )).
```

which could have been expressed, more concisely, also as:

```
reaction( out(p(_)), ( in_r(p(a)), in_r(p(X)), out_r(pp(a,X)) ))
```

Each time a new tuple is inserted in the tuple space with an **out**, this reaction checks for the presence of two **p/1** tuples (whose one should be **p(a)**) and, in the case they are found, it replaces them with one single **pp/2** tuple. If some reaction goal fails (possibly because there is only one **p/1** tuple instead of the two required), no tuples are actually removed from the tuple space, nor are any other side-effects ever produced. If the reaction succeeds, instead, all its associated side-effects (removal of two tuples, and addition of a third) are realised altogether: so, the simultaneous presence of the two p/1 tuples is perceived by the system as a single pp/2 tuple.

As shown in Subsection 2.1, a multiplicity of reactions can be triggered in response to the same communication event, both because the latter has been mapped onto multiple logical events, or because multiple reactions have been specified for the same logical event. In addition, further reactions may be triggered as a consequence of the successful completion of another reaction, as a reaction body can contain communication primitives in its turn. In order to guarantee the transaction semantics, all such further reactions are executed only *after* the triggering reaction has been successfully completed: accordingly, reaction nesting is not permitted.

In any case, all reactions following an agent-triggered communication event - both triggered *directly* by the event and *indirectly* by other reactions produced by the event - are actually executed *before* serving any other agent-triggered communication event. As a result, agents can only perceive the final result of the execution of the communication event and the set of all the reactions it triggered (directly and indirectly). For instance, if the following reaction has been defined:

```
reaction( out(p(s(X))), ( in_r(p(s(X))), out_r(p(X)) ))
```

a component suspended on an in(p(s(0))) operation will not be waked up, as normally expected, by an out(p(s(0))) operation, as this reaction will first replace the p(s(0)) tuple with a p(0) tuple. As a result, only the p(0) tuple is visible at the component's perception level, while the p(s(0)) tuple is not perceived.

This behaviour introduces a new kind of tuple space state transition at the component's perception level, and enhances the expressive power of the coordination model. In fact, thanks to the execution model of $\mathcal{ACLT}$ reactions described above, coordination entities still perceive the response of a tuple space to a communication event as a single-step transition of the tuple space state. However, such a transition is no longer bounded to be simple (adding/deleting one tuple) and fixed by the model, like in Linda, but can be made as complex as desired. ¿From a component perspective, for instance, the previous reaction

```
reaction( out(p(_)), ( in_r(p(a)), in_r(p(X)), out_r(pp(a,X)) ))
```

has the effect of making the simultaneous presence of the two p/1 tuples unperceivable, and of leading a single out operation to result both in the removal of a tuple and in the insertion of another. In addition, the inserted tuple is not the one specified in the out operation, but is related both to that one and to the tuple space state.

An $\mathcal{ACLT}$ tuple space is then an example of a programmable coordination medium, since its observable behaviour in response to communication events can be modified through reaction programming. By freeing the components from the charge of explicitly handling a (possibly complex) interaction protocol, a programmable coordination medium allows coordination entities to be designed according to a straightforward communication protocol, while charging the medium of most of the low-level coordination details. Next Section discusses the benefits of this approach in the context of multi-agent systems.

3 Building multi-agent systems around a programmable coordination medium

Being intrinsically interactive [15], multi-agent systems are naturally characterised by the model of component interaction, as well as by the observable behaviour of their components, rather than by the rules of agent inner computation [8]. As a result, agent architectures can be designed independently of agent internal models, focussing on agent observable behaviour. Due to this shifting focus from agents to agent interaction, the communication abstraction is asked to play a major role within the coordination model of choice. In particular, once the coordination model for the multi-agent system is given, the choice of the interaction policy should not affect the single agent architecture, which could then concentrate on agent observable behaviour and on its interface towards the outside. In fact, it seems desirable that agents are designed according to a quite abstract model, so as to delegate the required interaction protocol to the communication abstraction behaviour. From a conceptual viewpoint, this makes coordination media [6], where interaction actually takes place, be in charge of the interaction policy, instead of the single coordination entities, which are not required to have a view of the system as a whole. In practice, this is particularly useful because agents of a multi-agent system may often be difficult or even impossible to modify, especially when dealing with legacy software components, whose observable behaviour could not be easy to accommodate so as to accomplish the interaction strategy of choice.

In order to show how a programmable coordination medium could be exploited in a multi-agent system, in the rest of this Section we discuss three examples of simple multi-agent systems based on $\mathcal{ACLT}$. The first one (Subsection 3.1), the classical *dining philosopher* problem [9], shows how some global properties of a multi-agent system (like deadlock avoidance) can be embodied into the communication abstraction. The second one (Subsection 3.2), a slight variation of the previous problem, is meant to show how a more complex interaction policy can be achieved by simply re-defining how the communication device works, with no changes to the interaction protocols of the philosopher agents. The last one (Subsection 3.3) generalises the previous example, discussing how the interaction policy can be handled and modified by an agent, possibly as a result of an inferential process on the current coordination state of the multi-agent system.

3.1 The dining philosophers

As an example of the flexibility provided by the extensibility of the communication abstraction to the $\mathcal{ACLT}$ model, we discuss an implementation of the classical dining philosopher problem, based on reactions. A characteristic of this problem is that, in order to avoid deadlock situations, a philosopher should either get the two forks he needs to eat, or get none. This means that the two forks should be obtained through a transaction. In order to ensure fairness, moreover, fork release should be performed atomically. In fact, if both the left and the right neighbour of the currently-eating philosopher are waiting to eat, releasing one fork before the other would result in privileging one philosopher with respect to its colleague, which should be avoided.

When trying to express the solution to this problem in Linda, the main problem is that the natural choice of modelling the fork acquisition as a sequence of two *in* operations is not transactional, thus yielding a potential risk of deadlock. Similarly, a sequence of two *out* operations would not be atomic, thus not ensuring fairness. In such a framework, a safe solution requires that the user explicitly handles a locking mechanism, thus affecting the agent behaviour. Using $\mathcal{ACLT}$ reactions, instead, transactionality is guaranteed by suitably programming the tuple space behaviour, with no need for a more complex agent protocol. Thus, deadlock avoidance and fairness are obtained through the programmable coordination medium.

Philosopher agents are designed according to a very straightforward interaction protocol: when a philosopher wants to eat, he tries to acquire the two forks through an in(forks($F1,F2$)) operation; when he is satiated, and wants to start thinking, he gives the forks back by means of an out(forks($F1,F2$)) operation. So, all the charge of the interaction policy is up to the communication abstraction.

While resources are actually available singly in the tuple space (each fork is represented by a fork(F) tuple), philosophers view resources as pairs of forks (tuples forks($F1,F2$)): the tuple space is then programmed so as to bridge the two different perceptions - the system level (fork/1 tuples, representing single forks) and the agent level (forks/2 tuples, representing pairs of forks).

For instance, the forks($F1,F2$) tuple emitted by a philosopher agent when releasing forks is not perceived by the other agents, as it is immediately replaced with the two fork($F1$), fork($F2$) tuples by the following reaction:

```
reaction( out(forks(F1,F2)), (                              (1)
    in_r(forks(F1,F2)), out_r(fork(F1)), out_r(fork(F2)) )).
```

Handling fork requests, instead, is more complex, because the desired forks may not be immediately available. In this case, the in(forks($F1,F2$)) operation suspends, and the request should be recorded in the tuple space, so that it may be served later. Consequently, fork requests will be recorded in the tuple space by means of a reaction associated to the *pre* phase of the in(forks($F1,F2$)) operation. Such a tuple will then be retracted, by means of another appropriate reaction associated to the *post* phase of the same operation, when the philosopher has been served (after the proper forks have become available) and can start eating:

```
reaction( in(forks(F1,F2)), ( pre, out_r(required(F1,F2)) )).   (2)
reaction( in(forks(F1,F2)), ( post, in_r(required(F1,F2)) )).
```

Whenever a new fork request is recorded as a **required(*F1,F2*)** tuple, the tuple space is programmed so as to check whether the desired forks are immediately available, in what case it conquers the pair of resources by replacing the two **fork(*F1*)**, **fork(*F2*)** tuples with one single **forks(*F1,F2*)** tuple:

```
reaction( out_r(required(F1,F2)), (                              (3)
    in_r(fork(F1)), in_r(fork(F2)), out_r(forks(F1,F2)) )).
```

Obviously, if the two forks are not available, this reaction fails, the philosopher agent stays suspended, and the **required/2** tuple remains in the tuple space.

However, waiting philosophers will be served later, when new single forks are made available as a consequence of a fork release performed by other agents. For this reason, the fork-release event has to be intercepted, and handled trying to group the pairs of forks needed by still-waiting philosophers. Since each fork may be requested, in principle, by two distinct philosophers, two reactions are needed - one for the left agent, and another one for the right agent. Each reaction checks whether there is a corresponding dangling fork request, and tries to serve it if this is the case:

```
reaction( out_r(fork(F)), ( rd_r(required(F1,F)),
    in_r(fork(F1)), in_r(fork(F)), out_r(forks(F1,F)) )).
reaction( out_r(fork(F)), ( rd_r(required(F,F2)),          (4)
    in_r(fork(F)), in_r(fork(F2)), out_r(forks(F,F2)) )).
```

Since reactions are executed transactionally, forks are reserved only in pairs when they are both available and needed by some agent: so, no deadlock can occur.

Notice that the agent model does not need to be specialised in order to accomplish the competition protocol: a philosopher simply asks for forks when hungry, and sets them free when satiated. Agent design can then concentrate on modelling agent internal architecture, while agent interaction model results quite simple and intuitive. A good deal of the intelligence of the system lays then in the interaction protocol, which is only of little concern for the single agent. Thus, the communication abstraction is specialised through suitable reaction programming so that it makes the system behave correctly, independently of the agent internal model: the only requirement is that the emerging behaviour of philosopher agents (their interaction model) accomplishes the very straightforward *acquire/release* protocol.

3.2 Philosophers dining with labelled forks

In order to show how an interaction policy can be modified and made more complex by changing the behaviour of the coordination medium, without affecting the interaction protocol of the coordination entities, we discuss a slight variation of the Dining Philosopher example. The basic problem is changed in that now there are three forks for each position on the table, labelled differently according to the kind of meal for which it has to be used: breakfast, lunch, or dinner. At any time in the multi-agent system, it is either breakfast, lunch, or dinner time.

When it is lunch time, for instance, only lunch forks can be used to start eating: however, a slowly-eating philosopher is allowed to keep on having his meal as long as he needs. So, if he starts eating at dinner time, he will be given dinner forks, and will be allowed to keep them for eating even when breakfast time comes around.

Since philosophers are supposed to be totally unaware of this enhancement, the philosopher protocol is exactly the same as in the previous example: in particular, they still try to get their pair of forks through an in(forks(F1,F2)) operation, and still give them back by means of an out(forks(F1,F2)) operation. Here, however, two contiguous philosophers, sharing a fork position, can eat at the same time (using, obviously, different forks obtained at different meal times), thus exploiting the extra resources - three forks instead of one. Take for instance the case of a two-philosopher system, where both agents get hungry at breakfast time. Only one of them (the *lucky philosopher*) will be assigned the breakfast forks, while the other (the *unlucky philosopher*) will be forced to wait. But when lunch time comes, the unlucky philosopher may be allowed to start eating even though the lucky one is still eating, because the lucky philosopher is using breakfast forks, and the lunch forks are free.

In order to achieve this new behaviour, we just have to slightly modify the internal representation of forks in the tuple space, adding a representation of the meal time concept, and updating the reactions of Subsection 3.1 accordingly. More precisely, the tuple space representation of the forks is changed from fork(Fork) to fork(Meal,Fork), representing the fork *Fork* which can be used at *Meal* time. Moreover, a timefor(Meal) tuple is assumed to be always in the tuple space, indicating which forks to allocate to hungry philosophers at any time. Reactions, in their turn, should be modified so that:

- the reaction handling fork requests as required(F1,F2) tuples takes the meal time into account;
- the two reactions serving dangling fork requests take the meal time into account, too;
- an extra reaction takes care of serving dangling fork requests when the meal time changes and, therefore, new forks can be used.

So, reactions *(2)* remain untouched,

```
reaction( in(forks(F1,F2)), ( pre, out_r(required(F1,F2)) )).    (5)
reaction( in(forks(F1,F2)), ( post, in_r(required(F1,F2)) )).
```

while reaction *(1)* becomes

```
reaction( out(forks(F1,F2)), ( in_r(used(M,F1,F2)),              (6)
    in_r(forks(F1,F2)), out_r(fork(M,F1)), out_r(fork(M,F2)) )).
```

The used/3 tuple is needed to track which forks are currently being used, given that, as discussed above, different types of forks may be used at the same time. Correspondingly, reaction *(3)* becomes

```
reaction( out_r(required(F1,F2)), ( rd_r(timefor(M)),
    in_r(fork(M,F1)), in_r(fork(M,F2)),
    out_r(forks(F1,F2)), out_r(used(M,F1,F2)) )).
```
                                                                    (7)

and reactions *(4)* become

```
reaction( out_r(fork(M,F)), ( rd_r(required(F1,F)),
    rd_r(timefor(M)), in_r(fork(M,F1)), in_r(fork(M,F)),
    out_r(used(M,F1,F)), out_r(forks(F1,F)) )).
reaction( out_r(fork(M,F)), ( rd_r(required(F,F2)),
    rd_r(timefor(M)), in_r(fork(M,F)), in_r(fork(M,F2)),
    out_r(used(M,F,F2)), out_r(forks(F,F2)) )).
```
                                                                    (8)

The new reaction needed to handle meal time changes does basically the same, serving a dangling fork request when the new meal time allows new forks to be used:

```
reaction( out_r(timefor(M)), ( rd_r(required(F1,F2)),
    in_r(fork(M,F1)), in_r(fork(M,F2)),
    out_r(forks(F1,F2)), out_r(used(M,F1,F2)) )).
```
                                                                    (9)

As a result, new notions (like meal time and meal forks) are introduced in the system, new resources are made available (more forks), a new policy for resource assignment is adopted, but the philosopher agents can keep on using the same straightforward *acquire/release forks* protocol defined in the example of Subsection 3.1. So, reaction programming makes it possible for agents to maintain the same perception of the resource space as in the previous example, even though such a space has changed and made more complex. This feature is achieved by properly programming the communication abstraction so as to encapsulate changes and hide them from agents, actually embodying the new coordination policy into the coordination medium.

3.3 Agents requiring labelled resources

In the previous example, a new interaction policy is achieved by properly re-programming the communication abstraction. How such a re-programming is performed is not specified, so one could think that the designer has to deal with this. However, $\mathcal{ACLT}$ support for logic agents with inferential capabilities suggests that a specific agent may be charged of such a task. This example shows how the modification of the interaction policy can be achieved dynamically, likely as a result of a reasoning over the current state of the coordination medium performed by a logic agent, working as a meta-level "supervisor".

For this purpose, the example of Subsection 3.2 is generalised by replacing the notion of meal time (and meal-labelled forks) with a general resource labelling scheme. Resources are now grouped in classes, and represented by tuples of the form res(*Type,Name*), where *Type* represents the resource class and *Name* the resource name. Generalising the meal time notion of the previous example,

285

represented there by the tuple timefor(Meal), we no longer suppose that only one class of resources is made available at one given time. So, the tuple space may contain more than one class(Type) tuple at the same time, each representing one class Type of available resources.

Agents require groups of n homogeneous (i.e., of the same class) resources through in(resources(A,R1,...,Rn)) operations, then release them by means of out(resources(A,R1,...,Rn)) operations, where A is the agent identifier. Agents are free to ask for as many resources as they need ($\leq max$), so that agent a1 may ask for two resources r1, r2 through an in(a1,r1,r2), while agent a2 may ask for three resources r1, r3, r4 through an in(a2,r1,r3,r4).

While the agents perceive resources as groups of unlabelled items $R1$, ..., Rn, the system handles single labelled items in form of res(Type,Res) tuples. For this purpose, reactions (10-11) are defined, handling requests for groups of resources, and recording them as req(A,R1,...,Rn) tuples. In particular, the agent protocol allows now agents to ask for resources in either a blocking (reaction (10)) or a non-blocking way (reaction (11)).

```
reaction( in(resources(A,R1)), ( pre,
    out_r(req(A,R1)) )).
...
reaction( in(resources(A,R1,...,Rn)), ( pre,
    out_r(req(A,R1,...,Rn)) )).
```
(10)

```
reaction( in_noblock(resources(A,R1)), ( pre,
    out_r(req(A,R1)) )).
reaction( in_noblock(resources(A,R1)), ( post, failure,
    in_r(req(A,R1)) )).
...
reaction( in_noblock(resources(A,R1,...,Rn)), ( pre,
    out_r(req(A,R1,...,Rn)) )).
reaction( in_noblock(resources(A,R1,...,Rn)), ( post, failure
    in_r(req(A,R1,...,Rn)) )).
```
(11)

Resource release is handled by reaction (12), which is in charge of making resources released (as a group) by one agent available as single resources to all agents.

```
reaction( out(resources(A,R1)), (
    out_r(res(T,R1)),
    in_r(used(A,T,R1)), in_r(resources(A,R1)) )).
...
reaction( out(resources(A,R1,...,Rn)), (
    out_r(res(T,R1)), ..., out_r(res(T,Rn)),
    in_r(used(A,T,R1,...,Rn)), in_r(resources(A,R1,...,Rn)) )).
```
(12)

A new agent request can be served when either a new request is performed and all needed resources are free (reaction (13)), or one resource is released (in which case – reaction (14) – all permutations are to be considered), or a new class of resources is made available (in which case – reaction (15) – all pending requests are to be checked).

```
reaction( out_r(req(A,R1)), ( rd_all_r(class(T),TL),
   out_r(lreserve(req(A,R1),TL)) )).
...
reaction( out_r(req(R1,...,Rn)), ( rd_all_r(class(T),TL),
   out_r(lreserve(req(A,R1,...,Rn),TL)) )).
```
(13)

```
reaction( out_r(res(T,R)), ( rd_r(class(T)),
   rd_all_r(req(A,R),ReqL),
   out_r(lreserve(ReqL,class(T))) )).
...
reaction( out_r(res(T,R)), ( rd_r(class(T)),
   rd_all_r(req(A,R,...,Rn),ReqL),
   out_r(lreserve(ReqL,class(T))) )).
...
reaction( out_r(res(T,R)), ( rd_r(class(T)),
   rd_all_r(req(A,R1,...,R,...,Rn),ReqL),
   out_r(lreserve(ReqL,class(T))) )).
...
reaction( out_r(res(T,R)), ( rd_r(class(T)),
   rd_all_r(req(A,R1,...,R),ReqL),
   out_r(lreserve(ReqL,class(T))) )).
```
(14)

```
reaction( out(class(T)), ( rd_all_r(req(A,R1),ReqL),
   out_r(lreserve(ReqL,class(T))) )).
...
reaction( out(class(T)), ( rd_all_r(req(A,R1,...,Rn),ReqL),
   out_r(lreserve(ReqL,class(T))) )).
```
(15)

In any case, a **reserve(*Req, Type*)** tuple is produced through reaction *(16)* for any possible match between the available resources and the pending requests, and is then handled by reaction *(17)*).

```
reaction( out_r(lreserve(Req,T)), ( in_r(lreserve(Req,T)) )).
reaction( out_r(lreserve(Req,[T|TL])), ( out_r(reserve(Req,T))
   out_r(lreserve(Req,TL)) )). ...
reaction( out_r(lreserve([Req|ReqL],T)), ( out_r(reserve(Req,T))
   out_r(lreserve(ReqL,T)) )).
```
(16)

```
reaction( out_r(reserve(Req,T)), ( in_r(reserve(Req,T)) )).
reaction( out_r(reserve(req(A,R1),class(T))), (
   in_r(res(T,R1)),
   out_r(resources(A,R1))
   out_r(used(A,T,R1)), in_r(req(A,R1)) )).
...
reaction( out_r(reserve(req(A,R1,...,Rn),class(T))), (
   in_r(res(T,R1)), ..., in_r(res(T,Rn)),
   out_r(resources(A,R1))
   out_r(used(A,T,R1,...,Rn)), in_r(req(A,R1,...,Rn)) )).
```
(17)

Finally, reactions *(18–20)* handle the deletion of a class of resources, performed through either a blocking or a non-blocking *in* operation.

```
reaction( in(class(T)), ( post,
   out_r(noclass(T)) )).
```
(18)

```
reaction( in_noblock(class(T)), ( post, success,        (19)
    out_r(noclass(T)) )).
```

```
reaction( out_r(noclass(T)), ( in_r(noclass(T)) )).
...                                                      (20)
reaction( out_r(noclass(T)), ( in_r(class(T)),
    out_r(noclass(T)) )).
```

In this example, many sets of resources can be made available at the same time through the simultaneous presence of many class(*Type*) tuples in the tuple space. Classes of resources can then be added and removed by inserting (reaction *(15)*) and removing (reaction *(18)*) class(*Type*) tuples. This allows resources to be allocated according to arbitrarily complex strategies, possibly driven by the reasoning of a logic agent on the content of the tuple space. For instance, the supervisor may realise that the system load is too heavy, checking the number of pending resource requests (represented by req($A, R1, \ldots, Rn$) tuples) by properly combining $\mathcal{ACLT}$ *demo* primitives with side-effect communication primitives. Thus, it may decide to add a new resource set to the system through a set of res(*NewType, Name*) tuples, and make them available to the agents by simply adding a single class(*NewType*) tuple.

4 Related works and conclusions

The particular instantiation of the notion of programmable coordination medium presented here (the $\mathcal{ACLT}$ programmable tuple space) deeply relies on the concept of reaction, like many other different coordination models. For instance, the chemical metaphor of Gamma [1] uses reactions to specify very general coordination laws in terms of *reaction conditions* and consequent *actions*, but no communication abstraction is provided, nor is any agent interaction protocol. As it can be argued from the Dining Philosopher example shown in [2], reactions are the only means for the evolution of a multi-agent system based on Gamma, since the model does not account for agent deliberative activity.

Also the ESP coordination language [5] is based on the notion of multiple logic tuple space, and exploits reactiveness of the tuple space. However, the computational shift from the agents to the communication abstraction is even stronger than in $\mathcal{ACLT}$, as ESP reduces the notion of agent to a purely reactive execution thread.

According to our perception, coordination architectures may actually take advantage from being based on a programmable coordination medium, that is a communication abstraction whose behaviour is not fixed, but can be extended and tailored to accomplish the overall system goals. In this work, we have explored the benefits of this approach in the context of the Linda-based $\mathcal{ACLT}$ coordination model, where the Linda tuple space communication abstraction is enhanced through reaction programming. Indeed, we suggest that the same approach may also be successfully exploited in typical multi-coordinated architectures based on message passing and peer-to-peer communication, like World

Wide Web servers, where no global communication abstraction is a-priori available. This is particularly true when considering the increasing request for value-added services, calling for more flexible and intelligent system behaviours. By combining a programmable coordination medium with the agent capability of performing inferential activities over the state of the coordination, one could build multi-component software systems able to intelligently drive their own evolution by dynamically self-modifying the communication abstraction behaviour.

References

1. J.-P. Banâtre and D. le Métayer. The Gamma model and its discipline of programming. *Science of Computer Programming*, 15(1):55–77, November 1990.
2. J.-P. Banâtre and D. le Métayer. Programming by multiset transformation. *Communications of the ACM*, 36(1):98–111, January 1993.
3. Kraig Brockschmidt. *Inside OLE*. Microsoft Press, 1995. 2nd ed.
4. A. Brogi and P. Ciancarini. The concurrent language, Shared Prolog. *ACM Transactions on Programming Languages and Systems*, 13(1), January 1991.
5. P. Ciancarini. Distributed programming with logic tuple spaces. *New Generation Computing*, 12, 1994.
6. P. Ciancarini. Coordination models and languages as software integrators. *ACM Computing Surveys*, 28(2), June 1996.
7. E. Denti, A. Natali, A. Omicini, and M. Venuti. An extensible framework for the development of coordinated applications, 1996. First International Conference, COORDINATION'96, Cesena, Italy, April 15–17, 1996.
8. E. Denti and A. Omicini. Designing multi-agent systems around an extensible communication abstraction. In A. Cesta and P.-Y. Schobbens, editors, *Proceedings of the 4th ModelAge Workshop on Formal Models of Agents, Certosa di Pontignano, Italy, January 15–18, 1997*, pages 87–97. National Research Council of Italy, 1997. To be published by Springer-Verlag in the LNAI Series.
9. E.W. Dijkstra. *Co-operating sequential processes*. Academic Press, London, 1965.
10. D. Gelernter. Generative communication in Linda. *ACM Transactions on Programming Languages and Systems*, 7(1), January 1985.
11. D. Gelernter. Multiple tuple spaces in Linda. In *Proceedings of PARLE*, volume 365 of *LNCS*, 1989.
12. D. Gelernter and N. Carriero. Coordination languages and their significance. *Communications of the ACM*, 35(2):97–107, February 1992.
13. Object Management Group. The common object request broker: Architecture and specification. Technical report, OMG, July 1995. Rev. 2.0.
14. A. Omicini, E. Denti, and A. Natali. Agent coordination and control through logic theories. In *Topics in Artificial Intelligence - 4th Congress of the Italian Association for Artificial Intelligence, AI*IA'95*, volume 992 of *LNAI*, pages 439–450, Firenze, Italy, October 11–13 1995. Springer-Verlag.
15. P. Wegner. Interactive foundations of computing. Technical report, Brown University, Providence (RI), August 1996.

Safer Tuple Spaces

Roel van der Goot[1], Jonathan Schaeffer[2], and Gregory V. Wilson[3]

[1] Erasmus University Rotterdam, The Netherlands, vandergoot@few.eur.nl
[2] University of Alberta, Canada, jonathan@cs.ualberta.ca
[3] Visible Decisions, Canada, greg@vizbiz.com

Abstract. The simplicity and elegance of the Linda programming model is based on its single, global, typeless tuple space. However, these virtues come at a cost. First, the tuple space can be an impediment to scalable high performance. Second, the "black box" nature of the tuple space makes it an inherently dangerous data structure, prone to many types of programming errors.

Blossom is a C++ version of Linda with extensions. This paper introduces some of the novelties in Blossom, as they pertain to creating "safe" tuple spaces. These new features include multiple strongly typed tuple spaces, field access patterns, tuple space access patterns, and assertions.

1 Introduction

The computing literature is replete with programming models for writing parallel programs. Many of them are research prototypes that are good enough for a few academic papers and then quietly disappear. Few models attract sustained interest in the literature, or establish a large user community. Linda [7] is one of the rare parallel programming models that has managed to survive for over a decade, in spite of the discriminating (and critical) tastes of the parallel computing community.

Linda's strength is the simplicity of its programming model. In effect, Linda offers a blackboard (the *tuple space*) that processes can read from, write to, and erase portions of. To support Linda, languages (such as C, C++, and Fortran) need only have a library implementing a few calls to access the tuple space. Thus, a simple implementation is easily built. More sophisticated versions of Linda exist, relying on compiler techniques to understand the parallelism in the application and optimize accordingly [8].

Although the uniqueness of the Linda approach excited the parallel computing community in the late 1980's, with time the novelty waned. In part this was because Linda became a commercial product (with the resulting licensing fees), and free versions suffered in performance. Nevertheless there continues to be an active Linda user community.

Although there are many advantages to the Linda model (simplicity, ease of integration in a language, ease of expressing communication and synchronization), there are two major criticisms. First and foremost, the tuple space is often seen to be a bottleneck and an impediment to high scalable performance. For many applications, these performance concerns effectively rule out Linda as a viable tool. Second, an often overlooked point is that the tuple space has some dangerous design flaws that can give rise to serious programming errors. The tuple space is a generic shared data structure that can be viewed as a black box: one can read and write to it, but an application cannot see inside it. It is legal to put *anything* into the tuple space, including semantically invalid data. Furthermore, there is no way to peek into this black box to see its internal structure and check for errors. Thus, to make Linda a more attractive parallel programming model, two things must be addressed: improved program performance, and making the model safer, in the sense that the likelihood of programming errors is reduced.

This paper introduces Blossom, an extended version of Linda for the C++ programming language, designed to address the major concerns of Linda. This paper describes some of the innovations in Blossom that influence the structure of the tuple space. By appropriately specifying tuple space(s), the probability of introducing a programming error into a parallel Blossom program is greatly reduced. Parallel programs are notoriously difficult to design, implement, test, and debug. Anything that can be done to shorten the program development cycle is welcome. Although the enhancements described in this paper address the software engineering concerns of generating correct programs, most of them also can be used to improve program performance.

Since C-Linda and Fortran-Linda made their debut, there has been a major shift in programming language trends. Strong typing and class libraries (as in C++ and Java) have increased the expressive power available to the programmer. In particular, these features and C++ templates allow us to achieve many of the capabilities of a Linda compiler using just a standard C++ compiler, without introducing new syntax or changing the semantics of the programming language.

The Linda model can easily be integrated into an object oriented programming language [15]. Linda implementations for Eiffel [13] and Java [9] require the user to explicitly create objects of class Tuple. In C++ Linda [5] a precompiler is required to translate new syntax into C++. Our Blossom system neither needs explicit creation of objects of class Tuple, nor does it use a precompiler.

Section 2 describes the Linda model and introduces some of the proposed model enhancements in the literature. Section 3 describes four innovations in Blossom. The paper is restricted to discussing the design of the tuple space, since these enhancements are currently implemented and working. Section 4 illustrates programming using Blossom. Finally, Section 5 discusses Blossom work in progress, including the performance enhancements.

2   Linda

Linda was introduced in 1985. Although the Linda model was not in its final form, it contained the idea of a global memory accessible by multiple processes. The global memory contains a collection of data records, called *tuples*, and it is accordingly called the *tuple space*. Tuple space data is organized as an associative memory, meaning that data is retrieved by its value(s), not by an index.

Linda provides six simple operations to access the tuple space. Operation in gets a tuple from the tuple space (*in* the program), out puts a tuple (*out* of the program) into the tuple space, and rd replicates a tuple. The rd operation is semantically equivalent to an in immediately followed by an out (combined in one atomic action).

The following example illustrates how a program might manipulate the tuple space. An out("todo", 1); puts a tuple with two fields into the tuple space; the first field is a string with value "todo" and the second field is an integer with value 1. A variable with value 1 as the second field would have the same result.

An in("todo", 1); will get the same tuple out of the tuple space, if it is present. If there is no tuple with values equivalent to all the arguments, the operation will block until another process puts a matching tuple in the tuple space. Wild cards can be used to enhance the capabilities of the operations that read tuples. For example,

```
int i;
in("todo", ?i);
```

matches any tuple with two fields, the first being a string with value "todo" and the second an integer (with any value). Such a wild card field (?i) is called a *formal* parameter as opposed to an *actual* parameter (a value field). Tuples that contain formal fields are sometimes referred to as *anti-tuples*.

Linda provides an eval operation for spawning new processes. For example, eval("todo", sqr(5)); will spawn two processes, each evaluating one of the arguments in parallel with the spawning process. As soon as all the arguments of the eval are evaluated, the resulting tuple is put into tuple space (the tuple ("todo", 25) in this case).

The operations inp and rdp are nonblocking versions of in and rd, respectively. They query the tuple space for a match and return a boolean indicating whether they succeeded in that. If no match is found the operations will not wait (i.e., block) for another process to insert a matching tuple.

Because the model is so simple (and elegant), it is easy to find fault with it. Consequently, numerous extensions to the model have been proposed in the literature. Some of the more interesting ones include: having multiple tuple spaces [11], more powerful tuple space operations such as collect [4] and copy-collect [16], specifying access patterns on tuples [6], persistent tuple spaces [3], fault-tolerant tuple spaces [1], and open Linda [14]. In this paper we will use the extension of multiple tuple spaces.

This paper discusses Blossom, a C++-based implementation of Linda with extensions. Since we are using only the C++ compiler and not a Linda compiler, the syntax of Blossom differs slightly from that of Linda. In Blossom tuple spaces become objects, and the operations on tuple spaces become member functions. The original Linda operations are relative to the program; the Blossom member functions are relative to the tuple space. Hence new names for the operations had to be chosen: out becomes put, in becomes get, rd becomes copy, inp becomes get_nb, and rdp becomes copy_nb (where nb indicates the call is nonblocking). The eval operation is handled as a special case of put:

```
eval(5, sqr(5));
```

becomes

```
// "ts" is the name of a user-defined tuple space
ts.put(5, eval(sqr)(5));
```

indicating that only one process is created to evaluate the square of 5.

Formal parameters (?) are handled differently as well:

```
int i;
in(5, ?i);
```

becomes

```
Arg<int> i;
ts.get(5, i.var());
```

where Arg< *type* > is a Blossom class that enhances the *type* to include additional methods. The var() method allows the variable to be used as a wild card.

Blossom's tuple spaces are first class objects, which means that it is possible to have tuple spaces of tuple spaces.

3   Enhancements

The tuple space is a typeless black box. The user can put data of any type in it, and attempt to extract data of any type from it. But the wealth of programming language design experience suggests that this is a bad idea. The trend in computing today is towards strong typing. We have seen the evolution of BCPL to C to C++, motivated in part by the benefits of strong typing. These benefits are twofold: catching more errors at compile-time, and preventing some classes of run-time errors. Given the inherently difficult nature of parallel programming, any language enhancements that reduce the probability of error are welcome.

In this section, four new enhancements to the basic Linda model are presented. All of them have to do with either preventing or detecting parallel program errors at compile- or run-time. This is achieved by changing the definition of the tuple space: it is given structure, behavior, and is made accessible (see Figure 1). The user provides annotations that give the compiler and run-time system information as to the expected behavior of the program, and forces it to meet those constraints.

Blossom is a C++ class library. Unlike C-Linda and Fortran-Linda, it does not add new syntax, alter the semantics, or extend the host language, each of which tends to result in programmer confusion [17]. C++ is a modern programming language with a rich set of features. This enables Blossom to achieve many

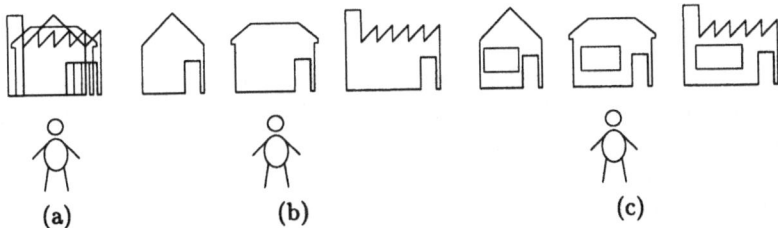

Fig. 1. Differences between tuple spaces; (a) Original Linda tuple space: It is a single collection of tuples of arbitrary structure. This implies that the user can try to insert/remove semantically incorrect tuples. The user cannot look inside the tuple space. (b) Strongly typed tuple space: Each tuple space can contain only one type of tuple. Hence a program cannot inadvertently insert/remove a wrongly typed tuple. (c) Strongly typed tuple space with assertions: It provides the user the additional benefit of being able to peek inside the tuple space.

of its objectives (including preventing programming errors) using only C++ syntax, without the need for a separate precompiler. To achieve the same benefits of a Linda precompiler (including error checking and run-time optimizations) , the user has to specify a small amount of additional detail in their program. This is reflected in the Blossom examples given later. They are (slightly) more verbose than their pure-Linda counterparts.

One issue not addressed in this paper is how to handle run-time errors generated by the new Blossom enhancements. Since we are using C++, a natural solution is to throw an exception whenever a run-time error occurs. The user can (at their discretion) catch the exception and handle it. Although this sounds good, it does have its problems. For example, do child processes throw exceptions in their parents? What if a process' parent is no longer around, but its grandparent is? Right now, all run-time errors result in aborting the application.

3.1 Strongly Typed Tuple Spaces

Linda's single tuple space can contain tuples of any type. Although this sounds conceptually simple, it has the disadvantage that it is easy to inadvertently introduce a bug in a program. Accidentally omitting a tuple field, introducing an additional field, changing a field, or reversing two fields is perfectly legal, yet may result in a semantically incorrect program. A sophisticated precompiler may be able to detect some but not all of these errors.

By having multiple tuple spaces, each strongly typed, these problems cannot occur. Each tuple space is created with a specification that gives the number, order, and type of each field of the tuples legally allowed (much like the parameters of a subroutine call). With this specification, many commonly occurring errors can be caught at compile time without the need for a Linda precompiler.

The advantages of strong typing can be summarized as follows:

1. Eliminate Errors. A strongly typed tuple space can eliminate many common errors.
2. Performance. Although this paper emphasizes the software engineering aspects of Blossom, it is important to realize that many of these enhancements can also be used to improve program performance. In effect, the typing partitions the tuple space into multiple disjoint address spaces. Hence, given a tuple of a particular type, the system knows exactly in what address space to look for the tuple.

The following example illustrates having multiple, strongly-typed tuple spaces in Blossom. The TupleSpace declarations each create new named tuple spaces, and specify the type of the tuples that are allowed inside them.

```
TupleSpace<Tuple<int, int> > square;
TupleSpace<Tuple<int, float> > sqrroot;

// Put values in the tuple spaces
for (int i = 1; i < MAX; i++) {
   square.put(i, i*i);
   sqrroot.put(i, sqrt(i));
}


// Take values out of the tuple spaces
Arg<float> answer;
sqrroot.get(4, answer.var()); // Succeeds
square.get(1, 1);             // Succeeds
square.get(2, 2);             // Blocks: no such tuple available
square.get("one", 1);        // Compile-time type error
square.get(1, 1.0);          // Compile-time type error
square.get(1.0, 1);          // Compile-time type error
```

3.2 Field Access Patterns

The philosophy behind typing a tuple space can be carried even further. A common programming scenario in Linda is to extract tuples using one of the fields as a discriminator. For example, one might have a producer-consumer computation where the tuples produced have to be processed in order. Every tuple contains a unique number which is more or less a time stamp. The smaller the number the older the tuple. The consumer gets the next tuple by increasing the time stamp field. In this case, this field is not only an integer, but it is always used as a *value*, not a wild card variable.

Every field in a tuple space declaration contains a declaration as to whether it is legal to use a wild card variable to retrieve a value or not. In other words, a field is designated as either Actual or Any. Actual indicates that a tuple field can only be retrieved by specifying a value, while Any extends this to include wild card variables.

This additional piece of information offers the user several advantages:

1. Eliminate Errors. By providing additional information about the intended behavior of the tuple space, the compiler can check whether the programmer always satisfies the specified requirements.
2. Performance. Specific fields can be used to determine (by hashing) on which machine to store or look for a tuple. Another method to distribute the tuple space is by broadcasting every change of the tuple space to all Linda processes. Hashing has the advantage that broadcasts are not necessary to distribute the tuple space. Instead a single communication is enough to put a tuple in a remote tuple space and only two communications are needed to get or to copy a tuple from a remote tuple space (the first sends the `get` or `copy` request to the remote tuple space; the second one when a matching tuple is found and how the formals are instantiated). An evenly distributed tuple space results in less tuples to be searched and removes possible bottlenecks of a big tuple space on one machine.

The following example illustrates field access patterns:

```
TupleSpace<Tuple<Actual<int>, Any<int> > > square;
Arg<int> sq;
for (int i = 1; i < MAX; i++)
    square.put(i, i*i);
square.get(1, sq.var());     // Succeeds
square.get(2, 2);            // Legal, but blocks
square.get(sq.var(), 4);     // Compile-time error
```

3.3 Tuple Space Access Patterns

The object-oriented community has recently embraced the concept of *design patterns* [10]: generic, frequently occurring programming paradigms. Similar ideas have played a prominent role in parallel computing, with common parallel structures such as master-slave and pipelines. Recent studies have shown that there are commonly occurring access patterns[1] on objects [2]. As part of program design, the user knows the intended access patterns on their objects. The first two columns of Table 1 gives these access patterns and their description, as defined in the Munin system [2].

The access patterns on objects are easily translated to access patterns on tuples [6]. In Blossom the access patterns are applied to tuple spaces instead of tuples. There are several reasons for doing this. First, in a good design, every tuple space has a unique purpose. All members of that tuple space are there to fulfill the design goals of the tuple space and should be handled similarly. Tuples with different access patterns in one tuple space are an indication of a poor design. Second, access patterns can be used to influence the (hidden) implementation of the tuple space, affecting program performance. For example, the choice of design pattern can effect the placement of the tuple space, the distribution of the tuple space, and whether data should be replicated.

---

[1] The original name is type-specific coherence mechanisms.

If a tuple space were annotated with an access pattern specification, then that might impose a constraint on how the tuple space is accessed at run-time (as shown in the third column of Table 1). Note that not all access patterns result in constraints on the tuple space. Read-mostly, write-many, and general read-write all allow an arbitrary combination of reads/writes to the tuple space. The only difference is the relative frequency with which the reads/writes occur. Hence these are too general to allow constraints to be imposed.

Table 1. Access patterns for tuple spaces

ACCESS PATTERN	DESCRIPTION	RESTRICTIONS
write-once	written during initialization, afterwards only read	no puts after a get or copy
private	local accesses only	only one process is allowed access
write-many	frequently modified	—
result	not needed until all data is collected	—
synchronization	semaphores	no copy or copy_nb allowed
migratory	accessed by a single process at a time	—
producer-consumer	written by one process, consumed by other processes	only one process is allowed to put
read-mostly	read far more often read than written	—
general read-write	general access pattern	—

There are a number of important advantages for having the user declare the access pattern of a tuple space:

1. Eliminate Errors. If the access pattern of a tuple space does not match the access pattern in the user's code, then warnings or errors can be given at compile- and run-time. For example, if the access pattern is producer-consumer and there are two or more processes putting tuples in the tuple space, the program can detect this at run-time. (Not at compile-time because we do not use a precompiler.) If the program has to run efficiently this run-time check can be turned off.

2. Performance. A programmer usually knows the intended use of a tuple space. Depending on these intentions, a distribution strategy could be selected by the user. For example a producer-consumer tuple space is best located in the data space of the producer process. It does not make sense that the producer first distributes the tuples over several processes, and next the consumer gathers the tuples from all these processes. The former approach

needs less communications to ship the data to the place it is used (consumed) and is thus faster.

3. Awareness of access patterns results in better designs. A good design never uses an object for more than one reason. This general rule applies to tuple spaces too. Access patterns can help the programmer distinguish different functionalities more easily.

It is important to realize that the access pattern attribute only changes the semantics of a tuple space if a restriction is encountered; if this is not the case access pattern attributes only change the implementation and not the semantics.

The following example illustrates the use of access patterns:

```
TupleSpace<Tuple<Any<int> >, ProducerConsumer> buffer;

// PRODUCER...
while(1) {
    int number = ...;
    buffer.put(number);        // Succeeds
}

// CONSUMER...
while(1) {
    Arg<int> number;
    buffer.get(number.var()); // Succeeds
    // ...
    buffer.put(16);            // Run-time error
}
```

3.4   Tuple Space Assertions

The simplicity of the Linda programming model comes, in part, from the capabilities of the tuple space; it is a black box with all the structure and implementation details hidden from the user. However, when looking for a bug, you want to be able to look inside the black box. This cannot be done in Linda, unless you extract each of the tuples one at a time and then put them back.

Tuple space assertions allow the user to peek into the tuple space. A problem with assertions in parallel programming is that several processes have access to the same tuple space. This means that if you put a tuple in the tuple space and then, for example, immediately assert that the number of tuples in the tuple space is greater than zero, the assertion can fail because another process removed the tuple. So either you have to make the assertion general (i.e., it takes other processes into account) or the assertion should form an atomic action with the other Linda operations. We chose the latter kind of assertion, because it better meets the needs of concurrent debugging.

Assertions act on an entire tuple space, which may be very inefficient if the tuple space is distributed. This is mainly because the whole tuple space should be locked during the evaluation of an assertion; no other processes are allowed to change its state. Assertions on tuple spaces should only be used to debug a program. However after fixing the bug you want to be able to recompile the program without removing the assertions again. Inclusion of another library (a compile-time option) can achieve this.

If the user wants to define an assertion on a tuple space, he has to derive a new class from class `Assertion`. In this class he can define two methods, `foreach()` and `exit()`. The constructor call initializes the object, the `foreach()` call is performed for every tuple in the tuple space, and the `exit()` call should return a boolean, indicating whether the assertion succeeded (`true`) or failed (`false`). If the `exit()` call returns false the program terminates. Blossom provides the (hidden) code to ensure that `foreach()` and `exit()` are called correctly.

Assertions are illustrated in the next section.

4 Example

The following example illustrates the usage of the concepts introduced in this paper. A (distributed) sieve of Eratosthenes calculates all primes smaller than a certain upper bound LIMIT. The function is_prime decides whether a number (the first argument) is a prime or not by trying to divide the number by all smaller primes (passed in the tuple space in the second argument). The strongly typed tuple space checks at compile-time that all accesses (here put and copy) have a tuple of the correct type (put only allows actual fields and copy only allows the specified fields). The SizeAssertion checks that the number of tuples in the tuple space is correct after all the primes are calculated.

```
#include <iostream.h>
#include "ts.h"

typedef TupleSpace<Actual<int>, Any<bool> > PrimesTS;

const int LIMIT = 5000;

class SizeAssertion: public Assertion {
   int size;
   int expected_size;
public:
   SizeAssertion(int s): expected_size(s), size(0) {}
   ~SizeAssertion() {}
   void foreach(int, bool) {
      size++;
   }
   bool exit() {
      return size == expected_size;
   }
```

```
};

bool is_prime(int number, PrimesTS primes) {
   int limit = sqrt(number);
   for (int i = 2; i < limit; i++) {
      Arg<bool> prime;
      primes.copy(i, prime.var());
      if (prime && (number%i == 0))
         return false;
   }
   return true;
}

void main() {
   PrimesTS primes;
   Arg<bool> prime;
   for (int i = 2; i < LIMIT; i++) {
      primes.copy(i, prime.var());
      if (prime)
         cout << i << endl;
   }
}
```

5 Future Work

The four enhancements discussed in this paper have been implemented and are working. All four help the user eliminate and/or detect common parallel programming errors. By making the tuple space safer, the user will spend less time debugging and they can invest more time in the design of their program.

Regrettably, it is impossible for us to quantify the benefits of the safe tuple spaces of Blossom. There is no easy metric, such as speedup, to compare against. A fair evaluation would require users to implement solutions using C-Linda and Blossom, and then compare the time it takes to correctly implement their solutions. Although we have experience performing these type of experiments [17], it is too early in the life-cycle of Blossom to go to this effort. Once we have completed the full Blossom implementation, we will be very interested in quantifying the influence of safer tuple spaces on the program design and implementation time.

Blossom is an evolving system. The following performance enhancements are in various stages of completion:

Futures: Arguments to get and copy can be futures [12]. Futures allow asynchronous versions of the aforementioned operations.

Get-update-put operation: The equivalent of a get-update-put operation in Linda results in three communications: send get, receive result, (update value,) and put update. By combining the operations, a reduction of one communication can be achieved: send **get**, (update value and put,) and receive result.

Reduction operations: Without a reduction operation, reducing a tuple space requires the user to **get** each tuple and perform the reduction, resulting in a potentially large amount of communication. A reduction operator performs the reduction according to the *owner computes* paradigm. There is a strong similarity between tuple space assertions and reduction operations: both require access to the entire tuple space in an efficient manner. The user can specify the reduction operator and let Blossom do the rest.

Conditionals: Sending a conditional to the tuple space, indicating what tuples you are interested in, can reduce communication and improve parallelism. Blossom can apply the conditional to all tuples in a tuple space and return those that match. The alternative in Linda is to **get** tuples until you find one that meets your conditions, and then **put** back all unneeded tuples.

Tuple space attributes: Additional information can be associated with a tuple space. *Ordered vs. Unordered*: Tuple spaces in which the tuples are ordered (sorted) are better for database applications (faster searching), but unordered tuple spaces generally have better performance. *Fair vs. Unfair*: In a fair tuple space every matching tuple has an equal opportunity of being selected. Unfair tuple spaces have biases but may have more efficient implementations. *Persistence*: Persistent tuple spaces are kept in files, which means that they are still present after a program terminates. Databases are in general persistent. *Size*: Allowing the user to specify the maximum size of a tuple space allows Blossom to more efficiently organize the data.

We expect to have complete working system by the end of the year.

Acknowledgments

We would like to thank *Nederlandse Organisatie voor Wetenschappelijk Onderzoek* (NWO), National Sciences & Engineering Research Council of Canada (NSERC), and IBM Toronto Labs for their financial assistance. Furthermore, we thank Josée Lajoie (IBM) for her patience answering numerous ANSI C++ questions, Bill O'Farrell (IBM) for sharing some of his knowledge on C++, Steve MacDonald (University of Alberta), and Arie de Bruin (Erasmus University Rotterdam) for their comments on the article.

References

1. BAKKEN, D. E., AND SCHLICHTING, R. D. Supporting Fault-Tolerant Parallel Programming in Linda. *IEEE Transactions on Parallel and Distributed Systems* 6, 3 (1995), 287–302.
2. BENNETT, J. K., CARTER, J. B., AND ZWAENEPOEL, W. Munin: Distributed Shared Memory Based on Type-Specific Memory Coherence. In *Second ACM SIGPLAN Symposium on Principles & Practice of Parallel Programming (PPoPP)* (1990), pp. 168–176.

3. BROWN, T., JEONG, K., LI, B., TALLA, S., WYCKOFF, P., AND SHASHA, D. *PLinda User Manual.* http://merv.cs.nyu.edu:8001/~binli/plinda/manual.ps, 1997.

4. BUTCHER, P., WOOD, A., AND ATKINS, M. Global Synchronisation in Linda. *Concurrency: Practice and Experience 6*, 6 (Sept. 1994), 505–516.

5. CALLSEN, C. J., CHENG, I., AND HAGEN, P. L. The AUC C++Linda System. In *Linda-Like Systems and Their Implementation*, G. Wilson, Ed. Tech. Rep., EPCC TR91–13, Edinburgh Parallel Computing Centre, June 1991, ch. 4, pp. 39–73.

6. CARREIRA, J., SILVA, L., AND SILVA, J. G. On the design of Eileen: a Linda-like library for MPI. In *Proceedings of the 1994 Scalable Parallel Libraries Conference* (1995), pp. 175–184.

7. CARRIERO, N., AND GELERNTER, D. *How To Write Parallel Programs: A First Course.* MIT Press, Cambridge, MA, 1990.

8. CARRIERO, N., AND GELERNTER, D. *Tuple Analysis and Partial Evaluation Strategies in the Linda Precompiler.* Research Monographs in Parallel and Distributed Computing. Pitman, London, 1990, ch. 7, pp. 114–125.

9. CIANCARINI, P., AND ROSSI, D. Jada: Coordination and Communication for Java agents. In *Mobile Object Systems: Towards the Programmable Internet*, J. Vitek and C. Tschudin, Eds., vol. 1222 of *Lecture Notes in Computer Science*. Springer Verlag, 1997, pp. 213–228.

10. GAMMA, E., HELM, R., JOHNSON, R., AND VLISSIDES, J. *Design Patterns.* Addison-Wesley, 1995.

11. GELERNTER, D. Multiple Tuple Spaces in Linda. In *Proceedings PARLE'89: Parallel Architectures and Languages Europe* (June 1989), pp. 20–27.

12. HALSTEAD, A. MultiLisp: A Language for Concurrent Symbolic Computation. *ACM Transactions on Programming Languages and Systems 7*, 4 (1985), 501–538.

13. JELLINGHAUS, R. Eiffel Linda: An Object-Oriented Linda Dialect. *ACM SIGPLAN Notices 25*, 12 (Dec. 1990), 70–84.

14. KIELMANN, T. Designing a Coordination Model for Open Systems. In *Coordination Languages and Models, First International Conference COORDINATION '96* (1996), P. Ciancarini and C. Hankin, Eds., pp. 267–284.

15. MATSUOKA, S., AND KAWAI, S. Using Tuple-Space Communication in Distributed Object-Oriented Architectures. *Proceedings ACM Conference on Object-Oriented Programming Systems, Languages and Applications (OOPSLA) 23*, 11 (1988), 276–284.

16. ROWSTRON, A., AND WOOD, A. Solving the Linda Multiple rd Problem. In *Coordination Languages and Models, First International Conference COORDINATION '96* (1996), P. Ciancarini and C. Hankin, Eds., pp. 357–367.

17. SZAFRON, D., AND SCHAEFFER, J. An Experiment to Measure the Usability of Parallel Programming Systems. *Concurrency: Practice and Experience 8*, 2 (1996), 147–166.

Coordinating Action Systems

Eric J. Hedman[1], Joost N. Kok[2], and Kaisa Sere[1]

[1] Turku Centre for Computer Science
Department of Computer Science, Åbo Akademi University
Lemminkäinengatan 14, FIN-20520 Åbo, Finland
{Eric.Hedman,Kaisa.Sere}@abo.fi
[2] Department of Computer Science, Leiden University
P. O. Box 9512, 2300 RA Leiden, The Netherlands
joost@cs.leidenuniv.nl

Abstract. We develop an action systems based approach that supports the separation of design of the functional or computation aspects of a system under construction from the coordination and synchronization issues. The computation aspects are modelled as nondeterministic actions that work in parallel with the coordination actions, which impose some control on this nondeterministic part. We define a special form of action systems that models this type of coordination activity. Certain forms of real time scheduling and coordination as well as exception handling are shown to be special cases of our approach. We show how the coordinators can be stepwise brought about from a high-level specification of the target system and how the reasoning about their behaviours is carried out separately from the computation aspects of the system within the refinement calculus.

1 Introduction

Recently, several languages and models for coordinating the work of independent agents have been proposed in the literature [9]. Many researchers have designed dedicated languages for coordination, separate from the language to model computation [12]. For Gamma programs [8] for instance a construct called scheduler is introduced [11]. The purpose of a scheduler is to restrict the nondeterminism present in a Gamma program. Another construct is the RTsynchronizer [19], which is a special form of an actor [1]. Often there have been difficulties in incorporating the new constructs into a formal framework. For example, there is no formal semantics given to the RTsynchronizers neither do they come with a methodology to reason about them or develop systems that involve them. For the Gamma approach, a separate framework is introduced for reasoning about the schedulers. The main contribution of this paper is to show how coordination can be modelled within an existing formal framework where both computation and coordination aspects are treated equally and uniformly. We formalize our ideas within the action systems formalism.

The action system formalism [4] is a state based approach to distributed computing. A set of guarded actions share some state variables and may act on those variables. The two main development techniques we use on action systems are *refinement* and *prioritized decomposition*. Refinement allows us to replace abstract state variables with more concrete representations such that the behaviour of the refined action system satisfies the behaviour of the abstract action system. The recently introduced prioritizing composition between actions and action systems [20] turns out to be a convenient way of expressing coordination policies. Additionally, *parallel decomposition* allows us to split an action system into parallel sub-systems by partitioning state variables and actions.

Action systems are related to the UNITY programs of Chandy and Misra [10]. Reasoning about UNITY programs is done within an associated temporal logic. This relies heavily on the underlying fairness assumption in the execution model. For some applications this is convenient, but not always. No such assumptions are made for action systems. Gamma and Swarm [13] programs also work on a set of actions that are intended to be executed in a nondeterministic fashion.

At first sight the philosophy behind design approaches like UNITY and action systems does not seem to support the coordination paradigm with its separation of computation from coordination. However, the formalisms as such are suitable as basis for coordination languages with their sets of nondeterministic actions. In this paper we show that within the action systems formalism it is indeed possible and natural to distinguish the functional part of a specification from the coordination part. We define a form of action systems that models a coordinator and propose several ways to do the separation. As examples we study a set of typical coordination problems from the literature, where the coordinators impose some particular scheduling mechanisms onto the otherwise independent and nondeterministic agents.

The design and reasoning about action systems is carried out within the refinement calculus [2,5,17,18] that is based on the use of predicate transformers [14]. The main refinement technique used here is data refinement [7].

We show how the coordination part can be stepwise developed from a high-level task description of a system within the refinement calculus. The advantage we gain is that we are able to reason in a structured way about the two aspects, functionality and coordination, within the same framework. Moreover, we can develop and refine these two lines independently of each other due to the compositionality of our (de-)composition operators.

This paper extends our previous work on coordination [15] into several directions. Earlier we showed how a typical communication medium for coordination, the tuple space, is added into a UNITY like language, ImpUNITY [21], and how this form of communication is used with a UNITY style refinement. Here we extend this by considering coordination as a language construct and propose a general strategy to derive coordinators or schedulers. The only composition operator defined for ImpUNITY programs is the union operator which corresponds to our parallel composition operator. In this paper we extend to prioritized composition and consider data refinement as our main refinement technique.

Overview. We proceed as follows. In Section 2 we describe the action systems formalism and the operators needed to model coordination. In Section 3, the

coordination aspects of an action system are developed. Section 4 is devoted
to special types of coordinators, namely exception handlers. In Section 5, the
refinement calculus for action systems is briefly described. Special emphasis is
put on the compositionality aspects. Section 6 describes how action system coordinators are developed in a stepwise manner within the refinement calculus.
We end in Section 7 with some concluding remarks.

2 Action Systems

An *action system* is a set of actions operating on local and global variables:

$$\mathcal{A} \ \widehat{=} \quad |[\ \textbf{var} \ y^*, x := y0, x0;$$
$$\textbf{proc} \ p_1^* = P_1; \ \ldots; p_n^* = P_n;$$
$$q_1 = Q_1; \ \ldots; q_l = Q_l;$$
$$\textbf{do} \ A_1 \ | \ \ldots \ | \ A_m \ \textbf{od}$$
$$]|: z, r \ .$$

Action system $\mathcal{A}$ describes a computation, in which the local variables x and the
exported global variables y, marked with $*$, are first created and initialized. Then
repeatedly any of the enabled actions $A_1, \ldots, A_n$ is nondeterministically selected
for execution. The computation terminates if no action is enabled, otherwise
it continues infinitely. Actions operating on disjoint sets of variables can be
executed in any order or in parallel.

The local variables x are only referenced locally in $\mathcal{A}$. The exported global
variables, y, on the other hand, can also be referenced by other action systems.
The imported global variables, z, of $\mathcal{A}$ are mentioned in $A_1, \ldots, A_n$, but not
declared locally. The identifiers x, y and z are assumed to be pairwise distinct
lists of variables. Thus, no redeclaration of variables is permitted.

A procedure is declared as $p = P$ with a *procedure header* p and a *procedure
body* P. In action system $\mathcal{A}$ the procedures $p_1 \ldots p_n$ are declared as exported
procedures, also marked with $*$, that are called from other action systems, while
the procedures $q_1 \ldots q_l$ are declared as local procedures. The procedures imported into $\mathcal{A}$ are denoted r. These are called from actions in $\mathcal{A}$, but are declared
elsewhere. The local and global procedures are assumed to be distinct.

A statement or an action is said to be *local* to an action system, if it only
refers to local variables of the action system. The procedures and actions are
allowed to refer to all the state variables of an action system. Furthermore, each
procedure and action may have local variables of its own.

Actions are taken to be *atomic*, meaning that only their input-output behaviour is of interest. They can be arbitrary sequential statements. Their behaviour
can therefore be described by the weakest precondition predicate transformer of
Dijkstra [14], where $\text{wp}(A, P)$ is the weakest precondition such that action A
terminates in a state satisfying predicate P. As we are only interested in the
input-output behaviour of actions, we consider two actions to be equivalent if
they always establish the same postcondition:

$$A = B \ \ \text{iff} \ \forall P : \text{wp}(A, P) = \text{wp}(B, P) \ .$$

In addition to the statements considered by Dijkstra, we allow assumptions $[P]$, where P is a predicate, and nondeterministic choice, $A \parallel B$, between the actions A and B. The assumption $[P]$ can be thought of as stopping execution, if P does not hold.

$$
\begin{array}{llll}
\mathrm{wp}(abort, P) & \mathrel{\widehat{=}} & false & \mathrm{wp}([Q], P) & \mathrel{\widehat{=}} & Q \Rightarrow P \\
\mathrm{wp}(skip, P) & \mathrel{\widehat{=}} & P & \mathrm{wp}((A \parallel B), P) & \mathrel{\widehat{=}} & \mathrm{wp}(A, P) \wedge \mathrm{wp}(B, P) \\
\mathrm{wp}(v := e, P) & \mathrel{\widehat{=}} & P[v := e] & \mathrm{wp}((A; B), P) & \mathrel{\widehat{=}} & \mathrm{wp}(A, \mathrm{wp}(B, P))
\end{array}
$$

Other operators can also be defined. The restriction we impose is that all actions are (finitely) conjunctive, hence excluding angelic nondeterminism [7]:

$$
\mathrm{wp}(A, P \wedge Q) = \mathrm{wp}(A, P) \wedge \mathrm{wp}(A, Q) \ .
$$

All of the above operators are conjunctive or preserve conjunctivity. Conjunctivity implies monotonicity:

$$
(P \Rightarrow Q) \Rightarrow (\mathrm{wp}(A, P) \Rightarrow \mathrm{wp}(A, Q)) \ .
$$

Definition of Procedures. Procedure bodies and actions may contain procedure calls. The meaning of a call on a parameterless procedure $p = P$ in a statement S is determined by the *substitution principle*:

$$
S = S[P/p] \ ,
$$

i.e. the body P of procedure p is substituted for each call on this procedure in statement S.

If a procedure or action contains a call to a procedure that is not declared in the action system, then the behavior of the action system will depend on the way in which the procedures are declared in some other action system, which constitutes the environment of the action system as will be described later. The definition of procedures (with formal parameters) for action systems is studied more detailed elsewhere [6].

Enabledness of an Action. The actions contain arbitrary program statements. A statement that establishes any postcondition is said to be miraculous. We take the view that a statement S is only enabled in those initial states in which it behaves nonmiraculously, i.e. for which $\neg \mathrm{wp}(S, false)$ holds. The guard of a statement characterizes those states for which the statement is enabled:

$$
gdS \mathrel{\widehat{=}} \neg \mathrm{wp}(S, false) \ .
$$

The statement S is said to be *enabled* in a given state, when the guard is true in that state. The statement S is said to be *always enabled*, if $\mathrm{wp}(S, false) = false$ (i.e., $gd(S) = true$), and *always terminating*, if $\mathrm{wp}(S, true) = true$.

Actions will in general be *guarded commands*, i.e., statements of the form

$$
C = g \rightarrow S \ ,
$$

where g is a boolean condition and S is a program statement. The guarded statement $g \to S$ is defined using assumption as follows:

$$g \to S \mathrel{\widehat{=}} [g]; S \ .$$

In this case, the guard of C is $g \wedge \neg\mathrm{wp}(S, \mathit{false})$. Hence, a guarded statement $g \to S$ is only enabled when S is enabled and g holds. Moreover, the non-deterministic choice $A \parallel B$ is enabled when either A or B is enabled:

$$gd(A \parallel B) = gdA \vee gdB \ .$$

We assume that procedures are always enabled. If additionally the body of each action of an arbitrary action system is always enabled, action systems coincide with the language of guarded commands. The *body* sC of C is defined:

$$sC \mathrel{\widehat{=}} gdC \to C \parallel \neg gdC \to abort \ .$$

Prioritized Actions. The prioritizing composition on actions turns out to be very important when modelling the coordination aspects of a system. Consider two actions A and B. We have that the prioritizing composition defined as

$$A /\!/ B \mathrel{\widehat{=}} A \parallel (\neg gdA \to B) \ ,$$

selects the first component A for execution if it is enabled, otherwise B is selected. The prioritizing composition of A and B is enabled when at least one of the actions is enabled:

$$gd(A /\!/ B) = gdA \vee gdB \ .$$

Under the assumption that the two actions exclude each other, the prioritizing composition and choice coincide:

$$A /\!/ B = A \parallel B \quad \text{if } gdA \Rightarrow \neg gdB \ .$$

Furthermore, the prioritizing composition of actions distributes over choice to the right:

$$A /\!/ (B \parallel C) = (A /\!/ B) \parallel (A /\!/ C) \ .$$

Other properties of this operator are studied by Sekerinski and Sere [20].

Parallel Composition. Consider two action systems, $\mathcal{A}$ and $\mathcal{B}$:

$$
\begin{aligned}
\mathcal{A} \mathrel{\widehat{=}} \quad &[\![\ \mathbf{var} \ v^*, x := v0, x0; \\
&\quad \mathbf{proc} \ r_1^* = R_1; \ \ldots; r_m^* = R_m; \\
&\qquad\quad p_1 = P_1; \ \ldots; p_n = P_n; \\
&\quad \mathbf{do} \ A \ \mathbf{od} \\
&]\!]: z
\end{aligned}
$$

$$
\begin{aligned}
\mathcal{B} \mathrel{\widehat{=}} \quad &[\![\ \mathbf{var} \ w^*, y := w0, y0; \\
&\quad \mathbf{proc} \ s_1^* = S_1; \ \ldots; s_k^* = S_k; \\
&\qquad\quad q_1 = Q_1; \ \ldots; q_l = Q_l; \\
&\quad \mathbf{do} \ B \ \mathbf{od} \\
&]\!]: u
\end{aligned}
$$

where $x \cap y = \emptyset$, $v \cap w = \emptyset$, and $r \cap s = \emptyset$. Furthermore, the local procedures declared in the two action systems are required to be distinct.

We define the *parallel composition* $\mathcal{A} \parallel \mathcal{B}$ of $\mathcal{A}$ and $\mathcal{B}$ to be the action system

$$
\begin{aligned}
\mathcal{C} \; \hat{=} \quad &|[\; \mathbf{var} \; b^*, x, y := b0, x0, y0; \\
&\quad \mathbf{proc} \; r_1^* = R_1; \; \ldots; r_m^* = R_m; \; s_1^* = S_1; \; \ldots; s_k^* = S_k; \\
&\qquad p_1 = P_1; \; \ldots; p_n = P_n; \; q_1 = Q_1; \; \ldots; q_l = Q_l; \\
&\quad \mathbf{do} \; A \parallel B \; \mathbf{od} \\
&]| : a
\end{aligned}
$$

where $a = z \cup u - (v \cup r \cup w \cup s)$, $b = v \cup w$, $r = (r_1 \cup \ldots \cup r_m)$, and $s = (s_1 \cup \ldots \cup s_k)$.

Thus, parallel composition will combine the state spaces of the two constituent action systems, merging the global variables and global procedures and keeping the local variables distinct. The imported identifiers denote those global variables and/or procedures that are not declared in either $\mathcal{A}$ or $\mathcal{B}$. The exported identifiers are the variables and/or procedures declared global in $\mathcal{A}$ or $\mathcal{B}$. The procedure declarations and the actions in the parallel composition consists of the procedure declarations and actions in the original systems.

Parallel composition is a way of associating a meaning to procedures that are called in an action system but which are not declared there, i.e., they are part of the import list. The meaning can be given by a procedure declared in another action system, provided the procedure has been declared global in that action system.

The behaviour of a parallel composition of action systems is dependent on how the individual action systems, the *reactive components*, interact with each other. We have for instance that a reactive component does not terminate by itself: termination is a global property of the composed action system. More on these topics can be found elsewhere [3].

Prioritizing Composition. Let the action systems $\mathcal{A}$ and $\mathcal{B}$ be as above. We define the *prioritizing composition* $\mathcal{A}/\!/\mathcal{B}$ of $\mathcal{A}$ and $\mathcal{B}$ to be the action system

$$
\begin{aligned}
\mathcal{C} \; \hat{=} \quad &|[\; \mathbf{var} \; b^*, x, y := b0, x0, y0; \\
&\quad \mathbf{proc} \; r_1^* = R_1; \; \ldots; r_m^* = R_m; \; s_1^* = S_1; \; \ldots; s_k^* = S_k; \\
&\qquad p_1 = P_1; \; \ldots; p_n = P_n; \; q_1 = Q_1; \; \ldots; q_l = Q_l; \\
&\quad \mathbf{do} \; A/\!/B \; \mathbf{od} \\
&]| : a
\end{aligned}
$$

where a, b, r and s are as above.

The prioritizing composition, like the parallel composition, will combine the state spaces of the two constituent action systems, merging the global variables and keeping the local variables distinct.

The prioritizing composition behaves as the parallel composition except when an action of $\mathcal{A}$ is enabled, in which case it will immediately be taken.

3 Coordination and Coordinators

The action systems formalism can be used in two ways to coordinate the work among a set of objects: (i) the objects can participate in joint actions that are scheduled for execution when all the participating objects are enabled, or (ii) we can define special action systems, coordinators, that carry out this coordination without effecting the functionality of the participating objects. The former approach to coordination is the usual action systems approach where the coordination is not separated from the rest of the system. This form was also studied in our earlier work [15]. We will here concentrate on the latter form of coordination.

Coordinators. A typical action system to be coordinated has some autonomous activity of its own, below modelled by the action A. The coordination, however, takes place via procedure calls to $\mathcal{A}$:

$$\mathcal{A} = |[\textbf{ proc } coordination\ procedures \, ; \textbf{do } A \textbf{ od }]|$$

The coordinator $\mathcal{C}$ has typically only autonomous actions C that check the precense of tuples and call the appropriate procedures in other systems.

$$\mathcal{C} = |[\textbf{ do } C \textbf{ od }]|$$

Let $\mathcal{C}$ be a coordinating action system and $\mathcal{A}$ some other system. Then

$$\mathcal{A} \parallel \mathcal{C}$$

models a system where the coordinator is a reactive component of the system it is supposed to coordinate. Here the coordination is not enforced, whereas in

$$\mathcal{C} /\!/ \mathcal{A}$$

the coordinator has a higher priority than the other actions of the system and, indeed, enforces coordination. We call this form of coordination pre-emptive. The previous form of coordination is called non pre-emptive.

In both cases above we assume that the communication from $\mathcal{A}$ to $\mathcal{C}$ is asynchronous, via some tuple space. The coordinator, after the appearance of certain tuples in the tuple space, may signal its coordination commands to $\mathcal{A}$ using synchronous communication.

Since shared variables is the typical way to achieve asynchronous communicatinon in our framework we can realize such a tuple space by declaring (and exporting) one or more variables of suitable type. The tuple space can be defined explicitly as was proposed earlier for IMPUNITY [15]. In the examples below we assume the existence of a tuple space, i.e. variable of type bag, that all the reactive components have access to. Furthermore, a tuple will have the form $\langle t \rangle$ where t denotes its contents. The command $add(\langle t \rangle)$ places the tuple $\langle t \rangle$ in the bag, $rem(\langle t \rangle)$ removes it from the bag and $\langle t \rangle$ in a boolean expression will check for the precense of the tuple in the bag.

Another way of thinking about the pre-emptive coordination is to look at two actions A and C. We have that

$$C /\!/ A$$

gives preference to C whenever C is enabled. Hence, in case both A and C are enabled, C will always be taken. When A is enabled, but C is not, the action A can be taken. The effect of this is to make the behavior of A more deterministic. Examples of this type of coordination are shown later in Section 6.

Below we give a set of typical examples of coordination problems to illustrate the above aspects. The examples show only the coordination aspects of the problem at hand. They are inspired by similar examples on RTsynchronizers that were studied during a recent research school on Embedded Systems in Veldhoven, The Netherlands [19].

Event Coordination. In the first example we have two action systems that model the left and right hands of a robot. The purpose of the coordinator is to ensure that when the left hand wants to give an object to the right hand, the object does not fall, but is indeed transferred from left to righ.

Hence, the systems $\mathcal{L}$ and $\mathcal{R}$

$$\mathcal{L} \mathrel{\hat{=}} \quad |[\textbf{proc } LRel^* = (lhand.rel := true) ;$$
$$\textbf{do } \ldots \text{ ordinary actions } \ldots$$
$$[\!] \neg lhand.rel \wedge \neg \langle lhand.rel \rangle \rightarrow add(\langle lhand.rel \rangle)$$
$$\textbf{od }]|$$

$$\mathcal{R} \mathrel{\hat{=}} \quad |[\textbf{proc } RGrab^* = (rhand.grab := true) ;$$
$$\textbf{do } \ldots \text{ ordinary actions } \ldots$$
$$[\!] \neg rhand.grab \wedge \neg \langle rhand.grab \rangle \rightarrow add(\langle rhand.grab \rangle)$$
$$\textbf{od }]|$$

announce their willingness to transfer an object by placing the relevant event name, *lhand.rel* and *rhand.grab* respectively, into a tuple space.

When the coordinator C below sees these two events, it makes the transfer between the hands to take place in a single atomic action:

$$C \mathrel{\hat{=}} \quad |[\textbf{do } \ldots \text{ ordinary actions } \ldots$$
$$[\!] \langle lhand.rel \rangle \wedge \langle rhand.grab \rangle \rightarrow$$
$$LRel ; RGrab; rem(\langle lhand.rel \rangle, \langle rhand.grab \rangle)$$
$$\textbf{od }]| : LRel, RGrab .$$

We have that the parallel composition

$$\mathcal{L} \parallel C \parallel \mathcal{R}$$

models the requested behaviour.

Periodic Events. Periodic events occur in real-time applications. An action system $\mathcal{A}$ behaves periodically, when it sends itself a message as a response to a similar message. The coordinator C fixes the periodic invocation of the sending actions independently of the sender. Let the period be P time units.

$\mathcal{A} \cong$ |[**proc** $receive^*(mess) = (m := mess \,; send := true)$;
var $send := false$;
do ... ordinary actions ...
| $send \rightarrow add(\langle m \rangle)$; $send := false$
od]|

$\mathcal{C} \cong$ |[**var** $t := now$; $add(\langle mess \rangle)$;
do ... ordinary actions ...
| $\langle mess \rangle \wedge now = t + P \rightarrow$
$\qquad\qquad receive(mess)$; $rem(\langle mess \rangle)$; $t := now$
od]| : now

$\mathcal{T} \cong$ |[**var** $now * := ?$; **do** $true \rightarrow now := now + 1$ **od**]|

We model the passage of time by the action system $\mathcal{T}$ that continuously advances time with one time unit. The current time is stored in the variable now that is used in a read-only mode by the coordinator $\mathcal{C}$.

We now have that the system

$$\mathcal{C} /\!/ \mathcal{A} /\!/ \mathcal{T}$$

allows time to advance only when there is nothing else to do. Moreover, the coordinator, having the highest priority, will force the system $\mathcal{A}$ to receive a message at every P time units.

Time Bounded Buffer. In a time bounded buffer we have a producer-consumer pair communicating via a buffer. Every element in the buffer is not allowed to stay there for longer than P time units. The producer places some elements into the buffer B. At that point the element is stamped with the time of insertion now. The consumer receives elements from the buffer via its global procedure get. It is not aware of the boundedness of time which is completely handled by the coordinator. It transfers elements to the consumer by calling get before the elements get too old, i.e. when $now \leq T + P$ holds where T is the time the element was placed in the buffer.

$\mathcal{P} \cong$ |[...
do ... ordinary actions ...
| $put \rightarrow B := B \cup \langle b, now \rangle$; $put := false$
od]| : B, now

$\mathcal{Q} \cong$ |[**proc** $get^*(buf) = (b := buf)$; **do** ... ordinary actions ... **od**]|

$\mathcal{C} \cong$ |[**var** $B^* := \emptyset$;
do ... ordinary actions ...
| $\langle b, T \rangle \in B \wedge now \leq T + P \rightarrow get(b)$; $rem(\langle b, T \rangle)$
od]| : now

The requested behaviour is modelled by

$$\mathcal{C}/\!/(\mathcal{P} \parallel \mathcal{Q})/\!/\mathcal{T}$$

Here the action system $\mathcal{T}$ is as above.

Alternatively, we can model different types of products with different deadlines in the buffer as follows:

$\mathcal{P}' \;\hat{=}\;$ |[...
    do ... ordinary actions ...
    | $put1 \rightarrow B := B \cup \langle b, p1, now \rangle$; $put1 := false$
    | $put2 \rightarrow B := B \cup \langle b, p2, now \rangle$; $put2 := false$
    od]| : B, now

$\mathcal{C} \;\hat{=}\;$ |[...
    do ... ordinary actions ...
    | $\langle b, p1, T \rangle \in B \wedge now \leq T + P1 \rightarrow get(b)$; $rem(\langle b, p1, T \rangle)$
    | $\langle b, p2, T \rangle \in B \wedge now \leq T + P2 \rightarrow get(b)$; $rem(\langle b, p2, T \rangle)$
    od]|

Here the product of type $p1$ will stay in the buffer at most $P1$ time units whereas the product of type $p2$ is stored in the buffer for at most $P2$ time units.

4 Exception Handling

A special case of coordination is exception handling, where little or no coordination is enforced by the exception handler during normal mode of operation. Instead coordination is only required by the exception handler in order to get the rest of the system back on track when something has gone wrong. Our framework for coordinators also lends itself to the modelling of exception handling. As an example of this way of using coordinators we will outline a way of modelling exception handling in a real time system with deadlines.

The composition

$$\mathcal{C}/\!/\mathcal{A}/\!/\mathcal{T}$$

studied in the examples above, allows time to pass only when there is nothing else to do and thus has progress built into the model. There is no way of missing a deadline and no need for exception handling. There are, however, variations of the composition we think are worth discussing as they lead us into the topic of modelling exceptions. Also here we are influenced by the work on RTschedulers.

Using parallel composition instead of prioritizing composition yields

$$\mathcal{C} \parallel \mathcal{A} \parallel \mathcal{T}$$

where all three parts run in parallel. In such a system the coordinator may miss a deadline and moreover unbounded waiting may occur. In order to prevent unbounded waiting, but still have the flexibility of modelling a system where deadlines may be missed we introduce the concept of an exception handler. Such a handler is an action system $\mathcal{E}$ with actions

$$E_i \quad \hat{=} \quad now > (t + P_i) \rightarrow \ldots \, ; t := now \ .$$

In the following system

$$\mathcal{E} /\!/ (C \parallel \mathcal{A} \parallel \mathcal{T})$$

the coordinator C may miss some deadlines, which leads to the enabling of some action in the exception handler $\mathcal{E}$ which ensures that the system will eventually make progress.

Exception handlers can be "nested", or layered, so that some exception handlers have deadlines of their own which in turn may be missed. In order for the system to model a meaningful system there has always to be a top level exception handler that guarantees that the system will make progress if all intermediate deadlines are missed. A system with layered exception handlers is composed as follows:

$$\mathcal{E}_n /\!/ (\mathcal{E}_{n-1} \parallel \ldots \parallel \mathcal{E}_1 \parallel C \parallel \mathcal{A} \parallel \mathcal{T})$$

where we have $n + 1$ deadlines (the coordinator C included). Furthermore, the actions of the intermediate exception handlers $\mathcal{E}_{n-1} \ldots \mathcal{E}_1$ can either be of the form described above or of the form:

$$E_i \quad \hat{=} \quad now > (t + P_i) \wedge now \leq (t + P_i + E_i) \rightarrow \ldots \, ; t := now$$

where E_i is the deadline for the exception handler to take action. Which of the two forms is used depends on the situation.

We have referred to the action systems $\mathcal{E}_i$ as exception handlers, which is the commonly used term for such functionality. Obviously, there is no difference between them and our coordinators so they could just as well be called layered coordinators. A scenario where layered coordinators could be used is in a safety system for a traffic airplane. If the plane is about to stall the pilot could be given t_1 time units to respond to the situation. However, if the plane is still in the same critical state after t_1 time units has passed the safety system should be enabled to take the corrective actions.

5 Action System Refinement

Action systems are intended to be developed in a stepwise manner within the refinement calculus. Data refinement is often used as a main refinement tool. Here we briefly describe these techniques. Data refinement of action systems is studied in detail elsewhere [7,3].

Data Refinement. The refinement calculus for actions is based on the following definition. Action A is refined by action A', written $A \leq A'$, if, whenever A establishes a certain postcondition, so does A':

$$A \leq A' \text{ iff } \forall P : \mathrm{wp}(A, P) \Rightarrow \mathrm{wp}(A', P) \ .$$

Together with the monotonicity of wp this implies that for a certain precondition, A' might establish a stronger postcondition than A, i.e. reduce the nondeterminism of A, or even establish postcondition *false*, i.e. behave miraculously. Choice and sequential composition are both monotonic with respect to refinement in both operands. Moreover, the refinement relation itself is reflexive and transitive.

Let now A be an action that refers to the variables x, z, denoted $A : x, z$, and A' an action that refers to the variables x', z. Then action A is *data refined* by action A' using *abstraction relation* $R(x, x', z)$, denoted $A \leq_R A'$, if

$$\forall Q.(R \wedge \mathrm{wp}(A, Q) \Rightarrow \mathrm{wp}(A', \exists x.R \wedge Q)) \ .$$

Note that $\exists x.R \wedge Q$ is a predicate on the variables x', z.

Let **proc** $p = P$ and let $R(u, u', x, z)$ be an abstraction relation on the involved variables such that

$$P \leq_R P' \ ,$$

where u and u' are local variables to P and P', respectively and x and z are the state variables of the system where p is declared. We then have that a call on p with declaration **proc** $p = P$ is refined by a call on p with the declaration **proc** $p = P'$.

Data Refinement of Action Systems. Let A and A' be two action systems.

$$A \mathrel{\widehat{=}} \quad \begin{aligned} &|[\ \textbf{var } z^*, x := z0, x0; \\ &\quad \textbf{proc } p_1^* = P_1; \ \ldots; p_j^* = P_j; \\ &\quad \textbf{do } A \textbf{ od} \\ &]|: u, r \end{aligned}$$

$$A' \mathrel{\widehat{=}} \quad \begin{aligned} &|[\ \textbf{var } z^*, x' := z0, x'0; \\ &\quad \textbf{proc } p_1^* = P_1'; \ \ldots; p_j^* = P_j'; \\ &\quad \textbf{do } A' \ \| \ H \textbf{ od} \\ &]|: u, r \end{aligned}$$

Here the idea is, that some variables x are replaced by the variables x'. Due to this replacement, the action A is replaced with the action A'. Some new computation, in terms of the action H, is added into the system. Even the global procedures p have been modified. We assume that there are no local procedures around (they have been reduced using the substitution principle). The following theorem states the conditions under which we can consider the action system A to be data refined by the action system A', i.e. when we have that $A \leq_R A'$ holds for some R.

Theorem 1. *Let A and A' be action systems as above and $R(x, x', u, z)$ some abstraction relation. Then $A \leq_R A'$, if*

   (i) *Initialization:* $R(x0, x'0, u, z0)$,
   (ii) *Procedures:* $P_i \leq_R P_i'$,

(iii) *Main actions:* $A \leq_R A'$,
(iv) *Exit condition:* $R \wedge gdA \Rightarrow gdA' \vee gdH$,
(v) *Auxiliary actions:* $skip \leq_R H$, and
(vi) *Termination of auxiliary computation:* $R \Rightarrow \text{wp}(\textbf{do } H \textbf{ od}, true)$.

Furthermore, when A occurs in a parallel composition with another action system $\mathcal{E}$, then $A \parallel \mathcal{E} \leq_R A' \parallel \mathcal{E}$, if for every action E in $\mathcal{E}$:

(vii) *Non-interference:* $R \wedge \text{wp}(E, true) \Rightarrow \text{wp}(E, R)$.

Decomposition. One method of developing a prioritized or parallel program is to first specify it without consideration of priorities and parallelism, and then add these in subsequent development steps. If the specification is given as an action system the definitions of the two composition operators directly gives a way of doing so.

Theorem 2. *(Parallel Decomposition.) If action system A is of the form*

$$A \mathrel{\hat{=}} \lVert [\textbf{ proc } p*, q* ; \textbf{var } b, c, y*, z* := b_0, c_0, y_0, z_0; \textbf{do } B \parallel C \textbf{ od} \rVert] : x$$

where the variables c do not occur in p, B, and the variables b do not occur in q, C, then

$$A = B \parallel C$$

where

$$B \mathrel{\hat{=}} \lVert [\textbf{ proc } p* ; \textbf{var } b, y* := b_0, y_0; \textbf{do } B \textbf{ od} \rVert] : x \text{ , and}$$
$$C \mathrel{\hat{=}} \lVert [\textbf{ proc } q* ; \textbf{var } c, z* := c_0, z_0; \textbf{do } C \textbf{ od} \rVert] : x \text{ .}$$

This development method for action systems, originally proposed by Back and Sere [6], is also applicable to prioritized programs in a slightly different form [20]. We first introduce a shorthand for the case when action system A is refined by action system A' with same local and global variables as A via some refinement relation:

$$A \leq A' \qquad \text{iff for some } R : A \leq_R A' \text{ .}$$

Theorem 3. *(Prioritizing Decomposition.) If action system A is of the form*

$$A \mathrel{\hat{=}} \lVert [\textbf{ proc } p*, q* ; \textbf{var } b, c, y*, z* := b_0, c_0, y_0, z_0; \textbf{do } B \parallel g \rightarrow C \textbf{ od} \rVert] : x$$

where the variables c do not occur in p, B, variables b do not occur in q, C, and for some predicate I,

(a) *Initialization:* $I(b_0, c_0, y_0, z_0)$,
(b) *Main actions:* $(I \wedge \text{wp}(B, true) \Rightarrow \text{wp}(B, I))$ and $(I \wedge \text{wp}(C, true) \Rightarrow \text{wp}(C, I))$,
(c) *Exit condition:* $I \wedge \neg gd B \wedge gd C \Rightarrow g$

then

$$A \leq B/\!/C$$

where

$$B \ \widehat{=} \ [\![\ \textbf{proc} \ p* ; \textbf{var} \ b, y* := b_0, y_0 \textbf{do} \ B \ \textbf{od} \ ]\!] : x \ , \text{and}$$
$$C \ \widehat{=} \ [\![\ \textbf{proc} \ q* ; \textbf{var} \ c, z* := c_0, z_0; \textbf{do} \ C \ \textbf{od} \ ]\!] : x \ .$$

Moreover, we have the following result for two action systems A and B:

$$A \parallel B \leq A/\!/B \ . \tag{1}$$

Hence, we are always allowed to give preference to an action system.

Compositionality. Both parallel and prioritizing composition are compositional under the restriction that the abstraction relation R is only over the local variables of the refined system. When the variables declared global in a system are used in a read-only fashion by other reactive components, this is enough to guarantee compositionality. Hence, under these restriction we have that:

$$A \leq_R A' \Rightarrow A \parallel B \leq_R A' \parallel B \ . \tag{2}$$

In case R also depends on the global variables, we need the additional requirement (vii) in Theorem 1 about non-interference.

For the prioritizing composition we have:

$$A \leq_R A' \Rightarrow A/\!/B \leq_R A'/\!/B \ , \text{ and} \tag{3}$$
$$A \leq_R A' \Rightarrow B/\!/A \leq_R B/\!/A' \ . \tag{4}$$

In case the abstraction relation R only depends on the local variables of A the above holds immediately. If R also depends on the global variables we need the same side conditions as above.

6 Constructing Coordinators

We can develop and refine coordinators stepwise within the refinement calculus for instance using the strategies below. When developing a non pre-emptive coordinator we use parallel decomposition.

$$A \leq A_1 \parallel C \parallel A_2$$
$$C \leq C' \Rightarrow A_1 \parallel C \parallel A_2 \leq A_1 \parallel C' \parallel A_2$$

In case pre-emptive coordination is needed, the prioritizing decomposition is used.

$$A \leq C/\!/(A_1 \parallel A_2)$$
$$C \leq C' \Rightarrow C/\!/(A_1 \parallel A_2) \leq C'/\!/(A_1 \parallel A_2)$$

Here the systems $\mathcal{A}$, $\mathcal{A}_1$ and $\mathcal{A}_2$ are intended to be coordinated by the systems $\mathcal{C}$ and $\mathcal{C}'$. The first refinement step in both cases is a decomposition step. In practice, such a step is justified by appealing to Theorem 2 and Theorem 3, respectively. In the second step, the idea is that the coordinator $\mathcal{C}$ is refined and to compositionality rules imply that the entire system gets refined.

Below we give two different examples of coordinators derived within this framework. For the sake of brevity we omit the details of the refinement steps and only present the results.

A Phone System. In an earlier study [16] we developed an IMPUNITY specification for a system of phones. The initial specification was given in a UNITY style. The specification was refined into a parallel composition of a number of phones and a switch board:

$$SwitchBoard \parallel Phone_1 \parallel \ldots \parallel Phone_n \ .$$

The reactive components communicated asynchronously via a tuple space as well as synchronously via procedure calls.

When we look at the *SwitchBoard* as an action system, we observe that it conforms to the general form of a coordinator as defined in this paper. It consists of a set of actions that calls procedures in the *Phone$_i$* systems connecting phone calls the same way as the robot coordinator connects events in Section 3.

Relying on our refinement rule (1) we have that

$$SwitchBoard /\!/ (Phone_1 \parallel \ldots \parallel Phone_n)$$

is a refinement of the original specification. The effect of this refinement is that it forces the actions of the switch board to be taken whenever enabled.

Let now

$$SwitchBoard \leq EmergencyCalls \parallel NormalCalls$$

using Theorem 1 again. Here we can think of the system *EmergencyCalls* to model certain emergency calls that need immediate attention by the system. They can be modelled by adding into the system a list of callee numbers and when ever such a number is present in the tuple space, the switch board will connect the call immediately. The system *NormalCalls* models rest of the calls. The above effect is achieved with the following constructs

$$EmergencyCalls /\!/ (NormalCalls \parallel Phone_1 \parallel \ldots \parallel Phone_n)$$

or

$$EmergencyCalls /\!/ NormalCalls /\!/ (Phone_1 \parallel \ldots \parallel Phone_n)$$

both of which are refinements of the first specification. We have again used the refinement rule (1) to justify the steps.

A Message Passing System. The following case study uses a message passing system as a vehicle to demonstrate the benefits of developing coordinators in the same framework as the functional aspects of the system. The initial specification $\mathcal{M}$ stores all messages in a bag *mail* of messages from which the appropriate receiver will pick up messages. The network is of fixed size with a set *Node* of nodes, and messages are passed around in "envelopes" consisting of a designated receiver and the message itself. The type of envelopes is $Env \;\hat{=}\; Node \times Msg$.

$$\mathcal{M} \;\hat{=}\; \quad |[\;\; \textbf{var } mail* := \langle\rangle \;;$$
$$\textbf{proc } Send_n((r, m) : Env) =$$
$$mail := mail \cup \langle(r, m)\rangle \;\; \textbf{for } n \in Node$$
$$\textbf{proc } Receive_n((r, m) : Env) =$$
$$mail := mail \backslash \langle(r, m)\rangle \;;\; process(m) \;\; \textbf{for } n \in Node$$
$$\textbf{do } (\exists m \mid (r, m) \in mail) \rightarrow m := m'.(r, m') \in mail \;;$$
$$Receive_r(r, m)) \;\; \textbf{for } r \in Node \;\textbf{od} \;\;]|$$

Given a subset $PriNode \subset Node$ of prioritized nodes we can for example refine $\mathcal{M}$ by augmenting it with a coordinator $\mathcal{P}$ that favours messages destined for nodes in $PriNode$.

$$\mathcal{P} \;\hat{=}\; \quad |[\;\; \textbf{do } (\exists m \mid (p, m) \in mail) \rightarrow m := m'.(p, m') \in mail \;;$$
$$Receive_p(p, m)) \;\; \textbf{for } p \in PriNode \;\textbf{od} \;\;]| : mail$$

We have that

$$\mathcal{M} \leq \mathcal{P} /\!/ \mathcal{M}$$

is a valid refinement since the composed system is a more deterministic version of the abstract one. Another possibility is to favour certain messages instead of certain nodes. The coordinator $\mathcal{U}$ can be seen as a router that prioritizes messages that are recognized as being urgent by the function $urgent : Msg \rightarrow Bool$.

$$\mathcal{U} \;\hat{=}\; \quad |[\;\; \textbf{do } (\exists m \mid (n, m) \in mail \wedge urgent(m)) \rightarrow$$
$$m := m'.((n, m') \in mail \wedge urgent(m')) \;;$$
$$Receive_n(n, m) \;\; \textbf{for } n \in Node \;\textbf{od} \;\;]| : mail$$

The composition favouring urgent messages is defined

$$\mathcal{M}'' \;\hat{=}\; \mathcal{U} /\!/ \mathcal{M}$$

which is also a more deterministic version of $\mathcal{M}$ and thus also a proper refinement, i.e.

$$\mathcal{M} \leq \mathcal{M}'' \;.$$

Working in the framework of action systems turns out to be quite flexible. Assume we start with the refinement from $\mathcal{M}$ to $\mathcal{M}''$. We can now refine either component, the controller $\mathcal{U}$ or the computational part $\mathcal{M}$ separately. Since our prioritizing composition operator is monotonic in its right argument any refinement of $\mathcal{M}$ can be used in the composition, including $\mathcal{M}'$ described above, yielding

$$\mathcal{M} \leq \mathcal{U} /\!/ (\mathcal{P} /\!/ \mathcal{M}) \;.$$

Due to associativity we can also view the system as

$$(\mathcal{U}/\!/\mathcal{P})/\!/\mathcal{M} \; .$$

When doing further refinements we can choose any of the components $\mathcal{U}$, $\mathcal{U}/\!/\mathcal{P}$, $\mathcal{P}/\!/\mathcal{M}$, or $\mathcal{M}$ as a specification to refine further.

7 Conclusions

We proposed a uniform action system/refinement calculus based approach to reasoning about coordination. The formalism, originally designed for the derivation of parallel and distributed systems, was used as such even for this new aspect. The main tool used was the prioritizing composition operator on actions and action systems.

We exemplified our methodology using a collection of typical coordination problems from the literature. Only the highlights of the coordination aspects were shown. Moreover, we only gave an informal justification for the refinement steps we carried out. Every step can be formally verified using the data refinement rules and strategies given in this paper.

Even though our refinement rules are compositional, we do need the side conditions on the abstraction relation R as discussed in Section 5. This means that the coordination part and functional part cannot be refined completely independent. A change of data representation in either the coordinator or the functional part requires that the refinement conditions are checked for both parts to the extent that both parts refer to the changed variables. However, in practice this can be minimized by well chosen interfaces to the functional part of the system. Another point is that the coordinator need not be introduced at the most abstract level, but can be introduced at any time, even as a final step of the refinement process. Yet another benefit we have with our approach is the dual view of the coordinator that we can consider as either an ordinary action system or as a separate scheduler, and we can switch views as we see fit.

Acknowledgements. The work reported here is carried out within the projects Cocos and Formet. These projects are supported by the Academy of Finland and the Technology Development Centre of Finland (Tekes).

References

1. G. Agha. *Actors: A Model of Concurrent Computation in Distributed Systems.* MIT Press, Los Alamos, California, 1986.
2. R. J. R. Back. *On the Correctness of Refinement Steps in Program Development.* PhD thesis, Department of Computer Science, University of Helsinki, Helsinki, Finland, 1978. Report A–1978–4.
3. R. J. R. Back. Refinement calculus, part II: Parallel and reactive programs. In J. W. de Bakker, W.–P. de Roever, and G. Rozenberg, editors, *Stepwise Refinement of Distributed Systems: Models, Formalisms, Correctness. Proceedings.* 1989, volume 430 of *Lecture Notes in Computer Science.* Springer–Verlag, 1990.

4. R. J. R. Back and R. Kurki-Suonio. Decentralization of process nets with centralized control. In *Proc. of the 2nd ACM SIGACT–SIGOPS Symp. on Principles of Distributed Computing*, pages 131–142, 1983.

5. R.J.R. Back and K. Sere. Stepwise refinement of action systems. *Structured Programming*, 12:17–30, 1991.

6. R. J. R. Back and K. Sere. From modular systems to action systems. Proc. of *Formal Methods Europe'94*, Spain, October 1994. *Lecture Notes in Computer Science*. Springer–Verlag, 1994.

7. R. J. R. Back and J. von Wright. Trace Refinement of Action Systems In B. Jonsson, J. Parrow, editors, *CONCUR '94: Concurrency Theory. Proceedings.* 1994, volume 836 of *Lecture Notes in Computer Science*, pages 367–384. Springer–Verlag, 1994.

8. J.-P. Banâtre and D. Le Métayer. Programming by multiset transformation. *Communications of the ACM*, 36(1):98–111, January 1993.

9. N. Carriero and D. Gelernter. Coordination languages and their significance. *Communications of the ACM*, 35(2):97–107, February 1992.

10. K. Chandy and J. Misra. *Parallel Program Design: A Foundation*. Addison–Wesley, 1988.

11. M. Chaudron and E. de Jong. Towards a Compositional Method for Coordinating Gamma Programs. In [12].

12. P. Ciancarini and C. Hankin, editors. *Coordination'96: Coordination Languages and Models*, volume 1061 of *Lecture Notes in Computer Science*. Springer–Verlag, 1996.

13. H.C. Cunningham and G.C. Roman. A UNITY-style programming logic for a shared dataspace language. *IEEE Transactions on Parallel and Distributed Systems*, 1(3):365–376, July 1990.

14. E. W. Dijkstra. *A Discipline of Programming*. Prentice–Hall International, 1976.

15. H. J. M. Goeman, J. N. Kok, K. Sere, and R. T. Udink. Coordination in the ImpUNITY Framework. In [12].

16. H. J. M. Goeman, J. N. Kok, K. Sere, and R. T. Udink. *Coordination in the ImpUnity Framework*. TUCS Technical Report No 50, October 1996. Turku, Finland.

17. C. C. Morgan. The specification statement. *ACM Transactions on Programming Languages and Systems*, 10(3):403–419, July 1988.

18. J. M. Morris. A theoretical basis for stepwise refinement and the programming calculus. *Science of Computer Programming*, 9:287–306, 1987.

19. S. Ren and G. Agha. A Modular Approach for Programming Distributed Real-Time Systems. In *Hand-Out, European Educational Forum, School on Embedded Systems*, November 1996, Veldhoven, NL.

20. E. Sekerinski and K. Sere. A theory of prioritizing composition. *The Computer Journal*. To appear.

21. R.T. Udink. *Program Refinement in UNITY-like Environments*. PhD Thesis, Utrecht University, September 1995.

Approximating UNITY

Jürgen Dingel

School of Computer Science
Carnegie Mellon University
Pittsburgh, PA 15213, USA
E-mail: `jurgen@cs.cmu.edu`

Abstract. A framework for the stepwise refinement of UNITY programs with local variables is proposed. It is centered around two preorders. The first one compares program components with respect to a given context. Aside from being context-sensitive, this order also allows the introduction of local variables. The second preorder compares program contexts with respect to their discriminating power. Using these two relations, program refinement arises as a form of assumption/commitment reasoning. An example illustrates the use of the framework and presents some proof rules.

The simple syntactic and semantic structure of UNITY allows for a natural game-theoretic characterization of the preorders used in the framework.

1 Introduction

Since its invention UNITY [CM88] has been a popular design notation for concurrent programs. It features a simple syntax and semantics and yet exhibits all the intricacies of concurrent programming. The programming notation is complemented nicely by an equally simple specification logic and proof system. These features make UNITY a very appealing candidate for the study of program development through stepwise refinement in the presence of concurrency. Two characteristics seem essential for a useful stepwise refinement technique:

- It should be *context-sensitive*. Typically, refinement is carried out in context. That is, an abstract component is to be replaced by a more concrete one in a particular context. Using information about the specific nature of the context makes this replacement substantially more powerful and may provide information crucial for establishing the soundness of the refinement step.
- It should support *local variables*. On the specification level, computations are often described in very abstract terms. During the course of the refinement it is then necessary to flesh out the implementation details of these computations. This very often requires the introduction of local variables, which, for example, step over an array, or compute temporary results. The effect of the local variables should be given solely by their effect on global variables, that is, changes to local variables should be unobservable outside their scope.

Essentially, there are two ways to define a refinement relation for UNITY. The first one is based on properties over the UNITY logic [CM88,San90,Sin91,UK93a]. Roughly, program G refines program F if every property of G is also a property of F. However, none of the property-based refinement notions are context-sensitive or support local variables. The second route towards a refinement relation is to define a suitable notion of trace and to compare programs with respect to their traces. G refines F, if the traces of G are contained in those of F. Trace-based semantics for UNITY have appeared in the literature in several places [CM88,Liu89,dBKPR91,UK93a,UK93b]. Trace-based notions of refinement are proposed in [UK93a,UK93b]. In [UK93a], it is shown that trace-based notions are strictly finer grained (less abstract) than property-based notions. However, again, none of the proposed notions are context-sensitive or support local variables. We transfer ideas from [Din96,UK93a] to develop a framework that supports the specification and stepwise refinement of UNITY programs with local variables. We give a trace-based denotational semantics for UNITY programs, define a context-sensitive notion of approximation that supports the introduction of local variables, show how stepwise program refinement arises as a form of assumption/commitment reasoning, and illustrate our ideas by means of an example.

Recently, there has been a lot of interest in the application of game-theoretic ideas to the semantics of programming languages, e.g., [AJM94,McC96]. Most of this work is phrased in very abstract (category-theoretic) terms and it is not always clear how the concepts introduced relate to "everyday computing". In [Sti96], Stirling bridges this gap by demonstrating how the verification of labeled transition systems with respect to mu-calculus formulae can be recast using game theory. The present paper intends to add another facet to this work by showing how games can also provide an appealing metaphor for the *compositional* refinement or verification of concurrent systems. Suppose we want to prove that some component S satisfies a specification φ. The game-theoretic interpretation of the question "Does S meet φ?" is as follows. An adversary plays legal environment moves to cause S to deviate from its specification. If she succeeds, then S violates its specification. If she never succeeds, then S satisfies its specification. In sequential programming, for example, φ could be a Hoare-triple $\{P\}\ S\ \{Q\}$. The moves by the adversary would then be limited to the very beginning of the play where the adversary would try to find an initial state that satisfies P but still causes S to terminate in a state that does not satisfy Q. In the concurrent world, φ could be some kind of assumption/commitment specification that places assumptions on the behaviour of the environment of S and in turn makes certain guarantees about the behaviour of S whenever S is executing in an environment that meets these assumptions. The adversary now has substantially more means at her disposal to show that S violates the specification. She can not only interfere before but also during the execution of S and change the state arbitrarily as long as she observes the assumptions. We will show that our context-sensitive approximation matches this metaphor very nicely by giving a game-theoretic characterization.

The next section introduces our slight extension of UNITY together with a denotational semantics. Section 3 presents context-sensitive approximation and the discrimination ordering on contexts. Section 4 demonstrates how stepwise refinement can be achieved using these relations. A small example is presented together with the necessary proof rules. Section 5 defines a suitable notion of game and shows how context-sensitive approximation can be given a natural game-theoretic characterization. Section 6 concludes and outlines further work.

In [Din96], a trace model is used for the compositional verification of the shared-variable parallel language introduced by Owicki and Gries. Most of the definitions in Sections 2 and 3 are rather straightforward adaptations of those in [Din96]. UNITY's simpler syntactic and semantic structure, however, allows for a cleaner and richer theory and the development of the material presented in Sections 4 and 5.

2 UNITY

In the original definition of UNITY atomic state changes are described in terms of multiple assignment statements $x_1, \ldots, x_n := e_1, \ldots, e_n$. To be able to describe state changes in more general terms we extend UNITY slightly and adopt Morgan's specification statement [Mor89]. It is of the form $V : [P, Q]$, where V is a set of variables and P and Q are assertions. It is meant to describe a single atomic transition, which transforms a state satisfying P into one satisfying Q by just changing the variables in V. The specification statement thus allows for very general descriptions of atomic transitions which is very useful for specification purposes. For instance, a random assignment which may set x to any natural number can be described by $\{x\} : [tt, x \geq 0]$. To be able to refer to the values a variable held initially, that is, at the beginning of the transition, we reserve zero-subscripted variables x_0 in Q. The meaning of the multiple assignment statement $x, y := x + 1, 0$, for example, is thus captured by $\{x, y\} : [tt, x = x_0 + 1 \wedge y = 0]$. An idling, or stuttering, step is expressed as $skip \equiv \emptyset : [tt, tt]$. It is standard in UNITY that an atomic statement whose precondition fails in a state can always stutter in that state. The semantics of specification statements is conveniently captured by characteristic formulae.

Definition 1. The *characteristic formula* of a specification statement, $cf_{V:[P,Q]}$, is given by the following predicate

$$cf_{V:[P,Q]} \equiv (P[\vec{x_0}/\vec{x}] \wedge Q \wedge \bigwedge_{x \in Var-V} .x = x_0) \vee (\neg P[\vec{x_0}/\vec{x}] \wedge \bigwedge_{x \in Var} .x = x_0)$$

where $P[\vec{x_0}/\vec{x}]$ abbreviates the substitution of all variables in the list $\vec{x}$ by their zero-subscripted versions in P. We interpret transition predicates Q over pairs of states (s, s') where s assigns values to zero-subscripted variables and s' to the unsubscripted ones. More precisely, $(s, s') \models Q$ iff replacing the variables with zero-subscripts in Q by their values in s and replacing the variables without zero-subscripts in Q by their values in s' makes Q true. □

Two statements S_1 and S_2 can be composed by means of the fair parallel composition operator $S_1 \| S_2$. Intuitively, the executions of a parallel composition are given by fairly interleaving the executions of each of the components. This composition is often also called *union* to reflect the fact that it is commutative, that is, $S_1 \| S_2$ and $S_2 \| S_1$ have, as we will see, equivalent semantics. The composition of a number of specification statements

$$V_1 : [P_1, Q_1] \| \ldots \| V_n : [P_n, Q_n]$$

should thus be thought of as a multiset rather than a list.

Our second extension to UNITY involves labels. Suppose S is $S_1 \| S_2$. In order to be able to distinguish the transitions of S_1 from those of S_2, we allow for S_1 to be enclosed in angle brackets to form $\langle S_1 \rangle \| S_2$. A statement that contains exactly one substatement enclosed in angle brackets is called *labeled*. A statement that contains no angle brackets is *unlabeled*. The following grammar generates labeled and unlabeled statements:

$$S ::= V : [P, Q] \mid S_1 \| S_2$$
$$U ::= S \mid \langle S \rangle \mid U \| S$$

In the sequel, let S and T range over unlabeled statements and U range over labeled or unlabeled statements.

Definition 2. A *program* is a triple $H = (L, I, U)$ where L is a finite set of local variables, I is a boolean formula that describes the initial states, and U is a labeled or unlabeled statement. If U is labeled, then H is called labeled. Otherwise, H is called unlabeled. For each of the components we define a projection function that yields that component: $init(H) = I$ and $local(H) = L$ and $stmt(H) = U$. $\square$

Let F and G range over unlabeled programs and H over labeled or unlabeled programs.

Transition Traces Let $s, s', s_i \in \Sigma$ denote states, that is, mappings from the finite set of program variables *Var* to values. Transition traces[1]

$$(s_0, s_0')(s_1, s_1') \ldots (s_i, s_i') \ldots$$

have proven very useful for the definition of compositional models of shared-variable concurrency [dBKPR91,Bro93,UK93b]. One such trace represents a possible "interactive" computation of a command in which state changes made by the command (from s_i to s_i') are interleaved by state changes made by its environment (from s_i' to s_{i+1}). The meaning of a program is given by a set of transition traces. To describe the meaning of a labeled statement $\langle S_1 \rangle \| S_2$ we will consider *labeled* transition traces of the form

$$(s_0, l_0, s_0')(s_1, l_1, s_1') \ldots (s_i, l_i, s_i') \ldots$$

---

[1] Sometimes also called *extended sequences* or *potential computations*.

where each transition carries a label l from the set $\Lambda = \{pro, env\}$. A transition labeled with *pro* was caused by a statement inside the angle brackets, that is, by S_1, and is called *program transition*. A transition with *env* is due to S_2 and is called *environment transition*. By describing a labeled statement by means of labeled transition traces we thus regard it as an *open system* while singling out the transitions made by a specific part of the statement. In other words, $\langle S_1 \rangle \| S_2$ can be thought of as an open system whose environment is known to at least comprise S_2.

A trace is *connected* if we have $s'_i = s_{i+1}$ for all $i \geq 0$. Following [UK93b], [UK93a], we use the operator $\natural$ to remove subsequences of finite, connected stuttering from a trace. More precisely, given a trace α, $\natural\alpha$ denotes a trace like α except that all maximal finite, connected subsequences of stutterings

$$(s_i, l_i, s_i)(s_i, l_{i+1}, s_i) \ldots (s_i, l_j, s_i)$$

have been removed. For instance,

$$\natural(s_0, l_0, s_1)(s_1, l_1, s_1)(s_1, l_2, s_2)(s_3, l_3, s_3)(s_3, l_4, s_3)(s_4, l_5, s_5) \ldots$$
$$= (s_0, s_1)(s_1, s_2)(s_3, s_3)(s_4, s_5) \ldots$$

where $s_0 \neq s_1$, $s_1 \neq s_2$ and $s_4 \neq s_5$. Note that the labels are also removed. While this operator may remove stuttering segments at infinitely many places in a trace, the length of each stuttering segment removed is always finite. We write $\alpha =_\natural \beta$ to abbreviate $\natural\alpha = \natural\beta$. Trace sets are closed under *stuttering equivalence*. Given a set X of transition traces, the closure of X, denoted $X^\natural$, is the smallest set which contains X and satisfies:

$$\text{if } \alpha \in X^\natural \text{ and } \alpha =_\natural \beta \text{ then } \beta \in X^\natural.$$

Note that the same closure condition was adopted in [UK93b,UK93a]. Let $\mathcal{P}^\natural(X)$ denote the set of all subsets of X that are closed under stuttering equivalence.

Before the denotational semantics of programs is presented, we introduce some notation and define a few operations on traces and sets of traces.

Parallel composition Given a set X, let X^* and X^ω denote the set of finite and infinite concatenations of elements in X respectively. X^∞ stands for $X^* \cup X^\omega$. Given $\alpha, \beta \in (\Sigma \times \Lambda \times \Sigma)^\infty$, let $\alpha\|\beta$ be the set of all traces built by fairly interleaving α and β. Following [Bro93], one way to define $\alpha\|\beta$ formally is:

$$\alpha\|\beta = \{\gamma \mid (\alpha, \beta, \gamma) \in fairmerge\}$$

where

$$
\begin{aligned}
fairmerge &= (L^* R R^* L)^\omega \cup (L \cup R)^* A \\
L &= \{(s, \epsilon, s) \mid s \in \Sigma \times \Lambda \times \Sigma\} \\
R &= \{(\epsilon, s, s) \mid s \in \Sigma \times \Lambda \times \Sigma\} \\
A &= \{(\alpha, \epsilon, \alpha) \mid \alpha \in (\Sigma \times \Lambda \times \Sigma)^\infty\} \cup \{(\epsilon, \beta, \beta) \mid \beta \in (\Sigma \times \Lambda \times \Sigma)^\infty\}
\end{aligned}
$$

where concatenation is extended to sets and triples of traces in the obvious way: $AB = \{\alpha\beta \mid \alpha \in A \wedge \beta \in B\}$ and $(\alpha_1, \alpha_2, \alpha_3)(\beta_1, \beta_2, \beta_3) = (\alpha_1\beta_1, \alpha_2\beta_2, \alpha_3\beta_3)$. Fair interleaving of closed sets of traces can now be defined by:

$$X_1 \| X_2 = \bigcup \{\alpha_1 \| \alpha_2 \mid \alpha_1 \in X_1 \wedge \alpha_2 \in X_2\}^{\natural}.$$

Local variables $[s|x_1 = n_1| \ldots |x_i = n_i]$ denotes the state that is like s except that the values of x_1 through x_i have been changed to n_1 through n_i respectively. Let $\vec{x}$ and $\vec{n}$ be two lists of variables $[x_1, \ldots, x_i]$ and values $[n_1, \ldots, n_i]$. $[s|\vec{x} = \vec{n}]$ abbreviates $[s|x_1 = n_1| \ldots |x_i = n_i]$. Let $\alpha = (s_0, l_0, s_0')(s_1, l_1, s_1') \ldots (s_i, l_i, s_i') \ldots$ be a transition trace. The trace $\langle \vec{x} = \vec{n}\rangle\alpha$ is like α except that the variables in $\vec{x}$ have values $\vec{n}$ in the first state and that the values of $\vec{x}$ are retained across points of possible interference. More precisely,

$$\langle \vec{x} = \vec{n}\rangle\alpha =$$
$$([s_0|\vec{x} = \vec{n}], l_0, s_0')([s_1|\vec{x} = s_0'(\vec{x})], l_1, s_1') \ldots ([s_i|\vec{x} = s_{i-1}'(\vec{x})], l_i, s_i') \ldots$$

where $s(\vec{x})$ stands for $[s(x_1), \ldots, s(x_i)]$.

Given a list of variables $\vec{x}$, the trace $\alpha \backslash \vec{x}$ on the other hand describes a computation like α except that it never changes the values of variables in $\vec{x}$. That is, $\alpha \backslash \vec{x}$ is

$$(s_0, [s_0' \mid \vec{x} = s_0(\vec{x})])(s_1, [s_1' \mid \vec{x} = s_1(\vec{x})]) \ldots (s_i, [s_i' \mid \vec{x} = s_i(\vec{x})]) \ldots.$$

We are now ready to give a denotational semantics of programs in terms of the above operations.

Definition 3. The semantic function $\mathcal{C}$ maps labeled and unlabeled programs and statements to $\mathcal{P}^{\natural}((\Sigma \times \Lambda \times \Sigma)^{\omega})$ and is defined as $\mathcal{C}_e[\![\_]\!]$ where $\mathcal{C}_l[\![\_]\!]$ for $l \in \Lambda$ is given by

$$\mathcal{C}_e[\![(L, I, U)]\!] = \{\alpha \backslash \vec{x} \mid \langle \vec{x} = \vec{n}\rangle\alpha \in \mathcal{C}_e[\![U]\!] \wedge [fst(\alpha)|\vec{x} = \vec{n}] \models I \wedge set(\vec{x}) = L\}^{\natural}$$
$$\mathcal{C}_e[\![\langle S\rangle]\!] = \mathcal{C}_p[\![S]\!]$$
$$\mathcal{C}_l[\![U_1 \| U_2]\!] = \mathcal{C}_l[\![U_1]\!] \parallel \mathcal{C}_l[\![U_2]\!]$$
$$\mathcal{C}_l[\![V : [P, Q]]\!] = \{(s_0, l, s_0')(s_1, l, s_1') \ldots \mid (s_i, s_i') \models cfv_{:[P,Q]} \text{ for all } i \geq 0\}^{\natural}$$

where $fst(\alpha)$ denotes the first state of α and $set(\vec{x})$ stands for the set of variables in $\vec{x}$. $\square$

The first semantic equation is central to our work and deserves a brief explanation. Let α be a trace and H be a program. Undoing the changes to the local variables of H along α yields a trace of H, if α is a trace of the statement of H assuming that the local variables are properly initialized and the environment is prevented from changing them. Note that [UK93a] contains an operational, yet compositional, definition of a variant of $\mathcal{C}$ without account for local variables. Furthermore, no explicit definition of the fair merge operation is given.

Definition 4. The *executions* of a program or statement are the connected transition traces. Let U be a labeled or unlabeled statement and let H be a labeled or unlabeled program.

$$\mathcal{E}[\![U]\!] = \{\alpha \in \mathcal{C}[\![U]\!] \mid \alpha \text{ is connected}\}$$
$$\mathcal{E}[\![H]\!] = \{\alpha \in \mathcal{C}[\![H]\!] \mid \alpha \text{ is connected}\}$$

□

Note that this notion coincides with Chandy and Misra's notion of execution [CM88].

Having presented the semantics, we can now give a more precise account of the impact of labels $\langle \ldots \rangle$ on the inequational theory of programs and statements. Trace inclusion between two labeled programs implies trace inclusion between their unlabeled versions. However, labeling a pair of programs does provide us with more distinguishing power: Trace inclusion between two unlabeled programs does not imply trace inclusion between their labeled versions.

Given a statement S' and a program $F = (L, I, S)$, we can regard F as defining the *context* or *environment* that S' is executing in. Placing S' in the context of program F yields a new program $F[S'] \equiv (L, I, S\|S')$. Very often, we will consider a labeled statement $\langle S' \rangle$ in the context of F, that is, $F[\langle S' \rangle]$ yields the labeled program $(L, I, S\|\langle S' \rangle)$. Let $S_1 \subseteq_{\mathcal{C}} S_2$ abbreviate $\mathcal{C}[\![S_1]\!] \subseteq \mathcal{C}[\![S_2]\!]$. Similarly for $\mathcal{E}$.

Proposition 5. *Let S range over unlabeled statements and U range over labeled or unlabeled statements.*

1. $U_1 \subseteq_{\mathcal{C}} U_2$ *implies* $U_1 \subseteq_{\mathcal{E}} U_2$
2.a. $F[\langle S_1 \rangle] \subseteq_{\mathcal{C}} F[\langle S_2 \rangle]$ *implies* $F[S_1] \subseteq_{\mathcal{C}} F[S_2]$
2.b. $F[\langle S_1 \rangle] \subseteq_{\mathcal{E}} F[\langle S_2 \rangle]$ *implies* $F[S_1] \subseteq_{\mathcal{E}} F[S_2]$
3.a. $F[S_1] \subseteq_{\mathcal{C}} F[S_2]$ *does not imply* $F[\langle S_1 \rangle] \subseteq_{\mathcal{C}} F[\langle S_2 \rangle]$
3.b. $F[S_1] \subseteq_{\mathcal{E}} F[S_2]$ *does not imply* $F[\langle S_1 \rangle] \subseteq_{\mathcal{E}} F[\langle S_2 \rangle]$

Proof. 1, 2.a and 2.b follow directly from the definitions. 3 follows from the fact that a program transition cannot be matched by an environment transition and vice versa. For a counterexample for 3.a let

$$F[\langle S_1 \rangle] \equiv \langle x : [tt, x = 1] \rangle \ \| \ x : [tt, x = 2]$$
$$F[\langle S_2 \rangle] \equiv x : [tt, x = 1] \ \| \ \langle x : [tt, x = 2] \rangle.$$

Then, $F[S_1] \subseteq_{\mathcal{C}} F[S_2]$, but $F[\langle S_1 \rangle] \not\subseteq_{\mathcal{C}} F[\langle S_2 \rangle]$. Similarly for 3.b.   □

3   Approximation

A very natural notion of program approximation arises through transition trace inclusion. Given a set of variables V, let *inv* V abbreviate $Var - V : [tt, tt]$. That is, *inv* V is the most general statement that leaves all variables in V unchanged, but can change all other variables arbitrarily.

Example 6. A statement S always leaves the values of the variables in V unchanged in all contexts iff $S \subseteq_C inv\ V$.

Trace inclusion between atomic statements is characterized by implication of their characteristic formulae.

Proposition 7. $V_1 : [P_1, Q_1] \subseteq_C V_2 : [P_2, Q_2]$ *iff* $cf_{V_1:[P_1,Q_1]} \Rightarrow cf_{V_2:[P_2,Q_2]}$.

The following proposition states that trace inclusion is a congruence. This is due essentially to the definition of C in terms of monotone operations on trace sets.

Proposition 8. $S_1 \subseteq_C S_2$ *implies* $F[\langle S_1 \rangle] \subseteq_C F[\langle S_2 \rangle]$ *and* $F[S_1] \subseteq_C F[S_2]$ *for all programs* F.

Trace inclusion between two statements S_1 and S_2 is a very strong property in the sense that it implies that in *all* possible contexts the executions of S_1 are contained in those of S_2 in the same context. Thus, whenever we want to do refinement in a specific context, trace set inclusion is too strong, because it does not incorporate information about that particular context. In other words, $\subseteq_C$ is not context-sensitive. We now present a notion of approximation that is context-sensitive and that will form the basis of our stepwise refinement method.

Definition 9. Let S_1 and S_2 be unlabeled statements and F be an unlabeled program. $S_1 \leq_F S_2$ iff $F[\langle S_1 \rangle] \subseteq_\mathcal{E} F[\langle S_2 \rangle]$. ☐

$S_1 =_F S_2$ abbreviates $S_1 \leq_F S_2$ and $S_2 \leq_F S_1$. Although F in the above definition formally is a program, we will often refer to it as the context of the approximation.

Example 10. We have

$$x : [tt, x = x_0 + y] \leq_{(\emptyset, y=1, inv\ y)} x : [tt, x > x_0],$$

but

$$x : [tt, x = x_0 + y] \not\leq_{(\emptyset, y=1, inv\ y \| y:[tt,y=0])} x : [tt, x > x_0].$$

Also,

$$x : [tt, x = x_0 + 1] \not\leq_F x : [k = 0, x = x_0 + 1] \parallel k : [tt, k = 1]$$

where $F \equiv (\{k\}, k = 0, \emptyset)$. Due to fairness, the program on the right can only do a finite number of increments.

The above definition together with Proposition 5.2.b imply the following corollary.

Corollary 11. $S_1 \leq_F S_2$ *implies* $F[S_1] \subseteq_\mathcal{E} F[S_2]$.

3.1 A discrimination ordering on programs

Once we have a context-sensitive notion of approximation, it seems natural to attempt to distinguish contexts with respect to their "discriminating" power. For CCS, for example, this was done in [Lar87]. The program $F_1 \equiv (\emptyset, tt, Var : [tt, tt])$, for instance, can do any transition at any time. The program $F_2 \equiv (\emptyset, tt, inv\ x)$, however, can only do those transitions that leave the value of x unchanged. Every approximation that holds with respect to F_1 will also hold with respect to F_2, whereas the converse is not true. F_1 is more general and thus has more discriminating power.

Definition 12. F_2 is *at least as discriminating* as F_1, $F_1 \sqsubseteq F_2$ for short, if for all statements S_1 and S_2, $S_1 \leq_{F_2} S_2$ implies $S_1 \leq_{F_1} S_2$. □

Example 13. We have $(\emptyset, y = 1, inv\ \{x, y\}) \sqsubseteq (\emptyset, y = 1, inv\ y)$. Using Example 10 this allows us to conclude $x : [tt, x = x_0 + y] \leq_{(\emptyset, y=1, inv\ \{x,y\})} x : [tt, x > x_0]$.

All three components of a program F influence its discriminating power. Reducing the number of local variables $local(F)$, or augmenting the set of initial states $init(F)$ or the capabilities of the statement $stmt(F)$ makes F more discriminating.

Proposition 14.

1. $(L, I, S) \sqsubseteq (L', I, S)$ *iff* $L' \subseteq L$
2. $(L, I, S) \sqsubseteq (L, I', S)$ *iff* $I \Rightarrow I'$
3. $(L, I, S) \sqsubseteq (L, I, S')$ *if* $S \sqsubseteq_c S'$

In [Lar87], Larsen introduces a discrimination ordering on CCS contexts and presents a characterization result. Unfortunately, the fairness requirement prevented us from obtaining a similar result for our setting. Note, however, that Proposition 14.3 can be strengthened to an equivalence in case S_1 and S_2 contain only one atomic statement each.

4 Stepwise refinement

We now present a few rules that allow the replacement of statements by equivalent or more refined ones. Statements are equal to themselves in every context. *skip* is the neutral element with respect to composition.

REFL: SKIP:

$$\overline{S =_F S} \qquad \overline{S[\![skip =_F S}$$

Implication of characteristic formulae of atomic statements implies trace inclusion and thus context-sensitive approximation. The soundness of this rule follows from Propositions 7, 8 and 5.1.

ATOM:

$$\frac{}{V_1 : [P_1, Q_1] \leq_F V_2 : [P_2, Q_2]} \qquad cf_{V_1:[P_1,Q_1]} \Rightarrow cf_{V_2:[P_2,Q_2]}$$

Adding $V : [P, Q]$ to a program F will not change the behaviour of F, if all variables in V are local and none of the variables in V are mentioned in the statement of F.

LOCAL:

$$\frac{S_1 =_{(L,I,S)} S_2}{S_1 \| V : [P, Q] =_{(L \cup V, I, S)} S_2} \qquad V \cap vars(S_1 \| S) = \emptyset$$

where $vars(S)$ denotes the set of *all* variables mentioned in S.

Let W be a set of variables and let P_W be a unary state predicate with free variables W. Remember that $inv\ W$ is the most general statement that always leaves the variables in W unchanged. Thus, all transitions of $inv\ W$ also leave P_W unchanged. Given a program F with some atomic statement $A \equiv V : [P, Q]$ in $stmt(F)$, strengthening the precondition of A from P to $P \wedge P_W$ may allow F to diverge, that is, stutter forever without ever changing the state again. However, if we can show that in a context that leaves P_W invariant, P_W will eventually be true forever, then it is safe to conclude that the strengthening will not introduce divergence.

STRENGTH:

$$\frac{S \| V : [P \wedge P_W, Q] \leq_{(L,I,inv\ W)} Var : [\neg P_W, tt] \| Var : [tt, P_W]}{S \| V : [P \wedge P_W, Q] \leq_{(L,I,inv\ W)} S \| V : [P, Q]}$$

If the initial condition of a program F implies P_V and the statement of F contains S, which will always preserve P_V while the remaining statements in F leave the variables in V unchanged, then P_V will hold throughout every execution.

INV:

$$\frac{S \leq_{(L,I,inv\ V)} Var : [tt, P_V] \qquad I \Rightarrow P_V}{S =_{(L,I,inv\ V)} S[P_V/tt]}$$

where $S[P/tt]$ abbreviates the replacement of tt by P in S. Since rule ATOM can be used to replace an occurrence of P by $P \wedge tt$ and vice versa, the above rule allows for both the introduction and elimination of nontrivial predicates. Note that it plays the same role as the substitution axiom in [CM88,San91].

The next rule offers a formalization of assumption/commitment reasoning. Suppose we want to show that S_1 approximates S_2 in context F_1. First, we show that the approximation holds in some possibly very general and thus more discriminating context F_2. F_2 reflects the assumptions required for the approximation to hold. Then, we show that F_1 meets those assumptions by arguing that F_2 is at least as discriminating as F_1. By Definition 12 it is then sound to conclude that S_1 approximates S_2 in context F_1.

ENV:
$$\frac{S_1 \leq_{F_2} S_2 \qquad F_1 \sqsubseteq F_2}{S_1 \leq_{F_1} S_2}$$

4.1 Example

We now show how the theory developed so far can be applied for the step-wise derivation of UNITY programs. The following example was inspired by [AS82,QJ91]. Suppose $n \geq 1$ bank accounts are represented by an array $A[1..n]$. We want to develop a program which computes the sum s over all entries in A and concurrently also transfers \$20 from account a to account b while leaving the array A and the variables a, b and n unchanged. We will develop a sequence of increasingly detailed programs G_i by applying the rules above. In step i, G_i will be refined into G_{i+1} as follows: We first identify statements S_i, S_i' and a program F_i such that $G_i = F_i[S_i]$ and $G_{i+1} = F_i[S_i']$. Then, we argue that $S_i' \leq_{F_i} S_i$ by means of the above rules. $G_{i+1} \sqsubseteq_{\mathcal{E}} G_i$ then is implied by Corollary 11. For better legibility we will write a program (L, I, S) as **local** L **with** I **in** S. Remember that the atomic statements in S are executed in an infinite loop.

We start with a very coarse specification G_0 which is easily seen to be correct. Let

$$G_0 \equiv \textbf{local } \emptyset \textbf{ with } tt \textbf{ in}$$
$$s : [tt, s = \textstyle\sum_{i=1}^{n} A[i]] \;\|$$
$$A : [tt, Q]$$

where $Q \equiv (A[a] = A[a]_0 - 20 \wedge A[b] = A[b]_0 + 20)$. In our first refinement step we introduce local variables k and t.

$$G_1 \equiv \textbf{local } \{k, t\} \textbf{ with } k = 1 \wedge t = 0 \textbf{ in}$$
$$\{k, t\} : [k \leq n, t = t_0 + A[k]_0 \wedge k = k_0 + 1] \;\|$$
$$s : [tt, s = \textstyle\sum_{i=1}^{n} A[i]] \;\|$$
$$A : [tt, Q]$$

We prove $G_1 =_{\mathcal{E}} G_0$ as follows: Let

$$S_0 \equiv s : [tt, s = \textstyle\sum_{i=1}^{n} A[i]]$$
$$S_0' \equiv \{k, t\} : [k \leq n, t = t_0 + A[k]_0 \wedge k = k_0 + 1] \;\| \; S_0$$
$$F_0 \equiv (\emptyset, tt, A : [tt, Q]).$$

Then,

$$\cfrac{\cfrac{\rule{3cm}{0.4pt}}{S_0 =_{F_0} S_0} \text{ REFL}}{\cfrac{S_0' =_{(\{k,t\}, tt, A:[tt,Q])} S_0}{S_0' =_{(\{k,t\}, k=1 \wedge t=0, A:[tt,Q])} S_0} \text{ ENV}} \text{ LOCAL}$$

where the ENV rule uses

$$(\{k, t\}, k = 1 \wedge t = 0, A : [tt, Q]) \sqsubseteq (\{k, t\}, tt, A : [tt, Q])$$

which follows from Proposition 14.2. Corollary 11 then implies $G_1 =_\varepsilon G_0$. Next, we restrict the transition that sets s to the sum over A to a state in which $k > n$.

$$G_2 \equiv \textbf{local } \{k,t\} \textbf{ with } k = 1 \wedge t = 0 \textbf{ in}$$
$$\{k,t\} : [k \leq n, t = t_0 + A[k]_0 \wedge k = k_0 + 1] \; \|$$
$$s : [k > n, s = \textstyle\sum_{i=1}^{n} A[i]] \; \|$$
$$A : [tt, Q]$$

We need to show that this strengthening of the precondition does not introduce divergence. Let

$$S_1 \equiv \{k,t\} : [k \leq n, t = t_0 + A[k]_0 \wedge k = k_0 + 1] \; \| \; s : [tt, s = \textstyle\sum_{i=1}^{n} A[i]]$$
$$S_1' \equiv \{k,t\} : [k \leq n, t = t_0 + A[k]_0 \wedge k = k_0 + 1] \; \| \; s : [k > n, s = \textstyle\sum_{i=1}^{n} A[i]]$$
$$F_1 \equiv (\{k,t\}, k = 1 \wedge t = 0, A : [tt, Q]).$$

Then,

$$\cfrac{\cfrac{S_1' \leq_{(\{k,t\}, k=1\wedge t=0, inv\{k,n\})} \; Var : [k \leq n, tt] \; \| \; Var : [tt, k > n]}{S_1' \leq_{(\{k,t\}, k=1\wedge t=0, inv\{k,n\})} S_1} \text{ENV}}{S_1' \leq_{F_1} S_1} \text{STRENGTH}$$

where the **ENV** rule uses

$$F_1 \sqsubseteq (\{k,t\}, k = 1 \wedge t = 0, inv \{k,n\})$$

which follows from Proposition 14.3 together with the fact that $stmt(F_1) = A : [tt, Q]$ does not change k or n, that is, $A : [tt, Q] \sqsubseteq_C inv \{k,n\}$.

We now want to approximate $s : [k > n, s = \sum_{i=1}^{n} A[i]]$ by $s : [k > n, s = t_0]$. In other words, we have to argue that the loop correctly stores the sum in t. If there was no interference then this would be easy to do. In this case, however, parallel components may interfere such that replacing the computation of the sum via an atomic transition by a loop may yield results violating the specification. Therefore, we need to restrict the transitions of the interfering components such that they cannot "disturb" this computation. This is achieved by postulating that the transition which transfers \$20 from account a to account b does not change $\sum_{i=1}^{k-1} A[i]$. To this end, it is sufficient to restrict this transfer to states in which

$$P \equiv (a < k \wedge b < k) \vee (k < a \wedge k < b).$$

Let

$$G_3 \equiv \textbf{local } \{k,t\} \textbf{ with } k = 1 \wedge t = 0 \textbf{ in}$$
$$\{k,t\} : [k \leq n, t = t_0 + A[k]_0 \wedge k = k_0 + 1] \; \|$$
$$s : [k > n, s = \textstyle\sum_{i=1}^{n} A[i]] \; \|$$
$$A : [P, Q]$$

and

$$S_2 \equiv A : [tt, Q] \; \| \; k,t : [k \leq n, t = t_0 + A[k]_0 \wedge k = k_0 + 1]$$
$$S_2' \equiv A : [P, Q] \; \| \; k,t : [k \leq n, t = t_0 + A[k]_0 \wedge k = k_0 + 1]$$
$$F_2 \equiv (\{k,t\}, k = 1 \wedge t = 0, s : [k > n, s = \textstyle\sum_{i=1}^{n} A[i]]).$$

We show $S_2' \leq_{F_2} S_2$ using exactly the same rules as in the previous step together with the fact that $1 \leq a, b \leq n$.

Now that all interference is "benign", $s : [k > n, s = \sum_{i=1}^{n} A[i]]$ can be replaced by $s : [k > n, s = t_0]$.

$$G_4 \equiv \text{local } \{k, t\} \text{ with } k = 1 \wedge t = 0 \text{ in}$$
$$\{k, t\} : [k \leq n, t = t_0 + A[k]_0 \wedge k = k_0 + 1] \,\|$$
$$s : [k > n, s = t_0] \,\|$$
$$A : [P, Q]$$

Let

$$S_3 \equiv \{k, t\} : [k \leq n, t = t_0 + A[k]_0 \wedge k = k_0 + 1] \,\|$$
$$s : [k > n, s = \sum_{i=1}^{n} A[i]] \,\|$$
$$A : [P, Q]$$
$$S_3' \equiv \{k, t\} : [k \leq n, t = t_0 + A[k]_0 \wedge k = k_0 + 1] \,\|$$
$$s : [k > n, s = t_0] \,\|$$
$$A : [P, Q]$$
$$F_3 \equiv (\{k, t\}, k = 1 \wedge t = 0, \emptyset)$$
$$P_{k,t,n} \equiv (t = \sum_{i=1}^{k-1} A[i] \wedge (k \leq n \vee k - 1 = n)).$$

The approximation $S_3' \leq_{F_3} S_3$ is shown in several steps. First, $k > n$ in S_3 is replaced by $k > n \wedge tt$ using ATOM. Then, we show $S_3[P_{k,t,n}/tt] =_{F_3} S_3$ using INV and ENV. Note how the precondition of $A : [P, Q]$ ensures the preservation of $P_{k,t,n}$. Finally, $S_3' \leq_{F_3} S_3[P_{k,t,n}/tt]$ is established through ATOM using

$$cf_{s:[k>n \wedge P_{k,t,n}, s=t_0]} \Rightarrow cf_{s:[k>n \wedge P_{k,t,n}, s=\sum_{i=1}^{n} A[i]]}$$

and by replacing $k > n \wedge P_{k,t,n}$ by $k > n$ with INV and ATOM. With some obvious syntactic sugar the final program G_4 thus is

$$G_4 \equiv \text{local } \{k, t\} \text{ with } k = 1 \wedge t = 0 \text{ in}$$
$$k, t := k + 1, t + A[k] \qquad \text{if } k \leq n \,\|$$
$$s := t \qquad\qquad\qquad\quad \text{if } k > n \,\|$$
$$A[a], A[b] := A[a] - 20, A[b] + 20 \quad \text{if } a, b < k \vee k < a, b.$$

5 Game semantic interpretation

In order to be able to define games we need to set up an operational semantics for statements and programs. A *configuration* is a tuple of a state s and either an unlabeled statement S or an unlabeled program F. We now define three transition relations between configurations.

Strong transitions There is a strong transition between two configurations, $\langle S, s \rangle \longrightarrow \langle S, s' \rangle$, if S contains an atomic statement that can transform s into s' and $s \neq s'$. Similarly for programs.

$$\frac{}{\langle V : [P,Q], s \rangle \longrightarrow \langle V : [P,Q], s' \rangle} \qquad s \neq s' \wedge (s, s') \models cf_{V:[P,Q]}$$

$$\frac{\langle S_1, s \rangle \longrightarrow \langle S_1, s' \rangle}{\langle S_1 \| S_2, s \rangle \longrightarrow \langle S_1 \| S_2, s' \rangle} \qquad \frac{\langle stmt(F), s \rangle \longrightarrow \langle stmt(F), s' \rangle}{\langle F, s \rangle \longrightarrow \langle F, s' \rangle}$$

Silent transitions A silent transition does not change the state.

$$\frac{}{\langle V : [P,Q], s \rangle \stackrel{\tau}{\longrightarrow} \langle V : [P,Q], s \rangle} \qquad (s, s) \models cf_{V:[P,Q]}$$

$$\frac{\langle S_1, s \rangle \stackrel{\tau}{\longrightarrow} \langle S_1, s \rangle}{\langle S_1 \| S_2, s \rangle \stackrel{\tau}{\longrightarrow} \langle S_1 \| S_2, s \rangle} \qquad \frac{\langle stmt(F), s \rangle \stackrel{\tau}{\longrightarrow} \langle stmt(F), s \rangle}{\langle F, s \rangle \stackrel{\tau}{\longrightarrow} \langle F, s \rangle}$$

Weak transitions A weak transition is given by a strong transition enclosed in an arbitrary but finite number of silent transitions. $\langle S, s \rangle \Longrightarrow \langle S, s' \rangle$ iff

$$\langle S, s \rangle \stackrel{\tau}{\longrightarrow}{}^* \langle S, s \rangle \longrightarrow \langle S, s' \rangle \stackrel{\tau}{\longrightarrow}{}^* \langle S, s' \rangle.$$

Similarly for programs. Note that contrary to the denotational semantics all changes to local variables are exposed along a transition. Additionally, there is no account for fairness.

A program F *diverges* in a state s, $\langle F, s \rangle \Uparrow$ for short, F it can perform infinitely many stuttering steps from s. $\langle F, s \rangle \Uparrow$ iff $\langle F, s \rangle \stackrel{\tau}{\longrightarrow} \langle F, s \rangle \stackrel{\tau}{\longrightarrow} \ldots$. We say a trace α diverges if α ends with infinite stuttering.

Games Our notion of games is inspired by [Sti96]. Let S and T be unlabeled statements and F be an unlabeled program. A game is a triple $\mathcal{G}(S, T, F)$ for which there are two players. The role of Player I is to try to show that $S \leq_F T$ fails whereas Player II attempts to frustrate this. A *play* π of $\mathcal{G}(S, T, F)$ is a possibly infinite sequence of triples

$$\pi = (s_0, t_0, l_0)(s_1, t_1, l_1) \ldots$$

where $l_i \in \{pro, env\}$, $s_0 = t_0$, and $s_0 \models init(F)$. If part of the play is

$$(s_0, t_0, l_0)(s_1, t_1, l_1) \ldots (s_i, t_i, l_i)$$

then the next move is one of

env: Player I chooses $\langle F, s_i \rangle \Longrightarrow \langle F, s_{i+1} \rangle$ and then Player II chooses $\langle F, t_i \rangle \Longrightarrow \langle F, t_{i+1} \rangle$ such that $s_{i+1} =_{local(F)} t_{i+1}$, or

pro: Player I chooses $\langle S, s_i \rangle \Longrightarrow \langle S, s_{i+1} \rangle$ and then Player II chooses $\langle T, t_i \rangle \Longrightarrow \langle T, t_{i+1} \rangle$ such that $s_{i+1} =_{local(F)} t_{i+1}$, or

div: Player I chooses $\langle S, s_i \rangle \Uparrow$ and then Player II chooses $\langle T, t_i \rangle \Uparrow$

where $s =_V t$ iff s and t agree on all variables *not* in V, that is, $x \notin V$ implies $s(x) = t(x)$ for all $x \in Var$. In case of an env-move the new play is

$$(s_0, t_0, l_0)(s_1, t_1, l_1) \ldots (s_i, t_i, l_i)(s_{i+1}, t_{i+1}, env).$$

In case of a pro-move the new play is

$$(s_0, t_0, l_0)(s_1, t_1, l_1) \ldots (s_i, t_i, l_i)(s_{i+1}, t_{i+1}, pro).$$

In both cases the play resumes with a next move. In case of a div-move the new play is

$$(s_0, t_0, l_0)(s_1, t_1, l_1) \ldots (s_i, t_i, l_i)(s_i, t_i, l_{i+1}) \ldots$$

where $l_j = env$ and $l_k = pro$ for infinitely many $j, k > i$. A div-move terminates the play.

Player I wins a play if she chooses a transition $(S, s_i) \Longrightarrow (S, s_{i+1})$ or $(F, s_i) \Longrightarrow (F, s_{i+1})$ or divergence that Player II cannot match. In the first two cases we say that the play π was decided by (s_i, pro, s_{i+1}) or (s_i, env, s_{i+1}) respectively. Note that a play won by Player I is not necessarily finite. For an example, consider the last approximation in Example 10 where Player II can match only finitely many moves. Player II wins a play if she can match every move of Player I. A game won by Player II is always infinite. An infinite play π is *fair* if every statement in both $F[S]$ and $F[T]$ is executed infinitely often. More precisely, for all $A \in stmt(F[S])$ and $B \in stmt(F[T])$ there are infinitely many indices i and j along π such that $(s_i, s_{i+1}) \models cf_A$ and $(t_j, t_{j+1}) \models cf_B$. Player I has a winning strategy for game $\mathcal{G}(S, T, F)$, $S \not\preccurlyeq_F T$ for short, if there is a fair play that she wins. Player II has a winning strategy for game $\mathcal{G}(S, T, F)$, $S \preccurlyeq_F T$ for short, if she wins every fair play.

Our goal is to show that context-sensitive approximation $\leq$ coincides with $\preccurlyeq$. We introduce some notation first. Let $\alpha = (s_0, l_0, s_0')(s_1, l_1, s_1') \ldots$ and let $\vec{x}$ and $\vec{n}$ be two lists of equal length of variables and values respectively. Then, $\ll \vec{x} = \vec{n} \gg \alpha$ is like α except that variables in $\vec{x}$ are set to the values in $\vec{n}$ throughout α. That is,

$$\ll \vec{x} = \vec{n} \gg \alpha = ([s_0|\vec{x} = \vec{n}], l_0, [s_0'|\vec{x} = \vec{n}])([s_1|\vec{x} = \vec{n}], l_1, [s_1'|\vec{x} = \vec{n}]) \ldots$$

Let $\pi = (s_0, t_0, l_0)(s_1, t_1, l_1) \ldots$ be a finite or infinite play of some game $\mathcal{G}(S, T, F)$. Then, α_π abbreviates

$$\alpha_\pi = (s_0, l_0, s_1)(s_1, l_1, s_2) \ldots.$$

The set of executions corresponding to π is

$$exec(\pi) = \{\ll \vec{x} = \vec{n} \gg \alpha_\pi \mid set(\vec{x}) = local(F)\}^{\natural}.$$

where $set(\vec{x})$ denotes the set of variables in $\vec{x}$.

Given a finite play $\pi = (s_0, t_0, l_0)(s_1, t_1, l_1) \ldots (s_i, t_i, l_i)$ decided by (s_i, l_i, s_{i+1}) the corresponding set of executions is

$$exec_{(s_i, l_i, s_{i+1})}(\pi) = \{\ll \vec{x} = \vec{n} \gg (\alpha_\pi(s_i, l_i, s_{i+1})) \mid set(\vec{x}) = local(F)\}^\natural.$$

Given a finite execution α and a program F, we say that α can be extended to an execution of F, if there is β such that $\alpha\beta \in \mathcal{E}[\![F]\!]$. α cannot get extended to an execution of F, if for all β we have $\alpha\beta \notin \mathcal{E}[\![F]\!]$. If x and y are sequences over some alphabet, then $x \leq y$ expresses that x is a prefix of y.

Lemma 15. *1. Let π be an infinite fair play of $\mathcal{G}(S, T, F)$. π is won by Player II iff all α in $exec(\pi)$ are executions of $F[\langle S \rangle]$ and $F[\langle T \rangle]$.*

2.a. Let π be finite play of $\mathcal{G}(S, T, F)$ and $\alpha \in exec(\pi)$. If there is α' such that $\alpha \leq \alpha'$ and α' can be extended to an execution of $F[\langle S \rangle]$ and $F[\langle T \rangle]$ then there exists a play π' of $\mathcal{G}(S, T, F)$ such that $\pi \leq \pi'$ and $\alpha' \in exec(\pi')$.

2.b. Let π, π' be finite plays of $\mathcal{G}(S, T, F)$. If $\pi \leq \pi'$ then for all $\alpha \in exec(\pi)$ there exists $\alpha' \in exec(\pi')$ such that $\alpha \leq \alpha'$.

3. There is a trace α that is an execution of $F[\langle S \rangle]$ but not of $F[\langle T \rangle]$ such that all finite prefixes of α can be extended to executions of $F[\langle S \rangle]$ and $F[\langle T \rangle]$ iff there exists an infinite fair play of $\mathcal{G}(S, T, F)$ won by Player I.

4. Let π be play of $\mathcal{G}(S, T, F)$. If π is decided by (s_i, l_i, s_{i+1}), then for all $\alpha \in exec_{(s_i, l_i, s_{i+1})}(\pi)$, α can be extended to an execution of $F[\langle S \rangle]$ but not of $F[\langle T \rangle]$.

Proof. We only sketch the proof of 3. "$\Rightarrow$": Case: α does not diverge. Let α_i be the prefix of α of length i. $\langle \alpha_i \rangle_i$ is a ascending sequence under the prefix ordering with $\alpha = lub\langle \alpha_i \rangle_i$. Using Lemma 15.2.a $\langle \alpha_i \rangle_i$ defines a sequence of plays $\langle \pi_i \rangle_i$ such that $\alpha_i \in exec(\pi_i)$ for all i. Let $\pi = lub\langle \pi_i \rangle_i$. Since α is fair, π is too. The non-divergence of α implies $\alpha \in exec(\pi)$. Since α is an execution of $F[\langle S \rangle]$ but not of $F[\langle T \rangle]$, Lemma 15.1 implies that π is won by Player I. Case: α diverges. Let α_1 be the maximal finite prefix of α that does not end in stuttering. With Lemma 15.2.a there is a play π_1 of $\mathcal{G}(S, T, F)$ such that $\alpha_1 \in exec(\pi_1)$. Then, Player I can play a div-move that Player II cannot match. For a contradiction, suppose Player II can match this div-move. The resulting play π extends π_1, is infinite and won by Player II. Moreover, $\alpha \in exec(\pi)$. With Lemma 15.1 we then get a contradiction. "$\Leftarrow$": Similar using Lemma 15.2.b. $\qquad\square$

Proposition 16. $S \leq_F T$ *iff* $S \preccurlyeq_F T$.

Proof. "$\Leftarrow$": Let $S \nleq_F T$, that is, there is α such that α is an execution of $F[\langle S \rangle]$ but not of $F[\langle T \rangle]$. Case: α has a maximal finite prefix α_1 that can be extended to an execution of $F[\langle S \rangle]$ and $F[\langle T \rangle]$. Note that in this case α cannot diverge. With Lemma 15.2.a there exists a maximal play π_1 of $\mathcal{G}(S, T, F)$ such that $\alpha_1 \in exec(\pi_1)$. Let (s_i, l_i, s_{i+1}) be the first transition in α after α_1 and let s_i' be the last state in π_1. Note that $s_i =_{local(F)} s_i'$. Subcase: $l_i = pro$. Then, Player I can make a pro-move by choosing $(S, s_i') \Longrightarrow (S, s_{i+1}')$ for some s_{i+1}'

such that $s_{i+1} =_{local(F)} s'_{i+1}$ which Player II cannot match. Subcase: $l_i = env$. Then, Player I can make an env-move $(F, s'_i) \implies (F, s'_{i+1})$ for some s'_{i+1} such that $s_{i+1} =_{local(F)} s'_{i+1}$ which Player II cannot match. In each case, Player I wins the play and thus $S \not\preceq_F T$. Case: All finite prefixes of α can be extended to executions of $F[\langle S \rangle]$ and $F[\langle T \rangle]$. Lemma 15.3 implies $S \not\preceq_F T$. "$\Rightarrow$": Let $S \not\preceq_F T$, that is, there is a play π of game $\mathcal{G}(S, T, F)$ won by Player I. Case: π finite and decided by (s_i, l_i, s_{i+1}) for some s_i, s_{i+1} and l_i. Lemma 15.4 implies $S \not\sqsubseteq_F T$. Case: π infinite. Lemma 15.3 implies $S \not\sqsubseteq_F T$. $\qquad\qquad\square$

In the light of the above characterization, Proposition 14 can be interpreted as follows: Both, augmenting the set of initial states $init(F)$ and the capabilities of statement $stmt(F)$, enlarge the "repertoire" of moves of an adversary and thus put her in a better position to refute the approximation and thus win the game. Reducing the number of local variables makes it harder to match the moves of an adversary and thus also put her in a better position. The discrimination ordering $\sqsubseteq$ can be viewed as comparing the strength of these "repertoires".

6 Conclusion and further work

We have presented a refinement framework for UNITY that allows the formal derivation of programs from more abstract specifications. It is centered around a context-sensitive notion of approximation which supports the use of local variables. Derivations in the framework take on the form of assumption/commitment reasoning. A game-theoretic characterization of context-sensitive approximation is given.

Further work As indicated in Section 4, there is a connection between the rules presented there and the UNITY logics in [CM88,San91]. It would be interesting to investigate this connection further. In particular, this might be helpful for identifying additional useful rules for our proof system. Whereas our work concentrates on traces, [CK95] demonstrates how the UNITY logic can be extended using the assumption/commitment paradigm to achieve compositionality. This work also seems particularly relevant in this context.

There is some hope that games might fruitfully be applied to the verification of concurrent systems. Assuming that even novice users of verification systems have some intuitive understanding of simple game-theoretic concepts, games might offer a natural and powerful illustration of the intricacies of concurrent programs and their verification. As an example, we mention the work in progress on the Edinburgh Concurrency Workbench. Games as presented in [Sti96] are incorporated into the system to illustrate branching time temporal logic and model checking [Ste96]. There is some hope that our work might be applicable for similar purposes.

Acknowledgments We thank Steve Brookes for his support and the anonymous referees for their comments.

References

[AJM94]   S. Abramsky, R. Jaghadeesan, and P. Malacaria. Full abstraction for PCF (extended abstract). In *TACS '94*, volume LNCS 789, pages 1–15. Springer Verlag, 1994.

[AS82]   G. R. Andrews and F.B. Schneider. Concepts and notations for concurrent programming. Technical Report 82-520, Cornell University, Department of Computer Science, 1982.

[Bro93]   S.D. Brookes. Full abstraction for a shared-variable parallel language. In *Proceedings 8th Annual IEEE Symposium on Logic in Computer Science*. IEEE Computer Society Press, June 1993.

[CK95]   P. Collette and E. Knapp. Logical foundations for compositional verification and development of concurrent programs in UNITY. In *AMAST '95*, LNCS 936, pages 353–367. Springer Verlag, 1995.

[CM88]   K.M. Chandy and J. Misra. *Parallel program design: a foundation*. Addison Wesley, 1988.

[dBKPR91] F.S. de Boer, J.N. Kok, C. Palamidessi, and J.J.M.M. Rutten. The failure of failures in a paradigm of asynchronous communication. In *CONCUR '91*, pages 111–126. Springer Verlag, 1991.

[Din96]   J. Dingel. Modular verification of shared-variable concurrent programs. In *CONCUR '96*, pages 703–718. Springer Verlag, 1996.

[Lar87]   K. G. Larsen. A context dependent equivalence between processes. *Theoretical Computer Science*, 49(2):185–216, 1987.

[Liu89]   Z. Liu. A semantic model for UNITY. Technical report, Computer Science Department, University of Warwick, 1989.

[McC96]   G. McCusker. Games and full abstraction for FPC. In *Proceedings 11th Annual IEEE Symposium on Logic in Computer Science*. IEEE Computer Society Press, June 1996.

[Mor89]   C. Morgan. The specification statement. *ACM Transactions on Programming Languages and Systems*, 10(3), January 1989.

[QJ91]   X. Qiwen and H. Jifeng. A theory of state-based parallel programming: Part I. In J. Morris, editor, *4th BCS-FACS Refinement Workshop*, 1991.

[San90]   B.A. Sanders. Stepwise refinement of mixed specifications of concurrent programs. In M. Broy and C.B. Jones, editors, *Proceedings of IFIP Working Conference on Programming and Methods*, pages 1–25. Elsevier Science Publishers (North Holland), May 1990.

[San91]   B.A. Sanders. Eliminating the substitution axiom from UNITY logic. *Formal Aspects of Computing*, 3(2), 1991.

[Sin91]   A.K. Singh. Parallel programming: Achieving portability through abstraction. In *11th International Conference on Distributed Computing Systems*, May 1991.

[Ste96]   P. Stevens, December 1996. Private communication.

[Sti96]   C. Stirling. Games and modal mu-calculus. In *Tools and Algorithms for the Construction and Analysis of Systems*. Springer Verlag, 1996. LNCS 1055.

[UK93a]   R.T. Udink and J.N. Kok. On the relation between UNITY properties and sequences of states. In *Semantics: Foundations and Applications*, pages 594–608. Springer Verlag, 1993.

[UK93b]   R.T. Udink and J.N. Kok. Two fully abstract models for UNITY. In *CONCUR '93*, pages 339–352. Springer Verlag, 1993.

Mobile UNITY Coordination Constructs Applied to Packet Forwarding for Mobile Hosts *

Peter J. McCann and Gruia-Catalin Roman

Department of Computer Science, Washington University, One Brookings Drive,
St. Louis MO 63130

Abstract. With recent advances in wireless communication technology, mobile computing is an increasingly important area of research. A mobile system is one where independently executing components may migrate through some space during the course of the computation, and where the pattern of connectivity among the components changes as they move in and out of proximity. Mobile UNITY is a language and logic for specifying and reasoning about mobile systems, the components of which must operate in a highly decoupled way. In this paper it is argued that Mobile UNITY contributes to the modular development of system specifications precisely because of the decoupled and declarative fashion in which coordination among components is specified. The packet forwarding mechanism which is at the core of the Mobile IP protocol for routing to mobile hosts is taken as an example. A Mobile UNITY specification of packet forwarding and the mobile system in which it must operate is developed. Mobile hosts are the components that can disconnect from one location in the network and reconnect to another at any point during system execution. Finally, the role of formal program verification in the development of protocols like Mobile IP is discussed.

1 Introduction

Mobile computing represents a major point of departure from the traditional distributed computing paradigm. The potentially very large number of independent program units, a decoupled computing style, frequent disconnections, continuous position changes, and the location-dependent nature of the behavior and communication patterns present designers with unprecedented challenges in the areas of modularity and dependability. So far, the literature on mobile computing is dominated by concerns having to do with the development of protocols and services for this environment. These services are characterized by more dynamic binding and weaker consistency than traditional distributed applications.

* This paper is based upon work supported in part by the National Science Foundation under Grant No. CCR-9217751. Any opinions, findings, and conclusions or recommendations expressed in this paper are those of the authors and do not necessarily reflect the views of the National Science Foundation. The authors thank Toni Reiss for the illustrations in figures 1 and 3.

For example, the components needed to carry out a service are often not determined until runtime, as in the location-dependent services provided by a mobile web browser [12]. Other work has pointed out the importance of context other than location [9], such as the presence or absence of other components. Weak consistency protocols for filesystems and databases [8, 10, 11] are motivated by the low bandwidth and frequent disconnections typical of a wireless network with mobile nodes. These systems trade consistency for availability under the assumption that in some cases, dealing with the consequences of inconsistencies is cheaper than denying access to a resource.

Some researchers have focused on toolkits and abstractions for building mobile applications. Badrinath and Welling [1] describe a C++ abstraction for delivering events such as bandwidth variations, disconnections, and battery measurements to applications. Noble, Price, and Satyanarayanan [6] present the *Odyssey* application library for managing changing resources and emphasize the importance of application- and data type-specific policies for reacting to changes in the environment. Both emphasize the need to present information about connectivity directly to applications, which violates traditional notions of abstractions and encapsulation of the network. Such information is necessary, however, to build applications that behave properly under changing circumstances, such as responding to diminished connectivity by changing to a lower-resolution video stream.

In this paper we focus on new kinds of abstractions for interprocess communication in the mobile setting. Mobile UNITY [5] provides a notation for mobile system components and a coordination language for expressing interactions among the components. Once expressed in our notation, a system can be subjected to rigorous formal verification against a set of requirements expressed as temporal properties of executions. Mobile UNITY is based on the UNITY model of Chandy and Misra [2], with extensions to both the notation and logic to accommodate specification of and reasoning about mobile programs. In Mobile UNITY, each program is a unit of mobility and all variables are locally owned. We capture movement by augmenting the program state with a location attribute whose change in value is used to represent motion. The new language supports a declarative style of communication that allows a component program to be written in a modular fashion, without regard to the identities of the other components with which it must later interact. This is accomplished with a novel construct, transient variable sharing. This allows mobile programs to share data when in close proximity, i.e., a variable owned by one program may be shared in a transparent manner with different programs at different times depending upon their relative location in space. This implies that a value written to one variable of such a pair must be propagated to the other variable as a side-effect of an assignment. The basic constructs of Mobile UNITY that allow us to express this idea also allow for other coordination constructs, such as transient statement synchronization. However in this paper we deal only with transient sharing, which suffices for the examples presented.

Mobile UNITY is designed to accommodate mobile applications and services that exhibit dynamic reconfiguration and weak consistency, like the ones discussed earlier. Perhaps the most basic service that can be provided in the mobile setting is simple packet routing. The Mobile IP protocol [7] is designed to deliver this service to mobile hosts that are transiently connected to the Internet. In this paper we give a formal description of the packet forwarding mechanism at the core of the Mobile IP protocol and begin to investigate some of its formal properties. Eventually, we hope to formally describe other packet routing algorithms, such as those for ad-hoc networks [4], which provide routing services to a group of mobile hosts that may be completely disconnected from the Internet. Such situations may arise at a conference, for instance, where it would cost too much to install a fixed routing infrastructure for a short-duration event, or in an urban setting after a natural disaster had wiped out the fixed infrastructure. These kinds of networks must rely on the individual hosts for control and routing functions. For now, however, we concentrate on the current version of Mobile IP, which assumes that mobile hosts connect to the Internet at specific points designated by network administrators.

Section 2 gives a simple description of a network that allows hosts to disconnect but not to move to another point of connectivity. This serves as an introduction to the Mobile UNITY notation and offers an example of how mobile, transiently-connected systems may be specified. Section 3 refines the example to model packet forwarding inside the fixed network, which allows mobile nodes to migrate from one point of connectivity to another and to receive packets there. Section 4 shows how UNITY-style program verification is still feasible in Mobile UNITY. Several correctness properties of the packet forwarding system are stated and outlines of their proofs are discussed—the presentation style is accessible to a broad audience. Finally, conclusions appear in Section 5.

2   A Notation for Mobile Programs

We favor a state-based model, axiomatic reasoning, and explicit representation of space and its properties. While the choice of underlying model may be a matter of personal taste, we contend that modeling the space explicitly is desirable when one hopes to take into account the physical reality of moving objects and its implications on the behavior of the software that they carry. Because the behavior exhibited by a component is affected by what other components are in its proximity, location is likely to play an important role in reasoning about mobile computations. This is why we treat mobility as a change in the location of a component—a mobile program. In this paper we use the UNITY [2] notation to express the computation taking place within the mobile components of a system and the UNITY proof logic to reason about mobile computations. Both are extended appropriately to account for the effects of movement and transient interactions. To introduce the reader to the UNITY notation we first consider a standard UNITY program which models a network. A picture of the network is shown in Fig. 1.

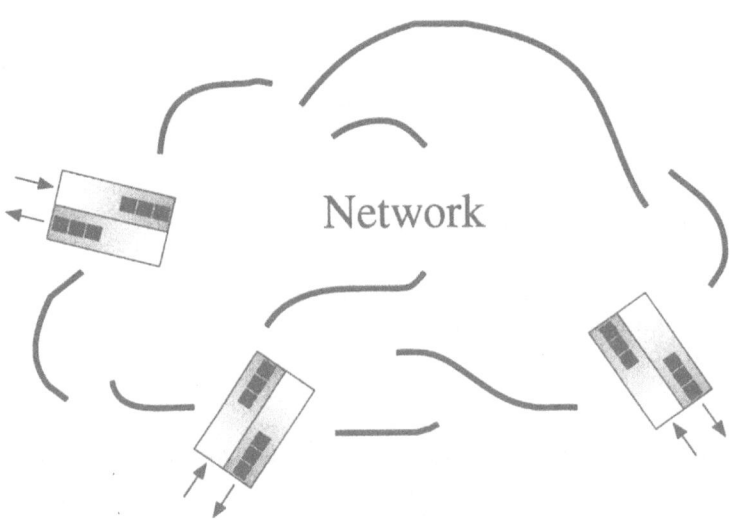

Fig. 1. The simple packet router modeled by the program network, below.

The simplified network consists of *NPorts* input queues and *NPorts* output queues. The index of each queue is a network address that can be assigned to some host. The state of the network is completely defined by the contents of the queues. Each queue contains one or more packets (the *msg* type in the program below) which are assumed to be tuples of the form (A, D), where A is the destination address of the packet and D is the data contents. The destination address of a message m can be accessed by writing $m.A$. Execution of the network corresponds to taking some packet out of an input queue and delivering it to the appropriate output queue. Execution of the network continues forever.

The program below expresses these ideas formally. The **declare** section contains variable declarations, here the two arrays of queues. The **always** section defines convenience functions to be used later in the program text and in proofs. Here it contains the definition of the parameterized function $dest(i)$ which returns the address of the packet on the head of queue i. The **initially** section is a set of state predicates defining the allowed set of initial states. The predicates are separated by the symbol $[]$ which is used as the quantifier in three-part notation[1].

---

[1] The three-part notation ⟨op quantified_variables : range :: expression⟩ used throughout the text is defined as follows: The variables from *quantified_variables* take on all possible values permitted by *range*. If *range* is missing, the first colon is omitted and the domain of the variables is restricted by context. Each such instantiation of the variables is substituted in *expression* producing a multiset of values to which *op* is applied, yielding the value of the three-part expression. If no instantiation of the variables satisfies *range*, the value of the three-part expression is the identity element for *op*, e.g., *true* when *op* is ∀.

```
program network
  declare
    in, out : array[NPorts] of queue of msg
  always
    dest(i) = in[i].head.A
  initially
    ⟨[] i : 0 ≤ i < NPorts :: in[i] = InitialPort(i)⟩
  assign
    ⟨[]  i : 0 ≤ i < NPorts :: out[dest(i)], in[i] :=
      out[dest(i)] ∘ in[i].head, in[i].tail if in[i] ≠ φ⟩
end
```

Each initialization predicate makes use of the function $InitialPort(i)$, which simply returns some initial state for input queue i. The network will execute as a closed system for now, performing routing only for those packets which are initially in the input queues. The **assign** section contains the "code" for the program. It contains a set of assignment statements, one for each port, each guarded with an **if**. Each assignment is a multiple assignment, that is, each has an equal number of left and right hand sides. When a statement is selected for execution, all right hand sides (and left hand side array indices) are completely evaluated before any assignment takes place. Concurrent execution is modeled as a non-deterministic fair interleaving of the statements from this set. In the **assign** section, the notation $q.head$ is used to refer to the element on the front of queue q, and $q.tail$ refers to a queue formed by removing the first element of q. The operator '∘' appends an element to a queue; the expression $(q \circ e)$ is equivalent to the queue q with element e added to the end. Thus, if input port i is non-empty $(in[i] \neq \phi)$ the assignment takes the packet from the head of input queue i and places it on the end of the output queue given by the packet's destination address.

This model of the network has no interaction with the outside world. The initial conditions place packets on the input links. Packets are routed to the appropriate output links where they remain forever. Once all packets have been routed, the program is said to have reached *Fixed Point*, i.e., no further state changes take place. However, we would like to compose this program with others that model hosts connected to the network. These hosts would insert packets into input queues and remove packets from output queues. In standard UNITY, this composition would be accomplished with statically shared variables. Any two variables with the same name are considered shared, and the relationship is not allowed to change over the course of execution. However, we would like to model the intermittent kinds of system relationships characteristic of mobile computing. The first step towards this goal is to isolate the namespaces of each program. Thus, in Mobile UNITY variables are not shared unless explicitly allowed to by the circumstances of the current state; this leads to a less tightly coupled system where relationships between components change dynamically. The program *mobile-node* contains two queues, one for input to the node and one for output from the node. The first two statements in the **assign** section consume and generate messages on these links. Messages are generated from the function *NextMessage(address)* which is simply assumed to return the next message that the host wants to transmit.

```
program mobile-node(k) at λ
  declare
    in, out : queue of msg
    [] address : integer
  initially
    address = k
  assign
    in := in.tail if in ≠ φ
    [] out := out ∘ NextMessage(address)
    [] λ := Move(λ)
end
```

The factors leading to interaction are likely to include location, so we add this as a distinguished variable λ which models the physical placement of the node in space. This program contains one assignment statement that modifies λ, which uses the function Move(λ) to determine the new location. Implicit in our notational conventions is the notion that a program and its variables are co-located and move as a single unit. Assignments to λ are not compiled as assignment statements but instead model physical movement. In this case, the statement simply models the fact that the program may move at some point in its execution, most likely due to a user walking away from the network. Such statements must represent a correct reflection of the physical world, accurate enough to facilitate reasoning about both functional and mobility aspects of the program's behavior. Even though movement is continuous, the movement statements must be viewed as atomic state changes associated with the arrival at the new location in order to make them fit with the interleaved model of concurrency used by UNITY. This has interesting implications on the statement scheduling strategy in the runtime system supporting the execution of Mobile UNITY programs, e.g., a guard on a movement statement ought not to change during the unit of time it takes to complete the move. In this paper we simply assume that the implementation maintains the appearance of an interleaved atomic execution and we use this fact when reasoning about such programs. The type of λ was left unspecified. Throughout the paper we assume the existence of a global declaration for the spatial context in which the programs move.

In general, restrictions on how such a location variable is accessed and updated must reflect the mobility characteristics of the computation. In a cellular network, for instance, the location of the mobile unit is determined by the car or person carrying the computer but is constrained to movements from one cell to a neighboring one (as long as the unit is on). The verification of any hand-off algorithm must rely on this assumption. Protocols involved in reestablishing connectivity at the time a mobile computer is powered up may have to assume that initial locations are arbitrary. In some applications a program may have to know its own location while not in others. In the former case the location is directly accessible by the program while in the latter the location plays a role only in reasoning about the computation. In a robot application it is also conceivable that a program may actually have the ability to control the movement of its carrier. In this case, movement is no longer under the control of the environment but planned by the program which could request future data delivery at specific locations to be reached along the movement path.

To compose this program with the network program given earlier, we need to formally declare the components and specify the interactions between them using a specialized abstract coordination language built on top of three primitive structures not discussed in this paper (see [5] for details). In the following system specification, we declare one network component, one mobile-node component for each port, parameterized by the port number, and one sharing interaction for each mobile node input and output queue.

> **System** network-and-nodes
> **Components**
> network
> $[] \langle []i : 0 \le i < \text{NPorts} :: \text{mobile-node(i)} \textbf{ at } \lambda_i \rangle$
> **Interactions**
> $\langle []i : 0 \le i < \text{NPorts} ::$
>   mobile-node(i).in $\approx$ network.out[i]
>   **when**   mobile-node(i).$\lambda = \lambda_i$
>   **engage**   mobile-node(i).in
>   **disengage**   current, ϕ
>
> $[]$ mobile-node(i).out $\approx$ network.in[i]
>   **when**   mobile-node(i).$\lambda = \lambda_i$
>   **engage**   network.in[i]
>   **disengage** ϕ, current
> $\rangle$
> **end**

Consider the first sharing interaction. It names two variables, *mobile-node(i).in* and *network.out[i]*. The first is a variable from an instance of a parameterized program, while the second is an array element from the fixed program network. The two variables are treated as shared when the mobile node i is co-located with port i at λ_i. By "shared" we mean that any change to one copy is atomically propagated to the other copy, just as if the variables were statically shared as in standard UNITY. In this system, only node i can be connected to port i (a node has no connectivity when away from its home port). The **engage** expression is used to specify what value the newly shared variable should take when the sharing predicate transitions from *false* to *true*. In this case, we use the value *mobile-node(i).in* because the shared queue is actually physically located on some network interface hardware present on the mobile node (we assume that the network interface has on board a queue of messages that have not yet been processed by the mobile node). We must also specify what values the shared variables should take when the sharing predicate transitions from *true* to *false*. This is the **disengage** value, which in this case states that the variable *mobile-node(i).in* should retain the current shared value, while the variable *network.out*[*i*] should be cleared. Packets might be placed on this output queue during the period of disconnection, but they will be dropped by the **engage** specified here once the connection is re-established. We share the mobile node's output queue with the appropriate network input queue in a similar fashion.

The notion of transient shared variables is an interesting generalization of a well established computing paradigm. The engagement and disengagement protocols are closely tied to the notions of cache coherence and reconciliation among multiple versions of a database or filesystem. Our experience to date indicates that transient data sharing can contribute significantly to decoupling among the components of a mobile system. Individual programs have no knowledge of the identity of other programs in the system. Changes in the design of individual components often have effects limited only to the definition of the interactions. The same programs work in a multitude of configurations using varying numbers of components. Finally, by hiding the communication behind what amounts to be a set of declarative rules the programming task is greatly simplified; all communication responsibilities are relegated to the runtime support system.

3   Packet Forwarding in Mobile IP

In the previous section, we modeled the network as a simple packet router, and the hosts were mobile but could only be connected when present at the home location. In this section, we would like to refine this abstract program so that it captures important aspects of the Mobile IP protocol [7]. This is an extension to IP version 4 that attempts to deal with host mobility at a network level by forwarding those packets that arrive at the mobile node's home address to the foreign subnetwork on which the host happens to be. The goal of Mobile IP is to accomplish this without introducing changes to the bulk of the Internet routing fabric or nodes that want to communicate with mobile hosts. In what is expected to be the most common mode of operation, implementation of the protocol requires a *home agent*, which accepts packets on behalf of the mobile node and performs forwarding, a *foreign agent*, which receives the forwarded packets and delivers them to the mobile node, and a *mobile node* that detects movement and initiates the appropriate registration with the home agent so that packets can be forwarded. Figure 2 illustrates a mobile node away from home and the "tunnel" through which the home agent sends packets. The mobile node is allowed to transmit packets normally as long as it can find an appropriate outgoing router (often the foreign agent itself).

In this section, we introduce some modifications to the abstract program presented earlier that let it capture the packet forwarding idea from Mobile IP. To keep the presentation short, the protocol is modeled at a very high level

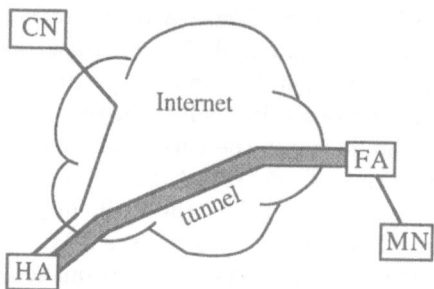

Fig. 2. A high-level picture of the Mobile IP protocol. Packets arriving at the home agent (HA) from some correspondent node (CN) are tunneled using some form of packet encapsulation to the foreign agent (FA), which then delivers them to the mobile node (MN).

and we make many simplifying assumptions. We make no modifications to the *mobile-node* program; this program corresponds to the interface presented by the operating system to applications. Our modifications will thus be confined to the *network* program and the system declarations. The resulting new system is named *mobile-ip*. Because our modifications are to the *network* program, this is where we are modeling the functionality provided by home and foreign agents. As before, each port i is considered to be "at" location λ_i, and a mobile node can be connected only when it is co-located with some port—*any* port in this refined example. The mapping from agents to ports is not defined; each port could correspond to a separate mobility agent or one mobility agent could manage several ports. The function of the agents is completely encapsulated inside the network. Figure 3 illustrates this away-from-home connectivity.

Our modified network program is shown below. It now contains two additional arrays, *address* and *binding*.

```
program network
  declare
    in, out : array[NPorts] of queue of msg
    [] address, binding : array[NPorts] of integer
  always
    dest(i) = binding[in[i].head.A]
  initially
    ⟨[] i : 0 ≤ i < NPorts :: binding[i] = i⟩
    [] ⟨[] i : 0 ≤ i < NPorts :: address[i] = i⟩
  assign
    ⟨[] i : 0 ≤ i < NPorts :: out[dest(i)], in[i] :=
        out[dest(i)] o in[i].head, in[i].tail if in[i] ≠ φ⟩
    [] ⟨[] i : 0 ≤ i < NPorts :: binding[address[i]] := i if address[i] ≥ 0⟩
  end
```

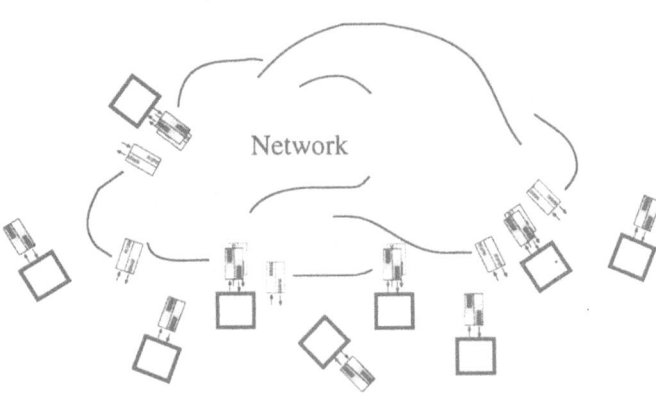

Fig. 3. A network supporting mobile hosts in the style of Mobile IP. The packet forwarding scheme is modeled as a modification to the routing functionality so that packets at any input are routed immediately to the correct output.

The value in *address*[i] is set to the address of the mobile node that is currently connected to port i, or -1 if no mobile node is present. The system specification given later will accomplish this. The value in *binding*[i] will be set to the forwarding address of node i. This will be accomplished by the program network itself when it detects a mobile node at some port (using the value of *address*[i]). The code for the network now has two sets of quantified actions. The first accomplishes routing and is very similar to the routing action of the previous version, except that it now uses the forwarding address of the destination, instead of the destination itself, to determine the final endpoint of the communication. This models correct execution of the home agent and foreign agent as they collaborate to deliver a packet to the mobile node. The second set of actions establishes a forwarding address for a mobile node when it is connected away from home and also clears this forwarding address when it is re-connected to the home port. This models registration of the mobile node as it moves from subnetwork to subnetwork. As the reader can readily observe, the program required very few modifications to capture the essential nature of the packet forwarding scheme. The basic structure of the program remains the same. We simply modified the routing to account for forwarding, and added one statement to model remote registration.

The system *mobile-ip* is shown below. In it, we rely on interactions given in the system specification to update the address array. As before, the system is composed of one *network* program and as many *mobile-nodes* as there are ports.

System mobile-ip
  Components
  network
  $[]\langle\ []i : 0 \leq i < \text{NPorts} :: \text{mobile-node}(i) \text{ at } \lambda_i\rangle$
  Interactions
    $\langle\ []i, j : 0 \leq i < \text{NPorts} \wedge 0 \leq j < \text{NPorts} ::$
      mobile-node(i).address $\approx$ network.address[j]

when	mobile-node(i).$\lambda = \lambda_j \wedge \text{Alone}(\lambda_j)$
engage	mobile-node(i).address
disengage	current, -1

      $[]$ mobile-node(i).in $\approx$ network.out[j]

when	mobile-node(i).$\lambda = \lambda_j \wedge \text{Alone}(\lambda_j)$
engage	mobile-node(i).in
disengage	current, ϕ

      $[]$ mobile-node(i).out $\approx$ network.in[j]

when	mobile-node(i).$\lambda = \lambda_j \wedge \text{Alone}(\lambda_j)$
engage	network.in[j]
disengage	ϕ, current

  $\rangle$
  end

The transient sharing conditions now support away-from-home interaction, however, so there are now $O(\text{NPorts} \times \text{NPorts})$ interactions. For each pairing of
mobile node to port, there are three interactions. The first shares the mobile
node's address with the appropriate network port when connected. This models
the acquisition of a foreign agent upon entering a new subnetwork. The actual
registration with the home agent was modeled by assignment to the binding
array given previously, based on this address. The second and third interactions
are the same as the ones given earlier that share the input and output queues
of the current port with the mobile node. As before, the actual state of any
queue is considered to reside on the receiving side, as reflected by the **engage**
values. Because a mobile node can now be connected to any port, not just the
port with the same index, we must be careful that no two nodes are connected
to the same port. This would lead to undefined behavior of the queues as both
nodes tried to access them. We can think of the locations as corresponding to
physical network connections that can accommodate only one node at a time.
Therefore, even if two mobile nodes are co-located, neither has connectivity to
the port at that location. This is reflected in the semantics of the *Alone* predicate which is true if and only if there is only one node at the given location. This
system is an abstract program that ignores many of the details of the Mobile
IP protocol. However, it does capture the essence of the protocol at a similar
level of abstraction to the single point of connectivity example presented earlier.
The modifications did not affect the mobile-node program in the least, which

is indicative of the amount of decoupling among components provided by our notation.

Throughout the examples, the manner in which we have modeled the links among programs (as shared message queues) is an abstraction from the physical reality of a wired or wireless data link between hardware devices where each receiver maintains a queue of unprocessed messages. In reality, each program has "append-only" access to a remote queue. This restriction is in fact satisfied by the above programs as they are composed here, but our notation does not explicitly protect the queues from remote access. Mobile UNITY is intended to be a general model helpful in the design, modeling, and verification of mobile computations and not a programming language supporting implementation. Consequently, it allows one to model undesirable structures and subject them to analysis.

In the next section we discuss the appropriateness of the level of abstraction presented so far and the role of formal verification in the design process.

4 Verification Strategy and Issues

The brevity of this paper does not allow us to give a complete description of the Mobile UNITY notation or its proof logic, e.g., we omitted the transient action synchronization mechanism among others. Neither can we provide a complete formal verification of the Mobile IP protocol, even at this abstract level. The purpose of this section is to show how one might approach this task and the benefits one can expect from such an exercise. We hope to convince the reader that Mobile UNITY makes the task manageable even for programs involving mobility. Formally, the key to accomplishing this is the fact that Mobile UNITY inherits most of the proof logic of UNITY, along with its inference rules. This is because we were able to encapsulate the impact of mobility to very few low level axioms, e.g., a reformulation of the Hoare triple and of the concept of basic progress.

Typically, a designer starts out with informal ideas for what a protocol is expected to accomplish, and then proposes an operational solution (a program) to meet those goals. The process of protocol verification entails formalizing the correctness criteria and verifying that the proposed program meets these conditions. The program that is verified is usually an abstraction of the actual implementation—it contains fewer details than a running implementation would. This simplifies the verification process and does not adversely affect the correctness of a final implementation, as long as a correctness-preserving mechanical transformation of the abstract program into an implementation can be performed. Of course, the abstract program must contain enough detail so that all interesting and difficult aspects of the protocol are captured within it.

The Mobile UNITY program notation offers a simple means to specify operational solutions, provides a means to verify properties of such programs, and is sufficiently abstract so as to be compatible with many implementation architectures. In formalizing the correctness expectations of a protocol, the UNITY logic can be used to write down properties that will later be proven of a specific program. These properties are called assertions. They are of two kinds, *safety* and *liveness* properties. In the UNITY logic, which is based on a restricted form of temporal logic, an assertion must hold in every state along every execution sequence. This allows us to distance ourselves from reasoning about execution sequences explicitly. Basic properties are derived from the program text and are combined using a battery of inference rules.

Simple program properties are built from state predicates and simple relations on them. A state predicate is constructed using boolean algebra, the names of variables from the program text, quantification, and ordinary relational operators, as in

$$\text{network.address}[3] = 5 \land \text{network.binding}[5] = 3$$

which states that the program variable *network.address*[3] (the third element of the *address* array from program *network*) has the value 5, and the variable *network.binding*[5] (the fifth element of the *binding* array from program *network*) has the value 3. For any given state (an assignment of values to the program variables), this predicate might be *true* or *false*. Those states for which the predicate is true are said to be the set of all states that "satisfy" the predicate. Note that there are many such states that satisfy the above predicate, because it fixes only two of the program variables, while the others can take on any value.

An execution is a sequence of states the program passes through starting from an acceptable initial state. All executions are assumed to be infinte in length and weakly fair. Relations over predicates can be used to express properties of executions. For example, the relation **co** (short for constrains)

$$p \, \mathbf{co} \, q$$

asserts that if a state satisfying p occurs anywhere in the execution, the next state must satisfy q. This expression is now a predicate over state sequences (executions) and defines a set of executions that satisfy it. This kind of property is called a safety property because if it is not true, there is a finite place in the execution where it breaks down. A safety property states that "bad things do not happen." The **co** relation for two predicates p and q with respect to some program F can be proven by considering all the statements of F and showing that if each is executed in a state satisfying p, it will terminate and leave the program in a state satisfying q. Well known methods from sequential programming can be used to carry out this proof [3]. Invariant properties, those that are true throughout execution, can be expressed simply as

$$\mathbf{invariant} \, p \; \equiv \; \text{Init} \Rightarrow p \land p \, \mathbf{co} \, p$$

which states that the initial conditions satisfy p and also every action preserves p if executed from a state satisfying p.

For example, consider one desirable property of the Mobile-IP protocol, *NO-MISDELIVERY*, which states that a message (A, D) is never delivered to the wrong node, i.e., to a node i different from the address A. We can express this property as a predicate over the input queue for node i, stating that the queue can only contain messages addressed to node i.

NO-MISDELIVERY ≡
invariant (A, D) ∈ mobile-node(i).in ⇒ A = i

By convention, all free variables (i.e., A, D and i) are assumed to be universally quantified over the appropriate ranges.

In a standard UNITY program, we would prove the above by showing first that it was satisfied by the initial conditions, and then that every statement preserved it. In Mobile UNITY, we follow the same basic procedure, except that some of the statements have side-effects due to the variable sharing. These side-effects propagate changes to variables that are currently shared and also establish **engage** and **disengage** values whenever a state change causes a transition in the value of a sharing predicate. A formal proof logic for the transient sharing construct as well as other coordination constructs can be found in [5]. For the purposes of this short paper, we reason about the packet forwarding system somewhat informally, at a level that might be undertaken by a system designer while thinking about the code presented so far. This is done by enumerating the system transitions that may affect the truth of the invariant and proving that the invariant is preserved in each case. There are two actions that could potentially modify the variable *mobile-node(i).in*. The easiest to consider is the statement inside *mobile-node* that removes messages from the queue. Clearly, this statement preserves the invariant, because if no errant messages are in the queue before a removal there will be none afterwards.

The other statement that modifies the queue is the routing statement inside network, under the condition that the mobile node is attached and the queue is shared. Note that we cannot prove that this action preserves the above invariant: the routing statement might be directing packets meant for another node j (which hasn't yet updated its binding address *binding[j]*), to the outgoing queue currently shared with node i. To prevent this from happening, we need to strengthen the guard on the routing statement so that the network checks to see that the right node is currently attached. That is, we should change the statement to read

out[dest(i)], in[i] := out[dest(i)] ∘ in[i].head, in[i].tail
if in[i] ≠ ϕ∧ address[dest(i)] = in[i].head.A

This is an example of how formal thinking helps reveal program errors even when proof outlines are substituted for the actual formal treatment.

The movement statements might also affect the value of the variable *mobile-node(i).in*, because it is a transiently shared variable that could be affected by engagement and disengagement. Careful inspection of the **Interactions** section reveals that the input queue is always preserved intact for both engagement and disengagement.

In most cases, safety properties are not sufficient to fully specify the desired behavior of a program. In addition to not doing a bad thing, a program is usually expected to accomplish some good thing. Without a liveness property as part of the specification, the empty program would trivially satisfy the correctness criteria. In UNITY, we can express basic liveness properties using **ensures**. Again, this is a relation over state predicates:

$$p \text{ ensures } q$$

is written to mean that if a state satisfying p occurs anywhere in the execution, and q is not also satisfied in this state, then p will continue to be true from that state forward until a state satisfying q occurs. In addition, there is some statement that is guaranteed to establish q if selected for execution. Due to the weak fairness assumption of the UNITY statement scheduler, this statement cannot be denied forever and will eventually establish q. More complicated progress properties such as leads-to can also be expressed. The property

$$p \text{ leads-to } q$$

means that if a state satisfying p occurs, then eventually a state satisfying q will occur. Here there is no requirement that p is maintained until q is established. This property is usually proven using induction on a well-founded integer metric that is shown to eventually decrease (by inductive use of **ensures** or another **leads-to**) to zero, at which point q is established.

For example, consider the property *EVENTUAL-DELIVERY*, which states that a message on an output queue of some node is eventually delivered to the input queue of the node to which it was addressed.

EVENTUAL-DELIVERY ≡
  (A, D) ∈ mobile-node(i).out **leads-to** (A, D) ∈ mobile-node(A).in

where again, free variables are quantified over the appropriate ranges. To prove this property, we might break it up into separate leads-to conditions and then chain these together using the standard transitivity rule for leads-to which states

$$\frac{p \text{ leads-to } q \land q \text{ leads-to } r}{p \text{ leads-to } r}$$

We can take p to be $(A, D) \in$ *mobile-node(i).out*, r to be $(A, D) \in$ *mobile-node(A).in*, and q to express the property $(A, D) = $ *mobile-node(i).out.head*. Then, we have broken the overall property into two parts. The first part says that any message in the output queue of a mobile node eventually reaches the head, and the second part says that a message on the head of an output queue is eventually delivered to the correct mobile node.

Note that we can prove neither of these from the text of the program as it was given. If a mobile node becomes disconnected, its output queue is not shared with the network and any packets placed there will be lost. Similarly, if the destination mobile node becomes disconnected, it will miss packets directed towards it. The protocol satisfies *EVENTUAL-DELIVERY* only with very strong guarantees on the movement patterns and connectivity of nodes, e.g., if mobile nodes are connected to the same foreign agent for "long enough." A UNITY mechanism called a *conditional property* allows us to formalize such assumptions and to carry out the necesssary proofs. This illustrates another benefit of formal reasoning, the identification and formal characterization of the assumptions made by the protocol.

5 Conclusions

Mobile UNITY consists of a notation for specifying abstract programs and an assertional style proof logic, both aimed at the specification and verification of mobile computations. Coordination among components is specified separately from the components involved. This can be viewed as a way to manage connectivity changes in a declarative fashion. Our transient sharing abstraction is closely related to weak consistency policies in filesystems and databases, and allows explicit specification of re-integration values for disconnected variables. By adding location explicitly to the formal model (but not constraining the semantics or type of this location except on an as-needed basis) we can reason about context-dependent applications as well. Despite its stylized treatment, the packet forwarding example is representative of the verification strategies we inherited from UNITY and of the decoupled style of programming promoted by Mobile UNITY. Using Mobile UNITY, abstract programs that provide an operational characterization of some mobile computing task can be verified against formally stated assertions. We hope that, after further evaluation of the approach, some of the lessons we learned so far will make their way into the programming practice in the form of packages supporting high level coordination languages for mobile systems. The potential is here to simplify the application development effort by providing the right programming abstractions along side a semantic model supportive of formal verification.

References

1. B. R. Badrinath and G. Welling, "Event Delivery Abstractions for Mobile Computing," Rutgers University, New Brunswick, NJ 08903, Technical Report LCSR-TR-242, 1995.
2. K. M. Chandy and J. Misra, *Parallel Program Design: A Foundation.* Addison-Wesley, 1988.
3. D. Gries, *The Science of Programming.* Springer-Verlag, 1987.
4. D. B. Johnson, "Routing in Ad Hoc Networks of Mobile Hosts," *Proceedings of the Workshop on Mobile Computing Systems and Applications,* Santa Cruz, CA, pp. 158-163, 1994.
5. P. J. McCann and G.-C. Roman, "Mobile UNITY: A Language and Logic for Concurrent Mobile Systems," Washington University in St. Louis, Technical Report WUCS-97-01, 1997.
6. B. D. Noble, M. Price, and M. Satyanarayanan, "A Programming Interface for Application-Aware Adaptation in Mobile Computing," *Computing Systems,* vol. 8, no. 4, pp. 345-63, 1995.

7. C. Perkins, "IP Mobility Support," ftp://ds.internic.net/rfc/rfc2002.txt, Request for Comments 2002, October 1996.
8. M. Satyanarayanan, J. J. Kistler, L. B. Mummert, M. R. Ebling, P. Kumar, and Q. Lu, "Experience with Disconnected Operation in a Mobile Computing Environment," *Proceedings of the USENIX Symposium on Mobile and Location-Indepedent Computing*, Cambridge, MA, pp. 11-28, 1993.
9. B. N. Schilit, N. Adams, and R. Want, "Context-Aware Computing Applications," *Proceedings of the Workshop on Mobile Computing Systems and Applications*, Santa Cruz, CA, pp. 85-90, 1994.
10. C. D. Tait and D. Duchamp, "An Efficient Variable Consistency Replicated File Service," *Proceedings of the USENIX File Systems Workshop*, Ann Arbor, MI, pp. 111-126, 1992.
11. D. Terry, M. Theimer, K. Petersen, A. Demers, M. Spreitzer, and C. Hauser, "Managing Update Conflicts in Bayou, a Weakly Connected Replicated Storage System," *Operating Systems Review*, vol. 29, no. 5, pp. 172-83, 1995.
12. G. M. Voelker and B. N. Bershad, "Mobisaic: An Information System for a Mobile Wireless Computing Environment," *Proceedings of the Workshop on Mobile Computing Systems and Applications*, Santa Cruz, CA, pp. 185-90, 1994.

From Layer to Layer —
Object-Oriented Protocol Refinement in Kannel

Kari Granö and Jukka Paakki

Department of Computer Science
P.O.Box 26, FIN–00014 University of Helsinki, Finland

Abstract. The refinement of communication in protocol engineering is studied by analyzing the relation between a peer-to-peer communication scheme and its service-level counterpart, a characteristic that is well-known in practice but rarely studied in detail. It is shown how an abstract protocol can be developed towards a concrete implementation by gradually refining the abstract messages and the involved state machines, moving systematically from layer to layer over the subject application. The characteristics of the refinement are formalized, and an example is given showing how the method can be applied in practical protocol development. The object-oriented language Kannel is introduced as an advanced tool for protocol engineering providing special support for the refinement technique.

1 Introduction

Protocol engineering is a systematic discipline for the development of communications software. The communicating systems are typically organized as layers with modular interfaces. A communication *protocol* defines how messages are exchanged through a common interface, either between two peers residing at the same layer n in two different end systems or between two adjacent layers n and $n-1$ within the same system. There is a close conceptual coupling between these two: A layer(n)-to-layer$(n-1)$ protocol can be regarded as an implementation of the peer(n)-to-peer(n) communication protocol.

From a software engineering point of view, this coupling is most valuable when moving from protocol design into protocol implementation. A peer-to-peer protocol specifies abstractly how the end systems shall communicate in general, whereas the corresponding layer-to-layer protocol defines concretely how the upper-layer communication is actually realized in terms of the services provided by the lower layer. Hence, the step from design into implementation can be taken by transforming the peer-level protocols (and interfaces) to the corresponding service-level protocols (and interfaces).

In this paper we present a constructive technique of systematically implementing abstract communication protocols. Our approach is based on the *refinement* of the peer(n)-to-peer(n) protocol into protocols of more concrete functionality: a layer(n)-to-layer$(n-1)$ service protocol and a peer$(n-1)$-to-peer$(n-1)$ communication protocol.

The technique is supported by the *Kannel* language [GHP94,GHJ95] in terms of object-oriented inheritance and formal refinement of communication patterns. Kannel is a full-fledged protocol engineering language, providing application-oriented support for the central aspects of protocol engineering. We will omit a detailed description of Kannel in this paper and concentrate on the protocol refinement mechanism only.

We proceed as follows. The characteristics of protocol refinement are presented in Sect. 2, followed by a formal study in Sect. 3. In Sect. 4 a constructive approach to protocol refinement is presented with an example application written in Kannel. Finally, conclusions are drawn in Sect. 5.

2 The notion of protocol refinement

Let us study a typical abstract communication scheme illustrated in Fig. 1. Here A and B are (probably distributed) entities (usually processes) that communicate according to their common protocol AB to provide the required services to their clients, *User_A* and *User_B*.

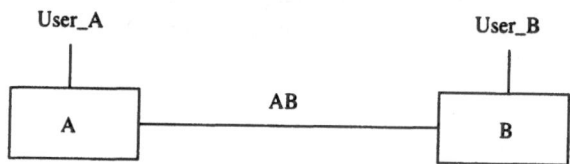

Fig. 1. Abstract communication.

In simple applications the communication might be carried out in this straightforward manner, but in realistic cases the functionality of A and B is so complex that some form of modularity is needed, as illustrated in the refined scheme of Fig. 2. Now the protocol AB is realized by making use of entities C and D residing at a "lower layer" of functionality. That is, the AB protocol is implemented by using the services of C and D following the protocol CD of their own. From the viewpoint of message-flow, a message from *User_A* to *User_B* does not go directly via A and B as the abstract scheme in Fig. 1 suggests, but indirectly along the path $A' - C - D - B'$. Still, from the client's point of view, the external functionality of the system is the same irrespective of the system's architecture (Fig. 1 or Fig. 2).

Notice that the scheme in Fig. 2 is more detailed than that in Fig. 1: (1) The peer-to-peer protocol AB (at layer n) has been replaced by three new protocols, the service-level protocols $A'C$ and DB' (between layers n and $n-1$) and the peer-to-peer protocol CD (at layer $n-1$); (2) the entities C and D have been introduced (at layer $n-1$); and (3) the entities A and B (at layer n) have been replaced by A' and B', respectively, since their direct mutual communication

357

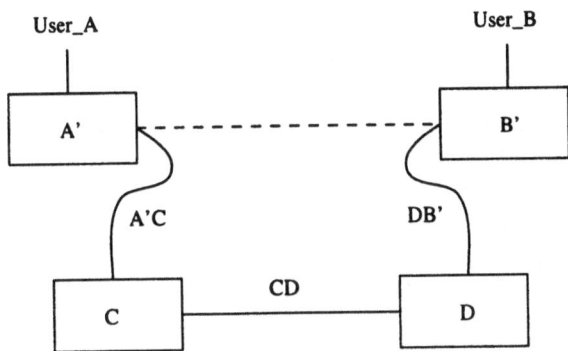

Fig. 2. Communication by refinement of AB.

scheme has been changed into an indirect one. Thus we can regard the scheme in Fig. 2 as an implementation or a *refinement* of that in Fig. 1.

The term "refinement" suggests that the two communication schemes shall be semantically related: (1) The external behaviour with respect to User_A and User_B shall remain the same; and (2) the abstract peer-to-peer protocol AB shall be retained, that is, the refinement shall still follow the communication rules captured in protocol AB. Intuitively, this means that even under the refinement, (1) User_A and User_B shall be able to exchange the same set of message sequences as originally; and (2) for each message sequence transmitted between A and B, there must be a corresponding (refined) exchange between A' and B'. Notice, however, that in addition to the messages covered by the abstract protocol AB, A' and B' typically process a number of implementation-oriented messages, at least those captured in protocols $A'C$ and DB' as services provided by the entities C and D.

Since the scheme in Fig. 2 still applies a peer-to-peer protocol, CD, the refinement process can be continued. By iteratively following the same principle, an abstract communication scheme can be developed into a suitable layered architecture and a proper level of precision. The refinement process typically continues until a layer providing direct physical communication services has been encountered.

3 Formal properties of protocol refinement

3.1 Possible solutions

Consider the refining step from Fig. 1 to Fig. 2 in more detail. What kind of techniques are possible to revise the abstract communication scheme of Fig. 1 into the more concrete setting of Fig. 2 and still retain the behaviour externally the same? At least the following solutions are possible:

1. The whole system is rewritten, by informally making sure that the refined scheme does not introduce any communication mismatches with respect to the clients.

2. A formal *program refinement* strategy is applied, as described e.g. in [Bac88]. In this case the refinement step from Fig. 1 to Fig. 2 is formally proven correct by showing that the latter scheme preserves the behaviour of the former one.

3. A *protocol conversion* methodology can be used. In protocol conversion [Gre86], two different protocols are merged together by automatically producing a special intermediate machine that "translates" the messages sent by the machine of one protocol into messages accepted by the machine of the other protocol.

4. One can apply the general concept of *software / interface adaptors* [YeS94] to glue together protocols at different layers of the communication architecture. This strategy resembles protocol conversion, especially if the adaptation is based on communicating state machines. The main difference is that the software adaptation technique is more general than protocol conversion, due to accepting the distribution of parameters into several different services, and to being based on advanced software engineering principles such as object-orientation [Tha94].

The first alternative is hopeless in nontrivial cases since the matching has to be done totally by human means without any formal support. The formal step-wise refinement strategy is rather laborous since then the protocol designer has to (a) formally specify the abstract scheme, (b) formally specify the concrete scheme, and (c) formally prove that the latter correctly implements the former. Finally, the related techniques of protocol conversion and software adaptation introduce additional components to the communication architecture, typically one converter/adaptor for each pair of integrated processes; this soon leads to an exhaustive number of components when devising a layered protocol implementation. Moreover, these techniques need some additional information for generating the converter/adaptor, such as a service specification over the client protocols or a description of the synchronized behaviour of the integrated components.

Due to such shortcomings with the conventional solutions, our approach to protocol refinement is based on *object-oriented* techniques: *incremental modification*, *subtyping*, and *code reuse*. The central idea is to avoid the introduction of new system components upon protocol refinement, and instead reuse as much of the existing framework as possible. With regard to our example transition from the abstract scheme in Fig. 1 to the more concrete one in Fig. 2, this means the following:

- The process A' is a modification of the process A. This means that the program code written for A is reused when producing the code for A'. This applies most notably to the (communicating) state machine for A that is incrementally modified to cope with the new protocol scheme. Likewise, the process B' is a modification of the process B.

- The structured layer architecture in Fig. 2 and the flat layer in Fig. 1 (excluding in both cases the external clients *User_A* and *User_B*) are subtypes of the same virtual layer and hence compatible.
- The message flow along the path $A' \rightarrow C \rightarrow D \rightarrow B'$ following the protocols $A'C$, CD, and DB' in Fig. 2 is a refinement of the flow along the path $A \rightarrow B$ by the protocol AB in Fig. 1. Likewise, the message flow along the path $B' \rightarrow D \rightarrow C \rightarrow A'$ in Fig. 2 is a refinement of the flow along the path $B \rightarrow A$ in Fig. 1.

The relation of inheritance and refinement has been analyzed, e.g., in [Cus91]. The notion of refinement is more restrictive than the notion of inheritance: For a component C to be a refinement of a component D, C must guarantee the same behaviour whenever substituted for D. In [WeZ88] such a property of an incremental modification mechanism is called *behavioral compatibility* which is usually not guaranteed by inheritance in object-oriented languages—they usually satisfy just a weaker property, *signature compatibility*. The Kannel refinement mechanism lies between these two notions, since it is based on message signatures, but at the same time imposes an *ordering* for the legal message sequences and allows disciplined transformation of these messages during refinement.

3.2   Definitions

Definition 1. We assume conventionally that the communication between processes is specified as communicating finite state automata (machines), one for each process. A *communicating finite state automaton* $\mathcal{A}$ is a 5-tuple: $\mathcal{A} = (S, s_0, F, M, \delta)$, where S is a finite set of *states*, $s_0 (\in S)$ is the *initial state*, $F (\subseteq S)$ is the set of *final states*, M is a finite set of *messages*, and δ is the *transition function*: $\delta : S \times M \rightarrow S$. The message set M is divided into two subsets: $M = M^i \cup M^o$, where M^i denotes the set of *input* messages (events) and M^o denotes the set of *output* messages. $\mathcal{A}_P$ denotes the finite state automaton associated with the process P. M_P, M_P^i, and M_P^o denote respectively the message set, the input message set, and the output message set of the automaton associated with the process P.

Since state automata are expressed as statecharts in Kannel (see Sect. 4), a transition from a state S to a state T can be associated with an input message $i \in M^i$ and a sequence of output messages $o_1, o_2, \ldots, o_n; \forall i \in [1, n] : o_i \in M^o$, standing for the reception of an incoming event and the immediate sending of the outgoing messages: $\delta(S, (i o_1 o_2 \cdots o_n)) = T$. Such a situation is interpreted as introducing intermediate states S_i for splitting the multi-message transition into singletons: $\delta(S, i) = S_1$, $\delta(S_1, o_1) = S_2$, $\ldots$, $\delta(S_n, o_n) = T$.

Definition 2. Let P and Q be processes associated with a (communicating) finite state automaton. Then M_{PQ}^o denotes the set of *messages from P to Q*, and M_{PQ}^i the set of *messages to P from Q*. These define the communicated message set between P and Q, that is, the set of output messages of the automaton for P (Q) that are also input messages of the automaton for Q (P): $M_{PQ}^o = M_{QP}^i = M_P^o \cap M_Q^i$. The total communication between P and Q is denoted by $M_{PQ}^{io} = M_{QP}^{io} = M_{PQ}^o \cup M_{PQ}^i$. To be able to communicate in both directions, P and Q must have the sets M_{PQ}^o and M_{PQ}^i (M_{QP}^i and M_{QP}^o) nonempty. For notational simplicity, we assume that the communicated message set is different for each different pair of target processes: $M_{PQ}^{io} \cap M_{PR}^{io} = \emptyset$ whenever $Q \neq R$.

Consider the example in Fig. 1. The communication between the processes A and B is specified by two finite state automata, $\mathcal{A}_A$ for A and $\mathcal{A}_B$ for B. Since the process A is communicating with its client $User\_A$ (denoted U) and with its peer B, the set of messages A is processing is divided into the following subsets: $M_A = (M_A^i \cup M_A^o) = (M_{AU}^{io} \cup M_{AB}^{io}) = (M_{AU}^o \cup M_{AU}^i \cup M_{AB}^o \cup M_{AB}^i)$. Likewise, $M_B = (M_B^i \cup M_B^o) = (M_{BV}^{io} \cup M_{BA}^{io}) = (M_{BV}^o \cup M_{BV}^i \cup M_{BA}^o \cup M_{BA}^i)$, where V denotes $User\_B$. Furthermore, $M_{AB}^o = M_{BA}^i$, and $M_{BA}^o = M_{AB}^i$.

As usual, we model the behaviour of a distributed system as sequences of messages, or traces, between the processes in the system (see e.g. [Jon89]). Since the functionality of communicating processes is defined in our approach as finite state automata, we can apply the standard concepts and techniques of automata theory for specifying and analyzing the trace-behaviour of protocols.

Definition 3. Let $\mathcal{A} = (S, s_0, F, M, \delta)$ be a communicating finite state automaton. A *trace* in $\mathcal{A}$, denoted $\mathcal{T}_A$, is a sequence of (input or output) messages associated with a path from the initial state of $\mathcal{A}$ to a final state of $\mathcal{A}$. That is, a message sequence $m_1 m_2 \cdots m_n$ ($\forall i \in [1, n] : m_i \in M$) is a trace, if $\delta(s_0, m_1) = s_1, \delta(s_1, m_2) = s_2, \ldots, \delta(s_{n-1}, m_n) = s_n$ such that $s_n \in F$. The *language* of $\mathcal{A}$, denoted $\mathcal{L}_A$, is the set of traces in $\mathcal{A}$.[1] If the automaton $\mathcal{A}$ is associated with the process P, we denote by $\mathcal{T}_P$ a trace in P and by $\mathcal{L}_P$ the *language* of P.

Definition 4. Let $\mathcal{A} = (S, s_0, F, M, \delta)$ be a communicating finite state automaton, and let $\mathcal{T}_A = m_1 m_2 \cdots m_n$ be a trace in $\mathcal{A}$. Let $N \subseteq M$ be a set of messages. The *projection* of $\mathcal{T}_A$ with respect to N, denoted $\mathcal{T}_A/N$, is a subsequence of $\mathcal{T}_A$ consisting of just the messages in N. That is, $m_i (i \in [1, n])$ is in $\mathcal{T}_A/N$ only if $m_i \in N$.

The refinement of a protocol between processes P and Q is achieved by refining the messages exchanged between P and Q into more concrete ones, by introducing a new protocol layer to implement the abstract protocol, and by modifying the communicating automata associated with P and Q to cope with the new architecture.

---

[1] This corresponds to the concept of language in automata theory. Therefore it is necessary for our automata to have final (accepting) states. Notice that while reactive systems usually do not have a fixed final state from where no progress is possible, even they always have "logical" final states closing a main event loop. Typically a reactive automaton contains a cycle with the initial state as entry; in that case the initial state must be regarded as a final state as well.

To specify this, we give the necessary definitions below. Intuitively, mapping functions are needed for translation between an abstract message and a more concrete one (usually achieved in practice by composing a protocol data unit from a service data unit and embedded local control information, and by decomposing it later on), for splitting a concrete message into several abstract ones (in practice by segmenting a service data unit into a set of protocol data units), and for joining several messages into a single one (in practice by concatenating several protocol data units into a single service data unit).

Definition 5. Let P, Q, and R be processes, such that $\mathcal{A}_P$ and $\mathcal{A}_R$ both communicate directly with $\mathcal{A}_Q$. P and R are *trace-equivalent* with respect to Q, if the following conditions hold: (1) $M_{PQ}^o = M_{RQ}^o$; (2) $M_{PQ}^i = M_{RQ}^i$; (3) $\{\mathcal{T}_P/M_{PQ}^{io} \mid \mathcal{T}_P \in \mathcal{L}_P\} = \{\mathcal{T}_R/M_{RQ}^{io} \mid \mathcal{T}_R \in \mathcal{L}_R\}$.

This definition stands for the fact that the refinement of one communication protocol shall not affect the system's behaviour with respect to the other protocols. When considering the situation in Figs. 1 and 2, the processes A and A' must be trace-equivalent with respect to $User\_A$, and the processes B and B' must be trace-equivalent with respect to $User\_B$.

Definition 6. Let $P_1, P_2, \ldots, P_n, n \geq 2$, be processes such that P_i communicates directly with P_{i+1} via state automata $(i = 1, \ldots, n-1)$. Then $(P_1 P_2 \cdots P_n)$ is called a *configuration*.

For instance, $(User\_A \; A \; B \; User\_B)$ and (AB) are configurations in Fig. 1, and $(User\_A \; A' \; C \; D \; B' \; User\_B)$ and $(A'CDB')$ are configurations in Fig. 2.

Definition 7. Let $\mathcal{T}_P = m_1 m_2 \cdots m_n$ be a trace, let $f : M \to N$ be a function where M and N are sets of messages, and let $S \subseteq M$. Then the *transformation* of $\mathcal{T}_P$ by f and S, denoted $t(\mathcal{T}_P, f, S)$, is the trace $p_1 p_2 \cdots p_n$ where $p_i = f(m_i)$ if $m_i \in S$, and $p_i = m_i$ otherwise; $i = 1, 2, \ldots, n$.

Definition 8. (See Figs. 1 and 2). Let (AB) be a configuration, and let M be a message set. Let $Com(P)$ denote the set of processes with which process P communicates directly. The configuration $(A'CDB')$ is a *refinement* of (AB) if there exist *mapping functions* f_1 (total), f_2, f_3, f_4, g_1 (total), g_2, g_3, and g_4 (M^+ denotes a set whose elements are M-sequences with one or more elements):[2]

$f_1 : M_{AB}^o \to M_{A'C}^o \; (= M_{CA'}^i)$
$f_2 : M_{CA'}^i \to (M_{CD}^o)^+ \; (= (M_{DC}^i)^+)$
$f_3 : (M_{DC}^i)^+ \to M_{DB'}^o \; (= M_{B'D}^i)$
$f_4 : M_{B'D}^i \to M_{BA}^o \; (= M_{AB}^o)$
$g_1 : M_{BA}^o \to M_{B'D}^o \; (= M_{DB'}^i)$
$g_2 : M_{DB'}^i \to (M_{DC}^o)^+ \; (= (M_{CD}^i)^+)$
$g_3 : (M_{CD}^i)^+ \to M_{CA'}^o \; (= M_{A'C}^i)$

---

[2] For more extensive configurations, the definition is similar but involves a larger number of mapping functions.

$$g_4 : M^i_{A'C} \rightarrow M^i_{AB} \; (= M^o_{BA})$$

such that the following conditions hold:

1. $\forall m \in M^o_{AB} : m = f_4(f_3(f_2(f_1(m))))$
2. $\forall n \in M^o_{BA} : n = g_4(g_3(g_2(g_1(n))))$
3. $Com(A') \setminus \{C\} \supseteq Com(A) \setminus \{B\}$, and A' and A are trace-equivalent with respect to every process $P \in Com(A) \setminus \{B\}$
4. $Com(B') \setminus \{D\} \supseteq Com(B) \setminus \{A\}$, and B' and B are trace-equivalent with respect to every process $P \in Com(B) \setminus \{A\}$
5. Each trace in $\{t(T, g_3 \circ g_2 \circ g_1, M^i_{AB}) \mid T = t(\mathcal{T}_A/M^{io}_{AB}, f_1, M^o_{AB})\}$ is a subsequence of a trace in $\{\mathcal{T}_{A'}/M^{io}_{A'C}\}$.
6. Each trace in $\{t(T, f_3 \circ f_2 \circ f_1, M^i_{BA}) \mid T = t(\mathcal{T}_B/M^{io}_{BA}, g_1, M^o_{BA})\}$ is a subsequence of a trace in $\{\mathcal{T}_{B'}/M^{io}_{B'D}\}$.

An example of applying this definition using the Kannel language can be found in Sect. 4.3. The definition of refinement captures the fact that the abstract communication pattern shall remain the same, even when the concrete message path changes. Conditions 1 and 2 above guarantee that each message in the original protocol and process configuration reaches its destination in the corresponding format in the refined protocol/configuration even when having different intermediate representations during the transmission. Conditions 3 and 4 state that the refinement of a protocol shall not affect the external client-wise behaviour of the end processes. Finally, conditions 5 and 6 guarantee that the state automata of the refined processes (A' and B' in Fig. 2) retain the abstract communication protocol with respect to the original processes (A and B in Fig. 1) even when introducing concrete representations for the messages as well as additional communication with the new lower-layer processes (C and D in Fig. 2). In other words, the extended communication must preserve the original traces by the following mapping of messages:

- a message sent as m from $\mathcal{A}_A$ to $\mathcal{A}_B$ is represented as $f_1(m)$ in $\mathcal{A}_{A'}$ (condition 5);
- a message from $\mathcal{A}_B$ received as n in $\mathcal{A}_A$ is represented as $g_3(g_2(g_1(n)))$ in $\mathcal{A}_{A'}$ (condition 5);
- a message sent as o from $\mathcal{A}_B$ to $\mathcal{A}_A$ is represented as $g_1(o)$ in $\mathcal{A}_{B'}$ (condition 6);
- a message from $\mathcal{A}_A$ received as p in $\mathcal{A}_B$ is represented as $f_3(f_2(f_1(p)))$ in $\mathcal{A}_{B'}$ (condition 6).

In general, finding the mapping functions f_i and g_i is very hard without any discipline on the structure of the refinement. Consequently, the refinement mechanism in Kannel involves certain syntactic and semantic restrictions to make it possible to *automatically* find the mapping functions and to verify the refinement conditions.

4 Protocol refinement in Kannel

Kannel is a special-purpose, object-oriented programming language for engineering protocols. In addition to the extensible object-oriented model, the language provides support for such largely protocol-specific issues as distribution, automata, the transfer representation of objects and layering. These mechanisms are difficult to be consistently supported with frameworks only. For example, a Kannel compiler is able to perform strong typing in a distributed context while still retaining freedom for representing the data in various transfer-time formats. Furthermore, support for verifying the correctness of the refinement of a protocol layer can be provided as the supporting mechanisms are built into the Kannel type system. The Kannel protocol engineering environment consists of a number of tools, most significant of which are a graphical editor and a compiler. The graphical editor supports the visual syntax of Kannel and allows textual representation to be merged in for the nonvisual program elements.

A Kannel program consists of a set of communicating objects that are divided into two categories: *local* objects are sequential and may create and hold references to other objects. These properties do not hold for *processes* (distributable objects) as they are allowed to reside in different address spaces during execution. Distributable objects model protocols: they have a concurrent body (given as a Harel statechart [Har87]) that declares the synchronization of processed messages. In effect, the body defines the language accepted by the process. Processes can have several communication points that are called *ports*. The messaging via ports is strongly typed as each associated port pair refers to a *channel* definition that enumerates the allowed message classes.

Processes are used to specify the system on a larger level of granularity, whereas local objects perform conventional computation. Recognizing this, Kannel provides a *visual syntax* for the distributable parts of the language.

The refinement concept is realized in Kannel with mechanisms for grouping and subtyping processes, combined with constructs for layer refinement and event mapping within state machines.

We illustrate the refinement mechanism with a Kannel model of a weather reporting system that consists of a set of sensors connected to a control terminal. The sensors send status reports to the control terminal which keeps track of them and informs the system user about them. First, a generic model is derived which assumes errorless channels between the sensors and the terminal. This model is then refined to use an alternating bit transport service for the sensor reports. We aim to show that (a) this refinement allows maximal reuse of the original model and that (b) although message traces inside the refined system differ from the original model, an analyzer can automatically prove that the original communication scheme is preserved. Due to space limitations, the complete source code for the example is omitted. It is included in the full version of this paper which can be found from `http://www.cs.helsinki.fi/research/kannel/refine.ps`.

4.1 A generic specification of WeatherSystem

Process interfaces The control terminal and the sensors are abstracted into a
WeatherSystem process interface which is used as the basis for subtyping. The
interface specifies the externally visible properties of a process but lacks an
implementation:

> **process interface** WeatherSystem **is**
>   service : CONTROL(**in** Requests, **out** Results);
>   protocol SENSOR **separate**
> **end**

The interface states that its concrete subtypes are prepared to receive any message in the Requests view and may generate any message within the Results
view of the CONTROL channel (views denote sets of unidirectional messages). In
addition, the interface contains a *protocol assertion* that abstracts the kind of
service it internally provides. The assertions are crucial for process refinement,
as we shall see: any channel to be refined must be specified with a protocol
assertion.

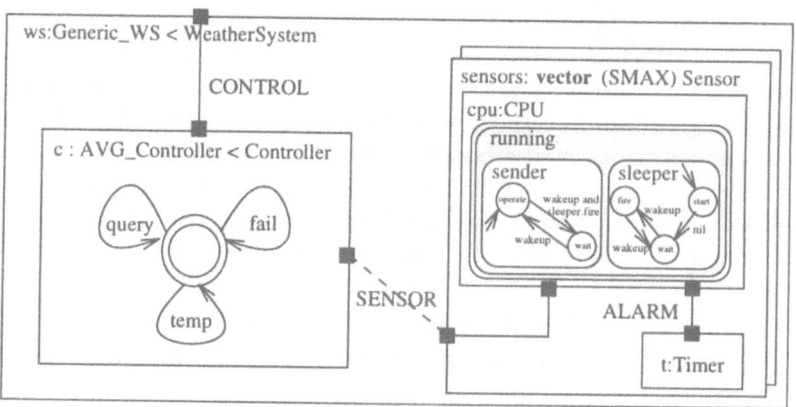

Fig. 3. The Generic_WS process.

The Generic_WS process in Fig. 3 is an architectural description of Weather-
System. The channels connecting the components are depicted as lines between
ports (e.g, SENSOR). Generic_WS groups together a Controller process together
with several Sensor processes. Each Sensor in turn contains a Timer and a CPU
process.

Generic_WS is an example of a (structured) *branch process* used to encapsulate entities that implement a protocol. Unlike *leaf processes* that contain a

controlling statechart, branch processes have no behaviour. Rather, they are used to encapsulate leaf processes and bind the channels between them. Fig. 3 contains three leaf processes: `AVG_Controller`, `CPU` and `Timer`.

Subtyping based on language equivalence An interface for a leaf process enumerates a set of service interfaces for the process. Kannel requires that the languages of the concrete subtypes of an interface are equivalent. For example, when a `Controller` receives a `query` message, it will respond with a `report` (Fig. 3 depicts only message receptions; see the source code for full details): this behaviour is required for all its concrete subtypes (here just `AVG_Controller`), as stated in Definition 8, Sect. 3.

Protocol assertions Every branch process has a *protocol assertion* that indirectly states the protocol implemented by the component processes. The assertion identifies a channel within a subtype of the process; for example, the `SENSOR` assertion within the `WeatherSystem` interface must appear within every concrete subtype of `WeatherSystem`.

Protocol assertions are not just labels; they carry significant semantic weight by imposing the requirement that the endpoints of the channel identified by the assertion *become part of the service interface* of the process for the purposes of type checking. Naturally, the endpoints are not visible to the clients of the process; rather, the language at the endpoint must be the same for every subtype of the process. Protocol assertions are reminiscent to the concept of *structural conformity* in [HaG96]; however, they are more flexible by allowing the designer to leave out the components that are "uninteresting" with regard to layer behaviour (e.g., endpoints of the `ALARM` channel within `Sensor`).

```
process Generic_WS < WeatherSystem is
    c : AVG_Controller;
    sensors : vector (SMAX) Sensor;
        ...
assoc
    SENSOR: c.peer and separate sensors.all.peer;
        c.up and service
    end Generic_WS
```

The (abbreviated) textual definition for `Generic_WS` above specifies its components (`c` and `sensors`) and the channels connecting component ports together. The channels are given in an `assoc` section which specifies all the channels managed by the enclosing process, effectively determining the flow of data within the process. In the example above the first channel (labeled `SENSOR`) connects the controller with all the sensors. The channel is tagged **separate**, implying that the endpoint processes will reside in separate address spaces during execution. The second channel connects the controller to the service interface of the `Generic_WS` process. The port names (e.g. `up`) do not appear in Fig. 3, only the channels connecting the ports are visible. The subtype relation is indicated with

366

a < symbol. Note the required assertion label before the channel between the
sensors and the controller.

4.2 The refinement of Generic_WS

Now we are ready for the refinement of the **SENSOR** channel over an alternating
bit transport service layer. It is important to realize that this involves deriving new versions of the processes connected by **SENSOR**. This is necessary as
the transport layer might introduce additional messages that need to be processed. Furthermore, all communication activity on the **SENSOR** channel must be
adapted to use transport services instead. However, refinement ensures that type
compatibility is retained at the enclosing layer **Generic_WS**.

The mechanisms we are going to present are based on the observations that
(a) the *behaviour* of the processes to be refined does not change at all on service
interfaces except for the one being refined and that (b) the actual structure of
the automata within the original and refined processes does not really matter if
the *language* of the processes (the set of accepted traces) remains the same.

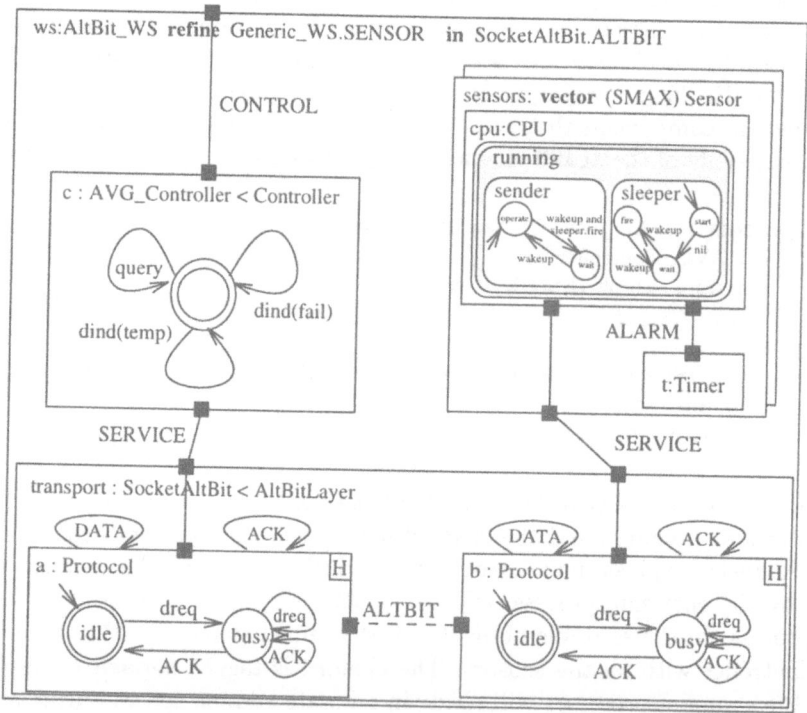

Fig. 4. The refined **AltBit_WS** process.

WeatherSystem

Generic_WS   AltBit_WS

Fig. 5. Subtypes of WeatherSystem.

Figure 4 illustrates the refinement of the Generic_WS process with respect to protocol SENSOR within an alternating bit transfer service (cf. the corresponding abstraction in Fig. 2). Its description is omitted in order to keep the presentation compact. We proceed by presenting the textual form of the mechanisms and by discussing their semantics and effects on code reuse.

Branch process refinement Refinement is done based on a protocol assertion that identifies a channel within a branch process. Thus, the assertion enables stepwise extension of a process' components. The structure of the refined AltBit_WS process is shown below:

```
process AltBit_WS
    refine Generic_WS.SENSOR
          in SocketAltBit.ALTBIT
is
    transport : SocketAltBit
assoc
    transport.up1 and c.peer;
    transport.up2 and sensors.all.peer
end AltBit_WS
```

The subtyping section of the process is replaced with a *refine* clause that names two protocol assertions, the original and its replacement. Note that both assertions are on peer level—we thus establish a binding between two adjacent layers of which the latter is less abstract than the former. The effects of the mechanism are as follows:

- The AltBit_WS process becomes a subtype of the process to which the SENSOR assertion belongs and for which Generic_WS must be a subtype; in this case WeatherSystem.
- The channels and other code (including component names) are reused as is within the AltBit_WS process except for the channel to be refined.
- The leaf processes residing at the endpoints of the refined channel (in this case AVG_Controller and CPU) become undefined and must be superimposed into AltBit_WS as explained below.

Note that the transformed channel endpoints remain unassociated and must be explicitly bound. In our case a new process **transport** is connected with the endpoints. This also resolves any potential ambiguity about the refining component (there might exist more than a single **SocketAltBit** component within **AltBit_WS**).

The resulting type hierarchy is shown in Fig. 5. Note that **AltBit_WS** is *not* a subtype of **Generic_WS** but rather a subtype of its interface—this is in harmony with the Kannel type system which builds on the idea that all type relations are abstract and should not be confused with code reuse.

The leaf processes at the endpoints of the refined channel remain to be respecified. Here the situation is more complex, since their automata are populated with receptions and transmissions of messages that are part of the abstract protocol.

Superimposing leaf processes The types of the original leaf processes and their refinements do *not* remain compatible, since one service interface changes. However, there is still significant similarity that we wish to reuse. By inspecting the leaf processes **CPU** and **AVG_Controller** in Figs. 3 and 4 we find that the send statements in the former and the message receptions in the latter have been changed and must be remapped in order to obtain the refined version:

```
process CPU in AltBit_WS map          process AVG_Controller
  s1 : peer ! dreq(temp.create(unit, t.read));    in AltBit_WS map
  s2 : peer ! dreq(fail.create(unit))             temp,fail in dind
is action                              is action
  running                                AVG_Controller
end CPU;                               end
```

A further consideration in the refinement is that both the original and the refined process definition must coexist within the source code. The formal definitions in the beginning of this paper use naming (e.g. A and A') to solve this, but Kannel uses scoping: the superimposed processes are only defined within the context of the refined branch process. As a result, identical names may be used, providing a more syntactically tractable mechanism.

Specifically, the refinement of leaf processes involves that the subtyping section of the refined process is replaced with a *superimposition* clause **in** α **map** β, where α names the branch process into which the refined leaf process will be superimposed and β provides a transformation mapping for all messages travelling in the abstract channel being refined. As a result of superimposition, the code for the original process (which is identifiable since we know the channel being refined) is reused by inserting it into the refined process definition. During this, those parts of the automaton dealing with the abstract service interface are replaced with parts from the transformation mapping.

The type of the refined leaf process is set identical to the type of the original process except for the single service interface that gets transformed. For **CPU**, the port declaration **peer:SENSOR** is automatically changed into **peer:SERVICE**.

369

The transformation mapping The automata in Kannel are granularized on the
level of message *receptions*: one reception may result in several transmissions
(depending on the transition action). This is a convenient notation for specifying
the behaviour since one does not have to clutter the state space with states which
immediately fire by transmitting a message.

In the context of transformation mappings this extra convenience has a price:
the designer must give explicit labels for all message transmissions into the abstract peer channel; these labels are then used within the mapping to provide
the refined transmission statement. For example, the message transmissions into
the SENSOR channel within the CPU process are wrapped as dreq messages into
the SERVICE channel within the refinement; the original CPU definition contains
the labels s1 and s2 referred to in the mapping. For message receptions the situation is simpler, since they can use the originating state as a natural label. In
our example the receptions within AVG_Controller are all wrapped into dind
messages.

4.3   Ensuring the preservation of behaviour

The notion of branch processes allows one to have type relations between refinements, which is useful in practice. However, a more fundamental issue concerns
the amount of checking a Kannel analyzer can do when confronted with a refinement. The statechart model augmented with the notion of final states allows
us to speak about the language of a process, and subsequently we have more
freedom in modifying the statecharts.

In order to prove the conditions of Definition 8 (Sect. 3) a Kannel analyzer
must first compute the mapping functions $f_1, \ldots, f_4, g_1, \ldots, g_4$. The following
table enumerates these functions for the weather system example:

From AVG_Controller to CPU	From CPU to AVG_Controller
$f_1 : \emptyset \to \emptyset$	$g_1 : \{\text{temp,fail}\} \to \{\text{dreq}\}$
$f_2 : \emptyset \to \{\text{DATA,ACK}\}^+$	$g_2 : \{\text{dreq}\} \to \{\text{DATA,ACK}\}^+$
$f_3 : \{\text{DATA,ACK}\}^+ \to \{\text{dind}\}$	$g_3 : \{\text{DATA,ACK}\}^+ \to \{\text{dind}\}$
$f_4 : \{\text{dind}\} \to \emptyset$	$g_4 : \{\text{dind}\} \to \{\text{temp,fail}\}$

The transformation mapping in refined AVG_Controller provides the analyzer the total functions f_1 and g_4; symmetrically, the transformation mapping
in CPU provides the functions g_1 and f_4. Note that in our example f_1 is an empty
mapping since the communication is unidirectional.

The remaining mappings $f_{2,3}$ and $g_{2,3}$ are defined implicitly by the constraints set upon refinement. They do require, however, that the analyzer can
perform data-flow analysis in order to reveal the mappings. For instance, consider the SENSOR channel of Fig. 3 which is refined in Fig. 4. Assume process
CPU receives message wakeup from Timer and consequently sends message temp
to AVG_Controller. How can we ensure that CPU' (denoting the refined version of CPU) accomplishes the equivalent task? First note that the refinement
provides the transformation mappings M_1 from CPU to CPU' and M_2 from
AVG_Controller' to AVG_Controller.

- By inspecting M_1 we find that **temp** is actually transmitted within **dreq** into the **SERVICE** channel.
- The refinement captures the fact that **SENSOR** is transformed into **ALTBIT**. By performing data-flow analysis for **dreq** within **Protocol** and by inspecting the messages transmitted into its **ALTBIT** channel we can ensure that **dreq** actually gets sent into **ALTBIT** within **DATA.contents** where **DATA** is one of **ALTBIT** messages. This procedure effectively computes g_2.
- By inspecting the refinement we find that the **SERVICE** channel must be followed to reach the other end of the refinement. By performing data-flow analysis for **DATA.contents** within **Protocol** and by inspecting the messages transmitted into its **SERVICE** channel we can ensure that **DATA.contents** actually gets sent into **SERVICE** within message **dind**. This procedure effectively computes g_3.
- By inspecting M_2 we find that a **dind** within **AVG_Controller'** is actually a **temp** within **AVG_Controller**; this accomplishes the checking.

Functions $f_{2,3}$ in the reverse direction are obtained similarly. With the mapping functions ready, the next task for an analyzer is to check that the refinement fulfills the conditions 1–6 of Definition 8. For notational convenience, we abbreviate $A =$ **AVG_Controller**, $B =$ **CPU** and $C = D =$ **Protocol**. As before, A' and B' denote the refined versions of A and B, respectively.

- Condition 1: all messages sent from A to B arrive intact in the refinement. Since $M_{AB}^o = \emptyset$ the condition is trivially met in this case.
- Condition 2: all messages sent from B to A arrive intact in the refinement. Since $M_{BA}^o = \{$temp,fail$\}$ we need to show that $m = g_4(g_3(g_2(g_1(m))))$; $m \in \{$temp,fail$\}$. By performing data-flow analysis, an analyzer can ensure that $m \in \mathrm{ran}(g_4 \circ g_3 \circ g_2 \circ g_1)^3$, i.e. that there exists a data path from B to A. However, proving that the message received by A equals the one sent by B is beyond the capabilities of static analysis.
- Condition 3: the client-visible behaviour of A must not change in the refinement. Since $Com(A') \setminus \{C\} = \{$User$\} \supseteq \{$User$\} = Com(A) \setminus \{B\}$ we have to show that A and A' are trace-equivalent with respect to User.[4] This is easily confirmed by examining the definition of A'. An analyzer, however, must be prepared for the general case and prove the equivalence of traces. Conceptually, this is done as follows. $\mathcal{A}_A$ and $\mathcal{A}_{A'}$ are stripped from all statements not related to communication with $\mathcal{A}_{\mathrm{User}}$. The languages of the resulting automata are then compared for equality (applicable procedures for performing this can be found in e.g. [AhU72]).
- Condition 4: the client-visible behaviour of B must not change in the refinement. Since $Com(B') \setminus \{D\} = \{$Timer$\} \supseteq \{$Timer$\} = Com(B) \setminus \{A\}$ we have to show that B and B' are trace-equivalent with respect to Timer. A procedure similar to the one in the previous item can be applied here.

---

[3] ran$f$ denotes the range of function f.

[4] The User process represents the weather system user connected to the **CONTROL** channel in Fig. 4.

– Condition 5: the abstract communication between A and B is retained between A' and C. In other words, each trace in $t(\mathcal{T}_A/M_{AB}^{io}, g_3 \circ g_2 \circ g_1,$ {temp, fail}) is a subsequence of a trace in $\{\mathcal{T}_{A'}/M_{A'C}^{io}\}$. An analyzer can perform the check as follows. $\mathcal{A}_A$ and $\mathcal{A}_{A'}$ are stripped from all statements not related to communication with $\mathcal{A}_B$ and $\mathcal{A}_C$, respectively. Next, all receptions for a message m in $\mathcal{A}_A$ are renamed as $g_3(g_2(g_1(m)))$.[5] The resulting automata are compared for subset equality, that is $\mathcal{L}_{\mathcal{A}_A} \subseteq \mathcal{L}_{\mathcal{A}_{A'}}$.

– Condition 6: the abstract communication between B and A is retained between B' and D. In other words, each trace in $t(\mathcal{T}_B/M_{BA}^{io}, g_1,$ {temp,fail}) is a subsequence of a trace in $\{\mathcal{T}_{B'}/M_{B'D}^{io}\}$. A procedure similar to the one in the previous item can be applied here; the required renamings in this case are $g_1(m)$ for the transmissions and $f_3(f_2(f_1(m)))$ for the (in this case nonexisting) receptions, respectively.

4.4 Discussion

The distinction between subtyping and code reuse extends quite naturally in Kannel from local classes to processes. With processes, subtyping considers the language induced by their state automata. Since the concept of language has no forced relation with any fixed automaton, subprocesses of a process interface may use any means whatsoever to implement it. Consequently, the reuse mechanism is quite liberal, allowing practically any modifications to a reused state machine. This differs from approaches that use inheritance for automata reuse and hence have to place severe restrictions on the set of allowed modifications [HaG96,McM93,CHB92].

A precondition for comparing the languages induced by the statecharts using conventional methods (e.g. [AhU72]) is that they can be transformed into regular state automata. Our recent work suggests that this is indeed feasible with the possible exception of the statechart history mechanism.

5 Conclusions

We have presented a systematic methodology for developing distributed applications by stepwise refinement of communication protocols over a layered architecture. The central characteristics of the problem of protocol refinement have been formalized and potential solutions have been outlined.

As a practical approach to protocol refinement, we have shown how the mechanism can be expressed and implemented using object-oriented principles in the protocol engineering language Kannel. As far as we know, similar facilities are not provided in any other (protocol engineering) language. Most notably, the popular standard languages for distributed applications, SDL [BeH89] (or its object-oriented dialect SDL-92 [FæO92]), Estelle [BuD87], LOTOS [BoB87], and ASN.1 [Ste90] do not provide refinement as a built-in mechanism.

---

[5] Similarly, all transmissions of a message m in $\mathcal{A}_A$ are renamed as $f_1(m)$; however, this does not apply here since our example only uses unidirectional communication.

With regard to other suggested approaches, the main novelty of ours is being *constructive* rather than theoretical. Unlike the formal refinement approaches (e.g. [Bac88]) whose main objective is to employ formal specifications to formally prove the correctness of system evolution, we have developed a programming language by which a protocol designer can express the system evolution on a proper level of preciseness. The task of verifying the refinement is laid on the Kannel system, not on the designer. Most notably, the verification ensures that the abstract and refined protocols have compatible behaviour where the notion of behaviour means the equivalence of languages over communicated messages.

Being object-oriented in general, Kannel shares some features with general-purpose object-oriented programming languages, such as Eiffel [Mey92] and Sather [SOM93]. The key difference to these is that Kannel is a special-purpose language with a number of facilities tuned towards protocol engineering. For instance, the refinement mechanism presented in this paper is not intended for applications of arbitrary kind but for the development of distributed systems with a communication protocol in the core. By focusing refinement on one ("peer") side of a process interface at a time, our approach shares some ideas with dividing the interface of a class into two distinct categories, a client interface and a specialization interface [Lam93].

From the applications' point of view, Kannel is closely related to the formal language family of telecommunications, in particular to the object-oriented variant of SDL, *SDL-92* (OSDL) [FæO92]. With respect to the theme of this paper, these two languages differ in that Kannel considers incremental refinement as a semantic mechanism of special kind, whereas a similar effect has to be simulated in SDL-92 using conventional object-oriented inheritance and virtuals without formal support.

An implementation of the core constructs of Kannel is complete, as a translator into C++. The refinement mechanism described in this paper is currently under implementation. In addition to the translator, the Kannel system currently contains a visual program editor and a graphical simulator.

References

[AhU72] A.V. Aho, J.D. Ullman: *The Theory of Parsing, Translation and Compiling.* Volume I:Parsing. Prentice-Hall, 1972.

[Bac88] R.J.R. Back: A Calculus of Refinements for Program Derivations. *Acta Informatica* 25, 1988, 593–624.

[BeH89] F. Belina, D. Hogrefe: The CCITT Specification and Description Language SDL. *Computer Networks and ISDN Systems* 16, 4, 1989, 311–341.

[BoB87] T. Bolognesi, E. Brinksma: Introduction to the ISO Specification Language LOTOS. *Computer Networks and ISDN Systems* 14, 1, 1987, 25–59.

[BuD87] S. Budkowski, P. Dembinski: An Introduction to ESTELLE: A Specification Language for Distributed Systems. *Computer Networks and ISDN Systems* 14, 1, 1987, 3–23.

[CHB92] D. Coleman, F. Hayes, S. Bear: Introducing Objectcharts or How to Use Statecharts in Object-Oriented Design. *IEEE Transactions on Software Engineering* 18, 1, 1992, 9–18.

[Cus91] E. Cusack: Refinement, Conformance and Inheritance. *Formal Aspects of Computing* 3, 1991, 129–141.

[FæO92] O. Færgemand, A. Olsen: Introduction to SDL-92. *Computer Networks and ISDN Systems* 26, 1994, 1143–1167.

[Gre86] P.E. Green, Jr.: Protocol Conversion. *IEEE Transactions on Communications* 34, 3, 1986, 257–268.

[GHJ95] K. Granö, J. Harju, T. Järvinen, T. Larikka, J. Paakki: Object-Oriented Protocol Design and Reuse in Kannel. In: *Proc. 21st EUROMICRO Conf. on the Design of Hardware/Software Systems* (EUROMICRO'95), Como, Italy, 1995. IEEE Computer Society Press, 1995, 465–472.

[GHP94] K. Granö, J. Harju, J. Paakki, T. Järvinen: Proposal for a Protocol Engineering Language. Technical Reports TR-6, Department of Computer Science and Information Systems, University of Jyväskylä, 1994.

[HaG96] D. Harel, E. Gery: Executable Object Modeling with Statecharts. In: *Proc. 18th International Conf. on Software Engineering* (ICSE-18), Berlin, Germany, 1996. IEEE Computer Society Press, 1996, 246–257.

[Har87] D. Harel: Statecharts: A Visual Approach to Complex Systems. *Science of Computer Programming* 8, 1987, 231–274.

[Jon89] B. Jonsson: On Decomposing and Refining Specifications of Distributed Systems. In: *Stepwise Refinement of Distributed Systems*. Lecture Notes in Computer Science 430, Springer-Verlag, 1989, 361–385.

[Lam93] J. Lamping: Typing the Specialization Interface. In: Proc. OOPSLA'93, Washington, DC. *ACM SIGPLAN Notices* 28, 10, 1993, 201–214.

[McM93] J.D. McGregor, D.M. Dyer: A Note on Inheritance and State Machines. *ACM SIGPLAN Notices* 18, 4, 1993, 61–69.

[Mey92] B. Meyer: *Eiffel — The Language*. Prentice-Hall, 1992.

[SOM93] C. Szyperski, S. Omohundro, S. Murer: Engineering a Programming Language: The Type and Class System of Sather. In: J. Gutknecht (ed.): *Programming Languages and System Architectures*. Lecture Notes in Computer Science 782, Springer-Verlag, 1993, 208–227.

[Ste90] D. Steedman: *ASN.1 — Tutorial & Reference*. Technology Appraisals Ltd., 1990.

[Tha94] S.R. Thatté: Automated Synthesis of Interface Adapters for Reusable Classes. In: *Conf. Record 21st ACM SIGACT-SIGPLAN Symp. on Principles of Programming Languages* (POPL'94), Portland, Oregon, 1994, 174–187.

[WeZ88] P. Wegner, S.B. Zdonik: Inheritance as an Incremental Modification Mechanism or What Like Is and Isn't Like. In: *Proc. Second European Conf. on Object-Oriented Programming* (ECOOP'88), Oslo, Norway, 1988. Lecture Notes in Computer Science 322, Springer-Verlag, 1988, 55–77.

[YeS94] D.M. Yellin, R.E. Strom: Interfaces, Protocols, and the Semi-Automatic Construction of Software Adaptors. In: Proc. OOPSLA'94, Portland, Oregon. *ACM SIGPLAN Notices* 29, 10, 1994, 176–190.

An Asynchronous Model of Locality, Failure, and Process Mobility

Roberto M. Amadio

Université de Provence (LIM), Marseille *

Abstract. We present a model of distributed computation which is based on a fragment of the π-calculus relying on *asynchronous* communication. We enrich the model with the following features: the explicit distribution of processes to locations, the failure of locations and their detection, and the mobility of processes. Our contributions are two folds. At the specification level, we give a synthetic and flexible formalization of the features mentioned above. At the verification level, we provide original methods to reason about the bisimilarity of processes in the presence of failures. *Keywords:* π-calculus. Bisimulation. Asynchronous communication. Locations. Models of distributed systems. Failures and failures' detection. Mobility of processes.

1 Introduction

Traditional process calculi such as CCS and CSP lie their foundations on a reduced set of concepts and therefore do not provide direct support for the modeling of certain relevant aspects of systems such as the distribution of resources on different locations, the impact of failures on the behaviour of the system, the detection of failures, and the mobility of processes (the exact meaning of these terms will become clearer, as we progress in our discussion). This paper pursues a research line initiated in [4], in which an explicit modeling of the features mentioned above is specified, and then a reduction to a more basic model is sought.

In carrying on this programme, we rely on a π-calculus formalism [13]. In first approximation, the π-calculus models systems of asynchronous processes which interact by message passing. The calculus embodies features such as dynamic process creation, dynamic channel creation, transmission of channel names, and a static scoping discipline. The blending of these features has led to a calculus which is quite expressive and close to programming issues, while having a tractable semantic theory.

We select a variety of π-calculus as the basic model on which additional features are added. The advantage of this approach is that notions and results can be inherited and stated, respectively, within the theory of the π-calculus. The

* CMI, 39 rue Joliot-Curie F-13453, Marseille, France. amadio@gyptis.univ-mrs.fr. This work was partially supported by CTI-CNET 95-1B-182, Cefipra project 1502-1, and Working group Confer.

disadvantage is that to understand this paper some knowledge of the π-calculus is required.

The variety of π-calculus we consider is a fragment of the *asynchronous π-calculus* [11, 6]. In this calculus, the sending of a message is non-blocking, that is a process can deliver a message without waiting for a receiving process (think of e-mail). This communication model implicitly relies on a non-bounded buffer in which messages can be stocked. Messages in the buffer can be reordered in arbitrary ways (the buffer does not obey a FIFO discipline).

We consider a fragment of the asynchronous π-calculus in which every channel name is associated with a *unique* (persistent) process which may receive messages addressed to that name (communication becomes point-to-point). To emphasize the unicity of the receptor, we will refer to this fragment as the π_1-calculus. Technically, the π_1-calculus is formalized by means of a simple typing discipline which enjoys a suitable subject reduction property. We show that the π_1-calculus is sufficiently expressive to simulate the asynchronous π-calculus (with multiple receivers). We also observe that by restricting the syntax to "functional" processes, we can define an expressive sub-calculus where (internal) reduction is *confluent*.

Starting from the π_1-calculus, we specify in an incremental way the features we are interested in: (1) We explicitly distribute processes to *locations*. Locations are our unit of distribution and they can be generated dynamically. (2) Locations are also our unit of *failure*. A location can fail, entailing the failure of all processes running on it. (3) We specify an operator to *spawn* a process at a remote location. It is then possible to compute a process with an environment (a closure) at a location, and start its execution at another location. (4) We specify an operator to *detect the failure* of a location.

There is a variety of choices to be made concerning the model of failures (halting, transient, byzantine,...), the exact kind of mobility of processes which is allowed and its impact on message routing, and the power of the failure detectors. We will not try to cover all possible combinations of these choices, instead we will study in depth a simple model while hinting to possible variations.

In first approximation, we will consider a system of asynchronous processes which interact by asynchronous message passing. Processes are distributed to locations which can stop (halting failure), they can spawn processes at remote locations (possibly under certain conditions which keep the routing problem simple), and they can consult a perfect oracle which will eventually say if a location has failed or not.

Related work Our previous work on Facile [4], is based on a synchronous communication model with multiple receivers. Hence a communication may require a synchronization between processes distributed to three different locations: the location of the sender, the location of the receiver, and the location of the channel manager (which is a process which has to resolve concurrent requests for reading or writing on a channel). The work on the join calculus [9], suggests that a simplification of the communication primitive (asynchronous communication with a unique receiver) can considerably simplify reasoning about a system where failures can occur. Technically, the π_1-calculus can be regarded as a way to capture some basic features of the join calculus, e.g. unicity of the receptor, by imposing a type discipline rather than by modifying the π-calculus. One advantage of this approach, is that it is possible to reuse technical insights already developed for the (asynchronous) π-calculus such as labelled transition system, and proof techniques based on bisimulation [2].

Besides Facile, other programming languages which address (some of) the issues of locations, failures, and process mobility include CML, Erlang, Java, Pict, Obliq, Oz, and Telescript. Like Facile, they lack a complete formal definition, and a fortiori any serious technique to reason about program equivalence.

The definition and analysis of systems where failures can occur, has also been the subject of a number of studies in the *distributed algorithms* community in the last decade. In these studies, a system is roughly the (asynchronous) product of a *finite* number of labelled transition systems. The way the labelled transition systems are generated is either ignored or informally specified. It follows that it is impossible to study issues such as process equivalence, model-checking, scoping, and process mobility.

Although this was not our initial aim, it appears that our model can be regarded as a "coordination model", at least as long as the goal of a coordination model is to abstract the behaviour of individual modules (software or hardware components) and concentrate on their "interaction" in the overall system organization. Certainly, one level of interaction is the exchange of information between modules. Thus "coordination primitives" are quite close to the "communication primitives" considered in concurrency theory. There are other aspects of interaction which have been brought to the limelight by advances in network computing. These aspects certainly include the distribution, fault-resilience, and mobility of network resources. We provide a synthetic and flexible specification of these features.

Paper organization The rest of this paper is organised as follows. In sections 2 and 3, we define our model and illustrate its expressiveness. In particular, in section 2 we present the π_1-calculus, and study its typing system (theorem 1), and in section 3, we incrementally define the π_{1l}-calculus as an enrichment of the π_1-calculus where locations, failures, mobility of processes, and failure detectors are explicitly modelled.

In section 4, we turn to semantic issues. Our goal is to develop techniques to prove the bisimilarity of processes. In particular, we study characterizations of contextual equivalences, and calculi translations. We define an adequate translation (theorem 10) from the π_{1l}-calculus to the π_1-calculus. Next, we characterize barbed equivalence (a contextual equivalence) for the π_1-calculus (theorem 15). The tool we use is a recently introduced notion of asynchronous bisimulation [2]. We also show that there is a fragment of the π_{1l}-calculus for which the translation into the π_1-calculus is fully abstract, and we formalize the fact that in our model distribution is *transparent* in the absence of failures. Because of space limitations we will omit proofs and examples. They can be found in [1].

2   The asynchronous π_1-calculus

We start by considering a polyadic, asynchronous π-calculus whose processes are specified as follows (we often omit parentheses):

$$p ::= a(\mathbf{b}).p \mid \bar{a}\mathbf{b} \mid p \mid p \mid 0 \mid \nu a\, p \mid (\mathbf{rec}A(\tilde{a}).p)(\tilde{b}) \mid A(\tilde{a}) \mid [a = b]p, q \qquad (1)$$

We collect here some basic conventions. We denote with $a, b, \ldots$ channel names, with $\mathbf{a}, \mathbf{b}, \ldots$ vectors of channel names, with $\tilde{a}$ two vectors of channel names separated by a ";", say $\mathbf{a_1}; \mathbf{a_2}$ (either vector can be empty), and with $p, q, \ldots$ processes. The sets $fn(p)$, $bn(p)$ contain, respectively, the names free and bound in the process p. If $\mathbf{a}$ is a vector of names, we denote with $\{\mathbf{a}\}$ the corresponding set. If $\tilde{a} = \mathbf{a_1}; \mathbf{a_2}$ then we let $\tilde{a}_{io} = \mathbf{a_1}$, $\tilde{a}_o = \mathbf{a_2}$, and $\{\tilde{a}\} = \{\mathbf{a_1}\} \cup \{\mathbf{a_2}\}$. Intuitively, in a recursive definition, we distinguish between the names $\tilde{a}_{io}$ that can be used in input and output, and the names $\tilde{a}_o$ that can be used in output only. Correspondingly, every process identifier A has two arities $ar_{io}(A)$ and $ar_o(A)$: $ar_{io}(A)$ is the number of parameters that can be used in input and output, whereas $ar_o(A)$ is the number of parameters that can be used only in output. In a well-formed process, actual and formal parameters agree, and all process identifiers are bound. In a recursive definition $(\mathbf{rec}A(\tilde{a}).p)(\tilde{b})$, we suppose that $fn(p) \subseteq \{\tilde{a}_{io}, \tilde{a}_o\}$. To define recursive processes, we will also rely on parametric equations as an equivalent notation. The equivalence $\equiv$ stands for syntactic identity up to renaming of bound names.

Sorts are defined as follows: $s ::= Ch(s_1, \ldots, s_n)$, where $n \geq 0$. A channel of sort $Ch(s_1, \ldots, s_n)$ can carry a tuple $c_1, \ldots, c_n$, where c_i has sort s_i, for $i = 1, \ldots, n$. We suppose that every name a has a sort s which we denote with $st(a)$, that there are infinitely many names for every sort, and that terms are well-sorted. The basic reduction rule of this calculus is: $a(\mathbf{b}).p \mid \bar{a}\mathbf{c} \to [\mathbf{c}/\mathbf{b}]p$. The behaviour of a process is completely described by a labelled transition system (lts), whose actions α are specified as follows: $\alpha ::= \tau \mid ab \mid \nu\{c\}\,\bar{a}b$. In $\nu\{c\}\,\bar{a}b$, we suppose that $a \notin \{c\} \subseteq \{b\}$. Conventionally, we set $n(\alpha) = fn(\alpha) \cup bn(\alpha)$ where: $fn(\tau) = \emptyset$, $fn(ab) = \{a\} \cup \{b\}$, and $fn(\nu\{c\}\,\bar{a}b) = \{a, b\}\setminus\{c\}$, $bn(\tau) = \emptyset$, $bn(\bar{a}b) = \emptyset$, $bn(\nu\{c\}\,\bar{a}b) = \{c\}$.

The labelled transition system is specified in figure 1, following an early instantiation style. The notion of *weak* transition is defined as usual: $p \stackrel{\tau}{\Rightarrow} p'$ iff $p(\stackrel{\tau}{\to})^*p'$, and, for $\alpha \neq \tau$, $p \stackrel{\alpha}{\Rightarrow} p'$ iff $p \stackrel{\tau}{\Rightarrow} \cdot \stackrel{\alpha}{\to} \cdot \stackrel{\tau}{\Rightarrow} p'$.

The π_1-calculus   The π_1-calculus is a *typed* version of the asynchronous π-calculus. A typing context Γ, is a set of names $\{a_1, \ldots, a_n\}$. In figure 2, we introduce a system to prove when a process p is well-typed in the context Γ. The typing rules rely on the following intuitions: (1) If $a \in \Gamma$ then there is *exactly* one (persistent) process that is allowed to receive on a. (2) Property (1) has to be preserved by labelled transitions. (3) Whenever we create a name, we have to make sure that a unique receiving process is associated to that name.

The typing rules apply to processes with free process identifiers, as to type a recursive definition we need to type a process where the related process identifier is free. The actual parameters of a recursive definition provide a kind of

$$(in) \quad \overline{a(b).p \xrightarrow{\;ac\;} [c/b]p} \qquad\qquad (out) \quad \overline{\overline{ab} \xrightarrow{\;\overline{ab}\;} 0}$$

$$(out_{ex}) \quad \frac{p \xrightarrow{\;\nu\{c\}\,\overline{ab}\;} p' \quad a \neq d \quad d \in \{b\}\setminus\{c\}}{\nu d\,p \xrightarrow{\;\nu\{d,c\}\,\overline{ab}\;} p'} \qquad (\nu) \quad \frac{p \xrightarrow{\;\alpha\;} p' \quad a \notin n(\alpha)}{\nu a\,p \xrightarrow{\;\alpha\;} \nu a\,p'}$$

$$(cp) \quad \frac{p \xrightarrow{\;\alpha\;} p' \quad bn(\alpha) \cap fn(q) = \emptyset}{p \mid q \xrightarrow{\;\alpha\;} p' \mid q} \qquad (cm) \quad \frac{p \xrightarrow{\;\nu\{c\}\,\overline{ab}\;} p' \quad q \xrightarrow{\;ab\;} q' \quad \{c\} \cap fn(q) = \emptyset}{p \mid q \xrightarrow{\;\tau\;} \nu c\,(p' \mid q')}$$

$$(rec) \quad \frac{[recA(\tilde a).p/A, \tilde b/\tilde a]p \xrightarrow{\;\alpha\;} p'}{(recA(\tilde a).p)(\tilde b) \xrightarrow{\;\alpha\;} p'} \qquad (cg) \quad \frac{p \equiv p' \quad p' \xrightarrow{\;\alpha\;} q' \quad q' \equiv q}{p \xrightarrow{\;\alpha\;} q}$$

$$(m_t) \quad \frac{p \xrightarrow{\;\alpha\;} p'}{[a=a]p,q \xrightarrow{\;\alpha\;} p'} \qquad\qquad (m_f) \quad \frac{q \xrightarrow{\;\alpha\;} q' \quad a \neq b}{[a=b]p,q \xrightarrow{\;\alpha\;} q'}$$

Fig. 1. Labelled transition system for the asynchronous polyadic π-calculus

declaration of the channel names on which the defined process intends to perform input/output actions, and output actions, respectively. The typing system makes a "linear" use of the names in the context, and in this respect it has some points in common with other typing systems which have been proposed for the π-calculus (cf., e.g., [12]). What appears to be original, is the handling of the input prefix and of the recursive definitions. Note that in a recursive definition we require that the number of distinct actual io-parameters equals the io-arity of the process identifier ($\#\{\tilde b_{io}\} = ar_{io}(A)$). Hence, the typing under a process identifier is performed under the hypothesis that all actual io-parameters are distinct.

Suppose $\Gamma \vdash p$, where p cannot be decomposed in the parallel composition of other processes (p is a thread). Then Γ can be considered as the "interface" of the process p, that is the names of the channels on which p may receive messages. There are two natural variations on this idea: (i) We can ask that an interface is composed of exactly one channel name. This variation makes programming a bit more cumbersome as a process receives all its messages through one channel and it has to filter them after reception. (ii) We allow non-empty intersections of the interfaces, thus introducing multiple receivers. This may ease programming, on the other hand it complicates a bit the mobility issue. If we want to keep the idea that a communication depends only on the location of the receiver then, when a process moves, it should move with all processes whose interfaces intersect the one of the moving process (and so on recursively).

We can show that typing is preserved by labelled transitions. Typing contexts are not affected by labelled transitions but in the case of scope extrusion. We note that a context never shrinks, this is because the π_1-calculus always keeps a trace of the running processes, even when they are virtually terminated as in the process $Idle(a)$ (cf. figure 3). This entails that if two processes are typed with respect to the same context, then this property is preserved by labelled transitions. [2]

$$\overline{\emptyset \vdash 0} \qquad\qquad \overline{\emptyset \vdash \overline{a}b}$$

$$\frac{\Gamma_1 \vdash p_1 \quad \Gamma_2 \vdash p_2 \quad \Gamma_1 \cap \Gamma_2 = \emptyset}{\Gamma_1 \cup \Gamma_2 \vdash p_1 \mid p_2} \qquad \frac{\Gamma \cup \{a\} \vdash p \quad a \notin \Gamma}{\Gamma \vdash \nu a\, p}$$

$$\frac{\Gamma \vdash p \quad a \in \Gamma \quad \Gamma \cap \{b\} = \emptyset}{\Gamma \vdash a(b).p} \qquad \frac{\{\tilde{a}_{io}\} \vdash p \quad \sharp\{\tilde{b}_{io}\} = ar_{io}(A)}{\{\tilde{b}_{io}\} \vdash (recA(\tilde{a}).p)(\tilde{b})}$$

$$\frac{\sharp\{\tilde{a}_{io}\} = ar_{io}(A)}{\{\tilde{a}_{io}\} \vdash A(\tilde{a})} \qquad \frac{\Gamma \vdash p \quad \Gamma \vdash q}{\Gamma \vdash [a = b]p, q}$$

Fig. 2. Typing rules for the π_1-calculus

Let σ be a name substitution which is the identity almost everywhere. We say that σ is injective on a context Γ, if σ restricted to Γ is injective. We write $\sigma\Gamma$ for $\{\sigma a \mid a \in \Gamma\}$, and σp for the application of the substitution σ to the process p. We observe that: (1) If $\Gamma \vdash p$, and σ is an injective substitution on Γ, then $\sigma\Gamma \vdash \sigma p$, and (2) If $\{\tilde{a}_{io}\} \vdash p$ and $\sharp\{\tilde{b}_{io}\} = ar_{io}(A)$ then $\{\tilde{b}_{io}\} \vdash [recA(\tilde{a}).p/A, \tilde{b}/\tilde{a}]p$. From this, we can prove the following theorem by induction on the derivation of the transition $p \xrightarrow{\alpha} p'$ and analysis of the last typing rule applied.

Theorem 1 subject reduction. *If $\Gamma \vdash p$ and $p \xrightarrow{\alpha} p'$ then $\Gamma \cup bn(\alpha) \vdash p'$.*

Barbed bisimulation We provide some insight on the way π_1-processes can be observed. For the time being, we will just introduce a notion of barbed bisimulation which is sufficient to argue about the *adequacy* of various encodings. In section 4, we will develop a notion of (asynchronous) bisimulation for the π_1-calculus based on the lts in figure 1.

As for the asynchronous π-calculus, we should suppose that only output actions are visible. Intuitively, since communication is asynchronous the observer has no way of knowing when an input action is carried on (we refer to [11, 2] for a more extended discussion). There is also an additional hypothesis that

---

[2] In the typing system in figure 2 we make a *linear* use of hypotheses. One may consider a slightly more liberal system which includes a *weakening* rule. In this case, we can replace the "bizarre" process *Idle* with **0** and still type all definitions in figure 3. In this paper we stick to linear typing because it gives us directly the "least" context needed to type a process, and thus makes the definition 12 of bisimulation simpler.

should be made, namely we suppose that an output action is visible only if the corresponding receptor is not defined in the observed process (otherwise the resulting process would not be well-typed). The context Γ tells us exactly what are the receptors defined in the process p. Hence if $\Gamma \vdash p$, then we can only observe output commitments on names which are not in Γ.

Definition 2 commitment. Suppose $\Gamma \vdash p$. We write $p \downarrow \bar{a}$ if $p \xrightarrow{\alpha} p'$, $\alpha \equiv \nu\{c\}\,\bar{a}b$, and $a \notin \Gamma$. We also write $p \Downarrow \bar{a}$ if $p \xRightarrow{\tau} p'$ and $p' \downarrow \bar{a}$.

Definition 3 barbed bisimulation. A symmetric relation S on π_1-terms is a strong *barbed bisimulation* if whenever pSq the following holds: (1) If $p \downarrow \bar{a}$ then $q \downarrow \bar{a}$. If $p \xrightarrow{\tau} p'$ then $q \xrightarrow{\tau} q'$ and $p'Sq'$.

Let $\overset{\bullet}{\sim}$ be the largest barbed bisimulation. The notion of weak barbed bisimulation is obtained by replacing everywhere the commitment $\downarrow$ with $\Downarrow$, and the reduction $\xrightarrow{\tau}$ with $\xRightarrow{\tau}$. We denote with $\overset{\bullet}{\approx}$ the largest weak barbed bisimulation.

Derived operators Our next goal is to provide evidence for the expressiveness of the π_1-calculus. Towards this end, we introduce in figure 3 a few *derived* operators which allow for a more handy notation. For each operator, we show the derived typing and (internal) reduction rules. In the following, we give some intuition, and state some properties of these operators.

- The process $Idle(\mathbf{a})$ can be regarded as a process which declares the channels a for input/output but never actually uses them.

- Using the idle process, we can type a process that *receives only once* on a channel.

- The replicated input operator is particularly interesting. The process $a(\mathbf{b}) \triangleright p$ (if we had π-calculus replication, we could write this process as $!(a(\mathbf{b}).p)$) can be regarded as a *functional* or *stateless* process. This feature can be formalised as follows.

Definition 4 π_{1f}-calculus. Let the π_{1f}-calculus (f for functional) be the sub-calculus of the π_1-calculus in which we allow input prefix and recursion only as macro expansions of processes of the shape $a(\mathbf{b}) \triangleright p$.

Let $\equiv_1$ be a structural equivalence which includes besides α-renaming, the laws for the commutation of restriction with restriction and parallel composition, and the laws for the associativity and commutativity of parallel composition.

Proposition 5 confluence. *In the π_{1f}-calculus, τ-reduction is confluent modulo $\equiv_1$.*

We note that the typing rules forbid the nesting of replicated inputs on free names. Indeed, this would break the property that each channel has at most one receiver. Nevertheless, the π_{1f}-calculus is still quite expressive. For instance, one can adequately encode the simply typed call-by-value λ-calculus (it is enough to replicate all inputs in the coding described in [3]). Roughly, one can think of the

Idle
$$Idle(\mathbf{a}) \equiv (\mathbf{rec}A(\mathbf{b};).A(\mathbf{b};))(\mathbf{a};)$$

$$\frac{\sharp\{\mathbf{a}\} = ar_{io}(A)}{\{\mathbf{a}\} \vdash Idle(\mathbf{a})}$$

Input once
$$a(\mathbf{b}) : p \equiv a(\mathbf{b}).(p \mid Idle(a))$$

$$\frac{\Gamma \vdash p \quad a \notin \Gamma}{\Gamma \cup \{a\} \vdash a(\mathbf{b}) : p} \qquad a(\mathbf{b}) : p \mid \bar{a}\mathbf{c} \to [\mathbf{c}/\mathbf{b}]p \mid Idle(a)$$

Replicated input $a(\mathbf{b}) \triangleright p \equiv (\mathbf{rec}A(a;\mathbf{a}').a(\mathbf{b}).(A(a;\mathbf{a}') \mid p))(a;\mathbf{a}')$
$fn(p) \subseteq \{\mathbf{b}\} \cup \{\mathbf{a}'\} \cup \{a\}$, which are pairwise disjoint sets.

$$\frac{\emptyset \vdash p \quad a \notin \{\mathbf{b}\}}{\{a\} \vdash a(\mathbf{b}) \triangleright p} \qquad a(\mathbf{b}) \triangleright p \mid \bar{a}\mathbf{c} \to a(\mathbf{b}) \triangleright p \mid [\mathbf{c}/\mathbf{b}]p$$

Booleans
$$(\mathbf{if}\ c\ \mathbf{then}\ p\ \mathbf{else}\ q) \equiv [c_1 = c_2]p, q$$

$$\bar{a}\mathbf{t}, \mathbf{b} \equiv \nu c_1\,(\bar{a}c_1, c_1, \mathbf{b} \mid Idle(c_1))$$
$$\bar{a}\mathbf{f}, \mathbf{b} \equiv \nu c_1\,\nu c_2\,(\bar{a}c_1, c_2, \mathbf{b} \mid Idle(c_1, c_2))$$

$$\frac{\Gamma \vdash p \quad \Gamma \vdash q}{\Gamma \vdash \mathbf{if}\ c\ \mathbf{then}\ p\ \mathbf{else}\ q}$$

Internal choice
$$p \oplus q \equiv \nu a\,(a(c) : \mathbf{if}\ c\ \mathbf{then}\ p\ \mathbf{else}\ q \mid \bar{a}\mathbf{t} \mid \bar{a}\mathbf{f})$$

$$\frac{\Gamma \vdash p \quad \Gamma \vdash q}{\Gamma \vdash p \oplus q} \qquad p \oplus q \to \cdot \sim_a p \quad p \oplus q \to \cdot \sim_a q$$

Link
$$a \mapsto b \equiv Link(a;b) = a(c) \triangleright \nu d\,(\bar{b}d \mid Link(d;c))$$

$$\frac{}{\{a\} \vdash a \mapsto b} \quad (\bar{a}c \mid a \mapsto b) \to a \mapsto b \mid \nu d\,(\bar{b}d \mid d \mapsto c)$$

Fig. 3. Derived operators

join calculus [9] as the π_{1f}-calculus extended with the *join operator*. The join operator allows to receive two (or more) messages as an atomic operation. This feature is essential in programming non-functional processes; in particular using the join, one can represent a variant of the *channel manager* described in the following figure 5 (which can be understood as a process with two states).

• Boolean values **t** and **f** are coded as a pair of fresh names (equal for **t** and distinct for **f**). We use **bool** as an abbreviation for $Ch(), Ch()$ (which is a list of sorts). If c is a pair, we denote with c_1 the first component and with c_2 the second. An **if_then_else_** operator can then be simulated relying on the matching operator. Using the **if_then_else_**, we can code an internal choice operator (the equivalence $\sim_a$ stands for strong bisimulation and will be defined in 12). It is possible to code the if_then_else_ and the internal choice operators without using the matching operator, however in this case the typing rules are less general. [3]

Another useful translation, is the one into a monadic π-calculus where all transmitted vectors of names have length one. In the monadic calculus, we assume that all names have a sort s satisfying the recursive equation $s = Ch(s)$. By analogy with the untyped λ-calculus, we call this the *unsorted* monadic π_1-calculus. We observe that the translation presented in [7] from the polyadic to the monadic asynchronous π-calculus can be typed in our framework. We outline the translation in figure 4.

$$\langle \bar{a}b_1, \ldots, b_n \rangle \quad = \nu c \, (\bar{a}c \mid c(d).(\bar{d}b_1 \mid \cdots \mid c(d).(\bar{d}b_{n-1} \mid c(d) : \bar{d}b_n) \cdots))$$

$$\langle a(b_1, \ldots, b_n).p \rangle = a(c).(\nu d\, \bar{c}d \mid d(b_1).(\bar{c}d \mid \cdots \mid d(b_{n-1}).(\bar{c}d \mid d(b_n) : \langle p \rangle)) \cdots))$$

Fig. 4. From the polyadic to the unsorted monadic π_1-calculus

Translating the asynchronous π-calculus A test for the expressiveness of the π_1-calculus is its ability to simulate a calculus where a channel can have multiple receivers. As source language, we consider the core of an asynchronous polyadic π-calculus. The translation is presented in figure 5. We suppose that for every channel a with sort s of the source calculus there is a pair of names a_i, a_o (i for input and o for output) in the π_1-calculus such that a_i has sort $Ch(s)$ and a_o has sort s. Since we cannot have several receivers on the same channel, we associate to every (restricted) channel a channel manager $CM(a_i, a_o)$, which continuously receives input/output requests and matches them if possible. We note that $\emptyset \vdash \langle p \rangle$.

A first rough relationship between the source and target calculus can be stated by supposing that in the source calculus we consider processes such that: (i) all input names are restricted (so that the commitments $\bar{a}_i c$ in the translation are hidden), and (ii) input parameters cannot be used as the subject of an input action. The notion of barbed bisimulation is adapted in a straightforward way to this asynchronous π-calculus.

It is possible to give decidable conditions that guarantee properties (i-ii), for instance see the read/write sorting discipline in [14]. Moreover, property (ii)

---

[3] Another possibility, is to remove the matching operator and introduce a rule to type (a simulation of) the if_then_else_. In this case, internal choice can still be defined, but matching is not definable. There is an interesting translation of the calculus without matching into a sub-calculus where all transmitted names are new and which relies on the *link operator* [15]. The idea is to replace the message $\bar{a}b$, where b is free, with the process $\nu c\,(\bar{a}c \mid c \mapsto b)$.

$$\langle a(\mathbf{b}).p\rangle = \nu c\,(\overline{a_i}c\mid c(\mathbf{b}_o):\langle p\rangle)$$
$$\langle\overline{a}\mathbf{b}\rangle \quad = \overline{a_o}\mathbf{b}_o$$
$$\langle\nu a\,p\rangle \quad = \nu a_i\,\nu a_o\,(\langle p\rangle\mid CM(a_i,a_o))$$
$$CM(a_i,a_o) = a_o(\mathbf{b}_o).a_i(c).\,(\overline{a_o}\mathbf{b}_o\mid\overline{a_i}c\mid CM(a_i,a_o))\oplus$$
$$(\overline{c}\mathbf{b}_o\mid CM(a_i,a_o))$$
$$\langle p\mid q\rangle \quad = \langle p\rangle\mid\langle q\rangle$$

Fig. 5. From a π-calculus with multiple receivers to the π_1-calculus

is not so restrictive since Boreale [5] has defined an adequate translation from an asynchronous π-calculus into an asynchronous π-calculus satisfying condition (ii).

Proposition 6. *Let p, p' be processes of the asynchronous π-calculus satisfying properties (i) and (ii). Then: $p \overset{\bullet}{\approx} p'$ iff $\langle p\rangle \overset{\bullet}{\approx} \langle p'\rangle$.*

3   An enriched π_1-calculus

We extend the syntax of the π_1-calculus in order to model the distribution of processes to locations, the failure of a location, the spawning of a process at a remote location, and the detection of a failure. We start by defining the language of *configurations*. A configuration is a "solution" in which we can find processes running at a location, messages, and locations.

• A process p running at a location a is denoted with $\{p\}a$. New channels and new processes that might be created during the computation of p are located in a. To create processes at remote locations, a special operator $\mathbf{spawn}(\_)$ is applied.

• Messages (m) can be output particles $(\overline{a}\mathbf{b})$, stop of a location a $(\mathbf{stop}(a))$, spawning of a process p at a location a $(\mathbf{spawn}(a,p))$, and testing of a location a, with a return on b_1 if the location is running, and on b_2 otherwise $(\mathbf{ping}(a,b_1,b_2))$.

• We associate to every location name a *location process* which receives routing, $\mathbf{stop}(\_)$, $\mathbf{spawn}(\_)$, and $\mathbf{ping}(\_)$ messages. To this end, we introduce a new sort $\mathtt{loc}$, and a specific way of creating a location process which receives on a name a of sort $\mathtt{loc}$ $(Loc_T(a)$, where $T \in \{R, S\}$, R for run, and S for stop). Location names are just names of sort $\mathtt{loc}$, in particular location names are transmissible values. The typing rules will be extended to location processes as well. In this way, we will guarantee that for every location name there is at most one location process. We refer the reader to [4] for an alternative presentation in which the information about the status of the locations is maintained in a context.

Formally, we define the following syntactic categories. The languages for sorts and processes, include the respective languages defined for the π_1-calculus.

$$
\left\{
\begin{array}{lll}
\text{sort} & s ::= & \text{loc} \mid Ch(s_1,\ldots,s_n) \quad (n \geq 0) \\
\text{process} & p ::= & a(\text{b}).p \mid p \mid p \mid 0 \mid \nu a\, p \mid (\text{rec} A(\tilde{a}).p)(\tilde{b}) \mid A(\tilde{a}) \mid \\
& & [a = b]p, q \mid m \mid l \\
\text{configuration} & r ::= & \{p\}a \mid m \mid l \mid r \mid r \mid 0 \mid \nu a\, r \\
\text{message} & m ::= & \bar{a}\text{b} \mid \text{stop}(a) \mid \text{spawn}(a, p) \mid \text{ping}(a, b_1, b_2) \\
\text{location process } l & ::= & Loc_T(a) \quad T \in \{R, S\}
\end{array}
\right.
\tag{2}
$$

Reduction rules Next we define a few reduction rules which specify the possible interactions between the components of the solution. It is particularly appealing that all the rules share the same pattern: reduction happens when a message (possibly decorated with the name of its location) meets its destination.

$$
\left\{
\begin{array}{lll}
(\text{cm}) & \bar{a}c \mid \{a(\text{b}).p\}a' & \rightarrow \{[c/b]p\}a' \\
(\text{stop}) & \text{stop}(a) \mid Loc_R(a) & \rightarrow Loc_S(a) \\
(\text{route}) & \{m\}a \mid Loc_R(a) & \rightarrow m \mid Loc_R(a) \\
(\text{spawn}) & \text{spawn}(a, p) \mid Loc_R(a) & \rightarrow \{p\}a \mid Loc_R(a) \\
(\text{ping}_r) & \text{ping}(a, b_1, b_2) \mid Loc_R(a) \rightarrow \bar{b}_1 \mid Loc_R(a) \\
(\text{ping}_s) & \text{ping}(a, b_1, b_2) \mid Loc_S(a) \rightarrow \bar{b}_2 \mid Loc_S(a)
\end{array}
\right.
\tag{3}
$$

We describe the operational intuition behind these rules:

(cm) Processes are decorated with the location where they run. In the absence of failures, this decoration is *transparent* (cf. proposition 18), in particular to send a message to a process, we do not need to know its location. Later, we will add a few structural equivalences (equations (5)) to ease the manipulation of the decorations.

(stop) When a running location process $Loc_R(a)$ meets a stop message $\text{stop}(a)$ it becomes a stopped location process $Loc_S(a)$, and stays in that state for ever (halting failure). One should note the dual use of the stop command: it can be employed either to program the halt of a location, or to model the potential failure of a location.

(route) Once a location has stopped, all processes running at that location should be *virtually* stopped for an external observer. We model this requirement, by blocking the routing of the messages at location a: *a process that cannot route its messages is as good as a stopped one*. On the other hand, a process running at a failed location keeps receiving messages as stated by rule (cm). Since communication is asynchronous and messages are addressed to a unique process, we can never observe this receiving activity. It would be possible to actually stop all processes running at a failed location, as it is done in [4], however, in the model considered here, this is a needless complication.

(spawn) One should wonder if this extension is really necessary. Indeed, one alternative would be to stick to the π-calculus tradition of transmitting names only. In this case, we could imagine that each location is equipped with a sort of interpreter (a "universal π-calculus machine") which by some protocol receives a description of the process to run (as a sequence of channel names), and runs it locally. While this solution is theoretically possible, it would make the modeling of process mobility in distributed systems particularly heavy. It is a widespread belief that, in order to perform formal verification, the model has to abstract from inessential details. A model in which we have to take into account the details of the interpreter would probably defy formal treatment. The modeling solution which we adopt instead, is that of enriching the calculus with a $\mathbf{spawn}(a, p)$ operator that allows to start the execution of the process p at the location a. Hence, in our model the transmission of processes is regarded as a primitive and atomic operation whose implementation is left unspecified. An important restriction that one may impose on the spawning of processes, will be described next in the context of the typing rules.

(ping) The systems we model are fully asynchronous, a few non-trivial problems can be solved in this framework in the presence of failures (e.g. remaming algorithms). On the other hand, there are problems, consensus being the most famous, which cannot be solved in a fully asynchronous framework in the presence of failures. In order to cope with this limitation, the asynchronous model has been enriched in a number of ways including randomization, partial synchrony hypotheses, and failure detectors. We refer to [8] for an up-to-date discussion of these issues. The approach we follow here, is to enrich our model with a failure detector $\mathbf{ping}(\_)$ which eventually allows any process to know if a location runs or not. This solution can be integrated with little effort into our model. On the other hand, the handling of time or probabilities would require a major revision. In [1], we show: (i) how to implement a perfect failure detector using $\mathbf{ping}(\_)$, (ii) how to specify transient failures, and (iii) how to represent weaker failure detectors. In this paper, we concentrate on the model which enjoys the simplest formalization.

Typing rules The typing rules for processes and configurations are obtained by adding the rules in figure 6 to those in figure 2. We allow the creation and transmission of new location names. As for channels, whenever we create a new location name a, we have to associate with it a location process $(Loc_T(a))$. We omit the rules for typing the parallel composition or restriction of configurations. These rules are shaped after the corresponding rules for processes.

$$\frac{\Gamma \vdash p \quad st(a) = \mathtt{loc}}{\Gamma \vdash \{p\}a} \qquad \frac{\Gamma \cup \{a\} \vdash p \quad a \notin \Gamma \quad st(a) = \mathtt{loc}}{\Gamma \vdash \nu a\, r}$$

$$\frac{st(a) = \mathtt{loc}}{\{a\} \vdash Loc_T(a)} \qquad \frac{st(a) = \mathtt{loc}}{\emptyset \vdash \mathbf{stop}(a)}$$

$$\frac{st(a) = \mathtt{loc} \quad \Gamma \vdash p}{\Gamma \vdash \mathbf{spawn}(a, p)} \qquad \frac{st(a) = \mathtt{loc} \quad st(b_1) = st(b_2) = Ch()}{\emptyset \vdash \mathbf{ping}(a, b_1, b_2)}$$

Fig. 6. Additional typing rules for the π_{1l}-calculus

It is interesting to restrict the rule for **spawn(_)** by requiring that the context Γ is empty. In this way, we can make sure that by spawning we are not moving a process which can receive on some name, from a location to another, so that *each channel name can be seen as an absolute physical address which does not change during the computation.* It is still possible to express interesting mobility in this framework because the spawned process can create new channels and communicate them to the environment (e.g., in [1] we program a "migrating stack"). The unrestricted version of spawning is obviously more attractive from a programming view point: a process keeps its names while migrating. However in the unrestricted framework we hide a few problems under the carpet. At the implementation level one has to develop routing algorithms which adapt to changes in the network topology in the presence of failures, at the specification level one has to find an abstract description of the properties guaranteed by the routing algorithm. To the author's knowledge, there is no satisfying analysis of these issues. An attempt at defining a programming language where processes can migrate while keeping their identity has been recently proposed in [10], however that paper does not analyse the implementation level.

Labelled transition system The reduction rules (3), can be rephrased as labelled transitions, by including "location signals" among the actions:

$$\alpha ::= \tau \mid ab \mid \nu\{c\}\,\bar{a}b \mid a_t \mid \bar{a}_t \quad t \in \{R, S, P\} \tag{4}$$

Labelled transitions are defined on configurations and they are displayed in figure 7. Besides renaming of bound names we assume the following structural equivalences:

$$\{p \mid q\}a \equiv \{p\}a \mid \{q\}a \quad \{\nu b\,p\}a \equiv \nu b\,\{p\}a \ (a \neq b)$$
$$\{Loc_T(a')\}a \equiv Loc_T(a') \tag{5}$$

The rules specified for the π_1-calculus are trivially extended, moreover we add the labelled transitions for the location processes and the new messages. Subject reduction is proved by adapting the proof of theorem 1.

Proposition 7 subject reduction. *If $\Gamma \vdash r$ and $r \xrightarrow{\alpha} r'$ then $\Gamma \cup bn(\alpha) \vdash r'$.*

4 Tools to reason about equivalence

There is a simple translation $\lceil\_\rceil$ from the π_{1l}-calculus to the π_1-calculus. We are interested in this translation as a way of reducing verification problems for the π_{1l}-calculus to verification problems for the π_1-calculus (cf. [4]). The translation (bi-)simulates the π_{1l}-calculus in the π_1-calculus. A fortiori it has nothing to do with the way a program of the π_{1l}-calculus would actually be executed. Every name a of sort $st(a)$, is translated into the same name with sort $\lceil st(a)\rceil$, where:

$$\lceil Ch(s_1, \ldots, s_n)\rceil = Ch(\lceil s_1\rceil, \ldots, \lceil s_1\rceil) \quad \lceil \mathtt{loc}\rceil = Ch(\mathtt{bool}, \mathtt{bool}, Ch(), Ch())$$

The translation of configurations is displayed in figure 8, where we use a **case** statement (which can be easily coded with a nesting of **if_then_else_**'s) to make

$$
(in)\ \frac{}{\{a(b).p\}d \xrightarrow{ac} \{[c/b]p\}d} \qquad (out)\ \frac{}{\overline{a}b \xrightarrow{\overline{a}b} 0}
$$

$$
(out_{ex})\ \frac{r \xrightarrow{\nu\{c\}\,\overline{a}b} r'\ \ a \neq d\ \ d \in \{b\}\backslash\{c\}}{\nu d\, r \xrightarrow{\nu\{d,c\}\,\overline{a}b} r'} \qquad (\nu)\ \frac{r \xrightarrow{\alpha} r'\ \ a \notin n(\alpha)}{\nu a\, r \xrightarrow{\alpha} \nu a\, r'}
$$

$$
(cp)\ \frac{r \xrightarrow{\alpha} r_1\ \ bn(\alpha) \cap fn(r') = \emptyset}{r \mid r' \xrightarrow{\alpha} r_1 \mid r'} \qquad (cm)\ \frac{r \xrightarrow{\nu\{c\}\,\overline{a}b} r_1\ \ r' \xrightarrow{ab} r_1'\ \ \{c\} \cap fn(r') = \emptyset}{r \mid r' \xrightarrow{\tau} \nu c\,(r_1 \mid r_1')}
$$

$$
(rec)\ \frac{\{[recA(\tilde{a}).p/A, \tilde{b}/\tilde{a}]p\}d \xrightarrow{\alpha} r}{\{(recA(\tilde{a}).p)(\tilde{b})\}d \xrightarrow{\alpha} r} \qquad (cg)\ \frac{r \equiv r'\ \ r' \xrightarrow{\alpha} r_1'\ \ r_1' \equiv r_1}{r \xrightarrow{\alpha} r_1}
$$

$$
(m_t)\ \frac{\{p\}d \xrightarrow{\alpha} r}{\{[a=a]p, q\}d \xrightarrow{\alpha} r} \qquad (m_f)\ \frac{\{q\}d \xrightarrow{\alpha} r\ \ a \neq b}{\{[a=b]p, q\}d \xrightarrow{\alpha} r}
$$

$$
(RR)\ \frac{}{Loc_R(a) \xrightarrow{a_R} Loc_R(a)} \qquad (RS)\ \frac{}{Loc_R(a) \xrightarrow{a_S} Loc_S(a)}
$$

$$
(SS)\ \frac{}{Loc_S(a) \xrightarrow{a_R} Loc_S(a)} \qquad (stop)\ \frac{}{stop(a) \xrightarrow{\overline{a}_S} 0}
$$

$$
(spawn)\ \frac{}{spawn(a,p) \xrightarrow{\overline{a}_R} \{p\}a} \qquad (route)\ \frac{}{\{m\}a \xrightarrow{\overline{a}_R} m}
$$

$$
(ping_t)\ \frac{}{ping(a,b_1,b_2) \xrightarrow{\overline{a}_R} \overline{b}_1} \qquad (ping_f)\ \frac{}{ping(a,b_1,b_2) \xrightarrow{\overline{a}_F} \overline{b}_2}
$$

$$
(cm_t)\ \frac{r \xrightarrow{\overline{a}_t} r'\ \ r_1 \xrightarrow{a_t} r_1'}{r \mid r_1 \xrightarrow{\tau} r' \mid r_1'}
$$

Fig. 7. Lts for the π_{1l}-calculus

the control of the location process clearer. The translation of configurations relies on an auxiliary translation of processes which is parametric in a location name. This name represents the location where the process is running. We use the following codes: t, t to spawn or to route, t, f to ping, and f, f to stop.

Definition 8 complete configuration. Let $\Gamma \vdash r$ be a well typed configuration. We say that the configuration r is *complete* if $r \Rightarrow r'$ and $a \notin \Gamma$ implies that r' cannot perform a transition with label $\overline{a}_t$.

Intuitively, in a complete configuration all locations mentioned in the configuration have been defined and therefore transitions labelled with $\overline{a}_t$ are not visible. Let $\Gamma \vdash r$ be a complete configuration. This property is preserved by internal reduction, hence we can introduce a relation of barbed bisimulation on the π_{1l}-calculus, commitment being defined as follows. Let $\Gamma \vdash r$ be a complete configuration, then $r \downarrow \overline{a}$ if $a \notin \Gamma$, and $r \xrightarrow{\nu\{c\}\,\overline{a}b}$.

Definition 9. A symmetric relation S on well-typed, complete configurations is a strong *barbed bisimulation* if whenever rSr' the following holds: (1) If $r \downarrow \overline{a}$ then $r' \downarrow \overline{a}$. (2) If $r \xrightarrow{\tau} r_1$ then $r' \xrightarrow{\tau} r_1'$ and $r_1 S r_1'$.

$$\lceil m \rceil d = \nu c\,(\overline{d}\,\mathbf{t},\mathbf{t},c,c \mid c : \lceil m \rceil)$$
$$\lceil \overline{a}b \rceil = \overline{a}b$$
$$\lceil \mathbf{spawn}(d,p) \rceil = \nu c\,(\overline{d}\,\mathbf{t},\mathbf{t},c,c \mid c : \lceil p \rceil d)$$
$$\lceil \mathbf{ping}(d,c,c') \rceil = \overline{d}\,\mathbf{t},\mathbf{f},c,c'$$
$$\lceil \mathbf{stop}(d) \rceil = \overline{d}\,\mathbf{f},\mathbf{f},\_,\_$$

$$\lceil Loc_T(a) \rceil = L_T(a;\ ) \quad \text{where}$$
$$L_R(a;\ ) = a(b,b',c,c').\ \mathbf{case}\ (b,b',c,c')\ \mathbf{of}$$
$$\qquad (\mathbf{t},\mathbf{t},c,c) : \overline{c} \mid L_R(a;\ )$$
$$\qquad (\mathbf{t},\mathbf{f},c,c') : \overline{c} \mid L_R(a;\ )$$
$$\qquad (\mathbf{f},\mathbf{f},\_,\_) : L_S(a;\ )$$

$$L_S(a;\ ) = a(b,b',c,c').\ \mathbf{case}\ (b,b',c,c')\ \mathbf{of}$$
$$\qquad (\mathbf{t},\mathbf{f},c,c') : \overline{c'} \mid L_S(a;\ )$$
$$\qquad (\_,\_,\_,\_) : \overline{a}b,b',c,c' \mid L_S(a;\ )$$

$\lceil \nu a\,r \rceil$	$= \nu a\,\lceil r \rceil$	$\lceil \nu a\,p \rceil c$	$= \nu a\,\lceil p \rceil c\ \ a \neq c$
$\lceil p \mid q \rceil c$	$= \lceil p \rceil c \mid \lceil q \rceil c$	$\lceil r \mid r' \rceil$	$= \lceil r \rceil \mid \lceil r' \rceil$
$\lceil 0 \rceil$	$= 0$	$\lceil 0 \rceil c$	$= 0$

$$\lceil a(b).p \rceil c = a(b).\lceil p \rceil c \quad c \notin \{b\} \qquad \lceil (recA(\tilde{a}).p)(\tilde{b}) \rceil c = (recA(\tilde{a}).\lceil p \rceil c)(\tilde{b}) \quad c \notin \{\tilde{a}\}$$
$$\lceil [a=b]p,q \rceil c = [a=b]\lceil p \rceil c,\lceil q \rceil c \qquad \lceil \{p\}c \rceil = \lceil p \rceil c$$

Fig. 8. Translating the π_{1l}-calculus into the π_1-calculus

Let $\overset{\bullet}{\sim}_l$ be the largest barbed bisimulation. The notion of weak barbed bisimulation is obtained by replacing everywhere the commitment $\downarrow$ with $\Downarrow$ and the reduction $\overset{\tau}{\to}$ with $\overset{\tau}{\Rightarrow}$. We denote with $\overset{\bullet}{\approx}_l$ the largest weak barbed bisimulation.

Theorem 10 adequacy. *Let r,r' be complete well-typed configurations. Then:*

$$r \overset{\bullet}{\approx}_l r' \quad \text{iff} \quad \lceil r \rceil \overset{\bullet}{\approx} \lceil r' \rceil$$

Bisimulation for the π_1-calculus We undertake a deeper study of equivalence for the π_1-calculus. It is well known that barbed bisimulation fails to be a congruence, in particular it is not preserved by parallel composition. Barbed equivalence is the greatest equivalence which refines barbed bisimulation and is preserved by parallel composition.

Definition 11 barbed equivalence. We define a relation $\sim_b$ of barbed equivalence between well typed processes as follows: $p \sim_b p'$ iff for each q, such that $p \mid q$ and $p' \mid q$ are well-typed, $p \mid q \overset{\bullet}{\sim} p' \mid q$ holds. The notion of weak barbed equivalence $\approx_b$ is obtained by replacing $\overset{\bullet}{\sim}$ with $\overset{\bullet}{\approx}$.

In the following, whenever we compose two processes we implicitly suppose that their composition is well-typed. We also note that if $p \approx_b p'$, then there is a context Γ which types both processes. Suppose $\Gamma \vdash p$, $\Gamma' \vdash p'$ and $a \in \Gamma \backslash \Gamma'$, then $p \mid \overline{a}$ cannot be barbed bisimilar to $p' \mid \overline{a}$ as the second commits on $\overline{a}$ while the first does not. For instance, it can be shown that $Idle(a)$ is barbed equivalent to $a(\mathbf{b}) \triangleright \overline{a}\mathbf{b}$ but it is *not* barbed equivalent to $\mathbf{0}$.

In this section, we show that barbed equivalence can be characterized by a suitable (asynchronous) bisimulation over the labelled transition system. This supports the view that the π_1-calculus is not only an *expressive* calculus, but it has also a "tractable theory" of equivalence (at least in the sense the π-calculus has one!). For the sake of simplicity we will work with the monadic unsorted π_1-calculus (cf. section 2). Following standard notation [13], we write the action $\nu\{b\} \, \overline{a}b$ as $\overline{a}(b)$.

In defining the commitment relation, we have been careful to observe only those output commitments which relate to free channels whose receiver is not defined in the observed process. Following this idea, we introduce a restricted form of labelled transition. Let the function cmt be defined on actions as follows: $cmt(\tau) = cmt(ab) = \emptyset$ and $cmt(\overline{a}b) = cmt(\overline{a}(b)) = \{a\}$. The rule (cp) in the lts described in figure 1, is then replaced by:

$$(cp_{tp}) \quad \frac{p \stackrel{\alpha}{\to} p' \quad bn(\alpha) \cap fn(q) = \emptyset \quad \Gamma \vdash q \quad cmt(\alpha) \cap \Gamma = \emptyset}{p \mid q \stackrel{\alpha}{\to} p' \mid q} \tag{6}$$

Whenever we speak of transitions of typed processes, we will apply the rule (cp_{tp}). We can now define a notion of (asynchronous) bisimulation over the restricted lts. The following definition follows quite closely [2] modulo some type constraints.

Definition 12 bisimulation. A symmetric relation S on typed processes is a bisimulation if $p \, S \, q$ implies: (1) There is a context Γ such that $\Gamma \vdash p$ and $\Gamma \vdash q$. (2) If $p \stackrel{\alpha}{\to} p'$, $bn(\alpha) \cap fn(q) = \emptyset$, and α is not an input action, then $q \stackrel{\alpha}{\to} q'$ and $p' \, S \, q'$. (3) If $p \stackrel{ab}{\to} p'$ then either $q \stackrel{ab}{\to} q'$ and $p' \, S \, q'$, or $q \stackrel{\tau}{\to} q'$ and $p' \, S \, (q' \mid \overline{a}b)$.

We denote with $\sim_a$ the greatest bisimulation. The notion of weak bisimulation is obtained by replacing everywhere transitions with weak transitions. We denote with $\approx_a$ the greatest weak bisimulation.

It is shown in [2] that weak asynchronous bisimulation is preserved by all operators of the asynchronous π-calculus but matching. In particular, the fact that asynchronous bisimulation preserves parallel composition, suffices to show that asynchronous bisimulation implies barbed equivalence. This is stated as follows (in the weak case).

Proposition 13. *If $p \approx_a p'$ then (1) for each q, $p \mid q \approx_a p' \mid q$, and (2) $p \approx_b p'$.*

In the other direction, we rely on a proof technique introduced in [2] which is based on the definition of a countable collection of testing processes.

Definition 14. Let us fix a decidable structural equivalence relation. A lts is *image finite* (w.r.t. weak transitions), if for any process p and action α the set $\{p' \mid p \stackrel{\alpha}{\Rightarrow} p'\}$ is finite up to the structural equivalence relation. We say that a process p is image finite if the lts formed of the processes reachable from p by labelled transitions is image finite.

Image finite processes include "finite control" processes and therefore represent an interesting class. In the case of strong transitions, all processes of the π_1-calculus turn out to be image finite.

Theorem 15 characterization. *(1) If $p \sim_b q$ then $p \sim_a q$. (2) If p, q are image finite and $p \approx_b q$, then $p \approx_a q$.*

Full abstraction and transparency We concentrate on a non-trivial set of configurations which is defined as follows.

Definition 16. A *location closed* configuration is a configuration where transitions of the shape a_t or $\bar{a}_t$ are not observable, and such that this property is preserved by labelled transitions.

Of course, location closed configurations are complete configurations. Many systems resilient to failures can be formalized within this fragment (an example is in [1]). On location closed configurations, the translation described in figure 8 turns out to be *fully abstract*. Intuitively, the translation of a location closed configuration can interact with the environment without revealing any information about the internal representation of locations.

To state our result, one has to adapt the definition 12 of bisimulation so that it relates location closed configurations to processes of the π_1-calculus. By a little abuse of notation, we still indicate with $\approx_a$ the related greatest weak bisimulation.

Proposition 17 full abstraction. *Let r be a location closed configuration. Then $r \approx_a \lceil r \rceil$.*

We conclude with a formalization of the idea that in the absence of failure, the distribution of processes is *transparent*. Given a location closed configuration r, $er_l(r)$ is either (i) a process of the π_1-calculus where all the information on locations has been erased, or (ii) undefined if the configuration contains stopped locations, or **stop**(_) messages. The formal definition of the function $er_l(\_)$, on its domain of definition, is given in figure 9.

Proposition 18 transparency. *Let r be a location closed configuration. If $er_l(r)$ is defined, then $r \approx_a er_l(r)$.*

Acknowledgements In carrying on this work, I relied on previous joint work with Ilaria Castellani, Sanjiva Prasad, and Davide Sangiorgi. I also benefited from discussions with Gérard Boudol and members of the PARA project at INRIA-Rocquencourt. Thanks to Uwe Nestmann for pointing out a mistake in the definition of the lts in figure 7.

$$er_l(\texttt{loc}) \qquad = Ch() \qquad er_l(Ch(s_1, \ldots, s_n)) = Ch(er_l(s_1), \ldots, er_l(s_n))$$

$$
\begin{aligned}
er_l(Loc_R(a)) &= Idle(a) & er_l(\texttt{spawn}(a, p)) &= er_l(p) \\
er_l(\texttt{ping}(a, b_1, b_2)) &= \bar{b}_1 & er_l(\bar{a}b) &= \bar{a}b \\
er_l(\{p\}a) &= er_l(p) & er_l(\nu a\, r) &= \nu a\, er_l(r) \\
er_l(a(b).p) &= a(b).er_l(p) & er_l(p \mid p') &= er_l(p) \mid er_l(p') \\
er_l(\nu a\, p) &= \nu a\, er_l(p) & er_l(r \mid r') &= er_l(r) \mid er_l(r') \\
er_l(A(\tilde{a})) &= A(\tilde{a}) & er_l((\texttt{rec}A(\tilde{a}).p)(\tilde{b})) &= (\texttt{rec}A(\tilde{a}).er_l(p))(\tilde{b}) \\
er_l(0) &= 0 & er_l([a = b]p, q) &= [a = b]er_l(p), er_l(q)
\end{aligned}
$$

Fig. 9. Location erasure

References

1. R. Amadio. An asynchronous model of locality, failure, and process mobility. RR-INRIA 3109. Available at http://protis.univ-mrs.fr/~amadio/.
2. R. Amadio, I. Castellani, and D. Sangiorgi. On bisimulations for the asynchronous π-calculus. In *CONCUR 96, SLNCS. 1119*, 1996.
3. R. Amadio, L. Leth, and B. Thomsen. From a concurrent λ-calculus to the π-calculus. In *Proc. Foundations of Computation Theory 95, SLNCS 965*, 1995.
4. R. Amadio and S. Prasad. Localities and Failures (Extended Summary). In *Proc. of FST-TCS94 SLNCS 880*, 1994.
5. M. Boreale. On the expressiveness of internal mobility in name passing calculi. In *CONCUR 96, SNLCS 1119*, 1996.
6. G. Boudol. Asynchrony and the π-calculus. RR-INRIA 1702, 1992.
7. G. Boudol. Some chemical abstract machines. In *Proc. of REX School*, SLNCS 803, 1993.
8. T. Chandra and S. Toueg. Unreliable failure detectors for reliable distributed systems. *Journal of ACM*, 43(2):225-267, 1996.
9. C. Fournet and G. Gonthier. The reflexive CHAM and the join-calculus. *Proc. POPL*, 1996.
10. C. Fournet, G. Gonthier, J.-J. Lévy, L. Maranget, and D. Rémy. A calculus of mobile agents. In *CONCUR 96*, SLNCS 1119, 1996.
11. K. Honda and M. Tokoro. An object calculus for asynchronous communication. *Proc. ECOOP 91, Geneve*, 1991.
12. N. Kobayashi, B. Pierce, and D. Turner. Linearity in the π-calculus. *Proc. POPL*, 1996.
13. R. Milner, J. Parrow, and D. Walker. A Calculus of Mobile Process, Parts 1-2. *Information and Computation*, 100(1):1-77, 1992.
14. B. Pierce and D. Sangiorgi. Typing and subtyping for mobile processes. In *Proc. LICS*, 1993.
15. D. Sangiorgi. π-calculus, internal mobility and agent-passing calculi. In *Proc Tapsoft 95*, SLNCS 915, 1995.

A Component Calculus for Modeling the Olan Configuration Language

Jean-Yves Vion-Dury[1], Luc Bellissard[2] and Vladimir Marangozov[2]

[1] Rank Xerox Research Centre
6 Chemin de Maupertuis 38240 Meylan - France
E-mail: Jean-Yves.Vion-Dury@grenoble.rxrc.xerox.com

[2] INRIA Rhône-Alpes, SIRAC Project
655, avenue de l'Europe, 38330 Montbonnot Saint Martin - France
E-mail: {Luc.Bellissard,Vladimir.Marangozov}@inrialpes.fr

Abstract. *Components will certainly become a key concept for the next generation of software architectures because of their impact on effective software reuse, real interoperability and integration. Within the Olan project [15], we face the difficulty of defining an operational semantics able to reflect the diversity of execution models involved in real applications. Existing process calculi offer the required abstractions such as encapsulation and process equivalences, but they rely on the fundamental assumption that agents are active, i.e autonomously able to initiate communication. However, components, viewed as software pieces with explicit interfaces, require a notion of passive composition that allows, for instance, several components to be traversed by a same process. In this paper, we introduce a calculus, named ICCS, which extends the Milner's CCS calculus with (1) an operator for passive composition, and (2) selective interactions. While preserving the powerful theory of process equivalences established for CCS, this calculus provides an operational definition of passive components and allows thus to establish the basis of an operational semantics for the Olan Configuration Language.*

1 Introduction

Configuration languages such as Darwin [16] or Olan [1] aim at using components as the basic structure for programming distributed applications, and thus take full advantage of their properties: reusability of software at minimal cost, explicit rendering of the software architecture and clear separation of the communication code from the application specific code.

The first benefit of such an approach is to ease the distribution of component-based applications over various hardware platforms, and to significantly help the configuration, monitoring and administration tasks.

Other key issues for component technologies are related to software reuse, integration and interoperability. The reuse is addressed through the notion of *interfaces* which define offered services, as well as required services in order to make explicit the dependencies of the component, and thus allowing its use in various contexts. The first theoretical difficulty is to provide enough information at the interface level in order to allow compatibility checking, but to avoid too complicated specifications. The second difficulty, for component-based language designers, is to provide guidelines and methods for encapsulating heterogeneous pieces of code (possibly written in different programming languages) in order to make them work together. The "programmer in the large" [13] should be able to build up new applications from various primitive components, with no deep knowledge of their internal implementations. Here again, the interface definition must be able to provide relevant information concerning the semantics of the component. A third difficulty is related to interoperability, i.e. provide coordination and data transformation in order to adapt entities that were not initially designed to work together. The challenge here is to propose, as automatically as possible, the communication specific code that performs the adaptation [4].

Clearly, theoretical foundations are needed that allow the modeling of the behavior of components and offer effective methods for computing component compatibility as well as adaptations toward ad hoc or generic agents, specialized in communication and coordination tasks.

Process calculi, as CSP [6], CCS [9] and the π-calculus [10] offer formal tools for modeling general concurrent systems through the notion of communicating processes. The CCS calculus appears to be the closest to our requirements because:

1. CCS is based on an observational approach (as opposed to more specification-oriented calculi)
2. Basic hypotheses are weak (for instance processes are not forced to synchronize on communication channels), and also the calculus is general and concise (only one alternation operator, no specific termination actions)
3. Process equivalence theory is particularly developed, and leads to subtle and important criteria for behavioral compatibility. This last point is central to our requirements concerning component composition, because compatibility criteria must be defined, and interfaces must correctly reflect encapsulated behaviors.
4. Numerous extensions have been proposed which are of particular interest in our area, such as distributed real time processes calculi [2] [3].

The key issue addressed in this paper is the use of a formal calculus to model applications constructed and configured with Olan. Olan rely on a component-based model that describes applications as interconnections of components, with no restrictions on the execution model of those components. Indeed, components may encapsulate active entities or software (e.g. a multi-threaded server) as well as passive entities (e.g. a framework of non-active classes or a library). CCS as well as other calculi are all based on the hypothesis that components are processes and the problem of interconnecting components is thus addressed as process composition. The idea of the remaining sections is to adapt the CCS calculus to the Olan Component Model where the information about the execution model is exhibited at the interface level of components, thus allowing totally passive components to be interconnected to any kind of other components. Section 2 presents ICCS, an extension of CCS that allows the composition of active as well as passive entities. Section 3 details the applicability of such a calculus to Olan and finally, we conclude by comparing our proposition with related works and the existing approaches in this area.

2 ICCS: an Interconnected Component Calculus

2.1 Overview

We propose to refine the CCS calculus into a new calculus able to model the notion of *passive* components as well as *active* components, while preserving the powerful theoretical tools of process equivalence, needed for the definition of component composition. Therefore, we propose a new static composition operator ◁ that allows the combination of properly active components with passive components, by expressing the intuitive notion of *activity flow transfer*.

In CCS, the fundamental assumptions are message-passing exchanges (as opposed to shared memory models) and asynchrony across processes. The parallel composition is thus a construction which expresses the potential transfer of data *and* the concurrency among processes. But if more general composition relationships are needed, such as for assembling software pieces, then some different assumptions are required. For instance, a standard procedure call can be viewed as a construction that transfers both values *and* activity flow, since no action can be performed at the upper level by the calling activity.

The most common response to this difficulty is to model the synchronous call by two activities synchronized correctly. We argue that this is possible, but too general, and thus it does not exactly fulfill the requirements. The following example emulates a synchronous call in CCS:

$(\bar{a}.a.0|a.\bar{b}.b.\bar{a}.0) \setminus \{a\}$, which produces the derivation $\xrightarrow{\tau}\xrightarrow{\bar{b}}\xrightarrow{b}\xrightarrow{\tau}$.

By using the value-passing form of the calculus, it is possible to simulate a synchronous call with input parameter x and output parameter y:

$(\bar{a}x.a(y).0|a(w).\bar{b}w.b(z).\bar{a}z.0) \setminus \{a\}$, which produces the derivation $\xrightarrow{\tau}\xrightarrow{\bar{b}x}\xrightarrow{b(z)}\xrightarrow{\tau}$.

This last one is fully representative (it models data transfer), and correct, since the calling activity is suspended during the call. But the following expression is correct too, although not representative of the activity transfer:

$(\bar{a}x.\bar{c}y.a(y).0|a(w).b(z).\bar{a}z.0) \setminus \{a\}$, since the calling activity performs an output communication action c before the return of the call. Thus, in CCS, there is no *operational* distinction between these two cases: conditions for ensuring the validity of *passive composition* do not appear directly in the calculus. We propose to go even further and to make this difference explicit by proposing a new composition operator ◁ in order to model the activity transfer *and* the value passing.

The idea is to allow output communication actions on the left side of the operator and input actions on the right side, and to commute the operands when actions are performed. Of course, internal τ actions must be possible to express the passing of values between the two operands. Thus, the previous example becomes:

$$(\bar{a}.a.0 \vartriangleleft a.\bar{b}.b.\bar{a}.0) \setminus \{a\} \xrightarrow{\tau} (\bar{b}.b.\bar{a}.0 \vartriangleleft a.0) \setminus \{a\}$$
$$\xrightarrow{\bar{b}} (a.0 \vartriangleleft b.\bar{a}.0) \setminus \{a\}$$
$$\xrightarrow{b} (\bar{a}.0 \vartriangleleft a.0) \setminus \{a\}$$
$$\xrightarrow{\tau} (0 \vartriangleleft 0) \setminus \{a\}$$

and, more interesting, the previous "non-desired" example is now discriminated, since the passive composition produces a different derivation tree:

$$(\bar{a}.\bar{c}.a.0 \vartriangleleft a.\bar{b}.b.\bar{a}.0) \setminus \{a\} \xrightarrow{\tau} (\bar{b}.b.\bar{a}.0 \vartriangleleft \bar{c}.a.0) \setminus \{a\}$$

$$\xrightarrow{\bar{b}} (\bar{c}.a.0 \vartriangleleft b.\bar{a}.0) \setminus \{a\}$$

$$\xrightarrow{b} (\bar{a}.0 \vartriangleleft \bar{c}.a.0) \setminus \{a\}$$

$$\text{or} \xrightarrow{\bar{c}} (b.\bar{a}.0 \vartriangleleft a.0) \setminus \{a\}$$

However, this notion we can call *preemption* leads to difficulty if we want to preserve a reasonable level of concurrency.

What does the following composition mean if the entire left subtree is suspended while executing the preemptive communication with the right component: $(\bar{a}.a.0|(P_1|P_2)) \vartriangleleft a.\bar{b}.b.\bar{a}.0$?

In such a case, the concurrent sub-system $(P_1|P_2)$ cannot evolve asynchronously, even if $\bar{a}.a.0$ alone is involved in the passive composition. We propose to tackle this problem (in other terms, the problem of managing the compatibility between the two composition operators) by introducing the notion of *selective interaction*. The key idea is to refine the component composition by associating *paths* to action labels of the transition system, and to use these paths in order to bring more selectivity to the interaction.

The previous example could become $((\bar{a}.a.0)::p|(P_1|P_2)) \vartriangleleft_p a.\bar{b}.b.\bar{a}.0$, expressing the fact that $(\bar{a}.a.0)::p$ is concerned by the passive composition, but not $(P_1|P_2)$, which can run asynchronously. The following sub-sections make this precise and demonstrate that this approach solves the compatibility problem. Moreover, it also brings a new way of specifying static component interconnections, as opposed to the dynamic binding capabilities of the π-calculus, and eases the description of configuration languages such as Olan.

2.2 The syntax

The set $\mathcal{P}$ of ICCS formulae, ranged over by P_i or Q_i is defined by two sets of syntax rules. The first one is very similar to the original set proposed by Milner for CCS [9]:

$$
\begin{array}{lll}
P ::= & 0 & \textit{Nul component: do nothing} \\
& |\ X & \textit{Component variable} \\
& |\ \alpha_p.P & \textit{Prefix} \\
& |\ P + P & \textit{Alternate choice} \\
& |\ P \setminus L:M & \textit{Restriction} \\
& |\ P[f:g] & \textit{Relabeling} \\
& |\ P|_{mn}P & \textit{Concurrent composition} \\
& |\ recX:P & \textit{Recursive operator}
\end{array}
$$

The second set defines the new constructions:

$$
\begin{array}{lll}
P ::= & P::p & \textit{Path nesting} \\
& |\ P \vartriangleleft_{mn} P & \textit{Passive (or preemptive) composition}
\end{array}
$$

The priority level is given by the following list (binding from the higher to the lower priority): $\alpha_p.P < (P::p) < (P \triangleleft P) < (P\,|\,P) < (P+P) < (recX:P) < (P\backslash L:M), P[f:g])$. Thus, $\alpha.P_1 + P_2\,|\,P_3 \triangleleft P_4$ means $((\alpha.P_1) + P_2)\,|\,(P_3 \triangleleft P_4)$.

2.3 Transitional semantics

The transition system is based on the idea of actions and co-actions on the one hand, and the notion of *path* on the other hand. Paths can be viewed as the concatenation of sub-paths which are able to reflect hierarchical structures. *Selectors* are paths associated to composition operators which refine the potential interactions between components. Indeed, the rules that define the evolution of the system use a matching function over paths and selectors in order to evaluate the potential interactions. In CCS, if a process P can interact with a process Q, the expression $(P_1|Q_1|P_2|Q_2)$ allows P_1 to interact either with Q_1 or with Q_2, and also the same for P_2. Within our calculus, the expression $(P_1\,|_{\circ\circ}\,Q_2)\,|_{**}\,(P_2\,|_{\circ\circ}\,Q_1)$ prevents all interactions between P_1, Q_2 and P_2, Q_1, because the selector $\circ$ can't match any path while $*$ matches all paths. The following definitions make this precise.

The labeled transition system The transition system $\xrightarrow{\alpha:p}\subseteq \mathcal{P} \times \mathcal{P}$ is defined over the set $\mathcal{P}$ of ICCS terms, $(\alpha, p) \in Act \times S$; Act is the set of communication actions and S the set of *paths*.

Communication actions α. $\alpha \in Act = \mathcal{L} \cup \{\tau\}, \mathcal{L} = A \cup \bar{A}$. Here $A = \{a,b,c,\dots\}$ is a set of names, $\bar{A} = \{\bar{a}, \bar{b}, \bar{c}, \dots\}$ is a set of co-names, and $\bar{}$ is a bijection over A and $\bar{A}$ such that $\bar{\bar{a}} = a$. As in Milner's CCS, A represents input communication actions and $\bar{A}$: output communication actions. τ is a distinguished label that represents internal (unobservable) actions, possibly generated by "hand-shaking" among components.

Paths. Paths, usually written p or q are terms defined by the grammar (1) or are equal to $\circ$. The symbol $\circ$ is used as the void item of a matching function over S.

$$S ::= p_i S \mid *S \mid ?S \mid \varepsilon \tag{1}$$

p_i range over an alphabet $P_s = \{a, b, \dots\}$. For example a, abc, $a?c$, $*c$, ε are all in S.

Definition 1. Concatenation $(+)$

$+ : S^2 \longrightarrow S$ is such that whatever $s_1, s_2 \in S - \{\circ\}$, $s_1 + \varepsilon = \varepsilon + s_1 = s_1$ and $s_1 + s_2 = s_1 s_2$. S is made stable for $+$ by: $s_1 + \circ = \circ + s_1 = \circ = \circ + \circ$ $p_1 + p_2$ is written $p_1 p_2$ for convenience.

Definition 2. Matching function over S

We define a matching function $\simeq: S \times S \longrightarrow \{\text{true}, \text{false}\}$, by using the table:

$\simeq$	$p_2 S_2$	$*S_2$	ε	$\circ$
$p_1 S_1$	$(p_1{=}p_2 \vee p_1{=}? \vee p_2{=}?) \wedge (S_1 \simeq S_2)$	$(p_1 S_1 \simeq S_2) \vee (S_1 \simeq *S_2)$	$false$	$false$
$*S_1$	$(S_1 \simeq p_2 S_2) \vee (*S_1 \simeq S_2)$	$(S_1 \simeq S_2) \vee (*S_1 \simeq S_2) \vee (S_1 \simeq *S_2)$	$S_1 \simeq \varepsilon$	$false$
ε	$false$	$\varepsilon \simeq S_2$	$true$	$false$
$\circ$	$false$	$false$	$false$	$false$

This definition yields a natural matching function such that $a*d \simeq abcd$, $a?c? \simeq abcd$ or even $a*d \simeq a*?d$, $a?c? \simeq a*$

Note that $*^n$, $(n \geq 1)$ matches everything except o and that o matches nothing.

Inference rules

$$\frac{true}{\alpha_p.P \xrightarrow{\alpha:p} P} \text{[Prefix]} \tag{2}$$

It is the fundamental rule that expresses the sequential behavior of components: $\alpha_p.P$ performs the communication $\alpha{:}p$ and then behaves like P. In the rest of the paper, α_ε is written α for convenience.

$$\frac{P \xrightarrow{\alpha:p} P'}{P+Q \xrightarrow{\alpha:p} P'} \text{[Alt1]} \qquad \frac{Q \xrightarrow{\beta:q} Q'}{P+Q \xrightarrow{\beta:q} Q'} \text{[Alt2]}$$

The rules [Alt1] and [Alt2] describe the alternative, which can be indeterministic when both P and Q are able to perform transitions (the choice can be either the left operand or the right one).

$$\frac{P \xrightarrow{\alpha:p} P'}{P::q \xrightarrow{\alpha:pq} P'::q} \text{[Nesting]} \qquad \frac{P \xrightarrow{\alpha:p} P'}{P[f:g] \xrightarrow{f(\alpha,p):g(\alpha,p)} P'[f:g]} \text{[Relab]}$$

[Nesting] allows expansion by concatenation of the path associated to the initial transition. This can be seen as a way of coding some structural information into the communication itself. [Relab] is designed for allowing the relabeling of both action labels and paths. Note that the function f is such that $f : Act{\times}S \longrightarrow Act$ and g is such that $g : Act{\times}S \longrightarrow S$.

$$\frac{P \xrightarrow{\alpha:p} P' , \alpha \notin L \cup \bar{L}, p \notin M}{P \setminus L:M \xrightarrow{\alpha:p} P' \setminus L:M} \text{[Restr]} \qquad \frac{P\{recX : P \mid X\} \xrightarrow{\alpha:p} P'}{recX : P \xrightarrow{\alpha:p} recX : P'} \text{[Rec]}$$

[Restr] is the restriction operator, very similar to the CCS one, except that it can use a set of paths. It forces internal communication by forbidding any communication actions (L and M specify the forbidden sets), excepted τ, which is actually an unobservable action. It is also the way of forcing synchronization among components. Restrictions of the form $P \setminus \{a, b, \dots\} : \emptyset$ will sometimes be written $P \setminus \{a, b, \dots\}$ for simplification.

[Rec] is a recursive operator such that $recX : P$ behaves like $recX : P'$ if $P\{(recX : P)/X\}$ becomes P' after the transition. The notation $A\{x/y\}$ defines a component built by substituting all occurrences of y in A by x (for instance, if $A \equiv a.b.X$, then $A\{Y/X\} \equiv a.b.Y$).[1]

The concurrent composition (with selective interaction) is defined toward [Par1], [Par2] and [Par3]:

$$\frac{P \xrightarrow{\alpha:p} P'}{P \mid_{mn} Q \xrightarrow{\alpha:p} P' \mid_{mn} Q} \text{[Par1]} \qquad \frac{Q \xrightarrow{\beta:q} Q'}{P \mid_{mn} Q \xrightarrow{\beta:q} P \mid_{mn} Q'} \text{[Par2]}$$

---

[1] We consider in our language only guarded recursions, i.e recursions $recX : P$ were any occurrence of X in P is within some sub-expression $\alpha.X$ ($recX : X + E$ is an example of unguarded recursion).

$$\frac{P \xrightarrow{\alpha:p} P' , Q \xrightarrow{\beta:q} Q' , p \simeq m , q \simeq n}{P \mid_{mn} Q \xrightarrow{\tau:\varepsilon} P' \mid_{mn} Q'} \text{[Par3]} \tag{3}$$

The following equations define the (selective) preemptive operator. Note that in [Preemp1b], [Preemp2b] and [Preemp3] a, b and $\bar{a}$ (respectively $\in \mathcal{A}$ and $\bar{\mathcal{A}}$) are used instead of $\alpha, \bar{\alpha}$ (both in *Act*), because only matching co-labels emitted by the left operand (and also meeting matching labels from the right operand) can trigger the transition. The $\triangleleft_{mn}$ notation is used for making explicit this notion of orientation. Intuitively, this expresses that outgoing calls and returns are able to transfer the activity flow.

$$\frac{P \xrightarrow{\alpha:p} P' , p \neq m \text{ or } \alpha = \tau}{P \triangleleft_{mn} Q \xrightarrow{\alpha:p} P' \triangleleft_{mn} Q} \text{[Preemp1a]} \qquad \frac{P \xrightarrow{\bar{a}:p} P' , p \simeq m, \bar{a} \in \bar{\mathcal{A}}}{P \triangleleft_{mn} Q \xrightarrow{\bar{a}:p} Q \triangleleft_{nm} P'} \text{[Preemp1b]}$$

$$\frac{Q \xrightarrow{\beta:q} Q' , q \neq n}{P \triangleleft_{mn} Q \xrightarrow{\beta:q} P \triangleleft_{mn} Q'} \text{[Preemp2a]} \qquad \frac{Q \xrightarrow{b:q} Q' , q \simeq n, b \in \mathcal{A}}{P \triangleleft_{mn} Q \xrightarrow{b:q} Q' \triangleleft_{nm} P} \text{[Preemp2b]}$$

$$\frac{P \xrightarrow{\bar{a}:p} P' , Q \xrightarrow{a:q} Q' , p \simeq m , q \simeq n}{P \triangleleft_{mn} Q \xrightarrow{\tau:\varepsilon} Q' \triangleleft_{nm} P'} \text{[Preemp3]} \tag{4}$$

Note that in (4), both operands P', Q' and selectors m, n are exchanged after the τ transition. The following derivation illustrates the functioning of the $\triangleleft$ operator:

$$(\bar{a}.a.0 \triangleleft_{**} a.\bar{b}.b.\bar{a}.0) \setminus \{a\} \xrightarrow{\tau:\varepsilon} (\bar{b}.b.\bar{a}.0 \triangleleft_{**} a.0) \setminus \{a\} \text{ [Preemp3]}$$

$$\xrightarrow{\bar{b}:\varepsilon} (a.0 \triangleleft_{**} b.\bar{a}.0) \setminus \{a\} \text{ [Preemp1b]}$$

$$\xrightarrow{b:\varepsilon} (\bar{a}.0 \triangleleft_{**} a.0) \setminus \{a\} \text{ [Preemp2b]}$$

$$\xrightarrow{\tau:\varepsilon} (0 \triangleleft_{**} 0) \setminus \{a\} \text{ [Preemp3]}$$

The reader shall consider the following derivation produced by preemptive composition of a component which is not passive (P):

$$(\bar{a}.a.0 \triangleleft_{**} a.\bar{b}.\bar{c}.b.\bar{a}.0) \setminus \{a\} \xrightarrow{\tau:\varepsilon} (\bar{b}.\bar{c}.b.\bar{a}.0 \triangleleft_{**} a.0) \setminus \{a\} \text{ [Preemp3]}$$

$$\xrightarrow{\bar{b}:\varepsilon} (a.0 \triangleleft_{**} \bar{c}.b.\bar{a}.0) \setminus \{a\} \text{ [Preemp1b]}$$

The derivation ends at this point. The composition $(a.\bar{b}.\bar{c}.b.\bar{a}.0 \mid \bar{a}.a.0) \setminus \{a\}$ would produce a different (successful, and thus not representative) derivation tree:
$\xrightarrow{\tau:\varepsilon} \xrightarrow{\bar{b}:\varepsilon} \xrightarrow{\bar{c}:\varepsilon} \xrightarrow{b:\varepsilon} \xrightarrow{\tau:\varepsilon}$.

2.4 Bisimulations and observation equivalences

The definition of observation equivalences is very important for characterizing components. For a composite component, it establishes the validity of a specification (obtained by composition of sub-components) with respect to the behavorial description of its interface. It also opens perspectives for reusing existing components by finding equivalent components in a repository indexed by interface descriptions. This section shows that the labeled transition system of ICCS allows us to define the notions of strong and weak bisimulation, thus allowing the same definitions of observation equivalences as in CCS. Moreover, it proposes more specific bisimulations able to capture the features of ICCS, related to selective interactions.

Definition 3. Derivatives.
Let $t = (\alpha_1 : p_1) \cdots (\alpha_n : p_n) \in \text{Act}^*$. Then
(1) $\xrightarrow{t} \stackrel{\text{def}}{=} \xrightarrow{\alpha_1 : p_1} \cdots \xrightarrow{\alpha_n : p_n}$;
(2) $\hat{t} \in \text{Act}^*$ is the result of removing all $(\tau : p_i)$'s from t;
(3) $\stackrel{t}{\Longrightarrow} \stackrel{\text{def}}{=} (\xrightarrow{\tau : p_i})^* \xrightarrow{\alpha_1 : p_1} (\xrightarrow{\tau : p_j})^* \cdots \xrightarrow{\alpha_n : p_n} (\xrightarrow{\tau : p_k})^*$.

The first bisimulation is the *strong bisimulation*, that allows to state $a.(b.0 + b.0) \sim a.b.0 + a.b.0$, for instance, but also $a.\tau.b.0 \not\sim a.b.0$. It is the strongest equivalence proposed.

Definition 4. Strong bisimulation.
A binary relation $\mathcal{R} \subseteq \mathcal{P} \times \mathcal{P}$ is a strong bisimulation if $(P_1, P_2) \in \mathcal{R} \Rightarrow \forall(\alpha, p) \in \text{Act} \times \mathcal{S}$:
(1) Whenever $P_1 \xrightarrow{\alpha : p} P_1'$ then, for some P_2', $P_2 \xrightarrow{\alpha : p} P_2'$ and $(P_1', P_2') \in \mathcal{R}$
(2) Whenever $P_2 \xrightarrow{\alpha : p} P_2'$ then, for some P_1', $P_1 \xrightarrow{\alpha : p} P_1'$ and $(P_1', P_2') \in \mathcal{R}$

Definition 5. Strong equivalence.
P_1 and P_2 are strongly equivalent, written $P_1 \sim P_2$ if $(P_1, P_2) \in \mathcal{R}$ for some strong bisimulation $\mathcal{R}$. This can be expressed as:

$$\sim = \bigcup \{\mathcal{R} : \mathcal{R} \text{ is a strong bisimulation }\}$$

Definition 6. Weak bisimulation.
A binary relation $\mathcal{R} \subseteq \mathcal{P} \times \mathcal{P}$ is a weak bisimulation if $(P_1, P_2) \in \mathcal{P} \Rightarrow \forall(\alpha, p) \in \text{Act} \times \mathcal{S}$:
(1) Whenever $P_1 \xrightarrow{\alpha : p} P_1'$ then, for some P_2', $P_2 \stackrel{\hat{\alpha} : p}{\Longrightarrow} P_2'$ and $(P_1', P_2') \in \mathcal{R}$
(2) Whenever $P_2 \xrightarrow{\alpha : p} P_2'$ then, for some P_1', $P_1 \stackrel{\hat{\alpha} : p}{\Longrightarrow} P_1'$ and $(P_1', P_2') \in \mathcal{R}$

Definition 7. Weak equivalence.
P_1 is weakly equivalent to P_2, written $P_1 \approx P_2$ if $(P_1, P_2) \in \mathcal{R}$ for some weak simulation $\mathcal{R}$. This can be expressed as:

$$\approx = \bigcup \{\mathcal{R} : \mathcal{R} \text{ is a weak bisimulation }\}$$

The weak equivalence equates processes by ignoring τ actions. For instance, $\tau.a.b.0 + c.\tau.0 \approx (a.\tau.b.0 + c.0)$. But $\approx$ is not substitutive for $+$: $b.0 \approx \tau.b.0$, but $a.0 + b.0 \not\approx a.0 + \tau.b.0$.

As for CCS, the observation equality is the better equivalence of ICCS, because it equates more components than $\sim$, and because it is a congruence relation, i.e substitutive for all operators, $\lhd$ excepted (for instance $P = Q \Rightarrow (P \mid_{mn} R) = (Q \mid_{mn} R)$). In fact, for the operator $\lhd$, $=$ is not substitutive in the general case, due to the different way of processing matching τ actions at the left and the right side: $a.\bar{b}.\tau.b.\bar{a}.0 = a.\bar{b}.b.\bar{a}$, but $(0 \lhd a.\bar{b}.\tau.b.\bar{a}.0) \neq (0 \lhd a.\bar{b}.b.\bar{a})$. The full substitution is verified only if both components are in the same category, i.e *passive* or not *passive*. In the sub-section 2.7, definition (15) and proposition (16) will give the formal definition of *passive* components.

Definition 8. Observation equality.
P_1 and P_2 are equal, or observation congruent, written $P_1 = P_2$ if $\Rightarrow \forall (\alpha, p) \in \text{Act} \times \mathcal{S}$:
(1) Whenever $P_1 \xrightarrow{\alpha:p} P_1'$ then, for some P_2', $P_2 \overset{\alpha:\underline{p}}{\Longrightarrow} P_2'$ and $P_1' \approx P_2'$
(2) Whenever $P_2 \xrightarrow{\alpha:p} P_2'$ then, for some P_1', $P_1 \overset{\alpha:\underline{p}}{\Longrightarrow} P_1' and P_1' \approx P_2'$

As an example, we have $a.\tau.b.0 \not\approx a.b.0$, but $a.\tau.b.0 = a.b.0$, and $(\tau.a.0 + b.0) \neq (a.0 + b.0)$, but $(\tau.a.0 + b.0) \approx (a.0 + b.0)$.
The important point for equivalence laws is that $(P \sim Q) \Rightarrow (P = Q) \Rightarrow (P \approx Q)$. This is a general result that comes from definitions of the different equivalences. The following bisimulations take into account the richer composition possibilities of ICCS. The reader may consider for instance $A \equiv a.b.0$ and $B \equiv a.(b.0) :: p$, which are such that $A \not\approx B$, but $(A \,|\, \bar{b}.0) \sim (B \,|\, \bar{b}.0)$.

Definition 9. m-selective strong bisimulation.
A binary relation $\mathcal{R} \subseteq \mathcal{P} \times \mathcal{P}$ is a m-selective strong bisimulation if $(P_1, P_2) \in \mathcal{R} \Rightarrow \forall (\alpha, p) \in \text{Act} \times \mathcal{S}$:
(1) Whenever $P_1 \xrightarrow{\alpha:p} P_1'$ then, for some P_2', $P_2 \xrightarrow{\alpha:q} P_2'$, $(p \simeq m \Rightarrow q \simeq m)$ and $(P_1', P_2') \in \mathcal{R}$
(2) Whenever $P_2 \xrightarrow{\alpha:q} P_2'$ then, for some P_1', $P_1 \xrightarrow{\alpha:p} P_1'$, $(q \simeq m \Rightarrow p \simeq m)$ and $(P_1', P_2') \in \mathcal{R}$

The corresponding m-selective equivalences, written $\sim_m$, $\approx_m$ and $=_m$ are defined in a similar way. The example given previously now becomes: $A \sim_* B$ and $(A \,|_{**}\, \bar{b}.0) \sim (B \,|_{**}\, \bar{b}.0)$. A law that generalizes this proposition will be proposed at the end of the next sub-section.

2.5 Equational laws

We outline hereafter some equational laws, obtained by establishing strong bisimilarity. Other laws could be produced by specifying conditions on selectors and paths. Basic laws established for CCS are reusable due to the similarity of the transition system. In fact, the rule [Preemp3] shows that $P \,|_{**}\, Q$ is semantically equivalent to the original operator $P|Q$ of CCS (as long that $\varphi(P) \neq \{\circ\}$ and $\varphi(Q) \neq \{\circ\}$). This means that, in association with the semantic definition of the restriction [Restr] and the relabeling [Relab], ICCS can be viewed as a superset of CCS (however, some laws might be restricted by the path condition).

Definition 10. Sorts.
The (syntactic) sort $\phi(P) \subseteq \mathcal{L}$ of a component P, is a set defined recursively over the syntactic structure of P:

$$\phi(\alpha_p.P) = \phi(P) \cup \{\alpha\} - \{\tau\}$$
$$\phi(P_1 \mid_{mn} P_2) = \phi(P_1) \cup \phi(P_2)$$
$$\phi(P[f:g]) = f(\phi(P))$$
$$\phi(P :: p) = \phi(P)$$

$$\phi(P_1 + P_2) = \phi(P_1) \cup \phi(P_2)$$
$$\phi(P \setminus L:M) = \phi(P) - L \cup \bar{L}$$
$$\phi(recX : P) = \phi(P)$$
$$\phi(P_1 \triangleleft_{mn} P_2) = \phi(P_1) \cup \phi(P_2)$$

For example, $\phi(a.\bar{c}.\tau.0 + b.0) = \{a, b, \bar{c}\}$.

Definition 11. Path sorts.
The (syntactic) path sort $\varphi(P) \subseteq S$ of a component P, is the set built over P from the following definition:

$$\varphi(0) = \emptyset$$
$$\varphi(\alpha_p.P) = \{p\} \cup \varphi(P)$$
$$\varphi(P_1 \mid_{mn} P_2) = \varphi(P_1) \cup \varphi(P_2)$$
$$\varphi(P[f:g]) = g(\phi(P) \times \varphi(P))$$
$$\varphi(P :: p) = \oplus(p, \varphi(P))$$

$$\varphi(X) = \emptyset$$
$$\varphi(P_1 + P_2) = \varphi(P_1) \cup \varphi(P_2)$$
$$\varphi(P \setminus L:M) = \varphi(P) - M$$
$$\varphi(recX : P) = \varphi(P)$$
$$\varphi(P_1 \triangleleft_{mn} P_2) = \varphi(P_1) \cup \varphi(P_2)$$

Here, $\oplus$ is the function:
$$\oplus : S \times \{p_i \in S\} \to \{q_i \in S\} \text{ such that } \forall s \in S, \oplus(s, p_i) = q_i = p_i + s$$
For example, if $P \equiv a.(b.\tau.0 : p_1)$, then $\varphi(P :: p_2) = \{p_2, p_1 p_2\}$.

Definition 12. Path quotient.
The quotient of a path sort $\varphi(P)$ by a path q, written $\varphi(P)/q$ is the set $\{p_i \in \varphi(P) : p_i \backsimeq q\}$

Proposition 13. *Laws and relations for* $\mid_{mn}$, $\triangleleft_{mn}$, $\sim$ *and* $\sim_k$.
We shall use:
(a) $\parallel$ *instead of* $\mid_{oo}$ *and* $\triangleleft_{oo}$; **(b)** $\mid$ *instead of* $\mid_{..}$; **(c)** $\triangleleft$ *instead of* $\triangleleft_{..}$.

monoïd laws	
1. $(P+Q) \sim (Q+P)$	2. $((P+Q)+R) \sim (P+(Q+R))$
3. $(P+P) \sim P$	4. $(P+0) \sim P$

static laws
1. $(P \mid_{mo} Q) \sim (P \mid_{om} Q) \sim (P \triangleleft_{om} Q) \sim (P \triangleleft_{mo} Q) \sim (P \triangleleft_{oo} Q) \sim (P \mid_{oo} Q)$ $\quad \forall m, n, m', n' \in S$
2. $P \mid_{mn} Q \sim Q \mid_{nm} P$
3. $P \mid_{mn} (Q \mid_{m'n'} R) \sim (P \mid_{nm} Q) \mid_{m'n'} R)$ 4. $P \mid_{mn} 0 \sim P$
5. $P \setminus L:M \sim P$ if $\phi(P) \cap (L \cup \bar{L}) = \emptyset$ and $\varphi(P) \cap M = \emptyset$
6. $P \setminus L:M \sim 0$ if $\phi(P) \cap (L \cup \bar{L}) = \phi(P)$ or $\varphi(P) \cap M = \varphi(P)$
7. $P \setminus L:M \setminus K:N \sim P \setminus L \cup K:M \cup N$
8. $(P \mid_{mn} Q) \setminus L:M \sim (P \setminus L:M) \mid_{mn} (Q \setminus L:M)$ if $\phi(P) \cap \overline{\phi(Q)} \cap (L \cup \bar{L}) = \emptyset$ or $\varphi(P)/m \cap \varphi(Q)/n \cap M = \emptyset$
9. $(P \triangleleft_{mn} Q) \setminus L:M \sim (P \setminus L:M) \triangleleft_{mn} (Q \setminus L:M)$ if $\phi(P) \cap \overline{\phi(Q)} \cap (L \cup \bar{L}) = \emptyset$ or $\varphi(P)/m \cap \varphi(Q)/n \cap M = \emptyset$
10. $0 :: p \sim 0$ 11. $P :: \varepsilon \sim P$
12. $P :: p_1 :: p_2 \sim P :: p_1 p_2$ 13. $(P+Q) :: p_1 \sim P :: p_1 + Q :: p_1$
14a. $(P \mid_{mn} Q) :: p \sim (P :: p \mid_{mp\ np} Q :: p)[(\tau/\tau : \varepsilon):(p/\tau : \varepsilon)]$
14b. $(P \triangleleft_{mn} Q) :: p \sim (P :: p \triangleleft_{mp\ np} Q :: p)[(\tau/\tau : \varepsilon):(p/\tau : \varepsilon)]$
15. $\varphi(P)/o = \emptyset$ 16. $\varphi(P :: o)/* = \emptyset$
17. $\varphi(P :: o) = \{o\}$ 18. $0[f:g] \sim 0$
19. $P[f:g][f':g'] \sim P[f' \circ (f:g):g' \circ (f:g)]$

equational laws
1. $P_1 \vartriangleleft_{mn} (P_2 \| P_3) \sim (P_1 \vartriangleleft_{mn} P_2) \| P_3$ if $\varphi(P_3)/n = \emptyset$
2. $(P_1 \| P_2) \vartriangleleft_{mn} P_3) \sim (P_1 \vartriangleleft_{mn} P_3) \| P_2$ if $\varphi(P_2)/m = \emptyset$
3. $((P_1 + P_2) \vartriangleleft_{mn} P_3) \sim ((P_1 \vartriangleleft_{mn} P_3) + P_2)$ if $\varphi(P_2)/m = \emptyset$
4. $(P_1 \mid_{mn} P_2) \sim (P_1 \| P_2)$ if $\varphi(P_1)/m = \emptyset$ or $\varphi(P_2)/n = \emptyset$
5. $(P_1 \mid_{mn} P_2) \sim (P_1 | P_2)$ if $\varphi(P_1)/m = \varphi(P_1)$ and $\varphi(P_2)/n = \varphi(P_2)$
6. $(P \| Q) \setminus L : M \sim (P \setminus L : M) \| (Q \setminus L : M)$ 7. $(P \| Q) :: p \sim (P :: p) \| (Q :: p)$

$\sim$ is a congruence relation
1. $P \sim Q \Rightarrow (P \mid_{mn} R) \sim (Q \mid_{mn} R)$ 2. $P \sim Q \Rightarrow (P \vartriangleleft_{mn} R) \sim (Q \vartriangleleft_{mn} R)$
3. $P \sim Q \Rightarrow (R \vartriangleleft_{mn} P) \sim (R \vartriangleleft_{mn} Q)$ 4. $P \sim Q \Rightarrow (P :: p) \sim (Q :: p)$

$\sim_k$ and composition
1. $P \sim_k Q \Rightarrow (P \mid_{kn} R) \sim (Q \mid_{kn} R)$ 2. $P \sim_k Q \Rightarrow (P \vartriangleleft_{kn} R) \sim (Q \vartriangleleft_{kn} R)$
3. $P \sim_k Q \Rightarrow (R \vartriangleleft_{mk} P) \sim (R \vartriangleleft_{nk} Q)$
4. $P \sim Q \Rightarrow P \sim_k Q$ for some selector k 5. $P \sim_k Q \Rightarrow (P :: p) \sim_{kp} (Q :: p)$

2.6 Expansion Laws

Providing an expansion law, i.e a law that relates static constructors of ICCS, such as [Relab], [Restr], [Preemp] and [Par] to dynamic constructors ([Prefix] and [Alt]) is an important step for establishing an axiomatization of the process equality, as Robin Milner did for CCS restricted to finite state agents [9].

ICCS does not yet provide a notion equivalent to the *concurrent normal form* of CCS. A set of transformation laws could be investigated in order to define a normal form able to include the two composition operators. However, we propose four laws for all static operators, which can be recursively applied to any sequential component (without recursive operators), in order to bring them into standard form (prefix and summation):

Proposition 14. *Expansion laws for* $\vartriangleleft_{mn}, \mid_{mn}, ::, [f:g]$.

expansion law for $\vartriangleleft_{mn}$
If $R \equiv (P \vartriangleleft_{mn} Q) \setminus L : M$,   then
$R \sim \sum\{a_p.(Q \vartriangleleft_{nm} P') \setminus L : M$ if $P \xrightarrow{a:p} P', a \in \bar{A}, p \simeq m, a \notin \bar{L}, p \notin M\} +$
$\sum\{b_q.(Q' \vartriangleleft_{nm} P) \setminus L : M$ if $Q \xrightarrow{b:q} Q', b \in A, q \simeq n, b \notin L, q \notin M\} +$
$\sum\{\tau.(Q' \vartriangleleft_{nm} P') \setminus L : M$ if $P \xrightarrow{\bar{a}:p} P', Q \xrightarrow{a:q} Q', a \in A, p \simeq m, q \simeq n\} +$
$\sum\{\beta_q.(P \vartriangleleft_{mn} Q') \setminus L : M$ if $Q \xrightarrow{\beta:q} Q', q \neq n, \beta \notin L \cap \bar{L}, q \notin M\} +$
$\sum\{\alpha_p.(P' \vartriangleleft_{mn} Q) \setminus L : M$ if $P \xrightarrow{\alpha:p} P', (p \neq m, \alpha \notin L \cap \bar{L}, p \notin M)$ or $(\alpha = \tau)\}$

expansion law for $\mid_{mn}$
If $R \equiv (P \mid_{mn} Q) \setminus L : M$,   then
$R \sim \sum\{\tau.(P' \mid_{mn} Q') \setminus L : M$ such that $P \xrightarrow{\alpha:p} P', Q \xrightarrow{\bar{\alpha}:q} Q', p \simeq m, q \simeq n\} +$
$\sum\{\beta_q.(P \mid_{mn} Q') \setminus L : M$ such that $Q \xrightarrow{\beta:q} Q', \beta \notin L \cap \bar{L}, q \notin M\} +$
$\sum\{\alpha_p.(P' \mid_{mn} Q) \setminus L : M$ such that $P \xrightarrow{\alpha:p} P', \alpha \notin L \cap \bar{L}, p \notin M\}$

expansion law for ::
$(P :: q) \sim \sum\{\alpha_{pq}.(P' :: q)$ such that $P \xrightarrow{\alpha:p} P'\}$

expansion law for $[f : g]$
$P[f:g] \sim \sum\{f(\alpha, p)_{g(\alpha,p)}.(P'[f:g])$ such that $P \xrightarrow{\alpha:p} P'\}$

As an illustration, these laws allow the following: if $P \equiv \bar{a}.a.0 \vartriangleleft a.\bar{c}.(b.\bar{a}.0 + c.\bar{a}.0)$ then $P \setminus \{a\} : \emptyset \sim (\tau.\bar{c}.(b.\tau.(0 \vartriangleleft 0) + c.\tau.(0 \vartriangleleft 0)))$ (after removing identities in relabeling), and, by applying appropriate equational laws: $P \sim (\tau.\bar{c}.(b.\tau.0 + c.\tau.0))$. The direct application of expansion laws is to put ICCS expressions in full standard form (only prefix and alternation constructors) in order to reduce and compare them on the basis of a few primitive laws.

2.7 More on passive components and passive composition

This sub-section proposes a formal definition of passive components and gives examples that illustrate the concept.

Definition 15. Passive components (behavorial definition)
A component $P \in \mathcal{P}$ is passive iff:
for all derivative P' of P such that $P \xrightarrow{a:p} (\xrightarrow{\tau:p_i})^* P'$, then $((\exists P'' s.t. P' \xrightarrow{b:q} P'') \wedge (a, b \in \mathcal{A}) \wedge (P'' \text{ is passive}))$.

The following components are also passive: $0, a.\bar{a}.0, (a.\bar{b}.c.\bar{d}.0 + e.\bar{e}.0), a.\tau.recX : (\bar{b}.c.X + \bar{a}.0)$, as are the following: $(a.b.\bar{c}.0|\bar{b}.c.\bar{a}.0) \setminus \{b, c\} : \emptyset$ which can be equated to $a.\tau.\tau.\bar{a}.0$ by using the expansion and static laws. The following components are not passive: $\bar{a}.a.0, a.\bar{b}.\tau.b.\bar{a}.0$. Note that internal actions are allowed only after an input action and before an output action (this corresponds with the presence of the activity flow into the component).

The following proposition relates the preemptive composition operator to passive components:

Proposition 16. *Passive components (equational characterization)*
A component P ($\varphi(P) \neq \{\circ\}$) is passive iff $(0 \vartriangleleft P) \sim P$

The full modeling of any passive component requires the consideration of reentrance, which allows the modeling of the interleaving of activity flows inside a passive component, and thus concurrency conflicts or ordered schedules toward semaphores.
Consider the following example:
$A \equiv a.\bar{b}.b.\bar{a}.0$ and $B \equiv \bar{a}.a.0$. Then $((B\|B) \vartriangleleft A) \setminus \{a\} \sim (\tau.\bar{b}.b.\tau.0 + \tau.\bar{b}.b.\tau.0)$, by applying the expansion law. This does not correspond with a concurrent execution of A. Consider instead $A' \equiv recX : a.(\bar{b}.b.\bar{a}.0\|X)$.
Now, the reader might verify (by developing both derivation trees) that $((B\|B) \vartriangleleft A) \setminus \{a\} \approx (\bar{b}.b.0\|\bar{b}.b.0)$, which corresponds to the full activity flow interleaving that was expected. The following definition makes this precise, for components that can be expressed in a standard form $\sum \alpha_i.P_i$

Definition 17. Reentrant form of passive components
A passive component $P \equiv \sum \alpha_i.P_i$ is set in reentrant form P_r by:
$P_r \equiv recX : \sum \alpha_i.(P_i\|X)$

Although this definition is required for modeling general Olan components, it raises two problems: the component must be expressed in a standard form, and the recursive definition produces components which are not finite-state. The first hypothesis is acceptable in our context, where all component interfaces can effectively be rewritten in standard form (see section 3). For the second one, Robin Milner demonstrated that the process equality of infinite-state agents is not decidable in the general case. Anyway, some solutions exist for restricted cases: it is easy to show that $(P \sim Q) \Rightarrow (P_r \sim Q_r)$, and thus, assuming the constraint that any reentrant component must be composed of reentrant components, the component equality becomes decidable by using the initial standard form.

3 Applying ICCS to Olan

3.1 The Olan Component Model

The Olan project [15] investigates a "programming in the large" approach that allows the specification of applications as hierarchies of interacting components, glued together through *connectors*, which are agents specialized in communication and coordination tasks.

The Olan Configuration Language (OCL) belongs to the class of Module Interconnection Languages (MIL) [13] and aims at clearly separating the programming phase of individual components from the configuration phase of the application's structure and behaviour. An application is described and configured as a hierarchy of interconnected components, the leaves of which are basic software units encapsulated in the so-called *primitive components*. The nodes of this hierarchy are more complex components (namely *composite components*) which are constructed from interconnected components at a lower level of the hierarchy.

A component is made of an interface and an implementation. The interface describes the services that the implementation provides to other components, along with the services it requires at run-time. The implementation, either primitive or composite, fulfills the requirements expressed at the interface level; in other words, it maps the interface to the encapsulated pieces of software.

Within any composite implementation, the application designer describe the interconnections of components. The interconnections specify the way components should communicate with each other. At first, an interconnection is a binding of component's requirements to component's provisions by the means of a connector. More than just a "binding object" between components, connectors ensure the adaptation between compliant but not necessarily compatible interfaces, the control of the communication (for instance, in terms of coordination of the execution flows) and the effective transport of information through the use of a configurable communication protocol (e.g. TCP or UDP) and/or mechanism (e.g. an ORB or simple sockets).

The application designer which uses the Olan Configuration Language needs to specify the behavior of composite components, starting from a behavioral description of reusable sub-components (interfaces). At this level, the interface description needs some level of non-determinism in order to describe a large frame of possibilities: $a.P + \bar{b}.Q$ describes a component able to perform P after receiving a, or to perform the output action $\bar{b}$ and then Q, without providing any information concerning the internal or external mechanisms issuing the decision. As opposed to this descriptive level, the designer is expected to specify the behavior of connectors in a full deterministic way: behavioral variations of the new system must only depend on behavioral variations of sub-systems, otherwise, the designer will increase entropy rather than controlling the new functionalities.

3.2 Weak and strong determinism

This subsection introduces two notions of determinism that will be used respectively for interface descriptions and for connector specifications. The first one, called weak determinism, allows branching as long as it does not occur on the same communication action. This allows branching such as $a.0 + \bar{b}.0$ or $a.\tau.0 + b.0$, but prohibits $a.b.0 + a.c.0$, $\bar{a}.0 + \bar{b}.0$ or $\tau.a.0 + b.0$.

Definition 18. Weak determinism.
A component P is weakly deterministic if, for all derivatives P' of P:
$P' \xrightarrow{\alpha:p} Q$ and $P' \xrightarrow{\beta:q} Q'$ implies $(\alpha : p \neq \beta : q$ and $\alpha, \beta \neq \tau)$.

Definition 19. Strong determinism.
An component P is strongly deterministic if, for all derivatives P' of P:
$P' \xrightarrow{\alpha:p} Q$ and $P' \xrightarrow{\beta:q} Q'$ implies $(\alpha : p \neq \beta : q)$ and $\alpha, \beta \in \mathcal{A}$.

This means that branching is allowed only for distinct input labels. This specifies components for which outputs are determined by inputs only, and not by internal decisions. It is obvious that if P is strongly deterministic, then P is weakly deterministic.

3.3 Component interfaces

These first describe basic services, synchronous (**provide, require**) or asynchronous (**react, notify**); synchronous services can accept or raise a set of exceptions. Moreover, provided services can be protected against concurrent accessing toward semaphores of the form $Sem_i \equiv recX : u_i.\bar{u}_i.d_i.\bar{d}_i.X$.

The following table summarizes all possibilities:

services	ICCS form
provide p	$p.\bar{p}.P$
provide p [†]	$(p.\bar{u}_p.u_p.\bar{p}_0.p_0.\bar{d}_p.d_p.\bar{p}.P_1) \lhd (Sem_p \| p_0.\bar{p}_0.P_0)$
provide p [‡]	$p.(\bar{p}.P_1 + \sum e\bar{x}_i.P_i)$
provide p [††]	$(p.\bar{u}_p.u_p.\bar{p}_0.(p_0.\bar{d}_p.d_p.\bar{p}.P_1 + \sum(e\bar{x}_i.\bar{d}_p.d_p.P_i))) \lhd (Sem_p \| p_0.\bar{p}_0.P_0)$
require r	$\bar{r}.r.P_1$
require r [‡]	$\bar{r}.(r.P_1 + \sum ex_i.P_i)$
react r	$r.P$
notify n	$\bar{n}.P$

[†] : with synchronization for exclusive calls
[‡] : with exceptions $\sum ex_i$

Interface descriptions contain a behavior description specified by finite state, weakly deterministic expressions, built over the following sub-language:

$$P ::= 0 \mid X \mid \alpha.P \mid P + P \mid recX : P$$

where α_i are taken from the set of services defined.

All specifications S can be equated to some $\sum \alpha_i.P_i$ by using expansion laws. This last expression is then translated to $recX : \sum \alpha_i.(P_i \| X)$, if the component is declared as passive and reentrant; for active or passive components, the behavorial specification is translated to $recX : \sum \alpha_i.Q_i$, where $Q_i \equiv P_i\{X/0\}$.

3.4 Connectors

The connector functionalities are specified by finite and strongly deterministic components, either passive or active, of the form $\sum \alpha_i.P_i$. This means that any connector is specified through the transfer of input sequences into output sequences. The following sub-language covers the requirements: $P ::= 0|X|\alpha.P|P + P.$[2] The connector itself is finally defined by $recX : \sum \alpha_i.Q_i$, where $Q_i \equiv P_i\{X/0\}$, for active or passive connectors, and by $recX : \sum \alpha_i.(P_i \| X)$ for passive *and* reentrant connectors.

3.5 Specification correctness

The definition of correctness criteria, i.e. a set of theoretical tools that assert whether an interface specification or a composite implementation is correct or not, is a central issue in architectural description languages ([7], [4], [14]), because it permits taking full advantage of the explicit architectural specifications and to compensate the specification overhead. The following paragraphs detail the main criteria proposed here.

Interfaces In order to describe passive or reentrant components, an interface specification I_{itf} must verify $(0 \lhd I_{itf}) \sim I_{itf}$. It must always be weakly deterministic, and this can be checked by a simple syntactic analysis of branching.

Connectors Connectors can be either active or passive, and this can be checked in the same way as interfaces. Connectors must be strongly deterministic, and this can be verified by a static analysis of the syntax tree (branching).

Composite implementation This is the most important point. Here, the problem is to define the conformity of the implementation with respect to the interface specification. The component equality brings a powerful response: For active components, the specification S and the interface I_{itf} must verify $S =_k I_{itf}$ for some selector k such that $\varphi(S)/k \neq \emptyset$. This means that the implementation must present the same behavior as the interface, up to a (significant) selector k. For passive components, it is slightly different, due to the fact that $\lhd$ is not associative: $P \lhd (Q \star R)$ is not equal to $(P \lhd Q) \star R$ in the general case ($\star$ stands for $\lhd$ or $|$). Notably, this means that the specification must use a component variable E_{ext} for representing the external context, and a selector variable

---

[2] The composition operators might be usable

to parameter the left interaction. For instance: $((E_{ext} \vartriangleleft_{mn} P) \star Q \cdots) \setminus A \cup E_A$ (P, Q are not detailed here), and the effective behavior is given by a system of the form:

$$\left\{ \begin{array}{c} (E_{ext} \vartriangleleft_{mn} P) \star Q \cdots) \setminus A \cup E_A \\ m =? \\ E_{ext} = R \\ E_A = \{\ldots\} \end{array} \right.$$

In order to check the conformity, the system must be:

$$S \equiv \left\{ \begin{array}{c} ((E_{ext} \vartriangleleft_{mn} P) \star Q \cdots) \setminus A \cup E_A \\ m = * \\ E_{ext} = 0 \\ E_A = \emptyset \end{array} \right.$$

Now, as for active composite components, the equation $S =_k I_{itf}$ must hold for some significant selector k.

This equality is fine, because it covers very different cases. First, as the component equality is fully substitutive, it is ensured that an implementation will behave like its interface through any kind of composition. Secondly, it will check the divergences in the implementation, as well as deadlocks that might be introduced. For instance, if $I_{itf} \equiv a.\bar{b}.b.\bar{a}.0$, then $S \equiv (a.\bar{c}.d.0 \mid \bar{d}.c.\bar{b}.b.\bar{a}.0) \setminus c, d$ (deadlock on c, d) will not equate I_{itf}. Of course, the implementation cannot be correct if the interface is not so. But by minimizing the interface specification expressiveness (no composition), we make things easier in this direction. However, properties of component composition should be studied more deeply, in order to take full benefits of the hypothesis concerning determinism for interfaces and connectors, and in order to make weaker the constraints concerning the composition of reentrant components.

4 Conclusion and future work

The paper presents a calculus which preserves most of the theoretical contribution of CCS, while providing new possibilities for modeling *passive* components, of which we gave a formal definition (see def. 15).

The difficulty of combining the new operator for passive composition with the standard one is tackled toward the concept of selective interaction, which led as a side effect to refining the expressiveness concerning communication channels. This last issue is important for interconnection languages. Formal developments of section 2 show that the complexity overheads remain at an acceptable cost, and that the theory provides tractable issues. Moreover, selective interactions produce an elegant refinement of the notion of concurrency, making the repertoire of parallel composition richer by providing the $\|$ operator (which semantics expresses parallelism without interaction), and the $\mid$ operator (which semantics expresses parallelism with full interaction). Both of them appear natural to use within specifications.

Some calculi, such as OC [5], define a composition operator able to perform functional calls as well as remote calls (inter-processes). But the notion of passive composition we propose in this paper is different and more general, allowing the coordination of passive components owning a state, as well as the modeling of functional calls.

Authors such as Yellin and Strom [4] have shown the interest of behavorial specification at the interface level for automating the synthesis of software adaptors. But the formalism presented is not very tractable, and expressiveness of finite-state automatons is poor and probably too verbose for realistic applications. Moreover, this work does not clearly establish the relationship between the finite-state automaton model and the hypothesis concerning execution models.

Robert Allen and David Garlan have proposed in [7] the formalization of architectural interconnections toward ports and connectors, specified by using a subset of CSP [6]. Their work has put the emphasis on connectors which centralize most of the knowledge concerning the interconnection (using *roles* and *glue*), as opposed to the Olan approach, where behavioral specifications are shared between interfaces and connectors. They define compatibility checking toward deadlock free and conservative connectors, i.e. connectors that preserve the deadlock free property toward composition with any specified role. But their correctness criterion seems more complex, less concise and not stronger than ours. Moreover, here again the expressiveness of connectors and role specification is not addressed regarding the basic hypothesis concerning the execution model (connectors and ports are activities).

Magee, Eisenbach and Kramer [8] propose modeling the Darwin configuration language in the π-calculus. Darwin is close to Olan regarding the component model, but proposes few abstractions for capturing the primitive component behaviors. They argue that dynamic aspects of Darwin justify the choice of the π-calculus (which is more complex than CCS), but it is not clear whether dynamic component instantiations might be modeled in CCS or not. But the important point is that by attempting to clearly separate the operational behavior of Darwin architectures from the implementation behaviors, without any information on primitive behaviors, they only define the semantics of communication. Thus no architectural analysis is proposed, and the benefits of the architectural description seem restricted to easing the distribution.

It would be interesting to relate our work to some results in the software engineering field, such as the I-composition of Lam and Shankar [14], and to compare our correctness criteria, based on bisimulation, to their theorem for characterizing the Interface/Implementation correctness by using set oriented operations. However, the calculus developed in this paper seems more adapted to define operational semantics of interconnected systems.

ICCS will be used precisely for defining the operational semantics of the Olan Configuration Language, and for specifying specialized connectors. Moreover, by associating behavorial specifications to the Interface Description Language, it could be applied to a simulation tool (integrated within the Olan development environment), and to the generation of test sets from middle-level specifications. This last issue could take advantage of the modal logic proposed by Robin Milner [9][11], quite applicable to the transition system of ICCS. A small compiler and a simulator have been realized [12] which can be used for exploratory work.

Acknowledgements

The authors are thankfull to all members of the SIRAC Project and its contributors: Roland Balter, Sacha Krakowiak, Michel Riveill, Marie-Claude Pellegrini and Fabienne

Boyer. Sincere thanks are due to Jean-Marc Andreoli for his advices during the different stages of this work and to Irene Maxwell for her careful reading of various versions of the manuscript.

References

1. L. Bellissard, S. Ben Atallah, F. Boyer, M. Riveill, "Distributed Application Configuration", *Proc. 16th International Conference on Distributed Computing Systems,* pp. 579-585, IEEE Computer Society, Hong-Kong, May 1996.
2. Ichiro Satoh and Mario Tokoro, "A Timed Calculus for Distributed Object with Clocks" *Proceedings of the 7th European Conference on Object Oriented Programming,* pp. 326-345, Springer-Verlag, Kaiserslautern, Germany, July 1993.
3. Ichiro Satoh and Mario Tokoro, "A Formalism for Distributed Real-Time Processes with Temporal Uncertainties", *Proceedings of OOPSLA'92,* ACM, pp.315-326, October 1994.
4. Daniel M. Yellin and Robert E. Strom "Interfaces, Protocols, and the Semi-Automatic Construction of Software Adaptors", *Proceedings of OOPSLA'94 (Portland, Oregon USA),* ACM, pp.176-190, October 1994.
5. Oscar Nierstrasz, "Toward an Object Calculus", *Proceedings of ECOOP'91 Workshop on Object-Based Concurrent Computing - Geneva,* LNCS, pp 1-20, July 1991.
6. Hoare C.A.R., "Communicating Sequential Processes", *Communications of ACM,* 21(8), 1978.
7. Robert Allen and David Garlan, "Formal Connectors", *Technical Report CMU-CS-94-115,* School of Computer Science, Carnegie Mellon University, Pittsburgh, PA 15213, March 1994.
8. Jef Magee, Susan Eisenbach and Jeff Kramer, "Modelling Darwin in the π-calculus", *Theory & Practice in Distributed systems, Dagstuhl Castle, Germany,* Lecture Notes in computer Sciences 938, September 1994.
9. Robin Milner, *Communication and Concurrency,* Prentice Hall international, 66 Wood Lane End, Hemel Hempstead Hertfordshire, HP2 4RG UK, 1989.
10. Robin Milner, Joachim Parrow and David Walker, "A Calculus of Mobile Processes (Part 1 & 2)", *LFCS Laboratory for Foundation of Computer Sciences, University of Edinburgh,* June 1989.
11. Robin Milner, Joachim Parrow and David Walker, "Modal Logics for Mobile Processes", *LFCS Laboratory for Foundation of Computer Sciences, University of Edinburgh,* April 1991.
12. Jean-Yves Vion-Dury, 'http://pukapuka.inrialpes.fr/ICCS/', *Exploratory Compiler and simulator for ICCS,* January 1997.
13. De Remer F. and Kron H. "Programming-in-the-large versus Programming-in-the-small", *IEEE Transactions on Software Engineering,* Vol. 2 (No. 2), pp. 80-87, June 1976.
14. Simon S. Lam, A.Udaya Shankar, "A Theory of Interfaces and Modules I-Composition Theorem" *IEEE Transactions on Software Engineering,* Vol. 20, No. 1, January 1994.
15. Bellissard L., Ben Atallah S., Kerbrat A., and Riveill M. "Comonent-based Programming and Application Management with Olan", *Object-Based Parallel and Distributed Computation France-Japan Workshop, OBPDC'95,* Briot J.P., Geib J.M., Yonezawa A. (Eds.), LNCS, Vol. 1107, Springer-Verlag, 1996.
16. Magee J., Dulay N. and Kramer J. "A Constructive Development Environment for Parallel and Distributed Programs", *Proceedings of the International Conference on Configurable Distributed Systems,* Pittsburgh, PA, March 1994.

A Coordination Model for Distributed Object Systems

Mathieu Buffo and Didier Buchs

University of Geneva and Swiss Federal Institute of Technology
buffo@cui.unige.ch   buchs@di.epfl.ch

Abstract. Distributed systems have strong similarities with object systems. However, coordination models for these systems have slightly different requirements. This paper presents a specific coordination model for distributed object systems, built on hierarchical execution contexts. This model allows to refine object-oriented specifications into distributed software architectures.

1 Introduction

Quality and reliability are important themes of the software engineering community. With the increase of software importance, both in terms of demand and complexity, software deficiencies appear more and more acute, as pointed out by software engineers. Software quality may be increased by using appropriate programming paradigms and techniques. Among these, we can cite concurrent computing - and more particularly *distributed programming* - and *object-orientation*.

Distributed object systems are computer systems being at the same time distributed and descrubed using objects. Actually, both kinds of systems are composed of many loosely-coupled software components interacting for achieving a global goal. Merging both concepts is important [4], because it allows to develop suitable distributed software architectures by refining abstract and formal object-oriented specifications, as in this case specifications and software architectures share the same overall structures [6].

Distributed object systems must be coordinated for managing the dependencies of their components [9]. Preserving characteristics of objects systems imposes that in actual practice, the coordination features are not substituted but added to the traditional object coordination features; they are likely to be described as a suitable coordination layer surrounding a traditional object core, as depicted in figure 1.

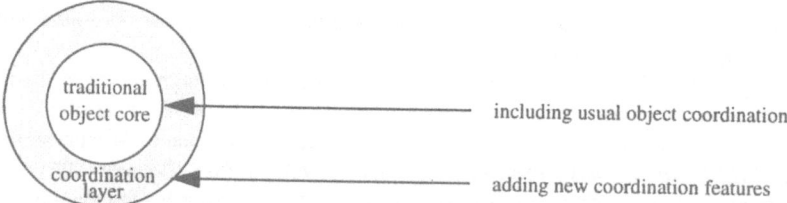

Fig. 1. structure of distributed object systems

Coordination models for distributed and for object systems have slightly different requirements [3]. In short, configurations of distributed object systems should:
- unify the description of the granularity of processes and the granularity of objects;
- add the notion of localization into the object system description;
- allow dynamic configurations by means of object migration.

Likewise, interactions in distributed object systems have following characteristics:

- the coordinated entities are the objects;
- the coordinating media is a multi-client multi-server model;
- the coordination rules are synchronization expressions managing message passing.

2 Contextual Coordination Model

This section presents a new coordination model specifically developed for distributed object systems, namely the contextual coordination model. Historically, it was mainly inspired by the complex associations [8], coping with structural object interactions, by the ActorSpace model [1], providing communication models based on destination patterns, and by the language Darwin [7], focusing on structural distributed system configurations. With regards to both its predecessors, the contextual coordination model allows complete hierarchical coordination of object-oriented systems, preserving total object encapsulation [3].

The basic idea behind the contextual coordination model is the separation between objects and their execution contexts. In consequence, objects can be considered as abstruse software entities defined in relation to their execution context. They are gaining sense when plunged into their context. On the other hand, contexts represent execution environments encompassing one or more objects.

Due to lack of space, we only sketch here the coordination model. Its complete description can be found in [3].

2.1 Configuration Structure

Contexts are encompassing actions, and actions can be described by active objects. However, a complex action can also be expressed as a set of coordinated objects, i.e. as a context encapsulating sub-actions. Therefore, contexts are allowed to contain objects *and* sub-contexts. As a result, coordinated systems are depicted as a hierarchy of contexts, allowing to unify the granularity of processes and objects.

Moreover, objects can be static or dynamic. Statics objects are encompassed in a context for the whole execution time of the system. On the contrary, dynamic objects can dynamically evolve in the system.

2.2 Interaction Structure

Interaction structures are described by means of connections propagating method calls. These connections are connecting so-called *gates* with methods. Gates are output ports and methods are input ports, both for objects and contexts. In fact, gates allow to handle messages when they cross the sender's membrane, while methods are used in a traditional way.

As connections are part of contexts, they can bind only ports belonging to the encompassing context, just as elements of a contexts are allowed to interfere only with other elements of the object. In other words, connections are respecting the configuration hierarchy. The resulting coordination medium is a hierarchical network of method calls between computation and coordination entities.

Non trivial coordination rules are allowed through the use of complex synchronization expressions in the connections. These expressions are build using simultaneous, sequential and alternate operators, as in CO-OPN$_{/2}$.

2.3 Contexts as Modelling Boundaries

Contexts are delimiting execution worlds; they are defining conditions of accessibility for components of models. Contexts are providing modelling boundaries. Actually, contexts encapsulate each of their components. As a result, sub-contexts as well as contained objects are invisible from the external world coordination. In addition, the encapsulation is extended to the coordination provided by traditional object layer; objects contained in different contexts cannot communicate directly by traditional message passing. Hence, contexts are defining modelling boundaries; components are protected from aggressions of external world.

Object migration is introduced into the contextual coordination model. Actually, the contextual coordination model allows objects to migrate along with a copy of their identifier, when messages are transiting into the coordination layer. The contextual coordination model allows two kinds of migrations, namely the definitive one and the temporary one. Using definitive migration, the involved objects are moving from the origin to the recipient at the time of the method call, i.e. at the time of the service fulfillment. On the other hand using temporary migration, the involved objects are moving from the origin to the recipient for the duration of service fulfillment only, i.e. objects move to the recipient and then return to their origins.

2.4 Contexts as High-Level Coordination Abstractions

Contexts are providing high-level coordination abstractions to the external world. Indeed, a context provides an abstraction of its internal components. Likewise, interacting with a context stands for an abstraction of many internal interactions. Accordingly, a contextual system is described by a unique main context, abstracting the whole system, and encompassing each of its components.

The contextual coordination model fulfil the requirements made in section 2 for coordinating distributed object systems.

- In terms of configurations, it allows to unify processes and objects granularities, through hierarchical abstractions, and it adds localization informations into object systems. Moreover, dynamic configurations are introduced through the underlaying object model and through the use of the high-level object migration mechanism.
- In terms of interactions, the contextual coordination model proposes a multi-client multi-server coordinating medium, consistent with the traditional object-oriented message passing mechanism. Complete coordination rules are provided through the use of synchronization expressions. Finally, it allows coordination of object systems without breaking encapsulation, through the use of gates.

3 Context and Objects Interface Language

According to the coordination model, we developed COIL [3], a coordination language suited for our object-oriented specification language CO-OPN$_{/2}$ [2]. The semantics of a COIL system is given by a translation to an equivalent CO-OPN$_{/2}$ system.

4 Conclusions

We tested the modelling capabilities of the model and the language by means of a case study of a cooperative hierarchical diagram editor, showing that contextual coordination actually can be used for describing a distributed software architecture respecting a set of user's requirements. We started with an existing object-oriented specification, and we derived, formally and progressively, a convenient distributed software architecture, with the same main properties. During this process, we exploited the software re-configuration and reuse capabilities of the model. This exercise is succeeded and can be found in [3].

Now, it seems to be fundamental to integrate the coordination model and language into an existing object-oriented development method. A first step in this direction is given by the current research about the integration of CO-OPN$_{/2}$ into the object-oriented analysis method proposed by Fusion [5]. We plan to extend this integration up to the design phase, by integrating COIL and contextual coordination to Fusion.

References

[1]   Gul Agha and Christian J. Callsen. ActorSpace: An open distributed programming paradigm. In *Proc. of the fourth ACM Symposium on Principles and Practice of Parallel Programming*, San Diego, Ca., 1993. Published in SIGPLAN Notices, Vol. 28, No. 7, 1993.

[2]   Olivier Biberstein, Didier Buchs, and Nicolas Guelfi. Coopn/2: A concurrent object-oriented formalism. In *Proc. IFIP Conf. on Formal Methods for Open Object-Based Distributed Systems (FMOODS)*, Canterbury , 1997. to appear.

[3]   Mathieu Buffo. *Contextual Coordination: a Coordination Model for Distributed Object Systems*. PhD thesis, University of Geneva, 1997. To appear.

[4]   Mathieu Buffo and Didier Buchs. Contextual coordination between objects. In José Carlos Maldonado and Paulo Cesar Masiero, editors, *Proceedings of the X SBES Brazilian Symposium on Software Engineering*, São Carlos, Brasil, 1996.

[5]   Derek Coleman, Patrick Arnold, Stephanie Bodoff, Chris Dollin, Helena Gilchrist, Fiona Hayes, and Paul Jeremaes. *Object-Oriented Development: the Fusion Method*. Prenctice-Hall, 1994.

[6]   D. de Champeaux, D. Lea, and P. Faure. The process of object-oriented design. In *Proceedings of OOPSLA'92*, 1992.

[7]   Jeff Kramer, Jeff Magee, Morris Sloman, and Naranker Dulay. Configuring object-based distributed programs in rex. *IEEE Software Engineering Journal*, 7(2):139–149, 1992.

[8]   B. B. Kristensen. Complex associations: Abstractions in object-oriented modeling. In *Proceedings of OOPSLA'94*, Portland, Oregon, USA, 1994.

[9]   Thomas W. Malone and Kevin Crowston. The interdisciplinary study of coordination. *ACM Computing Surveys*, 26(1):87–119, 1994.

Coordination Patterns for Parallel Computing

Bernd Freisleben and Thilo Kielmann

Dept. of Electrical Engineering and Computer Science, University of Siegen
Hölderlinstr. 3, D–57068 Siegen, Germany
{freisleb|kielmann}@informatik.uni-siegen.de

Abstract. The aim of this paper is to promote the idea of developing reusable *coordination patterns* for parallel computing, i.e. customizable components from which parallel applications can be built by software composition. To illustrate the idea, a fundamental *manager/worker* coordination pattern useful for programming a variety of parallel applications is presented.

1 Introduction

Although coordination models based on generative and anonymous communication allow to express complex process interactions in a straightforward manner, their programming interface is often felt to be rather low level. Therefore, higher–level abstractions on top of the basic communication operations would significantly ease concurrent program development. Instead of reinventing the wheel each time new concurrent programs have to be written, such *reusable coordination patterns* should provide basic abstractions common to frequently used settings in which concurrent processes have to interact in a coordinated manner. Developing concurrent programs from these reusable basic building blocks would then simply require to parameterize the behaviour of the patterns to the needs of the given problem and to compose the concurrent application out of these patterns. This approach follows the idea of *software composition* [4], i.e. producing new software by composing it from already existing components which can simply be "plugged together". This paper is intended to initiate the discussion and collection of suitable coordination patterns (in the sense of *design patterns* as initially introduced by Gamma et al. [2]) which may be reused in various areas of parallel programming. In order to illustrate the idea, we present a fundamental parallel computing paradigm useful in a variety of situations, namely a *manager/worker* pattern.

2 The Manager and Worker Patterns

The intent of these patterns is to decouple coordination–level issues such as task assignment strategies and worker termination from application–level issues such as task creation, task computation, and result combination. The Manager pattern is responsible for providing and assigning task units and for collecting results. The Worker pattern is responsible for acquiring and executing task units and for transmitting computed results to the manager.

2.1 Motivation

It is a very common situation in parallel programming to employ a specific manager process to divide a given problem into smaller tasks and to distribute these tasks among several worker processes. While workers repeatedly process such tasks and return the computed results to the manager process, the managerial task is much more complex. The manager not only has to operate on the application level by providing task units and later combining the received results to the overall result of the application. It also has to perform coordination–level tasks, such as assigning tasks to workers and terminating workers.

Although both levels of managerial tasks are independent of each other, they are typically intermixed in existing applications. They are hardly made explicit, but instead implicitly performed by the communication operations of manager and workers. Therefore, it is our motivation to provide clearly defined abstractions for both levels in the form of coordination patterns suitable for building reusable coordination components.

2.2 Structure and Participants

The structure of the participants in the **Manager** and **Worker** patterns are illustrated by the Booch diagram shown on the right. The figure is divided into two horizontal layers, one for coordination aspects and one for application aspects. Furthermore, the diagram is vertically divided into the manager role, the worker role, and the data exchanged between both, namely objects and object spaces.

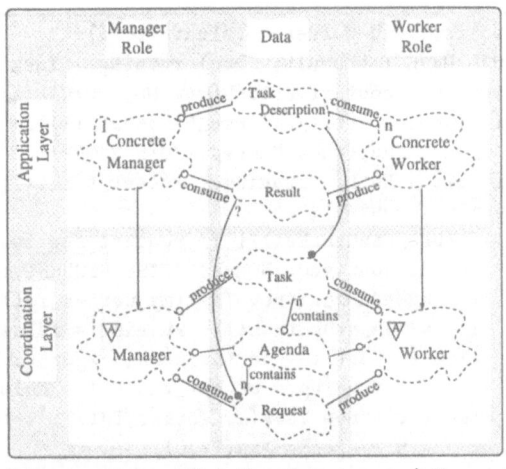

The **Agenda** is the central shared data structure (i.e. the object space) through which the abstract components in the coordination layer, **Manager** and **Workers**, communicate. The **Task** and **Request** objects exchanged in this layer are primarily used as containers for their application–specific counterparts, **Task Description** and **Result**, which are transparently transported via the coordination layer. **Concrete Manager** and **Concrete Worker** are instantiated by inheriting from **Manager** and **Worker**, respectively, while providing suitable implementations for their application–specific, abstract methods.

2.3 Implementation and Sample Usage

In the following, an implementation of **Manager** and **Worker** components implemented in the C++ language and using the Objective Linda coordination model [3] will be sketched. The presentation is restricted to the evaluate routines. These define the behaviour of the components once they are activated.

```
public: void Manager::evaluate(void){
 OIL_OBJECT *task_descriptor;  Request *r;  Task *t;  int workers = 0;
 bool still_work_to_do = true; agenda = new OBJECT_SPACE;
 context->out(*new OS_LOGICAL(agenda_id(),agenda));  setup_agenda();
 while ( still_work_to_do || (workers > 0) ){
  r = agenda->in(*new Request);
  switch (r->get_tag()){
   case JOIN_GROUP: workers++;  break;
   case LEAVE_GROUP: workers--;  break;
   case RESULT: still_work_to_do = process_result(r->get_result()); break;
   case TASK_REQUEST: still_work_to_do = process_result(r->get_result());
            task_descriptor = get_next_task(); t = new Task(r->get_id());
            if ( still_work_to_do )  t->assign_task(task_descriptor);
            else  t->set_stop_task(true);
            agenda->out(*t);  break;
 } delete r; } }
```

```
public: void Worker::evaluate(void){
 OIL_OBJECT *result;  bool running;  Task *t;
 agenda = context.attach(new OS_LOGICAL(agenda_id()));
 if (do_register() || use_handshake()) // register with manager
  agenda->out(*new Request(JOIN_GROUP));
 result = NULL;  running = accept_tasks();
 while (running){
  if (use_handshake()){ // request new task
   agenda->out(*new Request(TASK_REQUEST,my_worker_id(),result));
   t = agenda->in(*new Task(my_worker_id()));
   if (t->is_stop_task())  running = false;
   else {  result = do_the_work(t->get_task());
           running = accept_tasks();  delete t; } }
  else { t = new Task(my_worker_id()); t->match_valid_tasks_only(true);
         t = agenda->in(*t,0);
         if ( t == NULL )  running = false;
         else { agenda->out(*new Request(RESULT,my_worker_id(),
                do_the_work(t->get_task()); running = accept_tasks();
                delete t; } }
  if (do_register()||use_handshake())
    agenda->out(*new Request(LEAVE_GROUP)); } }
```

To illustrate the sample usage of the manager and worker components, a sophisticated technique taken from a raytracing application, adaptive scheduling [1] will be presented, where the concrete Adaptive_Manager performs adaptive load distribution by successive reduction of task sizes and hence by assignment of larger tasks to faster workers. The implementations of Adaptive_Manager and Adaptive_Worker show how the concrete instances parameterize the components' coordination protocol and implement the application–specific parts.

```
class Adaptive_Manager : public Manager{
private: int lines, lines_received, next_line_out;
protected: virtual OIL_OBJECT *get_next_task(void){  int size;
  range *result;  if ( next_line_out >= lines ) return NULL;
  else { size = next_size(); // compute the current task size
         result = new range(next_line_out,next_line_out+size-1);
         next_line_out += size; return result; } }
virtual bool process_result(OIL_OBJECT* imagelines) {
  // store contents of imagelines to file
  lines_received += (imagelines->end - imagelines->start + 1);
  return lines_received == lines; }
public: Adaptive_Manager (int size_of_image)
  { lines = size_of_image; lines_received = 0; next_line_out = 0; } };
```

```
class Adaptive_Worker : public Worker{  protected:
virtual bool do_register(void) { return true; }
virtual bool use_handshake(void) { return true; }
virtual char *my_worker_id(void) { return new uuid; }
virtual OIL_OBJECT *do_the_work(OIL_OBJECT* my_range)
  { return imagelines(my_range); }// compute imagelines from line range
};
```

3   Conclusions

The major benefit of employing the manager and worker patterns is the decoupling of the coordination layer from the application layer. Hence, application programs only need to provide application–specific code whereas all program code related to coordination between the manager and its workers can easily be "plugged in". This alleviates application programmers from coordination aspects, allowing them to focus on the application itself.

The decoupling of the application code from the control flow also enforces a "framework–like" structuring of the manager implementation. Typically, the manager implements the control flow of the application as a whole. But because the patterns take over this part, the application–specific methods of a concrete manager simply have to react whenever they are called. Therefore, the concrete manager's only duty is to produce one task after the other and to process incoming results when it is requested to do so.

References

1. B. Freisleben, D. Hartmann, and T. Kielmann. Parallel Raytracing: A Case Study on Partitioning and Scheduling on Workstation Clusters. In *Proc. of the 30th Ann. Hawaii Int. Conf. on System Sciences*, Vol. 1, pp. 596–605, IEEE Press, 1997.
2. E. Gamma, R. Helm, R. Johnson, and J. Vlissides. *Design Patterns, Elements of Reusable Object–Oriented Software*. Addison Wesley, 1994.
3. T. Kielmann. Designing a Coordination Model for Open Systems. In *Coordination Languages and Models*, LNCS 1061, pp. 267–284, Cesena, Italy, Springer, 1996.
4. O. Nierstrasz and T.D. Meijler. Research Directions in Software Composition. *ACM Computing Surveys*, 27(2):262–264, 1995.

Concurrent METATEM as a Coordination Language

Adam Kellett and Michael Fisher

Department of Computing, Manchester Metropolitan University
Manchester, United Kingdom, M1 5GD
EMAIL: {A.Kellett,M.Fisher}@doc.mmu.ac.uk

Abstract. In the area of concurrent and reactive system design, the use of temporal logic as a formal notation has become widespread. Concurrent METATEM is a language designed to support such systems by allowing the direct execution of temporal specifications. Programs in this language consist of asynchronous, concurrent objects which communicate via broadcast message passing. Each object executes its own temporal specification representing a required behaviour. In this paper we present work on the development of Concurrent METATEM as a coordination language. By using the temporal specifications as a high-level mechanism whereby properties required of coordinated applications can be concisely defined, we show how Concurrent METATEM can be extended to utilize the functionality of an underlying language.

1 Introduction

In this paper we consider the extension of Concurrent METATEM to act as a coordination language. Our aim is to extend the functionality of the language to provide a consistent link between formal specification using temporal logic and implemented systems. Temporal logic can be seen as classical logic extended with various modalities representing temporal aspects of logical formulae [2]. The propositional and first-order temporal logics we use (called PTL and FTL) are based on a linear, discrete model of time. Thus, time is modeled as an infinite sequence of discrete states, with an identified starting point, called 'the beginning of time'. Classical formulae are used to represent constraints *within* states, while temporal formulae represent constraints *between* states. As formulae are interpreted at particular states in a sequence, operators which refer to both the past and future are required. Examples of such operators and criteria for their satisfaction at a specific moment in time are given below.

$\Diamond \varphi$ is satisfied if φ is satisfied *sometime* in the future.
$\Box \varphi$ is satisfied if φ is satisfied *always* in the future.
$\bigcirc \varphi$ is satisfied if φ is satisfied in the next moment.
$\bullet \varphi$ is satisfied if in the previous moment in time φ was satisfied.
$\varphi \, \mathcal{U} \, \psi$ is satisfied if ψ is satisfied *until* a future moment when ψ is satisfied.

The past-time operators $\blacklozenge$ (sometime in the past), $\blacksquare$ (always in the past), and $\mathcal{S}$ (since) mirror those of the future given above. The operator **start** is introduced to represent the beginning to time.

Concurrent METATEM programs are, in effect, executable specifications. Programs express the properties required of an execution. Using the *Imperative Future* paradigm [1], program execution is a forward chaining process which dynamically reflects changes over time in a temporal model. This imperative approach means that an execution not only assesses the validity of events against the properties required, but actively take steps to ensure they as satisfied. In this paper, we present an overview of Concurrent METATEM and our approach to coordination.

2 Concurrent METATEM

Concurrent METATEM is a programming language for reactive systems [7] that has been shown to be particularly useful in representing and developing multi-agent systems [4]. It is based on the combination of two complementary elements: the direct execution of temporal logic specifications providing the behaviour of an individual object [5]; and a concurrent operational model in which such objects execute asynchronously, communicate via broadcast message-passing, and are organized using a grouping mechanism [3].

The basic elements of Concurrent METATEM are objects. These are considered to be encapsulated entities, executing independently, and having complete control over their own internal behaviour. An *interface definition* specifies messages an object may received and produce, while the internal definition of each objects is provided by a temporal formula. Execution corresponds to the construction of a model for an object's formula. At each moment in time, the formula is evaluated using information about the history of the object in order to constrain its future execution. As an example, the following forms a fragment of an object's description.

$$\mathbf{start} \Rightarrow \neg \texttt{moving}$$
$$\bullet \texttt{go} \Rightarrow \Diamond \texttt{moving}$$
$$\bullet (\texttt{moving} \wedge \texttt{go}) \Rightarrow \texttt{overheat} \vee \texttt{fuel}$$

Here, we see that moving is false at the start of execution and, whenever go is true in the last moment in time, a commitment to eventually make moving true is made. Similarly, whenever both go and moving are true in the last moment in time, then either overheat or fuel must be made true.

It is fundamental to our approach that all objects are (potentially) concurrently active. In particular, they may be asynchronously executing. Each object, in executing its temporal formula, independently constructs its own temporal sequence. Within Concurrent METATEM, communication between separate objects consists of a partition of each object's predicates into those controlled by the object and those controlled by its environment. To fit in with this logical view of communication, whilst also providing a flexible and powerful message-passing mechanism, *broadcast* message-passing is used to pass information between objects.

3 Coordination

Concurrent METATEM as a coordination language provides a formal mechanisms for defining the interaction between independent software modules. As a coordination language, the use of temporal logic, utilizing the declarative mechanisms of rules and constraints, provides a highly expressive formal mechanism for the abstract definition of compositional properties. It should also be noted that the use of temporal logic as the basis for the computation rules gives an extra level of expressive power over the corresponding classical logics.

A framework for coordination languages must support both *coordinators* and *participants* [8]. In our approach we regard each object in a Concurrent METATEM program as a coordinator for some independent software process. To support our object-based model, we define the participants of an application to be object-based software processes. Each object is continuously active and executes independently. The encapsulation of participants into active object frameworks provides the interface between the two languages. Each coordinator can only directly access operations provided by its own participant, with services of other objects accessed through the Concurrent METATEM coordinators controlling their behaviour.

To integrate coordinator and participant, initiation of a method belonging to a participant is associated with the satisfaction of an atomic formula in the coordinator. The behaviour of a participant consequently reflects the execution of coordinator's temporal formula. In this example, where of the proposition process is associated with a method, if a request is received, then in the next state process is satisfied:

$$\text{\Large\textbf{o}}\ \text{request} \Rightarrow \text{process}$$
$$\text{\Large\textbf{o}}\ \text{return} \Rightarrow \text{respond}$$

Atomic formulae are similarly associated with messages from the participant and as an extension to the existing operational framework, are satisfied in the temporal model when messages are received. In the above example, the proposition return indicates the completion of the method and specifies the subsequent behaviour. Using first-order temporal logic allows a transfer of data between coordinator and participant.

$$\text{\Large\textbf{o}}\ \text{request}(X,Y) \Rightarrow \text{process}(X,Y)$$
$$\text{\Large\textbf{o}}\ \text{return}(W,Z) \Rightarrow \text{respond}(W,Z)$$

The terms of a predicate are associated with the arguments of a method. Similarly for return values, predicate terms hold the results of a method's execution.

Used as a language for implementing multi-agent systems, Concurrent METATEM has provided an effective approach to specifying both *reactive* and *pro-active* behaviours. Pro-active applications, with the ability to influence their environment, have been demonstrated with a variety of cooperative and competitive behaviours [6]. While purely reactive systems are suitable for many applications, it has been proposed that pro-active behaviour is necessary to provide a framework for full coordination [8].

Using temporal logic as a specification language, applications are defined by properties which the execution must satisfy. These are categorized as *safety* properties, defining the parameters which an application must always satisfy to ensure correct execution, and *liveness* properties defining conditions which will at some time be realized. Safety properties constrain the execution to a set of acceptable circumstances. For example, the following temporal formula defines that at any moment in time read and write may not be simultaneously true:

$$\Box(\neg\text{read} \lor \neg\text{write})$$

421

Using the execution mechanism of Concurrent METATEM, liveness properties provide a goal directed behaviour so that such conditions are realized as soon as possible. This allows the direction of execution towards the most profitable sequence of actions within the constraints specified by safety properties. In the following example, two eventualities (represented by $\Diamond$) define that the I/O requests get and put are undertaken as soon as possible, with a safety property serializing their satisfaction:

$$\bullet \textbf{true} \Rightarrow \neg\texttt{read} \lor \neg\texttt{write}$$
$$\bullet \texttt{get} \Rightarrow \Diamond\texttt{read}$$
$$\bullet \texttt{put} \Rightarrow \Diamond\texttt{write}$$

4 Conclusions and Future Work

Concurrent METATEM as a coordination language presents a formal mechanism for defining the interaction between independent software modules. The use of temporal logic provides a highly expressive notation for the abstract definition of compositional properties. The association between coordinated system and temporal formulae allows the verification of coordination properties via temporal theorem-proving.

In this paper we have presented an extension to Concurrent METATEM to support the coordination of underlying software processes. The benefits of using the expressive power of temporal logic to define the integration of a coordinated system have been described. We propose that the ability of the language to define pro-active behaviours, demonstrated with multi-agent applications, can provide significant advantages for coordination. In our ongoing work, Concurrent METATEM is being developed to support larger applications and the integration of dynamic object creation.

References

1. H. Barringer, M. Fisher, D. Gabbay, R. Owens, and M. Reynolds, editors. *The Imperative Future: Principles of Executable Temporal Logics*. Research Studies Press, Chichester, United Kingdom, 1996.
2. E. A. Emerson. Temporal and Modal Logic. In J. van Leeuwen, editor, *Handbook of Theoretical Computer Science*, pages 996–1072. Elsevier, 1990.
3. M. Fisher. A Survey of Concurrent METATEM — The Language and its Applications. In *First International Conference on Temporal Logic (ICTL)*, Bonn, Germany, July 1994. (Published in *Lecture Notes in Computer Science*, volume 827, Springer-Verlag).
4. M. Fisher. Representing and Executing Agent-Based Systems. In M. Wooldridge and N. R. Jennings, editors, *Intelligent Agents*. Springer-Verlag, 1995.
5. M. Fisher. An Introduction to Executable Temporal Logics. *Knowledge Engineering Review*, 11(1):43–56, March 1996.
6. M. Fisher and M. Wooldridge. A Logical Approach to the Representation of Societies of Agents. In N. Gilbert and R. Conte, editors, *Artificial Societies*. UCL Press, 1995.
7. M. Fisher. Concurrent METATEM — A Language for Modeling Reactive Systems. In *Parallel Architectures and Languages, Europe (PARLE)*, Munich, Germany, June 1993. (Published in *Lecture Notes in Computer Science*, volume 694, Springer-Verlag).
8. J-M. Andreoli, H. Gallaire, and R. Pareschi. Rule Based Object Coordination. *Object-Based Models and Languages for Concurrent Systems* ed. P. Ciancarini, O. Nierstrsz, A. Yonezawa. LNCS 924. Springer-Verlag. 1994.

Control-Based Coordination of Human and Other Activities in Cooperative Information Systems

George A. Papadopoulos

Department of Computer Science
University of Cyprus
75 Kallipoleos Str, P.O.B. 537
CY-1678 Nicosia, Cyprus

E-mail: george@turing.cs.ucy.ac.cy

Farhad Arbab

Department of Interactive Systems
CWI
Kruislaan 413, 1098 SJ Amsterdam
The Netherlands

E-mail: farhad@cwi.nl

1 Introduction

Modelling of activities within an information system or between different information systems has become a complex task. Performing these activities (often known as *groupware, workflow, electronic commerce* and *enterprize reengineering*) is often done in conjunction with computer-based cooperative environments such as electronic mail, voice and video teleconferencing, electronic classrooms, etc. Modelling these activities has become a task which often is not possible to perform by single persons, but by groups of people, often even distributed over different organisations, countries, etc.

Recently, we have seen the use of coordination languages to model activities in information systems, and, in particular, variants of the so called Shared Dataspace Model, its most prominent member being Linda ([1]). Although Linda is indeed a successful coordination model, when it is evaluated from the point of view of acting as a framework for modelling human and other activities in information systems, it has some serious deficiencies which carry over to all the other related models that are based on it. These deficiencies are: (i) It is data-driven which may not be very natural since we are interested more in how the *flow of information* between the involved agents is set-up and how an agent *reacts* to receiving some information, rather than *what kind of data* it sends or receives. (ii) The shared dataspace as a metaphor may not be very intuitive since the sharing it encourages and imposes contrasts with how information actually flows within an organisation; people do not take the work to be done by others to common rooms where from other people pass by and pick the work up. (iii) Furthermore, the shared dataspace is not secure and it is possible for information posted there to be lost or forged.

In the next section we present a different approach for modelling such activities where: (i) communication between agents is done by means of point-to-point *stream* connections; (ii) the agents comprising a coordination pattern are defined by means of being in one of a number of predefined *states*, where a state is a set of observable stream connections; (iii) evolution of a community of coordinators is *event-driven* (or control based) in the sense that the agents in question observe the presence of events and react accordingly.

2 An Event-Driven Control-Based Modelling Framework

In this section we describe a framework for modelling activities in organisations based on MANIFOLD and its underlying coordination model IWIM ([2]). Our framework is essentially a three level one: (i) the top part is an easy to use visual interface which defines graphically the interrelationships and behaviour of the involved agents; (ii) the middle part is a verbal (semi-formal) description of the states defining each agent and how it reacts to receiving some event; (iii) the lower part is the actual implementation of the scenario to be modelled in MANIFOLD.

In our model, all entities participating in an activity (humans, devices, CSCW tools, shared resources such as active or passive documents, etc.) are *agents*. We distinguish two categories of agents: *worker* agents which perform computational work (whatever that may be according to the specific details of some particular scenario) and *manager* agents which are responsible for coordinating the activities of worker agents. Note that manager agents may themselves be seen as worker agents from other, higher up in the hierarchy, manager agents. However, the genuine worker agents (i.e. those performing some actual computational task) such as computer programs, CSCW tools, hardware devices, etc. form the bottom level of the layer and cannot be subdivided any further. We are not concerned with the internal details of these agents, only with their interaction with their environment.

Every agent, whether it is a manager or a worker agent, communicates with its environment by means of at least one *input port* and one *output port*. In general, an agent may have more than one input and/or output port. Furthermore, every agent observes a number of *events* and reacts to them accordingly. However, it should be made clear that the purpose of an event is to make one or more agents aware of some situation that must be handled and not to transfer actual data — this is the purpose of *streams*. More to the point, agents communicate actual data between themselves by means of connecting respective pairs of their input and output ports via *streams*. Finally, every agent is defined at any moment in time by means of being in some *state*. It is known beforehand which states an agent can be in during the lifespan of its activities. In order for some agent to change its state, it must observe the raising of a particular event. Reacting to an event (and therefore changing the current state) typically means establishing new stream connections between input and output ports and abandoning old connections.

The above general description of our model has some clear advantages over the traditional Linda-like approaches we have seen so far: (i) Every worker agent is only concerned with getting workload from its input port(s), performing the required work for which it is responsible, and putting the outcome to its output port(s). Its only other communication with its environment is by means of observing (if at all) any events. (ii) Every manager agent is only concerned with making sure that the output produced by some worker agents are sent to some other worker agents that require it. The manager identifies workers by means of their responsibilities and workflow interdependencies, not the actual work (data) they produce. (iii) The model is inherently secured and flexible (new agents can come and go dynamically).

As an example we model a scenario where (mainly) four agents are involved, as it happens all of them being humans, collaborating in the development of some document. The first agent is the *author* who is responsible for writing up the document as well as performing significant changes to it. The second agent is the *editor* who checks the document's validity, performs any corrections and, if necessary, returns the document back to the author for further substantial changes. The third agent is the *manager* (still a worker process though, as far as our model is concerned) which either approves the document or sends it back to the editor. The fourth agent is a true coordinator agent responsible for managing the workflow between the other three agents (it could represent a department's supervisor). We also assume the presence of other agents (especially atomic agents performing purely computational work). In the sequel and for reasons of brevity we present the code for levels ii and iii only and for three of the agents involved, namely author, editor and manager. Level ii is described in terms of the states an agent can be in and what event it must observe to make a transition to another state; level iii is the MANIFOLD code.

Author

State 0: Receive document in in-port. State 1: Produce or modify document. State 1a: Put document in out-port. State 2: Recur from the beginning. State 3: Request to be substituted.

```
manifold Author (event i_had_enough)
{
  event prod_amend_doc, doc_ready, send_doc, time_to_go, flushed.

  begin: (guard(input,full,prod_amend_doc),              // State S0
          terminated(void)).
  prod_amend_doc:(process writer is Word_Program(doc_ready).
                                                         // State S1
                    begin: (activate(writer),
                            input->writer,
                            terminated(void)).
                    doc_ready:(writer->output,           // State S1a
                               post(send_doc)).
                  }.
  send_doc:(post(begin)).                                // State S2
  time_to_go:{begin:(raise(i_had_enough),                // State S3
                     guard(output,a_disconnected,flushed),
                     terminated(void)).
              flushed:halt.
             }
}
```

Editor

State 0: Receive document in in-ports. State 1: Check document. State 1a: Send document to the manager. State 1b: Send document back to the author. State 2: Forward document back to the author.

```
manifold Editor (port in from_author, from_man, port out to_author,
to_man)
{
  event check_doc, doc_ok, doc_not_ok, send_doc_back, send_doc_man.

  begin: (guard(from_author,full,check_doc),           // State S0
          guard(from_man,full,send_doc_back),
          terminated(void)).
  check_doc:{process checker is Speller(doc_ok, doc_not_ok).
                                                       // State S1
              begin: (activate(checker),
                      from_author->checker,
                      terminated(void)).
              doc_ok: (checker->to_man,                // State S1a
                       guard(checker.output,empty,begin),
                       terminated(void)).
              doc_not_ok: (checker->to_author,         // State S1b
                           guard(checker.output,empty,begin),
                           terminated(void)).
            }
  send_doc_back: (from_man->to_author,                 // State S2
                  post(begin)).
}
```

Manager

State 0: Receive document in in-port. State 1: Verify and forward document. State S2: Ask for more work.

```
manifold Manager (event more_work, port out to_dept_head, to_editor)
{
  event verify_doc.

  begin: (guard(input,full,verify_doc),                // State S0
          terminated(void)).
  verify_doc: (if (document is ok)                     // State S1
               then input->to_dept_head
               else input->to_editor,
               guard(input,empty,begin).
  ... raise(more_work).                                // State S2
}
```

References

[1] S. Ahuja, N. Carriero and D. Gelernter, "Linda and Friends", *IEEE Computer* **19(8)**, Aug. 1986, pp. 26-34.

[2] F. Arbab, "The IWIM Model for Coordination of Concurent Activities", *1st International Conference on Coordination Models, Languages and Applications (Coordination'96)*, Cesena, Italy, 15-17 April, 1996, LNCS 1061, Springer Verlag, pp. 34-56.

Using Asynchronous Tuple-Space Access Primitives (BONITA Primitives) for Process Co-ordination

Antony Rowstron

Computer Laboratory, University of Cambridge, New Museums Site, Pembroke Street, Cambridge CB2 3QG, UK

Abstract. In this paper an interactive talk program is used to demonstrate the difference between the Linda primitives and the recently proposed BONITA primitives. Both use the concept of shared tuple spaces for inter-agent communication, but the BONITA primitives provide asynchronous tuple space access. The paper demonstrates the performance gains and the novel co-ordination patterns achievable using the BONITA primitives.

1 Introduction

The concept of shared tuple spaces is the foundation of the Linda[1] co-ordination language. Linda provides asynchronous process communication but synchronous tuple space access. The BONITA[3] primitives are a set of asynchronous tuple space access primitives. In distributed environments the need for such primitives is driven by both functionality and performance concerns. The implementation of the C-BONITA uses the run-time system used in the York Linda Kernel II[2] and the primitives are described in detail in Rowstron et al.[3]. A detailed description of Linda can be found in Carriero et al.[1].

In order to compare the use of the BONITA primitives and the Linda primitives the implementation of a talk tool is considered. The talk program requires an arbitrary number of people should be able to communicate concurrently (interactively) using the talk program and the text that makes the conversation should be stored for future reference. The people involved in the conversation can dynamically alter. An initialisation section displays the conversation to date, and the main section allows the user to participate in the conversation.

1.1 C-Linda version

This initialisation code (lines 1–9, Figure 1) assumes that each conversation uses a unique tuple space (in this case represented by a tuple space handle called con), and this has been initialised and a tuple representing a counter of the number of messages in the conversation is present. Each line of the conversation is a simple tuple of the form $[index_{integer}, name_{string}, textline_{string}]$, and the counter tuple contains the value of index for the next line to be inserted.

```
1     out(con, user_name);
2     in(con, ?num_lines); /* Get counter */
3     out(con, num_lines, user_name, "Joining");
4     out(con, ++num_lines);
5     init_window();      /* Set up the window */
6     for (pos = 0; pos < num_lines; pos++) {
7        rd(con, pos, ?name, ?text);
8        print_screen(name,text);
9     }
10    next = num_lines;
11    while (!exit_status) {
12       /* If available display next line */
13       if (inp(con, next, ?name, ?text)) {
14          print_screen(name,text);
15          next++;
16       }
17       if (ready_line(text)) {
18          in(con, ?num_lines);
19          out(con, num_lines+1);
20          out(con, num_lines, user_name, text);
21       }
22    }
23    in(con, user_name);
```

Fig. 1. The talk program using C-Linda.

The first operation is to insert a tuple containing the users name (line 1). This is so other users can ask who is currently active in a conversation. When a user exits the tuple containing the name is removed (line 16). A line in the conversation is inserted to indicate that the a new person has joined the conversation (lines 2–4). This is achieved by removing the counter tuple (line 2), and then inserting a new conversation line (line 3), and then replacing the incremented counter tuple (line 4). Then, each line of the conversation is read and printed on the screen (lines 6–9). The main section code (lines 10–23, Figure 1) of the C-Linda program uses polling for detecting the tuple containing the next line of the conversation in the tuple space and for getting user input text. An inp primitive is used to keep checking if a tuple containing a new line of the conversation has been inserted into the tuple space (line 13). If so, it is displayed and the local counter incremented thus enabling checking for the next tuple. The function ready_line manages the input of text from the keyboard and checks if a line of text is ready. If a line of text is ready it is inserted into the conversation by retrieving the counter tuple (line 18), reinserting it incremented (line 19), and then adding the tuple to the conversation (line 20).

1.2 C-Bonita version

The initialisation code (lines 1–12, Figure 2) for the C-Bonita version functionally does exactly the same as the C-Linda version. It should be noted that the Bonita primitives can emulate the Linda primitives, hence the Linda primitives are provided as macros. The second part of the initialisation code uses pipelining of tuple space accesses. The requesting of all tuples is achieved within the for loop (line 7) and the dispatch primitive (line 8). The *request identifier* for each of the dispatch primitives is stored, to be used when retrieving the results. The for loop (line 9) and the obtain primitive (line 10) retrieve the requested tuples. The C-Bonita main section code (lines 13–29, Figure 2) again uses polling to check if the next line of the conversation is available or if there is user input ready. The polling of the next line of the conversation *does not* use inp but instead requests the tuple using a dispatch primitive (lines 14 and 20) and checks for the tuples arrival using the arrived primitive (line 17).

```
1    dispatch(con, user_name); /* Place name in ts */
2    in(con, ?num_lines); /* Get the line counter */
3    dispatch(con, num_lines, user_name, "Joining");
4    dispatch(con, ++num_lines);
5    init_window(); /* Set up the window */
6    /* Get lines of text - pipelining the ts access */
7    for (pos = 0; pos < num_lines; pos++)
8      arr[pos] = dispatch(con, pos, ?n, ?text, NONDEST);
9    for (pos = 0; pos < num_lines; pos++) {
10     obtain(arr[pos]);
11     print_screen(n,text);
12   }
13   next = num_lines;
14   ref = dispatch(con, next, ?n, ?text, NONDEST);
15   while (!exit_status) {
16     /* If next line here then display it */
17     if (arrived(ref)) {
18       print_screen(n,text);
19       /* Request the next line of the conversation */
20       ref = dispatch(con, ++next, ?n, ?text, NONDEST);
21     }
22     if (ready_line(text_input)) {
23       in(con, ?num_lines);
24       dispatch(con, num_lines+1);
25       dispatch(con, num_lines, user_name, text_input);
26     }
27   }
28   in(con, user_name);
```

Fig. 2. The talk program using C-BONITA.

It should be noted that the dispatch primitive on line 14 is used to request the first tuple containing a text line that was not displayed during the initialisation section, and subsequent tuples containing text lines are requested by the one on line 20. If a conversation tuple is available then the arrived primitive retrieves it (line 17), and the text displayed (line 18). The function ready_line is used to manage and check the text input by the user. If a line of text is available, the counter is retrieved (line 23), and then incremented and reinserted (line 24) and then the tuple with the line of text is inserted (line 25). At the end the users' name is removed from the tuple space (line 28).

2 Comparison of the C-Linda and C-BONITA programs

By examining the two programs it is clear to see that the C-Linda version appears more compact and in some ways more elegant. The fundamental difference between the two initialisation sections is the way in which the tuples representing the text of the past conversation is retrieved. The C-BONITA version pipelines access to the tuple space, whereas the C-Linda version does not. This cannot lead to the C-BONITA version taking longer, and in most cases will provide a speed-up. This is because when using a rd primitive, a message is sent to the system managing the tuple spaces (kernel), the kernel processes the message, and a reply message is sent back. When this is received the rd has completed and the program continues to perform the next rd primitive. In the C-BONITA version the the request for the next tuple is *not* dependent on the receipt of the result for the previous request.

The results shown in Table 1 show the time taken to retrieve a number of tuples from a tuple space. These were produced using a network of Silicon Graphics Indy workstations connected by a non-dedicated 10Mbit/s Ethernet LAN network. The kernel used was the York Kernel II[2] but using it as a *single* centralised server, instead of using it as a distributed server (this favours the C-Linda version). The test programs were executed on a different Indy Workstation to the one which the kernel was executing on. The C-Linda test program was lines 6–9 of Figure 1, and the C-BONITA test program was lines 7–12 of Figure 2. The results for the C-BONITA version demonstrate the speed advantage of pipelining the tuple space accesses.

Number of tuples	C-Linda (seconds)	C-BONITA (seconds)	C-BONITA speedup
1	0.004	0.004	0 (0%)
10	0.033	0.019	0.014 (42%)
100	0.362	0.197	0.165 (46%)
1000	4.645	2.683	1.962 (42%)

Table 1. Timings for retrieving tuples.

The fundamental difference between the two main sections is the way in which the tuples representing the next line of text in a conversation are retrieved. In the C-Linda version this is achieved using the inp primitive and in the C-BONITA version this is achieved using a dispatch and arrived primitives. The C-Linda approach has a disadvantage over the C-BONITA approach due to the level of communication between the user process and the kernel. The C-BONITA approach requires two messages to pass between the user process and the kernel (dispatching the template and reply tuple). Arrived is simply a local check within the user process to see if the reply message has arrived, there is no extra communication with the kernel. An inp is two messages (a dispatch and a reply), but the reply will either contain a tuple or a value indicating no matching tuple was found. *Each time* an inp both messages are required. This also increase the load on the kernel, because it must process each message and create a reply.

3 Conclusions

We have briefly compared the Linda primitives and the BONITA primitives using a simple example, and shown that the BONITA primitives are better suited to the type of co-ordination required in agent systems. A full copy of the paper is available as Technical Report No. 422 from the Computer Laboratory, Cambridge University. The author would like to thank Dr. Andy Hopper and ORL Ltd, Cambridge for funding this work.

References

1. N. Carriero and D. Gelernter. Linda in context. *Communications of the ACM*, 32(4):444–458, 1989.
2. A. Rowstron and A. Wood. An efficient distributed tuple space implementation for networks of workstations. In *Euro-Par'96*, LNCS 1123, pages 510–513. Springer-Verlag, 1996.
3. A. Rowstron and A. Wood. BONITA: A set of tuple space primitives for distributed coordination. In *HICSS-30*, volume 1, pages 379–388. IEEE CS Press, 1997.

Berlinda: An Object-Oriented Platform for Implementing Coordination Languages in Java

Robert Tolksdorf

Technische Universität Berlin, Fachbereich Informatik, FLP/KIT, Sekr. FR 6–10,
Franklinstr. 28/29, D-10587 Berlin, Germany,
mailto:tolk@cs.tu-berlin.de, http://www.cs.tu-berlin.de/~tolk/

Abstract. Linda-like coordination languages are based on manipulating a shared coordination medium. A coordination language usually defines the kind of elements, operations to construct elements, and the actual coordination operations that manipulate the shared media. Berlinda is a model and a platform, on which coordination languages à la Linda and beyond can be implemented. As example coordination languages, a simple version of Linda and a subset of KQML have been implemented.

Coordination languages in the Linda family center around a coordination medium which is a multiset of elements shared amongst agents. The elements, the structure of the collection, and the operations defined vary. With a broader view one can also consider approaches without a shared multiset as the coordination medium ([Tol97]), like interface repositories in the OMA ([Sol93]), or the message exchange amongst agents in KQML ([FMM94]). An environment on which such languages can be compared, and integrated is of interest. Berlinda is an object-oriented platform capable of hosting a panorama of coordination languages.

1 Designing Berlinda

Coordination languages under consideration define a shared medium as the central abstraction from underlying issues like locations – let it be a multiset, or a space of directed messages. In the medium, elements of some characteristics are manipulated in some way by operations of the language. With the following concepts in our model we hope to cover a whole range of coordination languages:

The *coordination medium* is the structure shared amongst agents. It provides operations for its manipulation that define the type of the coordination medium and form the coordination language. The medium is a collection of *elements* that are kept in the coordination medium which restricts the type of elements via its operations. An element is a vector of fields from a set of supported types.

Elements can carry a *signatures* with meta information, which can be a type description of the element, a name, or a communication address of a receiver. Elements provide a *matching function* on two of them relating elements as given by the semantics of the coordination language. This can be a Linda-like matching, but might degenerate to test identity of communication addresses.

Agents are threads that manipulate the coordination medium. Berlinda is a platform on which a coordination language based on this model can be implemented in Java. For a coordination language, one Java package is implemented which uses classes from the berlinda package. Packages implementing specific coordination languages share the same functional kernel provided by berlinda. An application programmer working with a specific language uses classes from that package only, whereas the implementor of the language uses berlinda. The structure of the berlinda classes is depicted in the diagram in figure 1.

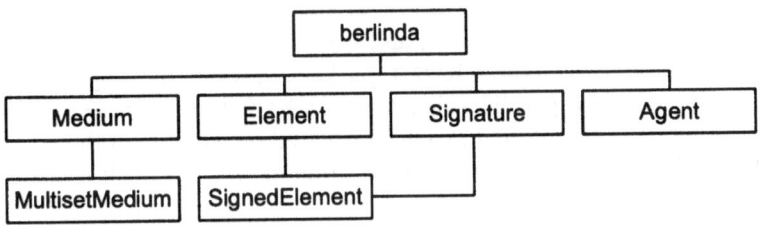

Fig. 1. The structure of berlinda

2 Linda and KQML on Top of **Berlinda**

Implementing Linda on top of berlinda requires the definition of classes that provide a tuplespace as a medium with the Linda operations, tuples as signed elements, and tuple signatures. Figure 2 shows the structure of our implementation wrt. berlinda. It turned out to be straightforward and to result only in a

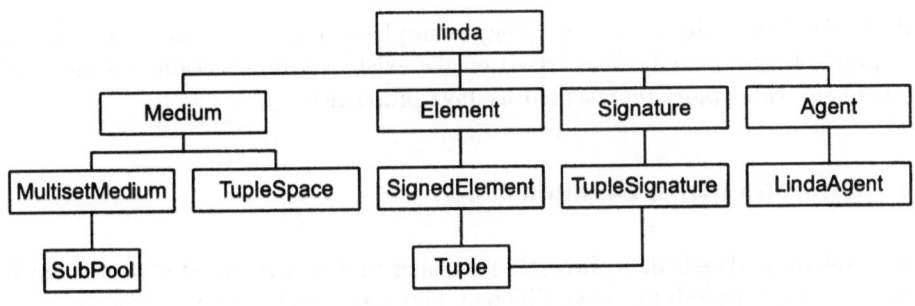

Fig. 2. Class structure of our Linda system

small set of classes. They are concerned with implementing the outform of elements as tuples, the according matching routines, and the addition of the aspects of suspending and resuming agents to support blocking operations.

We can use the Linda implementation as a starting point to study a set of variations to the Linda language. Candidates for future implementation are different matching routines, a different set of supported field types (like Object, Class, Tuple, and TupleSpace), nested tuplespaces, and extended primitives.

A language also focusing on the coordination of agents is KQML, which is based on speech acts ([FMM94]). It defines a set of types of directed messages and a semantics for these types. Each agent is assumed to possess a knowledge base with a specific language and ontology, about which agents perform a conversation. KQML abstracts from the representation language for knowledge and ontologies in the KB. Thus, KQML is a coordination language which focuses on the interaction amongst agents only, and leaves open the message content.

We instantiated berlinda to a KQML package in which messages are kept in a multiset of signed messages. The signature of a KQML message is a communication address of its recipient, and matching is based on equality of those signatures – thereby implementing directed communication. As KQML itself is abstract wrt.

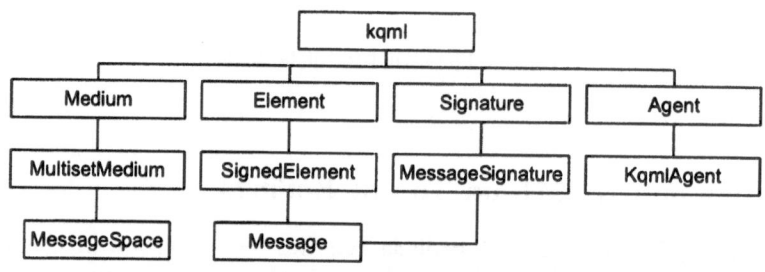

Fig. 3. The structure of the KQML implementation with berlinda

the kind of knowledge base underlying, we implemented a very simple one serving as proof-of-concept only. It is based on the existence, intersection and union of sets of key-value pairs represented as Java properties.

3 Implementing Berlinda

We implemented berlinda in Java, thus utilizing an object-oriented platform which promises high portability over different hardware- and operating system platforms. Java is a simple object-oriented language, which lacks several features known from other languages. Java turned out to be useful in facilitating a well structured implementation; however, limitations of the language became visible. We experienced several restrictions of the standard Java class packages. Most of the classes that would make natural superclasses for berlinda classes are marked as final in the JDK. Thus, the class structure is relatively flat. The implementation is comparably compact. The berlinda package consists of about 1200 lines of code with comments, the Linda package of about 3500 LOC (2500 lines for tuple constructors alone), and the KQML package needs 1200 LOC.

The current implementation of berlinda supports only local ensembles of agents within a single Java VM. A distributed berlinda cannot be achieved easily by just providing means of a distributed Medium. It is hard to find an abstract support for a distributed coordination language. The semantics of distributed behavior and policies to manage distributed agents are given by the coordination language implemented and difficult to move to the underlying platform.

4 Perspectives

The next step in developing berlinda will be the integration of the coordination language Laura ([Tol96]), which has been reimplemented in the PageSpace project ([CKTV96]) in Java. Amongst issues to be covered in the future are:

As berlinda offers coordination media as objects, we can allow for dynamic, heterogeneous, nested spaces – for example, a nested tuplespace which contains either tuplespaces, or KQML message-spaces as leaves. Thereby Berlinda can host multiple coordination languages, where an application is able to use several of them at a time. Thus, the agents in a berlinda application could use KQML for conversations about tasks to achieve and choose Linda for local knowledge bases in which inferences are drawn by sets of concurrent knowledge base agents.

How can agents that operate in multiple coordination environments agree dynamically on which environment to use? We termed that issue *metacoordination* in [Tol97]. The importance of metacoordination becomes visible, when integrating systems – such as legacy systems – that are built on different coordination platforms. Operations are needed to discuss the usage of coordination models amongst agents, forming a *metacoordination language*.

More on berlinda can be found at *http://www.cs.tu-berlin.de/~tolk/berlinda*.

References

[CKTV96] Paolo Ciancarini, Andreas Knoche, Robert Tolksdorf, and Fabio Vitali. PageSpace: An Architecture to Coordinate Distributed Applications on the Web. *Computer Networks and ISDN Systems*, 28(7–11):941–952, 1996. Proceedings of the Fifth International World Wide Web Conference.

[FMM94] Tim Finin, Fritzson Don McKay, and Robin McEntire. KQML as an Agent Communication Language. In *Proceedings of the Third International Conference on Information and Knowledge Management (CIKM'94)*, 1994.

[Sol93] Mark Soley, Richard. An object model for integration. *Computer Standards & Interfaces*, 15(2-3):149–166, 1993.

[Tol96] Robert Tolksdorf. Coordinating Services in Open Distributed Systems with Laura. In Paolo Ciancarini and Chris Hankin, editors, *Coordination Languages and Models, Proceedings of Coordination '96*, LNCS 1061, pages 386–402. Springer, 1996.

[Tol97] Robert Tolksdorf. Coordinative Applications, Structured Coordination, and Meta Coordination. In *Proceedings of the 30th Hawaiian International Conference of System Sciences, HICSS*, pages 391–392. IEEE Press, 1997.

Author Index

Lecture Notes in Computer Science

For information about Vols. 1–1211

please contact your bookseller or Springer-Verlag